THE ACHIEVEMENT OF AMERICAN LIBERALISM

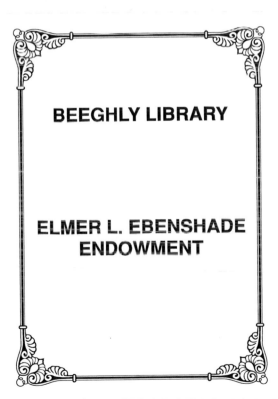

THE ACHIEVEMENT OF AMERICAN LIBERALISM

The New Deal and Its Legacies

Edited by William H. Chafe

COLUMBIA UNIVERSITY PRESS   NEW YORK

Columbia University Press
Publishers Since 1893
New York   Chichester, West Sussex

© 2003 Columbia University Press

Library of Congress Cataloging-in-Publication Data
The achievement of American liberalism : the New Deal and its legacies /
   edited by William H. Chafe.
         p.   cm.
      Includes bibliographical references and index.
      ISBN 0–231–11212-2 (alk. paper)—ISBN 0–231–11213–0
      1. United States—Politics and government—1933-1945. 2. New Deal,
   1933–1939. 3. World War, 1939–1945—Social aspects—United States.
   4. World War, 1939–1945—Influence. 5. Liberalism—United States—
   History—20th century 6. Political culture—United States—History—
   20th century. 7. United States—Social conditions—20th century.
   9. Social movements—United States—History—20th century
   I. Chafe, William Henry.

E806 .M63 2002
973.917—dc21
                                                          2002073366

Columbia University Press books are printed on permanent and durable
acid-free paper.
Printed in the United States of America
c 10 9 8 7 6 5 4 3 2 1
p 10 9 8 7 6 5 4 3 2 1

For William E. Leuchtenburg

CONTENTS

CONTRIBUTORS

William H. Chafe is the Alice Mary Baldwin Professor of American History and dean of the Faculty of Arts and Sciences at Duke University. He has published widely in the areas of race and gender history. His *Civilities and Civil Rights: Greensboro, North Carolina, and the Black Struggle for Freedom* (1980) was awarded the Robert F. Kennedy Book Award, and his *Never Stop Running: Allard Lowenstein and the Struggle to Save American Liberalism* (1993) received the Sidney Hillman Book Award.

Alan Brinkley is the Allan Nevins Professor of History at Columbia University. Among his publications are *Voices of Protest* (1982), *The End of Reform* (1994), and *Liberalism and Its Discontents* (1998).

Richard M. Fried is professor of history at the University of Illinois at Chicago. His most recent book is *The Russians Are Coming! The Russians Are Coming! Pageantry and Patriotism in Cold-War America* (1998).

Otis L. Graham Jr. is Distinguished Visiting Professor at the University of North Carolina, Wilmington, and emeritus professor at the University of California, Santa Barbara. He has been a fellow at the Center for Advanced Study in the Behavioral Sciences and the Woodrow Wilson International Center for Scholars and Distinguished Fulbright Lecturer at the University of Bologna, Italy. His most recent book (with Roger Daniels) is *Debating American Immigration, 1882–Present* (2001).

Alonzo L. Hamby is Distinguished Professor of History at Ohio University. His most recent books are *Liberalism and Its Challengers: F.D.R. To Bush* (1992) and *Man of the People: A Life of Harry S. Truman* (1995).

Cynthia Harrison is associate professor of history and women's studies at George Washington University. She is the author of *On Account of Sex: The Politics of Women's Issues, 1945–1968* (1988).

Steven F. Lawson is professor of American history at Rutgers University. He is the author of *In Pursuit of Power: Southern Blacks and Electoral Politics, 1965–1982* (1985), *Running for Freedom: Civil Rights and Black Politics in America Since 1941* (1997), *and Debating the Civil Rights Movement, 1945–1968* (1998), among other books.

Richard Polenberg is Goldwin Smith Professor of American History at Cornell University, where he has taught since 1966. In 1988–89 he served as Fulbright Visiting Professor at the Hebrew University in Jerusalem. He is the author of *The World of Benjamin Cardozo: Personal Values and the Judicial Process* (1997) and editor of *In the Matter of J. Robert Oppenheimer: The Security Clearance Hearing* (2002).

Harvard Sitkoff is professor of history at the University of New Hampshire. He is the author of *A New Deal for Blacks* (1978) and *The Struggle for Black Equality* (1993) and the editor of *Fifty Years Later: The New Deal Evaluated* (1985), among other books.

Melvin I. Urofsky is professor of history and public policy and director of the doctoral program in public policy at Virginia Commonwealth University. He is the author or editor of more than forty books, of which the most recent is *Religious Liberty* (2002).

INTRODUCTION

William H. Chafe

In the late 1960s, the British journalist and historian Godfrey Hodgson described the "liberal consensus" that had emerged after World War II in America as the paradigm that framed American politics in the decades that followed. The consensus, as Hodgson outlined it, consisted of a series of intersecting axioms: (1) capitalism, not socialism, provided the best economic system in the world; (2) capitalism and democracy worked together hand in hand, each indispensable to the other; (3) there was nothing organically or structurally wrong with American society as it currently existed (hence, incremental reform rather than radical change offered the most effective modus operandi for political action); (4) the best way to bring about reform and greater equality of opportunity was through growing further an already vibrant economy, thereby providing a larger pie to be divided up; and (5) what united Americans in support of the liberal consensus was implacable opposition to communism, the worldwide system that represented totalitarianism, sterility, and economic stagnation.

Hodgson's interpretive assessment crystallized the changes that had occurred in definitions of liberalism during the New Deal and World War II, and it suggested the degree to which these definitional changes shaped the politics of an era. Significantly, each axiom of the liberal consensus that Hodgson described had far-reaching import for what could or could not be considered an option within American political discourse; moreover, each axiom so thoroughly informed the others that none could be isolated or considered separately from the others. The anchor for everything was anticommunism, with implications for domestic as well as foreign policy. Thus, not only was it impossible for any American politician after 1948 to advocate striking a deal with Russia or pursuing a foreign policy that would accommodate socialist countries such as North Vietnam or Hungary lest he or she be labeled a communist sympathizer, but it also became impossible to advocate left-of-center domestic policies such as national health care or childcare services, inasmuch as these suggestions might be construed as "socialistic," collectivist, and hence sympathetic to communist ideology. In short, the ground rules established by the paradigm clearly limited the terms of political discourse.

The liberal consensus, as Hodgson described it, also constrained the ways in which reformers could seek change on issues like race or poverty. Given the premise that the American system was organically healthy, with no fundamental flaws, change had to be put forward as incremental reform. Civil rights advocates focused, therefore, on remedial legislation to improve voting rights or on lawsuits that would refine and enhance the meaning of equal protection under the law. All of this occurred within the context of embracing the American Dream and seeking to make it more inclusive; the underlying soundness of the American Dream never came into question. Similarly, antipoverty warriors concentrated on making opportunities more available to poor people, not on promoting structural change in the economy through redistribution of income, because to do so would presume that there was something wrong with the existing system.

Yet it had not always been the case that liberalism was so defined. Nor would it necessarily remain so in the future. Indeed, the ways that liberalism has changed in meaning provide a critical prism through which to understand twentieth-century American politics. Although Hodgson applied his definition of the liberal consensus specifically to the period from 1948 to 1968, it by no means exhausts the way the term *liberal* has altered over time. If we presume a longer time frame, from the New Deal through the beginning of the twenty-first century, the shifting definitions of liberalism provide an ideal vehicle through which to understand what has and has not taken place in American society. In this larger framework, each change in the conception of liberalism potentially represents a pivotal variable in shaping America's political history during this period.

Clearly, the New Deal constitutes the beginning point for any discussion of liberalism. The Great Depression had ushered in a period of unrelenting suffering for the American people. More than 25 percent of American workers were unemployed; factory wages had shrunk from $12 billion to $7 billion; more than five thousand banks had failed; nine million people had lost their life savings; and millions of mortgages were foreclosed. Whatever else the 1932 election accomplished, it signified frustration and dissatisfaction with a government that did nothing to respond to such suffering, and it mandated a new approach. Franklin D. Roosevelt's "New Deal," however embryonic and ambiguous it might have been in the rhetoric of the 1932 campaign, represented the starting point of a new kind of politics.

But what would liberalism mean? Was it antibusiness or probusiness? For agrarian reform and support of tenant farmers, or dedicated to the buttressing of big agriculture? In favor of government planning and state-owned enterprises, or devoted to private enterprise? For civil rights for minorities, or content with the persistence of white supremacy? A defender of civil liberties, or a foe? Committed to radically altering the existing distribution of wealth and income, or supportive of the status quo? Dedicated to using government as an agent to bring health, education, and security to average citizens, or committed more to individualism and self-determination?

The answer, it turned out, was all of the above. Like the multiple and contradictory themes of his 1932 campaign speeches, Roosevelt's administration represented a potpourri of policy initiatives, many of them seemingly unrelated to each other and at times in direct conflict. The National Industrial Recovery Act essentially represented a partnership of big government and big business, with the one colluding with the other in price-fixing and economic planning. The Agricultural Adjustment Administration did the same for big agriculture while displacing thousands of sharecroppers and tenant farmers—though the Tennessee Valley Authority foreshadowed what government ownership of utilities might mean.

Relief policies, on the other hand, brought money and jobs to millions of the unemployed while putting in place new schools, hospitals, roads, airports, and post offices that would benefit, at government expense, the society as a whole. Blacks found for the first time a reason to vote Democratic, largely because of Roosevelt's economic relief measures; yet Roosevelt would not support a federal antilynching bill, preferring to maintain his alliance with the white supremacist Democratic leadership of the South. Labor received new legitimacy and encouragement from the Wagner Act, which helped fuel the creation of mass industrial unions in auto, steel, rubber, and the electrical industry; yet Roosevelt came on board only at the end, when passage of the Wagner Act seemed a certainty. Social Security brought a measure of stability and support to millions of senior citizens, yet it was based on a regressive taxing system that in fact injured the economy. In short, far from representing a coherent ideological statement of what liberalism meant and where it should lead, the New Deal expressed in tantalizing and confusing ways the multiple possibilities implicit in government's playing a new and critical role in the nation's economy.

There were, however, significant themes, themselves often contradictory, that emerged from the New Deal: recovery, relief, and reform. Of the three, only relief could be called a significant success. With millions of the unemployed given public-works jobs and welfare payments, and with myriad new welfare measures from Social Security to disability and unemployment insurance, a floor of government support for the basics of existence became a foundational pillar of liberalism. Recovery proved less attainable, not really occurring until the huge defense buildups that accompanied World War II. Even though by 1936 agriculture and industry had come back, the cutback in federal spending implemented by Roosevelt in 1937 precipitated a new recession that in many ways went back to the worst days of the 1930s.

The New Deal legacy is most confusing in the area of reform. Arguably, signals existed that portended a reshaping of American society. In addition to the Wagner Act, which helped send union membership soaring from two million members in 1930 to sixteen million by 1944, antitrust actions increased during the second Roosevelt administration, there was some talk about national health insurance, and modestly progressive changes occurred in tax policy. The New Deal political coalition of urban ethnics, minorities, union members, and farmers also held the potential of coming together around a variety of social welfare measures. Most suggestive of change, perhaps, was Roosevelt's political rhetoric in 1936 and 1937. Denouncing "economic royalists" and "malefactors of wealth," Roosevelt pledged in his second inaugural to focus on the "one third of a nation that is ill-housed, ill-clothed, and ill-fed." Such words suggested, potentially at least, a rallying cry for change more systemic than incremental.

Yet it was not to be. Roosevelt's plan to pack the Supreme Court in 1937 precipitated construction of a new conservative coalition in Congress that persistently frustrated his quest for further reform legislation. The failure of Roosevelt's effort to purge Congress of its most reactionary members in 1938 represented another critical setback. The onset of war in Europe and the growing national preoccupation with World War II put domestic reform on a back burner, culminating in Roosevelt's 1943 proclamation that Dr. Win-the-War had now taken precedence over Dr. New Deal. All of this led historian Alan Brinkley to conclude that the era of reform was over and that liberalism had moved from a focus on the potential restructuring of society and from grappling with underlying social problems to an immersion in what he has called "administrative liberalism" and the construction of the modern social welfare state.

In the meantime other issues critical to the liberal agenda surged to the forefront. For the entire history of America, race has constituted the original sin staining the nation's profession to be a democratic republic. The constitutional protections erected after the Civil War to provide equal treatment before the law became a victim of a new alliance between northern economic interests and southern Democrats, with the infamous era of Jim Crow installing a system of economic, political, and social segregation that deprived African Americans not only of the opportunity for economic well-being, but also of all political and social rights. Now, with the growth of industrial unions, at least some of them committed to greater racial equality, and with a government making war on Hitler's racist regime, African Americans insisted that they would no longer be left out of the nation's democratic equation. From World War II all the way through to the end of the century, nothing would affect the fate of liberalism, or its definition, more than the issue of how Americans should come to grips with their oldest problem.

Simultaneously, the terms of the liberal debate became hostage to developments in foreign policy, and specifically the Cold War. For a generation, anticommunism shaped the options perceived as possible within the liberal agenda, as well as how they might be pursued. Moreover, the predominance of a Cold War mentality, particularly vis-à-vis the war in Vietnam, created a new crisis for the viability of liberalism. Radicals from the 1960s raised new questions about the soundness of the nation's social and economic system that had not been heard since the late 1930s. In a new era, shaped by the ideological values articulated by Richard Nixon and Ronald Reagan, older issues of the welfare state, minority group politics, and individual versus collective responses to social problems assumed a new and critical urgency. By 1988 the word "liberal" itself had become almost a smear, with confusion once again rampant within those political circles that remained part of the New Deal legacy.

In many respects the person who more than anyone else has framed our thinking about the New Deal and its legacy for liberalism is William E. Leuchtenburg. As author of the prizewinning classic *Franklin D. Roosevelt and the New Deal* (1964), Leuchtenburg set forth the parameters of all future discussions of the New Deal. A dedicated liberal in his own right—Leuchtenburg spent his first years after college working as a field agent for the Fair Employment Practices lobby and Americans for Democratic Action—he carefully and precisely dissected the political and methodological tensions that shaped New Deal policies. It was Leuchtenburg who described the New Deal as a "broker state" characterized by political leadership that sought to balance interest group against interest group. As a result, Leuchtenburg pointed out, the New Deal became a "parallelogram of pressure groups"—a political construction that inevitably doomed any direct challenge to vested interests in the society. Roosevelt might seek to balance the political influence of business and labor, but to do so ignored the fundamental disparity of power from which the two began.

Leuchtenburg's ultimate contribution to the liberal legacy of the New Deal was threefold. First, he showed with compelling insight that whatever its proponents and detractors said, the New Deal was at best a "half-way revolution." It may have dramatically extended the power of the state and created an irreversible model for government involvement in the economy, but it did little to alter the balance of forces within society. Social Security, Leuchtenburg pointed out, was "astonishingly inept and conservative," taking funds out of the economy, ignoring those most in need of help (farm laborers and domestic workers), and failing to deal with issues of health. Notwithstanding Roosevelt's rhetoric about "economic royalists" and aiding the poorest third of the nation, tenant farmers received little if any assistance, the wealthiest 1 percent of the population increased its share of the nation's resources, and only moderate steps were taken to address the underlying oppression of black Americans.

Second, Leuchtenburg provided the key answer to the question of where the New Deal had come from. In the midst of a sometimes interminable debate between those who traced part of Franklin D. Roosevelt's legislative initiatives to the New Nationalism of Theodore Roosevelt and part to the New Freedom of Woodrow Wilson, Leuchtenburg came forward with the critical intervention that the major prototype for the New Deal, both in theory and in personnel, was the massive federal intervention in the economy that had occurred in World War I. The same dollar-a-year executives who had run wartime agencies in 1917–18 came back to Washington to manage the NRA and AAA, latter-day parallels of the War Industries Board and the War Food Board; the rhetoric of the war against depression drew heavily on the precedent of the sloganeering of World War I; and the image of a nonpartisan wartime coalition government, including the overarching symbol of the NRA's "Blue Eagle," pervaded Roosevelt's approach to the national crisis. Leuchtenburg had found the critical ingredients—human as well as institutional—that more satisfactorily than anything else provided an explanation for where these ideas originated.

Third, Leuchtenburg has shaped a generation of scholarship on the New Deal and its legacies for liberalism by the students he has trained. Few American historians have so directly sculpted and trained successive generations of scholars. More than twenty of Leuchtenburg's students have published at least two books apiece. Many of these books have in turn defined the parameters of the political and social history of the last fifty years. A literary craftsman of exquisite taste, Leuchtenburg imparted to his students both the encouragement for each to find his or her own voice, and the insistence that, whichever voice was chosen, it must be expressed with clarity, conciseness, and elegance. "Writing," he has said, "is its own justification, the way a beautiful day is, or eating a peach. There is a feeling of joy when you have done something well."

As Leuchtenburg guided his students into the profession, he also empowered them to ask new questions about the liberal tradition. Although proud to be called a "political historian," even in an age when that label occasionally generated scorn rather than applause, Leuchtenburg pushed those he mentored to break new ground, studying such issues as gender, race, homosexuality, and the media. In his own scholarship, he incorporated some of these new insights, raising questions in such books as *A Troubled Feast* (1973) about the influence of economic prosperity and suburbanization on the liberal tradition, and noting the historical discontinuities in political history created by massive social movements led by women and blacks.

It is appropriate, therefore, that this set of inquiries into the legacy of the New Deal and American liberalism should come from those who have benefited most from William E. Leuchtenburg's mentorship. These essays deal with many aspects of liberalism's ever-changing definition. Alan Brinkley chronicles the experimental evolution of the New Deal, showing the powerful but competing pressures that made the New Deal into such a fascinating political potpourri. Alonzo Hamby traces the Democratic Party's evolving effort to incorporate the multiple traditions of the New Deal as it moved forward into the Cold War world. Richard Fried, in turn, assesses the impact of McCarthyism, one of the most important political realities for the liberal tradition, yet one that is not necessarily well comprehended. Richard Polenberg eloquently describes the impact of the liberal tradition, and its limitations, on the brilliant father of the atomic bomb, Robert Oppenheimer. And Mel Urofsky shows how the Roosevelt Court charted, in profound ways, the legal playing field on which the debate about the meaning of liberalism would be conducted. Significantly, four of the essays in this volume—by Harvard Sitkoff, William Chafe, Steven Lawson, and Cynthia Harrison—look at the legacy of liberalism from the perspective of issues of race, gender, and, to a lesser degree, class. In the ongoing attempt to develop a liberal ideology that incorporates both the rights of individuals and the importance of collective identities on people's lives and fortunes, questions of race and gender have been the most nagging and troublesome, forcing a reassessment of how and whether the liberal tradition speaks to our most fundamental social divisions. And Otis Graham, in a provocative overview of liberalism from the New Deal to the New Millennium, brings together all of these themes, suggesting just where and when liberalism may have lost its anchor.

The purpose of these essays is not to answer all questions about liberalism, but to engage these questions in ways that may prove helpful to delineating key issues for future scholars. We dedicate this book to William E. Leuchtenburg in tribute to all he has done to make twentieth-century political and social history such a vibrant and vital field of inquiry, and in gratitude for the model he has presented to all of us of how to research tirelessly, argue fairly and tenaciously, and write gracefully and elegantly.

THE ACHIEVEMENT OF
AMERICAN LIBERALISM

1

THE NEW DEAL EXPERIMENTS

Alan Brinkley

Historians have expressed impatience with Franklin Roosevelt at times. He was, they have complained, a man without an ideological core and thus unable to exercise genuine leadership. He was a compromiser, a trimmer. He "was content in large measure to follow public opinion," Richard Hofstadter once wrote, and thus charted no clear path. He allowed the existing political landscape to dictate his course, James MacGregor Burns lamented, instead of reshaping the Democratic Party to serve his own purposes. Such complaints were common among Roosevelt's contemporaries as well, most of all among those who had invested the greatest hopes in him. There seemed to be something almost slippery about the man—with his eagerness to please everyone with whom he talked, with his ability to persuade people expressing two opposing views that he agreed with them both, with his tendency to allow seemingly contradictory initiatives to proceed simultaneously. "When I talk to him, he says 'Fine! Fine! Fine!'" Huey Long once complained. "But Joe Robinson [one of Long's ideological nemeses] goes to see him the next day and again he says 'Fine! Fine! Fine!' Maybe he says 'Fine' to everybody." Henry Stimson, Roosevelt's secretary of war from 1940 on, was constantly frustrated by this enigmatic man—so much so that not long after Roosevelt died, Stimson privately expressed relief that in Harry Truman, the new president, he finally had someone willing to make a clear-cut and unequivocal decision. Roosevelt's fundamentally political nature—his rejection of all but a few fixed principles and his inclination to measure each decision against its likely popular reaction—may have been a significant weakness, as some of his critics have claimed, or his greatest strength, as others insist. But it was the essence of the man.[1]

So, too, was the New Deal a confusing amalgam of ideas and impulses—a program that seemed to have something in it to please everyone except those who sought a discernible ideological foundation. "Take a method and try it," Roosevelt liked to say. "If it fails, admit it frankly and try another. But above all, try something." Such statements have sometimes led critics and admirers alike to conclude that the New Deal reflected nothing but pragmatic responses to immediate problems; that it was, as Hofstadter described, little more than a "chaos of experimentation." "To look upon these programs as the result of a unified plan," Roosevelt's erstwhile advisor Raymond Moley wrote in a sour memoir published after his falling out with the president, "was to believe that the accumulation of stuffed snakes, baseball pictures, school flags, old tennis shoes, carpenter's tools, geometry books, and chemistry sets in a boy's bedroom could have been put there by an interior decorator." But it also reflected Roosevelt's instinct for action—his belief in, if nothing else, the obligation of the leaders of government to work aggressively and affirmatively to deal with the nation's problems.[2]

Roosevelt was no ideologue; but neither he himself nor the New Deal he created lived in an ideological vacuum. The blizzard of experiments that coexisted, and sometimes clashed, within the Roosevelt administration were the product not just of short-term, pragmatic efforts to solve immediate problems. They were the product too of the well of inherited ideologies that he and other New Dealers had derived from the reform battles of the first third of the century and from which they felt at liberty to pick and choose as they saw fit. The New Deal may have had no coherence, but it did have foundations—many of them.

Roosevelt entered office convinced that he faced three urgent tasks. He needed to devise policies to end the Great Depression. He needed to create programs to help the millions in distress weather hard times until prosperity returned. And he needed, most New Dealers believed, to frame lasting reforms that would prevent a similar crisis from occurring again. He made strenuous efforts to fulfill all of these tasks. And while he succeeded fully at none of them, he achieved a great deal in the trying.

Roosevelt's first and most compelling task was to restore prosperity. But in truth the New Dealers had no idea how to end the Depression because they had only the vaguest idea of what had caused it. Some believed the Depression was a result of overproduction, which had driven down prices and launched the spiraling deflation. Others sensed that it was a result of under-consumption, of the inadequate incomes of working people and hence the inadequate markets for industrial goods. Some believed the problem was the composition of the currency, others that it was a lack of "business confi-dence." Few people in any of these groups (and in many others, with differ-ent diagnoses still) had any persuasive prescriptions for how to solve the problems they cited. Virtually no one yet understood the Keynesian eco-nomic ideas that would in later years inspire concerted, and at times effec-tive, government efforts to fight recessions.

Just as the Federal Reserve Board in the first years of the Depression had raised interest rates at a time of massive deflation when rates should have gone down, Roosevelt entered office convinced that one of his most pressing tasks was to reduce federal spending to protect the government's solvency at a time when the most effective response to the crisis would have been sub-stantial deficits. His first week in office, he won passage of the Economy Act, which slashed the federal payroll and reduced veterans benefits. And while he never succeeded in actually balancing the budget, for more than five years he never stopped trying. In time-honored fashion, Roosevelt also tinkered with the currency First he sabotaged an international economic conference that was meeting in London to stabilize world currencies. (He sent his adviser, Raymond Moley, to represent him there. Then he repudiated the agreements Moley was attempting to forge by releasing what became known as the "bombshell" message, in which Roosevelt informed the conference that the United States would not abide by its results whatever they might be. The meeting quickly dissolved in failure.) Then he loosened the dollar's attach-ment to the gold standard. Later, he engaged in a fanciful program of buying gold on the international market in an effort to lower the value of the dollar and make American goods more attractive in world markets—an arcane panacea that may have done little harm but certainly did no good. Roosevelt did act effectively to stem the corrosive banking crisis that was his most im-mediate challenge on taking office. He declared a "bank holiday," passed emergency bank legislation to give the government authority to review the fi-nancial health of banks before allowing them to reopen, and then later won passage of more substantial banking reform that created federal insurance of banking deposits and strengthened the Federal Reserve System. That stopped the financial panic and saved the banks. But to the larger crisis in the nation's economy he had no effective solution.

Most historians and economists now agree that the best, perhaps the only, way to end the Great Depression quickly in 1933 would have been to increase total spending rapidly and substantially. And because the private sector was trapped in a deflationary spiral that made such increases virtually impossible for businesses and individuals, the only agent for doing so was the government. But during its first five years, most New Dealers recognized the need for public spending only dimly—and constantly sought to balance that recognition against their lingering commitment to fiscal orthodoxy. Not until 1938, after a premature effort to balance the budget had helped trigger a severe recession, did Roosevelt openly endorse the idea of public spending as a stimulus to economic growth—validating the core of what would soon be known as Keynesian economics in the process. Even then, the fiscal stimulus was much smaller than economic conditions required.[3] In the meantime, the New Deal had to content itself with a largely inadvertent contribution to purchasing power and total spending: its public works projects and its increasingly elaborate programs of relief to the distressed and the unemployed. Not until World War II did government spending increase dramatically enough to bring the Depression wholly to an end.

Perhaps Roosevelt's most important contribution to the nation's short-term economic fortunes was to dispel the broad sense of panic that was threatening to destroy not just the banking system, but the entire financial and industrial structure of the nation. He did so in part through the flurry of legislation he steered through a compliant Congress in his famous first "hundred days." But he did so as well by thrusting his own personality into the center of public life. His firm and confident inaugural address—with its ringing promise that "the only thing we have to fear is fear itself" and its stern warnings of quasi-military responses to the crisis if more conventional means did not work—established him as a leader determined to do whatever it took to avert disaster. His warm, comforting "fireside chats" over the radio, in which he patiently explained what the government was doing and what it meant to ordinary people, made him the first president whose voice and image became an ordinary part of everyday life. Soon portraits of Roosevelt were appearing in the living rooms and kitchens of farmers, working people, and others all over the country. Roosevelt did not end the Depression. But he challenged the despair that had gripped so many Americans in the last, lugubrious year of the Hoover presidency and helped them to believe that the government could do something about their problems.

In the absence of an effective program for ending the Depression, the New Deal's efforts to provide relief became all the more important. State, local, and private relief efforts were collapsing under the unprecedented demands

placed on them, and Roosevelt stepped into the void with a series of new programs. In his first months in office, he created the Civilian Conservation
Corps, which took young, unemployed, urban men and gave them jobs working in national parks and forests. This was a plan the president (who retained
a preference for rural life despite his many years in New York City and who
voiced his cousin Theodore's faith in the value of the "strenuous life"—a life,
of course, now barred to him) particularly liked. He created the Federal Emergency Relief Administration, which offered financial assistance to state relief
agencies, and some months later the Civil Works Administration, a federally
managed jobs program administered by the former social worker Harry Hopkins. The New Deal launched other programs as well, offering financial assistance to imperiled homeowners, farmers, and small businesses. Even taken together, these early relief programs were modest when measured against the
gravity of the problems they were trying to address. For the people they
helped, they were a godsend. For millions of others, they were simply an al-
luring but unattainable promise.

These early experiments in providing relief revealed both the extent and
the limits of the New Deal commitment to social welfare. Roosevelt and
those around him clearly rejected the rigid conservative views of those who
considered any aid to the poor dangerous and improper. In 1931, as governor of New York, Roosevelt had challenged that orthodoxy. Government had
a clear responsibility, he told the state legislature, "when widespread economic conditions render large numbers of men and women incapable of
supporting either themselves or their families because of circumstances beyond their control which make it impossible for them to find remunerative
labor. To these unfortunate citizens aid must be extended by government—
not as a matter of charity but as a matter of social duty."[4] As president, he
continued to reject the conservative argument against social assistance.

But Roosevelt, Hopkins, and most of the other critical figures in shaping
the New Deal welfare state also feared the debilitating effects of what was still
widely known as "the dole." Harry Hopkins, looking at the effects of the
FERA in 1933, said, "I don't think anybody can go on year after year, month
after month accepting relief without affecting his character in some way un-
favorably. It is probably going to undermine the independence of hundreds
of thousands of families. . . . I look upon this as a great national disaster." The
president himself proclaimed in 1934, "I do not want to think that it is the
destiny of any American to remain permanently on the relief roles."[5] Instead,
the New Deal turned to an approach with which it felt much more comfortable: work relief, providing the unemployed with jobs. "Give a man a dole,

and you save his body and destroy his spirit," Hopkins said. "Give him a job
. . . and you save both the body and the spirit. It saves his skill. It gives him a
chance to do something socially useful."[6] Both the CCC and the CWA had
been experiments in work relief. In 1935, with unemployment still a corrosive problem, the New Deal created a much larger experiment: the Works
Progress Administration.

The mission of the WPA was to fund public works programs all over the
country. Hopkins became its administrator; and while he hoped to provide
useful and necessary work, his first priority was to provide immediate assistance to the unemployed. Hopkins spent the money allotted to him lavishly,
rapidly, and with remarkable creativity. The WPA built hospitals, schools,
airports, theaters, roads, hotels in national parks, monuments, post offices,
and federal buildings all over the country. It created some of the most imaginative government projects in American history: the Federal Theater Project, which hired actors, directors, playwrights, and other unemployed theater people to write and produce plays, skits, and revues all across the
country; the Federal Arts Project, which recruited unemployed artists, paid
them a wage, and put them to work creating public art; the Federal Writers'
Project, which hired writers to produce state and city guidebooks and to collect oral histories from ordinary men and women (including former slaves).
Most of all, the WPA pumped desperately needed money into the economy.
In the process, it raised popular expectations of government and helped le-
gitimize the idea of public assistance to the poor. But it did not become the
model for a lasting federal role in social welfare. Congress abolished it in
1943, and federally funded jobs programs have been rare and generally modest in the years since.

What did become important and lasting parts of the American welfare
state were two forms of public assistance created by the Social Security Act of
1935, the single most important piece of social legislation in American history. The first was public assistance, which the framers of the Act considered
to be the less important of the two—a relatively small, limited commitment,
they believed, to help certain, specified categories of people who clearly were
unable to help themselves. It institutionalized, in effect, the longstanding distinction in American attitudes toward poverty between the deserving and
undeserving poor, or (as the New Dealers themselves described them) between employables and unemployables. New Dealers had opposed generalized relief because they feared giving a dole to people who could and should
work. But the Social Security Act identified groups of people who, its framers
believed, could not and should not work. Specifically, it provided direct as-

sistance to the disabled (primarily the blind), to the elderly poor (people presumably too old to work), and most important (although no one realized at the time how important it would be) to dependent children. The Aid to Dependent Children program (later Aid to Families with Dependent Children) eventually achieved dimensions far beyond even the wildest imaginings of those who created it and struggled constantly for real legitimacy for over sixty years until finally succumbing to conservative opposition in 1996.

The Act also set up two important programs of social insurance: unemployment compensation and the old age pensions that we now associate most clearly with the name Social Security. Unlike ADC, these insurance programs had little difficulty achieving political legitimacy. Indeed, they remained through the end of the twentieth century among the most popular, even sacrosanct, of all the functions of the federal government. Unemployment insurance and old-age pensions were able to entrench themselves so successfully in part because they were universal—because virtually everyone who worked eventually stood to benefit from them. But they were also popular because they represented such a safe and conservative approach to welfare that many people (including many New Dealers) did not consider them welfare at all. They were, Americans came to believe, "insurance," much like private-sector insurance and pension plans. They were funded not out of general revenues, but out of special, separate taxes on employers and workers, whose revenues into separate and presumably inviolable trust funds. (Social Security was not even included in the official federal budget until the late 1960s.) Recipients would, in theory, receive benefits they had earned and paid for (although in fact the program was more redistributive than its popular image suggested, and many people received either much more or much less in benefits than they had paid into it in contributions).

The Social Security Act, in other words, set up two forms of welfare—separate and highly unequal. Public assistance (most notably ADC) was the product of assumptions about the difference between the deserving and the undeserving, and it was both stingier in its benefits and much more vulnerable to public hostility than its social-insurance partner in birth. Social insurance, which rested on no such distinction, was more generous from the beginning and enjoyed much greater public support. It is no coincidence that one of these programs—public assistance—was a program whose benefits went disproportionately to women and that the other—social insurance—was a program whose benefits went, at least at first, principally to white men. That was not because the Social Security program was devised by men; many women were centrally involved in shaping these programs as well. It was be-

cause both the men and the women who devised these programs agreed that
women should be treated differently; that public policy should assume that
married women would be supported by their husbands and that only when
a man was absent from the home should a woman be eligible for assistance.
Women, unlike men, would need public assistance when left alone, particularly when left alone with children. This was a system (in both its public assistance and social insurance elements) that was designed to preserve the traditional family wage system. Unemployment insurance and old-age pensions
provided a safety net for the wage earner or retiree (although not, at first, to
all earners, since until the 1940s the program excluded large categories of
working people—including agricultural workers, domestics, and other
groups that were largely black or female or both). ADC provided assistance,
somewhat grudgingly, primarily to those unfortunate women and children
who found themselves outside the family wage system.[7]

The most ambitious effort of the first hundred days was a series of measures
to reshape the American economy in more basic and lasting ways. The reform effort took several different shapes. Some reflected the belief in government regulation of concentrated power that New Dealers had derived
from the progressive reform crusades of the early twentieth century and from
their suspicion of what Louis Brandeis had once called the "curse of bigness."
Their inspiration was Woodrow Wilson's New Freedom, or at least those elements of it (mostly rhetorical) that warned of the power of large corporate
institutions and envisioned a more decentralized and competitive economy.
At the instigation of such self-proclaimed Brandeisians as Felix Frankfurter,
Thomas Corcoran, and Benjamin Cohen, and with the enthusiastic support
of the inveterate antimonopolist Sam Rayburn in the House of Representatives, the New Deal created a new agency to regulate the stock and bond markets—the Securities and Exchange Commission, which set out to prevent the
kind of reckless speculation and occasional fraud that had created such in-
stability in the financial markets in 1929. It produced the Federal Communications Commission, the Civil Aeronautics Board, and other agencies to supervise sensitive areas of the economy. Later, the same forces helped inspire
a controversial (and only partially successful) effort in 1935 to break the
power of utilities monopolies: the Utilities Holding Company Act. Later still,
they won passage of the Fair Labor Standards Act of 1938, which created a
minimum wage, a forty-hour work week, and a ban on child labor; and they
pressed for the creation of the Temporary National Economic Committee—
a highly publicized inquiry into monopoly power run jointly by the White

House and Congress that ran from 1938 to 1943, produced mountains of data, but failed to inspire any concrete reforms.

Other New Dealers envisioned a much more forceful kind of national planning, rooted in the progressive-era faith in system, process, and expertise. Implicit in their efforts was an acceptance of large-scale organization as the basic feature of the modern economy and a belief in the need for some kind of centralized coordination and control. "The essential conditions of efficiency," Herbert Croly had written early in the century, "is always concentration of responsibility." Among the New Dealers who shared that belief was Rexford Tugwell. He was certain that new administrative structures could be created, new techniques of management and control devised, that would allow a modern society to achieve what Walter Lippmann had once called "mastery" over the forces that threatened to overwhelm it. Among his heroes was Theodore Roosevelt, who had begun in 1910 to articulate the ambitious vision of state supervision of the economy he called the "New Nationalism." "We should," the earlier Roosevelt had declared, "enter upon a course of supervision, control, and regulation of these great corporations—a regulation which we should not fear, if necessary to bring to the point of control of monopoly prices."[8]

No effective, centralized planning mechanisms ever emerged out of the New Deal, to Tugwell's lasting chagrin—despite the efforts of a series of committed but politically ineffective agencies charged with "planning" that survived within the government from 1933 to 1943. But the Roosevelt administration did launch some important, if limited, federal planning efforts. The most prominent of them was the Tennessee Valley Authority, a dramatic experiment in flood control and public power that was also for a time an ambitious effort to plan the future of an entire region.

The TVA's most ambitious planning efforts ultimately came to naught. Its more lasting significance may have been as a spur to another New Deal approach to political economy: a wide-ranging experiment in what the historian Jordan Schwarz has called "state capitalism" and what in contemporary political discourse is known as "public investment."[9] The commitment to public investment was not new to the Roosevelt administration, as New Dealers were quick to point out in response to their critics. The federal government had invested in roads, waterways, railroads, universities, and other public projects throughout its history. It had built the Panama Canal. Herbert Hoover, whom New Dealers spent a generation demonizing as a reactionary, had created the Reconstruction Finance Corporation in 1932, which included among its many missions government investment in public works and which remained under Franklin Roosevelt one of the government's most important economic instruments. But the New Deal went much further than any previous administration in making the state an instrument of capitalist development. It spent billions of dollars constructing highways and bridges, building dams and other hydroelectric projects, creating irrigation systems and other water projects in California and the Southwest. Its Rural Electrification Administration carried electrical power to millions of rural Americans.

Federally financed infrastructure projects provided short-term stimuli to the economy by creating jobs and markets for industrial goods. But they had an even more important long-term legacy. The New Deal's public works projects were concentrated disproportionately in the Southwest and the West, in part because men committed to the development of those regions played critical roles in allocating resources—among them Jesse Jones of Texas, chairman of the RFC. As a result (and by design), they laid the groundwork for the postwar transformation of the American Southwest from an arid, sparsely populated region with limited economic growth into a booming "Sunbelt."

But most New Dealers considered their most important initiatives to be their efforts to reform the two major segments of the modern economy: industry and agriculture. In that effort, the most powerful traditions were not the great progressive battles between Roosevelt and Wilson, between the New Nationalism and the New Freedom, but the more immediate and more resonant legacy of World War I.

The historian William Leuchtenburg was among the first to note the critical role the war played in shaping the New Deal's approach to the Depression. The war, he noted, became the Roosevelt administration's principal metaphor. In his inaugural address, the new president promised to treat the task of fighting the Depression "as we would treat the emergency of war," and he called on the "great army of the people" to embrace the effort "with a unity of duty hitherto invoked only in time of armed strife."[10] But the war was not just a metaphor; it was a model. For the wartime experiments in economic mobilization had inspired bright dreams among many reformers of an "ordered economic world" that might be recreated in peacetime. The War Industries Board of 1918, many liberals fervently (and not entirely accurately) believed, had rationalized and coordinated industrial activity under the supervision of the "super-manager" Bernard Baruch. Surely, influential New Dealers argued (just as many aspiring reformers had argued through the

1920s), something similar could work comparable miracles now. The most important result of such beliefs was the National Industrial Recovery Act of June 1933.[11]

The origins of the NIRA were inauspicious. It was drafted hastily and pushed through Congress suddenly—a response not just to longstanding visions of reform, although it was that, but also to several alternative industrial-recovery measures moving through Congress that the president did not like: a wages and hours bill, sponsored by Senator Hugo Black of Alabama, which proposed imposing a thirty-hour work week on industry as a way to spread work around and reduce unemployment; and a number of proposals for "vast public works programs," programs much vaster than Roosevelt was willing to consider. The NIRA was, in part, an effort by Roosevelt to forestall these measures.

It was, many New Dealers believed, the most important piece of legislation in American history. And it was packed with provisions designed to placate the many warring factions who had a stake in reform. It created the Public Works Administration, to satisfy the many demands for new job-creation measures—a large and important program that built dams and other major infrastructure projects, but that proceeded so carefully and punctiliously under the directorship of Secretary of the Interior Harold Ickes that it failed to provide much in the way of short-term economic stimulus. The NIRA also tried to protect small businesses from monopoly power, but with regulations too weak to have any real impact. And it provided a legal guarantee of organized labor's right to organize and bargain collectively with employers (Section 7a, the first such guarantee the government had ever provided, albeit one with no effective enforcement mechanisms). At its heart, however, was the effort to impose on the Depression economy the same kind of enlightened coordination that New Dealers liked to believe Baruch and his War Industries Board had imposed on the wartime economy. As such, it was a victory for an industry-led trade association movement, led by Gerard Swope of General Electric, which had been arguing for two years that if businesses could be released from antitrust pressures and allowed to cooperate in setting production levels, prices, and wages, they could break the deflationary spiral and restore prosperity.[12]

The act created a new federal agency, the National Recovery Administration, with authority to work with representatives of business and labor to produce wage and price codes to stabilize various industries. Within each major industry, a new code authority would set floors below which no one could lower prices or wages; it would also set quotas for production; and it would have the power to enforce compliance. Government administrators would play a role in the process, but the real authority would lie with the business leaders themselves. The NRA would, in effect, allow industries to operate as cartels. It has often been described, with considerable justification, as an effort to create an American form of corporatism. "Many good men voted this new charter with misgivings," Roosevelt said in signing the bill. "I do not share their doubts. I had a part in the great cooperation of 1917 and 1918 and it is my faith that we can count on our industry once more to join in our general purpose to lift this new threat."[13]

The NRA swung into action quickly and impressively. Within weeks, almost every major industry had drawn up a code and had agreed to abide by its provisions; and the agency's energetic director—General Hugh Johnson, former director of the World War I draft—succeeded in whipping up broad popular excitement about the experiment and its iconography. The famous NRA Blue Eagle seemed to be everywhere—in shop windows, and on posters, emblazoned on banners carried in "Blue Eagle" parades (one of which, in New York, was the largest parade in the city's history—larger than the great celebration that had greeted Charles Lindbergh on his return from Paris nearly a decade before). Thousands of school children in San Francisco celebrated the NRA by assembling on a playing field for photographers in the shape of an eagle. The owner of the Philadelphia professional football team renamed it the "Eagles" in honor of the NRA.

But the initial enthusiasm could not disguise the fundamental problems at the heart of the experiment. And within a year, the entire effort was a shambles. There were many reasons for this. The codes served the needs of large economic organizations reasonably well. They allowed big industrial firms to keep their prices up without having to fear being undercut by competitors. But small businesses often could not compete with larger firms *unless* they undercut them in price; forcing small businesses to charge the same as large ones, which the codes tried to do, often meant robbing them of their only access to the market. Despite Section 7a, the code authorities permitted labor virtually no role at all in setting their guidelines. Workers organized, but companies continued to refuse to bargain with them. And the codes, therefore, became vehicles not just for keeping prices up, but for keeping wages down. Perhaps most damningly, the NRA catered to industry fears of overproduction; and it became a vehicle that helped manufacturers move in the direction of lower production, lower wages, and higher prices at a time when the economy needed just the opposite. Criticism mounted, and the government attempted to correct the problems; but its efforts to intervene more forcefully in the process produced opposition from business leaders, who resented this government interference in their internal affairs and who were, in any case, becoming disillusioned with the codes, which didn't seem to be working as well as they had hoped. By the end of 1934, the NRA was in chaos. And in the spring of 1935, it was ruled unconstitutional by the Supreme Court and abolished. The administration made no attempt to replace it.

The NRA was a failure, but it was not without legacies. It had emerged out of the efforts of businessmen to achieve one of their most cherished goals (cartelization), and it did help create some longstanding cartels in a few particularly troubled sectors of the economy, including oil, lumber, and aviation. On the whole, however, the NRA ended up contributing to the development that many of its supporters from the corporate world had most feared: the creation of an organized movement of independent labor unions sanctioned and protected by the government. The one aspect of the NRA that Congress did move to revive after the 1935 Supreme Court decision was Section 7a—the provision guaranteeing collective bargaining rights to workers. In 1935, it passed the National Labor Relations Act (the Wagner Act)—along with Social Security one of the two most important pieces of New Deal legislation—which not only restored, but greatly strengthened that provision and added many others. It created the National Labor Relations Board to police labor-management relations and use federal authority to stop unfair labor practices. The framers of the NIRA had accepted the provisions that led to the mobilization of trade unions, assuming that within the harmonious economy they believed the NRA would create unions would work cooperatively with management. But once the NRA was gone, the unions remained—not as partners in an effort to coordinate the industrial economy, but as adversarial organizations challenging the prerogatives of business. The effort to create a cooperative economy had, inadvertently, contributed to creating a more competitive one: an economy increasingly characterized by the clash of powerful interest groups.

In May 1933, a month before Congress passed the NIRA, the administration won passage of legislation creating the Agricultural Adjustment Act. The agricultural economy had been in something like a depression since the mid-1920s. And in an age when agriculture played a much larger role in the nation's economy than it later would, and when farmers were a much more important political force than they would later become, the crisis of the agrarian economy seemed almost as urgent to New Dealers as the crisis of the industrial one. The principal problems facing farmers were excess production and falling prices. The AAA, therefore, was an effort to end the chronic

agricultural overproduction and lift inadequate prices by limiting production and subsidizing farmers. It embodied the demands of the so-called
McNary-Haugenites—representatives of agricultural interests who had battled throughout the 1920s to create federal protection for farm prices. But
it went in some ways much further than these earlier proposals had done.

The AAA paid farmers to take acreage out of production. In the meantime, the government would guarantee them an equitable price for the goods
they did produce. Like the NRA, the AAA included provisions for protecting
small producers (in this case family farmers, tenants, and sharecroppers);
and it contained provisions for guarding against excessive concentration or
monopoly. But also like the NRA, the AAA in practice largely ignored those
provisions. Roosevelt had insisted that farmers themselves take the lead in
designing and administering any effort at reform. And the AAA soon came
to be dominated by the American Farm Bureau Federation, which represented
larger farmers and whose leaders had, in fact, helped draft the bill. The Farm
Bureau played a major role in administering the AAA, (much as trade associations had inspired and later dominated the NRA). The National Farmers
Union, a rival organization representing mostly small producers, was largely shut out. Most landowners simply ignored the provisions requiring them
to keep tenants on the land and to share AAA benefits with them. The program was particularly hard on African Americans, who formed a large proportion of the landless farmers in the South and who had even less political
leverage than their white counterparts. The workings of the AAA became
part of the process that drove many black farmers off the land and into
towns and cities.

But in other respects the AAA was a striking success. It stabilized farm
prices; it limited production; it won and retained the support of most commercial farmers. By 1936, farm prices had risen significantly for most major
commodities, and American farmers had become a much better organized
and more powerful interest group than ever before. The American Farm Bureau Federation, in particular, had expanded dramatically and was able to
put great pressure on Congress on behalf of its demands. When the Supreme
Court struck down the AAA as unconstitutional in 1935 (at about the same
time it struck down the NIRA), farmers were able to get is major provisions
re-enacted in slightly different form to meet the Court's objections. The essential AAA programs thus survive and became the basis for the system of
federal subsidization of farming that continued into the 1990s.

The NRA and the AAA were efforts—very similar efforts in many ways—
to introduce order, harmony, and coordination into the two major sectors of

the American economy. Both tried to stabilize unstable economies through restrictions on production and floors under prices. Both relied heavily on representatives of the private sector (the NRA on trade associations, the AAA on the Farm Bureau) to design and administer the programs. Both gave the government authority to enforce cooperation and punish violations. Both contained provisions to protect weaker members of the economy: workers and small businessmen in industry; tenant farmers and sharecroppers in agriculture. And both largely ignored those provisions.

And yet the results of these two experiments were dramatically different. The NRA utterly failed to stabilize industrial prices and production; its administrative structure dissolved in chaos; its legal authority was struck down by the Supreme Court and never revived; and the most important remnant of the experiment was the one element that businessmen had most opposed: the elevation of organized labor. The AAA, on the other hand, succeeded impressively in stabilizing farm prices and production; its administrative bodies worked reasonably effectively and attracted wide support; when the Court struck them down, they were quickly replaced; and the one area where the AAA did not live up to its original goals was the only area where the NRA did: the protection of the working class of the agricultural world, the sharecroppers and tenant farmers.

There are several reasons for this difference in results. Perhaps the most basic was that the agricultural and industrial economies were not at all alike. American industry was highly diverse, deeply fragmented, with large and perhaps irreconcilable divisions between the interests of large organizations and small ones, and between management and labor. No one element within the industrial economy was capable of dominating and bringing order to it; big business, small business, labor were all too powerful to be subordinated entirely to the others and too diverse and internally divided to be entirely dominant on their own. The agricultural economy was considerably more homogeneous. There were important competing factions within the agricultural economy to be sure—between large and small farmers, between landlords and tenants—but the large interests were relatively more powerful, and the smaller interests relatively weaker, than their counterparts in industry. The agricultural economy could work reasonably harmoniously on the basis of cooperation among its most powerful members; the industrial economy could not.

Another difference, as Theda Skocpol, Kenneth Finegold, and other scholars have argued, was in the administrative capacities of the two agencies. Both the NRA and the AAA required elaborate bureaucracies to supervise the complex economic arrangements they envisioned. The NRA was established more or less from scratch, outside any existing department. There were no existing institutions, no experts, no reliable information on which those running the agency could rely. It really had no choice but to turn to the industries and their trade associations to run the program. But the industries were themselves so fragmented that they couldn't bring order to the economy either. Given the absence of administrative capacity within the government, it is difficult to imagine how the NRA could possibly have worked. The AAA, by contrast, was part of the Agriculture Department, and it benefited from the beginning from that department's elaborate institutional network of statisticians and administrators. Agriculture was the only sector of the American economy that had already developed a public-policy elite of government experts, schooled in agricultural economics, experts with long experience in various federal farm programs, some of which had been in existence for twenty or thirty years. There was a tradition of government involvement with agriculture, even if a limited one; and the AAA built on and profited from that tradition.[14]

In retrospect, the New Deal has often seemed as significant for its failures and omissions as for the things it achieved. It did not end the Great Depression and the massive unemployment that accompanied it; only the enormous public and private spending for World War II finally did that. It did not, the complaints of conservative critics notwithstanding, transform American capitalism in any genuinely profound way; except for relatively limited reforms in labor relations and the securities markets, corporate power remained nearly as free from government regulation or control in 1945 as it had been in 1933. The New Deal did not end poverty or produce any significant redistribution of wealth; there was a significant downward distribution of wealth and income between 1929 and 1945—the first in more than a century and, as of the 1990s at least, also the last. But virtually all of that shift occurred during (and as a result of) World War II. Many of the New Deal's most prominent and innovative efforts—its work-relief programs, its community and national planning initiatives, its community-building efforts, its public works agencies—did not survive the war.

Nor did the New Deal do very much to address some of the principal domestic challenges of the postwar era. Roosevelt was not unsympathetic to the problems of African Americans, and he made sure that his relief programs offered benefits (even if not always equal ones) to blacks as well as whites. But he was never willing to challenge the central institutions of racial oppression in American life, fearful that to do so would damage the Democratic Party in the South and lose him the critical support of powerful southerners in Congress. Nor did the New Deal make any serious effort to address problems of gender inequality. Roosevelt appointed the first woman cabinet member, Secretary of Labor Frances Perkins, and he named more women to secondary positions in government than any president had ever done. Eleanor Roosevelt, through the prominent role she played in her husband's administration, helped serve as a symbol to many women of the possibilities of active public service. But New Deal programs (even those designed by New Deal women) continued mostly to reflect traditional assumptions about women's roles and made few gestures toward the aspirations of those women who sought economic independence and professional opportunities. The interest in individual and group rights that became so central to postwar liberalism—the source of both its greatest achievements and its greatest frustrations—was faint, and at times almost invisible, within the New Deal itself.

For all its limitations, however, the Roosevelt administration ranks among the most important of any presidency in American history. The New Deal created a series of new state institutions that greatly, and permanently, expanded the role of the federal government in American life. The government was now committed to providing at least minimal assistance to the poor, the unemployed, and the elderly; to protecting the rights of workers and unions; to stabilizing the banking system; to regulating the financial markets; to subsidizing agricultural production; and to doing many other things that had not previously been federal responsibilities. As a result of the New Deal, American political and economic life became much more competitive ever before, with workers, farmers, consumers, and others now able to press their demands upon the government in ways that in the past had been available only to the corporate world. (Hence the frequent description of the government the New Deal created as a "broker state," a state brokering the competing claims of numerous groups.) The New Deal literally transformed much of the American landscape through its vast public works and infrastructure projects. It revolutionized economic policy (although not until near its end) with its commitment to massive public spending as an antidote to recession. And it created broad new expectations of government among the American people, expectations that would survive—and indeed grow—in the decades that followed.

The New Deal also produced a new political coalition that sustained the Democrats as the majority party in national politics for more than a generation after its own end. After the election of 1936, the Democratic Party could claim the support of its traditional constituencies in the white South and the urban immigrant cities of the East and Midwest. It could also claim a much larger share than in the past of the working-class and farm votes, the vast majority of the African American vote in the North, and the overwhelming support of liberals and progressives of all stripes—many of whom had once found a home in the Republican Party.

And the Roosevelt administration generated or gave new life to a broad set of political ideas. Some of them faded from the New Deal even before Roosevelt's death and have played a relatively small role in American political life in the years since—but they resonate, if perhaps only faintly, with the impulses of many Americans in the early twenty-first century. There were experiments in fostering new forms of community—through the Tennessee Valley Authority, the Farm Security Administration, the Resettlement Administration, and other agencies, that sought to provide alternatives to the harsh, competitive individualism of the staggering capitalist economy of their day. There were innovative forms of social assistance, most notably the work relief programs of the Works Progress Association, which rested on a notion of the government as employer of last resort. And there was the continuing and at times impassioned effort to control the effects of monopoly—to keep the issue of concentrated economic power where it had been, at least intermittently, since the late nineteenth century and where it would not be again for at least a half century after Roosevelt's death: at the center of American political life. Roosevelt was the last president to talk openly about the power of the "money-changers in the temple," the "economic royalists," and the "new industrial dictatorship." No leading political figure since has spoken so directly about the power of "organized money," who were—he said in his extraordinary speech accepting the Democratic nomination in 1936—"unanimous in their hatred for me, and I welcome their hatred." "I should like to have it said of my first Administration," he continued, "that in it the forces of selfishness and lust for power met their match. . . . I should like to have it said of my second Administration that in it these forces met their master."[15]

That language—a language only rarely dominant and more rarely decisive even within the New Deal itself—has since become almost entirely lost to American politics, even though the problems it attempted to address—the problems associated with highly concentrated economic power and widening disparities of wealth and income—have survived.

But the Roosevelt administration also produced other, more hardily enduring ideas—ideas known to later generations as New Deal liberalism, ideas that sketched a vision of a government that would compensate for rather than challenge the limitations of capitalism, ideas that embraced Keynesian economics and a vision of a sturdy welfare state—that remained a source of inspiration and controversy for decades and that helped shape the next great experiments in liberal reform in the 1960s. Roosevelt may have had no coherent philosophy of his own. The New Deal may have been an amalgam of inconsistent and even contradictory measures. Its experiments may have seemed no more than what Rexford Tugwell once dismissively described as "pitiful patches" on an inadequate government, an exercise in "planting protective shrubbery on the slopes of a volcano." But the cumulative effect of Roosevelt's leadership and the New Deal's achievements was a dramatically changed political world that continues, more than half a century later, to define our own.

NOTES

1. Richard Hofstadter, *The American Political Tradition and the Men Who Made It* (New York: Alfred A. Knopf, 1948), 316; James MacGregor Burns, *Roosevelt: The Lion and the Fox* (New York: Harcourt Brace Jovanovich, 1956), 287–288; Alan Brinkley, *Voices of Protest: Huey Long, Father Coughlin, and the Great Depression* (New York: Alfred A. Knopf, 1982), 58. 2. Hofstadter, *The Age of Reform: From Bryan to F.D.R.* (New York: Alfred A. Knopf, 1955), 307; Raymond Moley, *After Seven Years: A Political Analysis of the New Deal* (New York: Harper & Row, 1939), 369–370.

3. See Alan Brinkley, *The End of Reform: New Deal Liberalism in Recession and War* (New York: Alfred A. Knopf, 1995), chaps. 4–5.

4. Frank Freidel, *Franklin D. Roosevelt: The Triumph* (Boston: Little, Brown, 1956), 216.

5. Arthur M. Schlesinger Jr., *The Coming of the New Deal* (Boston; Houghton Mifflin, 1959), 267; Samuel I. Rosenman, ed., *Public Papers and Address of Franklin D. Roosevelt,* 13 vols. (New York: Random House, 1938), 3:420.

6. Anthony J. Badger, *The New Deal: The Depression Years, 1933–1940* (New York: Hill & Wang, 1989), 200–201.

7. Theda Skocpol, *Protecting Soldiers and Mothers: The Political Origins of Social Policy in the United States* (Cambridge, Mass.: Harvard University Press, 1992), and Linda Gordon, *Pitied but Not Entitled: Single Mothers and the History of Welfare* (New York: Free Press, 1994), are the two most important studies of the gendered quality of the early welfare state. Skocpol's study ends before the New Deal but describes the pre-1930s history of gendered social provision. Gordon's study includes the creation of the Social Security Act itself.

8. Alan Brinkley, "The New Deal: Prelude," *Wilson Quarterly* 6 (1982): 50–61.

9. Jordan Schwarz, *The New Dealers: Power Politics in the Age of FDR* (New York: Alfred A. Knopf, 1993).

10. William E. Leuchtenburg, "The New Deal and the Analogue of War," originally appeared in 1964 and has been republished in Leuchtenburg, *The FDR Years: On Roosevelt and His Legacy* (New York: Columbia University Press, 1995), 35–75.

11. See Robert D. Cuff, *The War Industries Board: Business-Government Relations during World War I* (Baltimore: Johns Hopkins University Press, 1973), and David M. Kennedy, *Over Here: The First World War and American Society* (New York: Oxford University Press, 1980), 126–143, for descriptions of the War Industries Board and its legacy.

12. The best account of the origins, structure, and operations of the NRA is Ellis Hawley, *The New Deal and the Problem of Monopoly: A Study in Economic Ambivalence* (Princeton: Princeton University Press, 1967), especially 19–146.

13. Rosenman, ed., *Public Papers and Addresses,* 2:252.

14. Kenneth Finegold and Theda Skocpol, "State Capacity and Economic Intervention in the Early New Deal," *Political Science Quarterly* 97 (1982): 255–278; Kenneth Finegold and Theda Skocpol, *State and Party in America's New Deal* (Madison: University of Wisconsin Press, 1995).

15. Rosenman, ed., *Public Papers and Addresses,* 5:568–569.

2

HIGH TIDE: ROOSEVELT, TRUMAN, AND THE DEMOCRATIC PARTY, 1932–1952

Alonzo L. Hamby

The modern Democratic Party, observers agree with near unanimity, emerged from the trauma of the Great Depression. For a twenty-year moment in history, beginning with Franklin Roosevelt's landslide victory over Herbert Hoover in 1932, it dominated American politics and served as a vehicle for an enormous social transformation that was abetted by an unprecedented growth in the functions and institutional structure of the national government. What with the Depression, World War II, the onset of the Cold War, and the social restructuring that accompanied these phenomena, it seems natural enough to call these two decades a watershed in American history.[1]

The Democratic high tide, however, might equally be considered a peak in which a long-established political party, with a polyglot constituency and an amorphous policy direction, displayed unexpected resources to lead the American nation through one of the most critical periods of its history. The special character of this era in Democratic history is illustrated by a telling statistic: in 1932, Roosevelt was the party's first candidate for president since Franklin Pierce (in 1852) to win more than 50 percent of the total popular vote. FDR would do it four times. Only two Democrats have managed it since—Lyndon Johnson in 1964 by an enormous margin and Jimmy Carter in 1976 by a scant half a percent. To an enormous degree, the Democratic success of the 1930s and 1940s was less a matter of national identity and organizational strength than the personal charisma and strong leadership of one president—who in the end valued policy achievement over party.

Begun in the 1790s as an alliance between southern agrarians and northern city politicians, the Democratic Party could locate both its greatest strength and greatest weakness in the diversity of its adherents. Its truly national base made it usually a force to be reckoned with in Congress but also caused it to appear frequently unfocused in presidential elections. Its diversity also contributed to a disjunction between presidential and congressional parties far more pronounced than among the more homogeneous Republicans. From Jefferson and Jackson on, the Democrats claimed one unifying theme—an identity as the party of "the people," representing the majority in a society permeated by democratic values. The electoral appeal of that claim could at times be overwhelming. More often, however, this identity was lost in discord among the party's disparate economic and ethnoreligious groups. Increasingly in the nineteenth century, the Democrats had difficulty mobilizing their purported majority in presidential contests precisely because of deep divisions. (When the party split in 1860, so, catastrophically, did the nation.) Without a charismatic president with a strong sense of direction (Jefferson, Jackson, Wilson), the party was less than the sum of its parts, lacking policy coherence and more devoted to forming firing squads in a circle than to attacking the presumed common enemy.

Franklin Roosevelt and the new liberalism to which he attached himself would initiate a moment of Democratic ascendancy in American politics until the generational change and new social-cultural values of the 1960s reshuffled American politics. The building of a new majority from diverse elements was briefly characterized by a group of unprecedented public policy innovations that we call the New Deal (a label that gives a misleading impression of unified coherence), a "transforming" or "realigning" election in 1936 that seemed to create an unbeatable coalition, then a reaction in which disunifying tendencies reasserted themselves. After Roosevelt, the Democrats would continue as the majority party in American politics, but more in congressional than presidential elections and at the cost of an internal gridlock that contained within itself elements of self-destruction.

THE DEMOCRATIC SPLIT PERSONALITY

In some respects, the Democratic Party of 1932 reflected the split personality that had resulted from the alliance between Jefferson and Burr 140 years earlier. Its most visible segment consisted of the predominantly rural-small town, white, Anglo-Saxon, Protestant South and West; it was here that, first, William Jennings Bryan, then, Woodrow Wilson had drawn the bulk of their electoral votes in their runs for the presidency. Its most dynamic and fastest-growing segment, however, was among the ethnoreligious, working-class minorities of the northeastern quadrant of the country. As yet, they had delivered few electoral votes to Democratic presidential candidates, but Wilson's paper-thin 1916 success in Ohio and Al Smith's 1928 victories in Massachusetts and Rhode Island were harbingers of the future.

The prevailing outlook of the southern-western wing was "Jeffersonian," a term of almost infinite malleability[2] variously interpreted in one or more of the following senses: (1) small, frugal government and states rights (often tied in with white supremacy), (2) an agrarian fundamentalism that stressed the importance of the small, family farmer as an anchor of social stability, (3) a more broadly based faith in the small enterpriser as the linchpin of society, (4) an often bitter hostility toward the large corporations and enormous financial power centered in the Northeast, (5) a related belief in free trade and resentment of the protective tariff as special-interest legislation, and (6) a generalized devotion to democracy and the essential virtue of "the common people," often defined as the "producing classes."

In this multiplicity of meanings, one could find a rationale for a conservatism that stood for as few public services as possible and rejected any interference in such quaint local customs as slavery, lynching or child labor; one equally could find a basis for certain types of government activism, especially antitrustism, the regulation of big business and finance, or help for the farmer. In one way or another, however, Jeffersonians looked backward, hoping to recreate a fondly remembered, mythic past in which America was less urbanized, less spoiled, less complicated, and less centralized. Many of them envisioned that world as characterized by a high degree of ethnic and cultural homogeneity in which their own norms were dominant. In the 1920s, facing the challenge of the urban-immigrant world, they resorted to such instruments of social control as prohibition and immigration restriction. Not a few looked to the revived Ku Klux Klan as a tribune of Americanism. With cultural issues at the forefront of American politics, they found themselves more in conflict with the urban wing of their own party than with the Republicans.

The outlook of the northeastern urban Democrats was far less well defined but clearly different in style and content. Based primarily upon the experience of belonging to a working class that was economically and culturally marginalized, frequently reflecting a day-to-day existence at or near the bottom rung in hierarchical systems of industrial authority, it possessed a quasi-Marxian (not communist, not even socialist) sense of the distribution of power and privilege in American society. Motivated by feelings of class differences far more intense than those ordinarily found among the southern-western Jeffersonians, the northeastern Democrats tended vaguely toward social democracy, or, as some then and since have called it, "bread and butter liberalism." They had far fewer qualms than many of the Jeffersonians about an activist state. Their politics was less about opportunity and support for the small enterpriser than about regulation of working conditions, wages, and hours; social welfare; and encouragement of labor unionism. If the Jeffersonians, in one fashion or another, put the free individual at the center of their philosophy, the northeasterners thought more in terms of the collective. The policy conceptualizers among them might have at least a foot in various ideological camps just to the left of the party structure, primarily in the democratic socialism of Norman Thomas, David Dubinsky, and Sidney Hillman. Stopping short of nationalization of industry, they tended to favor extensive government regulation and economic planning.

Throughout the 1920s, cultural conflicts fatally divided the party. The southern-western Democrats saw themselves as attempting to protect a traditional America against an alien attack; the northeastern Democrats perceived themselves as being under assault from bigots trying to force their ways upon people who wanted the freedom to continue their cultural traditions (whether the consumption of alcoholic beverages or the education of one's child in a parochial school) and the right to get a job without discrimination. By 1928, many southern-western Democrats envisioned Herbert Hoover as less offensive than their own party's candidate, Al Smith. In the Northeast, on the other hand, the scorn of traditional America drove Catholics and Jews, Irish and Italians, and numerous other ethnic and religious groups that previously had displayed little use for each other together behind Smith.

In truth, both sides to the Democratic conflict practiced what David Burner has called a "politics of provincialism"[3] during the 1920s, their conflicting cultures reflecting a near-even demographic balance between city and country. This situation illustrated a general tendency in the history of American politics—during periods of prosperity, ethnocultural and "social" issues loom large in the political dialogue; during periods of economic distress, they tend to be displaced by distributive questions. It took the Great Depression to refocus the Democratic Party and bring unity to it.

THE GREAT DEPRESSION AND THE NEW DEAL

It is all but impossible for the contemporary generation to grasp the seriousness of the economic trauma the Great Depression inflicted on the entire world. An international phenomenon with origins in World War I and its aftermath, the Depression demanded an international solution. Instead, it fostered feelings of go-it-alone nationalism in virtually every developed country and set in motion forces that culminated in World War II. Beginning in the United States as a relatively moderate recession after the stock market crash of 1929, it accelerated downward after mid-1930, partly as a result of the Hawley-Smoot tariff (the most protectionist U.S. trade legislation of the twentieth century) and egregiously mistimed credit tightening by the Federal Reserve, partly as a result of numerous errors and catastrophes in other countries.[4]

By the end of 1932, the U.S. gross national product and per capita personal income had fallen to approximately 56 percent of the 1929 total. Unemployment, estimated at an average 3.2 percent in 1929, was at 23.6 percent. Farm income was approximately one-third the 1929 level. In the three years 1930–32, some five thousand banks failed with estimated losses to depositors of about $800 million dollars (at least $8 billion in today's terms).[5] During the winter of 1932–33, thanks to the strong downward momentum already established and to widespread uncertainty about the direction of a new administration in Washington, things actually got worse. It would take volumes to describe the suffering summarized by such statistics.

However one wishes to apportion the blame, it is clear that the dominant Republicans, from President Herbert Hoover down, dealt with the economic crisis in a way that neither arrested its precipitous slide nor raised public morale. Hoover had begun as a vigorous activist, confident that presidential leadership could manage the economy into recovery, but despite some promising first steps he had been overwhelmed. His line-in-the-sand opposition to federal funding of individual relief payments or works projects had given him an unjustified appearance of indifference to the suffering of the unemployed. Shantytowns populated by the homeless began to spring up in one city after another, called, in time, "Hoovervilles." In 1932 the electorate swept Franklin D. Roosevelt and the Democrats into office in a landslide that was primarily a negative vote against Hoover and the Republicans.[6]

Roosevelt's inauguration on March 4, 1933, endures among the most compelling moments in American history. Tens of millions listened by radio; other millions saw highlights in the movie newsreels that were just beginning to achieve a level of maturity. The voice and the film images conveyed a firm confidence and radiated the authority of a man born to the leadership class. The speech was electrifying: "This is a day of national consecration. . . . This great nation will endure as it has endured, will revive and will prosper. . . . The only thing we have to fear is fear itself." It promised "action, and action now." Democracy would prevail. The people had "asked for discipline and direction under leadership." The new president continued: "They have made me the present instrument of their wishes. In the spirit of the gift, I take it." The specifics of Roosevelt's agenda were at best fuzzy, but no one could doubt that he would be a strong leader who stood for change.[7]

FDR had put forth no clear, coherent program during the campaign. In part conscious strategy, this policy fuzziness also reflected the unprecedented character of the emergency and the divided mind of his party. Clearly, however, the new president had trumped Hoover by stating not simply a commitment to policies of economic recovery, but also to relief and reform. Whether from Jeffersonian or northeastern urban perspectives, the Democrats had been, on the whole, a party of reform in American life since Bryan and *the* party of reform since Theodore Roosevelt's failed Bull Moose campaign. Precisely what kind of reform, however, remained a question. For Bryan, then Wilson, reform had meant government aid to farmers and small enterprisers, low tariffs, regulation of big business, some social legislation, and tentative ties to organized labor. Wilson's 1916 campaign had been waged on policies that established a basis for the grand coalition of interest groups that would be solidified by Franklin Roosevelt. Still, no observer in 1932 would have identified the party unequivocally with northeastern, working-class social democracy.[8]

Never firmly aligned with the northeastern wing of the party, Roosevelt had many personal and emotional ties to the Wilson administration, which had been heavily southern-western in tone while reaching out to the northeastern Democrats. Throughout the 1920s, while struggling with polio, he had kept a foot in both camps. Although he was in his fourth year as governor of New York in 1932, the northeasterners predominantly supported Al Smith. FDR owed his nomination largely to the southern and western Jeffersonians, whom he repaid by naming as his vice president John Nance Garner of Texas. His major advisers included northeastern social welfarists and economic planners, Ivy League lawyers and economists, a few regional businessmen, and a couple of turncoat Republicans. His congressional leadership was primarily from the South and West. His policies over the next six years reflected that diversity.[9]

The New Deal began as a relatively coherent economic recovery program based on "corporatist" planning. A loose concept of state management in the interest of all classes and occupational groups, corporatism was in vogue in Europe, where it had roots stretching back into feudal conceptions of society and could make use of already strong state bureaucracies. Its American antecedents lay in the New Nationalism of Herbert Croly and Theodore Roosevelt; in the institutional economics of FDR's "brains-trusters" Rexford Tugwell, Adolf A. Berle Jr., and Raymond Moley: and above all in the experience of World War I mobilization. Its closest working model was the political economy of Italy. Needless to say, Roosevelt did not envision himself as a Mussolini-style dictator. He and his advisors did hope that the guiding hand of government could coordinate business, labor, and agriculture in a way that would deliver benefits to all concerned and bring the nation out of the depression.

On paper, the blueprint seemed promising. A National Recovery Administration (NRA) would provide a mechanism by which industry could stabilize prices and production while labor received fair wages, hours, and working conditions. A separate Agricultural Adjustment Administration (AAA) would curtail the surplus of farm commodities and thereby put upward pressure on prices. In the meantime, limited relief payments and public works expenditures would combine with devaluation of the dollar and a large increase in the money supply to jump-start the economy.[10]

Alas, the history of the 1930s would demonstrate that a managed economy functioned much better under a totalitarian regime, whether Fascist, Nazi, or Communist, than under a democratic one. It was to the credit of the New Deal that compliance to NRA codes by businesses was in the beginning voluntary (although subject to the pressure of public opinion) and that labor unions retained the right to organize and to strike. These democratic safeguards, however, made implementation a slow and uneven process; the Ford Motor Company, for example, never signed on. The NRA soon made itself an unhappy example of imperial overstretch by trying to regulate everything from mom and-pop grocery stores to the New York "burlesque industry."[11] The green light for labor unionism, the wage and hour provisions, and the cumbersome bureaucratic character of most NRA codes engendered wide resentment among smaller businessmen. Labor unions soon discovered that the codes could not guarantee them organizing victories; a major drive built around the slogan, "President Roosevelt wants you to join the union," failed badly during the NRA's first year, a victim of management resistance, union ineptness, and worker indifference. In the end, the NRA was far more successful at raising prices than increasing wages or giving the average consumer more purchasing power.

Public-works spending, moreover, got underway far too haltingly because of caution on the part of Secretary of the Interior Harold Ickes and because most states lacked the matching funds they were required to contribute. It was for this reason that, much to the disgust of many progressives, a large chunk of PWA money went into a major naval building program that produced the aircraft carriers *Enterprise* and *Yorktown,* four cruisers, and numerous other warships.

Only agriculture experienced a significant measure of recovery. Although controversial in its initial use of crop destruction, the AAA (primarily employing acreage allotments) pulled up prices for its desperate clients. Supplemental loan programs provided relief from mortgage foreclosures. Farmers, who liked to think of themselves as independent, individualistic enterprisers, protested not a whit. In fact, no other group had so long a history of seeking (and receiving) government support. Before 1933 most of what was called "progressivism" had consisted of agrarian initiatives; the New Deal agricultural programs represented a fulfillment. Ruled unconstitutional in January 1936, the AAA was quickly resurrected in the guise of a soil conservation program; in 1938, after the Supreme Court had been tamed, it was reinstated openly.

On the other hand, when the Supreme Court declared the NRA unconstitutional on May 27, 1935, the agency had become unpopular and was generally judged a failure. Special ad hoc legislation continued corporatist-style planning in a few industries, most notably coal, at the behest of both labor and management. Several enactments, moreover, brought comprehensive federal regulation to trucking, the airlines, and inland waterways in much the same fashion that it already existed in railroads, thereby establishing a de facto corporate state for transportation.

Agreat outburst of legislation in mid-1935 brought the country the National Labor Relations Act (Wagner Act), important banking regulation, and the path-breaking Social Security system. In general, however, after the demise of the NRA, the New Deal possessed no consciously administered recovery plan worthy of the name. Instead, driven by political opportunism, intellectual exhaustion, and sheer frustration, its economic policies featured big-business bashing, attacks on the rich, and an intermittent, inconsequential, antitrustism.

All the same, in 1936, prosperity seemed to be roaring back; industrial production moved up sharply, and unemployment threatened to fall into single digits. In retrospect, this apparently strong recovery seems to have been in large measure the result of two developments: a greatly expanded relief program centered on the new Works Progress Administration (WPA), and congressional passage over FDR's veto of immediate payment of the World War I veterans bonus. Together, these measures, which many congressmen saw as reelection devices, injected enormous stimulus into the economy. The WPA reached into every county in the United States; its roads, buildings, and parks were useful additions to the national infrastructure. More often than not, its local operations were controlled by Democratic officials who employed it as a patronage device. It contributed enormously to Roosevelt's reelection.

In early 1937 the president, persuaded that the nation could no longer afford huge budget deficits, decided to cut back. He ordered draconian relief reductions for the fiscal year that began July 1. By then also, the one-time-only shot of the bonus payment had made its impact. Federal Reserve policy, as was the case throughout the thirties, did some inadvertent damage; fearing inflation, although unemployment was still at double-digit rates, the Fed pushed up interest rates. (Roosevelt's Federal Reserve chairman, Marriner Eccles, is usually remembered as a strong advocate of deficit spending; he was also a sound Mormon banker who spent much of his career fixated on the adverse consequences of loose monetary policies.)

The result was a recession that might fairly be styled a mini-depression. In a matter of months, unemployment rocketed toward 20 percent; as late as 1939, it averaged 17 percent.[12] Looking back, it appears that the Roosevelt administration almost inadvertently had set a recovery *process* in motion with no real *plan* for managing it. What could have been the crowning success of the New Deal became instead its most conspicuous failure.

THE PROBLEM OF ECONOMIC RECOVERY: WAS THERE AN UNTAKEN PATH?

In February 1938, as the "Roosevelt recession" was plumbing its depths, the president received a lengthy letter from the renowned English economist John Maynard Keynes. Stripped to its essentials, the communication had two central lines of advice: back off from unproductive fights with the business community and resume a program of strong government spending, especially in such socially desirable areas as working-class housing.[13] Roosevelt answered with a friendly, noncommittal reply. Two months later, after an in-

tense debate among his advisers, FDR initiated a period of higher relief expenditures; the move halted the downward economic spiral. But the renewed
spending was too little and too late to bring the country back to where it had
been in 1936, much less to full recovery; and neither the administration nor
Congress was prepared to go much farther.

A generation of scholars that had accepted Keynesian economics as a new
orthodoxy came rather too easily and naturally to the conclusion that Roosevelt had needlessly prolonged the Depression because he did not understand the emerging Keynesian formula for restoring prosperity. Intimidated
by Republican criticism of his "enormous" deficits, he failed to inject enough
fiscal stimulus into the economy to bring it back.[14] The argument is attractive
when one considers that the economy waxed and waned during the 1930s in
relatively direct proportion to the amount of federal spending. It is probable
that the largely unconscious Keynesian policies of 1935–36 amounted to the
right path. If WPA spending had tapered off more slowly over a period of a
few years, the country might have pursued an orderly course to prosperity. As
it was, the administration's go-stop fiscal policy created a second, and more
difficult, pit to climb out of. By the beginning of 1938, Germany had left the
Depression behind for two years—even before Hitler's massive military program had reached full development. Britain in many respects also had handled the Depression better than the United States. Despite enormous problems managing industrial decline at home and global interests abroad, its
predominantly Conservative government managed to avoid the depths
reached in Germany and the United States. It won enormous electoral victories in 1931 and 1935. As Roosevelt struggled with the economic collapse of
1937–38, the British were beginning rearmament in earnest and putting the
Depression behind them. America, by contrast, remained mired in its economic meltdown until the unrestrained spending of World War II finally
ended unemployment and laid the basis for postwar prosperity.[15]

Before then, however, massive federal spending on a scale beyond that of
1936, whether for dams and regional development authorities or for aircraft
carriers and tanks, was never a live option. Keynes himself had published his
major work, *The General Theory of Employment, Interest, and Money*, only in
1936. At best an influential policy gadfly in his own country, he had no wide
following among either academics or policy intellectuals for fiscal prescriptions that struck most economists as the rankest heresy. Roosevelt's moves to
pump up relief spending in 1938 were a product of political calculation and
social compassion, not economic strategy, and were limited by political realities. He had run enormous deficits all along when measured against any pre-

vious standard. In the first fiscal year (FY) of the New Deal (as well as the last two of the Hoover administration!), the budget deficit exceeded 50 percent of expenditures. Until FY 1938 deficits remained extraordinarily high, running from 33 to 46 percent of total outlays. The resumption of spending in FY 1939 brought the percentage back to 43 percent.[16]

Federal spending as a portion of the gross national product was, it is true, much smaller then than now, but in the climate of the Depression decade it seemed awesome. The pressure to cut back spending in 1937 was broadly based and widely felt. The political system likely would not have accommodated even greater "excess," especially after the Republicans made a strong comeback in the 1938 elections. And even if hyperdeficits had been possible, it is far from clear that in peacetime they would have had the same effect as when incurred under the necessity of war. It is fair to say that the Keynesian alternative was never fully tried—so long as one also notes that it, for all practical purposes, did not exist.

Neither did another route that would seem imperative not many years later—the expansion of world trade. The world of the 1930s had become irretrievably autarkic; New Deal planners and Keynesians alike assumed realistically that a recovery had to be driven by internal consumption. Thus, Roosevelt abandoned a traditional Democratic doctrine. The Hawley-Smoot tariff stayed on the books, altered a bit by numerous bilateral trading deals negotiated under the reciprocal trade program. In truth, however, reciprocal trade was as much a smokescreen to conceal the basic pattern of protectionism that persisted through the 1930s as an effort to return piecemeal to the openness of the Underwood tariff. The best that could be said in defense of such a policy was that Hawley-Smoot had let the genie out of the bottle and that it was too late to reverse the trend of protectionism that gripped every major economic power. Post–World War II Democrats, believing they had learned from the past and able to impress their vision upon a prostrate world, would see interwar protectionism as a leading cause of World War II and promote an open international political economy.

With the possibilities for spending mishandled and imperfectly understood, with the expansion of international trade impossible, with a totalitarian alternative unthinkable, no clear road to prosperity existed after 1936. Political power, however, had given the Democrats opportunities to pursue long-held reform impulses. The 1930s thus became an age of reforms that, as often as not, got in the way of recovery.

In no area does this conclusion seem more obvious than tax policy.[17] The Social Security payroll tax is usually cited as the primary example. It may, as

Roosevelt contended, have been a necessary method of institutionalizing the program. From the beginning it also had the peripheral function of providing a lot of forced savings to fund the public debt, thereby sucking money out of the private economy and discouraging a consumption-driven recovery. The processing tax that funded the original agricultural program effectively raised the prices of many ordinary consumer products and was likewise regressive.

The Wealth Tax Act of 1935 became emblematic of a New Deal commitment to income redistribution and "class warfare." It raised marginal tax brackets on incomes of more than $100,000 and increased taxes on gifts, inheritances, and the like, but in truth it was more symbol than substance. Proposed primarily to counter the "share the wealth" appeal of Huey Long, it was both a political ploy and an automatic expression of a traditional progressivism that equated soaking the rich with reform. By one estimate it raised taxes only for America's richest man, John D. Rockefeller. Nevertheless, the atmosphere of class conflict that swirled around it surely decreased the confidence of the investing classes. Perhaps the worst considered of the New Deal taxes was the Undistributed Profits Tax of 1936, a 7–27 percent surtax on retained corporate profits, apparently passed in the belief that business was stashing cash hordes under mattresses and thereby retarding recovery. An extraordinarily effective way of discouraging capital formation, it elicited intense, and mostly justifiable, protests from business. It was repealed in 1938 with Roosevelt's grudging assent.

The primary motive behind New Deal tax policy was an increasingly perceived need for revenues to fund new relief and social welfare programs. Here it ran up against the problem that all modern welfare states face: How much can be extracted from the haves in order to assist the have-nots, and by what methods, without damaging the engines of productivity that ultimately sustain any safety-net system? The issue is one of pragmatic judgment rather than fundamental morality, of finding ways to define and balance social responsibility with economic reality.

There was a strong secondary impulse, however. Partly cold political calculation but at least equally visceral emotion, it consisted of a desire to punish the rich and the business classes. And why not? "Business" (a term generally used to denote the large corporate interests and, by extension, the wealthy) had claimed credit for the prosperity of the 1920s, had been unable to cope with the Depression, and now bitterly criticized the New Deal as an assault on the American Way of Life. "Business" by the mid-1930s had become America's favorite scapegoat, whether in Hollywood films or in Washington.

By then, corporate leaders who could not bear to hear Roosevelt's name called him "That Man," accused him of communistic tendencies, and semi-privately relished rumors that he was syphilitic. In the campaign of 1936, Roosevelt responded by attacking "economic royalists," "the forces of organized selfishness and of lust for power," and advocates of "a new industrial dictatorship."[18] From the standpoint of political tactics, such rhetoric made a lot of sense. Roosevelt and his core constituencies, moreover, found it emotionally satisfying. Nonetheless, attacks on business did little to get the economy moving. Just as Roosevelt never understood Keynesian economics, neither did he follow another bit of advice he received from Keynes—to cultivate business leaders, treat their crankiness as that of household animals who had been badly trained, respond to it with kind words, ask for their advice, and elicit their support.[19] It was wise counsel, but by the time Roosevelt received it in early 1938 too many bridges had been burned.

Roosevelt and many of the New Deal policy makers had feelings about commerce that ran from simple disinterest to positive revulsion. The president himself, the product of an old-money family, derived his income from inherited wealth and had been brought up in the tradition of a socially responsible gentry. The New Deal brain-trusters and administrators were heavily drawn from an emerging policy intelligentsia of academics and social activists who had to one degree or another consciously rejected business as a livelihood. Many of the southern and western "Jeffersonians" in the Democratic Party were neopopulists who thrived on the traditional Jeffersonian-Jacksonian hostility toward big finance. The rapidly growing forces of organized labor were in some places led at the local level by Communists and almost universally prone to a militancy and sense of class conflict that appeared as natural in the hard times of Depression America as it seems alien to a more prosperous society.

New Deal policies of maximum support to organized labor may have brought a healthy balance to the economy by contributing to the establishment of a society in which an affluent working class could indulge in mass consumption. In the short run, they got in the way of recovery. Strikes and labor militancy in 1937–38 disrupted the economy. Union wage settlements (undergirded to a small extent by the Fair Labor Standards Act) gave employed workers a better income than they otherwise might have enjoyed but also gave employers a greater incentive to minimize employment.[20]

Neither Roosevelt nor those around him nor the Jeffersonians nor many of the labor leaders wanted to do away with capitalism; rather, they talked about humanizing it and finding a middle way. Still, one is forced to conclude, neither did they understand how it worked. There was a certain justice to the oft-repeated complaint that they were theorists who had never met a payroll. Alienated from commerce, they never found much common ground with the leaders of American business. They often proclaimed their sympathy for small business, saw it as a constructive force, and wanted to champion it. Few among them, however, understood that small businessmen as a group shared the worldview of big business leaders. Indeed they clung to it more tenaciously because they were usually entrepreneurs who had an investment of personal ego in their operations exceeding that of most corporate managers.[21]

Small enterprisers undoubtedly found the burdens of government regulation and the need to negotiate with labor unions harder to deal with than did large corporations. Nor did New Deal tax policy give them any relief. The Wealth Tax Act of 1935, according to William E. Leuchtenburg, "destroyed most of the Brandeisian distinction between big and small business,"[22] whatever the intentions of the administration. The Social Security payroll tax provided a new federal requirement at a time when federal taxes were not generally withheld from paychecks.

In the tumultuous 1930s, some degree of hostility and misunderstanding between the Roosevelt administration and the business community was probably inevitable. The outlook of both sides was characterized by prejudices and blind spots that made it practically impossible to find common ground. Still, one may wish the effort had been made—and must observe that it was, during World War II, with considerable benefit to the nation and to all the concerned social groups. In the absence of an obvious formula for restoring prosperity and promoting economic growth, the Roosevelt administration and many Democrats in Congress turned to class conflict and redistributionism, rhetorical antitrustism, generous relief programs, and a rudimentary social welfare state. Not productive as an economic program, this agenda emerged because it was a logical outgrowth of the Democratic Party's history.

In his 1938 letter to Roosevelt, Keynes had written, "I am terrified lest progressive causes in all the democratic countries should suffer injury, because you have taken too lightly the risk to their prestige which would result from a failure measured in terms of immediate prosperity."[23] The remark implicitly recognized the leadership that both the United States and Roosevelt himself *had* to provide for what remained of the liberal-democratic world. One can assess with a fair degree of precision the consequences of the economic failure of 1937 for the United States in terms of increased unemployment and unproduced GNP. It is not possible to gauge the impact on the wider world. One can imagine a United States as prosperous as Nazi Germany, able to look outward and present democracy rather than totalitarianism as the wave of the future. Just possibly, such a nation might have been able to provide leadership for demoralized European democracies at a time when the Nazi experiment might have been brought to a sudden halt. Instead, the New Deal was at best an ambiguous example to the rest of the world.

BUILDING A DEMOCRATIC MAJORITY: THE ROOSEVELT COALITION

If, then, the Democrats failed to solve the economic crisis they had been elected to meet, how did they emerge from the 1930s as a majority party?

A small part of the answer is that they were lucky in the opposition. The Republicans, shell-shocked by the Depression, produced no ideas, no vision, and no leadership. The emergence of Robert A. Taft as "Mr. Republican" and Thomas E. Dewey as Most Electable Candidate by the 1940s suggests a party not only in bankruptcy but also in a desperate search for a suitable receiver.

The parties of the left (Wisconsin Progressives, Minnesota Farmer-Laborites, La Guardia Fusionists, Socialists) never presented a significant challenge. They failed to develop a domestic program with mainstream appeal, were hopelessly split on foreign policy, and eventually were unable to resist the overwhelming gravitational pull of the Democrats.

Still, the shortcomings of the opposition provide only the beginning of an explanation. Politicians and parties become winners not just because they have some good breaks but because they know how to take advantage of them. Roosevelt and the Democrats did so superbly.

Roosevelt himself was the party's greatest asset. Political scientists may quibble about whether he was the founder of "the modern presidency," but he surely unlocked its potential. Above all, he demonstrated that a party of diversity requires strong, charismatic leadership to rise above its natural tendency to engage in interest-group squabbling. Evoking first the fight against the Depression, and then the struggle against fascism, he gave the Democratic Party and New Deal liberalism a vision of the national interest that legitimized it for a generation.

Influenced by the examples of his cousin Theodore and his old chief, Woodrow Wilson, FDR was a consummate master of the news media. He opened up the White House press conference, playing it like a virtuoso to get his message across while maintaining a rapport with most of the journalists who covered him regularly. He appeared in newsreels radiating confidence and fortitude. Above all, he emerged as a technical master of the newest and most direct medium of communication—radio.

Possessing an authoritative Harvard-accented voice that appealed to the sensibility of the age, gifted with a remarkable talent for rhetorical pacing, able to project a sense of empathy with ordinary people out beyond the micro-phone, he was his nation's first great communicator of the electronic media age.[24] Words, Roosevelt understood, were no substitute for policy, but they could serve as a powerful adjunct to it, bringing the political support of people who were convinced that he cared about them in a direct, personal way and who felt connected to a grander, larger vision. Accepting the Democratic nom-ination in 1936, he declared, "This generation of Americans has a rendezvous with destiny." More than a nice rhetorical flourish, the sentence was a declara-tion of national mission that made a lasting impact on millions of people.

Roosevelt's style and talent facilitated the policies that recreated the De-mocratic Party as a majority coalition. If ultimately he and the Democrats failed at achieving economic recovery, they would appear throughout his first term to be marching toward it with double-digit gains in GNP and a steady reduction in the unemployment rate. (Richard Vedder and Lowell Gallaway estimate that unemployment in March 1933, when Roosevelt took office, peaked at 28.3 percent and that in November 1936, when he was elected for a second term, it was down to 13.9 percent.[25]) Voters, moreover, benefited from numerous varieties of direct and immediate assistance.

The New Deal programs aimed at helping individuals in distress were so numerous as to defy a complete listing—home and farm mortgage refinanc-ing, work relief, direct relief (also known as the dole and constituting a far greater proportion of the total relief effort than is usually recognized), re-gional development, rural resettlement, farm price supports, wage and hour legislation, and the Social Security system. At one level, as many Republicans charged, this amounted to buying votes by playing Santa Claus. At another, however, it was an effort by an activist government to meet genuine human needs. Unsurprisingly, the political and the humanitarian motives might get mixed up with each other.

The most far-reaching of the work programs, the WPA, for example, pro-vided hundreds of thousands of jobs for desperate people and left behind tens of thousands of little monuments in the form of useful public works in almost every county in the United States. It also was, pure and simple, a source of patronage for many state and local political bosses. And, in the manner of today's welfare programs, it fostered a sense of dependency among its long-term clients, especially those who lived in low-wage rural areas with little manufacturing or construction.[26]

Yet while Republican criticism resonated with what was left of the comfortable middle class, it was less than devastating because the purposes of New Deal largesse were fundamentally conservative—to preserve a class of farm and home owners, to provide work for those who needed it, and to give handouts only to unemployables. Those who received benefits from the New Deal were generally intensely grateful, frequently reacting almost as if they were a personal gift from FDR himself. For millions of Americans the New Deal boiled down to two elements: Roosevelt and relief. All the rest was irrelevant.

Roosevelt's landslide victory of 1936 was a transforming event in American history, but a somewhat deceptive one. What we might call the "core Roosevelt coalition" lies within the 60 percent of the vote that FDR polled; it would be a dominant force in Democratic presidential politics but no more than a powerful minority in the larger electoral panorama. In taking forty-six of forty-eight states, Roosevelt carried virtually every significant group in America other than (for lack of a better term) "the business classes." He also carried in on his coattails the largest Democratic delegations ever in the House of Representatives (331) and the Senate (76). But much of this majority was produced by a surging economy and a weak, uninspiring Republican opponent. Like Ronald Reagan half a century later, the president could ask people if they were better off than four years earlier and get a happy response. The longer-term question as the economic upturn stalled in 1937 was just who would stay with him. A rough sorting-out of several overlapping categories follows.

OLD STOCK, WHITE, ANGLO-SAXON PROTESTANTS. Roosevelt carried only a bare majority of this predominantly middle-class, traditionally Republican group. In the future it would go against him and other Democratic candidates.

URBAN ETHNORELIGIOUS MINORITIES. Roosevelt won the normally Democratic Catholic and Jewish votes by large majorities. He had actively sought both. Catholics, personified by Democratic National Chairman Jim Farley, Securities Exchange Commission Chairman Joe Kennedy, or young White House aide Tommy Corcoran, were a highly visible part of his administration. Catholic constituencies at the local level included many national backgrounds—Italian, Polish, German, Portuguese, Eastern European, French-Canadian. These groups might have little use for each other in the cauldron of melting-pot politics, but as they became more assimilated they also became more class-conscious.[27] Moreover, they responded to a degree of attention they never had received from any previous president.

Jews who looked for representation in Washington would find, among others, Secretary of the Treasury Henry Morgenthau and Corcoran's good friend and White House colleague Benjamin V. Cohen. On the whole they were more likely than Catholics to be drawn to FDR by a liberal ideology. Despite some reluctance by New Deal administrators to take on too many Jews in visible positions, they were far more numerous, and more noticed, in the Roosevelt presidency than in any that had proceeded it.[28] Mutterings from the far right that the New Deal was a Jew Deal were grossly exaggerated but were also motivated by an unprecedented Jewish presence at the highest levels of government.

In the future, both groups would remain important parts of the coalition. Catholic representation, however, would be eroded by upward economic mobility and by concerns that the party was too soft on communism. Jewish representation would be increased by World War II and by Harry Truman's postwar policies on immigration and Palestine.

AFRICAN AMERICANS. Economically devastated by the Depression, weary of a half-century of benign neglect by the Republican Party, blacks were ready for a political alternative. As early as 1932, dissatisfaction with Hoover and his party was palpable among the black elite. Robert Vann, publisher of the nation's most influential black newspaper, the Pittsburgh *Courier*, shocked many Republicans when he declared, "My friends, go turn Lincoln's picture to the wall. That debt has been paid in full." Although Hoover still managed to carry the black vote in 1932, Vann had seen the future. Over the next four years, no demographic group benefited so greatly from New Deal programs. In 1936, the black vote was 3–1 for Roosevelt. Vann, who had received an appointment in the Department of Justice, became a prominent member of an informal administration black advisory group known as the "black cabinet." He and others like him spoke to a constituency that cared more about the food Roosevelt had put on the table than about his lack of interest in civil rights legislation. The time for the latter would come after World War II.[29]

LABOR. Organized labor, made a permanent part of the American political economy by the Wagner Act of 1935, emerged as a potent campaign force, a big contributor of money to the Democrats as well as a major source of organization and manpower. Its role would loom larger and larger as traditional urban machines decayed in one city after another over the next couple of decades. From 1948 through 1968 Democratic presidential campaigns would start with the nominee speaking to large union rallies on Labor Day in Detroit's Cadillac Square. For a time it appeared that the Democrats were well along the path to becoming a de facto counterpart of the British Labor Party, a prospect welcomed not simply by the unions but also by an increasingly influential liberal policy intelligentsia.

THE CITIES. Ethnoreligious minorities, working classes, and organized labor were of course all centered in the cities, which supported Roosevelt overwhelmingly. "Labor" included heavy representations of the white minority groups listed above, but old-stock working-class Americans also voted heavily for FDR. Roosevelt carried not only ethnic manufacturing centers like Lowell, Massachusetts, and Flint, Michigan, but also Tulsa and Oklahoma City, not just Cleveland and Chicago but also Kansas City and Los Angeles. Of the 106 cities in the country with a population over 100,000, Roosevelt carried 104.

THE "LIBERAL INTELLECTUALS." From the beginning of his presidency, Roosevelt had enjoyed the support of an emergent group of policy-oriented intellectuals who had rejected the conservative, business-oriented Republican dominance of the 1920s but who, unlike those on the independent left, wanted to work within the Democratic Party. Political journalists, lawyers, social workers, academic social scientists, "intellectuals" by virtue of education, some were egalitarian ideologues motivated by a social-democratic vision, others pragmatists dedicated to the use of human intelligence in solving practical social problems, and not a few (after the example of the great philosopher-activist John Dewey) were both.

Most wanted a society characterized by a more equitable distribution of wealth. Many saw strong government management of the economy as a means both of achieving that goal and of smoothing out the business cycle. Increasingly, they identified themselves with the causes of (racial) civil rights and expanded civil liberties. Inside the New Deal, they provided much of the management and policy conceptualization. Outside the administration, they might be writers for such left-liberal magazines as the *New Republic, The Nation,* or *Common Sense*; a few might be found on Capitol Hill working for liberal Democratic legislators.

Like all participants in the political process, they doubtless found the idea of power for themselves and their "class" attractive; all the same, they were less self-interested in the conventional sense than almost any of the groups attracted to the New Deal. Most deplored Roosevelt's compromises and saw

the New Deal as only a very partial realization of their blueprints for a perfect society. At bottom, however, most of them loved him as they would no
other politician. Numerically insignificant, they were important as idea people, publicists, and organizers. They would support FDR to the end, feel just
mild about Harry Truman, find a close approximation of their ideal in Adlai
Stevenson, be wary of John Kennedy, and reject Lyndon Johnson.

FARMERS. Perhaps the most volatile segment of the electorate, farmers constituted nearly a quarter of the population in the 1930s, and thus were an imposing voting bloc. (By 1960 they would be down to less than 9 percent.[30])
Roosevelt carried farm areas easily in a vote that reflected widespread gratitude for the way in which the New Deal had saved rural America from liqui-
dation. After that, however, the relationship would cool quickly. Farm prices
fell in the late 1930s because of the recession of 1937–38 and surpluses that
outpaced the government's ability to curtail them. Moreover, the administration's increasing identification with labor and the urban minorities made
it less attractive to what was, after all, a culturally traditional segment of the
population.

THE SOUTH. Still homogenous, overwhelmingly old-stock WASP, aggressively white supremacist, mainly rural and small-town, distrustful of labor
unions and outsiders, the South (that is, the states of the Confederacy) had
been reliably Democratic since Reconstruction, with the one exception of the
Smith-Hoover campaign of 1928. The most impoverished region of the
country, it had received a disproportionate amount of assistance from the
New Deal. In 1936 and subsequent years it would be solidly for Roosevelt,
but its ideological and cultural divergences from the overall trajectory of the
party raised serious doubts about the future.

   Stripped to its enduring essentials, the Democratic Party of 1936 looked a
lot like the bargain that Jefferson and Madison had made with Aaron Burr in
the 1790s, but now the order of power and influence was reversed. The center of gravity (intellectually as well as numerically) now lay not in the agrarian South but in the bustling cities of the industrial North. Roosevelt could
not have been reelected in 1940 and 1944 without his overwhelming urban
majorities; in both cases, he would have won without a single electoral vote
from the South.

PRESIDENTIAL PARTY VS. CONGRESSIONAL PARTY. Yet what he had created was a presidential electoral coalition that bore only a tenuous relation-

ship to the realities of power in Congress. In the American constitutional system, presidential and congressional electoral systems are not designed to be in sync; from the late 1930s into the 1960s, the divergence would become especially pronounced among Democrats, sharply divided between presidential and congressional parties.

The different balance of power in Congress was partly attributable to the underrepresentation of urban America still common in the state legislatures that redrew congressional districts every decade. It also stemmed, however, from the undeniable fact that minorities (whether ethnic, religious, or racial) were less able to leverage their voting power in 531 House and Senate races than in a national presidential election. The labor/social-democratic nature of the worldview that had attached itself to their political emergence was a hard ideological sell.

Roosevelt, probably more pushed by the pressure of events than purposefully leading, had created a coalition that made the Democrats a majority party without ending the divisions among its factions. Within a year of his astounding victory in 1936, his power was waning and American politics was headed toward a deadlock of democracy.[31]

The immediate precipitants were:

THE COURT-PACKING PLAN. This was the move that began the sharp slide in FDR's authority. He had neither made the Supreme Court an issue in the 1936 campaign nor discussed legislation with his leaders in Congress. He much too slickly presented the bill as a method of dealing with tired blood on the Court rather than of getting his way in a dispute with it. The public and many congressmen perceived an attempt to subvert the Constitution. The president had only himself to blame for the disaster that followed. By the time it was over, he had shown that he could be successfully opposed on an important issue.

THE RECESSION OF 1937–38. Here, Capitol Hill had to share the blame with the White House. Many safely reelected moderate to conservative Democratic legislators saw no more need for the WPA and allied programs. New Deal tax policy and the generally poisonous relations with the business community surely contributed to the economic debacle.

THE UPSURGE OF LABOR MILITANCY. Strongly identified with the unions, Roosevelt could not escape a widespread reaction against the tough, angry, class conflict-oriented organizing campaigns that began shortly after his reelection. The sit-down strikes, which captured the attention of the nation, were a special affront to the American middle-class ethic and drew a resolution of condemnation that nearly passed the Senate. Roosevelt's attempt to wash his hands of the issue by declaring "a plague on both your houses" satisfied almost no one.[32]

THE FAILED PURGE OF 1938. Never mind that Roosevelt had every right—constitutional, legal, and moral—to campaign against Democratic congressmen who had opposed him; never mind that as party leader he may even have had a duty to do so. He affronted the sense of localism that has always been a distinguishing feature of American political parties. Worse yet, he also did it very badly, striking openly at opponents he could not topple. After the dust had cleared, he was a more diminished president than ever.

The pattern of American politics that emerged from these events was at the most visible level one in which a liberal president found himself checked by a loose, informal coalition of conservative Democrats (primarily from the South) and Republicans. Accompanying and facilitating this development was the reemergence in somewhat different form of the ideological and cultural differences that had split the party before the New Deal. The argument, to be sure, was no longer about prohibition, immigration restriction, the alleged menace of a Catholic president, or the depredations of the Ku Klux Klan. Now it was about antilynching legislation, labor unions, and, in broad terms, the New Deal's threat to the conservative interpretation of Jeffersonianism as small, frugal, locally centered government. Yet the sides to the debate were much the same as in the 1920s, and the reciprocal sense of cultural hostility was rarely suppressed. By 1938 the Democrats were two parties at odds with each other behind a common facade.

Strong Republican gains in the 1938 elections left Roosevelt all but checkmated on Capitol Hill. FDR spent much of his second term working to institutionalize established programs through the creation of a stronger presidency and a much-enlarged continuing executive bureaucracy, or "administrative state," with considerable independence from congressional and electoral control. The Executive Reorganization Act of 1939, although extensively compromised before its narrow final passage, was a significant victory. Creating the Executive Office of the President, it gave Roosevelt an institutional base unlike any enjoyed by his predecessors and allowed him considerable authority to initiate administrative changes. In 1940 he secured passage of the Ramspeck Act, which extended civil service protection to some 200,000 mid- and high-level positions in the executive bureaucracy, most of them held by administration appointees.

These developments, the political scientist Sidney Milkis has brilliantly argued, signaled that Roosevelt's commitment to his programmatic legacy was greater than his devotion to party leadership.[33] FDR continued, of course, to accept the role of party leader—indeed, at election time, most Democrats pressed it on him—but he had little interest in being a party unifier. He would make the point unmistakably in 1940 when, under threat of refusing a third presidential nomination, he literally forced the Democratic convention to nominate the New Dealer Henry A. Wallace as his running mate.

But what was Roosevelt institutionalizing? Alan Brinkley, the most important historian of the New Deal's later years, has argued that the political outcome of FDR's second term was "the end of reform." Early visions of a major social-economic restructuring gave way to a style of Keynesian liberalism more interested in promoting mass consumption and developing a half-formed welfare state than in undertaking a major changeover of America. The ultimate result, he argues, was a deferral of festering social problems that plague us today.[34] As a description of what happened in the late 1930s and was confirmed by World War II, Brinkley's account is surely accurate. Whether real alternatives existed, or whether they would have been preferable, must remain a matter of individual judgment.

WORLD WAR II

The argument over the New Deal and a complex of domestic issues created the political coalitions of the 1930s, but foreign policy and World War II also affected them.[35] World War I had been a disaster for the Democrats, wrecking the nascent "Wilson Coalition" of 1916, breaking the health of their charismatic president, and leaving them bitterly divided. The party would emerge from World War II intact and legitimized as the vehicle of national leadership in foreign policy, yet also weakened by the corrosive effects of a total war. Moreover, the prosperity that the war made possible after 1945 created a society less amenable to the messages of class division and social reform that had served the Democrats so well in the 1930s.

However halting and inconsistent Roosevelt's pre-1939 foreign policy leadership may seem, it was in fact prescient and at times risky. Privately convinced that America could not remain isolated from the rest of the world, he did about as much as possible to prepare the country—intellectually, morally, and militarily—for the gathering storms he correctly discerned in Europe and Asia. True enough, he acquiesced in the Neutrality Acts of 1935–37, backed away from his 1937 "quarantine" speech after a strong backlash against it, and publicly praised the Munich agreement. These need to be understood, however, as Fabian tactics practiced by a leader who wanted to take the offensive but sensed that the correlation of forces was against him. Perhaps reaction would have been different if the quarantine speech (October 1937) had not taken place against the backdrop of a national economic slide and the Munich pact (September 1938) had not occurred with the unemployment rate hovering just below 20 percent. As it was, most Americans—whether conservative Republicans, militant independent progressives, or Democrats of any stripe—were isolationists, far more concerned with the continuing depression than with the follies of Europe.

The war came anyway in September 1939. After the collapse of France in mid-1940, Roosevelt took enormous chances to prevent a Nazi victory by funneling scarce American military resources to a shaky Britain. Although these actions were enormously controversial, the war's political impact was to propel FDR to a third term. The conflict made him seem an indispensable man, boosted the economy, and galvanized his core support. In November, he defeated Republican Wendell Willkie handily, winning nearly 55 percent of the vote, but not appreciably changing the party balance in Congress. The less committed support of 1936 had fallen away; more than ever, the working-class minorities in the big cities *were* the Roosevelt coalition.

In 1941, Roosevelt pushed ahead with Lend-Lease, aid to the Soviet Union after it was invaded, and an undeclared naval war with Germany. Most stunningly, he met with British Prime Minister Winston Churchill on the United Kingdom's newest battleship, *Prince of Wales,* off Argentia, Newfoundland, in August 1941. They issued a manifesto they called the Atlantic Charter, "a joint declaration of war aims" that declared their mutual allegiance to liberal and democratic values. Affirmations of good causes might lift British spirits, but it was beyond Roosevelt's power to give Churchill what he really wanted—an American declaration of war against Germany. In fact, the administration barely secured legislation to extend the terms of newly trained draftees in the U.S. Army.

It is hardly surprising then that Roosevelt at times was disingenuous, even guilty of outright deception, as he attempted to cope with a self-deceptive public opinion unwilling to accept either the triumph of Nazism or full American participation in the fighting. To criticize such behavior as among the many abuses of the "imperial presidency" strikes one as far less meaningful than recognizing it as a defense of the national interest—and indeed of the ideals of liberalism and democracy. Pearl Harbor,[36] a consequence of a policy toward Japan that got tougher as the Japanese allied themselves more closely to Nazi Germany and Fascist Italy, finally plunged the United States into a fight that Roosevelt correctly realized it could not avoid.

Roosevelt's World War II foreign policy, a presidential exercise that all but excluded Secretary of State Cordell Hull, is open to fair criticism.[37] It had serious contradictions that arose from his attempts to combine the approaches that had characterized the thinking of his two great political heroes—the power-driven realism of Theodore Roosevelt and the idealistic internationalism of Woodrow Wilson. The two themes were not wholly irreconcilable, but the tension was obvious and the practical difficulties of juggling them were great. Roosevelt was a magnificent rhetorical leader who justified the sacrifices of the war with visions of a worldwide democratic utopia—four freedoms (of speech, of religion, from want, from fear) "everywhere in the world." He named the wartime alliance "the United Nations," and consistently depicted it as a force fighting for democracy and the common man. Yet he also was capable of making deals with fascists and their sympathizers—especially if it would further such military gains as the capitulation of the French in North Africa or the surrender of Italy. Most glaringly, he accepted as senior partners in the alliance not only the broken-down, militaristic government of Chiang Kai-shek in China but also Stalin's Soviet Union, a totalitarian despotism capable of matching Nazi Germany evil for evil (and its ally for a critical twenty-two months at the beginning of the war).

Such inconsistencies were not the work of a flighty mind; they possessed the virtue of necessity. The Western democracies could not have won World War II without the Soviet alliance. Yet the difficulties of squaring sweeping idealistic objectives with the harder realities of power encouraged an ad hoc diplomacy that jumped nervously from issue to issue, postponed hard decisions about the postwar world, and placed excessive emphasis on friendly relations between the men at the top. Roosevelt mistakenly assumed the continued viability of Britain as a great power (even while pursuing an anticolonial policy that anticipated the dismemberment of the British empire) and never worked out a realistic scenario for postwar East Asia. Worried about American public opinion, he never engaged in the sort of frank realpolitik that alone might have established a satisfactory basis for dealing with Stalin and the USSR after the war. Despite his private understanding that balance and accord among the great powers would be the only basis for a postwar settlement, he found himself mortgaging American diplomacy to the establishment of a United Nations organization and the accompanying illusion that total war would bring in its wake total peace.

Nonetheless, FDR successfully mobilized the United States for total war, kept the Grand Alliance together, and protected American interests around the world. It was primarily geographical isolation and economic power that allowed the United States, alone among the major nations of World War II, to emerge with enhanced strength; but Roosevelt did much to establish the conditions for that development. When he died with ultimate victory in sight, a majority of Americans perceived him as a heroic leader who had brought the country through unprecedented ordeals with its ideals and institutions intact.

Yet, however much Roosevelt had established the Democrats as *the* party of leadership in crisis, the war also eroded the party's strength in significant ways. The casualty lists, high taxes (withheld from paychecks for the first time), and shortages of consumer goods—all affected about every American. The use of New Deal–style federal agencies to develop and enforce price control and rationing aroused considerable resentment among farmers and businessmen. Millions of ordinary Americans had episodic difficulty finding objects as mundane as razor blades, a new set of tires, or a decent cut of meat. Labor strikes, infrequent to be sure, aroused widespread popular outrage when they occurred, or even were threatened.

The congressional election of 1942 was a particularly grim experience for New Deal Democrats. The party barely maintained control of Congress. Roosevelt faced a hostile conservative majority on Capitol Hill and experienced a near-collapse of his personal leadership, even among many legislators who agreed with him on policy issues. In 1944, Alben Barkley dramatized the new situation by resigning as Senate majority leader in protest against FDR's veto of a tax bill. He was unanimously reelected by Democratic senators in a show of solidarity that amounted to a direct slap at the president, who had to respond with a conciliatory "Dear Alben" letter.

It is one of the ironies of World War II that the United States, which suffered less than any other major combatant and organized with supreme success to provide the wherewithal for victory, experienced the greatest backlash against big government and a powerful state. The classical liberal distrust of the state that permeated American history had much to do with the reaction. But so also did the American geographical isolation from the terrors of warfare. In nations under attack, whether Allied or Axis, the state was an all-powerful source of protection and sustenance, organizing defenses against the depredations of feared enemies, resettling the victims of bombings, overseeing the fair distribution of scarce rations, providing medical care for civilian and soldier alike, embodying the spirit of a national identity. In America, it was unnecessary for the government to provide such services; instead to millions of its citizens, it became a nuisance, exacting from them one petty sacrifice after another and at times laying claim on the life or limb of a loved family member. However justified the war might seem as an abstract matter, the sacrifices remained irritants, leading increasing numbers of citizens to wonder if the New Deal state was not too big and too meddlesome.

In the presidential election year of 1944, the Democrats turned once again to Roosevelt. Whatever the political setbacks of the war, whatever the restiveness among dissidents, he clearly was the only candidate who could lead the party to victory. All the same, the president was weakened enough that he consented to the dumping of Vice President Wallace, who had been a model of ineptness in his congressional relations and was widely disliked by party conservatives and moderates. The new running mate was Senator Harry S. Truman, a New Deal supporter who enjoyed widespread popularity in both houses of Congress. The Roosevelt coalition, tattered about the edges, held firm despite FDR's own visibly worn health, the multitude of resentments he had accumulated over twelve years, and all the strains of the war. It was bolstered by an important mobilization of organized labor. The Congress of Industrial Organizations established the CIO Political Action Committee, which provided resources and organization that may have been decisive in some large industrial states. On Election Day, Roosevelt defeated Thomas Dewey, polling about 53.3 percent of the vote and once again finding his decisive majorities in the cities.

The Democrats gained twenty-four seats in the House but lost two in the Senate. The conservative coalition and the divergent congressional party remained intact. The 1940 elections had left the party with 66 senators and 268 representatives; the 1944 elections returned 56 Democratic senators and 242 representatives.

Franklin Roosevelt at the top of his form would have found it necessary to yield much of his program to such a Congress. The Roosevelt who began his fourth term was suffering from the effects of chronic hypertension, an affliction for which, in those days, there was no good treatment. Chronically fatigued, he was in truth not physically fit to continue as president. A horrified Truman told a friend that FDR "had the pallor of death on his face."[38] His last overseas trip, a crucial meeting with Stalin and Churchill at Yalta in the Soviet Crimea, exacted a fearsome toll. On March 1, 1945, he reported on the Yalta conference before a joint session of Congress. Worn in appearance, unable to stand, he delivered a rambling speech in a tired voice. The performance failed to satisfy his critics and confirmed the worst fears of his friends. Six weeks later, April 12, 1945, he died suddenly at his Warm Springs, Georgia, retreat.

Roosevelt left behind not simply a record of victory in four presidential elections but also a transformed Democratic Party. What remained uncertain, however, was whether that party had an independent viability or whether it was, at bottom, a personal creation that would fly apart in his absence. Even if it could be held together, moreover, could any successor effect an ideological unification that would bring the Democratic congressional party back into line with the Democratic presidential party? It would be up to Harry S. Truman to provide the answers.

THE MAINTAINING PRESIDENCY OF
HARRY S. TRUMAN

Truman's presidency demonstrated that a chief executive lacking the assets that had meant so much to Roosevelt—style, charm, media charisma—could make much of his office.[39] Truman assuredly deserves credit for the virtues that made him one of the most important twentieth-century American presidents—hard work, determination, shrewd political judgment, and gutsy decision-making. For all his differences in style and personality from FDR, he also showed that individuals make a difference. Consider what likely would have happened to the Democratic Party under President Henry A. Wallace.

The Truman presidency demonstrated that the Roosevelt coalition, and the fact of a presumptive Democratic majority, possessed a social and political basis that extended beyond Roosevelt—and that it could be rallied by a midwesterner with a considerably different cultural identity. A product of an urban political machine, Truman understood the New Deal coalition and its imperatives. A committed ideological progressive from his earliest years, he moved naturally to a liberal course. He also showed that the party required a strong man in the White House in order to hold it together, shape its identity, and give it the leadership necessary to win national elections. Finally, his years in office confirmed that the Democratic presidential-congressional split was an enduring fact of national life.

If Truman demonstrated that there was life after Roosevelt for the Democrats, the roller-coaster ups and downs of his years in the White House equally displayed the party's continuing internal contradictions. By the end of 1946, Truman, pulled between one Democratic faction and another, seemingly ineffective in his management of the economy, looked like a failure. The Republicans especially capitalized on a failed attempt to control meat prices that had succeeded only driving supply off the market. Using the slogan "Had enough?" the GOP swept to victory in the mid-term elections, winning control of Congress for the first time since 1928. Once in power, they quickly realized their major objective, passing the antilabor Taft-Hartley Act over Truman's veto. With near unanimity, pundits proclaimed the Democratic era at an end.

Remarkably, it was not. The Truman years, by and large, constituted a maintaining period rather than a transforming one. Just how did Truman manage to hold together a party that seemed to be on the verge of flying apart?

CENTRIST LIBERALISM. Truman picked up the heritage of the New Deal and added to it a series of his own programs (which he would call the Fair Deal in his second term) that seemed logical extensions. The broad public was not ready for most of them (national health insurance, federal aid to education, comprehensive civil rights legislation, repeal of the Taft-Hartley Act, the Brannan Plan for agriculture). The one item that did get through Congress, large-scale public housing in 1949, is widely adjudged a failure.

All the same Truman had defined an agenda for the next generation of liberal activism. His Fair Deal appealed to a substantial majority of nonsouthern Democrats who engaged themselves with policy issues; it maintained the allegiance of such critical constituencies as organized labor, African Americans, and the liberal intelligentsia. What made it distinctive and gave it enduring significance was the way in which it adjusted Democratic liberalism to the new and apparently permanent prosperity that had emerged from World War II.

Truman's most momentous addition to the liberal agenda was civil rights.[40] His ideas about race—he thought in terms of "equal opportunity" rather than "social equality"—may seem primitive today, but in the immediate postwar years they were enlightened. Like Roosevelt before him, he preferred to dodge racial issues, but the end of the Depression made it impossible to satisfy African Americans with distributional politics. As fairness and constitutional rights became the primary objectives of blacks and their white liberal allies, Truman had no fundamental inhibitions about taking up their cause. He deserves more credit than he usually gets for his civil rights stand. Inevitably, however, it added considerably to the centrifugal forces within the Democratic coalition.

The first president to offer a comprehensive civil rights program, he was never able to get legislation past a southern filibuster in the Senate, but he took major steps in other ways. His Justice department submitted a series of path-breaking amicus curiae briefs to the Supreme Court; they placed the executive branch squarely in favor of reversing *Plessy* v. *Ferguson* and thus set the stage for the *Brown* decision of 1954. Despite determined opposition from the military bureaucracy, Truman desegregated the armed forces, thereby creating an integrated world that touched the lives of millions of Americans before desegregation became a norm in the 1960s.

GROWTH ECONOMICS. After his election victory in 1948, Truman adjusted Democratic liberalism to postwar prosperity in one other critical way. Under the leadership of Leon Keyserling, the second chairman of the Council of Economic Advisers, the administration abandoned Depression-era assumptions about an economy of scarcity.[41] Instead, it began to promote economic growth as a more fundamental objective of liberalism.

Because Truman's years in office were characterized by a full employment economy in every year save 1949, this change was more in the realm of rhetoric than of policy. Keyserling, an eclectic thinker who lacked a Ph.D. in economics, never developed an elegant theoretical formula. He simply asserted that the federal government should employ all the tools at its disposal to concentrate single-mindedly on enlarging the economy; other problems would take care of themselves. He understood that only economic growth could fund the major objective of Democratic liberalism—the steady development of a state with bigger and better social programs.

The "stagflation" of the Eisenhower years would give a special relevance to Keyserling's message and keep it at the top of the Democratic agenda. Walter Heller and other academic economists in the meantime developed a theoretical neo-Keynesian rationale for growth economics.[42] John F. Kennedy and Lyndon Johnson would adopt their proposals in the 1960s and pursue what appeared a promising growth program, built around the tax cut of 1964, before Vietnam overheated the economy. Thereafter, partly because of mounting concern over the environmental consequences, partly because of the party's difficulties in controlling inflation, rapid growth would lose its salience on the Democratic economic agenda. Amazingly, in the 1980s the issue would be captured by the Republicans under Ronald Reagan, talking Kennedy-style tax cuts but devoted to private investment and consumption rather than social democracy.

ANTICOMMUNISM. Leaving aside their substantial merits, Truman's Cold War policies had the tactical advantage of disconnecting the party from what had become an embarrassing alliance with the Soviet Union and American Communists. The Truman Doctrine and the Marshall Plan protected American interests in Europe and the Middle East while sustaining liberal democracy in such countries as France and Italy. The president's diplomacy also provided a focus for a debate on the left wing of the party that led to the expulsion of Communists and pro-Communist "Popular Fronters" from the organized liberal movement and leading labor unions. Henry Wallace and the 1948 Progressives probably did more good for Truman by running against him than by remaining a conspicuous pro-Soviet faction within the Democratic Party.

Truman's anticommunist policies were, to be sure, not perfect. His diplomacy was well crafted, thanks in no small part to a highly professional Department of State. Its domestic extensions, however, included an ill-conceived loyalty program for the entire federal civil service and the even worse decision to prosecute the leaders of the American Communist Party under the Smith Act. Truman himself came to realize that the loyalty program was a mistake, courageously (although unsuccessfully) vetoed the McCarran Internal Security Act of 1950, and emerged as a defender of civil liberties against the assaults of Senator Joseph McCarthy and others on the right.

In his diplomacy, as with his domestic reform program, Truman aligned himself with what Arthur Schlesinger Jr., characterized as Vital Center liberalism. Rejecting the totalitarianism of the left as well as that of the right, advocating civil liberties and democratic politics at home and abroad, renouncing full-scale socialism in favor of enhanced social welfarism, Vital Center liberalism could reach a wide audience within the Democratic Party, not least among them large ethnoreligious minorities that were bitterly anti-Soviet.

TRUMAN'S LEADERSHIP. In the end, it was Truman himself who defined what the Democratic Party meant in the immediate postwar years and then sold that definition to the American people in 1948. His foreign policy surely helped him. In his first term, by mutual understanding with the Republicans, it was bipartisan and not a matter of debate. During the campaign of 1948, Truman's authorization put U.S. military transports in the air around the clock to thwart the Soviet-imposed blockade of Berlin.

Another foreign policy issue had important political ramifications. The Arab-Jewish conflict in Palestine might seem a bit of a sideshow when contrasted to the U.S.-Soviet confrontation in Europe, but the electoral stakes were large. Here also there was no real difference between the two parties; leaders in both generally sympathized with the concept of some sort of Jewish political entity in Palestine. But with the Jewish population overwhelmingly committed to the Democratic Party and Jewish leaders wielding substantial influence within it, Truman faced the toughest pressures.

As president, he struggled desperately with the issue of Palestine throughout his first term, striving to make decisions that would reconcile the national interest with his political interests. In May 1948, over the protests of the State Department, he ordered recognition of the newly proclaimed state of Israel. For the rest of the year he would acquiesce in the department's resistance to further concessions, but what he had done was enough to hold the bulk of the Jewish vote. During his second term, the U.S.-Israeli relationship became closer, establishing a pattern of support for the Jewish state that became a sine qua non of Democratic foreign policy thereafter.

The campaign of 1948 was largely about competing visions of domestic policy, which meant it was about liberalism. In itself that did not necessarily bode well for the Democrats. Truman was smart enough to realize that his initiatives had limited appeal. A Congress controlled by Democrats in 1945–46 had been about as unwilling to do anything with them as had the Republican Congress of 1947–48. The Taft-Hartley Act had been supported by a majority of the Democratic delegation in the House. The civil rights program he had sent up to Congress in early 1948 attracted little public enthusiasm in the North and was fearsomely unpopular in the South.

The president never repudiated anything in his own agenda, although he would have soft-pedaled civil rights in the Democratic platform; as it was, a floor revolt led by Hubert Humphrey, the dynamic young mayor of Minneapolis, obtained a full-scale commitment to every point in the civil rights program. "The time has come," Humphrey declared on the convention floor, "for the Democratic Party to get out of the shadow of states' rights and walk into the bright sunshine of human rights."[43] He and his liberal allies nailed the banner of civil rights to the Democratic Party for once and for all. They also precipitated a walkout of delegates from Alabama and Mississippi. Shortly afterward, a new States Rights Party would nominate Governor J. Strom Thurmond of South Carolina for president. The "Dixiecrats" had only one raison d'être—to deny the South, and the presidency, to Truman. Realizing that conciliation of the South was impossible, the president had quickly issued an executive order desegregating the armed forces. During the campaign he became the first chief executive ever to speak in Harlem. African American leaders, who understood they were in a contest with the white South to determine who held the balance of power in a presidential election, took note. But the election was not primarily about civil rights.

Truman waged a grueling, fiery campaign in which he established himself as a plain-talking leader fighting for the common people against a fat-cat opposition. Leaving Washington on his first big swing around the country, he told his running mate, Senator Alben Barkley, "I'll mow 'em down Alben, and I'll give 'em hell."[44] Over the next several weeks, he described the Republicans as "gluttons of privilege" aching to oppress farmers and workers. If at times his rhetoric was excessive, many voters found the persona of the fighting underdog appealing. His campaign train drew large and friendly crowds at one stop after another.

A solid strategy lay behind the tactics. Truman made the election into a referendum on Roosevelt's New Deal. Crisscrossing the country, making hundreds of speeches, he repeatedly accused the Republicans of wanting to repeal the New Deal and turn the clock back to the 1920s. In a feat of political jujitsu, he converted the Democratic defeat of 1946 into a stroke of good fortune. No one, after all, could expect him to have gotten anything from a Republican Congress—even if he had done so brilliantly on foreign policy issues—and the Republicans, especially those in the House, had managed to appear inflexibly negative. Truman's opponent, Thomas E. Dewey—governor of New York, cool personification of the organization man, a sure winner—never stooped to answer the president's charges.

It is overly simple, of course, to describe any presidential election as merely an ideological plebiscite. Truman's intensive campaigning no doubt heated up the blood of a lot of Democratic partisans whose loyalty to the party had little to do with programs and platforms. His fighting underdog role surely enhanced his personal appeal. Still, in the end, all explanations come back to Truman's defense of the New Deal. Roosevelt's achievements were established beyond recall. Truman polled 49.5 percent of the popular vote, Dewey 45 percent. Thurmond and Wallace received about 2.4 percent each; Thurmond carried Alabama, Louisiana, Mississippi, and South Carolina for thirty-nine electoral votes. Wallace pulled enough votes away from the Democrats to throw Maryland, Michigan, and New York to Dewey. The count was close enough that numerous groups could claim some credit for the victory—African Americans motivated by civil rights, farmers who resented cuts in the agricultural program, labor in support of Truman's Taft-Hartley veto. The important question, however, was just what sort of a mandate Truman had.

The answer, to put it simply, was "not much." The public had voted *against* a largely fanciful threat to established New Deal programs they had come to cherish, not *for* a lot of new legislation. The Democrats had regained control of Congress, but by margins in the House almost the same as those of 1938, the election that had given birth to the conservative coalition; in the Senate, they had only a 54–42 edge. Truman would get some very significant enlargements of Social Security and other ornaments from the 1930s. However, aside from the Housing Act of 1949, the Fair Deal would run into a brick wall. What the president had done in 1948 was to arrest the disintegration of the party and just barely preserve the Roosevelt coalition, right down to maintaining its internal gridlock.

Perhaps most critically, the South emerged with more potential power within the party than in years, despite the apparent failure of the Thurmond candidacy. The South had been irrelevant to Roosevelt's four victories; Truman had won the election only because he had held on to most of it. If in addition to the four states he carried Thurmond had won Texas and any other two southern states, Truman would have failed to attain a majority in the Electoral College, leaving the contest to be decided by the House of Representatives.

If the Republicans could have laid claim to all those electoral votes, Dewey would have been elected. There already were plenty of stirrings of independence in Texas, where Governor Coke Stevenson had been friendly to the Dixiecrats and Houston publisher Jesse H. Jones, a leader of conservative Democrats in the Roosevelt years, had endorsed Dewey. The vision of a South, anti-civil rights and conservative in its broader outlook, voting Republican in presidential elections suddenly was by no means outlandish. It was probably the mathematics of his victory as much as anything that impelled Truman to avoid retaliation against the Dixiecrats and reject efforts to reduce southern influence in Congress after 1948.

Numerous developments cemented the gridlock—the fall of China, the Soviet A-bomb, the Hiss case, the Rosenberg case, and, above all, the Korean War. Truman faced the unexpected invasion of South Korea with decisiveness and fortitude. As soon as he was informed of North Korea's move across the thirty-eighth parallel, he told his secretary of state, Dean Acheson, "Dean, we've got to stop the sons of bitches no matter what."[45] The price was high— a stalled domestic program, a prolonged, stalemated war after China intervened, and a surge of hysterical anticommunism that engulfed the administration. By the end of 1950, McCarthyism had become a dominating force in American politics, the Democrats had given back some of their gains in Congress, and Truman was circling the wagons to defend his foreign policy. He had to unite the party behind a holding action in Korea, the dismissal of General Douglas MacArthur for insubordination, and a sharp military expansion to insure the defense of Europe. Revelations of small-bore corrup-

tion in the administration added to the damage. In 1952, a Republican strategist would describe the formula for his party's campaign as K-1, C-2: Korea,
Communism, corruption.

Truman was by then a spent force politically, although feistier and more vehement than ever in his campaigning. The Republican candidate, Dwight D.
Eisenhower, eclipsed Dewey in charisma and political savvy; significantly, he
went out of his way to reassure the voters explicitly that he would pose no
threat to the achievements of the Roosevelt era. This pledge, given with at least
a degree of reluctance, underscored Truman's accomplishment. If he had been
unable to achieve his Fair Deal program, he had demonstrated that a broad
national consensus supported the New Deal. Republicans from Eisenhower
on understood the lesson. Even the "Reagan Revolution" would be largely a reaction against the Great Society and the 1960s, not the New Deal.

Truman also had committed the Democratic Party to a foreign policy that
both Republicans and Democrats would follow for a generation—active involvement in the world with the objective of establishing a liberal international order while containing expansionist totalitarianism in the form of the
Soviet empire. Pursued with varying degrees of activism and passivity, skill
and ineptness by his successors, frequently denounced by utopians of both
the liberal left and the conservative right, containment nonetheless remained the guiding principle of American foreign policy until the collapse
of the Soviet Union.

Roosevelt and Truman between them had created a new Democratic Party one with nearly unlimited faith in activist government, social-democratic
policies, and a commitment to the rights of minorities, even those with black
skin; one that dedicated the United States to continuing international involvement against the menace of Communist totalitarianism; one that, whatever its
internal contradictions, was the dominant majority in American politics at the
level of Congress and the statehouses. In 1952, that achievement seemed about
as enduring as anything could be in American politics.

Vietnam, the New Left, and the counterculture were less than a decade
and a half away.

NOTES

This essay is a substantially revised and enlarged version of an article originally published in Peter B. Kovler, ed., *Democrats and the American Idea* (Washington, D.C.:
Center for National Policy Press, 1992).

1. There is a significant, if rather dated, literature about the issue of change and continuity during this period, focusing on the New Deal and the Great Depression. See, for example, Richard Hofstadter, *The Age of Reform: Bryan to F.D.R.* (New York: Alfred A. Knopf, 1955), chap. 7, parts 3 and 4; Carl Degler, *Out of Our Past* (New York: Harper & Row, 1959), chap. 12; William E. Leuchtenburg, *Franklin D. Roosevelt and the New Deal* (New York: Harper & Row, 1963), chap. 14; Richard S. Kirkendall, "The Great Depression: Another Watershed in American History?" in John Braeman et al., *Change and Continuity in Twentieth-Century America* (Columbus: Ohio State University Press, 1964); and Otis L. Graham, *Encore for Reform: The Old Progressives and the New Deal* (New York: Oxford University Press, 1967). The question is protean and ultimately irresolvable; still, it is an important one that forces one to think through fundamental issues of twentieth-century American history.

2. To attempt to divine the "true" meaning of the term *Jeffersonian* would be to embark on an endless tangent. Suffice to say that all the meanings in the text had acquired some currency by the early twentieth century. Those who would like to delve further into the problem should consult Merrill Peterson, *The Jefferson Image in the American Mind* (New York: Oxford University Press, 1960); Merrill Peterson, *Thomas Jefferson and the New Nation* (New York: Oxford University Press, 1986); and Noble E. Cunningham Jr., *In Pursuit of Reason: The Life of Thomas Jefferson* (Baton Rouge: Louisiana State University Press, 1987).

3. David Burner, *The Politics of Provincialism: The Democratic Party in Transition, 1918–1932* (New York: Alfred A. Knopf, 1967), a book of considerable merit and after thirty-five years the best single volume on its subject. See also Alan Lichtman, *Prejudice and the Old Politics: The Presidential Election of 1928* (Chapel Hill: University of North Carolina Press, 1979). Two classic works on American politics and society in the 1920s are William E. Leuchtenburg, *The Perils of Prosperity, 1914–1932* (Chicago: University of Chicago Press, 1958), and John D. Hicks, *Republican Ascendancy* (New York: Harper & Row, 1960); both are written from a "progressive" perspective that has much in common with the classic worldview of the Democratic Party. Ellis W. Hawley, *The Great War and the Search for a Modern Order*, 2d ed. (New York: St. Martin's Press, 1992), deemphasizes standard partisan ideology in favor of an "organizational-managerial" interpretation that stresses the growth of public and private bureaucracies, the emergence of specialized professional expertise, and consequent redefinitions of the nature of the state.

4. Two classic works on the causes and character of the Great Depression are Charles Kindleberger, *The World in Depression, 1929–1939* (Berkeley: University of California Press, 1973); and John A. Garraty, *The Great Depression* (New York: Harcourt Brace Jovanovich, 1986). For an interesting, albeit to my mind unconvincing, revisionist interpretation of Hawley-Smoot, see Alfred E. Eckes, *Opening America's*

Markets: U.S. Foreign Trade Policy since 1776 (Chapel Hill: University of North Carolina Press, 1995), chap. 4. On Federal Reserve policy, see Milton Friedman and Anna Jacobson Schwartz, *A Monetary History of the United States, 1867–1960* (Princeton: Princeton University Press, 1963), chap. 7.

5. *Historical Statistics of the United States* (Washington, D.C.: U.S. Government Printing Office, 1975) 1:135, 224, 483; 2:1038.

6. Martin L. Fausold, *The Presidency of Herbert C. Hoover* (Lawrence: University Press of Kansas, 1985), provides a thorough and authoritative account of Hoover's efforts and failures.

7. See Samuel I. Rosenman, ed., *The Public Papers and Addresses of Franklin D. Roosevelt*, vol. 2, *The Year of Crisis, 1933* (New York: Random House, 1938), 11–16, for the formal prepared text. For description of the event and for the text as actually delivered, see *New York Times,* March 5, 1933.

8. See, for example, David Sarasohn, *The Party of Reform: Democrats in the Progressive Era* (Oxford: University of Mississippi Press, 1989); Robert Cherney, *Righteous Cause: The Life of William Jennings Bryan* (Boston: Little, Brown, 1985); Le Roy Ashby, *William Jennings Bryan: Champion of Democracy* (Boston: Twayne, 1987); Paolo E. Coletta, *William Jennings Bryan*, 3 vols. (Lincoln: University of Nebraska Press, 1964–69); Arthur S. Link, *Woodrow Wilson and the Progressive Era, 1910–1917* (New York: Harper & Row, 1954), *Wilson: The New Freedom* (Princeton: Princeton University Press, 1956), and *Wilson: Campaigns for Progressivism and Peace* (Princeton: Princeton University Press, 1965); John Milton Cooper, *The Warrior and the Priest* (Cambridge, Mass.: Harvard University Press, 1983), and Cooper, *Pivotal Decades: The United States, 1900–1920* (New York: W. W. Norton, 1990), chap. 9 (note especially the illustration on p. 250).

9. The scholarly literature on Roosevelt and the New Deal is vast. David Kennedy, *Freedom from Fear: The American People in Depression and War, 1929–1945* (New York: Oxford University Press, 1999), is now the standard single volume work. William E. Leuchtenburg, *Franklin D. Roosevelt and the New Deal*, remains a classic interpretation. Other important interpretations include Anthony Badger, *The New Deal: The Depression Years* (New York: Hill & Wang, 1989); James MacGregor Burns, *Roosevelt: The Lion and the Fox* (New York: Harcourt, Brace & World, 1956), a thoughtful and provocative liberal critique; Frank Freidel, *Franklin D. Roosevelt: A Rendezvous with Destiny* (Boston: Little, Brown, 1990); Patrick Maney, *F.D.R.: The Roosevelt Presence* (New York: Twayne, 1992). Paul K. Conkin, *The New Deal*, 3d ed. (Arlington Heights, Ill.: Harlan Davidson, 1992) is a brief critique from the left in the pragmatic, social democratic tradition of John Dewey. Jordan Schwarz, *The New Dealers: Power Politics in the Age of Roosevelt* (New York: Alfred A. Knopf, 1993), examines the New Deal as a species of "state capitalism." Colin Gordon, *New Deals:*

Business, Labor, and Politics in America, 1920–1935 (New York: Cambridge University Press, 1994), approaches the topic from a perspective that combines the "organizational-managerial" interpretation with what appears to be a loose neo-Marxism reminiscent of the early work of Gabriel Kolko. On the World War I experience, see especially William E. Leuchtenburg, "The New Deal and the Analogue of War," in *The FDR Years: On Roosevelt and His Legacy* (New York: Columbia University Press, 1995), 35–75, an important pioneering essay. Arthur M. Schlesinger Jr., *The Age of Roosevelt*, 3 vols. (Boston: Houghton Mifflin, 1957–60), is a celebratory, scholarly, and near-definitive blending of history and biography covering the years 1929–36. John Braeman et al., eds., *The New Deal: The National Level* (Columbus: Ohio State University Press, 1975), is an important collection of original essays.

10. Among the many works on New Deal policy toward various sectors of the economy, the following are possibly the most useful: Ellis W. Hawley, *The New Deal and the Problem of Monopoly* (Princeton: Princeton University Press, 1966); Irving Bernstein, *Turbulent Years: The American Worker, 1929–1939* (Boston: Houghton Mifflin, 1969); and Theodore Saloutos, *The American Farmer and the New Deal* (Ames: Iowa State University Press, 1982).

11. Leuchtenburg, *Franklin D. Roosevelt and the New Deal*, 68.

12. *Historical Statistics* 1:135.

13. John Maynard Keynes to Franklin D. Roosevelt, February 1, 1938, reproduced in Howard Zinn, ed., *New Deal Thought* (Indianapolis: Bobbs-Merrill, 1966), 403–409.

14. For an early and very influential example, see Burns, *Roosevelt: The Lion and the Fox*, 328–336.

15. Garraty, *The Great Depression*, 197; R. J. Overy, *The Nazi Economic Recovery*, 2d ed. (Cambridge: Cambridge University Press, 1996).

16. *Historical Statistics* 2:1105.

17. On tax policy, the most comprehensive treatment is Mark Leff, *The Limits of Symbolic Reform: The New Deal and Taxation, 1933–1939* (New York: Cambridge University Press, 1984), a work that is, however, written from a social-democratic, redistributionist frame of reference quite different from my own.

18. Leuchtenburg, *Franklin D. Roosevelt and the New Deal*, 183–184.

19. Keynes to Roosevelt, February 1, 1938, in Zinn, ed., *New Deal Thought*, 403–409.

20. Richard Vedder and Lowell Gallaway, *Out of Work: Unemployment and Government in Twentieth-Century America* (New York: Holmes & Meier, 1993), especially chap. 7, is an important, although perhaps exaggerated, statement of the thesis that maximum employment occurs only when government lets the cost of labor fall to its natural market level. Along these lines, it is worth noting also that German full employment was achieved at the cost of lower worker real wages and living standards

than in the peak year of 1928. To be sure, part of this decline reflected Hitler's guns-over-butter decision to push military production at the expense of civilian goods after 1935, but it may be an irreducible fact that it is easier even (especially?) for a totalitarian regime to create many jobs with mediocre compensation than an equal number with good compensation. See Overy, *The Nazi Economic Recovery*, especially chap. 2.

21. On the administration incomprehension of small business, see, for example, Alan Brinkley, *The End of Reform: New Deal Liberalism in Recession and War* (New York: Alfred A. Knopf, 1995), 90–91.

22. Leuchtenburg, *Franklin D. Roosevelt and the New Deal*, 154.

23. Keynes to Roosevelt, February 1, 1938, in Zinn, ed., *New Deal Thought*, 403–409.

24. Roosevelt was perhaps foremost among a generation of political leaders that used the new media to great effect. Adolf Hitler in Germany is perhaps the most noted example, but Stanley Baldwin in Great Britain, who delivered his first radio address in 1924, was surely the pioneer and was far more formidable than generally remembered today. Each, it must be emphasized, was able to use the modern media as a vehicle of charisma because he spoke in the idiom of his own political culture, not only addressing its greatest concerns but also expressing its distinctive mood. See, for example, David Welch, *The Third Reich: Politics and Propaganda* (London: Routledge, 1993), 30–34, and Philip Williamson, *Stanley Baldwin: Conservative Leadership and National Values* (New York: Cambridge University Press, 1999), esp. 83–87.

25. Vedder and Gallaway, *Out of Work*, 77.

26. WPA workers often demonstrated and engaged in letter-writing campaigns in favor of continued appropriations for either their specific projects or for the agency in general. Occasionally they attempted to form labor unions. Sometimes they actually called strikes for better wages or working conditions; invariably these were put down with a decisiveness akin to that with which Ronald Reagan smashed the air-traffic controllers' walkout.

27. On this point see Lizabeth Cohen, *Making a New Deal: Industrial Workers in Chicago, 1919–1939* (New York: Cambridge University Press, 1990, a justly acclaimed melding of cultural and political history.

28. Schwarz, *The New Dealers*, discusses the issue of Jews in the New Deal at several points, esp. 146 and 181.

29. On African Americans and the New Deal, see Harvard Sitkoff, *A New Deal for Blacks* (New York: Oxford University Press, 1978); Raymond Wolters, *Negroes and the Great Depression* (Westport, Conn.: Greenwood, 1970); John B. Kirby, *Black Americans and the Roosevelt Era* (Knoxville: University of Tennessee Press, 1980); and Patricia Sullivan, *Days of Hope* (Chapel Hill: University of North Carolina Press, 1996).

30. *Historical Statistics* 1:457.

31. This phrase and the interpretive design are taken from James MacGregor Burns, *The Deadlock of Democracy* (Englewood Cliffs, N.J.: Prentice-Hall, 1963), a classic of popular political science.

32. Leuchtenburg, *Franklin D. Roosevelt and the New Deal*, 243.

33. Sidney M. Milkis, *The President and the Parties: The Transformation of the American Party System since the New Deal* (New York: Oxford University Press, 1993), vii–ix, chaps. 1–6.

34. Brinkley, *The End of Reform*, especially the introduction and epilogue.

35. The following surveys of American life in World War II are important general works: Richard Polenberg, *War and Society* (Philadelphia: Lippincott, 1972); Geoffrey Perrett, *Days of Sadness, Years of Triumph* (New York: Coward, McCann & Geoghegan, 1973); John M. Blum, *"V" Was for Victory* (New York: Harcourt Brace Jovanovich, 1976); William L. O'Neill, *A Democracy at War* (New York: Free Press, 1993); and John J. Jeffries, *Wartime America* (Chicago: Ivan Dee, 1996).

36. After sixty years one still sees new books and "documentaries" charging that Roosevelt knew of the Pearl Harbor attack plans and, for the sake of getting into the war, did nothing to stop them. Aside from the lack of convincing evidence for this thesis, it is inconceivable that Roosevelt, even if he wanted war, would have left the Pacific fleet exposed. Surely it is more likely that he would have deployed American air and naval power to beat off the attack and strike a surprise counterblow against the Japanese fleet. Such a stroke would have given him the war he *may* have wanted and would have started it with a U.S. victory.

37. Among the many works on Roosevelt as a diplomatist, Robert Dallek, *Franklin D. Roosevelt and American Foreign Policy, 1932–1945* (New York: Oxford University Press, 1979), remains standard. Other studies of considerable importance are James MacGregor Burns, *Roosevelt: The Soldier of Freedom* (New York: Harcourt Brace Jovanovich, 1970); John L. Gaddis, *The United States and the Origins of the Cold War* (New York: Columbia University Press, 1972); Waldo Heinrichs, *Threshold of War: Franklin D. Roosevelt and American Entry into World War II* (New York: Oxford University Press, 1988); Warren F. Kimball, *The Juggler: Franklin Roosevelt As Wartime Statesman* (Princeton: Princeton University Press, 1994); Frederick W. Marks III, *Wind over Sand* (Athens: University of Georgia Press, 1988).

38. Alonzo L. Hamby, *Man of the People: A Life of Harry S. Truman* (New York: Oxford University Press, 1995), 289.

39. The authoritative history of the Truman presidency is Robert Donovan's two-volume survey *Conflict and Crisis* and *Tumultuous Years* (New York: W. W. Norton, 1977, 1982). Donald R. McCoy, *The Presidency of Harry S. Truman* (Lawrence: University Press of Kansas, 1984), is a more selective account by a distinguished historian.

Alonzo L. Hamby, *Beyond the New Deal: Harry S. Truman and American Liberalism* (New York: Columbia University Press, 1973), pursues themes that may be of special interest to the readers of this work. Three biographies that focus as much on the man as his presidency are Robert H. Ferrell, *Harry S. Truman: A Life* (Columbia: University of Missouri Press, 1994); Hamby, *Man of the People*; and David McCullough, *Truman* (New York: Simon & Schuster, 1992).

40. Among the many works on civil rights and the Truman administration, the fullest and most balanced is Donald R. McCoy and Richard T. Ruetten, *Quest and Response* (Lawrence: University Press of Kansas, 1973).

41. Hamby, *Beyond the New Deal*, 297–303.

42. Walter Heller, *New Dimensions of Political Economy* (Cambridge, Mass.: Harvard University Press, 1966), is an accessible introduction to the New Economics.

43. Hamby, *Man of the People*, 448.

44. Hamby, *Man of the People*, 462.

45. Hamby, *Man of the People*, 534.

3

THE ROOSEVELT COURT

Melvin I. Urofsky

On August 12, 1937, after nearly four and a half years in office, Franklin D. Roosevelt finally named his first appointee to the U.S. Supreme Court. In a move that shocked supporters and opponents alike, the president sent to the Senate the name of Hugo LaFayette Black, the senator from Alabama who had been a vociferous proponent of the New Deal and of Roosevelt's controversial court-packing plan. After Black came one opening after another, and, in the end, Roosevelt made nine appointments to the nation's high court, more than any other chief executive save George Washington.

Contemporaries saw the long list of Roosevelt nominees as proof that the president had won the bitter fight with the Court that had erupted into a constitutional crisis in the spring of 1937. Although there is some recent scholarship to suggest that the Court was not as ideologically opposed to New Deal reform as had previously been assumed,[1] at the time both conservatives and liberals saw the Court as standing athwart Roosevelt's efforts to implement New Deal programs.

The Court, after narrowly approving two state reform measures, a Minnesota mortgage moratorium[2] and a New York milk-pricing statute,[3] seemingly turned against all efforts to deal with the economic crisis. First it invalidated a New York model minimum-wage law that even conservative newspapers and the Republican presidential candidate, Alf M. Landon, considered reasonable.[4] When the Court began to hear cases involving federal legislation in December 1934, the administration not only faced a hostile bench but also suffered the consequences of sloppy procedures, poor drafts-manship, and inadequate counsel.[5]

The pattern could be discerned in the first case the justices heard, *Panama Refining Company v. Ryan,* in which the Court exposed the administrative in-adequacies of section 9(c) of the National Recovery Act, an effort to control so-called hot oil from being sold in interstate commerce.[6] After narrowly and reluctantly approving the New Deal's cancellation of gold clauses,[7] the con-servative majority took a highly restrictive view of the interstate nature of railroads and voided the Railroad Retirement Act of 1934.[8] Then on "Black Monday," May 27, 1935, the Court struck at the heart of the New Deal, in-validating the National Industrial Recovery Act and the Frazier-Lemke Mort-gage Act and ruling that the president could not remove members of inde-pendent regulatory commissions.[9] The following January the Court, by a 6–3 vote, struck down what nearly everyone considered a well-planned and well-administered program, the Agricultural Adjustment Act.[10]

Roosevelt believed that the conservatives on the Supreme Court (the so-called Four Horsemen of James C. McReynolds, George Sutherland, Pierce Butler, and Willis Van Devanter, often joined by Chief Justice Charles Evans Hughes and Owen J. Roberts) based their judicial opinions not on a fair read-ing of the Constitution but on their own cramped and outmoded economic views. In his proposal to expand the number of justices on the bench, Roo-sevelt suffered one of the few political defeats of his career. But as countless teachers have told their classes, he lost the battle and won the war. His ap-pointees dominated the Court until the mid-1950s. One should bear in mind that five of the justices who heard and decided *Brown v. Board of Education* in 1954 had been appointed by Franklin Roosevelt, and two of them, Hugo Black and William O. Douglas, served on the high court into the 1970s.

To understand the Roosevelt legacy on the bench, we need to look briefly at the men he appointed and their judicial philosophies, because although they all agreed on the notion that courts should not second-guess the legislative and executive branches on matters of economic policy, they differed widely on oth-er matters, especially the role of the judiciary in protecting individual liberties.

Hugo LaFayette Black of Alabama (1886–1971), Roosevelt's first ap-pointee, joined the Court amid a cloud of controversy. At the time, many people believed Roosevelt had named Black to the Court for supporting the president's court-packing plan. Moreover, because the Senate would not turn down one of its own, Roosevelt in effect humiliated those in the Senate who had not backed the plan by foisting on them a man who apparently lacked credentials for the bench and whose populist political views irritated conservatives. Robert Jackson later recalled: "I had been rather amused at the President's maneuver, which enabled him to get even with the court and with the Senate, which had beat his plan, at the same time. He knew well enough that the Senate could not reject the nomination because of senatorial courtesy. He knew perfectly well it would go against their grain to confirm it. He knew it would not be welcomed by the court."[11] Then shortly after he had been sworn in, it turned out that Black had once belonged to the Ku Klux Klan. All in all, it hardly made for an auspicious start of a judicial career.[12]

Black grew up in rural Alabama, graduated first in his University of Alabama Law School class, and then, after practicing in his native Ashland for a few years, moved to Birmingham in 1907. To supplement his income, Black also served part-time as a municipal court judge and then for three years full-time as Jefferson County prosecuting attorney. In his most famous case, he investigated and prosecuted several police officers for beating and forcing confessions from black defendants. The experience marked him for life and gave him something no other member of the Court had—litigation experience in criminal law—and as a result he brought a discernible passion to those cases.

In his private practice Black tried hundreds of cases and honed his already considerable talents as a debater and orator, skills that led to his election to the U.S. Senate in 1926. In 1932 Black won a second term and immediately became a staunch defender of Franklin D. Roosevelt's New Deal policies, a position that often put him at odds with his fellow southerners. Most important, both on the Senate floor and as head of several important special committees, Black espoused a view that the federal government had sufficient authority under the commerce clause to enact legislation to deal with the Depression, that in fact Congress could regulate any activity that directly or indirectly affected the national economy, and that the judiciary had no power to interfere with these decisions.

Black went onto the Court with a fairly well-developed judicial philosophy, one that included a clear reading of the constitutional text, limited judicial discretion, the protection of individual rights, and broad powers for the government to address a wide range of economic and social problems. Someone once commented that Black's lasting influence on the Court grew out of his willingness to "reinvent the wheel." Like his friend and ally William O. Douglas, Black had little use for precedent, especially if he thought the case erroneously decided. In his first year alone Black issued eight solo dissents, including an almost unprecedented dissent to a per curiam decision.

At the heart of Black's philosophy lay a populist belief in the Constitution as an infallible guide. He opposed judicial subjectivity; the Constitution did not empower judges to select from competing alternatives. He distrusted experts, and leaving either legislative or judicial decision-making in the hands of so-called experts smacked too much of elitism. He offered instead the imposition of absolutes through a literal reading of the Constitution. This narrowed the scope of judicial discretion, but it also helped to make the judiciary the prime vehicle for guaranteeing the values of those absolutes.[13]

Throughout his career Black searched the text of the Constitution for guidance. He understood that one could not always read the document literally, but he sought the meaning he believed had been intended by the Framers. Thus, despite his populist political views and his strong defense of civil liberties, in many ways Black's was an extremely conservative approach, and indeed he saw himself as a strict constructionist. Black became the jurisprudential leader of the liberal bloc on the Court, a group whose ideas would triumph in the 1960s.

Part of Black's effectiveness derived from the considerable political skills he already possessed and had honed in the Senate. More than any other justice of his time, Black proselytized, "working" the other justices as he had once worked his senatorial colleagues in order to gain a majority. The columnist Irving Brant, an admirer of Black's, reported a story Black told that explained a good deal of his effectiveness. Black would talk about an unnamed senator who said that when he wanted to accomplish something he would introduce two bills—the one he wanted passed and another that made the first one seem conservative. Robert Jackson somewhat disdainfully noted that while these methods were appropriate in a legislative body where one dealt with adversaries, he considered them unsuited to a court where the members were supposed to be colleagues. Stone, according to Jackson, found Black's methods very unsettling, and they caused the chief justice "a great deal of discomfort and dissatisfaction."[14]

In January 1938 Roosevelt made his second appointment to the high court, Stanley Forman Reed of Kentucky (1884–1980). A genial man who lived to be ninety-five years old, he told Potter Stewart that he would not want to live his life over again, inasmuch as "it could not possibly be as good the second time." After graduating from Yale Law School, Reed had built a thriving law practice in Maysville, Kentucky, dabbled in state politics, and helped manage his friend Fred Vinson's congressional campaigns. Then in 1929 he moved to Washington when Herbert Hoover named him counsel to the Federal Farm Board, a position he retained in the Roosevelt administration. Reed's geniality as well as his passionate belief in the desirability of the federal government's playing a major role in the nation's social and economic life soon caught the attention of the president, who named Reed solicitor general. He performed that role in, at best, a lackluster manner, but in early 1938 Roosevelt named Reed to replace George Sutherland, the second of the Four Horsemen to retire.[15]

Once on the Court, Reed tended to defer to Congress, and a determination of what Congress had intended often proved dispositive for him, whether the issue concerned constitutional, administrative, or statutory interpretation. As with the other Roosevelt appointees, Reed could be considered liberal in that he believed the Court had no right to deny Congress full use of its commerce powers. He had less faith in state and local powers however, and seemed to have had little interest in the protection of individual liberties. One area did arouse his concern, and during his tenure Reed voted often but not in every case to broaden religious rights under the First Amendment. On the whole, his record is marked primarily by inconsistency, a not unfamiliar characteristic of many New Dealers.[16]

Roosevelt's third appointee, Felix Frankfurter (1882–1965), had been named to succeed Benjamin Nathan Cardozo in January 1939 amid high hopes that he would become the intellectual leader of the Court. Solicitor General Robert H. Jackson, in a sentiment echoed by Harlan Stone, claimed that only Frankfurter had the legal resources "to face Chief Justice Hughes in conference and hold his own in discussion." Upon news of his nomination, New Dealers had gathered in the office of Secretary of the Interior Harold Ickes to celebrate, and all those present heartily agreed with Ickes' judgment of the nomination as "the most significant and worthwhile thing the President has done."[17] There is, unfortunately, no way one can predict whether an appointee will be great or mediocre once on the bench, and Frankfurter ranks as one of the great disappointments in modern times.

Born in Vienna, Frankfurter had emigrated to the United States as a child, and his innate brilliance had shone first at the City College of New York and then at the Harvard Law School. Upon graduation he had briefly joined a Wall Street firm, but he soon fled to work with U.S. Attorney Henry L. Stimson; he then followed Stimson into the Roosevelt and Taft administrations. Short, exuberant, a brilliant conversationalist and an inveterate idol-worshipper, Frankfurter soon became the center of a group of young bureaucrats and writers who shared quarters on Nineteenth Street, a place they dubbed the "House of Truth." There Gutzom Borgum sketched his proposed presidential monument, Herbert Croly and Walter Lippmann expounded on contemporary problems, and Oliver Wendell Holmes and Louis Brandeis dropped by often.

Frankfurter and Holmes fell under each other's spell; the younger man adored Holmes, who reciprocated the sentiment. When Frankfurter accepted a position at the Harvard Law School after World War I, he took responsibility for choosing Holmes's clerks. Holmes appealed to Frankfurter for a number of reasons, but from a jurisprudential point of view, Holmes held high the banner of judicial restraint, a banner that Frankfurter in his own time would also carry.

In many ways, however, the relationship with Brandeis proved more decisive. Brandeis found in Frankfurter a surrogate to carry on his reform work; he urged Frankfurter to take the professorship at Harvard, and he provided a financial subsidy to enable Frankfurter, who lacked an independent income, to devote himself to reform efforts.[18] During the 1920s Frankfurter, through his defense of Sacco and Vanzetti and his writings for *The New Republic,* became a leading reformer in his own right, a man Brandeis called "the most useful lawyer in the United States."

His students also spread Frankfurter's influence. A brilliant teacher, he trained a whole generation of lawyers in administrative law, and when the Depression came and government burgeoned under the New Deal, Frankfurter became a one-man placement agency, staffing one federal office after another with his former students.[19] He also exerted a quiet but effective influence on several New Deal policies through his many contacts not only with leading administration figures but also with President Roosevelt. The two men had known each other since World War I, and during the 1930s Frankfurter became a frequent guest at the White House.[20]

Frankfurter, like Black, went onto the Court with a well-developed judicial philosophy, but one far different from the Alabaman's. Both men believed in judicial restraint, but Frankfurter took what Black considered a much too subjective approach, leaving too great a power in the hands of judges to "interpret" constitutional injunctions. Most importantly, however, Black drew a sharp distinction between economic legislation and restrictions on individual liberties, with judges carrying a special obligation to protect the latter; Frankfurter considered all legislation equal, and demanded that judges defer to the legislative will unless they found a clear-cut constitutional prohibition. The debate between these two views would define much of constitutional history in the last half of the twentieth century.[21]

One week after Frankfurter took his seat, Louis D. Brandeis retired, and to replace him Roosevelt named William Orville Douglas (1898–1980). A true product of the Pacific Northwest, Douglas had grown up in Yakima, Washington, where he contracted infantile paralysis as a child. Gradually he regained limited use of his legs, but he was still a sickly child at the time of his father's death. He later wrote that in the middle of the funeral he stopped crying only after he looked up and saw Mount Adams in the distance. "Adams stood cool and calm, unperturbed. . . . Adams suddenly seemed to be a friend. Adams subtly became a force for me to tie to, a symbol of stability of strength."[22] Between the strong will of his mother and his own self-determination, Douglas overcame his physical disabilities. He started to hike in the mountains, an experience that not only built up his strength but also turned into a lifelong devotion to the environment. The drive to build himself physically carried over into other areas of his life. The Yakima High School yearbook of 1916 noted that its valedictorian that year had been "born for success."

After graduation from Whitman College, Douglas headed east in the summer of 1922 with $75 in his pocket to attend Columbia Law School. Douglas entered Columbia at a time when its faculty had just begun to explore new areas of legal research that would eventually lead to the "Legal Realism" movement. The Realists believed that in order to understand the law and the behavior of legal institutions, one had to look at individual behavior and use the social sciences to find the real causes of particular actions. Douglas became a devoted adherent to this new philosophy, and after a miserable two years working in a Wall Street law firm, he returned to Columbia as a teacher in 1927. Within a year, however, he resigned to accept a position at the Yale Law School, which, under the leadership of its brilliant young dean Robert M. Hutchins, quickly became the center of Legal Realism, and Douglas one of its star exponents.[23]

His tenure at Yale may have been the most peaceful in his life, but beneath a surface tranquility he remained restless, especially when he looked to Washington and saw the dynamic activities going on under the New Deal umbrella. In 1934 Douglas accepted an assignment from the newly created Securities and Exchange Commission to study protective committees, the agency stockholders use during bankruptcy reorganization to protect their interests. He began commuting between New Haven and Washington, and soon came to the attention of the SEC chair, Joseph P. Kennedy, who arranged for the thirty-seven-year-old Douglas to be named to the commission in 1935. Two years later President Roosevelt named Douglas chair of the SEC.[24]

During these years in Washington, Douglas became part of Franklin D. Roosevelt's inner circle, often joining the weekly poker games at the White

House. Many people speculated that the bright, handsome westerner might have a future in politics. In fact, Douglas had already tired of the game and wanted to return to Yale. When a messenger interrupted a golf game on March 19, 1939, to tell Douglas that the president wanted to see him at the White House, Douglas almost did not go, for he fully expected that Roosevelt was going to ask him to take over the troubled Federal Communications Commission. But after teasing him for a few minutes, Roosevelt offered Douglas the seat on the Supreme Court vacated by Brandeis a month earlier. Roosevelt naturally wanted to make sure that his appointees would support his program, and in Douglas he had a confirmed New Deal liberal, someone who could mix it up with the conservatives, a quick mind, a westerner, and a loyal personal friend.

Douglas, the youngest person ever appointed to the Supreme Court, would establish a record of longevity for service before illness forced him to retire in late 1975. Moreover, no other justice ever engaged in so extensive and public a nonjudicial life. Douglas always claimed that the work of the Court never took more than three or four days a week; he read petitions rapidly, rarely agonized over decisions, could get to the heart of an issue instantly, and wrote his opinions quickly. This left him time for other activities, such as travel, lecturing, writing, climbing mountains, and, as some critics claimed, getting into trouble.

Douglas and Frankfurter had been friends, and friendly rivals, from their days as law school professors, and the younger Douglas had often looked to the more established Frankfurter for advice. Jurisprudentially, the two seemed to share the same basic values, but the shifting agenda of the Court soon highlighted the fact that on the crucial issues to confront the judiciary in the 1940s and 1950s they differed significantly. During his first years on the bench Douglas allied himself with Black, but he eventually proved far more willing and activist than his friend. Douglas, however, provided an able second to Black in the battles shaping up over which direction the Court should take.[25]

Roosevelt made his next appointment to the Court in early 1940, when he named Francis William Murphy (1890–1949) to replace Pierce Butler, and with that appointment sealed the constitutional revolution triggered by the New Deal. After more than two decades of conservative domination, the Court now had a majority committed to the idea that the political branches should determine economic policy, and that courts had no right to pass judgment on the wisdom of those policies. Roosevelt, of course, wanted men on the bench who would endorse New Deal policies, but as the Court's agenda changed in the later 1940s, several of his appointees seemed to grow more conservative. With Frank Murphy, however, Roosevelt got a thoroughgoing liberal, one who had little use for technical questions and believed that the objectives of law should be justice and human dignity. Even more than Douglas and Black, Murphy cared little for precedents and openly relied on what one commentator has called "visceral jurisprudence." The law knows no finer hour, Murphy wrote, "than when it cuts through formal concepts and transitory emotions to protect unpopular citizens against discrimination and persecution."[26]

Murphy inherited his radical politics from his father, who had been jailed in his youth for Fenian sympathies, and his devout Catholicism from his mother. From the beginning, he had seen law and politics as intertwined, with law the avenue to political success. In 1923 he won election as a criminal court judge in Detroit, and reformed an antiquated system. Labor and minority groups propelled him into the mayor's office in 1930, and he set about creating a welfare system to help those thrown out of work by the Depression. Roosevelt named Murphy, one of his early backers, as governor-general of the Philippines, but although Murphy proved popular and effective in that job, he saw it as a detour on the way to the White House.

Murphy returned to the country to run for and win the Michigan gubernatorial race in 1936, and shortly after he took office the auto workers began the sit-down strikes of 1937. Company officials immediately went to court to seek injunctions against the strikers, but Murphy refused to enforce the orders. He called out the national guard to maintain peace while he worked behind the scenes to avert outright bloodshed. He succeeded, but both sides accused him of favoring the other, and he lost his reelection bid in 1938. Roosevelt owed Murphy for taking the heat off Washington during the strikes, and so named him attorney general in 1939. Murphy was in that office less than a year, but during his tenure he set up a civil liberties unit that for the first time employed the power of the federal government to protect individual rights. This activity did not sit well with many people, especially southerners, and to some extent Roosevelt kicked Murphy upstairs to the Court. Murphy recognized this and did not really want to go. He still had his sights set on the presidency, and no one had ever gone from the bench to the Oval Office. Murphy also thought he would be on the sidelines, away from the real action. "I fear that my work will be mediocre up there while on the firing line where I have been trained to action I could do much better."[27]

Even Murphy's admirers make no claim that he had special talents as a jurist, and he recognized his own limitations. He felt inferior in the company of Stone and Black, Douglas and Frankfurter; he knew little constitutional law, and his prior judicial experience had been on a municipal criminal bench. But he learned, and relied on bright clerks to draft his opinions.

Murphy, however, did develop a jurisprudence, one based on the notion that restrictions on individual liberties required strict scrutiny by the courts, and he also adopted Hugo Black's notion that the liberties protected by the First Amendment held a "preferred position" in the constitutional firmament. Murphy's first opinion indicated the path he would take. New justices may pick their first opinion, and Murphy chose a case overturning a state law that banned virtually all picketing by union members. Although Brandeis had earlier suggested that picketing might be a form of protected speech, this notion did not become law until Murphy's opinion in *Thornhill v. Alabama* (1940). There the new justice extended First Amendment protection to peaceful picketing, and forcefully cited the *Carolene Products* footnote to justify the judiciary's overturning of a law that invaded civil liberties. In 1969 Justice Tom Clark wrote that the opinion was "the bedrock upon which many of the Court's civil rights pronouncements rest."[28] Although Murphy initially appeared willing to follow Frankfurter's lead and joined him in the first flag salute case, he soon gravitated to his natural moorings on the liberal side of the Court, and along with Black and Douglas consistently fought for greater protection of the individual.

On June 2, 1941, Chief Justice Charles Evans Hughes informed Roosevelt of his decision to retire, and, for a number of reasons, Roosevelt had to act quickly in filling not only the Court's center chair but also the seat vacated by James C. McReynolds a few months earlier. Speculation on Hughes's successor had quickly focused on Associate Justice Harlan Fiske Stone and on Attorney General Robert H. Jackson. Roosevelt had in fact promised the next vacancy on the Court to Jackson, one of the most widely respected members of the administration and a member of the president's inner circle of poker friends and advisors. But he had not expected that vacancy to be the center chair, and in the summer of 1941 sound political reasons supported the elevation of Stone, who had first been named to the Court in 1925.

Harlan Fiske Stone (1872–1946), after a brief stint in private practice, had served for many years as dean of the Columbia Law School. In 1923 he returned to private practice with a prestigious Wall Street form, but a year later an old college friend, Calvin Coolidge, named Stone as attorney general and gave him a mandate to clean out the corruption in the Justice Department left from the tenure of Harding's crony, Harry M. Daugherty. Stone won plaudits for his work and according to some sources, his very success led to his being kicked upstairs to the Supreme Court in 1925. Stone was the first nominee to the high court to appear in person before a Senate committee to answer questions. Liberal senators objected that Stone was too probusiness and that he had been J. P. Morgan's lawyer (Sullivan & Cromwell did count the House of Morgan among its clients). But Stone handled the questions easily, and the Senate confirmed the appointment by a vote of 71–6.

Despite the fears of progressives, Stone soon aligned himself with the liberals on the bench, Holmes and Brandeis in the 1920s, and then with Cardozo when he took Holmes's seat. In the 1920s Stone tended to let Holmes and Brandeis write the stinging dissents against the judicial activism of the Taft Court, but he believed just as passionately as they did in judicial restraint, the idea that courts should not try to second-guess the wisdom of the legislature and that legislation should not be struck down unless it violated a clear constitutional prohibition.

With the retirement of Holmes and the aging of Brandeis, Stone took a more vocal position in the 1930s, and by the time Hughes retired Stone had emerged as the chief opponent of judicial conservatism. During the constitutional struggles over New Deal legislation, Stone had consistently defended the administration's efforts to deal with the Depression, and his views on the proper role of the judiciary and the necessity for judges to practice self-restraint can be found in his dissenting opinion in *United States v. Butler* (1936). There Stone objected to the majority's striking down the Agricultural Adjustment Act, and in his dissent claimed that "the power of courts to declare a statute unconstitutional is subject to two guiding principles of decision which ought never to be absent from judicial consciousness. One is that courts are concerned only with the power to enact statutes, not with their wisdom. The other is that while unconstitutional exercise of power by the executive and legislative branches is subject to judicial restraint, the only check upon our own exercise of power is our own sense of self-restraint. For the removal of unwise laws from the statute books appeal lies not to the courts but to the ballot and to the processes of democratic government."[29]

Following the constitutional crisis of 1937 (in which Stone opposed Roosevelt's court-packing plan), the fight over economic legislation began to diminish, to be replaced by a concern for civil liberties. One of Stone's great contributions to American constitutional jurisprudence came in what appeared to be a minor case, *United States v. Carolene Products Co.* (1938). A federal law prohibited interstate transportation of "filled milk," skimmed milk mixed with animal fats. The Court had no trouble sustaining the legislation, but in his opinion for the majority Stone wrote what has since become the most famous footnote in the Court's history. In that note Stone erected the foundation for separate criteria in which to evaluate legislation embodying economic policy and laws that affected civil liberties. The latter restrictions, he declared, are to "be subjected to more exacting judicial scrutiny under the general prohibitions of the 14th Amendment than are most other types of legislation." Moreover, "statutes directed at particular religious . . . or national . . . or racial minorities" as well as "prejudice against discrete and insular minorities may be a special condition . . . which may call for a correspondingly more searching judicial inquiry."[30]

Stone's footnote, which has been cited in hundreds of cases ever since, ratified the change that had taken place following the Court-packing plan; economic legislation would henceforth receive a minimal level of scrutiny, with the justices relying on what came to be known as a rational basis test. As long as the legislature had the power and a reasonable justification for its use, courts would not question the wisdom of that legislation. But when statutes impinged on personal rights, there would be a much higher standard of review. With the *Carolene Products* footnote, the Court underwent a major sea change that would climax with the due process revolution and the civil rights decisions of the Warren Court in the 1950s and 1960s.[31]

While his jurisprudence appealed to the Democrats, Stone's opposition to the court-packing plan and his support of the Supreme Court's prerogatives won approval from conservatives. Newspapers across the political spectrum called for Stone's elevation to the center chair. Then over lunch at the White House, Felix Frankfurter urged his friend the president to name Stone, and to do so at once rather than wait until the fall when the Court convened. Frankfurter had a number of practical Court-related reasons, but his strongest argument concerned not matters of jurisprudence but of politics and international affairs. "It doesn't require prophetic powers," Frankfurter argued, "to be sure that we shall, sooner or later, be in war—I think sooner. It is most important that when war does come, the country should feel that you are a national, the Nation's president, and not a partisan President. Few things would contribute as much to confidence in you as a national and not a partisan President than for you to name a Republican, who has the profession's confidence, as Chief Justice."[32]

Confronted on all sides by this demand, Roosevelt sent Stone's name to the Senate on June 12 and was immediately rewarded with a wave of public approval. *Time* magazine caught the country's mood when it noted: "Last week the U.S. realized how much it liked the idea of a solid man as Chief Justice to follow Charles Evans Hughes. And solid is the word for Chief Justice Stone—

200 lb., with heavy, good-natured features and a benign judicial air. . . . [He] is almost as impressive as a figure of justice as were Taft and Hughes before him."[33] When the nomination came before the Senate on June 27, it received unanimous approval. The redoubtable George W. Norris of Nebraska, who had led the fight against Stone in 1925, now in 1941 made the only speech before the Senate's confirmation of Stone as chief justice. Noting that he had opposed Stone's original appointment to Court, Norris said, "I am now about to perform the one of the most pleasant duties that has ever come to me in my official life when I cast a vote in favor of his elevation to the highest judicial office in our land. . . . It is a great satisfaction to me to rectify, in a very small degree, the wrong I did him years ago."[34]

On the same day that Roosevelt sent Stone's nomination to the Senate, he named two other men to the high court, Robert Houghwout Jackson (1892– 1954) to replace Stone as an associate justice, and James Francis Byrnes (1879–1972) to take the seat vacated by the last of the Four Horsemen, James C. McReynolds.

Jackson is, in some ways, one of the least known members of the Court, even though he had a notable career and a facile pen and helped create the modern doctrinal rules for judicial review of economic regulation. Although Jackson did not share the First Amendment views of Black and Douglas, he wrote one of the outstanding defenses of the First Amendment right to free exercise of religion.[35] Jackson was also among the better stylists on the Court in this century. Following one of his early opinions, Judge Jerome Frank, himself a brilliant writer, told Jackson: "I've never admired you as much as now. . . . And I am tickled silly that you spoke in good plain American, just as you did before you became a judge. Ordinary folks like me can understand you."[36]

Born on a western Pennsylvania farm, Robert Jackson was self-educated; he briefly attended Albany Law School, but then qualified for the bar by reading law as an apprentice in a lawyer's office, the last Supreme Court justice to do so. He set up a thriving and varied practice in western New York, and as a fourth-generation Democrat became active in state politics and an advisor to Governor Franklin Roosevelt. After Roosevelt entered the White House in 1933, he brought Jackson to Washington, where the New York lawyer advanced from general counsel at the Bureau of Internal Revenue to solicitor general and then attorney general. Jackson later described his tenure as solicitor general as the happiest part of his life, and he won high marks for his role as the government's chief litigator; Louis Brandeis once commented that Jackson should have been named solicitor general for life.

Many people considered Jackson a possible presidential candidate, and his name was frequently mentioned for the 1940 Democratic nomination until Roosevelt decided to run for a third term. The president had promised Jackson a seat on the Supreme Court when he asked him to head the Justice Department; the next vacancy, however, arose with the resignation of Charles Evans Hughes and Roosevelt felt he had to name Stone to the center chair. A loyal supporter of the president, Jackson agreed, but it appears that Roosevelt may have also assured Jackson that he would elevate him to be chief upon Stone's departure from the Court. Both men assumed that the sixty-nine-year-old Stone would probably not stay on the Court more than five or six years, and that would leave Jackson, then only fifty, a fair amount of time to lead the high court.

Had Jackson been chief justice, he might have been happier on the Court, but his activist nature chafed at the restrictions of judicial propriety. During the war he felt cut off from the great events going on around him, and remarked that the Monday after Pearl Harbor the Court heard arguments about the taxability of greens fees. Although he, like Frankfurter and Douglas, continued secretly to advise Roosevelt,[37] he wanted to do more. Thus he leaped at the opportunity when President Harry S. Truman asked him to head the American prosecutorial team at the Nuremberg trial of Nazi war criminals.

Although Jackson tended to join Frankfurter on many issues, he could not be considered a predictable vote for the conservatives. He parted from Frankfurter, for example, in the second flag salute case; his decision in *Wickard v. Filburn* (1942) is a ringing endorsement of an all-encompassing congressional power over commerce,[38] yet he took a far more restricted view of presidential power during the Korean conflict.[39] Some of his opinions seem quirky, such as his dissent in *Beauharnais v. Illinois* (1952), in which he endorsed the idea of treating racist speech as group libel yet argued that the defendant had a right to a jury trial to prove the truth of the libel.[40]

Jimmy Byrnes sat on the Court for only one term, then resigned to become the so-called assistant president, Roosevelt's special aide during the war. Born in Charleston, South Carolina, Byrnes had little formal schooling, and, like Jackson, had learned his law by reading as an apprentice. Byrnes loved politics; he served in the House of Representatives from 1910 to 1925 and then in the Senate from 1931 to 1941. While in the Senate he became a trusted ally and adviser of the president and was one of the few southern senators besides Black to be fully committed to the New Deal. He also earned Roosevelt's gratitude for working out a face-saving compromise in the aftermath of the court-packing debacle. He urged Roosevelt not to push the bill, especially after Willis Van Devanter resigned. "Why run for a train after you caught it?" he asked.

Byrnes's main contribution to the Court appears to have been social; he regularly had the justices over to his house for dinner and then led them in postprandial songs. He wrote only one major opinion, *Edwards v. California* (1941),[41] and fifteen other minor rulings, with no dissents or concurrences, thus leaving a virtually uncharted jurisprudence. Byrnes, like other members of the Stone Court, felt isolated from the great events happening around them. The Court's slow and deliberative pace frustrated him, and he declared, "I don't think I can stand the abstractions of jurisprudence at a time like this." When Roosevelt intimated that he needed Byrnes off the bench, the South Carolinian jumped at the chance.

To replace Byrnes, Roosevelt named his ninth and last appointment to the Court, Wiley Blount Rutledge Jr. (1894–1949). Born in Kentucky, Blount made his home in the Midwest, taught law, and served as dean first at Washington University in St. Louis and then at the University of Iowa. While at Washington in the early 1930s, he solved a tense racial situation at a conference of white and black lawyers. Because Missouri enforced segregation, the African American lawyers could not sit at the same tables as the white participants; Rutledge invited all the minority members to join him at the dean's table. A few years later he gained national attention as being one of the few law school deans to support Roosevelt's court-packing plan, a position that won him more than a little notoriety in conservative Iowa.

Rutledge's name had figured prominently in 1938 and 1939 when vacancies opened on the Supreme Court, but Roosevelt used those opportunities to name Frankfurter and Douglas. However, the president did name Rutledge to the prestigious Court of Appeals for the District of Columbia, which heard many of the cases arising under the National Labor Relations Act. There Rutledge consistently voted on the pro-labor side and also endorsed other New Deal measures. When Byrnes stepped down, Rutledge was a natural choice as his successor.

Unfortunately, Rutledge died of a cerebral hemorrhage at the age of fifty-five after serving on the Court for only six years. During that time he carved out a consistently liberal position, one that took its cue from the double standard enunciated in Stone's *Carolene Products* footnote. Joining Stone, Black, Douglas and Murphy, Rutledge provided the fifth vote necessary to begin the expansion of protected freedoms under the First Amendment. Moreover, he was willing to go beyond Black's position regarding the meaning of the Fourteenth Amendment's due-process clause. Where Black believed the clause encompassed only the protections enunciated in the Bill of Rights, Rutledge tended to agree with Murphy and Douglas in arguing that it included at least those protections and possibly more. The area in which he had the most impact involved the religion clauses of the First Amendment, and Rutledge played a key role in the several Jehovah's Witnesses cases the Court heard during the early 1940s.

At his death in 1949, just a few months after that of Frank Murphy, articles appeared in the law reviews in a quantity one would associate with a justice with far longer service on the bench. Part of this resulted from Rutledge's friendly and open character; he treated his law clerks well and debated them as democratic equals, and he invited a friend, a Republican who owned a small Jewish delicatessen, to sit with the justices at Harry Truman's inauguration. But another part grew out of the belief that had Rutledge lived longer, he would have been a great justice. As two of his former clerks put it, "Death met him . . . after he had completed his apprenticeship but before he had proceeded far in a master's work."[42] Certainly Rutledge and the other Roosevelt appointees strike one as of a higher level of competence and craftsmanship than those appointed by Harry Truman to take their place.

Jurisprudentially, two things need to be noted about the so-called Roosevelt Court. First, it expanded the reach of the federal commerce power and repudiated any judicial role in economic policy making. Second, and more important, it started the Court on the road to expanding the definition of constitutionally protected rights, and it established the Court not only as the chief interpreter of the Constitution but also as the primary guarantor of individual liberties.

Nearly everyone assumed that the Roosevelt appointees would share his philosophy of government and interpret the Constitution broadly to give Congress and the president, as well as state legislatures, adequate power to meet the nation's needs. In this they did not disappoint the president and his followers. Perhaps the best example of the Roosevelt Court's broad view of the commerce clause is its sustaining the New Deal's agricultural program.

No case had better exemplified the antagonism of the Court conservatives against the New Deal than *United States v. Butler*,[43] in which the majority had struck down the popular agriculture act of 1933. In the act, Congress had intended to do away with the large crop surpluses that depressed farm prices by placing limits on how much individual farmers could grow. In return for their participation in the scheme, farmers would receive a subsidy financed through a tax on the first processor. In his opinion for the majority Justice Roberts had taken an extremely narrow view of both the commerce and the taxing powers.

Congress "cured" the tax problem in the second AAA by financing the plan through general rather than particular taxes, and following the Court fight in 1937, the new Court had little problem in sustaining the act in *Mulford v. Smith* (1939).[44] In the next few years the Court continued to sustain New Deal legislation, and in 1941, in *United States v. Darby,* Justice Stone effectively killed off the idea of "dual federalism," by which the conservatives had created a no-man's land in which neither the states nor the federal government could act.[45] The question remained, however, whether the states themselves retained any control over local commerce, and the answer appeared to be no.

Roscoe Filburn ran a small chicken farm in Ohio, and each year he planted a few acres of wheat to feed his poultry and livestock. Under the Agricultural Marketing Agreement Act of 1937 (which had been sustained by the Court in 1942), Filburn had signed an allotment agreement allowing him 11.1 acres of wheat, but he actually planted 23 acres and grew 239 bushels beyond his assigned quota. The Agriculture Department invoked the penalty provisions of the law and brought suit to collect the fines.

Filburn defended himself on the grounds that the regulations exceeded the federal powers granted by the commerce clause because the excess wheat had not gone into interstate commerce, but had been grown for and used by his chickens. This argument caused some doubt among at least five justices—Jackson, Murphy, Roberts, Byrnes, and Frankfurter—who were also dissatisfied with the presentations of both the government and Filburn's attorneys. Three members of the Court saw no problem, but for different reasons. Black and Douglas took an extremely expansive view of the commerce power, claiming it had no limitations except those explicitly mentioned in the Constitution. Stone, while agreeing that the constitutional arguments had not been well presented, nonetheless believed that sufficient precedent existed to sustain the law.[46] Interestingly, Robert Jackson, who would eventually write the opinion in the case, disagreed, and, in language that Stone's biographer terms "reminiscent of the Old Guard," complained that he did not see it as a simple matter. "The Constitution drew a line between state and federal power," Jackson wrote, "and here the Congress wants to cross that line admittedly."[47]

After rehearing that fall, Stone assigned the case to Jackson, who proceeded to write one of the Court's strongest opinions upholding the federal commerce power. Even though Farmer Filburn's wheat had been intended for his own chickens, "such wheat overhangs the market and if induced by rising prices tends to flow into the market and check price increases. Even if it never did enter the market, it supplies a need of the man who grew it which would otherwise be reflected by purchases in the open market. Home-grown wheat in this sense competes with wheat in commerce."[48]

Jackson, despite his earlier doubts, did have precedent on which to rely. Charles Evans Hughes, in his first tenure on the bench, had written in the *Shreveport Cases* that Congress could regulate intrastate rates of railroads if these rates had a substantial effect upon interstate rates.[49] Later, using a similar argument, Chief Justice Taft—whom no one would accuse of being overly sympathetic to federal regulation—had upheld congressional control over the Chicago Board of Trade, since its activities had an impact on interstate commerce.[50] But Jackson's opinion went further, since in the earlier cases Hughes and Taft had required some evidence that the intrastate activities did in fact have an interstate effect, other than that Congress merely said so. "If we are to be brutally frank," Jackson wrote shortly after the opinion came down, "I suspect what we would say is that in any case where Congress thinks there is an effect on interstate commerce, the Court will accept that judgment. All of the efforts to set up formulae to confine the commerce power have failed. When we admit that it is an economic matter, we pretty nearly admit that it is not a matter which courts may judge."[51]

In fact, the notion of an expansive commerce power was hardly new; it had been put forward by Chief Justice John Marshall in the early days of the Republic. But as Paul Murphy points out, in an era of minimal government Marshall had used a broad interpretation of the commerce clause to block out state interference without assuming that the federal government necessarily would act; the New Deal Court, on the other hand, intended to clear the path of state regulation so Congress could legislate far-reaching programs. Nonetheless, when Justice Frank Murphy declared that the government's regulatory power under the commerce clause "was as broad as the economic needs of the nation," commentators praised the statement as being particularly "Marshallian."[52]

But did the states have anything left to control, or had the Court really put an end to the whole notion of federalism? The answer came in the same term, and involved a challenge to California's Agricultural Prorate Act. California farmers grew nearly all of the raisins consumed in the United States, and about 90 percent of the crop entered interstate commerce. The Prorate Act created a state-sponsored monopoly for the marketing of raisins, and all growers had to comply with its provisions. Each grower could market only 30 percent of his crop in the open market and had to turn over the remainder to a central committee, which controlled the amount of raisins let into the market so as to stabilize prices.

The challenge to the Prorate Act raised three questions for the Court: Did the measure violate the Sherman Antitrust Act? Did it run afoul of the 1937 Agricultural Marketing Agreement Act? Did it transgress the commerce clause? In an opinion for a unanimous Court, Chief Justice Stone upheld the California statute, and in doing so completed the work he had begun in the *Darby* case the previous term. The Sherman Act had no applicability because it applied only to private companies, not to the states. In a federal system, Stone warned, courts should not infer applicability of federal legislation to the states in the absence of an explicit congressional directive. The law also did not interfere with the federal statute; Congress had not totally preempted the field, and the Secretary of Agriculture had testified that the federal and state plans worked harmoniously together.

The key question of course, was whether California's plan crossed into terrain reserved for Congress by the commerce clause. Stone noted that the state plan dealt primarily with regulation of raisins before shipment into interstate commerce and could legitimately be described as a local activity. But that would have been a mechanistic reading of the Constitution and the situation, since the scheme clearly affected interstate commerce. The courts, Stone declared, had to take a realistic view of the facts:[53]

> When Congress has not exerted its power under the commerce clause, and state regulation of matters of local concern is so related to interstate commerce that it also operates as a regulation of that commerce, the reconciliation of the power thus granted with that reserved to the state is to be attained by the accommodation of the competing demands of the state and national interests involved.
>
> Such regulations by the state are to be sustained, not because they are "indirect" rather than "direct" ... not because they control interstate activities in such a manner as only to affect the commerce rather than to command its operations. But they are to be upheld because upon a consideration of all the relevant facts and circumstances it appears that the matter is one which may appropriately be regulated in the interest of the safety, health, and well-being of local communities, and which, because of its local character and the practical difficulties involved, may never be adequately dealt with by Congress.

In some ways, Stone resurrected a "dual federalism" with this opinion, but one quite different from that used by conservatives in the 1920s and 1930s to strike down both state and federal measures. The conservatives had defined an area of activities that had both a local and an interstate character that in essence could be regulated by neither the states nor the federal government. Stone had put an end to that version of dual federalism in *Darby*, which had given the federal government the power to regulate goods made in local business and then shipped in interstate commerce.

Under Stone's version, the no-man's land became neutral territory, subject to regulation by either the state or federal government. Obviously, and especially after *Wickard v. Filburn*, federal control took precedence, but until Congress acted, the states remained free to establish whatever measures they saw fit. In many ways, Stone did little more than to return to the common sense rule of the nineteenth century, which the Court had enunciated in *Cooley v. Board of Wardens of the Port of Philadelphia* (1851).[54] That case made the Tenth Amendment what the Framers had intended it to be, a statement of the partnership between the states and the federal government, not a means to paralyze both.

In fact, in only two nonunanimous opinions during the Stone years did the Roosevelt Court invalidate state regulation of commerce as impinging on federal authority. In *Southern Pacific Railroad v. Arizona* (1945) the majority voided a state law limiting the size of trains operating within Arizona borders to no more than fourteen passenger cars or seventy freight cars in length. Evidence indicated that the railway unions backing the proposal saw it as a means of increasing jobs, but the official justification emphasized safety concerns, with the hazards to trainmen allegedly greater on overly long trains. The majority deemed the safety rationale slight and dubious, and outweighed by a "national interest in keeping interstate commerce free from interferences which seriously impede it and subject it to local regulation which does not have a uniform effect on the interstate train journeys which it interrupts." If there were to be limits on train size, the Court concluded, they would have to come from Congress.[55] The opinion elicited a strong dissent from Justice Black, joined by Douglas, who condemned the majority for attempting to evaluate the probable dangers to trainmen, a task that properly belonged to the state legislature.[56]

For the most part, the Court did not denigrate the role of the states, and in its role as umpire of the federal system, paid more deference to state prerogatives than some critics thought it would.[57] The only area in which the Court seemed to go too far involved insurance, which since 1869 had been held to be a matter of state regulation.[58] Then in 1942 the Justice Department secured antitrust indictments against the 196 members of the South-Eastern Underwriters Association, charging them with conspiracies to fix rates. The district court that heard the initial case felt constrained by precedent and dismissed the case, ruling that since insurance fell under state regulation it could not be prosecuted under a federal law. The government brought suit.

Despite internal dissension as to whether the Court should be bound by the 1869 precedent, it seems clear that of the seven members who heard the case, nearly all did in fact consider insurance as part of interstate commerce, and in the end Hugo Black managed to eke out a 4–3 majority to that effect. Rather than look at decisions regarding state power, under which *Paul v. Virginia* would have controlled, Black looked at the record in determining federal authority, and over the years the Court had consistently expanded that power. Black concluded that "no commercial enterprise of any kind which conducts its activities across state lines has been held to be wholly beyond the regulatory power of the Congress under the Commerce Clause. We cannot make an exception to the business of insurance."[59]

The decision triggered a chorus of protest, not so much at Black's rationale but at the chaos many people believed would follow. The expected turmoil, however, did not materialize. Congress declined to make insurance regulation a federal function, and in the McCarran Act permitted the states to continue regulation and taxation of the insurance business despite its interstate character. In addition, the act exempted the industry from any federal statute not specifically covering insurance, with the exception of the Sherman Antitrust Act and three other laws. In 1946 the Court unanimously upheld the McCarran Act's premise that insurance, even though interstate in nature, could be jointly governed by the states and the federal government.[60]

As a final note on the ending of the old economic regime, while the Roosevelt Court certainly expanded the meaning of interstate commerce and found that Congress had a wide-ranging authority in this area, it also sustained state regulatory legislation of the type that under the old Court would have been voided through the imposition of dual federalism. The Roosevelt appointees took very seriously the notion of judicial restraint and believed that unless a specific constitutional prohibition existed, Congress and the state legislatures should be free to act. The courts should defer to the wisdom of the legislative choice and not impose their own views; should the legislature be wrong, recourse lay with the people acting through the ballot.

As a result, state legislatures now had a much broader range of authority than they had enjoyed before, and how little the justices saw review of this

authority as within their responsibility can be witnessed in a 1955 opinion by
William O. Douglas. The Court by then had indicated it would no longer apply due-process criteria to economic issues. In *Williamson v. Lee Optical Co.*
Douglas announced what remains as the judicial standard for review of regulatory legislation. If the legislature had any "rational basis" to warrant the
controls, and if the statute did not violate a specific constitutional prohibition, the courts would not intervene.[61] With this case, it could be said that
Franklin Roosevelt had completely triumphed over the Four Horsemen.

The Roosevelt Court proved to be one of the most contentious in history,
marked by intense personality conflicts[62] as well as by a major jurisprudential dispute. By the time Hugo Black took his seat on the bench a majority of
the Court had agreed that the due-process clause of the Fourteenth Amendment "incorporated" at least some of the guarantees in the Bill of Rights and
applied them to the states. In *Palko v. Connecticut,* Justice Benjamin N. Cardozo had articulated a philosophy of limited or "selective" incorporation, in
which only those rights most important to a scheme of" ordered liberty"
would be enforced against the states.[63] Black originally accepted the *Palko*
doctrine but gradually came to believe that all of the rights enumerated in
the first eight amendments should be incorporated; moreover, he believed
that the First Amendment, protecting freedom of expression, held a "preferred" position.

Black objected to the Cardozo position, which Frankfurter championed,
because it smacked of natural law and relied too much on the justices' sense
of fairness and decency. In criminal cases Frankfurter would ask whether the
police conduct "shocked the conscience." Black wanted to know "whose conscience?" and charged that Frankfurter's approach left too much discretion in
the hands of the courts to expand or contract rights belonging to the people.
Frankfurter, on the other hand, objected to Black's position as historically as
well as logically flawed. Much of the language in the Bill of Rights could not
be interpreted in a strictly objective manner. What, for example, constituted
an "unreasonable" search? Judges had to interpret these words, and such interpretation was a proper judicial function.[64]

Black and Douglas also began developing a new jurisprudence that put
First Amendment rights in a "preferred" position, and argued for an "abso-
lutist" interpretation of the prohibition against the abridgment of speech.
The First Amendment, in their view, barred all forms of governmental restriction on speech; any other interpretation, they claimed, "can be used to
justify the punishment of advocacy." Frankfurter believed that individual lib-

erty and social order had to be balanced in First Amendment cases, and the yardstick would be the Holmes rule of "clear and present danger." Black, on the other hand, saw that doctrine as "the most dangerous of the tests developed by the justices of the Court."[65]

For Frankfurter, the evaluation and balancing implicit in the clear and present danger test fit perfectly with his conception of the judicial function. By rigorously applying the tools of logical analysis, judges would be able to determine when such a danger existed and thus justified state intervention, and when it did not. In this view, explicating First Amendment issues differed not at all from any other constitutional question. In a letter to Stanley Reed, Frankfurter asked, "When one talks about 'preferred,' or 'preferred position,' one means preference of one thing over another. Please tell me what kind of sense it makes that one provision of the Constitution is to be 'preferred' over another. . . . The correlative of 'preference' is 'subordination,' and I know of no calculus to determine when one provision of the Constitution must yield to another, nor do I know of any reason for doing so."[66]

These debates, between selective and total incorporation and between a preferred and nonpreferred reading of the First Amendment, would split the bench throughout the 1940s and 1950s. During the last two decades of the nineteenth century and the first four of the twentieth, the Court had confronted primarily economic issues; starting in the late 1930s, more and more cases involving individual liberties and civil rights appeared on the docket. Although in general the Roosevelt appointees favored such rights, they differed significantly over how the Bill of Rights should be interpreted, which provisions should apply to the states, and how far the Court should be involved in the emerging civil rights struggle.

In 1938, in his famous footnote 4 in the *Carolene Products* case, Justice Stone had suggested that while the courts should defer to the legislature in economic matters, it should impose higher standards of review in cases involving individual liberties and rights. With the significant exception of the Japanese relocation cases, in which the justices blindly deferred to the military,[67] the Court began to implement Stone's test in World War II.

In terms of economic regulation, the justices easily found constitutional justification for every federal measure brought before it, including price controls, rent controls, and restrictions on profiteering.[68] As the Court noted in the *Willingham* case, "A nation which can demand the lives of its men and women in the waging of a war is under no constitutional necessity of providing a system of price controls on the domestic front which will assure each landlord a 'fair return' on his property."[69] Justices willing to sustain strong governmental power in peacetime could hardly have been expected to rein even stronger policies in the midst of total war.

But what about individual liberties? How would the protection of civil liberties fare with the nation at war? Many people remembered the excesses of the Wilson administration and the willingness of the Court to acquiesce in severe limitations of free speech and press. Fortunately, so did the justices, and two of them, Frank Murphy and Robert Jackson, had taken steps during their terms as attorney general to ensure that such excesses would not be repeated if the United States entered a new war.[70] At the same time, the justices also recognized the government's legitimate need to protect itself.

Nonetheless, with the exception of the Japanese cases, the Court proved extremely reluctant to bless federal measures that impinged on individual rights. It struck down efforts at denaturalization,[71] upheld the rights of pacifists to become citizens,[72] prevented the states from establishing alien control laws,[73] and supported freedom of speech, even by communists and fascists.[74] But when it came to real and not alleged threats, such as the Nazi saboteurs, the justices had no trouble finding sufficient executive authority for a secret military trial.[75]

The Court also began the expansion of religious freedom with the several Jehovah's Witnesses cases, and in a landmark decision the Court reversed itself and found that a mandatory flag salute violated the First Amendment. Justice Jackson, who normally sided with the government on most issues, wrote one of the most ringing declarations of freedom ever penned in the Court: "If there is any fixed star in our constitutional constellation, it is that no official, high or petty, can prescribe what shall be orthodox in politics, nationalism, religion or other matters of opinion or force citizens to confess by word or act their faith therein."[76]

And during the war the Court took a few more steps, begun in the late 1930s, to reject the racist practices that had been condoned since the 1880s. In 1935 the Court had apparently validated black exclusion from primaries,[77] but the new appointees reversed this decision. In *United States v. Classic* (1941), the justices held that Congress could regulate a primary where it constituted part of the overall machinery for selecting federal officials.[78] Classic had been decided on narrow grounds and looked more like a voting fraud case than a civil rights decision. But Thurgood Marshall, the head of the NAACP Legal Defense Fund, gambled that with the more liberal makeup of the Roosevelt Court, he could use it as a weapon against the white primary itself, and the gamble paid off. In 1944 all the justices save Owen Roberts voted to overturn the 1935 *Grovey* decision and to invalidate southern laws preventing blacks from voting in the primaries.[79]

The most notorious civil rights decision involved the activities of Sheriff Claude Screws of Baker County, Georgia, who, with two of his deputies, had taken Robert Hall into custody, handcuffed him, and then beat him to death. Frank Murphy, then attorney general, had been unable to get Georgia authorities to prosecute under state law, so the Justice Department went into court and secured convictions that "under color of law" Screws and his deputies had deprived Hall of rights guaranteed to him by the Fourteenth Amendment.

The case split the Court, not because the justices approved of Screws's behavior, but rather because the underlying legal foundation rested on Reconstruction-era statutes, some of which had been narrowly interpreted by the Court in the 1880s, and even later interpretations had not given the government the scope of authority it claimed in this case.[80] Roberts, Frankfurter, and Jackson, although clearly shocked by the killing and having considered Screws guilty of murder, nonetheless thought the statute unconstitutionally vague; to permit its use would open a Pandora's box of federal interference in matters clearly within the jurisdiction of states. Stone thought the statute so vague as to "incorporate a law library" into it. Only Murphy seemed fully convinced of the statute's constitutionality.[81]

Stone assigned the case to Douglas, who wrote a careful and limiting opinion. The old law could be upheld as constitutional, but only if applied to state officials acting "under color of law." To save the statute from vagueness grounds, Stone suggested that they center the case on the question of whether Screws had acted "willfully." Douglas agreed, and in his opinion held that the law could be applied but he sent the case back for a new trial under clearer criteria of whether the sheriff had acted "willfully" and under "color of law."[82]

Because the Court had not struck the statute down as unconstitutionally vague, it remained alive and on the books for use by the government in later years. Congress corrected many of the defects in the 1964 and 1965 civil rights acts. Scholars have differed on the meaning of the case, with some heralding it as a distinct victory for civil rights and others claiming that it set up significant barriers to racial progress. Years later Thurgood Marshall, by then a member of the high court, said that much as he admired William O. Douglas, he could never forgive him for the *Screws* decision.[83]

Opinions on the Court and its protection of civil liberties during the war vary. While conceding that wartime often abridges individual liberty, Alpheus Mason declared, "Even in the time of greatest stress, the Justices upheld the citizen's liberty to think, speak, and act to an extent that the nation at peace has sometimes felt it could ill afford to maintain. In this realm Stone's Court almost brought a miracle to pass."[84] At the other end of the spectrum, John Frank claimed that the "dominant lesson of our history in the relation of the judiciary to repression is that the courts love liberty most when it is under pressure least."[85]

The truth may lie somewhere between these poles, but in terms of the Roosevelt Court, we can better understand the war record as part of the changing agenda from economic to individual liberties. All of the president's appointees cared fervently about rights, although they disagreed on how far the Constitution intended the Court to protect those rights or expand their meaning. In the years after the war, that tension continued to play itself out until well into the Warren years.

Initially, the pendulum swung to the Frankfurter side of limited judicial involvement and a restrictive view on incorporation. What had been a conservative bloc of Frankfurter, Reed, and Jackson found itself strengthened by the Truman appointees, Fred Vinson (as chief justice), Harold Burton, Tom Clark, and Sherman Minton—all decent men but intellectually and jurisprudentially far inferior to the Roosevelt appointees. From 1946 until illness forced his retirement in 1962, Frankfurter was able to impose his views of judicial restraint and limited expansion of individual rights on the Court. It was Frankfurter who wrote the 4–3 opinion in 1946 that put off reapportionment of state legislatures for nearly a generation. It was Vinson, supported by Frankfurter, who wrote the speech-restrictive decision in the landmark Cold War case *Dennis v. United States*. And after the generally pro-labor attitude of the New Deal and the Court in the early 1940s, the conservatives began imposing limits on labor, taking their cue from the 1946 Taft-Hartley bill.

But the story is far from one-sided, and in the postwar era one of the great jurisprudential battles of modern times played out as Frankfurter battled Black and Douglas for what they all recognized as the soul of the Court. It is this debate, and its continuing impact, that is the greatest legacy of the Roosevelt Court.

Ever since they had come onto the Court, Hugo Black and Felix Frankfurter had carried on a debate on the meaning of the Fourteenth Amendment's due-process clause. Both men started from the same place—their opposition to the use of substantive due process by earlier courts to strike down reform legislation. For Frankfurter, the answer to this abuse of power lay in judicial restraint and appropriate deference to the policy decisions of the political branches. But the due-process clause obviously meant something, and as interpreters of the Constitution, judges had to define what this "something" meant.

Black had just gone onto the Court when the *Palko* decision came down and at first subscribed to it. But he grew increasingly uncomfortable with the philosophy and method of selective incorporation and the great power it lodged in the courts. The heart of Black's differences with Frankfurter centered on the great discretion the Frankfurter-Cardozo approach vested in the judiciary. If judges could strike down state laws that failed to meet "civilized standards," then the courts had reverted to a "natural law concept whereby the supreme constitutional law becomes this Court's view of 'civilization' at a given moment." This philosophy, he declared, made everything else in the Constitution "mere surplusage," and allowed the Court to reject all of the provisions of the Bill of Rights and substitute its own idea for what legislatures could or could not do.[86] Black, however, still had difficulty articulating the standards he would apply.

The answer for Black came in a California murder case. Admiral Dewey Adamson, a poor, illiterate black, had twice served time for robbery. He had, however, been out of prison for seventeen years when police arrested him for the murder of an elderly white widow. The only evidence linking Adamson to the crime consisted of six fingerprints on a door leading to the garbage container in the woman's kitchen, which police identified as his. On the advice of his attorney, a veteran of the Los Angeles criminal courts, Adamson did not take the stand in his own defense. Had he done so, the prosecutor could have brought up Adamson's previous record and that would have resulted in a sure conviction. But the prosecutor, as he was allowed to do under California law, pointed out to the jury Adamson's failure to testify, and claimed that this surely proved his guilt. If he had been innocent, the prosecutor declared, it would have taken fifty horses to keep him off the stand. The jury convicted Adamson, and his lawyer on appeal challenged the California statute as violating the Fourteenth Amendment. Allowing comment on the failure to testify was equivalent to forcing a defendant to take the stand; both violated due process.[87]

In conference Frankfurter convinced a majority of his colleagues that the issue had already been decided, and correctly. In *Twining v. New Jersey* (1908) the Court had ruled that a state law permitting comment on a defendant's refusal to testify did not violate procedural fairness.[88] Justice Reed, assigned the opinion, conceded that such behavior by the prosecutor in a federal proceeding would be unacceptable and a violation of the Fifth Amendment. But it was "settled law" that the self-incrimination law did not apply to the states; it was not "a right of national citizenship, or . . . a personal privilege or immunity secured by the Federal Constitution as one of the rights of man that are listed in the Bill of Rights." In short, it was not one of the fundamental principles inherent in "the concept of ordered liberty" test of *Palko*. "For a state to require testimony from an accused," Reed concluded, "is not necessarily a breach of a state's obligation to give a fair trial."[89]

Black dissented and set forth his belief in the "total incorporation" of the first eight amendments by the Fourteenth. He would consider it the most important opinion of his career. "There I laid it all out. . . . I didn't write until I came to the complete conclusion that I was reasonably sure of myself and my research. It was my work from beginning to end."[90] Just as the Bill of Rights applied objective standards to the behavior of the federal government, so the application of the first eight amendments to the states would provide equally ascertainable criteria by which to judge state action. In a lengthy appendix he presented the historical evidence he had assembled to support this position, an essay most scholars find less than convincing. As might be expected from a former senator, Black relied entirely on the congressional history of the Fourteenth Amendment, the account of what Congress did in drafting it. But amending the Constitution requires ratification by the states, and Black neglected to look at the debates there; neither did he look at the abolitionist antecedents of the amendment.

What is most interesting in Black's rationale is that in many ways it resembled Frankfurter's own views on limiting judicial power. Black rejected Cardozo's criteria as too vague, in that phrases such as "civilized decency" and "fundamental liberty and justice" could be interpreted by judges to mean many things. This "natural law" theory of the Constitution "degrade[s] the constitutional safeguards of the Bill of Rights and simultaneously appropriate[s] for this Court a broad power which we are not authorized by the Constitution to exercise." The only way to avoid this abuse of judicial power would be to carry out the original intent of the framers of the Fourteenth Amendment, and apply all the protections of the Bill of Rights to the states.[91]

Douglas joined Black's opinion, but Murphy filed a separate dissent in which he attempted to combine elements of both the Frankfurter and Black approaches. He had found Black's essay "exciting reading," but added, "I think you go out of your way—as you always do—to strike down natural law." Murphy wanted to incorporate all of the Bill of Rights, as Black proposed, but he objected to what he saw as the rigidity in Black's approach. There were times when one had to be flexible, when a strict reading of the first eight amendments would not suffice to provide justice. In those instances Frankfurter's use of due process would allow judges to secure justice. Murphy's reading of Black's opinion was not that wrong. Although Black would later adopt some of Frankfurter's views regarding due process as fundamental fairness, at the time of the Adamson case he told a group of clerks with whom he was having lunch that the due-process clauses of the Fifth and Fourteenth Amendments had "no meaning, except that of emphasis."[92]

Relying on his own historical research, Frankfurter denied that the framers of the Fourteenth Amendment had intended to subsume all of the Bill of Rights.[93] Frankfurter also responded to what he took as the most serious of Black's charges, that the vague criteria of *Palko* left judges too much discretion and protection of rights relied on the mercy of individual subjectivity.[94] He portrayed judging as a process removed from the fray of daily pressures. Protected in their sanctum, justices may engage in that process of discovery that will yield the right answer—not an objective, eternally fixed answer, but the right answer for the time.

Frankfurter did not espouse a moral relativism, but believed that judges in their decisions should reflect the advances that society has made, so that the due-process clause does not mean fairness in terms of 1868, but fairness today. Courts thus help keep the Constitution contemporary, but they must do so cautiously, always following strict intellectual processes and always deferring to those who are in the thick of the battle—the state courts and legislatures—who must in turn be left free to reform their procedures according to their standards of fairness. As Frankfurter noted in another case: "Due process of law requires an evaluation based on a disinterested inquiry pursued in the spirit of science, on a balanced order of facts exactly and fairly stated, on the detached consideration of conflicting claims, on a judgment not ad hoc and episodic but duly mindful of reconciling the needs both of continuity and change in a progressive society."[95] Thus if the judge adheres to certain methods and standards, it does not matter what the result will be in a particular case, because the process will assure ultimate fairness across the spectrum of cases. "Whatever shortcut to relief may be had in a particular case," Frankfurter wrote a year after *Adamson*, "it is calculated to beget misunderstanding and friction and to that extent detracts from those imponderables which are the ultimate reliance of a civilized system of law."[96] The process and not a particular result is the desideratum of judging.

The great appeal of process jurisprudence is that it attempts to remove idiosyncrasy and individuality from judicial decision-making and replace them with objectivity and consistency. Public faith in the judicial process is enhanced if the public believes the judges are acting fairly and adhering to a common set of methods and principles in all cases, regardless of the results in specific instances.

Yet can judging ever be quite this impersonal? Would scientific analysis really produce the right results? Oliver Wendell Holmes had declared that the prejudices of judges had as much if not more to do with determining the law than the logic of the syllogism. As Black asked, how did one objectively determine the "canons of decency and fairness" that everyone accepted? Moreover, although one might say that due process is meaningful over a whole gamut of cases, individuals are on trial; individuals must cope with the criminal justice system; individuals must pay the penalties if found guilty; individuals suffer if deprived of their rights.

For Black, total incorporation provided at least a partial answer, in that judges would no longer subjectively determine what rights met the "canons of decency and fairness." There were still questions to answer. Even if one applied the Fourth Amendment to the states, for example, one still had to determine what constituted an "unreasonable search." But the basic rights, the ones enshrined in the Constitution, would be in force and not dependent on whether a handful of judges determined that they met the canon.

Neither approach is without merit, and neither is without flaw. If Frankfurter's method refused to face up to the fact that process jurisprudence involved subjective evaluation, it did have the virtue of recognizing an acceptable diversity in a federal system, and acknowledging that one could have more than one model of a fair and workable system. Its open-ended approach to fairness also permitted judges, always exercising caution, to help keep basic constitutional guarantees current with the times.

Black's approach did do away with some but not all subjectivity, and debates over the reach of the exclusionary rule and expectations of privacy show that interpreting the "canons of decency and fairness" is an ongoing judicial function. Moreover, in many ways Black's rigid adherence to the text led to a cramped view of individual liberty. He would take an uncompromising stand that the First Amendment permitted no abridgement of speech, but because he could find no mention of privacy in the Constitution, he could not support the judicial claim that such a right existed.[97]

In the end Frank Murphy's approach, almost ignored in the battle between Black and Frankfurter, prevailed, and it came into effect in the landmark 1965 case of *Griswold v. Connecticut,* which established a right to privacy that eventually came to be embedded in due process. Although the Court adopted the Cardozo-Frankfurter approach of selective incorporation, during the Warren years nearly all of the first eight amendment guaranties were applied to the states. But Black's approach proved too rigid, as Murphy had argued, and Frankfurter's notion of due process as fundamental fairness became a useful tool for judges confronting new and unusual situations in the Warren, Burger, and Rehnquist eras.

Adamson did not resolve the issue, but merely raised the curtain on what would be an ongoing debate within the Court. While the debate raged, the Roosevelt appointees, who still constituted a majority of the Court until 1955, had to deal with a variety of issues. In the late 1940s and early 1950s they decided a series of cases that began the dismantling of legally sanctioned race discrimination, and which culminated in the landmark decision in 1954 of *Brown v. Board of Education*. During the Cold War, with the exception of Hugo Black and William O. Douglas, the Court proved less than protective of free speech rights, and in the Dennis case it handed down one of the most speech-restrictive decisions of the century. But even as they debated the meaning of incorporation, the Roosevelt Court expanded the meaning of the First Amendment in other areas, notably religion, and laid the basis for the rights explosion of the 1960s and 1970s.[98]

The great steps to protect civil rights and civil liberties would not have been possible without the Frankfurter Black debate and without the decisions handed down by the Roosevelt appointees. Although it may not have been quite the judicial legacy that Franklin Roosevelt envisioned when he made his choices, it is hard to think of any other group of presidential nominees to the high court that has had such an enduring impact.

NOTES

1. Barry Cushman, *Rethinking the New Deal Court: The Structure of a Constitutional Revolution* (New York: Oxford University Press, 1998).

2. *Home Building and Loan Association v. Blaisdell*, 290 U.S. 398 (1934).

3. *Nebbia v. New York*, 291 U.S. 502 (1934).

4. *Morehead v. New York ex rel. Tipaldo*, 298 U.S. 587 (1936).

5. On the matter of poor counsel and draftsmanship, see Peter H. Irons, *The New Deal Lawyers* (Princeton: Princeton University Press, 1982).

6. U.S. 388 (1935).

7. *Norman v. Baltimore & Ohio R.R. Co., Perry v. United States*, 294 U.S. 330 (1935).

8. *Retirement Board v. Alton Railroad Company,* 295 U.S. 330 (1935).

9. *Schechter v. United States,* 295 U.S. 495 (1935); *Louisville Joint Stock Land Bank v. Radford,* 295 U.S. 555 (1935); *Humphrey's Executor v. United States,* 295 U.S. 602 (1935).

10. *United States v. Butler,* 297 U.S. 1 (1936).

11. Robert H. Jackson Memoir, Columbia Oral History Collection, Columbia University Library.

12. William E. Leuchtenburg, "A Klansman Joins the Court," in *The Supreme Court Reborn* (New York: Oxford University Press, 1995), chap. 7; Roger K. Newman, *Hugo Black: A Biography* (New York: Pantheon, 1944), chaps. 6 and 17.

13. For an excellent discussion of Black's judicial philosophy, see Mark Silverstein, *Constitutional Faiths: Felix Frankfurter, Hugo Black, and the Process of Judicial Decision Making* (Ithaca, N.Y.: Cornell University Press, 1984), especially chap. 4. See also Black's *A Constitutional Faith* (New York: Alfred A. Knopf, 1968).

14. Robert H. Jackson Memoir.

15. Daniel L. Breen, "Stanley Forman Reed," in Melvin I. Urofsky, ed., *The Supreme Court Justices: A Biographical Dictionary* (New York: Garland, 1994), 367. The only full-scale biography, John D. Fassett, *New Deal Justice: The Life of Stanley Reed of Kentucky* (New York: Vantage, 1994), is by a former clerk and is completely uncritical.

16. See William O. Brien, *Justice Reed and the First Amendment: The Religion Clauses* (Washington, D.C.: Georgetown University Press, 1958), and an unpublished dissertation by Mark J. Fitzgerald, "Justice Reed: A Study of a Center Judge" (University of Chicago, 1950).

17. Eugene Gerhart, *America's Advocate: Robert H. Jackson* (Indianapolis: Bobbs-Merrill, 1958), 166; Alpheus T. Mason, *Harlan Fiske Stone: Pillar of the Law* (New York: Viking Press, 1956), 482; Harold L. Ickes, *The Secret Diaries of Harold L. Ickes,* 3 vols. (New York: Simon & Schuster, 1954), 2:552.

18. There has been a great deal made of this relationship, especially by Bruce Murphy in *The Brandeis/Frankfurter Connection* (New York: Oxford University Press, 1982). A somewhat different picture emerges from the correspondence contained in Melvin I. Urofsky and David W. Levy, eds., *"Half Brother, Half Son": The Letters of Louis D. Brandeis to Felix Frankfurter* (Norman: University of Oklahoma Press, 1991).

19. G. Edward White, "Felix Frankfurter, the Old Boy Network, and the New Deal: The Placement of Elite Lawyers in Public Service in the 1930s," *Arkansas Law Review* 39 (1986): 631.

20. Their friendship and interaction can be seen in Max Freedman, ed., *Roosevelt & Frankfurter: Their Correspondence, 1928–1945* (Boston: Atlantic/Little, Brown, 1967).

21. For Frankfurter's pre-Court career and the influences that would shape his jurisprudence, see Michael Parrish, *Felix Frankfurter and His Times: The Reform Years*

(New York: Free Press, 1982); for the Court years, see Melvin I. Urofsky, *Felix Frankfurter, Judicial Restraint and Individual Liberties* (New York: Twayne, 1991).

22. William O. Douglas, *Of Men and Mountains* (New York: Harper & Row, 1950), 29.

23. Laura Kalman, *Legal Realism at Yale, 1927–1960* (Chapel Hill: University of North Carolina Press, 1986), especially chaps. 3 and 4.

24. For Douglas's tenure at the SEC, see Michael E. Parrish, *Securities Regulation and the New Deal* (New Haven: Yale University Press, 1970).

25. Douglas wrote what amounted to a three-volume autobiography, consisting of *Of Men and Mountains; Go East, Young Man: The Early Years* (New York: Random House, 1974); and *The Court Years: 1939–1975* (New York: Random House, 1980). The best biography is James F. Simon, *Independent Journey: The Life of William O. Douglas* (New York: Harper & Row, 1980).

26. Quoted in Peter Irons, "Frank Murphy," in Urofsky, *Supreme Court Justices,* 331.

27. Frank Murphy to Bishop William Murphy, 8 January 1940, in Sidney Fine, *Frank Murphy: The Washington Years* (Ann Arbor: University of Michigan Press, 1984), 133.

28. *Thornhill v. Alabama,* 310 U.S. 88 (1940); the Brandeis suggestion is in *Senn v. Tile Layers Protective Union,* 301 U.S. 468, 478 (1937). The *Thornhill* opinion proved to be both influential and enduring; it has been cited in more than three hundred subsequent opinions.

29. U.S. 1, 78–79 (1936).

30. U.S. 144, 152-53 (1938).

31. According to Daniel P. Currie, in his twenty years on the bench Stone "had done more perhaps than any other justice to bring constitutional law into the twentieth century. We are indebted to him for one of the most effective protests against the old order [his *Butler* dissent] and for the authoritative program of the new." *The Constitution in the Supreme Court: The Second Century, 1888–1986* (Chicago: University of Chicago Press, 1990), 334.

32. Felix Frankfurter, memorandum on the chief justiceship cited in Mason, *Stone,* 566–567; see also Frankfurter to Stone, 3 July 1941, Harlan Fiske Stone Papers, Manuscript Division, Library of Congress, Washington, D.C.

33. *Time,* 23 June 1941; for a sampling of the overwhelming approval that met the nomination, see Mason, *Stone,* 568–573.

34. *Congressional Record,* 77th Cong., 1st Sess. (27 June 1941), 5618.

35. *West Virginia State Board of Education v. Barnette,* 319 U.S. 624 (1943).

36. Frank to Jackson, 27 November 1941, Robert H. Jackson Papers, Manuscript Division, Library of Congress, Washington, D.C. See also the appraisal by Arthur Krock in his column in the *New York Times,* 15 June 1943. For an example of Jack-

son's style and wit, see his apology for a previous error in *McGrath v. Kristensen,* 340 U.S. 162, 177–178 (1950).

37. For the extrajudicial activities of Jackson and other justices during the war, see Melvin I. Urofsky, "*Inter Arma Silent Leges*: Extrajudicial Activity, Patriotism and the Rule of Law," in Daniel R. Ernst and Victor Jew, eds., *Total War and the Law: New Perspectives on World War II* (East Lansing: Michigan State University Press, in press).

38. U.S. 111 (1942).

39. *Youngstown Sheet & Tube Co. et al. v. Sawyer,* 343 U.S. 579 (1952).

40. U.S. 250 (1952).

41. U.S. 160 (1941), upholding as fundamental the right to travel within the country.

42. Victory Brudney and Richard F. Wolfson, "Mr. Justice Rutledge: Law Clerks' Reflections," *Indiana Law Journal* 25 (1950): 455.

43. U.S. 1 (1936).

44. U.S. 38 (1939). Roberts, in fact, wrote the opinion in this case, another example of his reversing prior positions. He later noted, "Looking back, it is difficult to see how the Court could have resisted the popular urge for uniform standards throughout the country—for what in effect was a unified economy." Owen J. Roberts, *The Court and the Constitution* (Cambridge, Mass.: Harvard University Press, 1951), 61.

45. U.S. 100 (1941)

46. Stone, Memorandum to the Court, 25 May 1942, Jackson Papers; Reed took no part in the discussion or decision of this case.

47. Mason, *Stone,* 594; Jackson to Stone, 25 May 1942, Stone Papers. Douglas believed there were sufficient precedents to uphold the law. Douglas to Jackson, 25 May 1942, William O. Douglas Papers, Manuscript Division, Library of Congress, Washington, D.C.

48. Wickard v. Filburn, 317 U.S. 111, 128 (1942).

49. U.S. 342 (1914).

50. *Chicago Board of Trade v. Olsen,* 262 U.S. 1 (1923).

51. Jackson to Sherman Minton, 21 December 1942, Jackson Papers. Stone evinced a similar sentiment; see Stone to Sterling Carr, 11 January 1943, Stone Papers.

52. Paul L. Murphy, *The Constitution in Crisis Times, 1918–1969* (New York: Harper & Row, 1972), 168; *American Power & Light Co. v. S.E.C.,* 328 U.S. 90, 141 (1946).

53. *Parker v. Brown,* 317 U.S. 341, 362–363 (1942).

54. How. 299 (1851).

55. U.S. 761, 776 (1945).

56. *Id.* at 784 (Black dissenting).

57. See Melvin I. Urofsky, *Division and Discord: The Supreme Court under Stone and Vinson, 1941–1953* (Columbia: University of South Carolina Press, 1997), chap. 4.

58. *Paul v. Virginia*, 8 Wall. 168 (1869).

59. *United States v. South-Eastern Underwriters Association*, 322 U.S. 533, 553 (1944); Reed and Roberts took no part in the decision.

60. *Prudential Insurance Co. v. Benjamin*, 328 U.S. 408 (1946); *Robertson v. California*, 328 U.S. 440 (1946).

61. U.S. 483 (1955).

62. See Urofsky, *Division and Discord*, 33–46.

63. U.S. 319 (1937).

64. For a fuller discussion of the debate and of Frankfurter's views, see Melvin I. Urofsky, *Felix Frankfurter: Judicial Restraint and Individual Liberties* (New York: Twayne, 1991), especially chap. 6.

65. Black, *Constitutional Faith*, 50, 52.

66. Frankfurter to Reed, 7 February 1956, Felix Frankfurter Papers, Manuscript Division, Library of Congress, Washington, D.C.

67. The classic work on the Japanese cases is Peter H. Irons, *Justice at War* (New York: Oxford University Press, 1983). See also the U.S. Commission on Wartime Relocation, *Personal Justice Denied* (Washington, D.C.: U.S. Government Printing Office, 1983), and for a less hostile approach, Page Smith, *Democracy on Trial: The Japanese-American Evacuation and Relocation in World War II* (New York: Simon & Schuster, 1995).

68. *Yakus v. United States*, 321 U.S. 414 (1944); *Steuart and Co. v. Bowles*, 322 U.S. 398 (1944); *Bowles v. Willingham*, 321 U.S. 503 (1944); *Lichter v. United States*, 334 U.S. 742 (1948).

69. U.S. at 518.

70. Murphy, *Constitution in Crisis Times*, 176–178; Frank Murphy's tenure as attorney general is detailed in Fine, *Murphy*, chaps. 1–7.

71. *Schneiderman v. United States*, 320 U.S. 119 (1943); *Baumgartner v. United States*, 322 U.S. 665 (1944); *Bridges v. Wixon*, 326 U.S. 135 (1945).

72. *Girouard v. United States*, 328 U.S. 61 (1946).

73. *Hines v. Davidowitz*, 312 U.S. 52 (1941).

74. *Hartzel v. United States*, 322 U.S. 680 (1944); *Viereck v. United States*, 318 U.S. 236 (1943); *Keegan v. United States*, 325 U.S. 478 (1945).

75. *Ex parte Quirin*, 317 U.S. 1 (1942).

76. *West Virginia Board of Education v. Barnette*, 319 U.S. 624, 642 (1943). For an analysis of the various Witness cases, see Edward F. Waite, "The Debt of Constitutional Law to Jehovah's Witnesses," *Minnesota Law Review* 28 (1944): 209.

77. *Grovey v. Townsend*, 295 U.S. 45 (1935).

78. U.S. 299 (1941).

79. *Smith v. Allwright*, 321 U.S. 649 (1944).

80. *Civil Rights Cases,* 109 U.S. 3 (1993); *Logan v. United States,* 144 U.S. 263 (1892); *United States v. Powell,* 212 U.S. 564 (1909).

81. Conference notes, 4 November 1944, Jackson MSS; Frankfurter to Stone, 30 November 1944, Frankfurter MSS, Harvard Law School; Fine, *Murphy,* 396–403.

82. Stone to Douglas, 25 November 1944, Stone MSS; *Screws v. United States,* 325 U.S. 91 (1945). The federal government was unsuccessful in its second attempt to convict Screws, who had in the meantime become something of a local hero. He later won election to the state senate.

83. Robert Carr, *Federal Protection of Civil Liberties* (Ithaca, N.Y.: Cornell University Press, 1947), 114; Herman Belz et al., *The American Constitution,* 7th ed. (New York: W. W. Norton, 1991), 597; author's interview with Justice Marshall, 17 May 1988.

84. Mason, *Stone,* 698. Paul Murphy joins in this judgment (*Constitution in Crisis Times,* 247) but adds the caveat that this was the most popular war in the nation's history; thus the type of civil liberties challenges present in the Civil War, World War I, and Vietnam were absent.

85. John P. Frank, "Review and Basic Liberties," in Edmond Cahn, ed., *Supreme Court and Supreme Law* (Bloomington: Indiana University Press, 1954), 114.

86. Black to Conference, 23 March 1945, Felix Frankfurter Papers, Harvard Law School.

87. *Adamson v. California,* 332 U.S. 46 (1947).

88. U.S. 78 (1908).

89. U.S. at 50–51, 54.

90. Roger K. Newman, *Hugo Black: A Biography* (New York: Pantheon, 1994), 3552.

91. U.S. at 68, 70.

92. Fine, *Murphy,* 503–504; the Murphy dissent is at 332 U.S. at 123.

93. For a brilliant exposition of the argument that the men who drafted the Fourteenth Amendment did, in fact, mean to incorporate all of the Bill of Rights, see Akhil Reed Amar, *The Bill of Rights: Creation and Reconstruction* (New Haven: Yale University Press, 1998).

94. U.S. at 67–68.

95. *Rochin v. v. California,* 342 U.S. 165, 172 (1952).

96. *Uveges v. Pennsylvania,* 335 U.S. 437, 449–450 (1948).

97. See Black's dissent in *Griswold v. Connecticut,* 381 U.S. 479, 507 (1965).

98. Urofsky, *Division and Discord,* chaps. 6–9.

4

VOTING AGAINST THE HAMMER AND SICKLE: COMMUNISM AS AN ISSUE IN AMERICAN POLITICS

Richard M. Fried

Since the Bolshevik Revolution, there has seldom been a time when some American politician has not accused another of loyalty to or softness on communism. Yet while the specter of communism has haunted US politics since 1917 (and even before), it never prowled full-time. The issue of communist influence in American life became a core political issue only when a perceived threat of communism from abroad converged with a conservative reaction against liberal initiatives at home. These conditions existed most palpably through stretches of the period 1938–1954.

Red-baiting has produced casualties aplenty in state and national politics, as well as a number of beneficiaries, but its use did not always guarantee political success for the long—and sometimes not even the short—term. Of all who strove to harness it, only one, Richard M. Nixon, rode it to the White House. Even he was a rather different figure in 1968, when he achieved his ambition, than in 1948–1954, the peak of his anticommunist prowess. Still, his career also embodied the persistence of the communist issue in the American political culture.[1]

Other anticommunists enjoyed electoral advantage or earned livelihoods by lecturing, writing, and testifying before investigative bodies. Yet their triumphs were mostly brief. Over the *longue durée*, anticommunism has occasionally operated as a dominant, but more often as a secondary, theme, sometimes little more than a rasping hum backgrounding other political tones. That conclusion depends on whether we stress the brevity of the moments of glory enjoyed by each exploiter of the issue or the recurrent frequency of these brief life cycles. Nor should a minimalist assessment over-look the fact that anticommunism expressed itself in many forms. It operated on at least three different levels: in claims that specific individuals followed communist discipline; in charges that political opponents pursued econom-ic policies that would lead toward communism or socialism; and in cultural expressions of anticommunism. Lenin had hardly won power before Ameri-can politicians sensed that anticommunism might yield a profit. Mitchell Palmer, Woodrow Wilson's attorney general and instigator of the Palmer Raids, hoped to parlay antiradical vigilance into a presidential nomination in 1920. He had the second-highest delegate total on the first ballot at the De-mocratic convention, but, stymied, had to release his delegates. Similarly, Ole Hanson had as mayor of Seattle helped break a 1919 general strike led by rad-icals, after which he launched a lucrative lecture tour, his topic the Red Men-ace. The anticommunists' excesses produced a counterreaction. Palmer had clearly overplayed his hand. No less than Warren G. Harding, the candidate of "normalcy" in 1920, declared that "too much has been said about Bolshe-vism in America."[2]

In 1924 Republicans, fearing damage from Robert M. La Follette's third-party presidential candidacy, labeled him a radical and all but ignored the De-mocrats. The senator's proposal to curb the Supreme Court's jurisdiction made him vulnerable, and his opposition to entering the world war raised doubts about his loyalty. Though he disavowed the communists, and they him, he was still red-baited.[3] One Republican activist proposed neutralizing La Follette with "a patriotic appeal against the Reds and Socialists." Charles Gates Dawes, President Calvin Coolidge's ebullient running mate, termed the third party "a heterogeneous combination, the largest portion of which are the Socialists, opposing the existing order of things and flying the red flag." Republicans warned that if the La Follette vote threw the decision to the House of Representatives, a deadlock there might enable Senate Democrats to pick Charles Bryan, William Jennings Bryan's younger brother, as vice presi-dent—and, in effect, president. The options were "Coolidge or Chaos." GOP orators claimed that communists were aiding La Follette; one even asserted that the Soviets had funded his campaign. However, Dawes expounded the more common theme, a choice between "Coolidge, who stands for the rock of the Constitution, or the shifting sand of socialism."[4] Republicans overrated La Follette's potential. His own party's organizational weaknesses and limited appeal, a divided Democratic Party, and prosperous times begat a Coolidge landslide. In the 1920s anticommunism had limited electoral use but some purchase when mobilized against particular policies. Conservatives discredited reform through red-baiting. Progressive senators fighting to expose the Teapot Dome scandals were linked with Bolshevism. So were feminism and social-welfare causes such as the Sheppard-Towner Act, which funded a program to improve the health of infants and expectant mothers. The metaphors of anticommunism were developing. Thus, the "spiderweb network" by which a set of prominent reformers might be associated, through common memberships or other ties, could be used to imply a sinister link between them and some Soviet leader. Efforts to end the policy of diplomatic non-recognition of the Soviet Union also attracted insinuations of procommunism, the labor movement was vulnerable to red-baiting, and so were such causes dear to an increasingly weak and fragmented Progressive movement as settlement houses and campaigns to improve the lot of workers.[5]

In 1932, despite the desperate throes in which capitalism found itself, the communist issue barely surfaced. In July, World War I veterans petitioning Congress for early payment of their service bonus had been routed out of Washington. General Douglas MacArthur, the Army Chief of Staff, and Secretary of War Patrick J. Hurley justified setting troops upon the ex doughboys on grounds that Reds had won influence among them and revolution impended. Although he knew better, President Herbert Hoover endorsed MacArthur's rationale —and further discredited his candidacy. At campaign's end a spent, beaten Hoover exclaimed, "Thank God, you have a government in Washington that knows how to deal with a mob." He charged that Franklin D. Roosevelt championed "the same philosophy of government which has poisoned all of Europe" and urged voters to avoid "the fumes of the witch's caldron which boiled in Russia." This blast was an exception; more typically Republicans said FDR had *no* views at all—offering, as one put it, only "glittering generality" and "slickness."[6] The New Deal's fast-breeding alphabet agencies, emphasis on planning, and growing control over the economy soon alienated conservatives, some of whom insinuated that FDR was in cahoots with or dominated by communists. Postwar investigations and trials would indicate that communists had found a first point of entry into the New Deal via the Agricultural Adjustment Administration, but in the 1930s suspicions of Red infiltration remained undocumented and were expressed in quarters so identified with diehard antagonism to the New Deal, then at its greatest popularity, that they were discounted. In 1934 the first investigation of charges that communists were at work in the administration owed its motivation to a critic of the New Deal's proposal to regulate the stock exchanges. Testifying against the measure, he claimed that one William A. Wirt had knowledge of a scheme by New Dealers to drive the country toward communism. Summoned before a House committee, Wirt testified so out-landishly as to discredit such charges.[7]

Other charges of procommunism emanated from spokesmen for the ultra-right American Liberty League, including some conservative Democrats displaced when FDR took over the party. The aggrieved Al Smith made a furious attack on the New Deal before a Liberty League audience. Democrat and Liberty Leaguer Joseph B. Ely charged that Roosevelt's viewpoints "constitute a great stride toward actual communism." Al Smith declared that Roosevelt was "neither a Communist nor a Socialist . . . but something has taken place in this country—there is some certain kind of foreign 'ism' crawling over this country," and FDR was oblivious to it. In 1936 Republican campaigners, conservative Democrats, and the president's sometime ally, the radio priest Father Charles E. Coughlin, warned of the New Deal's red coloration. Vice-presidential nominee Frank Knox and John D. M. Hamilton, chairman of the Republican National Committee, charged that the New Deal was careening toward communism. The RNC also declared that some of Roosevelt's closest advisors had "calmly discussed the amount of 'blood that ought to be shed' " in the coming revolution. Later, that body labeled FDR "the Kerensky of the American revolutionary movement"; although "the poor lamb" did not know where his disastrous policies led, Communist backers such as Earl Browder and Joseph Stalin did. Bainbridge Colby, a former secretary of state and now a disaffected Democrat, charged that Roosevelt had deserted "the time-honored doctrines of the Democratic Party" and was receiving Communist support that might prove decisive in New York and so determine "the character of government which we will have for the future." Al Smith accused his former protégé of leading an administration in which "even a Communist with wire whiskers and a torch in his hands is welcome."[8]

The White House felt the sting of such barbs. It preemptively denounced an attack in William Randolph Hearst's papers naming FDR "the real candidate—the unofficial candidate of the Comintern." In a major speech, Roosevelt rejected support from adherents of "communism or of any other alien 'ism,' " decried contrary imputations as a "red herring," and argued that while the Republicans had created conditions that nourished radicalism, his program had starved it. Thus, he was "the true conservative." In a radio talk sponsored by the Democratic National Committee, Monsignor John A. Ryan disavowed charges of communism against the New Deal and suggested that their purveyors had suspended the eighth commandment's strictures against bearing false witness. In the 1936 landslide, no accusations by FDR's foes won much traction.[9]

Charges of communism also greeted third-party and other radical movements such as Philip and Robert M. La Follette Jr.'s Wisconsin Progressives, the Minnesota Farmer Labor Party, and Upton Sinclair's End Poverty in California Movement. Sinclair's 1934 gubernatorial campaign stirred massive opposition from business interests and led a frightened Hollywood to create fanciful "documentary" short subjects suggesting that his program had lured a flood of hoboes into the state. All his critics in both major parties warned that he would usher the Golden State toward communism. Similarly, the La Follettes were red-baited within the Republican Party and again after they launched a third party. One Republican accused their newspaper of spreading "communist propaganda" just as did the *Daily Worker*.[10] That many attacks on the New Deal and movements to its left originated with Democrats initially muddled anticommunism's partisan implications. The first sustained charges that the New Deal gave refuge to communists issued from Congressman Martin Dies, the Texas Democrat who in 1938 launched a special investigation of un-American activities. (The Dies Committee was precursor to the House Un-American Activities Committee, or HUAC, formally constituted in 1945 through the efforts of Congressman John Rankin, also a Democrat.) Dies infused his anticommunism with a nativist viewpoint along with a growing distaste for the New Deal and the labor activism of CIO unions.[11]

Though he had once been a New Deal enthusiast, by the fall of 1938 Dies was allowing committee witnesses to suggest that several candidates, but especially Governor Frank Murphy of Michigan, furthered communist aims, in his case by coddling sit-down strikers the year before, as Murphy's Republican opponents were arguing. Dies also heard criticisms of Elmer Benson, Minnesota's Farmer-Labor governor, and Culbert L. Olson, the Democratic gubernatorial candidate in California. In New York, both Governor Herbert H. Lehman and his Republican challenger Thomas E. Dewey pledged to ban communists from state jobs. In Montana, the topic punctuated the effort (joined by the Democratic Party establishment as well as the Republicans) to unseat the left-wing Democratic Congressman Jerry O'Connell. A flyer supporting O'Connell's challenger enjoined Montanans to "Crush Communism."[12]

Charges of communism also echoed through New York's Sixteenth Congressional District. The incumbent, John J. O'Connor, a target of FDR's effort to "purge" the Democratic Party of conservatives, faced a primary challenge from his former campaign manager James H. Fay. He identified Fay's backers as the Communist Party, which did in fact oppose O'Connor; the left-wing Workers Alliance, which sought to corral the votes of WPA workers; and meddling New Dealers. He warned that success for FDR's purge would mean "one-man dictatorship" followed by communism. Fay denounced the charges and shunned Red support; his campaign manager accused the O'Connor forces of spreading bogus circulars purporting to show communist support for Fay. O'Connor lost the Democratic primary. Running as the Republican and "Andrew Jackson" Democratic candidate, he was defeated again in November.[13] Republicans scored broad gains in the U.S. House and Senate. The results probably owed most to an increasingly conservative electorate's fatigue with the New Deal, the 1937–38 recession, voter discontent with local political corruption, and low farm prices. Although off-year election losses are normal for the party in power, these were a sharp rebuff to the New Deal. Columnist Arthur Krock noted presciently that a bipartisan conservative "Congressional coalition" might well "prevent any further advance of New Deal programs."[14]

Yet beyond simple conservatism lay more corrosive, nasty electioneering. Some campaigns aggravated religious and ethnic divisions. Ominous events abroad bred a sense of crisis that led many Americans to fear for their security and to question the loyalty of others. In his pre-election appeal, FDR called for recovery "without attempting to commit the nation to any ism or ideology except democracy, humanity and the civil liberties which form their foundations" or paying the price imposed for economic growth by "dictators." Not everyone absorbed the civics lesson. In New York, foes of incumbent governor Herbert Lehman called on voters to "Save Our State for Americans" and tacked up posters urging: "Keep the American Way." (His challenger Thomas E. Dewey repudiated such devices.) Anticommunism's cultural dimension sometimes dovetailed with nativism, anti-Semitism, and other symptoms of social dislocation.[15]

Amid fears of foreign threats, electoral red-baiting heated up in 1940. The term "fifth column," coined in Spain's civil war, entered the political vocabulary, as did the phrase "Trojan horse." Politicians applied them to Nazi and Communist threats, a convergence suggested by the tactics of Hitler's allies in countries he menaced and the Nazi-Soviet Pact, which made the Soviets and their American allies at least temporary bedmates of the Nazis. Republicans and Democrats gleefully slung this coinage at each other, the right using it against the left and the Roosevelt administration against its isolationist foes.[16] GOP standard-bearer Wendell Willkie less often decried communism than warned that a third term for FDR would bring "dictatorship" closer. The Republican platform condemned the New Deal's "encouragement" of those seeking extra-constitutional change and the access of "such un-American groups" to high federal posts. Governor Harold E. Stassen charged that the weak and divisive New Dealers "just smiled and reached over and patted the flanks of the Trojan Horse." FDR riposted that "something evil is happening in this country" when "organizations that make no secret of their admiration" for dictatorship circulated Republican campaign materials and when a GOP ad appeared, "of all places," in the Communist *Daily Worker*. His running mate Henry A. Wallace charged that "appeasers" opposed Roosevelt, in whose defeat Hitler would "rejoice." He claimed "Nazi agents" and "friends of the totalitarian powers" aided the Republicans.[17] Such tit-for-tat tainting of the opposition's loyalties marked politics throughout the 1940s and may have helped sharpen the bitterness of electoral McCarthyism in its mature phase.

Anticommunist rhetoric mushroomed in 1944. The fourth-term issue prompted more cries of "dictatorship," and the wartime alliance with the USSR and tolerance of domestic communists irked conservatives. When FDR pardoned Communist Party leader Earl Browder, then in jail for passport fraud, and expressed hope that the action would "promote national unity," he stirred suspicion and anger. A "shocked" Catholic cleric passed on the comment that "Washington is growing to be a 'little Moscow.' " The worrisome future of the Eastern European lands in the Red Army's path troubled Catholics and ethnic groups and gave further poignancy to concerns about communist influences.[18]

Republicans belabored the CIO Political Action Committee's vigorous support for FDR. Heading the CIO's political arm was Sidney Hillman, a foreign born Jew who could be yoked to the Communists felt to be potent in the CIO. When FDR told aides to "clear it with Sidney" whether Senator Harry S. Truman was an acceptable vice-presidential nominee, he gave enemies a brickbat and anticommunists (and anti-Semites and nativists) a mantra. A Cleveland paper editorialized that "the complacency of the Roosevelt administration toward the communism-statism sympathizers within the government, and the cooperativeness of Hillman and the CIO fourth-term campaign committee toward the U.S. Communist leaders" had created a "Communist issue."[19]

From governors Thomas E. Dewey and John W. Bricker on the national ticket down through the ranks, Republicans rushed to seize the Browder and Hillman corollaries. Bricker speculated that Browder had been freed to electioneer for Roosevelt, who was now the Reds' "political prisoner." Dewey contrasted normal Soviet Communists with their sinister U.S. brethren. "In Russia, a communist is a man who supports his Government. In America a communist supports the fourth term so our form of government may more easily be changed." Dewey termed FDR "indispensable" to New Deal hangers-on, corrupt city machines, Hillman and the CIO-PAC, and "Earl Browder, the ex-convict and pardoned Communist leader." A GOP handbill in rural Illinois declared that voters looked to Dewey and Bricker to "drive Communism from Government."[20]

Such charges nettled the Democrats. Their adversaries were all "isolationists," doing the Fascists' work by Hitlerian methods, sowing dissent among ethnic groups, imperiling U.S.-Soviet relations. Tart-tongued Secretary of the Interior Harold Ickes termed it "better to be a foreign born American" like Hillman than "an American born foreigner" like the pro-Dewey isolationists. Author John Gunther exclaimed that "the Nazi radio actually came out for Dewey . . . saying flatly that his election would be providential for the Germans." Dewey and company were trying to "drag in such completely extraneous issues as the Communist bogey" and to "stir up the ugliest possible passions on a racist level." Actor Orson Welles recalled that "the Nazis rose to power" with lies about communism. He wondered if "the Deweyites might even attempt their own equivalent of the Reichstag fire." (Some FDR backers did fret that Republicans might spring a last-minute "Zinoviev letter" ploy, referring to a forgery allegedly written by a Soviet leader that, published on the eve of the 1924 election, shattered the British Labor Party's chances.) On another radio show, comedian Jimmie Durante mockingly warbled, "That man in the White House is Moscow Joe, it's regimentation from the top to the middle, it's totalitariorriorism for each individdle." Roosevelt disavowed any communist aid. Citing Republican mailings warning of a "Red Specter of Communism," he stated that such "fear propaganda is now new among rabble-rousers and fomenters of class hatred" and had been used by Mussolini, Hitler "and others on the lunatic fringe."[21]

The communist issue had bite in 1944. Certainly spokesmen for both parties thought so. October soundings by pollster Elmo Roper identified three factors explaining defections from FDR. One was worry over his " 'close tie-up' to Communism." Political scientist and one-time Roosevelt advisor Charles E. Merriam warned that some Americans held intense feeling against Blacks, Jews, labor, foreigners "inflamed by what they call radicalism, socialism, communism. Hillman makes their ideal target." Responding to such sentiments, FDR declared that he "never sought the support of any person or group which would undermine the American system of government." (Why then, asked one hostile newspaper, did he free Browder?[22])

The 1946 campaign promised still more salience for anticommunism. Relations with the USSR had grown prickly. Truman's dismissal of Secretary of

Commerce Henry A. Wallace for criticizing his anti-Soviet policies created disarray on the left and a target for the right. The postwar strike wave and fears of the expanded power of labor unions suggested a reprise for pertinent motifs from 1944.Republicans rushed to rescue America from "statism," "socialism," and Red influences. Their national chairman, Congressman B. Carroll Reece, labeled Democrats an unlovely coupling of descendants of slaveocrats and sovietizers. "The basic political issue before this nation is that of liberalism versus State absolutism"—or "communism and republicanism." House Minority Leader Joe Martin pledged that his party would give priority to "cleaning out the Communists, their fellow travelers and parlor pinks from high positions in our Government." Republicans gleefully played up a Soviet radio commentator's advice that voters support "progressive," CIO-PAC-backed candidates and oppose the GOP. To John W. Bricker it proved that the CIO-PAC campaign "is being directed from communistic Russia." A Wisconsin candidate for Congress declared that Republicans wanted no "Russia Firsters, the pinkos, the fellow travelers, the Red [Sen. Claude D.] Peppers and the Two World Wallaces." In California, Richard M. Nixon charged that Congressman Jerry Voorhis had been endorsed by the Political Action Committee. The CIO-PAC had not embraced the liberal Democratic incumbent, but a local chapter of its cousin, the National Citizens Political Action Committee, had. Though anticommunist himself, Voorhis never got off the defensive against this charge. Just before the election, a phone bank of anonymous callers intimated to constituents that Voorhis was a Communist.[23]

In Wisconsin, Judge Joseph R. McCarthy ran for the U.S. Senate as an anti–New Deal yet "modern" internationalist Republican. In the primary he taxed incumbent Robert M. La Follette Jr.: "By your failure to do anything to promote peace you are playing into the hands of the Communists." Seeking to reenter the Republican Party, La Follette stressed his opposition by Communists in the state's CIO (he had condemned Soviet policy in East Europe) and by Tom "Boss" Coleman, leader of the conservative Republicans, he rejected both extremes of "colemanism" and "communism." In the general election, McCarthy called his Democratic opponent "communistically inclined."[24] As the election neared, more mundane issues crowded forward. The turmoil of postwar reconversion brought on a meat shortage. When beef reappeared in stores a week before the elections, harassed shoppers were too busy queuing up for now-scarce sugar. Blessed with such issues, Republicans found their best slogan to be "Had Enough?" Their smashing victory drew on so many discontents that it is impossible to disaggregate the weight of the communist issue. Nixon's victory, columnist Tom Wicker suggests, owed less to red-baiting than to a changing electorate, the host of enemies rallied by Voorhis's liberal stands over ten years, the Congressman's inept campaign and the fact that his previous foes had been pushovers. A broader array of concerns than communism also elected McCarthy and many other Republicans. Nevertheless, the anticommunist speechifying prompted Speaker of the House Sam Rayburn to exclaim in a nationally broadcast radio talk: "if I were the kind of Moscow follower the Republicans are talking about, I would be cheering for the Republicans on Nov. 5." The 1946 elections suggested that there was mileage in the issue.[25]

Trends suggested a bull market for anticommunism in 1948. Great Power relations had further soured. The Iron Curtain was a fact of life. The doubts thus raised promised a harvest of Republican votes. The Democrats scrambled to defend their record on communism. Initially, that seemed to entail red-baiting the Progressive Party—"Henry Wallace and his Communists," as Truman labeled them on St. Patrick's Day. But as the Progressives foundered, Truman paid them less heed. He now stated that a vote for Wallace would only help the Republicans, and the latter, if returned to power, would foster communism through the hard times and isolationism that would ensue. This was an embellishment, not the main Democratic election theme.[26]

Whittaker Chambers's testimony implicating New Deal bureaucrats—most notably Alger Hiss—in pro-Soviet conniving prefaced the fall campaign. Both the FBI and the Central Intelligence Agency were keen to stir the pot, to provide grist for the Republicans, and the loyalty issue appeared to portend trouble. A White House staffer deemed the "spy" issue "the Administration's weakest link." Truman and his aides responded with an emphatic speech in Oklahoma City on September 28 in defense of his administration's vigilance. Some southern Democrats, alienated by the party's liberalism, notably its embrace of the civil-rights issue, also toyed with anticommunism. Thus, Texas Governor Beauford H. Jester listed among threats to the South "communistic agitators and a shallow-minded fringe of Henry Wallace liberals," and Truman's agitation of civil rights. While the Truman Doctrine helped people abroad to "preserve their institutions from being subverted by outside influences," apparently this credo was "too good for the Southern States."[27]

His 1944 apprenticeship had given candidate Dewey a solid grounding in the communist issue. A group of anticommunist activists backing him met in the summer of 1948 to canvass "the 'Communist Problem' " and its relation to the campaign. They labeled their project "Operation Polecat," reflecting Dewey's hope "to make communism as popular as a polecat." Members were businessman (and "China Lobby" leader) Alfred Kohlberg, publisher William Loeb, journalists Frederick Woltman, George Schuyler, Isaac Don Levine, Robert Humphreys, and, notably, Whittaker Chambers, who had just testified before HUAC. The group believed that Dewey could assail Democratic failures on that score and oust communists, yet preserve civil liberties and raise the issue "from the mire of rumor-mongering, smear-ladling, abuse and counter abuse" by promising to appoint a long-term presidential commission to "make an exhaustive study."[28]

However, Dewey did not embrace Operation Polecat. Urged to stress the communist issue, he said he would "fleck it lightly." He had already taken a moderate stance in debate with rival Harold Stassen in the Oregon primary, when he opposed outlawing the Communist Party; though Stassen claimed that policy would "coddle" the Reds, Dewey had won the primary. He regretted his dalliance with the issue in 1944. Dewey and his running mate Governor Earl Warren did raise the topic, but not as a primary theme. His reticence may have spawned an unhappy irony. More stress on the issue might have averted defeat, one that, according to some observers, so embittered many Republicans as to lead them to tolerate, if not encourage, McCarthy's excesses for their potential for partisan gain. Perhaps an inoculation with a light case of red-baiting in 1948 might have prevented the epidemic that arrived in 1950.[29]

If indeed 1948's frustrations led to 1950's full-blown electoral McCarthyism, the 1949 special U.S. Senate race in New York between John Foster Dulles and Herbert H. Lehman provided a preview. Dulles asserted that all the Reds were backing Lehman. Dewey, who had appointed Dulles to the Senate, stumped for him—and echoed the anticommunist emphasis. Lehman in turn accused Dulles of anti-Semitism for his remark upstate that "if you could see the kind of people in New York City making up this bloc that is voting for [Lehman] . . . I know that you would be out, every last man and woman of you on election day." Dulles insisted that the "bloc" he meant was "Communist American Labor Party voters" and rejected the "ugly charge of bigotry." Lehman proposed that the Communists attacked him harder than his foe, aware that only Democratic policies could prevent "the economic crash which Marshall Stalin so anxiously awaits." Lehman won.[30]

The year 1950 opened red-baiting's golden age. Joe McCarthy had captured newspaper headlines since February, convincing many Americans that his charges of communism in the State Department had not been fairly reviewed. The Cold War had grown more menacing, with China's "loss" in 1949, Alger Hiss's trials and conviction, the Soviet A-bomb, arrests and confessions of "atom spies," and then the Korean War. Even before Korea, these developments made South Dakota Republican Senator Karl Mundt optimistic about campaign prospects. "Certainly, the Communist issue is in the front as it has never been before."[31] The autumn began on an upnote for Democrats as UN forces drove the North Korean armies up the peninsula, but then China's intervention darkened the atmosphere as Americans went to the polls.

Since spring, the communist issue appeared to rack up victims. Southern liberal Senators Claude D. Pepper of Florida and Frank P. Graham of North Carolina lost to Democratic primary foes who termed them soft on communism (as wall as shaky on the race question). Senatorial primary rivals plied the communist issue against other Democrats on the party's left wing, notably Senator Glen Taylor of Idaho and Congresswoman Helen Gahagan Douglas of California. Taylor lost to a conservative; Douglas survived, but the communist issue was now teed up for her Republican foe, Richard M. Nixon, who, in light of the conviction of Alger Hiss and other events, would in any case have exploited it.[32]

Communism saturated the 1950 campaign. Republicans had a field day, but Democrats too, strove to flex their muscles. Congressman A. S. "Mike" Monroney held that his rival in Oklahoma's Senate race, by "making a political football out of the Korean war to win an election, and blaming our elected leaders for war guilt" parroted the Communist Party line. Candidates melded the topic deftly with collateral issues. Colorado Republican Senator Eugene Millikin used it to flavor a disparagement of Truman administration bungling: "The background music against which these clowns play their parts is too often 'The Internationale' rather than 'The Star Spangled Banner.' " It also meshed with the emergent issue of organized crime. Thus, Bob Considine, who often devoted his newspaper column to these topics, found them linked. A "subtle black stain of hoodlum super-government, well protected politically," was spreading in American cities. Like communism, "it is superbly concealed, well organized."[33]

The communist issue tinted Senate contests in Utah, Colorado, Oklahoma, Pennsylvania, Idaho, Iowa, and Ohio, governor's races in Pennsylvania, Michigan, and Wisconsin, and a spectrum of House campaigns. Informed that the topic was harvesting votes, Senator Mundt advised candidates like Nixon and Everett McKinley Dirksen to press it hard. The Mundt-Nixon bill, calling for the registration of communist groups, came up for debate in the tense weeks of late summer and passed by lopsided majorities in the harsher version offered by Senator Pat McCarran. If Truman vetoed it (as he did), Mundt predicted it would be "the best political issue in more than a decade."[34]

McCarthy starred in the campaign, speaking in some fifteen states. He aimed especially at senators Scott Lucas of Illinois, the majority leader; Brien McMahon of Connecticut, a critic of his assault on the State Department; and Millard Tydings of Maryland, the hostile chairman of the panel that investigated his charges. Lucas lost to ex-congressman Dirksen, whose campaign featured anticommunist rhetoric. Tydings, who had survived FDR's 1938 purge attempt, suffered a stunning defeat. These and other results prompted observers to credit McCarthy and his anticommunist barnstorming with striking influence on voters and his colleagues, drawing similar conclusions, to give the Wisconsinite a wide and fearful berth.[35]

Yet journalists and politicos overrated McCarthy's grassroots appeal. As an Administration spokesman, Lucas may have been vulnerable to the charges leveled at it, including softness on communism, but he was more grievously wounded by a local crime scandal involving Chicago's Democratic machine. Tydings, McCarthy's most prominent victim, may have been weakened by insinuations of having "whitewashed" McCarthy's charges. However, he had plural vulnerabilities: Maryland Democrats were in disarray; his ticket mate the governor was deeply unpopular; black voters were responsive to Republican appeals; Tydings had grown distant from his constituents; and a long-term Republican trend was operating in Maryland. At the time, however, the 1950 election induced a sense among political elites that a powerful anticommunism had settled firmly upon the electorate. Previously, McCarthy seemed to survive by nimble-footed evasiveness; it now appeared that his politics carried a heavy punch.[36]

In 1952, with the Korean War stalemated, Truman weakened on other fronts, and McCarthy a fixture in public life, anticommunism again loomed as an electoral catalyst. Republicans endorsed that surmise by naming Richard Nixon as General Dwight D. Eisenhower's running mate, and soon after the convention, the Republican National Committee proposed to Ike a campaign that would italicize the communist issue.[37] The fact that the Democratic nominee, Adlai E. Stevenson, had once served as a character witness for Alger Hiss gave further promise that the subject would get a full airing. Nixon credentialed the Illinois governor with a "Ph.D. from [Secretary of State] Dean Acheson's cowardly college of Communist containment." Senator William Jenner, a McCarthy ally, predicted: "If Adlai gets into the White House, Alger gets out of the jail house." Aside from one nationally televised speech, McCarthy played a secondary role in the national campaign, but he intervened on behalf of fellow-Republicans in thirteen states and seemed still to be an important political force.[38] The talk in 1952 suggested the importance of anticommunism, but politicians' rhetoric is not always an accurate guide to voting behavior. In most public opinion samplings, communism did not rank as a top concern. A May 1952 Roper poll found 27 percent of Americans preoccupied with the issue of government spending and taxes, 24 percent with inflation and the cost of living, 13 percent with "corruption and dishonesty," and 8 percent with allegations of communism and socialism. In September Gallup asked respondents to list reasons to vote Republican: the number citing communism was too small to be itemized. In 1952 as in 1950 there was a disconnect between the grounds on which politicians urged citizens to make their decision and the voters' actual reasons. Such a disjunction makes it hard for political elites to function. They find it easier to merge an election's rhetoric with its outcome. This temptation had much to do with a central fact of the age: the tendency of fellow politicians and the media to exaggerate McCarthy's political clout. In part the "McCarthy era" lasted as long as it did because of this conflation of appearances and reality.[39]

In 1954 many observers anticipated new excesses of political roughhousing. Democratic Party Chair Stephen A. Mitchell expected Republicans to "use the President to smile and McCarthy to smear." The nonpartisan Fair Campaign Practices Committee feared that campaigns would "descend to new and distressingly low levels." However, Republicans had now come to perceive McCarthy as a liability and isolated him from the campaign, a move whose wisdom the polls confirmed. In Illinois, for example, 16 percent of respondents would favor a McCarthy-backed candidate, but 35 percent would oppose him.[40] It is impossible to measure the extent to which his decline in status was linked to the distribution among political leaders of *Influences in the 1954 Mid-Term Elections*, a pamphlet by the statistician and political prognosticator Louis Bean. Subsidized by foes of McCarthy, the booklet claimed that Democrats against whom he had campaigned in 1950 and 1952 had not suffered damage and had even (in 1952) run ahead of Democrats he had ignored. Possibly this knowledge made some Democrats less timid and some Republicans less eager to rely on McCarthy or his campaign style. His censure was under consideration by a select committee, whose report, issued during the campaign, would be acted upon after the election. Democrats in Congress still fretted about the communist issue, as their support for the Communist Control Act, passed late in the session, made apparent. Two months later, according to veteran reporter William S. White, on the campaign trail "the 'Communist issue'—indeed, any kind of reference to communism—is vastly less on the people's lips than it was two years and four years ago."[41]

That situation would soon alter, especially in the West, as the worried GOP revisited the communist issue, albeit without McCarthy. Periodically the Eisenhower administration had trumpeted the ever-growing numbers of security risks it had ousted from federal jobs. In October 1954 the Civil Service Commission reported dismissing 6,926 security risks in roughly a year. (Earlier, when a reporter asked Ev Dirksen if some such new total could be expected at this opportune date, the Illinois senator broke into a "broad grin.") Ohio GOP Senate candidate George Bender asserted that "the Communists know that they can count on a far more favorable atmosphere under Democrats than under Republicans."[42]

Nixon bore the main burden of the 1954 Republican campaign. Slightly less stridently than in 1952, he thrust at Democratic laxity. Under Ike, "the threat of communism within our walls is no longer pooh-poohed and brushed off as a 'red herring.'" "We have driven Communists, the fellow travelers and the security risks out of the Government by the thousands." Nixon redoubled emphasis on the Democrats' economic radicalism. If they won, "left wingers" would control their party and the nation would veer back to a "socialist tradition." Republicans, he claimed, had found in government files a "blueprint for socializing America." He tethered Democrats to the ADA again, picturing the latter group as blasé about communism and keen for socialism.[43]

Democrats, even southerners, responded in irritation and, presumably, some confidence. South Carolina Senator Olin D. Johnson charged the vice president with leading a "fascist-type attack" utilizing "the big lie," noting that while Nixon spoke of thousands of ousted Communists, the chairman of the Civil Service Commission had confessed "he knew of no single Government employee who had been fired because he was a Communist" or "fellow traveler." In Wisconsin, Adlai Stevenson accused the campaigning Nixon of purveying "McCarthyism in a white collar."[44]

Insinuations of procommunism still materialized, particularly in western-state senate races. In Colorado, handbills asked, "How Red is John Carroll?" Pamphlets warned of "Senator [James] Murray and the Red Network over Congress," depicting the Montanan as a red spider. In Illinois, Paul Douglas was termed "Mr. Capital 'S' of Socialism." Some charges retained a sting, but a number seemed on the fringe. In a futile Texas primary challenge to Senator Lyndon B. Johnson, Dudley T. Dougherty advocated an exit from the UN, ending diplomatic ties with all communist nations, aggressive congressional

investigation of Reds, and outlawing the Communist Party. With ample conservative support, Johnson lost little sleep over Dougherty.[45]

Narrowly the Democrats recaptured the House and Senate, but off-year
electoral gains by the party out of power were normal, and these were slight.
Economic issues cut for the Democrats. Polling evidence suggested that a
more visible McCarthy would have harmed his party's prospects and that
Republican devotion to expelling Reds from the federal bureaucracy was a
theme that appealed to but 3 percent of one sample. Did Nixon's combative
campaigning also cost votes? Not according to the savvy analyst Louis Bean,
who reportedly concluded that Nixon's and Eisenhower's exertions may have
saved their party twenty House seats.[46] The 1956 election revealed how passé
McCarthy and his style had become. The senator was persona non grata in
his party's activities, reportedly once even hustled from the stage when
Nixon spoke in Milwaukee. (Nixon's office denied any repudiation, noting
that McCarthy accompanied him around the state and once called him "one
of the great men in America."[47]) There was some talk of Hiss and red job-
holders, but ex-president Truman triggered much of it with an eruption
against Nixon for having in 1952 labeled him a "traitor." (Nixon actually
called Truman, Acheson, and Stevenson "traitors to the high principles in
which many of the nation's Democrats believe.") Truman also commented
that he did not think Hiss had been a Communist or spy. To Republicans the
outburst became fair game. They challenged Stevenson to respond. When he
reavowed his view of Hiss's guilt, Nixon applauded, implying that the issue
was no longer germane. His hint that his party would stress positive themes
may have been a response to Stevenson's gibe that he and other Republicans
were "back on the same low road" they pursued in 1954. Stevenson also listed
among Ike's leadership failures the phase when McCarthy "conducted, un-
hampered, his career as a national bully." These exchanges measured how far
the nation had traveled in two years.[48]

In 1958 the theme was radicalism, not softness on communism. Again his
party's featured orator, Nixon warned that Democratic gains in Congress
would empower the party's "radical wing," or, as party chair Meade Alcorn
put it, the "left-wing extremists." After a conference at the White House, a
group of Republican leaders warned that "nationalization and socialization
of industry" would follow a Democratic win. The Fair Campaign Practices
Committee received reports of fourteen cases around the country of "imputations of softness on communism or shallow patriotism." The most bizarre
instance may have been an anonymous Arizona handbill on which a leering
Stalin (then dead five years) asked: "Why Not Vote for Goldwater?"[49]

By 1958, amid spreading discourse on the national purpose, the Democrats called for closing the missile gap and regaining lost momentum in the face of the Soviet challenge. Senator John F. Kennedy, seeking reelection and eyeing a presidential race, so embroidered these themes that RNC chair Alcorn urged him to "discard your all-is-lost, Russia-is-the-best speech," which might provoke the communists into "the most dangerous of miscalculations." The communist threat continued to punctuate political rhetoric, but it increasingly moved offshore. Thus, while J. Edgar Hoover told Nixon that the latter's riot-torn South American trip "made anti-Communism respectable again in the United States," there too the stimulus was an event abroad.[50]

By 1960, the communist threat as a personnel matter was dead. (There had been spy arrests under Eisenhower, and in 1960 two cryptanalysts defected to the USSR, but Democrats rarely addressed the topic.) Hard-nosed anticommunism was coming to be identified with a new political genus, the "extremists" or "ultra-right." One might still ask which party could more effectively resist the Soviet juggernaut. Indeed, the Democrats increasingly resorted to such attacks in Ike's second term, holding Republicans responsible for losing the race to orbit a satellite, for the missile gap and bomber gap, for the waning of U.S. prestige abroad and other evidence of "second-class" status, and, delicious irony, for the "loss" of Cuba to Castro.[51]

At a cultural level, hard-shell anticommunists still found reason to castigate Senator John F. Kennedy, the Democratic standard bearer. Extremist anticommunism and anti-Catholicism could even fuse. One ill-wisher, warning that under JFK "the White House would turn into a nunnery," endorsed a Protestant evangelist's handbill titled "The Pink, Punk, Pro-Red Record of Senator Jack Kennedy." That preacher found Kennedy soft on communism and prematurely counter-cultural in how he "sneered" at the loyalty oath, "shaking his head so violently, after the fashion of Elvis Presley doing his version of St Vitus dance, that his shaggy, uncut, uncombed hair spilled down into his eyes." On the other hand, some Democrats still feared Nixon would "lick Kennedy by use of the Communist issue. A leopard never changes its spots."[52]

Yet domestic communism was a nonstarter in 1960. After years of prosecutions, FBI infiltration, Khrushchev's disillusioning 1956 de-Stalinization speech and other blows, real Reds were scarce. Nixon did not wish to be cast solely as the man who got Hiss, and surely not as a red-baiting hatchet man. The communist threat had assumed an increasingly foreign aspect—in far-flung trouble spots and in a broad competition for prestige and supremacy. Nixon's "positives" stemmed from his foreign-policy expertise and experience, and from "standing up" to Khrushchev in the 1959 Kitchen Debate. An advisor cited a public mood of "no appeasement" to explain why Nixon got "a good crowd response with the line that no President should ever apologize to the Russians [as Kennedy had proposed after the Soviets downed a U-2 spy plane in May]."[53]

Republicans argued that Democratic laments of second-place status furthered Soviet ends, and this worried some Democratic strategists: "So long as the Republicans are unethical enough to play on the 'disloyalty' theme, foreign affairs will have a built-in disadvantage for the Democrats." A GOP congressman blamed partisan detractors for the riots in Japan protesting Ike's projected visit, labeling them "America second-class powerists" and "crawl on our bellies to Moscowites." However, charges that they were "running down" America enabled Democrats to respond, as did Senator Henry M. Jackson, chairman of their national committee, that Nixon sought to "deny the American people even a part of what Mr. Khrushchev knows already through his vast spy network." Voters "are not going to allow Mr. Nixon to hide the Republican record behind Nikita Khrushchev's baggy pants."[54]

Though "McCarthyism" had been exorcized from public life, both sides shot occasional cautionary glances at the past. "Now that the scourge of McCarthyism has become simply an embarrassing national memory, and the 'New Nixon' is professedly driving only on the center of the high road," red-baiting was apparently passé, but the Democratic National Committee warned of ongoing "tired distortions" of Roosevelt-Truman foreign policies.[55] Some Republicans expected Democrats to assail Nixon's campaigns against Voorhis and Douglas.[56] Nixon reproved his New Hampshire campaign chairman for calling JFK soft on communism. He differentiated his "constructive conservatism" from Democratic radicalism largely in economic terms. He warned of features of the Democratic platform "that would lead to socializing or nationalizing basic institutions" and highlighted Kennedy's as "the most radical program ever advocated by a Presidential candidate." He charged that JFK's farm program called for controls "which even Henry Wallace has said are as severe as those imposed in many Communist countries." He labored to ensure that news stories did not convey lines such as "Nixon hints Kennedy soft on Communism." There was little of the raw meat his fans had once enjoyed. Columnist Westbrook Pegler warned that he was repeating Dewey's error. "Communism is your dish."[57]

Kennedy had an analogous problem: convincing liberals that *he* had distanced himself from McCarthyism. He had claimed credit for having a Communist witness cited for contempt a year before Nixon confronted Alger Hiss.

He passed Nixon a contribution from his father for the campaign against Helen Douglas. Liberals had never heard him rebuke McCarthy; indeed, the two were friendly. Ill during the censure fight, JFK later peddled a speech that would have urged censure at an early stage of the battle, and he reiterated that stand to peevish liberals. His subsequent fight against the loyalty oath required of applicants for loans under the National Defense Education Act served to buff his liberal credentials. As he geared up to run for president, Eleanor Roosevelt stated her qualms about his silence in the McCarthy era. Boosters of his rival Senator Hubert H. Humphrey noted that much of Kennedy's Wisconsin presidential primary vote came from places that once "provided huge majorities for Joe McCarthy."[58] Thus, political circumstances prompted both candidates, but especially Nixon, to finesse the communist issue.[59]

When used, the old formula seemed quaint. A right-wing pamphlet exposed Lyndon Johnson's "left-wing voting record" and the praise he won from "extreme left-wingers" (namely the *Washington Post*). An Arizona congressman asserted that the Democrats' platform came "straight out of Marx's manifesto." Congressman Alvin Bentley, a Michigan Republican long enamored of the communist issue, charged Democratic Senator J. William Fulbright with blocking a bill "to stop the flow of Communist agents . . . by tightening passport laws." Frederic W. Airy assailed New Mexico's Democratic Senator Clinton P. Anderson for having "consistently voted with the 'soft-on-Communism' bloc." Airy did not survive even the Republican primary. As Anderson suggested to a home-state publisher, he had just spoken at the launching of the *Patrick Henry* and had been styled "Godfather" of this weapons system, so "surely the Navy would not have asked me to commission its newest submarine had this Administration felt I was soft on communism."[60]

A slight uptick in anticommunism accented the 1962 campaign. Running against Governor Edmund G. "Pat" Brown, Nixon declared "fighting Communism within California" a key problem. A bumper sticker asked: "Is Brown Pink?" Others were nastier. The campaign showed how anticommunism had moved rightward. Conservative senate candidate Howard Jarvis attacked the ex-Democrat Ronald Reagan, leagued with one of his Republican rivals, for using "so many procommunist people on his General Electric show." Canvassing for Nixon, Reagan himself described mainstream liberals as "more dangerous than outright Communists." Dewey—the 1944, not the 1948, model—consoled the defeated Nixon that "you had the undying enmity of the Communists and their allies." In his famous "last" press conference, Nixon pointed to press hostility "ever since the Hiss case."[61] In Florida, the far right resuscitated the Red issue by circulating a pamphlet entitled (as in

1950) "The Red Record of Senator Claude Pepper," but Pepper won a congressional seat even so.[62] Nixon's defeat suggested that his advisors and he were out of touch with the political culture.

Identification with "extremism" limited anticommunism's electoral utility. Barry Goldwater seemed to sense this early in his 1964 presidential campaign, when he let down a conservative audience by saying he was "not overly concerned" about communists in government, though he feared the "fuzzy-wuzzy" minds of their sympathizers and those who did not "understand Communists." But in the fall his running mate William Miller and he struck themes evocative of a decade back. Congressman Miller scored Democratic vice-presidential nominee Hubert Humphrey's voting record as "clearly one of the most radical in Congress." Goldwater termed the Johnson administration "soft on Communism"; he said Humphrey wanted "to drag our nation into the swampland of collectivism." "Well, shades of Nixon," Humphrey riposted, recalling the "witch-hunting days of McCarthyism." Though Nixon denied counseling Goldwater on the matter and declared LBJ's anticommunism above reproach, Goldwater reiterated the charge. The Democratic landslide suggested that intimations of softness on communism carried scant weight outside the circle of true believers.[63]

The last noisy gasp of election anticommunism arose as dissent over the war in Vietnam began to stir. New Jersey Republicans nominated Wayne Dumont Jr. for governor in 1965. He was given little chance to beat popular incumbent Richard J. Hughes. His chief issue was his zeal to fire Rutgers University historian Eugene D. Genovese for declaring at an antiwar teach-in that he welcomed "the impending Vietcong victory in Vietnam." Hughes dismissed the idea, upheld academic freedom, and said that Dumont's advocacy of a measure to make the Pledge of Allegiance mandatory "smacks of the McCarthy syndrome." He accused Dumont of seeking political profit from the deaths of American boys in Vietnam and of opening "a Pandora's box for the extremists." Bumper stickers appeared emblazoned "Rid Rutgers of Reds." A pro-Dumont handbill juxtaposed Genovese's remark, Hughes's position, and a depiction of tank-led Vietcong troops defiling a row of crosses over American graves. Several GOP leaders stumped for Dumont, but only Nixon endorsed his call to oust the professor. Hughes's easy victory convinced his party's state chairman "that elections can't be won by exploiting the unsubstantiated issue of soft on Communism."[64]

The jolts of the late 1960s triggered a conservative reaction, but anticommunist politics did not revive. That genre was now so discredited that occasional breaches of the new consensus were promptly punished. In 1968

Governor Spiro Agnew termed the deeply anticommunist Democratic presidential candidate Hubert Humphrey "squishy soft on communism." Hostile editorial reaction compelled the Republican vice-presidential nominee to regret and withdraw his crack. In 1972, Senator Henry M. Jackson charged that the "left-wing extremism" of Senator George S. McGovern, the front-runner for the Democratic presidential nomination, would lead to an ignominious defeat. He criticized McGovern's support for Henry A. Wallace in 1948. Americans for Democratic Action, liberal foes of Wallace in 1948, nevertheless blasted this "smear." A Democratic congressman insinuated that Jackson thought to salvage his sinking candidacy "by becoming the Democratic Party's Spiro Agnew."[65] McGovern was nominated anyway— and whipped by Nixon.

By 1972, with scattered exceptions, the Red Menace had outlived its electoral usefulness by nearly twenty years. It never elected a president. Though it eroded FDR's support in 1944 and generated bombast in 1952, it proved decisive in neither year. Perhaps its greatest influence came, backhandedly, in 1948, when it was the dog that didn't bark. It may have been more pivotal in off-year contests—certainly in particular races, and in 1938, 1946, and 1950. Though anticommunism gave Republicans a way to nationalize the rhetoric of these clusters of local campaigns, in no instance was it a controlling national issue. Still, for what it lacked in weight it compensated in noise.

Several factors explained the issue's rise and decline. It blended snugly with conservative politics in either major party—it gave point to onslaughts against bureaucrats, excessive and remote central authority, and "socialistic" programs. It could be used to attack any reform cause, from labor and feminism to civil rights to fluoridation of water. It served to validate objections to change—offering a shorthand means to oppose such trends as the shift from a rural and small-town to an urban society, from a nation governed near at hand to one run from Washington, from an existence ruled by tradition to a life bent by stressful change.[66] The New Deal made conservatives fear that traditional American values of localism, individualism, and limited government were crumbling; it was natural for many to ascribe such changes to un-American influences around Roosevelt.

To be salient, however, the communist issue required a convergence of circumstances. First, a plausible Soviet threat was required. The brief first Red Scare collapsed in 1920 as the menace failed to meet Attorney General Palmer's dire predictions. In the late 1930s, notably during the Nazi-Soviet Pact, the totalitarian danger underpinned a new drive against subversives of the left and the right. The machinery of later anticommunist activism—the

Smith Act and the earliest federal loyalty program, for example—originated in this era. The Cold War naturally prompted further anticommunist disquiet, and the Hiss case, the Rosenberg trial, and other episodes suggested that there was a basis for concern. It was no happenstance that the peak of anticommunist activism occurred in the period of most sustained East-West tension, that McCarthy's run in the national spotlight coincided with the Korean War and that his political demise came soon after the Korean armistice. In its long turn on the national stage, anticommunism bulked up conservative attacks against the New Deal and liberalism generally. It combined well with other oppositional themes in an age of growing state power, urbanization, and societal complexity. Small-town legislators often saw Reds as a big-city, "eastern" phenomenon. Assuredly simple and genuine countryside ways clashed with urban sophistication. Thus, the conservative *Indianapolis Star* identified the "shrillest criticism of Nixon" in 1952 as originating among "the 'liberal' martini sipping set in New York, Washington and Hollywood."[67] These cultural connections with anticommunism were always relevant, but, save when reinforced by the presence of a sense of crisis engendered by the dangers of the late 1930s and the first decade of the Cold War, they lacked force to dominate American politics.

NOTES

1. Another leader, J. Edgar Hoover, though never elected to office, plied the communist issue so astutely as to secure preferred status for the Federal Bureau of Investigation and himself. See Athan G. Theoharis and John Stuart Cox, *The Boss: J. Edgar Hoover and the Great American Inquisition* (Philadelphia: Temple University Press, 1988); and Richard Gid Powers, *Secrecy and Power: The Life of J. Edgar Hoover* (New York: Free Press, 1987).

2. Stanley Coben, *A. Mitchell Palmer: Politician* (New York: Columbia University Press, 1963), 261–262; Robert K. Murray, *Red Scare: A Study in National Hysteria* (Minneapolis: University of Minnesota Press, 1964 [1955]), 66; M. J. Heale, *American Anticommunism: Combating the Enemy Within, 1839–1970* (Baltimore: Johns Hopkins University Press, 1990), 76.

3. The Conference for Progressive Political Action, the organizational vehicle for La Follette's candidacy, refused at a 1922 meeting to seat delegates from the Workers Party, which stood for an "un-American" political tendency. Kenneth Campbell MacKay, *The Progressive Movement of 1924* (New York: Columbia University Press, 1947), 80, 87–88.

4. E. C. Stokes to Dwight Morrow, September 13, 1924, Morrow MSS, Robert Frost Library, Amherst College; *New York Times,* September 12, 1924, p. 1, September 19, 1924, p. 4, September 24, 1924, p. 4; MacKay, *Progressive Movement,* 164, 166.

5. On red-baiting in the Teapot Dome controversy, see Richard Gid Powers, *Not Without Honor: The History of American Anticommunism* (New York: Simon & Schuster, 1995), 70–72; of feminists, see J. Stanley Lemons, *The Woman Citizen: Social Feminism in the 1920s* (Urbana: University of Illinois Press, 1973), chap. 8 and passim; of settlement houses, see Heale, *American Anticommunism,* 90.

6. *New York Times,* November 6, 1932, pp. 25, 30; Donald J. Lisio, *The President and Protest: Hoover, Conspiracy, and the Bonus Riot* (Columbia: University of Missouri Press, 1974), 56–59, 197–199, 218–219, 229–230, 234.

7. Philip L. Cantelon, "In Defense of America: Congressional Investigations of Communism in the United States, 1919–1935" (Ph.D. diss., Indiana University, 1971), 264–280. On '30s anticommunism see Powers, *Not Without Honor,* 129–132.

8. George Wolfskill, *The Revolt of the Conservatives: A History of the American Liberty League, 1934–1940* (Boston: Little, Brown, 1962), 208, 209; *New York Times,* September 20, 1936, p. 26, September 22, 1936, p. 11, October 7, 1936, p. 7, October 2, 1936, p. 5, October 16, 1936, p. 18. Cf. Arthur M. Schlesinger Jr., *The Politics of Upheaval* (Boston: Little, Brown, 1960), 622–625.

9. *New York Times,* September 20, 1936, pp. 1, 29, September 30, 1936, p. 17, October 9, 1936, p. 1; Max Lerner, "Roosevelt and His Fellow-Travelers," *Nation* 143 (October 24, 1936): 471. For newspaper claims of Soviet support for FDR, see W. Cameron Meyers, "The Chicago Newspaper Hoax in the '36 Election Campaign," *Journalism Quarterly* 37 (Summer 1960): 356–364.

10. George H. Mayer, *The Political Career of Floyd B. Olson* (Minneapolis: University of Minnesota Press, 1951), 177, 240, 243, 250; Greg Mitchell, *Campaign of the Century. Upton Sinclair's Race for Governor and the Birth of Media Politics* (New York: Random House, 1992); John B. Chapple to Daniel W. Hoan, April 4, 1936, 1936 General Folder, Hoan MSS, Milwaukee County Historical Society.

11. The crusade against radicalism always had a strong nativist streak (though less so in the hands of Joe McCarthy). An early probe of communism led by Rep. Hamilton Fish (R., N.Y.) defined the threat largely as of foreign origin. The 1931 inquiry took place as the Depression deepened and energized those who wanted to tighten an already restrictive immigration policy. See Cantelon, "In Defense of America."

12. *New York Times,* November 5, 1938, pp. 4, 7; November 6, 1938, pp. 4, 10; Sidney Fine, *Frank Murphy: The New Deal Years* (Chicago: University of Chicago Press, 1979), 502–516; Robert E. Burke, *Olson's New Deal for California* (Berkeley: University of California Press, 1953), 29–31; *Nation* 147 (November 26, 1938): 464–465.

13. *New York Times,* September 1, 1938, p. 4, September 10, 1938, p. 2, September 13, 1938, p. 9, September 21, 1938, p. 20, November 9, 1938, p. 13.

14. Krock later advised critics of this coalition that FDR's following had once itself been a union of "former Republicans, former Socialists, Farmer-Laborites, descendants of the Populists and Free Silverites . . . and roving labor and intelligentsia groups" and occasional "Communists and fellow travelers." *New Republic* 97 (November 23, 1938): 57; *New York Times,* November 10, 1938, p. 1; March 10, 1946, p. 4.

15. *New York Times,* November 5, 1938, p. 5, November 6, 1938, p. 8; *Nation,* 147 (November 19, 1938): 525. Similar charges sometimes roiled intraparty battles. In a race for the Wisconsin Progressive Party nomination for the U.S. Senate, the more centrist Herman Ekern charged that the economic planning system proposed in Congressman Thomas R. Amlie's industrial expansion bill resembled a Soviet Five-Year Plan. John E. Miller, *Governor Philip F. La Follette, the Wisconsin Progressives, and the New Deal* (Columbia: University of Missouri Press, 1982), 152.

16. On the habit of terming foreign-policy foes a fifth column, see Wayne S. Cole, *Roosevelt and the Isolationists, 1932–1945* (Lincoln: University of Nebraska Press, 1983), 397–411, 456; Richard W. Steele, "Franklin D. Roosevelt and His Foreign Policy Critics," *Political Science Quarterly* 94 (Spring 1979): 15–35.

17. *New York Times,* June 25, 1940, p. 17, August 30, 1940, p. 1, October 26, 1940, p. 1, November 1, 1940, p. 1, November 2, 1940, p. 8; Samuel I. Rosenman, ed., *The Public Papers and Addresses of Franklin D. Roosevelt* (New York: Random House, 1938), 8:532.

18. Press release, May 16, 1942, Official File (OF) 3997, Franklin D. Roosevelt Library (FDRL); Rev. Joseph F. Scannel to [Stephen Early], May 17, 1942, ibid; Father J. Hamel to FDR, October 23, 1944, OF 299, FDRL; William D. Hassett to Hamel, October 31, 1944, ibid. See generally George Sirgiovanni, *An Undercurrent of Suspicion: Anti-Communism in America during World War II* (New Brunswick, N.J.: Rutgers University Press, 1990).

19. Clipping, *Cleveland News,* September 27, 1944, OF 3997, FDRL.

20. *New York Times,* September 26, 1944, October 8, 1944, p. 1, October 26, 1944, p. 15; handbill, "Dewey . . . Bricker for Victory Peace Unity," Box 7, OF 4070, FDRL.

21. Ickes speech, September 24, 1944, Box 1163, Democratic National Committee Papers; "Address of Hon. Oscar R. Ewing," October 27, 1944, Box 1159, ibid.; Publicity Bureau press release, Blue Network, NBC, Nov 1, 1944, Box 1163, ibid.; DNC radio script, CBS, November 6, 1944, Box 33, Stephen T. Early Papers, all FDRL; *New York Times,* October 6, 1944, p. 14. On the "Zinoviev Letter," see "Notes on Republican National Committee October strategy," n.d., with Robert E. Hannegan to Hopkins and Rosenman, September 30, 1944, Box 138, Harry H. Hopkins Papers, FDRL;

clipping, Robert G. Spivack, "Look for Last-Ditch Blast by G.O.P. to Scare Voters," New York *Post*, October 17, 1944, Box 6, Rosenman Papers, ibid.

22. Unsigned note, n.d. [October 1944] from Roper, attached to "Bill" [Hassett] to "Grace" [Tully], filed October 27, 1944, President's Secretary's File (PSF): Public Opinion Polls; Merriam to Hopkins, October 30, 1944, Box 211, Hopkins Papers, FDRL; clipping, "Repudiation?" *New York Daily Mirror,* October 7, 1944, Box 25, Samuel N. Rosenman Papers, FDRL; cf. Richard Polenberg, *War and Society: The United States, 1941–1945* (Philadelphia: J. B. Lippincott, 1972), 208–209.

23. *New York Times,* April 12, 1946, p. 17, May 29, 1946, p. 2, September 22, 1946, p. 53, October 21, 1946, p. 1, October 22, 1946, p. 2; *Milwaukee Journal,* October 2, 1946, p. 20; Roger Morris, *Richard Milhous Nixon: The Rise of an American Politician* (New York: Henry Holt, 1990), chaps. 10–11.

24. Milwaukee *Journal,* August 7, 1946, August 8, 1946, p. B2, October 17, 1946, p. B1; Patrick J. Maney, *"Young Bob" La Follette: A Biography of Robert M. La Follette, Jr., 1895–1953* (Columbia: University of Missouri Press, 1978), 298 and passim.

25. *New York Times,* October 13, 1946, p. D6, November 1, 1946, p. 1; Tom Wicker, *One of Us: Richard Nixon and the American Dream* (New York: Random House, 1991), 41, 48. Patrick Maney notes that during the fall ex-candidate La Follette spent more energy on the communist issue (in his writings) than did candidate McCarthy. *"Young Bob,"* 303. On the campaign generally, see James Boylan, *The New Deal Coalition and the Election of 1946* (New York: Garland, 1981).

26. Richard M. Fried, *Nightmare in Red: The McCarthy Era in Perspective* (New York: Oxford University Press, 1990), 81–82; but cf. Ken Hechler, *Working with Truman: A Personal Memoir of the White House Years* (Columbia: University of Missouri Press, 1982), 96.

27. Hechler, *Working with Truman,* 97; unsigned memorandum [George M. Elsey], "Random Thoughts 26 August [1948]," Internal Security—Congressional Loyalty Investigations, Subject File, Elsey Papers, Harry S. Truman Library, Independence, MO; address by Beauford H. Jester, Texas Democratic Barbecue, April 20, 1948, Box 5, Famous Names File, Lyndon Baines Johnson Archive, LDJ Library, Austin, Texas. Two years later, South Carolina Governor Strom Thurmond, the States' Rights presidential candidate of 1948, attacked Truman's program as "un-American, Communistic and anti-Southern." *Milwaukee Sentinel,* February 14, 1950, p. 2.

28. Memorandum, Robert Humphreys et al., n.d. [1948], Box 7, Humphreys Papers, Dwight D. Eisenhower Library; William Loeb to Dewey, August 26, 1948, Box 1, ibid.; Charles D. Breitel to Loeb, September 7, 1948, Box 3, ibid. Truman's Justice Department also pondered referring the issue of "Soviet espionage in the Federal Government" to a high-level bipartisan commission. George M. Elsey, memorandum for

Clark M. Clifford, August 16, 1948, Subject File, Internal Security— Congressional Loyalty Investigations, Elsey Papers, Harry S. Truman Library.

29. Richard Norton Smith, *Thomas E. Dewey and His Times* (New York: Simon & Schuster, 1982), 492–494, 507–508, 515; George S. Schuyler, *Black and Conservative* (New Rochelle, N.Y.: Arlington House, 1966), 311–312; Richard M. Fried, *Men against McCarthy* (New York: Columbia University Press, 1976), 15–17; Irwin Ross, *The Loneliest Campaign: The Truman Victory of 1948* (New York: New American Library, 1968), 54–57, 187–188; Earl Latham, *The Communist Controversy in Washington from the New Deal to McCarthy* (Cambridge, Mass.: Harvard University Press, 1966), 396.

30. Dulles to Lehman, October 30, 1949, Special File, Lehman MSS, Columbia University; Independent Citizen's Committee for Election of Herbert H. Lehman as U.S. Senator, "Sample Three-Minute Speech for Sound Truck," October 22, 1949, ibid.; Lehman speech, September 22, 1949, "Elections—New York—1949" folder, ibid. Dulles thought Lehman's charge of anti-Semitism pivoted on his need, in the prevailing balance of New York ethnic politics, to "get, to all intents and purposes 100% of the Jewish vote." Dulles to Richard Stone, February 13, 1952, Folder 1, Box II (Correspondence, 1952-1054), Dulles MSS, Princeton University.

31. Mundt to Raymond Hieb, May 29, 1950, Political Campaigns DB 5, U.S. Senate 1950, Mundt MSS, Dakota State College.

32. Fried, *Men against McCarthy,* 95–101; Morris, *Nixon,* 555, 560, 580.

33. *Daily Oklahoman,* October 21, 1950, p. 1; *Denver Post,* October 7, 1950, p. 2; *Milwaukee Sentinel,* February 15, 1950, p. 1. Considine praised two senators "jabbing" at the octopus—Estes Kefauver and Joe McCarthy.

34. Mundt to Nixon, May 8, 1950; to Dirksen, August 4, September 13,1950; to John M. Butler, September 30, 1950, all in "Political Campaigns US Senate 1950," Mundt MSS.

35. Robert W. Griffith, *The Politics of Fear: Joseph R. McCarthy and the Senate* (Lexington: University Press of Kentucky, 1970), 124–127, 131; Fried, *Men against McCarthy,* chaps. 4–5. A Truman aide noted that the Democrats' loss of five Senate and twenty-eight House seats was "far less than the usual mid-term trend throughout history." Kenneth Heckler memorandum, "The 1950 Elections," November 15, 1950, George Elsey Papers, HSTL.

36. Griffith, *Politics of Fear,* 126, 129–131; Fried, *Men Against McCarthy,* 118–121, 136–140; Caroline H. Keith, *"For Hell and a Brown Mule": The Biography of Senator Millard E. Tydings* (Lanham: University Press of America, 1991), chap. 2.

37. How firmly Eisenhower committed himself to this strategy is unclear. Jeff Broadwater, *Eisenhower and the Anti-Communist Crusade* (Chapel Hill: University of North Carolina Press, 1992), 38–39.

38. Fried, *Men against McCarthy*, 233–234; *Indianapolis Star*, September 7, 1952, p. 16.

39. "What the Opinion Surveys Said in May, 1952," Folder 3, Box 6, Hugh B. Mitchell MSS, University of Washington; *Indianapolis Star*, September 20, 1952, p. 4; Fried, *Men against McCarthy*, 232–234, 240; Griffith, *Politics of Fear*, 195. On the slight salience of the communist issue, also see Broadwater, *Eisenhower*, 44, 51–52.

40. Harry Louis Selden (Fair Campaign Practices Committee) to Bruce Barton, Box 20, Barton MSS, State Historical Society of Wisconsin; *New York Times*, June 28, 1954, p. 13, September 19, 1954, p. 7, October 3, 1954, p. 7; International Research Associates, Inc., State Poll, 11954, Illinois, Misc. Box 2, Paul Douglas MSS, Chicago Historical Society (CHS).

41. Louis H. Bean, *Influences in the 1954 Mid-Term Elections* (Washington, D.C.: Public Affairs Institute, 1954), 18–32; Griffith, *Politics of Fear*, 241–242; *New York Times*, October 10, 1954, IV, 5.

42. *New York Times*, October 12, 1954, pp. 1, 21, October 25, 1954, p. 18, October 27, 1954, p 19.

43. *New York Times*, June 27, 1954, p. 37, September 18, 1954, p. 11, September 29, 1954, p. 19, October 2, 1954, p. 9, October 14, 1954, p. 26, October 21, 1954, p. 22.

44. *New York Times*, October 1, 1954, p. 13, October 23, 1954, p. 1.

45. Fried, *Men against McCarthy*, 303; Joseph T. Meek, speech, Republican State Convention, June 12, 1954, Box 1, Meek MSS, CHS; Willis Ballinger, "The Texas Story," Committee for Constitutional Government, *Spotlight for the Nation*, No. D-269 [1954]; Herman Brown to Committee for Constitutional Government, June 2, 1954, both Box 13, Selected Names File, LBJ Archive, Lyndon Baines Johnson Library. Carroll lost; Murray was reelected.

46. CIO poll, "1954 Opinion Survey," n.d., Paul H. Douglas MSS, CHS; Angus Campbell and Homer Cooper, *Group Differences in Attitudes and Votes* (Ann Arbor: University of Michigan Press, 1956), 66; Leonard W. Hall to Nixon, Dec. 13, 1954, Box 313, Gen. Corres., Nixon Papers, National Archives and Records Administration—Laguna Niguel. Cf. Broadwater, *Eisenhower*, 163.

47. Robert L. King to Edward F. Mahon, October 22, 1956; King to Kermit W. Lueck, October 30, 1956; clipping, *Minneapolis Star*, "Nixon Snubs Sen. McCarthy," n.d., all Box 490, Gen. Corres., Nixon Papers, NARA—Laguna Niguel.

48. *New York Times*, September 4, 1956, pp. 1, 18, September 5, 1956, p. 20, September 13, 1956, p. 1, September 15, 1956, p. 8, September 18, 1956, pp. 1, 20, September 19, 1956, p. 1, September 27, 1956, p. 28.

49. *New York Times*, October 9, 1958, p. 31, October 11, 1958, p. 14, October 12, 1958, p. 71, October 13, 1958, p. 17; Fair Campaign Practices Committee, Inc., "Report: The State-by-State Study of Smear: 1958" (September 1959), "Political Ques-

tions" folder, Box 24, Civic Interests, Papers of John D. Rockefeller Jr., Rockefeller Archives Center, Pocantico Hills, N.Y.; Rice R. Rice, "The 1958 Election in Arizona," *Western Political Quarterly* 12 (March 1959): 271.

50. Meade Alcorn, press release, September 25, 1958, Box 25, Gen. Corres., Nixon Papers; Nixon to Murray Chotiner, June 23, 1958, Box 119, ibid.

51. Mary C. Brennan, *Turning Right in the Sixties: The Conservative Capture of the GOP* (Chapel Hill: University of North Carolina Press, 1995), 50–51; Powers, *Not Without Honor,* chap. 10; Kent M. Beck, "Necessary Lies, Hidden Truths: Cuba in the 1960 Campaign," *Diplomatic History* VIII (Winter 1984): 44–55.

52. ——— to Lyndon Baines Johnson, June 2, 1960, Box 76, Senate Political File, LBJL; Dan Gilbert, "Inside Election Report—No. 1," (Upland, Calif., 1960), ibid.; Clarence C. Dill to Sen. Henry M. Jackson, August 22, 1960, Folder 15, Box 249, Jackson MSS, Accession No. 3560-3, University of Washington.

53. Claude Robinson to Nixon, September 1, 1960, Box 646, Gen. Corres., Nixon Papers. For Nixon's "self-education" during his vice presidency, see Anthony R. Maravillas, "Nixon in the Fifties" (Ph.D. diss., University of Illinois at Chicago, 2001).

54. Unsigned memorandum, "Foreign Affairs as a Campaign Issue," n.d. [1960], Folder 26, Box 247, Jackson MSS; Rep. William G. Bray, press release, June 18, 1960, Box 99, Gen. Corres., Nixon papers; Jackson speech, Clarksburg, W.Va., October 1, 1960, Folder 11, Box 23, Jackson MSS.

55. Democratic National Committee, "FACTS for Victory in 1960," (August 1960), Box I-42, Wayne Morse MSS, University of Oregon.

56. Poll data, revealing how few voters knew of these episodes, discouraged such a step. Unsigned memorandum, n.d. [1960], "The Nixon Imagery," Folder 26, Box 247, Jackson MSS; Warren E. Miller to "George" [Belknap?], January 22, 1960, Box 30, Charles S. Murphy Papers, HSTL. For one attempt to raise the subject, see party chair Paul Butler in transcript, CBS "Face the Nation," January 3, 1960, Box 2, Famous Names File, LBJ Archive, LBJL.

57. *New York Times,* March 8, 1960, pp. 1, 25; memorandum, Neil Cotter to Robert H. Finch, "Campaign Tactics," January 6, 1960, Box 183, Gen. Corres., Nixon Papers; Nixon to Claude Robinson, April 9, 1960, Box 1, 1960 Campaign Series, Nixon Papers; Nixon speech copy, Tampa, Florida, October 18, 1960, Box 2, ibid.; memorandum, Nixon to Fred Seaton, September 21, 1960, Box 1, ibid.; Pegler to Nixon, October 4, 1960, Box 585, Gen. Corres., ibid.

58. Christopher Matthews, *Kennedy & Nixon: The Rivalry That Shaped Postwar America* (New York: Simon & Schuster, 1996), 70, 88, 108–109; *New York Times,* March 31, 1958, p. 11; JFK to Frank Altschul, May 20, 1960, Folder 450b, Herbert H. Lehman MSS; Orville L. Freeman to Sen. Mike Mansfield, April 22, 1960, XIV/48, Folder 1, Mansfield MSS, University of Montana.

59. Economist John Kenneth Galbraith rightly predicted that Nixon would not re-visit old haunts. "We must assume that he has learned better." Some more fearful Democrats found comfort that "Johnson on the ticket ha[d] taken away from the GOP the charge of 'radicalism.' " Galbraith memorandum, "Campaign Strategy, 1960," n.d. [July, 1960], Box 996, John F. Kennedy Pre-Presidential File, JFKL; un-signed "Memorandum for the Press," n.d. [1960], Reference File, 1960 Campaign, LBJ Archive, LBJL.

60. Handbill, "How Can the South Support Lyndon Johnson for President? Sena-tor Johnson's Left-Wing Voting Record," *The Independent American* [n.p., 1960], Box 16, VIP File, Nixon Papers; clipping, *Phoenix Gazette,* August 8, 1960, Box 76, Senate Political File, LBJL; RNC Press Release, October 31, 1960, Box 77, Gen. Corres., Nixon Papers; Airy press release, April 7, 1960, Box 421, Clinton P. Anderson MSS, Library of Congress; clipping, *Albuquerque Tribune,* April 4, 1960, ibid.; Anderson to Floyd B. Rigdon, April 12, 1960, ibid.

61. Nixon said Brown was anticommunist, but ineffectual. Stephen E. Ambrose, *Nixon; The Education of a Politician, 1913–1962* (New York: Simon & Schuster, 1987), 656, 658–661, 665, 670–671; "Murray Chotiner telephone call to rmw [Rosemary Wood], April 17, 1962, Box 147, Gen. Corres., Nixon Papers; Dewey to Nixon, Box 214, ibid. Dewey also noted public outrage over the fact that Alger Hiss was invited to offer televised comment on Nixon's political demise.

62. "Art" [H. Courshon] to Hubert H. Humphrey, April 23, 1962, Box 593, Humphrey MSS, Minnesota Historical Society; Harry LaFontaine to Claude D. Pep-per, April 17, 1962, ibid.

63. *New York Times,* February 15, 1964, p. 11, September 6, 1964, pp. 1, 44, Sep-tember 30, 1964, pp. 1, 22, October 1, 1964, p. 22, October 3, 1964, p. 14, October 9, 1964, p. 26, October 27, 1964, p. 21.

64. *New York Times,* July 30, 1965, p. 29, July 31, 1965, p. 18, October 13, 1965, p. 60, October 17, 1965, p. 84, October 25, 1965, pp. 1, 31, November 1, 1965, p. 46, No-vember 3, 1965, p. 1.

65. Clipping, *Washington Daily News,* April 27, 1972, Folder 4, Box 4, Sterling Munro MSS, University of Washington; telegram, Joseph L. Rauh Jr. to Jackson, May 2, 1972, ibid.; Herman Badillo to Jackson, May 2, 1972, ibid.

66. For suggestive discussion of some of these connections, see David A. Horowitz, *Beyond Left & Right: Insurgency and the Establishment* (Urbana: University of Illinois Press, 1997).

67. *Indianapolis Star,* September 22, 1952, p. 14.

5

THE ETHICAL RESPONSIBILITIES
OF THE SCIENTIST: THE CASE OF
J. ROBERT OPPENHEIMER

Richard Polenberg

In the spring of 1946, J. Robert Oppenheimer delivered a series of six lectures on atomic energy at Cornell University. He was a guest of the physics department, among whose members he counted several friends, veterans of the wartime Manhattan Project he had directed. For his efforts in developing the atomic bomb, Oppenheimer had recently been awarded the United States Medal for Merit, the highest honor the government can bestow on a civilian. Within the year he would accept a prestigious position as director of the Institute for Advanced Study at Princeton. When he visited Cornell, Oppenheimer was at the very pinnacle of his career.

Despite this public esteem, Oppenheimer's whereabouts were profoundly interesting to the Federal Bureau of Investigation. So much so, in fact, that the FBI obtained a detailed report on his comings and goings during the two weeks he spent at Cornell. The FBI learned how he spent his time on campus, how much he was paid for giving the lectures, what he said in them, how large an audience he had, who he met at various social functions, where he was housed, and to whom he made long distance telephone calls. The report concluded with assurances that Oppenheimer was "not contacted by any radical individuals" or "by any faculty members who were regarded as leftists," and that, fortunately, there were no "active . . . Soviet agents in the vicinity of Ithaca."[1]

This information was provided by "Confidential Informant T-1," who was identified only "as an official of Cornell University." The informant, it turns out, was Edward K. Graham, secretary of the university, who was, sad to say,

a former graduate student in history—later described by one of his professors as "a wild sort of chap . . . not an ounce of sense in his head"—who had
moved on into administration.[2] He was only one of many agents and in-
formants who spent their time shadowing Oppenheimer. When his FBI file
was released under the Freedom of Information Act, it became evident that
Oppenheimer was periodically monitored from 1941 until his death in 1967.
One of the last documents in the file is the obituary in the *New York Times*.

The files reveal that the FBI not only trailed Oppenheimer but also tapped
his home telephone. There are transcripts of conversations with Undersecre-
tary of State Dean G. Acheson, United States Supreme Court Justice Felix
Frankfurter, Atomic Energy Commissioner David E. Lilienthal, and Wall
Street financier Bernard Baruch, none of whom would seem to qualify as
dedicated agents of the international communist conspiracy. Oppenheimer
surely suspected that his phone was tapped. Calling his wife, Katherine, from
Cornell, he heard a clicking sound and joked, "The FBI must just have hung
up." Katherine, the transcript reports, merely giggled.[3]

As it turns out, the government did far more to Oppenheimer than subject him to surveillance and eavesdrop on his conversations. In December
1953 President Dwight Eisenhower erected a "blank wall" between Oppenheimer and classified information, and in June 1954 the Atomic Energy
Commission stripped him of his consultant's contract on the grounds that he
was a poor security risk. Many observers believed that the physicist was being punished because since 1949 he had opposed U.S. efforts to build a hydrogen bomb. He therefore came to be viewed with some reason as a tragic
hero, victimized for voicing honest doubts about the escalating arms race.

Yet Oppenheimer's tale is not merely one of injustice and persecution.
Rather, his career illustrates the dilemma that confronts a scientist faced
with the prospect of making ever more destructive weapons available to the
state, and faced with the problem, therefore, of deciding whether it is ever
appropriate to refuse such cooperation and, if so, on what grounds. Oppenheimer's dilemma was especially acute because he cared so deeply about
ethical issues. His role as a leader in his generation of physicists derived not
only from his brilliance as a theorist of quantum mechanics, but also from
his sensitivity to the ethical implications of nuclear and thermonuclear warfare, from his conviction, that is, that science and moral responsibility were
somehow inseparable.

In his marvelous memoir *Disturbing the Universe*, Freeman Dyson, who
was a friend of Oppenheimer's, writes: "The best way to approach the ethical
problems associated with science is to study real dilemmas faced by real sci-

entists."[4] I believe Dyson is right, and so my approach in this essay will be to discuss the religious, philosophical, and political influences that shaped Oppenheimer's outlook; then to examine the divergent ways in which that outlook shaped his decisions regarding the atomic bomb and the hydrogen bomb; and finally to speculate about how certain unresolved ambiguities in that outlook may have undermined his ability to defend himself at the 1954 security-clearance hearing.

ETHICAL CULTURE: THE LEGACY OF FELIX ADLER

J. Robert Oppenheimer was born in New York City in 1904. His father, Julius, had emigrated to the United States from Germany in 1888 at the age of seventeen and in 1903 married Ella Friedman. They had two sons, Robert and Frank, who was born in 1912. (A third child died in infancy.) Julius Oppenheimer, an importer of fabrics and textiles, became quite wealthy, and so the family enjoyed comfortable surroundings: a luxurious, beautifully furnished apartment on Riverside Drive and Eighty-eighth Street: servants, including a butler, a maid, and a chauffeur; and a private art collection with works by Van Gogh, Cezanne, and Gauguin. Summers were spent at Bay Shore, Long Island, where the family had a vacation home. When Julius died in 1937 (his wife had died in 1931), he left his sons an inheritance of nearly $400,000, a considerable fortune in those days

Although they were Jewish, the Oppenheimers were not practicing Jews. Instead they belonged to the Society for Ethical Culture, founded by Dr. Felix Adler in 1876. Julius Oppenheimer, who served for many years on the board of the society, was a friend of Adler's. Once, writing a poem in honor of his father's fiftieth birthday, Robert commented that "he swallowed Dr. Adler like morality compressed."[5] Both Oppenheimer boys attended the Ethical Culture School on Central Park West near Sixty-third Street, Robert from September 1911, when he entered the second grade, until his graduation from high school in 1921. The Ethical Culture movement, therefore, was profoundly important in the shaping of Robert Oppenheimer's moral universe.

Felix Adler had originally intended to enter the rabbinate, following in the path of his father, who presided over Temple Emanu-El, a reform synagogue in New York City. Upon graduating from Columbia College in 1870, he went to Germany to study theology and literature. During the three years he spent in Berlin and Heidelberg, however, he was exposed to the "Higher Criticism" of the Bible, a field of inquiry then flourishing under the intellectual leadership of Julius Wellhausen and Adler's teacher, Abraham Geiger. Applying modern techniques of textual analysis to the Old Testament, these scholars concluded that the Torah had been composed by different individuals at different times, and therefore could not have been inspired by divine will. Their findings contradicted fundamental tenets of Judaism—that the children of Israel had a special covenant with God, for example, and that the Ten Commandments expressed eternal truths.[6]

Felix Adler had begun to experience religious doubts even before arriving in Germany; now, the Higher Criticism fatally undermined his faith in Judaism. When he returned to the United States, he recalled, he attended a Sabbath service. After the reading of the Torah, the scrolls were lifted for all to see and the congregation chanted: "And this is the Law which Moses set before the people of Israel." But Adler no longer believed in the Torah's authenticity: "Was I to repeat these words?" he asked, and answered his own question: "It was impossible. I was certain that they would stick in my throat."[7]

After briefly teaching Oriental and Hebrew literature at Cornell University, Adler returned to New York City to found the Society for Ethical Culture, to which he devoted the rest of his life. Adler maintained that men and women had the capacity and the duty to lead morally righteous lives. To behave ethically required treating other people as ends in themselves, not as a means to one's own ends. Such behavior, "first-rate conduct" Adler liked to call it, would elicit the best in others and therefore in oneself. But the duty to behave ethically did not exist because God had ordained it and would reward those who obeyed His will and punish those who did not. Rather, Adler followed Immanuel Kant in asserting that human beings had an innate moral faculty capable of distinguishing right from wrong. "The moral law lives," Adler said, "whether there is a God or not."[8]

The Ethical Culture movement neither affirmed nor denied the existence of God, but it surely denied the existence of what most people mean by the word. If there were a God, Adler explained, it was not an omniscient God who provided meaning to the universe; or a personal God to whom one should pray; or an omnipotent God, since, as Adler wrote, "one cannot love infinite power and majesty." Most important, if there were a God it was not an ineffable God whose existence required belief in anything that offended reason. Adler wanted to create a "religion for adults" that would "satisfy [the] intellect," would be consistent with observable scientific truth, and would stress the performance of good deeds not adherence to a creed.[9]

The Ethical Culture School therefore fostered a "social and ethical outlook" through "the inculcation of the democratic spirit," "the awakening of serious intellectual interests and enthusiasms," "the awakening of the spirit of social service by enlisting the interest of the students in the work of the Settlements," and "the building up of a largely humanitarian and ideal purpose by placing at the focus of the entire educational scheme toward which all lines converge the idea of human progress." In addition to a demanding academic curriculum, students received "direct moral instruction." In the earlier grades, ethics was taught through fables and biblical tales, but by the seventh grade students were using selections from Greek history illustrating the virtues of temperance, intellectual striving and moral attainment; the readings included Plutarch's lives of Lycurgus, Pericles, Themistocles, Aristides, and Socrates. By the eighth grade students had progressed to "Biographical subjects drawn from Roman history. The conflict of Patricians and Plebeians, and the lessons to be derived from it."[10]

J. Robert Oppenheimer, then, was raised in an environment and attended a school that placed a great emphasis on ethical conduct. The necessity for such conduct, however, did not derive from a set of scriptural commandments that, in Felix Adler's view, were "unverifiable" but rather from one's own powers of logical understanding, one's own reason. Oppenheimer's memories of the Ethical Culture School, which he often shared with his brother Frank, remained with him all his life. So did the friendship he formed with one of his English teachers, Herbert Winslow Smith. In August 1945, Oppenheimer wrote to him about the role of the atomic bomb in ending the war and his own role in building the bomb. "This undertaking has not been without its misgivings; they are heavy on us today, when the future, which has so many elements of high promise, is yet only a stone's throw from despair. Thus the good which this work has perhaps contributed to make in the ending of the war looms very large to us, because it is there for sure."[11]

THE BHAGAVAD GITA: "I AM BECOME DEATH . . ."

Following his graduation from the Ethical Culture School, Oppenheimer took a summer trip to Europe. Unfortunately, he contracted a severe case of dysentery, followed by colitis. His convalescence took the better part of a year, and so he did not enter Harvard College until the fall of 1922. Making up for lost time, he completed the four-year course of study in only three by taking six courses a term; in his senior year, he enrolled in five courses and audited five more. In 1925 he went to England to continue his studies in physics but soon moved to Germany, to the University of Göttingen, where he studied with Max Born and James Franck. Oppenheimer received his Ph.D. in 1927, was awarded a National Research Council fellowship, and in 1929 accepted a joint appointment in physics at the University of California, Berkeley, and the California Institute of Technology. Within a short time he established himself as a leading theorist in the emerging field of quantum mechanics.

But Oppenheimer was more than a brilliant physicist. His intellectual interests encompassed poetry, literature, philosophy, and languages. He eventually became fluent in eight languages, lecturing in Dutch, for example, after studying it for only six weeks. He once asked his Berkeley colleague Leo Nedelsky to give a lecture for him, explaining that the preparation would be easy because "it's all in a book"; when Nedelsky located the book and reported that it was written in Dutch, Oppenheimer replied, "But it's such *easy* Dutch!"[12] In 1931 Oppenheimer began the study of Sanskrit with Arthur W. Ryder of the Berkeley faculty. "I am learning sanskrit," he told his brother, "enjoying it very much, and enjoying again the sweet luxury of being taught." Soon he was reading the Bhagavad Gita with Ryder in the original. "It is very easy," he reported, "and quite marvellous."[13] It would, in fact, become a determining influence on Oppenheimer's outlook on ethics.

Written between the fifth and second centuries B.C.E., the Bhagavad Gita, an epic poem of seven hundred stanzas, is a centrally important text of Hinduism.[14] The path to salvation, it asserts, lies in holy knowledge, the intuitive knowledge of a supreme truth. The perfected self may gain this knowledge and achieve union with the One through righteousness, asceticism, devotion, and karma yoga: that is, by engaging in disciplined activity, the task for which one is suited without concern for worldly rewards. The Bhagavad Gita, or "the song of the Lord," contains many other concepts central to Hinduism, but the crucial portion involves a dialogue within a dialogue: the charioteer Sanjaya is describing a conversation between Krishna, an incarnation of the god Vishnu who has assumed human form, and his disciple, Arjuna, who is contemplating going into battle.

Although destined to be a warrior, Arjuna, seeing the opposing forces lined up, shrinks from the fight. "My mouth becomes dry" thinking of the fearful cost in lives, he says, "nor surely can good ever come from killing my kinsmen" for once having slain them, "could we be happy?" Because even victory would be hollow, "should we not know enough to turn away from this havoc?" War produces only chaos, lawlessness, and corruption, he continues: "Far better that I remain / Unresisting and unarmed / And that the armed sons of Dhrita-rashtra / Should kill me in the struggle." Seating himself in his chariot, Arjuna "dropped his arrows and his bow / His heart brought low in sorrow." "I see nothing to drive away Grief," he tells Krishna, "I will not fight."

To dispel these corrosive doubts, Krishna instructs Arjuna to "shake off this petty weakness." "For a warrior there is no better thing / Than to fight out of duty." To refuse to do battle, Krishna says, will lead only to shame and disgrace. Then, Krishna gives Arjuna "the eye of a god," divine vision that allows him to behold Krishna in all his mystery, in the form of a god as bright as "a thousand suns." Blinded, overawed, overwhelmed, Arjuna, trembling with fear, begs for mercy: "Your dreadful rays fill the whole universe, Vishnu, and scorch it with their brightness." "Tell me, you of awful form, who are you?" And Krishna replies: "I am time, destroyer of worlds, grown old / Setting out to gather in the worlds." Krishna then instructs Arjuna: "Strike them down. Do not falter. Fight! You will beat your rivals in battle."

Nothing more clearly illustrates the influence of the Bhagavad Gita on Oppenheimer than his references to it at Alamogordo, the site in the New Mexico desert where the first atomic bomb was detonated. On July 14, as the bomb was being readied, Oppenheimer quoted a few lines to Vannevar Bush, who headed the federal Office of Scientific Research and Development: "In battle, in the forest, at the precipice in the mountains / On the dark great sea, in the midst of javelins and arrows / In sleep, in confusion, in the depths of shame / The good deeds a man has done before defend him."[15] Oppenheimer recalled that when he actually saw the bomb explode in a brilliant burst of light and the fireball ascend to the heavens: "There floated through my mind a line from the Bhagavad Gita in which Krishna is trying to persuade the Prince that he should do his duty: 'I am become death, the shatterer of worlds.'"[16]

Three months earlier, when Franklin D. Roosevelt died and thoughts of earthly mortality were much on Oppenheimer's mind, he had also instinctively turned to the Bhagavad Gita. Speaking to the scientists at Los Alamos in a memorial tribute, he said: "In the Hindu scripture, in the Bhagavad-Gita, it says, 'Man is a creature whose substance is faith. What his faith is, he is.'" Roosevelt's faith, Oppenheimer continued, was shared by millions of people around the world. "For this reason it is possible to maintain the hope, for this reason it is right that we should dedicate ourselves to the hope that his good works will not have ended with his death."[17]

Perhaps his most suggestive invocation of the Bhagavad Gita had occurred years before, in 1932, while Oppenheimer was studying Sanskrit with Arthur Ryder. In a letter to his brother Frank he cited the poem and other religious texts. "I believe that through discipline, though not through discipline alone, we can achieve serenity, and a certain small but precious measure of freedom from the accidents of incarnation, and charity." Self-discipline allows us "to preserve what is essential to our happiness" and abandon what is not, he went on, so "that we come a little to see the world without the gross distortion of personal desire." He then added a sentence that, as Freeman Dyson has observed, holds a key to understanding Oppenheimer's character: "Therefore I think that all things which evoke discipline: study, and our duties to men and to the commonwealth, war, and personal hardship, and even the need for subsistence, ought to be greeted by us with profound gratitude; for only through them can we attain to the least detachment; and only so can we know peace."[18]

Placing war on a short list of things for which to be grateful certainly reflected Oppenheimer's immersion in the Bhagavad Gita, which, at some level, he may have read as a sustained argument against pacifism. The work required of a warrior, faced with the prospect of fighting a holy war, was to fight. "Do the work that is required," Krishna counsels: "It is better to act than be still." For all the profound differences between Hinduism and Ethical Culture, this admonition resembled one of Felix Adler's. "The object of life is activity, work," Adler wrote: "We are here to do a certain work, to do it as faithfully, as efficiently and in as social a spirit as we may."[19] As it developed, the particular kind of work Oppenheimer was most capable of doing was precisely the kind needed by a nation in the midst of a world war.

THE POPULAR FRONT: THE GHOST OF JOE DALLET

"Tell me," Oppenheimer asked a friend in the early 1930s, "what has politics to do with truth, goodness and beauty?"[20] The remark captured the studied lack of interest in public affairs of a man who did not own a radio or read the newspapers. He did not know that the stock market had crashed in October 1929 until months afterward. He did not even bother to vote in 1932. But in 1936 his outlook changed dramatically. He plunged headlong into politics, and left-wing politics at that. Although he never became a member of the Communist Party, Oppenheimer supported its positions, subscribed to the daily *People's World,* joined several of its "front" organizations, and contributed substantial sums to its coffers. "I liked the new sense of companionship," he later explained, "and at the time felt that I was coming to be part of the life of my time and country."[21]

Oppenheimer offered various explanations for his political awakening: he read Sidney and Beatrice Webb's *Soviet Communism: A New Civilization?,* which led him "to make much of the economic progress and general level of welfare in Russia, and little of its political tyranny"; he felt a "continuing, smoldering fury about the treatment of Jews in Germany," where he still had relatives; he "saw what the depression was doing to my students," many of whom were unable to obtain jobs commensurate with their training. In the fall of 1936, moreover, he began courting Jean Tatlock—they twice were close enough to marriage to consider themselves engaged—who was an "on again, off again" member of the Communist Party and "a friend of many fellow travelers and Communists."[22] In 1937, Oppenheimer added, his brother Frank and his wife Jacquenette Quann both joined the Communist Party.

At the time, Oppenheimer noted, the Communist Party was supporting many "humanitarian objectives." The late 1930s was the era of the Popular Front, when communists emphasized the need for all progressive forces to unite in the struggle against fascism. The party avoided talk of revolution, endeavored to project an image of Americanism, and supported a broad range of social reforms, especially the building of a strong labor movement. Oppenheimer's involvement was typical of many people who were close to the party but not card-carrying members: he contributed to strike funds of left-leaning unions, helped establish a teacher's union, and joined the American Committee for Democracy and Intellectual Freedom. Above all, he supported the Republican cause during the Spanish Civil War. It was, he said, "the matter which most engaged my sympathies and interests."[23]

Oppenheimer did more than attend fund-raising events to aid the anti-Franco forces; he also dipped liberally into his own ample resources. During the winter of 1937–1938 he would, when asked, make cash donations of "probably never much less than a hundred dollars, and occasionally perhaps somewhat more than that." He gave the money to a friend, Dr. Thomas Addis, a medical researcher at Stanford, who assured him that it would go "straight to the fighting effort, and that it would go through Communist channels."[24] Addis eventually introduced Oppenheimer to Isaac "Pop" Folkoff, a Communist Party functionary. A legendary figure in left-wing circles, a former garment presser and self-taught Marxist philosopher, Folkoff specialized in fund-raising for party causes. Even after the Spanish Civil War ended in the spring of 1939, Oppenheimer continued his payments to Folkoff, now, presumably, for the relief of refugees from Franco's rule.

At this juncture, an unpredictable turn in his personal life strengthened Oppenheimer's commitment to the lost cause of Republican Spain as well as his connection to the Communist Party. In the summer of 1939 he met Katherine Harrison. They soon fell in love, and in the fall of 1940 she went to Reno where she obtained a divorce from her husband, Dr. Stewart Harrison; on November 1 she and Oppenheimer were married. Katherine had once been a member of the Communist Party, and she had formerly been married to a party leader, Joe Dallet, who had been killed in the Spanish Civil War, fighting as a volunteer in the Abraham Lincoln Brigade. By the time she met Oppenheimer she had ended her affiliation with the party but she had not, and could not, sever her personal ties to Steve Nelson, a communist who had been Dallet's comrade-in-arms. Disengaged as Katherine was from radical politics, Oppenheimer recalled, "when I met her I found in her a deep loyalty to her former husband."[25]

Nothing in Joe Dallet's background suggested the direction his life would later take. Raised by well-to-do, conservative parents, he attended a private academy, studied French, took piano lessons, toured Europe, and enrolled at Dartmouth. But in his junior year he left college, repudiated his past, and moved to New York City, where he became a longshoreman. In 1929, at the age of twenty-two, he joined the Communist Party. For the next five years he worked as an organizer, first in Chicago and then with steelworkers in Pennsylvania and Ohio. In Youngstown, he ran as the Communist candidate for mayor and congressman. In 1934 he met Katherine and they were married. She joined the party and for two years did general office work, typing letters and running mimeograph machines. By June 1936, tired of this Spartan routine, Katherine left Joe and returned to England to live with her parents. But she never stopped loving him, and in March 1937, when Joe arrived in France on his way to Spain, Katherine met him at the dock. They spent a week or ten days together, rekindling their romance. Katherine wanted to go with Joe to Spain, perhaps to work in an ambulance unit, but the Lincoln Battalion did not permit wives to accompany their husbands.

In Spain, according to a friend, Dallet affected "a tough proletarian style," "a 'hard' manner," a "way of speaking that was deliberately profane and deliberately ungrammatical."[26] He earned a reputation as a strict disciplinarian and was so ardent an ideologue that the Communist Party appointed him a political commissar. Even letters to his wife sometimes had a propagandistic tone. He wrote that those who "can feel the warm bonds and heart-throbs with and of the masses, can never never get seriously demoralized and never lose faith in the ability of the masses to triumph over all difficulties and obstacles," boasted that "the people's army of Spain is rounding into a first-rate war machine," and denounced "the counter-revolutionary role of the Trotskyites." Noticing a volunteer who was "short, built like a gorilla with a chest like a barrel, covered from head to toe with marvelous tatooes," Dallet exclaimed, "of such stuff is the proletariat made." In one of his last letters he wrote: "It's a bloody interesting country, a bloody interesting war and the most bloody interesting job of all the bloody interesting jobs I've ever had, to give the fascists a real bloody licking."[27]

While Dallet was training in Spain, Katherine continued to seek a way to join him. At long last a job was arranged for her, and on July 19 Dallet wrote: "Wonderful news. You can come." Katherine was to go to Paris where she would meet someone who would "put you through." But she then underwent an emergency appendectomy from which it took a while to recuperate. On September 15 Dallet wrote, "I hope to be seeing you soon."[28] In October, however, when Katherine got to Paris, Dallet's unit was already involved in the Battle of Fuentes de Ebro, in which eighty Americans were killed and 150 wounded. On October 17 Dallet died a hero's death, leading his men in a charge against vastly superior odds and being cut down by machine-gun fire.

Arriving in Paris, Katherine heard the tragic news from Steve Nelson. A Communist Party official whom she had met in Youngstown, Nelson had gone to Spain with Dallet and had himself been seriously wounded at Belchite. He was in Paris because he was trying to obtain a visa to go to Moscow for a celebration marking the twentieth anniversary of the Russian Revolution, at which he was supposed to bring greetings from the volunteers in Spain. Nelson spent most of a week with Katherine, comforting her, reminiscing about Joe, and explaining that her desire to go to Spain—even after her husband's death, she said, "I was emotionally involved in the Spanish cause"—was no longer feasible. Asked later what she had talked about with Nelson, she replied, "Joe, himself, myself."[29]

Katherine Dallet's bond with Steve Nelson, knit by grief and perhaps remorse, ensured that they would remain close friends. In the winter of 1938, Nelson recounted, when he and his wife were living in New York City, "Kitty Dallet moved in with us. Her life was in turmoil then, but she knew she could stay with us as long as need be." Eventually she moved to the West Coast, as did Nelson who went there on Communist Party business in the fall of 1939. Attending a rally for Spanish refugee relief, Nelson heard Robert Oppenheimer give "a good talk about the significance of the Spanish fight." Afterward, Oppenheimer approached him and said: "I'm going to marry a friend of yours, Steve." Later, Oppenheimer invited Nelson to his home "to get together with some of his friends from the academic community who wanted to meet someone who had been in Spain." In the fall of 1941, Nelson remembered, on his daughter's second birthday, there was a knock on the door, "and there was Robert, his blue eyes twinkling under the porkpie hat he always wore, with a birthday present."[30]

Oppenheimer attended his last rally in support of Spain on December 6, 1941, the Saturday evening before the attack on Pearl Harbor. But his emotional investment in the Loyalists and, more broadly speaking, in the cause of antifascism never waned. How could it? By making his contributions to Spanish relief directly to the Communist Party, Oppenheimer was in a sense paying homage to his wife's former husband. Yet however generous his financial sacrifice, it could never compare with Joe Dallet's ultimate sacrifice. Early in 1943, when Oppenheimer was about to leave Berkeley for Los Alamos, he sought out Dallet's comrade Steve Nelson. "He appeared excited to the point of nervousness," Nelson recalled: "He couldn't discuss where he was going, but would only say that it had to do with the war effort. We chatted, mostly about Spain and the war, and exchanged good-byes. His last comment was that it was too bad that the Spanish Loyalists had not been able to hold out a little longer so that we could have buried Franco and Hitler in the same grave."[31]

When Oppenheimer moved to Los Alamos to direct the Manhattan Project he brought with him a set of deeply rooted convictions—that ethical judgments had rational foundations, that the highest form of virtue consisted of accepting one's destiny, and that the war against fascism was a conflict of good against evil. Those beliefs would quiet whatever doubts he might otherwise have felt about unlocking the secret of the atom, harnessing its power for military purposes, or unleashing its destructive force.

THE ATOMIC BOMB: "A FIRECRACKER OVER A DESERT"

In September 1942 the United States Army placed General Leslie R. Groves in charge of the top-secret project to build an atomic bomb. In October Groves met J. Robert Oppenheimer in Berkeley, quickly concluded that he was "a real genius," and decided he was the right person to oversee the scientific effort.[32] Groves offered him the directorship of the laboratory despite the reservations of Army Counter Intelligence officials who knew all about his left-wing background and associations. In November Oppenheimer selected Los Alamos as the site for the laboratory, and he moved there in March 1943. Eventually, more than ten thousand people would be employed on the Manhattan Project.

According to Hans Bethe, who headed the Theoretical Division at Los Alamos, the success of the project "grew out of the brilliance, enthusiasm and charisma with which Oppenheimer led it."[33] Oppenheimer recruited the top-flight scientists whose services he considered essential through an artful blend of cajolery and flattery. He appealed not only to their patriotism but also to their intellectual curiosity, their desire, that is, to share in the excitement of doing a kind of physics that had never been attempted. Once he had persuaded them to move to Los Alamos, Oppenheimer inspired such strong feelings of camaraderie that many physicists would remember the Manhattan Project as a "magnificent" or a "golden" time. "I found a spirit of Athens, of Plato, of an ideal Republic," one of them recalled.[34]

Because he regarded Oppenheimer as indispensable, Groves defended him even when his nonchalance regarding security arrangements drove Counter Intelligence officers to despair. In mid-June 1943, for example, Oppenheimer met his former lover, Jean Tatlock, in San Francisco, had dinner with her, and spent the night at her apartment. Because she had been (and might still be) a Communist Party member, Army Counter Intelligence, which had been trailing Oppenheimer, wanted him removed as director. But Groves maintained in July that "he is absolutely essential to the project."[35] (Oppenheimer never saw Tatlock again; six months later she committed suicide.)

Again, in August 1943 Oppenheimer advised Counter Intelligence officers that he had been told that George Eltenton, an English chemical engineer, had means of getting technical information to Russian scientists. Oppenheimer had heard this from Haakon Chevalier, an old friend who taught French literature at Berkeley and who belonged to a number of Communist front organizations. To avoid implicating Chevalier, Oppenheimer concocted a confusing tale, or as he later called it, a "cock and bull story," alleging that three other scientists had also been approached. Not until December, at Groves's explicit order, did Oppenheimer provide Chevalier's name, and even then he did not tell the full truth about the incident. To Groves, however, Oppenheimer's behavior merely showed that he had "the typical American schoolboy attitude that there is something wicked about telling on a friend."[36]

Groves later recalled that when he was assigned to the atomic bomb project he was instructed "to produce this at the earliest possible date so as to bring the war to a conclusion . . . any time that a single day could be saved," Groves remembered being told, "I should save that day."[37] His loyalty to Oppenheimer can be explained largely by his belief that no other physicist could get a bomb built as quickly. In time, however, Groves discovered something else about Oppenheimer: he was a forceful advocate of the need to use the bomb, and to use it in such a way as to exhibit its awesome power.

This became evident in October 1944 when Captain William S. Parsons, a navy officer who headed the Ordnance Division at Los Alamos, wrote to Oppenheimer complaining that some of the physicists seemed to be more interested in experiments that had purely theoretical implications than they were in developing a deliverable weapon. Oppenheimer forwarded Parsons's memorandum to General Groves, adding: "I agree completely with all the comments of Captain Parsons' memorandum on the fallacy of regarding a controlled test as the culmination of the work of this laboratory. The laboratory is operating under a directive to produce weapons; this directive has been and will be rigorously adhered to." The only reason to schedule a test, Oppenheimer added, was that it "appears to be a necessary step in the development of a weapon."[38]

Once it was clear that the laboratory would indeed produce an atomic bomb, it was necessary to choose a target, or targets, in Japan. On May 10–11, 1945, a newly formed Target Committee met at Los Alamos. Oppenheimer prepared the agenda, which, along with various technical matters, included a consideration of "Psychological Factors in Target Selection" and the bomb's "Radiological Effects." The committee specified that it wanted "important targets in a large urban area of more than three miles diameter" that were "capable of being damaged effectively by blast" and were "likely to be unattacked by next August." The Air Force had agreed to reserve five targets that met these criteria, among them Kyoto, Japan's ancient capital and cultural center. The Committee concluded: "There is the advantage that Kyoto is an intellectual center for Japan and the people there are more apt to appreciate the significance of such a weapon as the gadget." Hiroshima offered different advantages: "There are adjacent hills which are likely to produce a focusing effect which would considerably increase the blast damage. Due to rivers it is not a good incendiary target." Oppenheimer endorsed these recommendations, although, in the end, Secretary of War Henry L. Stimson decided to spare Kyoto because of its historical and cultural significance.[39]

Oppenheimer also agreed with the need for "making the initial use sufficiently spectacular for the importance of the weapon to be internationally recognized when publicity on it is released." Warning that dangerous doses of radiation would necessarily accompany such a blast, he urged that sensible precautions be taken. His concern, however, extended only to the well-being of American airmen: "The basic recommendations of this memo are (1) for radiological reasons no aircraft should be closer than 2 1/2 miles to the point of detonation (for blast reasons the distance should be greater) and (2) aircraft must avoid the cloud of radio-active materials."[40]

Three weeks later Oppenheimer attended a crucial meeting of the Interim Committee of the War Department and its Scientific Advisory Panel. Besides Oppenheimer, the panel members were Arthur H. Compton, Enrico Fermi, and Ernest O. Lawrence. Meeting in Washington on May 31 and June 1, they recommended that the atomic bomb be used without prior warning. The scientists explained that "the visual effect of an atomic bombing would be tremendous. It would be accompanied by a brilliant luminescence which would rise to a height of 10,000 to 20,000 feet. The neutron effect of the explosion would be dangerous to life for a radius of at least two-thirds of a mile." Oppenheimer favored several simultaneous strikes, but his proposal was rejected partly because it was thought that the use of one bomb would make for a more dramatic contrast with the regular pattern of Air Force bombardment.[41]

A final opportunity to reevaluate the use of atomic bombs came on June 16, when the Scientific Advisory Panel considered a report presented to the secretary of war by James Franck of the University of Chicago's Metallurgical Laboratory, itself a division of the Manhattan Project. Acutely sensitive to the political implications of atomic energy, Franck urged that nuclear weapons "be considered as a problem of long-range national policy rather than of military expediency." Because it was impossible to safeguard atomic secrets forever, he reasoned, the only way to prevent an uncontrolled arms race was to foster an atmosphere of international trust. To accomplish that, a demonstration of the bomb "might best be made, before the eyes of representatives of all the United Nations, on the desert or a barren island." After such a test, if Japan still refused to surrender, "the weapon might perhaps be used against Japan if the sanction of the United Nations (and of public opinion at home) were obtained, perhaps after a preliminary ultimatum to Japan to surrender or at least to evacuate certain regions as an alternative to their total destruction." The report was signed by Franck, Leo Szilard, Eugene Rabinowitch, Glenn T. Seaborg, and three other prominent physicists.[42]

Even as he transmitted the Franck Report to Secretary Stimson, Arthur H. Compton expressed serious doubts about its conclusions: a failure to use the bomb might lengthen the war and cost American lives, he explained, and without a military demonstration the world would never understand "what was to be expected if war should break out again."[43] Compton soon discovered that Fermi and Lawrence agreed with him—and so did Robert Oppenheimer. The panel of scientists declared that they had "no claim to special competence in solving the political, social, and military problems which are presented by the advent of atomic power." They feared that a "purely technical demonstration" might fail, thereby exposing the United States to ridicule; and even if it succeeded, it would use up one of the few bombs likely to be ready. Accordingly, "we can propose no technical demonstration likely to bring an end to the war; we see no acceptable alternative to direct military use."[44]

Oppenheimer later described what was running through the minds of the advisory panel: "We did say that we did not think that exploding one of these things as a firecracker over a desert was likely to be very impressive."[45] To appreciate the destructive power of the bomb, that is, one had to let it do its destructive work. Oppenheimer shared the view, widely held by his fellow physicists, that the ultimate justification for creating such a terrible weapon was that it promised, by its very destructiveness, to usher in a new age in which war would be unthinkable. That is why he came to view the atomic bomb as "a great force for peace." The existence of such weapons, he said, ultimately "intensifies the urgency of our hopes—in frank words, because we are scared."[46]

Robert Jay Lifton has argued that physicists during the war were highly susceptible to "nuclearism," which he defines as "the passionate embrace of nuclear weapons as a solution to death anxiety and a way of restoring a lost sense of immortality. Nuclearism is a secular religion, a total ideology in which 'grace' and even 'salvation'—the mastery of death and evil—are achieved through the power of a new technological deity. The deity is seen as capable not only of apocalyptic destruction but also of unlimited creation." As a description of Oppenheimer's outlook this undoubtedly goes too far. Yet Oppenheimer surely exhibited, as Lifton says, a "reliance on the weapon to demonstrate its massive evil on behalf of ultimate good." His vision "was the vision of a gifted scientist who had in a sense merged with the weapon he had done so much to bring about."[47]

The merger was not fully complete until mid-July 1945. As the final preparations were being made for the test at Alamogordo, Oppenheimer learned of a petition that had been drafted by Leo Szilard and signed by sixty-nine physicists at the Metallurgical Laboratory. The petition was addressed to President Harry S. Truman. Written in measured yet certain tones, it urged him not to use the atomic bomb "unless the terms which will be imposed upon Japan have been made public in detail and Japan knowing these terms has refused to surrender," and, in any event, not to use it "without seriously considering the moral responsibilities which are involved." On July 10, Szilard wrote to Oppenheimer explaining that although a petition might not have much actual effect, "from a point of view of the standing of the scientists in the eyes of the general public one or two years from now it is a good thing that a minority of scientists should have gone on record in favor of giving greater weight to moral arguments." Szilard sent the petition to Los Alamos hoping to attract additional signatures; Oppenheimer refused to permit its circulation.[48]

Only after the bombing of Hiroshima and Nagasaki did Oppenheimer voice the fears, possibly even the doubts, he had suppressed during the war. The development of nuclear energy, he said in a farewell speech to the staff at Los Alamos, meant that the great powers must come to their senses. If nations did not agree to control atomic weapons but simply added them to their arsenals, he remarked, "then the time will come when mankind will curse the names of Los Alamos and of Hiroshima."[49] In October 1945, meeting President Truman for the first time, Oppenheimer said despairingly, "I feel we have blood on our hands;" Truman merely replied: "Never mind. It'll all come out in the wash."[50] But Oppenheimer was not easily reassured. As late as 1948 he was asserting: "In some sort of crude sense which no vulgarity, no humor, no overstatement can quite extinguish, the physicists have known sin; and this is a knowledge which they cannot lose."[51]

THE HYDROGEN BOMB

Although Japan surrendered in August 1945, Oppenheimer continued to direct the Los Alamos laboratory until November, when he returned to his professorship at the California Institute of Technology. Soon thereafter he arranged to resume his joint appointment at the University of California at Berkeley. In the spring of 1947 he accepted the directorship of the Institute of Advanced Study and that October moved to Princeton. Earlier in the year he was appointed to the General Advisory Committee (GAC) of the Atomic Energy Commission and was elected chairman, a position he held until mid-1952. No longer involved in theoretical research, Oppenheimer during this period acted as a public advocate for science, an administrator, and a high-level policy advisor. He served on so many advisory bodies and wrote so many official reports, Alice Kimball Smith and Charles Weiner explain, that in some instances "Oppenheimer was reporting to Oppenheimer."[52]

Oppenheimer recognized that his radical activities before the war, his "indiscretions" he called them, represented a potential threat to his public position. "I am worried about the wild oats of all kinds which I have sown in the past," he confessed in September 1945, and his worries naturally increased as Cold War tensions escalated, anticommunist hysteria mounted, and some of his former associates were dragged before congressional investigating committees.[53] Consequently, he carefully steered clear of any involvements that might prove in the least embarrassing. In August 1947, for example, he was asked to sign a manifesto marking the twentieth anniversary of the executions of Nicola Sacco and Bartolomeo Vanzetti, the Italian anarchists who were widely assumed to have been framed on a murder charge and sent to the electric chair for their radical views. The manifesto used the occasion to "appeal for resistance to all attempts through propaganda and demagogic politicians to create mob hysteria against Communist methods while at the same time we declare our unceasing opposition to those methods." Eleanor Roosevelt signed the document, as did Reinhold Niebuhr, Walter Reuther, and many others, but Oppenheimer begged off. Although he agreed with it, he said, "Please do not urge that I sponsor the manifesto: it deals with things very far from my field of competence, & where my word neither should nor would have weight. But if my encouragement is of any help, that you have."[54]

In his acknowledged field of competence, where his word carried immense weight, Oppenheimer could not so easily avoid controversy. This was especially true after the Soviet Union exploded an atomic device on August 29, 1949, ending the existing American monopoly. On September 23, after analysis of the radioactive debris confirmed that it was indeed a nuclear explosion, the Truman administration announced the frightening news to the public. The question then became whether the United States should embark on a crash program, analogous to the wartime Manhattan Project, to build a hydrogen or "super" bomb. That question came before the General Advisory Committee when it met in Washington on October 29–30, 1949. Eight of the nine members, all except Glenn T. Seaborg, were present, with Oppenheimer in the chair.

Advocates of the crash program—and there were many, both inside government and without—made two key arguments: first, Russia would surely attempt to develop such a weapon, and if the attempt succeeded and was not matched by the United States, the balance of military power would shift decisively in favor of Russia; second, the development of a "super" posed no ethical problem because the difference between atomic bombs and hydrogen bombs was only a matter of degree, not kind. In an ideal world, perhaps, such a weapon would not be required. But in the real world, the United States needed a weapon sufficient to deter Russia because "total power in the hands of total evil will equal destruction."[55]

The problem with this view from the standpoint of opponents of the crash program was that, as Herbert F. York has observed, "no one then knew how to make a 'super.' About all that was then known for certain was that, in principle, the energy was there."[56] Consequently, an all-out effort to determine the feasibility of a thermonuclear bomb ran the very real risk of diverting resources from the ongoing, successful nuclear program. Finally, critics asserted, the difference between atomic and hydrogen weapons was, indeed, a difference in kind, because the superbomb, by virtue of its enormously destructive power, could not be limited to use against a military target.

This last argument profoundly influenced Oppenheimer and his colleagues on the GAC, who unanimously recommended against the crash program. Because "the weapon is from a technical point of view without limitations with regard to the damage that it can inflict," it would necessarily destroy countless innocent people: "Its use therefore carries much further than the atomic bomb itself the policy of exterminating civilian populations." The GAC report proposed two alternatives: a "booster" program to support further research into the thermonuclear process and the feasibility of producing a superbomb; and "an intensification of efforts to make atomic weapons available for tactical purposes, and to give attention to the problem of integration of bomb and carrier design in this field." By expanding its arsenal of nuclear weapons, the report explained, the United States could adequately protect itself.

The report also noted that the scientists were "somewhat divided as to the nature of the commitment not to develop the weapon," and some of those divisions emerged in two addenda. One, signed by Enrico Fermi and Isadore I. Rabi, restated some of the report's conclusions regarding the development of a thermonuclear bomb, but more unequivocally: "By its very nature it cannot be confined to a military objective but becomes a weapon which in practical effect is almost one of genocide. It is clear that the use of such a weapon cannot be justified upon any ethical ground which gives a human being a certain individuality and dignity even if he happens to be a resident of an enemy country." Because the release of radioactivity would contaminate large areas, and because there were no inherent limits to the weapon's destructiveness, "It is necessarily an evil thing considered in any light." To avoid putting the United States in "a bad moral position," Fermi and Rabi thought the president should tell the American people "that we think it wrong on fundamental ethical principles to initiate a program of development of such a weapon."

Oppenheimer and the five other members of the GAC shared most of these sentiments, but not all of them. Like Fermi and Rabi, they maintained that a thermonuclear bomb posed dangers that far outweighed any military advantage, that it differed fundamentally from an atomic bomb because of its limitless power, that it created a grave risk of radioactivity, and that "its use would involve a decision to slaughter a vast number of civilians" and so it "might become a weapon of genocide." They also believed that if Russia succeeded in making a superbomb and used it against the United States, "reprisals by our large stock of atomic bombs would be comparably effective to the use of a super." They concluded, therefore, that "a super bomb should never be produced." But that conclusion derived from practical considerations, a rational balancing of pros and cons, rather than from abstract moral imperatives. Strikingly absent were references of the kind Fermi and Rabi had made to evil, morality, and ethics.[57]

So Oppenheimer certainly took a considerably more disapproving view of the hydrogen bomb than he had of the atomic bomb. He noted that a decision not to proceed with the superbomb offered "a unique opportunity of providing by example some limitations on the totality of war and thus of limiting the fear and arousing the hopes of mankind," a comment he would never have made about the atomic bomb.[58] Yet while opposing a crash program in 1949, Oppenheimer was perfectly willing to support a booster program of basic research. Indeed, on the eve of the October meeting he wrote that it would be "folly to oppose the exploration of this weapon. We have always known it had to be done; and it does have to be done."[59] Moreover, while he believed the world would be better off if the super were never developed, he did not ground his objections, as Fermi and Rabi did, in "fundamental ethical principles."

In any event, the scientists' recommendations were not followed. Although the five members of the Atomic Energy Commission voted against a crash program by a three-to-two margin, President Truman decided to go ahead with it. On January 31, 1950, after consulting with AEC Chairman David Lilienthal, Secretary of Defense Louis Johnson, and Secretary of State Dean Acheson, and finding only Lilienthal opposed to the superbomb, Truman announced that he was directing the AEC to explore the feasibility of developing thermonuclear weapons. Learning of the decision, Oppenheimer was heard to remark, "This is the plague of Thebes."[60]

For more than a year, efforts by Edward Teller, Stanislaw Ulam, and physicists at Los Alamos and elsewhere to construct a superbomb were unsuccessful. Although Oppenheimer did nothing to retard their work, neither did he offer any encouragement. His influence among physicists was such, however, that some proponents of the crash program thought his reservations dissuaded scientists from working on the project, although no evidence of such a negative influence was ever produced. What is certain is that Oppenheimer continued to believe that the ever-growing stockpile of atomic weapons adequately equipped the United States, if the need arose, "to engage in total war, to carry the war to the enemy and attempt to destroy him."[61]

Not until February and March 1951 did Ulam and Teller discover the principle that made possible the building of a hydrogen bomb. It was Ulam who conceived "a dramatically new approach to designing a thermonuclear weapon," and Teller who proposed the necessary refinements. In May the "Greenhouse" tests proved beyond any doubt that it was possible to produce a thermonuclear reaction. And so in June the General Advisory Committee reassembled, this time at Princeton, along with members of the Atomic Energy Commission, the Joint Committee on Atomic Energy, the Los Alamos staff, and knowledgeable physicists to learn about the recent developments.

As Teller and his associates explained their concept, which gave every indication of solving problems that had hitherto been insoluble, Oppenheimer, like everyone else, was caught up in a wave of excitement. Captivated, indeed entranced by the sheer beauty of the physics, Oppenheimer, according to Freeman Dyson, said that the Ulam-Teller formulation was "a sweet and lovely and beautiful job."[62] Gordon Dean, the chairman of the AEC, noted that Oppenheimer was "enthusiastic" and "almost thrilled" at the breakthrough.[63] Oppenheimer later characterized his own feelings at the time: the explanation was "technically so sweet that you could not argue" because "when you see something that is technically sweet, you go ahead and do it."[64]

On November 1, 1952, the United States went ahead and did it, testing a thermonuclear device that exploded with a force of 10.4 megatons, a thousand times more powerful than the bomb that leveled Hiroshima. The mushroom cloud, which reached a height of twenty-seven miles, "really filled up the sky," an observer reported: "It was awesome. It just went on and on." A sailor on a ship thirty miles away wrote home: "You would swear that the whole world was on fire." The blast obliterated the Pacific island of Elugelab. As Richard Rhodes explains: "The fireball had vaporized the entire island, leaving behind a circular crater two hundred feet deep and more than a mile across filled with seawater, a dark blue hole punched into the paler blue of the shallow atoll lagoon."[65]

By then, however, Robert Oppenheimer was no longer in a policy-making position. In July his term on the GAC expired and he did not seek reappointment. Though never an enthusiastic supporter of the hydrogen bomb, he had not been an outright opponent, either. He had voted against a crash program, but had backed a booster program; he had based his reservations on practical considerations, but had not endorsed Fermi's and Rabi's ethical objections; he had let it be known that he was opposed to thermonuclear weapons, but in the end had shown unbounded enthusiasm for the physics that made them possible. He viewed the hydrogen bomb much differently than he had once viewed the atomic bomb, but not differently enough, it turned out, to spare him the anguish that awaited him at his security clearance hearing.

THE ATOMIC ENERGY COMMISSION HEARING: THE CONFESSION

On May 12, 1953, Federal Bureau of Investigation director J. Edgar Hoover received a visit from Senator Joseph McCarthy, chairman of the Government Operations Committee, and his counsel Roy Cohn. According to Hoover, McCarthy said "that he wanted to discuss confidentially with me the matter of his Committee taking up for investigative purposes the activities of J. Robert Oppenheimer, the scientist." Hoover immediately replied that "I thought he had a number of problems to consider before embarking upon this project." Chief among them were that Oppenheimer had performed crucial work for the nation during the war and had maintained extensive contacts with scientists all around the world. All things considered, Hoover added, "whatever the Senator's Committee did concerning Oppenheimer should be done with a great deal of preliminary spade work so that if and when the Committee moved into the open it would have substantive facts upon which to predicate its actions. The Senator said he shared these views also."[66] It was not the kind of case, Hoover warned, "which should be prematurely gone into solely for the purposes of headlines."[67]

Over the next few months, however, Oppenheimer's position grew increasingly precarious. In August the Soviet Union tested its own hydrogen device. Although less powerful than the American model and not as yet in deliverable form, it nevertheless frightened American policymakers who had not expected the Russian program to advance so quickly. In November Senator McCarthy began directing his fire at the Eisenhower administration, charging that it with a failure to recognize the gravity of the communist threat. In November, also, William E. Borden, formerly the executive director of the Joint Congressional Committee on Atomic Energy, wrote to the Federal Bureau of Investigation, claiming that "more probably than not"

Oppenheimer is "an agent of the Soviet Union."[68] The FBI forwarded Borden's letter to the Atomic Energy Commission, the Defense Department, and the White House. On December 3, with these allegations swirling about, and with a McCarthy-led attack on the administration's failure to weed out subversives a distinct possibility, President Dwight D. Eisenhower erected a "blank wall" between Oppenheimer and information pertaining to national security.

The chairman of the Atomic Energy Commission, Lewis Strauss, although no friend of Oppenheimer's, urged him to resign his consultant's contract quietly, without any public fuss. (The contract had been renewed for a year in June, just before Strauss was named chairman.) But Oppenheimer refused to take the easy way out. Determined to clear his name and confident that he could, he insisted on a formal hearing. On December 23, Strauss sent Oppenheimer a letter containing twenty-four allegations, twenty-three of them relating to his radical associations and affiliations before 1946, and one pertaining to his having "slowed down" the development of the hydrogen bomb; all of these raised questions "about your veracity, conduct, and even your loyalty."[69] As he prepared for the hearing, Oppenheimer told a friend, the physicist Lee DuBridge, "the whole thing is damn nonsense," adding "the main thing that I have to do is going through the rigamarole and it's a major and complicated rigamarole."[70]

Just how complicated Oppenheimer had no way of knowing.[71] The hearing was held from April 12 to May 6 before a Personnel Security Board made up of Gordon Gray, president of the University of North Carolina; Ward Evans, a retired professor of chemistry; and Thomas Morgan, the retired chairman of Sperry Gyroscope. Breaking with precedent, the AEC retained an outside lawyer, Roger Robb, to present its case and permitted him to meet privately with the three board members to review Oppenheimer's security file in advance of the hearing. Oppenheimer selected a prominent attorney, Lloyd K. Garrison, to represent him, but Garrison lacked the needed security clearance and on several occasions had to leave the hearing room when sensitive matters were being discussed.

Then, too, the AEC did not have to prove beyond a reasonable doubt that Oppenheimer was a security risk; rather, Oppenheimer had to persuade the board that he was not one. To do this, he thought, required that he be cooperative, even to the extent of answering questions about the political affiliations of friends and former students. In effect, he played the role of an informer, however distasteful he found it. At one point, after listing a number of names, he was asked, "Would you break them down? Would you tell

us who the Communists were and who the fellow travelers were?" Oppenheimer finally exclaimed, "Is the list long enough?"[72] His testimony became
public knowledge when the AEC suddenly decided to publish the full text
of the hearings, which Oppenheimer and all concerned had assumed would
remain secret. In June, when one of the commissioners misplaced a summary of the hearing and of some files on a train, the AEC, fearing an unauthorized leak to the press, decided to publish the hearings in their entirety.
(Actually, by then the lost documents had been recovered and so no danger
of a leak existed.)

In his opening statement, Oppenheimer admitted that in 1943 he had not
told security officials the truth about the Haakon Chevalier incident. "It has
long been clear to me that I should have reported the incident at once," he
said. But Roger Robb was not satisfied with that admission. Relying on the
transcripts of Oppenheimer's conversations with an Army Counter Intelligence officer, Lt. Col. Boris T. Pash, Robb made it appear that Oppenheimer
was a habitual, inveterate liar. Robb's first question: "Did you tell Pash the
truth about this thing?" "No," Oppenheimer said. Robb's second question:
"You lied to him?" "Yes," Oppenheimer replied. Robb's third question: "What
did you tell Pash that was not true?" Oppenheimer answered truthfully: "That
Eltenton had attempted to approach members of the project—three members
of the project—through intermediaries." Robb's fourth question: "What else
did you tell him that wasn't true?" When Oppenheimer said, "That is all I really remember," Robb, referring to the transcript, asked a fifth question: "That
is all? Did you tell Pash . . ." and then implied that Oppenheimer's failure to
remember everything he had said in a decade-old interview amounted to purposeful deception. When Oppenheimer again admitted making up the story,
Robb asked: "Why did you do that, Doctor?" One would have thought Oppenheimer's reply—"Because I was an idiot"—would have sufficed. But Robb
was not done: "Is that your only explanation, Doctor?"[73]

Robb then moved to another subject designed to cause Oppenheimer acute
embarrassment—his visit to Jean Tatlock in the spring of 1943. Although Oppenheimer had admitted seeing her, he had not mentioned staying overnight
at her apartment. Now he said that Tatlock had wanted to see him "because she
was still in love with me." Robb's follow-up questioning was relentless: "You
have no reason to believe she wasn't a communist, do you? . . . You spent the
night with her, didn't you? . . . That is when you were working on a secret war
project? . . . Did you think that consistent with good security? . . . You didn't
think that spending a night with a dedicated Communist?" On one level,
Robb's questions were designed to show that Oppenheimer was careless about

security; on another, by reiterating the phrase, "spending the night," he was characterizing Oppenheimer as an adulterer.[74]

Yet Robb wanted more from Oppenheimer than an admission that he had once lied to security officials or had behaved indiscreetly. He also wanted Oppenheimer to confess that, having worked on the atomic bomb, he could not have had moral scruples about the hydrogen bomb. Robb's implication was clear: if Oppenheimer's reservations about the hydrogen bomb were not ethically derived, they must have been politically motivated, motivated, that is, by pro-Russian sentiment. Robb wanted Oppenheimer to concede that Hiroshima and Nagasaki proved that there are, in fact, no moral limits to what a scientist should do in the interests of the state, no ethical considerations that a scientist should place above the nation's security. And so Robb began:

> Q. . . . Doctor, you testified, did you not, that you assisted in selecting the target for the drop of the bomb on Japan?
> A. Right. . . .
> Q. You knew, did you not, that the dropping of that atomic bomb on the target you had selected will kill or injure thousands of civilians, is that correct?
> A. Not as many as turned out.
> Q. How many were killed or injured?
> A. 70,000.
> Q. Did you have moral scruples about that?
> A. Terrible ones.
> Q. But you testified the other day, did you not, sir, that the bombing of Hiroshima was very successful?
> A. Well, it was technically successful.
> Q. Oh, technically.
> A. It is also alleged to have helped end the war.
> Q. Would you have supported the dropping of a thermonuclear bomb on Hiroshima?
> A. It would make no sense at all.
> Q. Why?
> A. The target is too small.
> Q. The target is too small. Supposing there had been a target in Japan big enough for a thermonuclear weapon, would you have opposed dropping it?
> A. This was not a problem with which I was confronted.
> Q. I am confronting you with it now, sir.

A. You are not confronting me with an actual problem. I was very relieved when Mr. Stimson removed from the target list Kyoto, which was the largest city and the most vulnerable target. I think this is the nearest thing that was really to your hypothetical question.

Q. That is correct. Would you have opposed the dropping of a thermonuclear weapon on Japan because of moral scruples?

A. I believe I would, sir.

Q. Did you oppose the dropping of the atom bomb on Hiroshima because of moral scruples? . . .

A. We set forth our—

Q. I am asking you about it, not "we."

A. I set forth arguments against dropping it. . . . But I did not endorse them.

Q. But you supported the dropping of the atom bomb on Japan, didn't you?

A. What do you mean support?

Q. You helped pick the target, didn't you?

A. I did my job which was the job I was supposed to do. I was not in a policymaking position at Los Alamos. I would have done anything that I was asked to do, including making the bombs in a different shape, if I had thought it was technically feasible.[75]

Even as shrewd an inquisitor as Roger Robb may not have expected that a man of Oppenheimer's formidable intellect would appear so befuddled. The problem was that, when asked whether he had had moral scruples about using the atomic bomb, he replied, "terrible ones." But Oppenheimer had given no sign of having had such scruples before August 1945. To the contrary, his religious, philosophical, and political convictions had made him into a resolute, indeed zealous nuclearist. Why, then, did he answer Robb's question as he did? Perhaps he was reading back into the war years the very real doubts that assailed him after August 1945, when the immense human tragedy of Hiroshima and Nagasaki became known, doubts he expressed in his famous remark about the physicists having known sin. Then again, perhaps Oppenheimer was, whether consciously or not, seeking to establish a credible basis for having opposed the hydrogen bomb by claiming he had experienced moral qualms about the atomic bomb, thereby demonstrating his consistency.

Moreover, as we have seen, his reservations about the hydrogen bomb were not, like Fermi's and Rabi's, based on its incompatibility with "fundamental ethical principles" but rather on pragmatic considerations. The true continuity in Oppenheimer's view of nuclear and thermonuclear weapons was between his statement to Robb that he would have done anything he was asked to do during the war if it was "technically feasible" and his remark about the Teller-Ulam formulation for the hydrogen bomb: when you see something that is "technically sweet" you go ahead and do it.

CONCLUSION: THE TRAGEDY

One inevitably comes away from the story of J. Robert Oppenheimer with a profound sense of tragedy. An inexcusable injustice was done to a loyal, patriotic American when the Atomic Energy Commission voted to deny him security clearance on the grounds that his associations with radicals revealed "fundamental defects in his character" that passed the "tolerable limits of prudence and self-restraint."[76] The vote came on June 28, 1954, two days before his consultant's contract would have expired. An ideal opportunity to rectify the injustice was lost when in December 1963 the government presented Oppenheimer with the Fermi Award, thereby tacitly admitting its mistake, and yet did not restore his security clearance, which, in Oppenheimer's view, may well have been the more important thing to do.

Oppenheimer was also a tragic figure because of how he responded to the ethical dilemmas he faced as a scientist. His outlook was shaped by the Ethical Culture movement's emphasis on reason, the Bhagavad Gita's teachings on the duties of a warrior, and the Popular Front's passionate antifascism. That outlook led Oppenheimer to commit himself to the atomic bomb project, but to commit himself so completely that he opposed the efforts of James Franck, Leo Szilard, and others to ensure that adequate attention was paid to the moral implications of using the bomb. Oppenheimer's lack of enthusiasm for developing a hydrogen bomb derived chiefly from fears that a crash program would probably fail and would almost certainly disrupt the nation's nuclear buildup. Once it was shown that a hydrogen bomb could be built, Oppenheimer was drawn, magnetically, to the sheer "beauty" of the physics. It was, therefore, understandable why he would be so vulnerable to Roger Robb's barrage of questions on the relationship between science and ethics

In 1966 Oppenheimer, a chain smoker most of his life, developed throat cancer. He died in February 1967 at the age of only sixty-three. During the war he had been reading John Donne's *Holy Sonnets*, which provided the inspiration for naming the Alamogordo test site, "Trinity." Perhaps a fitting epitaph may be found in another of those poems:

Thou hast made me, and shall Thy worke decay?
Repair me now, for now mine end doth haste,
I run to death, and death meets me as fast,
And all my pleasures are like yesterday.

NOTES

1. H. B. Fletcher to Director, May 14, 1946; Donald E. Roney Report, August 5, 1946, FBI Security File: J. Robert Oppenheimer (Scholarly Resources). (Hereafter cited as FBI File.)

2. Interview with Professor Frederick G. Marcham, June 10, 1979.

3. Fletcher to Director, May 14, 1946, FBI File.

4. Freeman Dyson, *Disturbing the Universe* (New York: Harper & Row, 1979), 6.

5. Alice Kimball Smith and Charles Weiner, eds., *Robert Oppenheimer: Letters and Recollections* (Cambridge, Mass.: Harvard University Press, 1980), 3. See also S. S. Schweber, *In the Shadow of the Bomb: Bethe, Oppenheimer and the Moral Responsibility of the Scientist* (Princeton: Princeton University Press, 2000), 42–53.

6. Benny Kraut, *From Reform Judaism to Ethical Culture: The Religious Evolution of Felix Adler* (Cincinnati: Ktav Publishing, 1979). See also Horace L. Friess, *Felix Adler and Ethical Culture: Memories and Studies* (New York: Columbia University Press, 1981).

7. Felix Adler, *An Ethical Philosophy of Life* (New York: D. Appleton, 1918), 26.

8. Henry Neumann, *Spokesmen for Ethical Religion* (Boston: Little, Brown, 1951), 45.

9. David S. Muzzey, *Ethics As a Religion* (New York: Simon & Schuster, 1951), 94, 134.

10. *The Ethical Culture School Curriculum* (1921): 5–7, 66.

11. Smith and Weiner, *Oppenheimer*, 297.

12. Smith and Weiner, *Oppenheimer*, 149.

13. Smith and Weiner, *Oppenheimer*, 143.

14. All quotations are from *The Bhagavad Gita: A New Verse Translation*, edited by Ann Stanford (New York: Continuum, 1970). See also James A. Hijiya, "The *Gita* of J. Robert Oppenheimer," *Proceedings of the American Philosophical Society* 144 (June 2000): 123–167.

15. Vannevar Bush, *Pieces of the Action* (New York: William Morrow, 1970), 148.

16. Cited in Richard Rhodes, *The Making of the Atomic Bomb* (New York: Simon & Schuster, 1986), 676.

17. Smith and Weiner, *Oppenheimer*, 288.

18. Smith and Weiner, *Oppenheimer*, 154–156; Freeman Dyson, *Weapons and Hope* (New York: HarperCollins, 1984), 125.

19. Muzzey, *Ethics As a Religion*, 249.

20. Smith and Weiner, *Oppenheimer*, 195.

21. *In the Matter of J. Robert Oppenheimer: Transcript of Hearing before Personnel Security Board* (Washington, D.C.: U.S. Government Printing Office, 1954), 8. (Hereafter cited as *Hearing.*)

22. *Hearing*, 8–10.

23. *Hearing*, 8–9.

24. *Hearing*, 9.

25. *Hearing*, 10.

26. Steve Nelson, James R. Barrett, and Rob Ruck, *Steve Nelson: American Radical* (Pittsburgh: University of Pittsburgh Press, 1981), 197.

27. Joe Dallet, *Letters from Spain* (New York: International Publishers, 1938), 21, 38–39, 22, 57.

28. Dallet, *Letters from Spain*, 53, 56.

29. *Hearing*, 573–574.

30. Nelson, *Steve Nelson*, 268.

31. Nelson, *Steve Nelson*, 269.

32. Cited in Rhodes, *Making of the Atomic Bomb*, 448.

33. Cited in Rhodes, *Making of the Atomic Bomb*, 539.

34. Nuel Pharr Davis, *Lawrence and Oppenheimer* (New York: Da Capo, 1968), 185–187.

35. James W. Kunetka, *Oppenheimer: The Years of Risk* (Englewood Cliffs, N.J.: Prentice-Hall, 1982), 35; *Hearing*, 170.

36. *Hearing*, 167.

37. *Hearing*, 171.

38. Smith and Weiner, *Oppenheimer*, 276.

39. Rhodes, *Making of the Atomic Bomb*, 630–633.

40. Rhodes, *Making of the Atomic Bomb*, 632.

41. "Notes of the Interim Committee Meeting, May 31, 1945," in Martin J. Sherwin, *A World Destroyed: Hiroshima and the Origins of the Arms Race* (New York: Vintage Books, 1987), 295–304.

42. "The Political Implications of Atomic Weapons: Excerpts from the Franck Report, June 11, 1945," in Sherwin, *A World Destroyed*, 323–333.

43. Sherwin, *A World Destroyed*, 213.

44. "Science Panel: Recommendations on the Immediate Use of Nuclear Weapons, June 16, 1945," in Sherwin, *A World Destroyed*, 304–305.

45. *Hearing*, 34.

46. Cited in Sherwin, *A World Destroyed,* 213.

47. Robert Jay Lifton, *The Broken Connection: On Death and the Continuity of Life* (New York: Simon & Schuster, 1979), 369–381, 419–432.

48. William Lanouette with Bela Silard, *Genius in the Shadows: A Biography of Leo Szilard* (New York: Scribner, 1992), 269–273.

49. Smith and Weiner, *Oppenheimer,* 311.

50. Richard Rhodes, *Dark Sun: The Making of the Hydrogen Bomb* (New York: Simon & Schuster, 1995), 205.

51. J. Robert Oppenheimer, "Physics in the Contemporary World," *Bulletin of the Atomic Scientists* IV (March 1948): 66.

52. Smith and Weiner, *Oppenheimer,* 329.

53. Smith and Weiner, *Oppenheimer,* 307.

54. Oppenheimer to Gardner Jackson [August 1947], Gardner Jackson MSS (Franklin D. Roosevelt Library).

55. Senator Brien McMahon, cited in Richard G. Hewlett and Francis Duncan, *Atomic Shield, 1947–1952* (University Park: Pennsylvania State University Press, 1969), 402.

56. Herbert F. York, *The Advisers: Oppenheimer, Teller, and the Superbomb* (Stanford: Stanford University Press, 1976), 154.

57. For the text of the GAC Report, see York, *The Advisers,* 154–162.

58. York, *The Advisers,* 160.

59. Oppenheimer to James B. Conant, October 21, 1949, in *Hearing,* 242–243.

60. Davis, *Lawrence and Oppenheimer,* 330.

61. Oppenheimer to General Board of the Navy, April 14, 1948, in *Hearing,* 46–47.

62. Dyson, *Disturbing the Universe,* 53.

63. *Hearing,* 305.

64. *Hearing,* 251.

65. Rhodes, *Dark Sun,* 508–509.

66. J. E. Hoover to Tolson and Ladd, May 19, 1953, FBI File.

67. J. E. Hoover to Tolson and Ladd, June 24, 1953, FBI File.

68. For the text of the letter, see *Hearing,* 837–838.

69. *Hearing,* 3–7.

70. Transcript of Oppenheimer-DuBridge phone conversation, March 12, 1954, FBI File.

71. Important accounts are Barton J. Bernstein, "In the Matter of J. Robert Oppenheimer," *Historical Studies in the Physical Sciences* 12 (1982): 195–252; John Major, *The Oppenheimer Hearing* (New York: Stein and Day, 1971); and Philip M. Stern, *The Oppenheimer Case: Security on Trial* (New York: Harper & Row, 1969). See also

Richard Polenberg, ed., *In the Matter of J. Robert Oppenheimer: The Security Clearance Hearing* (Ithaca, N.Y.: Cornell University Press, 2002).

72. *Hearing,* 155.

73. *Hearing,* 137.

74. *Hearing,* 154.

75. *Hearing,* 235–236.

76. *Decision and Opinions of the United States Atomic Energy Commission in the Matter of Dr. J. Robert Oppenheimer* (Washington, D.C.: U.S. Government Printing Office, 1954), 51–54.

6

RACE IN AMERICA:
THE ULTIMATE TEST OF LIBERALISM

William H. Chafe

No issue has more severely challenged the liberal tradition in America than that of race. Whatever else liberalism has meant at different points in time—more or less equitable distribution of wealth, larger or smaller programs of social welfare, a stronger or weaker role for the federal government—there has always been at the heart of liberalism a belief in the goal of equal opportunity, a conviction that *individuals,* whatever their background or starting point in life, should be able to compete with each other and maximize their *individual* talents. Within such a framework, group identity ultimately does not count. The norm is one of assimilation, each man or woman developing his or her abilities within a social and economic system presumably capable of, and committed to, individual rights. Within such a paradigm, every person enjoys equal protection and similar chances to make it, or not make it, in the competition for success.

The critical question, of course, is whether a viable opportunity to achieve equal opportunity can ever exist in a society that from its inception has made race a dividing line separating people with black skin from those with white skin—with blacks having almost no rights, and whites having lesser or greater rights depending on their class, gender, and ethnicity. From Martin Delaney to Frederick Douglass, Booker T. Washington to W. E. B. DuBois, Marcus Garvey to Walter White, African Americans have differed profoundly on how to answer that question. Only in the years since the 1930s, however, have changes occurred that put the issue to a test.

During that period, two kinds of dialectic have taken place. The first has been between those who wield power in government and society, and others in established positions of civil rights leadership who have sought entry into the corridors of power on behalf of the previously disenfranchised. The second has been between people at the grass roots for whom experience is the best teacher, and whose vision has been less constrained by the customs or perquisites of power, and those who determine public policy. Occasionally, the two types of dialectic have overlapped and found some common ground. That happened in America during the late 1940s and the early 1960s. But more often, the two have diverged, calling into severe doubt whether the dream of liberalism can ever accommodate the reality of race.

THE DEPRESSION AND WAR YEARS

Only by contrast with what had gone before could anyone speak of the 1930s as a time of positive change for American blacks. The system of Jim Crow remained deeply entrenched. Lynchings continued to occur, gruesomely testifying to the degree that physical terrorism reinforced the customs of segregated jobs, schools, and social spaces. More than 75 percent of black Americans lived in the South. Fewer than 5 percent had the right to vote. White schools received more than five times the funding per student that black schools received. Richard Wright summarized the effect of growing up black in such an environment in his autobiographical novel *Black Boy*. Working as a domestic in a white person's home, he was asked by his employer why he was still going to school. "Well, I want to be a writer," he replied. "You'll never be a writer," she responded. "Who on earth put such ideas into your nigger head?" In spite of such experiences, blacks found myriad ways to sustain their communities and families, and even on occasion engaged in resistance—but always within a context of pervasive control.

Yet the New Deal also offered some reason to hope. Federal relief checks came to blacks as well as whites. Some jobs existed in the Works Progress Administration. African Americans were appointed to federal offices, and there was even a "black" cabinet of highly placed officials who advocated change in race relations. Although the president would not support an antilynching law, he acknowledged, with regret, the reality of white terrorism. And his wife, Eleanor Roosevelt, became a champion of civil rights, supporting black women leaders such as Mary McCleod Bethune, resigning from the Daughters of the American Revolution when they denied the black opera singer

Marian Anderson the right to sing at Constitution Hall—even testifying by her physical actions to her convictions about equal rights. When told at a Birmingham meeting of the Southern Conference on Human Welfare that she would have to take her seat on the "white" side of the room, separated from black delegates, she carefully placed two of the four legs of her chair on each side of the dividing line, showing her contempt for the whole concept of Jim Crow. By 1941 even her husband was ready to sign an executive order creating a Fair Employment Practices Commission barring discrimination against blacks in defense industries—especially when threatened by A. Phillip Randolph, the black union leader, with a massive march on Washington were he not to do so. It was World War II, however, that set in motion more dynamic and long-lasting grassroots change. The war jolted all Americans into new roles and responsibilities. More than two million blacks left the South for the North and West. The number of African Americans employed in manufacturing more than doubled, from 500,000 to 1.2 million. Black ballots were counted and mattered in the North, and politicians inevitably became champions of those who voted for them. Blacks enlisted at a rate 60 percent higher than their proportion in the population, and experienced, especially in posts such as England, France, and Hawaii, a warmth of reception and level of respect that gave credibility to the notion that a better world of race relations might someday exist.

The very existence of some progress, on the other hand, made all the more infuriating the persistence of white racism, both inside and outside the military. Blood supplies were segregated, notwithstanding the fact that a black physician, Dr. Charles Drew, had perfected the means of preserving blood plasma. A black soldier was lynched in Georgia. When a black army nurse violated Jim Crow seating regulations on a Montgomery bus, she was brutally beaten. A black soldier in Durham was shot and killed by a bus driver when the soldier protested the discourteous way in which the driver treated him. Symptomatic of the grinding tenacity of racism was the experience of black soldiers in Salina, Kansas, who sought service at a lunchroom. "You boys know we don't serve colored here," they were told. Indeed they did, so they walked away while inside the restaurant German prisoners of war sat at a table eating their lunch. "It was no jive talk," they noted. "The people of Salina served these enemy soldiers and turned away black American GIs." Precisely because of this chemistry—small, but important breakthroughs existing side by side with pervasive reminders of second-class citizenship—black Americans intensified their protest. The government's sophisticated propaganda campaign against fascism and for democracy highlighted America's vulnerability to the charge that it was the most racist country of all. "Our war is not against Hitler and Europe," one black columnist wrote, "but against the Hitlers in America." The black press united behind a "Double V" campaign—victory at home for democracy as well as victory abroad, increasing the militancy of its demands, even as circulation soared by 40 percent. Membership in the NAACP skyrocketed to 500,000 nationwide—a 900 percent increase, with local chapters increasing threefold. Racial tensions mounted, with race riots breaking out in Detroit, Harlem and elsewhere—only this time with black reprisals as well as white provocation and aggression. Black protest organizations, as well as average black citizens—and especially returning black soldiers—were determined that after this war, change would happen and happen quickly.

POSTWAR AMERICA, 1945–1960

Black hopes hinged on pricking the conscience of white America, generating new resilience and determination on the part of a biracial liberal coalition of northern urbanites, union members, and minorities, and sustaining black insurgency in the face of inevitable and overwhelming oppression. The last proved the easiest to achieve. More than a million black veterans came back from the war, many of them intent on remaking the world they had left. Medgar Evers and Amzie Moore returned to Mississippi and immediately went to register to vote. In Columbia, Tennessee, blacks insisted that there be a "new deal" in their community based on respect and dignity for blacks. Atlanta saw a registration effort that brought eighteen thousand new blacks to the polls in 1946, while in cities such as Greensboro and Winston-Salem a new black presence in politics resulted for the first time in aggressive candidacies for office. Overall, the number of blacks registered to vote in the South grew sixfold from 1945 to 1947, from 2 percent to 12 percent.

None of this came easily, and all of it occurred in the face of white terrorism. Medgar Evers and his associates were met by white men with pistols when they sought to register. The only black man to cast a ballot in one Georgia district was murdered immediately thereafter, his assailants never tried. When Isaac Woodward got off the bus in his hometown in South Carolina proudly wearing his uniform, policemen beat him with billyclubs and blinded him. A race riot greeted the efforts of blacks in Columbia, Tennessee, to forge a "new deal" there, and the response of white politicians to black voter registration drives was epitomized by Mississippi's Theodore Bilbo, who told a cheering throng: "If there is a single man or woman serving [as a registrar] who cannot think up questions enough to disqualify undesirables, then write Bilbo [because] there are a hundred good questions which can be furnished . . . but you know and I know what is the best way to keep the nigger from voting. You do it the night before the election. I don't have to tell you any more than that. Red-blooded men know what I mean." Bilbo then winked and left.

The key was whether the black insurgency could evoke a positive response from politicians across the nation. There the message was equivocal. On issues such as vigorous support for the Fair Employment Practices Commission, the new Truman administration provided more verbal than substantial backing, particularly on cases where a strong stance could have made a difference, as in hiring black operators for the Washington, D.C., transit system. After forty religious and civil rights groups visited him in the White House to protest the rise of racial violence, on the other hand, Truman seemed surprised (perhaps inappropriately so, given his Missouri background) at the degree of violence that had occurred. "My God," he said, "I had no idea it was as terrible as that. We have to do something."

In a dramatic follow-through, Truman appointed a blue-ribbon Committee on Civil Rights, featuring such luminaries as Charles Wilson, the head of General Electric, and Frank Porter Graham, the president of the University of North Carolina. Its report, "To Secure These Rights," boldly acknowledged the severity of the crisis and recommended a series of changes, including a permanent FEPC, creation of a Civil Rights Commission, desegregation of the armed forces, abolition of the poll tax, and support for the legal assault on segregated housing. As a follow-up, Harry Truman became the first U.S. president to address a national meeting of the NAACP, pledging to close the gap between black and white. "Every man," he declared, "should have the right to a decent home, the right to an education . . . the right to a worthwhile job, the right to an equal share in making public decisions through the ballot. . . . We must assure that these rights—on equal terms—are enjoyed by every citizen." In support of his words, Truman sent a special message to Congress in February 1948 embracing virtually all the recommendations of the Civil Rights Committee he had appointed.

Political self-interest also weighed in. Facing an extraordinarily difficult reelection campaign, Truman knew his political success hinged on winning the support of labor and urban minorities. Clark Clifford, one of Truman's chief political advisors, created a campaign blue print premised on such a strategy. Although Truman himself seemed reluctant to commit himself too overtly to a biracial liberal coalition, liberals in the Democratic Party forced him to become more assertive. Led by Minneapolis Mayor Hubert Humphrey, they generated a platform revolt at the convention that placed civil rights at the heart of the Democratic message. Although rabid segregationists such as South Carolina's Strom Thurmond walked out and formed their own party, Truman used the energy of his new coalition to lambaste the forces of reaction and bring to fruition, on election day, the successful political coalition that Clifford and Humphrey had made possible.

Other political developments, however, proved less promising, in terms of both implementing the party's new commitment to civil rights and narrowing the options for pursuing change. Progressive industrial unions in the auto, electrical, rubber, and textile industries were key to the success of a biracial coalition. Many of their most effective organizers, however, were either Communists or individuals significantly to the left of the mainstream Democratic Party. A number of their organizing successes had promoted the idea of using interracial solidarity as a vehicle for creating major economic changes, both in social welfare programs such as national health insurance, and in the sharing of decision-making power between unions and industry. In the face of the rapidly escalating Cold War, these radical union leaders were attacked as Communist sympathizers and purged from the labor movement. As a result, the focus on economic and systemic change as a solution to racial inequality faded into oblivion, and more and more of the energies of civil rights groups went into legal challenges, within the constitutional structure, to patterns of segregation.

At the same time, little was being done to enforce the new policies politicians had embraced. Though he won reelection, Truman seemed relatively powerless to secure enactment of progressive legislation. Although he ordered the desegregation of the armed forces in the summer of 1948, it was not really until after the Korean War ended in 1953 that integration took place. A permanent FEPC remained a dream; southern politicians seemed more racist than ever, with the "liberal" Frank Porter Graham defeated in a sordid campaign for the U.S. Senate in North Carolina where his opponent circulated (cropped) pictures of Graham supposedly dancing with a black woman and accused him of being a communist; and average black citizens continued to suffer terrorist repression. When Isaac Nixon, a black veteran, ignored white warnings and cast his ballot in 1948, he was murdered, with an all white jury acquitting his assailant. Blacks who stood up for justice consistently found themselves victims of economic reprisal. Much, therefore, rested on the degree to which the legal assault against segregation would prove successful, both in theory and in substance

In principle, there seemed good reason for optimism about the legal fight. Led by the irrepressible Thurgood Marshall (the NAACP's Herbert Hill noted, "he was a very courageous figure. He would travel to the court houses of the South, and folks would come from miles, some of them on muleback . . . to see the 'nigger lawyer' who stood up in white men's courtrooms"), the NAACP's legal team had strung together a series of victories eroding the impact of the infamous *Plessy v. Ferguson* decision in 1896 upholding segregation. In *Missouri ex.rel Gaines* (1939) the court mandated that equal treatment for a black law student required construction of a fully equipped and staffed black law school in Missouri. Two 1950 cases extended the court's dissatisfaction with how *Plessy* was implemented, one winning the Supreme Court's endorsement of the idea that equality could be measured by psychological as well as physical evidence so that a student made to feel "inferior," even in equal physical facilities, could still secure redress. Now, Marshall and his colleagues determined to take on the core of *Plessy*, arguing for its invalidation on the grounds that segregation, by definition, represented a denial of equality. The Court agreed in a 9–0 opinion masterfully orchestrated by new Chief Justice Earl Warren in order to signal the decisive reversal that had just occurred. Marshall and others predicted that within less than a decade all segregated schools would disappear, with other forms of mandated separation soon to follow. "We have won," black newspapers exulted.

Yet the ruling meant nothing, or almost nothing, without enforcement. "The law is a landing force [of change]," one legal scholar wrote at the time. "It makes the beachhead. But the breakthrough, if it is it to be significant, [must be] broadened by forces from behind which take advantage of the opening to go the rest of the way." Those forces were not there. In the dialectic between those in power who had the authority to create change, and those out of power seeking admission to the system, deafening silence greeted the petitioners. President Dwight Eisenhower disliked the *Brown* decision. He believed that changing racial customs by force "is just plain nuts," and that the federal government should "avoid any interference" in local racial situations. As a result, he did virtually nothing to make desegregation of the nation's schools a reality, sending troops into Little Rock on 1957 only because the governor there, Orval Faubus, had directly challenged Ike's authority as commander-in-chief. Although the White House had been known since Teddy Roosevelt's days as a "bully pulpit," it was, according to historian William E. Leuchtenburg, "an empty pulpit" when Eisenhower was president. "It is not too much to say," he has written, "that a great deal of the violence, as well as the fearfully slow rate of compliance after 1954, may be laid at Eisenhower's door."

That left the battle back in the hands of the people, many of them average black citizens who had experienced the resurgent hopes borne of war and protest, now angered and frustrated by the failure of those in charge to open the corridors of power for equal participation or to follow through with actions consistent with their words. One of those people was Rosa Parks, a seamstress in Montgomery, Alabama. In December 1955 she did what countless black people had done before her—refused to abide by the Jim Crow regulations that required black customers to give up their bus seats to whites if the whites were left standing while blacks were seated. On most other occasions, those who protested were arrested, forced off the bus, or in some cases beaten or even murdered. But the time was different and Mrs. Parks was different. "She was decent," one leading Montgomery black noted. "And she was committed . . . nobody could point no dirt at her. . . . And when she did something, people just figured it was the right thing to do." So when Mrs. Parks was arrested, the community reacted as one. Within hours a mass church meeting was called, a committee was put in place, and the Montgomery bus boycott—which lasted for 381 days and involved well over 90 percent of Montgomery's black citizenry—began.

Significantly, the bus boycott brought together themes that spoke to the long history of black organization and resistance, even during the worst days of Jim Crow. Mrs. Parks was no newcomer to protest. A secretary of the Montgomery NAACP, she had long participated in black protest activities and had attended a workshop on race relations at the Highlander Folk Institute in Tennessee, a major incubator for social activism. Other actors in the drama carried similar credentials. Jo Ann Robinson, a leader of the local Women's Political Council (an organization in the black community similar to the segregated and all-white League of Women Voters) had developed a political network of women activists with a phone tree, ready to put into place a plan for community mobilization whenever necessary. She, in turn, had an additional ally in E. D. Nixon, head of the Montgomery chapter of the all-black Brotherhood of Sleeping Car Porter's Union (of which A. Phillip Randolph was president). Nixon was prepared to call out his troops on a moment's notice as well. Not even the idea of a bus boycott was new. Black leaders in Montgomery had been discussing the need to take action to end callous and discourteous treatment from white bus drivers for years and were just waiting for the right moment to express their grievances.

Thus when the protest began, it represented the crystallization of social forces already in place. Black institutions, headed by experienced activists who had thought through their agenda, were prepared to mobilize their resources. The genius—and difference—of the bus boycott was its ability to provide a vehicle for so many people to express their discontent; *and* the emergence of a vibrant young leader named Martin Luther King Jr., who discovered in his ruminations about how to justify breaking the law the philosophy of nonviolent resistance, rooted in the Christian Gospel, and informed by the impulse to speak truth to power through love. If the president of the United States was unwilling to expand the beachhead secured by the *Brown* decision, the average citizens of Montgomery would help transform that "landing force" of change into a real breakthrough.

A few short years later, a new generation of African Americans would carry that beachhead still further, once again using their experience and the training they received from the all black institutions in their community to forge a new language of protest and insistence on self-determination. The four first year students at Greensboro's North Carolina A&T University who began the sit-in movement had come of age at the time of the *Brown* decision. They grew up with the expectation that the world would change around them, but it did not. They also grew up with teachers, ministers, and parents who taught them the importance of standing up for their beliefs. Members of an NAACP Youth group, they met weekly to talk about events such as the Montgomery bus boycott. They also went to all-black schools where teachers like Nell Coley and Vance Chavis imparted a message of empowerment, Chavis by having his homeroom pupils address voter registration envelopes at the beginning of the day, Coley by using the texts in her English class to transmit the values of courage, honor, and sacrifice. The students went to a church pastored by a young minister who himself had led civil rights activities at all-black Shaw University in Raleigh, and who preached his own version of liberation theology—that the Gospel of Jesus was a Gospel of freedom and justice.

Using that framework of teaching and institutional strength as a departure point, the four freshmen started to debate their own responsibility to bring change where change had not yet happened. Lest they become complicit in perpetuating segregation, they concluded, they must do something to combat it. And so they struck on the simple but elegant tactic of highlighting the moral absurdity of segregation by being customers at the local five and dime, and demonstrating the immorality of being treated one way at one counter and a totally different way when they tried to buy food. They purchased paper and toilet products alongside other customers in the main part of the Woolworth's, then, with their receipts in hand, sat down at the lunch counter and asked for a cup of coffee. "We don't serve Negroes here," they were told. "But you served us over there," they pointed out.

Refusing to leave, the sit-in demonstrators took out their books and began to study. Four hours later the store closed. The next day, they were back, this time with twenty others. The day after that there were sixty-six, then the next day a hundred. And on the fifth day there were a thousand. Within eight weeks, sit-ins had erupted in fifty-four cities in nine states. In April the Student Non-Violent Coordinating Committee was founded—at Shaw University. The student phase of the civil rights revolution had begun—all as a product of growing up with clear values, strong teachers, and a sense of community support.

Rosa Parks, the Montgomery Bus Boycott, and the Greensboro sit-in movement represented the entry of new actors onto the stage of racial protest. Significantly, they were actors who accepted the values and principles of the American Dream and the American political system. Like the NAACP attorneys before them, they wished to join, not destroy or subvert, the existing structures of society. Integration, not separatism, represented their goal. They believed that by making their case fairly, showing their good faith as citizens, they could prove the merits of being accorded equal opportunity. All they wanted was the right to be treated as individuals, regardless of their race. In the opening dialectic between those who held power and the organizational representatives of the disenfranchised, the failure of those with authority to respond to legal petitioning created circumstances where others had to find new ways of expressing themselves. With voices of average people, even if taking the form of a new language, the protestors initiated a new dialectic. But it was one born out of conservative instincts and innocent faith in the capacity of the larger society to respond in a just and progressive way. If the first round of dialectical interaction had failed to generate consensus about a common ground, perhaps the second round would lead to clearer, more direct communication and a new and better understanding of how equality of opportunity could come to exist within a liberal tradition.

THE 1960S

On three occasions during the first half of the 1960s, there seemed moments of possibility that such understanding could emerge.

The first came shortly after the Kennedy administration took office in January 1961. Although neither John nor Robert Kennedy had ever spent much time thinking or worrying about civil rights, the issue had in fact played a pivotal role in John F. Kennedy's defeat of Richard Nixon. A black aide to Kennedy had written him a memo early in the campaign urging a "bold, national gesture" that would speak emotionally to black Americans. When Martin Luther King Jr. was arrested and sentenced to two months of hard labor in an Alabama jail, the opportunity suddenly emerged for precisely such a gesture. John Kennedy called Mrs. King to express his personal concern, and a day later his brother Robert called the sitting judge in the case and successfully sought King's release. The tide of the black vote suddenly shifted, and Kennedy rode to his narrow victory largely on the basis of African American votes.

Although Kennedy never mentioned civil rights in his inaugural address or followed through on his campaign pledges to take immediate executive action on civil rights issues such as desegregated housing, the Freedom Rides in the spring of 1961 provided another opportunity for the convergence of black aspirations and government response. Robert Kennedy immediately became intimately involved in the Freedom Ride protests. Enraged that the governors of Alabama and Mississippi refused to provide protection for civil rights pro testors who were simply exercising their right to ride integrated interstate buses, he worked the phones night and day. "After all," he said in one call, "these people have tickets and are entitled to transportation. . . . I am—the government is—going to be very much upset if this group does not get to continue their trip." Kennedy personally persuaded a bus driver to get behind the wheel so that the Freedom Rides could continue, and then, when further violence met the demonstrators when they arrived in Montgomery, he called out federal marshals to protect them. To be sure, Kennedy also berated the demonstrators for criticizing the government just when the president was ready to go abroad for the first time, but in this, the first domestic crisis of the Kennedy presidency, there seemed evidence of a growing passion and commitment on the part of at least some people in government for the cause of racial justice.

The second moment of possibility occurred in the spring and summer of 1963. Although the Kennedy administration had severely disappointed blacks with its failure in 1961 and 1962 to advance civil rights legislation or protect civil rights workers engaged in voter registration activities, the Justice Department had increased fivefold the number of voting rights suits, and had increased ten times its number of black attorneys. Still, until the spring of 1963, Martin Luther King Jr. was accurate when he stated that "if tokenism were the goal, the [Kennedy administration] has moved us adroitly toward it." Now, the explosion of demonstrations in Birmingham ("Bombingham," as it was known in the black community) changed all that. As Bull Connor's police dogs attacked women and children and firehoses pinned peaceful demonstrators against storefronts and walls with the force of their water pressure, the world—and Washington—awakened to both the searing brutality of racism and the moral imperative of bringing racial change.

The Kennedys finally understood that they had no choice but to join the cause. Mobilizing the entire administration, they lobbied with business and political leaders to promote desegregation. Between May and July, the president met with more than 1,600 leaders from religious, labor and business organizations, while Robert Kennedy orchestrated the day-to-day response of federal law enforcement officials to the ongoing crisis of the demonstrations. Culminating the administration's new sensitivity to the issue of civil rights, President Kennedy went on television in June, and in an extemporaneous address (his text was not ready by air time), for the first time embraced civil rights as "a moral issue, as old as the Scriptures and . . . as clear as the American Constitution." Who among us, he asked, "would be content to have the color of his skin changed and stand in the [Negro's] place? Who among us would then be content with the counsels of patience and delay?" Finally delivering on what he had so long promised, Kennedy proposed a major civil rights bill that would mandate desegregation of public accommodations, promote school integration, and outlaw discrimination in hiring based on race or sex. It was a major step forward, reinforced when the Kennedys ended up supporting the civil rights movement's March on Washington in August 1963, with the president hosting the leaders of the march after its conclusion.

The third moment of possibility—and perhaps the most symbolic—came in the spring of 1965 when Lyndon B. Johnson, who inherited the presidency after John F. Kennedy's assassination, personally embraced the civil rights cause as his own when he advocated transformative voting rights legislation before the U.S. Congress. Once again, of course, the precipitating cause was massive civil rights demonstrations. Thousands of civil rights protestors had descended on Selma, Alabama—with Sheriff Jim Clark playing the role that Bull Connor had played in Birmingham—to petition peacefully for the right to vote. Vicious beatings, and a near stampede of dogs and state police horses as peaceful demonstrators tried to cross the Pettis Bridge in Selma, brought the same kind of national outrage against white state authorities that had occurred two years earlier in Birmingham. Although the federal government had avoided full support of the demonstrators before and had in fact secured injunctions to prevent them from marching, Lyndon Johnson now changed his position. In language worthy of Lincoln, he told the Congress and the American people that for more than a hundred years blacks had been suppressed in their desire to become full citizens, and that the time had now come to right that wrong once and for all. Expressing his complete identification with the movement, Johnson closed his address by using the movement's slogan as his own, telling the nation, "We shall overcome."

Even as the apparent convergence of civil rights insurgents and administration officials reached a new high, however, the disconnect between grassroots experience and political power was already eroding the possibility of civil rights advocates finding satisfaction and fulfillment within the liberal tradition. The decade had begun with optimism and faith on the part of civil rights protestors. They believed that by simply pointing out the wrongs and dramatizing their absurdity and immorality, they would cause lasting and meaningful reform. Instead, all too often, government officials defaulted on promises, waffled on implementation of policies, and, on occasion, even actively opposed civil rights insurgents. Even those who epitomized white liberalism failed repeatedly to come through, acting as though they had the right and authority to dictate the pace of change and the terms under which it would occur. By mid-decade, a significant segment of the civil rights movement had determined that liberalism itself was the problem, and that only by taking charge—defining their own agenda—could they achieve true self-determination.

Part of that evolution reflected the daily frustration of the student portion of the civil rights movement with the failure of government officials to protect them. Some were already disillusioned with what they saw as the effort of adult leaders like Dr. King and Roy Wilkins to manipulate them, expressing, in Ella Baker's words, anger "when the prophetic leader turns out to have heavy feet of clay." But that frustration paled beside the rage they felt when local law enforcement officers oppressed them, and federal agents stood by and did nothing. After Hartman Turnbow tried to register to vote in Mileston, Mississippi, his home was attacked with a Molotov cocktail and his family fired upon. The next day, Turnbow was arrested, not the perpetrators. The charge: that he had burned his own home. When Fannie Lou Hamer went to fill out voter registration forms, she was evicted from her home, then later taken from a bus, jailed, and viciously beaten.

To all of this, the federal government seemed to turn a deaf ear. After whites in Ruleville, Mississippi, fired into the homes of local blacks who were assisting the civil rights movement, FBI agents suggested that the civil rights workers were trying to extort money and that *they* had done the shooting. State troopers in Selma brutally jabbed voter registration applicants with cattle prods and billyclubs, and all the FBI did was stand and watch. Even after repeated phone calls for federal assistance, it took hours for FBI officials to come and investigate imminent threats of violence to civil rights advocates. In Albany, Georgia, the federal government even sought indictments against some civil rights advocates for conducting a boycott of businesses that discriminated against blacks.

Symptomatic of the underlying grievance many blacks felt was the way that white liberals, at both the March on Washington and the Democratic national convention in 1964, insisted on depriving blacks of their own, independent voice and making them conform to white terms and standards. After white labor and religious leaders saw SNCC leader John Lewis's speech attacking established politicians of both parties for failing to address black grievances, they censored his remarks and threatened to abandon the platform unless Lewis accepted their revised language. In Atlantic City, at the Democratic convention of 1964, black insurgents tested the resolve of white liberals by seeking, through the Mississippi Freedom Democratic Party, to replace the all-white, segregated Mississippi delegation. They had collected reams of affidavits; they proved, by using the rules of the party, that they had been unfairly excluded; and they won the support of enough members of the credentials committee to send the issue to the floor for debate and resolution— until Lyndon Johnson concluded that this would upend *his* convention and threaten *his* control. Using every political weapon at his disposal, including threats to take federal jobs away from delegates, and having union leader Walter Reuther call in favors owed him and Johnson—and Hubert Humphrey, who was told a solution was the only way he could become vice president—Johnson eventually forced a "compromise" that allocated only two out of forty-eight delegate seats to the MFDP, and then did not even allow the MFDP to choose the two. The MFDP said no. "We didn't come all this way for no two votes," Fannie Lou Hamer said.

Finally, a growing economic radicalism took root among young activists in the movement. The more students from colleges, southern and northern, saw firsthand the poverty facing black southerners and the ways that credit, loans, and insurance policies were used to whip blacks into conformity with white expectation, the more they saw the economic system, as well as the political system, as part of the explanation for racism. Some, at least, began to ask why anyone would want to be integrated into a social and economic system that perpetuated such inequality. What was it worth to be able to eat at a Holiday Inn if one could not afford the meal? The desire for control over their own movement reinforced the evolving conviction that systemic, not incremental, change was the only answer. "In earlier days," Roger Wilkins, nephew of the NAACP leader Roy Wilkins, wrote, "the overwhelming majority of Negroes retained their profound faith in America [and] her institutions. . . . [Now] there is a growing view . . . that white people have embedded their flaws so deeply in the institutions that those institutions are beyond redemption."

Out of such experience emerged the political doctrine of the Black Power movement. More an expression of frustration than a coherent program of economic and social policies, Black Power spoke powerfully to the desire of many African Americans to be in charge of their own movement and aspirations. America, Stokely Carmichael declared, "does not function by morality, love and non-violence." So why should blacks wish to become assimilated into such a nation. Occurring, as it did, at the same time that race riots broke out in areas as different as Watts in Los Angeles and inner city ghettoes in Newark, Cleveland, and Detroit, Black Power—and companion developments such as the emergence of the Black Panther Party—signified the degree to which the hopeful optimism of the early 1960s had been displaced by voices of anger that saw little if any hope for finding common ground with the larger liberal tradition.

THE POST-1960S

Even if the development of Black Power reflected the sentiments of only a portion of the African American population, the experiences that shaped its emergence suggested a degree of fragmentation and division that made unlikely the convergence around a set of common policies that had once seemed possible in the late 1940s and early 1960s. Instead, it seemed, race remained a reality within American society that the liberal tradition could accommodate, at best, only partially. Notwithstanding remarkable gains, both politically and economically, for a segment of the black population, race conferred a group identity that did not easily give way to an ethos of individualism and equal opportunity. Controversy after controversy heightened sensitivity on the part of blacks as well as whites about the underlying resonance of race as a social dividing line. And the degree to which poverty, housing segregation, and educational experience still revolved around racial variables suggested that the dream of a liberal coalition that would transcend race was a long time away from being a possibility.

No one used the political volatility of race better than Richard Nixon. Although in the 1950s Nixon was one of the chief supporters of civil rights in the Eisenhower White House, by 1968 he had become a specialist in using racial code words as a rallying cry for a conservative political resurgence. Issuing scathing denunciations of forced busing to desegregate schools, Nixon not too subtly suggested that he would cease heeding black America's call for change by focusing on the "restoration of law and order" as his chief priority. "As we look at America," he proclaimed, "we see cities enveloped in smoke and flame. We hear sirens in the night. We see Americans hating each other. And . . . millions of Americans cry out in anger: Did we come all this way for this?" Nixon pledged to speak on behalf of "the non-shouters, the non-demonstrators . . . those who do not break the law," the great silent majority. He did not have to use the words "black" or "Negro." It was all too clear who he was talking about, who his foil was. And blacks as well as whites got the message.

As another measure of the ongoing and divisive salience of race for both blacks and whites, affirmative action became—with abortion—the single most polarizing issue in American society. Started in the mid-1960s by JFK and LBJ as a policy of seeking the inclusion of blacks in employment pools, affirmative action by the 1970s had come to mean, for whites, quotas, preferential treatment, and mandated violations of equal employment procedures in order to give blacks something they did not deserve; for blacks, on the other hand, affirmative action was a critical and necessary intervention to reverse centuries of discrimination by making employers look carefully at qualified black candidates for positions that were open. The courts for the most part upheld affirmative action policies, especially where a history of proven discrimination existed, but the larger battle was in the symbolism of using race as a category of political decision-making. Even though for centuries laws had been made solely based on race—slavery and Jim Crow as prime examples—now it became un-American to use the same criterion for seeking to redress injustice. When in the 1970s network news anchors first started to use the phrase "reverse discrimination" as a synonym or descriptor of affirmative action, the cultural war was over. Blacks had lost, and they knew it, even if the policy of affirmative action itself had made a significant difference in the jobs many middle-class blacks, in particular, now occupied.

Perhaps the most enduring manifestation of race as a shaping issue in America was the dividing line that separated those African Americans who

enjoyed new opportunities to move to the suburbs, hold good jobs, and secure a decent education, and those who remained totally outside the mainstream, isolated by their race, class, and gender from even a chance to make
it in America. On the one hand, the proportion of blacks earning a middle-
class income increased 250 percent from 1960 to the mid-1970s. Black enrollments in colleges leaped fivefold. But on the other hand, the unemployment rate for blacks in inner city ghettoes was more than 30 percent, high
school dropout rates approached 50 percent, and the number of children
born out of wedlock in the black community went from 17 percent in 1950
to nearly 60 percent by 1990. Almost a third of black America lived in poverty
in the 1970s and '80s, with a new category of black female-headed households providing the major reason.

None of these trend lines shifted during the '80s and '90s. The bifurca-
tion of the black community by income and education accelerated rather
than diminished over time, with nearly two-thirds of black births in 2000
taking place in single-parent households. Affirmative action—or "reverse
discrimination," as most whites called it—continued to divide the population providing a lightning rod for both white conservatives such as Pat
Buchanan on one hand and black protestors such as Al Sharpton on the other
George Bush's use of the Willie Horton ad in the 1988 election—a black
convict, given weekend leave in Mike Dukakis's Massachusetts, who subsequently raped a white woman in Maryland—demonstrated the political
capital that could be seized by, once again, making race a dividing point in
political decision making.

Although many social scientists now talked about the "declining significance of race"— William Julius Wilson's phrase—two events in the 1990s
suggested that announcing the demise of race as a pivotal issue in America
was premature. In the early 1990s, Rodney King, a black man with a record
of minor criminal violations, was chased by Los Angeles police for a speeding violation. Subsequently, as recorded by an amateur photographer using a
new video camera, police officers with billyclubs subdued King on the
ground and struck him sixty-five times. When the officers were put on trial,
an overwhelmingly white jury decided that no brutality had occurred, despite the videotape.

A few years later, O. J. Simpson, the famous black football player and commentator, was arrested and charged with brutally murdering his ex-wife and
her companion. A record of previous domestic violence was established, with
911 calls from Nicole Simpson. Most important, DNA evidence directly linked
Simpson with the murder. Yet an overwhelmingly black jury acquitted Simp-

son, convinced that white police had framed him. Two-thirds of black Americans thought Simpson was innocent. Two-thirds of white Americans thought he was guilty. Two cases, one with videotape, one with DNA—both the equivalent of eyewitness testimony—each decided on the basis of race. It was not necessarily a good omen for those who believed in the liberal tradition.

CONCLUSION

What would have been required for liberalism to have passed successfully the test posed by the issue of race? Clearly, the total elimination of race as a category conferring group identity represents a utopian idea. Given the plethora of ethnic traditions in the United states, the persistence of cultural differences and collective pride in one's origins should be a source of strength, not weakness. Nor is there an inherent inconsistency between embracing the values of individualism and equal opportunity on one hand and celebration of group identity on the other. The key, then, is not the elimination of race as a concept conferring difference and identity, but rather the elimination of race as an automatic signifier of inequality and invidious treatment.

For that to have happened, the chasm between white leaders and black activists would have to close, and the disconnect between the average black person's daily experience and the pronouncements of public policymakers come to an end. There appeared to be moments in the post-1930s world when that kind of bridging might have been possible. The rhetoric surrounding President Truman's Committee on Civil Rights, and the strength of biracial liberalism at the 1948 Democratic convention offered hope. But then action failed to follow words, and in an age permeated by anticommunism and the fear that any criticism of America might be punished as giving aid to the enemy, that moment passed, with reliance on the courts the only viable means of seeking change.

Then again in the early 1960s, particularly in 1961, 1963, and 1965, there were occasions when white and black political leaders came together, and when even the dialectic between average insurgents and public policymakers seemed on the path to open communication, trust and synthesis. The Kennedy administration's responsiveness to the Freedom Rides and the Birmingham demonstrations—although only partial—provided hope that there could be more follow-through in the future and that a new coalition might be born. The same sense of optimism seemed warranted when Lyndon Johnson made voting rights a cause that he personally embraced, even though the foundations of a liberal coalition were already crumbling.

But in the end, the follow-through proved inadequate, leaders faltered under the ongoing temptation to use race as a negative wedge that would bring temporary political advantage, and the disconnect between average people's daily experience and the words that supposedly guided government policy became deeper and wider. Persistence, consistency, and vision were all necessary if the promise of incorporating racial equality within a liberal tradition were to be realized. If there had been agreement to "keep your eye on the prize," and that prize were defined as making race a positive value within a commitment to equal opportunity, the test that race posed for liberalism might have been passed. Instead, the moments of brightness became shadowed by longer periods of darkness, and the gap between leaders and the experience of average citizens widened. Ultimately, race was the Achilles heel of the liberal tradition, challenging its capacity to grow and to evolve organically in service to democratic values. It remains so in a new century, still challenging leaders and average citizens to redeem the original sin of American democracy.

7

AFRICAN AMERICANS, AMERICAN JEWS, AND THE HOLOCAUST

Harvard Sitkoff

African Americans and Jewish Americans have together journeyed a long, twisted path of enmities and empathies. Jews who currently oppose black goals as well as those who bemoan the dissolution of the civil rights alliance each have their antecedents to emulate, much as anti-Semitic African Americans and blacks who decry such prejudice each have their precedents to employ. Their joint, disjointed history points in no single direction. Today the media trumpet the views of African Americans praising Adolf Hitler or those claiming for themselves a greater victimization than that suffered by Jews during what we now call the Holocaust [1] Today Jews loudly condemn blacks for trivializing the Holocaust, for not recognizing its uniqueness. Little is heard of the 1930s and 1940s, a time when there was more black anti-Semitism and more Jewish racism among the mass of blacks and Jews as there is now, yet when leaders of both communities, despite being shaped by different historical and personal experiences, sought to make common cause against the common enemy of intolerance and hatred. Both saw themselves as objects of persecution and each other as means to ends. As opportunistic as they were dissimilar, they developed an organizational alliance to achieve acceptance and equality of opportunity in American society.[2]

Nazi and Fascist anti-Semitism in the 1930s, and especially the horrors of the Holocaust, proved central to that development and the coming of age of the modern civil rights movement. Jews became more sensitive to cries of injustice, more ready for alliances with other underdogs. News of the Holocaust also made some other Americans uneasy or guilty about their own racist beliefs and practices. And all the condemnations of Hitlerism by American government officials and shapers of public opinion, all the Allied talk of fighting a war against doctrines of racial superiority, fueled the righteous insistence of African Americans to end racism in the United States. African American leaders, particularly in the National Association for the Advancement of Colored People (NAACP), used Hitlerism and the Holocaust to generate concern for the plight of blacks and support for the cause of civil rights. They repeatedly pointed to what was happening to European Jewry as a means of advancing their own domestic agenda. They established an analogy between racial practices in Nazi Germany and those in the Jim Crow South to clarify and dramatize the nature of American racism to their fellow Americans. By linking the odious Nazism with Jim Crowism, these African Americans sought to make racial discrimination and segregation similarly anathema and to convince the white majority of the justness of their cause.[3]

Benito Mussolini helped them considerably. Regarding Africans as "inferior beings" and seeing himself as defending "western civilization against the colored races," Il Duce's forces attacked Ethiopia in October 1935, slaughtering defenseless children and women in the country many African Americans regarded as the "Black Zion." Mussolini then issued a Manifesto of Fascist Racism declaring theories of racial equality "absolutely inadmissible," branding the so-called Semitic and Hamitic (that is, black) races as inherently inferior, and insisting that the purity of the blood of the superior white race not be polluted by miscegenation with blacks or Jews. The Italian Ministry for Africa claimed proudly: "Italy is the first European nation to uphold the universal principle of the superiority of the white race."[4]

If not quite first, Hitler and the Nazis went even further to avoid "racial contamination" by inferiors. Coming to power in 1933, they used the power of the state and their own paramilitary organizations to assault German Jews, boycott their businesses, and discriminate against them. Then the Law for the Protection of German Blood and Honor and the Third Reich Citizenship Law (the Nuremberg Laws of September 1935) defined Jews by ancestry rather than religion, outlawed marriages and sexual intercourse between Jews and non-Jews, stripped Jews of most rights of German citizenship, and increased earlier restrictions on Jews in all spheres of German educational, social, and economic life. The Nazi government also established an Office for Racial Policy to see that the master race of Aryans was not contaminated by racial inferiors; and, on November 9–10, 1938, unleashed *Kristallnacht* (Night of the Broken Glass), a pogrom of arson, destruction, and looting against Jews. Following the invasion of the Soviet Union in 1941, Hitler authorized the creation of *Einsatzgruppen* (special mobile units) to accompany the German army and execute Jews. By year's end they had systematically murdered more than half a million "racial inferiors" in occupied Russia. By then, as well, the Nazis had begun to experiment at Chelmno in Poland with mass executions carried out by means of gas. In January 1942 Nazi officials met at Lake Wannsee, near Berlin, to coordinate the *Endlosung*, the "Final Solution of the Jewish Question." The gassing of prisoners at Auschwitz-Birkenau, Belzec, Majdanek, Sobibor, and Treblinka now became a round-the-clock phenomenon, murdering more than three million people, mostly Jews. Not till the approach of the Soviet armies from the east did the Nazis abandon their Polish "death camps" and march the surviving Jewish, Gypsy, Jehovah's Witnesses, Serb, homosexual, and other "antisocial" prisoners to concentration camps in Germany, where millions more died of disease, exposure, and starvation en route to and in Bergen-Belsen, Buchenwald, Dachau, Mauthausen, Nordhausen, and Sachsenhausen. It was the ultimate triumph of racism in practice.[5]

As soon as Hitler and the Nazis began their harassment of German Jewry, African American newspapers began highlighting the similarities of discriminations and oppressions in the United States and in Germany. Most of their editorials prior to 1936, however, were not at all sympathetic to the plight of German Jewry. The Great Depression engendered enormous anti-Semitism in the United States—by whites and blacks. Well over a hundred new anti-Semitic organizations were established in the second half of the 1930s alone, compared to just fourteen between 1915 and 1933. Indeed, throughout the 1930s and World War II most Americans were neither deeply touched nor troubled by the news about Jews coming out of Europe. A majority believed that Nazi persecution of the German Jews was either partly or entirely the Jews' own fault—their being too powerful, their running the economy, their being too radical. Few considered the plight of European Jewry their plight too. Until May 1945 many remained unaware, did not care, or thought the killing of European Jews a Jewish problem for Jews to solve. Most African Americans, accepting the dominant culture's values and prejudices concerning Jews, followed suit. An amalgam of religious folk beliefs and economic woes compounded their antipathy. Like many Germans and white Christian Americans, blacks viewed Jews as infidels, usurers, Christ-killers. Moreover, to the average African American tenant the Jew was the landlord, to the black worker he was the boss, to the black customer the Jew was the shopkeeper, and to the black domestic the Jew was the stingy woman whose house she cleaned. Still others condemned Jewish organizations in the United States for being blind to American racism, resented the attention paid to German Jewry while the plight of African Americans went ignored, and feared that a focus on anti-Semitism drew energy away from the struggle against Jim Crow.

Anti-Semitism also allowed African Americans to give vent to pent-up hostilities and indulge a sense of imaginary superiority. Thus, the *Philadelphia Tribune* warned its readers that "most of what is told about Jewish treatment in Germany is propaganda since the Jews control to a great extent the international press" and opined that to "be a Jew in Germany is hell," but "to be a Negro in America is twice as bad." The *New York Age* added: "If the Jewish merchants in Germany treated German workers as Blumsteins treat the people of Harlem, then Hitler is right." Not surprisingly, in September 1933, W. E. B. Du Bois responded with what he called "unholy glee" to the treatment of Jews by his beloved Germans: "When the only 'inferior' peoples were 'niggers' it was hard to get the attention of *The New York Times* for little matters of race, lynching and mobs. But now that the damned included the owner of the *Times,* moral indignation is perking up."[6]

More explicitly anti-Semitic than Du Bois were the black nationalist "don't buy where you can't work" campaigns. Marcus Garvey and Carlos Cooks, the leader of the neo-Garveyite African Nationalist Pioneer Movement, blamed the Jews, as lovers of money, for their own persecution. Sufi Abdul Hamid (labeled "a black Hitler" by Adam Clayton Powell Jr.), became a regular fixture on Harlem street corners in the 1930s, fulminating against Jewish merchants and employers while sporting a Nazi-like uniform. The Negro tabloid *Dynamite* declared: "What America needs is a Hitler and what the Chicago Black Belt needs is a purge of the exploiting Jew." In Baltimore, at an African American forum on Germany's treatment of the Jews, the audience burst into applause when a speaker praised Hitler's actions. And when Harlemites rioted in 1935, and then again in 1943, Jewish merchants were the chief target of their wrath.[7]

Indeed, much of the black press initially put the onus of Nazism on the Jews themselves, claimed that German Jewry suffered less than African Americans, argued against aiding Hitler's victims since Jews did not assist blacks, and, most emphatically, emphasized the hypocrisy of those denouncing Germany's treatment of Jews but not the oppression of blacks in the United States. Because Jews would not hire Negroes in their stores, opined the *Baltimore Afro-American*, in those stores "you will find Hitlerism in its most blatant form exercised by those who are being Hitlerized in Germany." American Jews, wrote the *St. Louis Argus,* use "the same tactics and methods to persecute and discriminate against Negroes" that Hitler uses against German Jews. "Why shed crocodile tears over the fate of the Jews in Berlin when here in America we treat black folk in the same manner every day?" the *Oklahoma City Black Dispatch* asked. "Why the comparison is so definite and clear," it added, "we are almost wont to feel Germans secured the pattern of Nazi violence visited upon the Jews from white America." The *Cincinnati Union* had no doubt that in segregating Jews Germany was "taking a leaf from the book of many American cities." Complaining that African Americans had to endure greater persecution "under American Hitlers," the *Amsterdam News* sneered at those rallying to save Europe's Jews "while Negroes were lynched, beaten and burned." "Just how we can charge and snort about Fascism abroad and practice it here" disgusted the *Des Moines Iowa Bystander*. The *Louisiana Weekly* insisted that, given the racism in the United States, Germany had "a right to look askance at any criticism leveled at its persecution of unfavored people." "We're tired of reading our favorite dailies and their editorials about Hitler and his Nazis," the *New York Age* chimed in: "It's about time that the papers stayed out of the internal affairs of other nations and that they help the United States first sweep its own doors clean." All too commonly in the 1930s, Chandler Owen summed up, Negroes could be heard saying "well, Hitler did one good thing: he put these Jews in their place."[8]

The black nationalist J. A. Rogers and the scholarly Kelly Miller reiterated these views in newspaper column after column. So did conservative George Schuyler. Traveling in Mississippi in 1935, Schuyler found "that Negroes of all classes from peons to planters are quite unconcerned about either the spread of fascism or the fate of the Jews. Indeed I am not at all exaggerating when I state that a surprising number of articulate Negroes seem to derive a sort of grim satisfaction from the Nazi persecution of the Jews. They contend that their local jews have been indistinguishable from the 'crackers' in their attitude toward Negroes. . . . They cannot see why, they contend, that under the circumstances they should get excited about the fate of German Jews." Neither did Schuyler. He remained indignant that the American press paid more attention to the persecution of German Jews than to the lynchings of Negroes and wrote in the *Courier*: "I would be able to wail a lot louder and deeper if American Jews would give more concrete evidence of being touched by the plight of Negroes. . . . If my Hebrew friends were only as quick to employ capable Negroes as they are other people and did not get so excited when a decent family moves in their districts, I could pray even harder for Hitler to let up on them." Adam Clayton Powell Jr. concurred. He termed Jewish merchants "the criminals of Harlem," and challenged "Jews to stop crying over German Jews and get an anti-lynch law passed." In response to an appeal from the Central Conference of American Rabbis for a "reconciliation of the proverbial friendship of our two peoples," he retorted that Negro anti-Semitism was regrettable "but the Jew himself was its author." And criticizing President Franklin Roosevelt's decision to admit some additional Jewish refugees in 1938, Powell complained that as soon as they "were off the boat most of them would settle in the Bronx Alps" and take the jobs that Negroes deserved to have.[9]

Various officials of the NAACP echoed such sentiments. Roy Wilkins thought that Jews were paying too much attention to "exaggerated charges of Nazi persecution and not enough to persecuted Negroes," and that the government was doing too much to help European Jews instead of African Americans. "Our sometimes friends," Wilkins said of Jews, "ask us to fight Nazism." But too many Jews, he continued, "never gave a dollar bill to fight lynching or break down prejudice in employment." Walter White, the NAACP's executive secretary, privately considered African American anti-Semitism "legitimate," a justified response to Jewish exploitation of and discrimination against blacks. He chided Jews for "doing to Negroes what they object to others doing to them." He denied the notion that the increasingly prosperous and prominent Jews were "in the same boat" as the poor, isolated Negroes. And he scorned those who protested against Hitlerism but failed to demand that the United States first end its own persecution of minorities. As late as December 1948, in a letter to a friend, White reiterated that Jewish merchants cheat blacks, that Jewish-owned theaters segregate them, that Jews in Hollywood stereotype African Americans, and that Jews contribute charitably only to atone for their anti-Negro prejudices. White ended the letter with a reminder that he had been candid because the correspondence was private: "I would not want to say such things publicly."[10]

Publicly, White and the NAACP expressed dramatically opposite views. Almost from the very start of Hitler's persecution of German Jews, when the Association was virtually alone in the black community in supporting campaigns to boycott German goods and the 1936 Olympics in Berlin, the NAACP focused on the plight of the Jews as a way of drawing attention to racial practices in the American South. The "unholy glee" of Du Bois lost out to the strategy enunciated in 1933 by William Pickens that the NAACP use a condemnation of Hitlerism to condemn Jim Crow, draw an analogy between the Ku Klux Klan and the Nazi Party, and demand of the American people whether or not they favor maintaining racial practices in the South just like Hitler's racist practices in Germany. Official NAACP resolutions and editorials in the NAACP's *The Crisis* as early as mid-1933 denounced the vicious prejudice directed against Jews by Hitler and equated Nazism with American racism, intending that those who abhorred the former would detest the latter. Pickens hoped that Americans would not favor maintaining racial practices at home that were just like Nazism. Added Walter White: the NAACP needs "to utilize the present and wise concern over anti-Semitism to call attention more vigorously than ever before to bigotry against the Negro here."[11]

Accusing the Nazis of "barbarism" over and again in the 1930s, White publicly expressed "wholehearted contempt for, and condemnation of, the unspeakable terror now being inflicted upon the Jewish people in Germany by the sadistic Nazi government." Again and again he pointed to developments in Germany to fortify his case for abolishing racial discrimination in the United States. To arouse opposition to Jim Crow he emphasized the fundamental similarity between racial practices in both countries, scorned the "counterpart of Hitlerism existing in the United States," and called upon all Americans, especially minorities, to fight fascism abroad and atrocities at home. "We Negroes know what this means since it has happened to us," White said of *Kristallnacht*, "what happens to one minority can happen to others—a lesson which Jews, Negroes, and all minorities must learn." While frequently associating himself and the NAACP with those protesting Hitler's treatment of the Jews, White never ceased equating Nazi anti-Semitism with American racism, with demands that Americans "clean up our own backyard." When New York City Mayor LaGuardia called for a protest rally at Carnegie Hall to denounce Hitler's persecution of Jews, White telegraphed him and the announced participants about the upsurge of lynchings against blacks, expressing his hope "you and other speakers will stress need of simultaneous American action to wipe out bigotry or racial hatred no matter who are the victims nor where such bigotry and oppression exist, including our own country." He publicly mocked Senator William King of Utah for failing to support antilynching legislation while wanting the United States to sever relations with Germany to protest Nazi atrocities. And concerning the admission of Jewish refugees, White wrote Secretary of State Cordell Hull that the NAACP shared the President's "reported indignation at the outrages being perpetrated upon minorities by the Nazi government. But we would be even more enthusiastic if our government could be equally indignant at the lynching, burning alive, and torture with blowtorchers of American citizens by American mobs on American soil which have shamed America before the world for a much longer time than persecution under Adolf Hitler."[12]

Resolutions adopted at the NAACP annual conferences throughout the decade mirrored White's efforts to equate the oppression of Jews and African Americans and to use events in Europe to change public attitudes in the United States. Numerous articles and editorials in *The Crisis* did so as well. Far more than most non-Jewish publications, *The Crisis* forthrightly expressed "profound and poignant sympathy" for the plight of European Jewry, as well as claiming that blacks felt that way more than most Americans because "they have known the same type of persecution ever since the beginning of America," because "Negroes are persecuted here in much the same manner that 'non-Aryans' are persecuted in Central Europe." Both are "segregated, humiliated, and terrorized." African American "feelings go out to the Jews. They know what Hitler means because they have known slave overseers, plantation riding bosses, high sheriffs." And: "Maybe some day we will see that until a Negro can freely study medicine at, say, the University of Michigan, we cannot make a convincing argument as to why Jews should be permitted to study at Heidelberg; or that until we stamp out the rope and the faggot as amusements for sections of our population, we cannot make a good case against the cruelties of Storm Troopers." And: "The tales of humiliation, terror and cruelty have a familiar ring to us. We know all about being driven off the streets, having our women kicked and beaten, being barred from public places, being at the mercy of hoodlums and bloodthirsty mobs, having 'scientists' prove us something less than human, being restricted in employment and residence, having separate schools set up for us, having our youth put on a quota basis in colleges and universities, and hearing and reading violent tirades against our race." And: "The only essential difference between a Nazi mob hunting down Jews in Central Europe and an American mob burning black men at the stake in Mississippi is that one is actually encouraged by its national government and the other is merely tolerated." Thus, to highlight the harms done by American racism *The Crisis* spotlighted Nazi terrorism. And, by emphasizing the shared oppression of Jews and African Americans, *The Crisis* message, explicitly and implicitly, was that minorities must "unite to fight the spread of Hitlerism."[13]

To underscore that tenet, *The Crisis* published numerous articles in the 1930s by prominent American Jews. Most, like Rabbi Stephen S. Wise's address to the 1934 NAACP Annual Meeting, centered on the common plight of the two minorities. A series by Jacob J. Weinstein spelled out the need for the two to work together against discrimination and prejudice in the United States. And to illustrate that they had done just that in the past, another series featured rabbis who had championed the cause of freedom and citizenship for black slaves, Jewish abolitionists, and Jews who fought alongside John Brown in Kansas. It concluded: "Jews and Negroes, because they often face identical problems and because they embrace a common destiny as victims of prejudice and bigotry," should therefore stand together—"the struggle for racial equality is indivisible." *The Crisis* also made the argument for an African American–Jewish American alliance by reprinting editorials from the Jewish press that called upon Jews to shed their racist prejudices and to fight with blacks for their common goals. In "We Must Stand Together," the *Jewish Frontier* acknowledged the need for African Americans to give voice to their own grievances while condemning German anti-Semitism, and emphasized that Jews and blacks should struggle together against racial discrimination and bigotry. Likewise, *The Reconstructionist* proclaimed that now was the time for blacks to insist that the United States put its "own house in order and wipe out every last vestige of anti-Negro discrimination," and that "If the injustices inflicted upon Jews in Germany will arouse the conscience of America to do justice to the Negro racial minority, it will be some consolation to us Jews." The Jewish editorial concluded: "Both self-interest and our holiest traditions demand our making common cause with the Negro in his fight for equality."[14]

Despite the widespread prejudices among the masses of both African Americans and American Jews, opposition to Hitlerism by their leaderships, to help their own causes, had begun to forge a commonality of purpose. Especially in New York City, which had large communities of blacks and Jews and was home to most of the major betterment and rights organizations of both groups, a common agenda emerged. The *American Hebrew* newspaper asked, "If Mussolini's fascism and Hitler's Nazism can join forces, why shouldn't their joint victims, Negroes and Jews ally to fight them?" And no less than the NAACP, National Urban League director Lester Granger, and the League's journal, *Opportunity,* answered affirmatively for such an alliance to "erase the shadow of the Swastika from our land." Utilizing the same analogies and arguments as the NAACP, the NUL condemned Nazi actions against German Jews while emphasizing the similarity of oppression of Jews and African Americans. Never failing to remind its readers that racial prejudice was just as sordid and cruel when directed against Mississippi blacks as against German Jews, the League also condemned black anti-Semitism, urging African Americans to combat it wherever it appeared.[15]

So did many other African American community leaders. Adam Clayton Powell Jr. was among those who took the lead in fighting anti-Semitism. He announced that the same psychology underlay prejudice against blacks and

Jews and that Hitler's persecution of Jewry and the plight of African Americans were inextricably intertwined. And he called repeatedly for a black-Jewish alliance "to stop Fascism." Ralph Bunche similarly assailed black anti-Semitism while stressing that the problems of both Jews and African Americans, "their grievances and their fears are cut to a common pattern." Many followed in linking Hitler's actions with the need for Jews and blacks to, in William Pickens phrase, "stand with unbroken ranks side by side."[16]

To underscore its necessity and the similarity of persecution, African Americans took to labeling racism in the United States as just a variant of Hitlerism. The *Baltimore Afro-American* termed the white South and Nazi Germany as "mental brothers," the oppression of blacks as "American Nazism," and the exclusion of African Americans from a college as "Nazis at Williams." "From the way Hitler talks," it editorialized, "one would think he is a member of the Ku Klux Klan and a native of Alabama." Indeed, the *Afro-American* christened Hitler as the Imperial Wizard of the German Ku Klux Klan, and columnist Kelly Miller termed him "the master Ku Kluxer of Germany."

Numerous editorial cartoons depicted Hitler as a Klansman and Klansmen as wearing swastikas, much as Nazis were transformed into "Crackers" and southern racists into Nazis (different names, said the *Afro-American*, but the "same result"). In like manner, the *Amsterdam News* called the exclusion of blacks from the major leagues "Nazism in Baseball," racial segregation as "Nazism in America," and the refusal of the Daughters of the American Revolution to permit Marian Anderson to sing in Constitution Hall as "Nazism in Washington." Lynch mobs, added *The Crisis*, were storm troopers; terrorist attacks on Negroes who sought to vote in Brownsville, Tennessee, the "work of Himmler's Gestapo;" and such terms as "Gestapo in Memphis," "the Himmler of the U.S.A.," and "Fuehrer Crump" were the way a *Crisis* writer referred to the police of Memphis, its police chief, and mayor. Despite the estrangement between the mass of African Americans and the mass of American Jews, despite the disparity of their progress into the American mainstream, their mutual identification as victims of discrimination and oppression now held sway. As Scottsboro lawyer Samuel Leibowitz exclaimed to a Harlem Elk's Convention, in urging them to reject anti-Semitism: "Both of us, Negroes and Jews are in the same boat together."[17]

Once the war in Europe began, censorship in Germany and the lands it occupied, as well as its desire to keep its mass murder of Jews secret, brought a diminution in news of Nazi persecution in both the Negro press and mainstream American press. But what was known, however fragmentary and piecemeal, caused some African American organizations and periodicals to increase their efforts to place the black struggle for justice and equality in an international context and to solidify the emerging leadership alliance of Jews and African Americans. Even more than in the 1930s, *The Crisis* employed the imagery of odious Nazism to call attention to American racism, to convince the white majority of the justness of the NAACP's reform cause. Segregation in the armed forces was "America's Mein Kampf," violence against black servicemen was Hitlerism or the work of "cracker Fascists," anti-black rioters in Detroit were referred to as "Nazi-minded mobsters," and, almost without fail, Mississippi's white supremacist Senators Bilbo and Eastland were labeled "America's Hitler and Goebbels." Similarly, the Urban League's *Opportunity* entitled an article on Governor Eugene Talmadge "A Georgia Hitler." More than a year after the war ended *The Crisis* continued to describe the KKK as Nazis and to accuse it of trying to build "an American *Volkstaat*." The monthly kept labeling white supremacists as fascists or Nazis, and described violence against African Americans as "Southern *Schrecklichkeit*."[18]

Knowing well the claim of the *Amsterdam News* in 1942 that "there never has been such general anti-Semitic sentiment in Harlem as exists right now," and the 1943 warning of the *Pittsburgh Courier* of "the dangerous and disastrous spread of anti-Semitism among Negroes," those African Americans engaged in the wartime crusade for civil rights nevertheless sought to exorcise prejudice against Jews. Describing anti-Semitism in the United States as "doing Hitler's work here at home," *The Crisis* observed that anti-Semitic actions in Boston and New York seemed "like something out of Berlin and Warsaw." The cause of each minority is the cause of all minorities, it continued, and "every beating of a Jewish child is an invitation to the lyncher of Negroes." At its 1944 annual conference, the NAACP adopted a resolution to eliminate anti-Semitism among Negroes. Among other prominent African Americans, Langston Hughes, Paul Robeson and Adam Clayton Powell Jr. concurred with Walter White's assertions that anti-Semitism and racism are the same kinds of bigotry, and that blacks indulging in anti-Semitism are playing Hitler's game. So did the Urban League, which established volunteer Service Councils to better relations between blacks and Jews." No Negro is secure from intolerance and race prejudice," summed up A. Philip Randolph at a Madison Square Garden rally of the March-on-Washington Movement, "as long as one Jew is a victim of anti-Semitism."[19]

Shortly after the United States entered the war, the NAACP Board of Directors pledged "its unqualified and unlimited effort on behalf of the persecuted Jews of the world, which includes anti-Semitism in the United States as well as slaughter in Poland." Little more was said or done for almost a year, until December 1942 when a delegation of representatives from major Jewish organizations submitted a memorandum to President Franklin Roosevelt on the deliberate, systematic annihilation of European Jewry. Using the information supplied by the World Jewish Congress, the American Jewish Congress (AJC) publicized news of the Holocaust and communicated hurriedly with the NAACP concerning it. As Rabbi Stephen Wise wrote Walter White in mid-December, there will be no Jews left in Europe at the end of the war unless the NAACP "associate itself with the action to prevent Hitler from accomplishing his purposes." At its next meeting, the NAACP Board adopted a resolution that it stands "appalled at the cold-blooded campaign of extermination of the Jews," and that it will do whatever it could to end this slaughter. Thereafter, White and other prominent African Americans joined with major labor, religious, and liberal spokesmen at emergency conferences to save the Jews of Europe and appealed for action to stop the extermination of the Jews. They pledged "to do whatever we can to help rescue Jews from the clutches," knowing, as White wrote the AJC that "if Jews can be slaughtered today," Negroes will be tomorrow. And they contributed financially toward the relief of Jews overseas, knowing, in Lester Granger's words, its importance "as another means of building goodwill between American Negroes and their fellow-citizens of Jewish faith."[20]

As the Holocaust intensified the insecurity felt by African American and American Jewish leaders, both reached out to the other. Jewish publications featured articles by and about African Americans. Editorials in the Jewish press, like "Defend the Negro," sent by the Independent Jewish Press Service to all its subscriber newspapers, made the case for the civil rights of blacks. Numerous essayists stressed the commonality of African American and Jewish needs and goals, as did editorial cartoons, such as the *Jewish Survey*'s "Help Wanted—No Negroes, No Jews." That magazine similarly featured a picture of a Negro and a Jewish soldier, arms intertwined, in the battle against Nazism. Also in 1942, the Central Conference of American Rabbis began to adopt annual resolutions deploring discrimination against blacks and promising support in the struggle for black equality. In 1942 it issued a "Justice for Negroes" message calling upon Jews, "who ourselves have been victims of injustice," to combat African American inequities. American rabbis then inaugurated an annual "Race Relations Sabbath." The Bronx Rabbinic Council joined with the National Council of Jewish Women to campaign for the fair treatment of Negro domestics. American Jewish Congress youth groups sponsored interracial forums and prepared petitions protesting racial discrimination. Numerous Jewish and black organizations featured speakers from the other race. Interracial Committees, Councils Against Intolerance in America, and Committees for Racial and Religious Understanding, largely composed of Jews and African Americans, became ubiquitous.[21]

Both black and Jewish leaders endorsed what Louis Reddick called "the establishment of an all out alliance." W. H. Jernigin, national chairman of the Fraternal Council of Negro Churches, urged African Americans and Jews "to unite in a common cause against Hitlerism," striking hard and quickly against racial and religious discrimination. So did the editors of the *Jewish Forward* and the *Jewish Survey*, arguing that "both their fates were becoming inextricably intertwined" and they needed to overcome their mutual oppressors. Jointly discussing the possibility of alliance, Rabbi Lou Silberman and Walter White agreed on the necessity of blacks and Jews pooling "our intelligence and idealism not only to defeat the Hitlers and the Rankins of the world, but to root out the prejudices from our own hearts." And in addresses to the NAACP, an American Jewish Congress officer described how the fate of Jews and African Americans "dovetailed," requiring that they work together to challenge their common oppressors.[22]

In 1944 the American Jewish Congress established a Commission on Community Interrelations, under social psychologist Kurt Lewin, to eliminate conflict between minority groups. It worked with the NAACP, as did the AJC's Commission on Law and Legislation (changed to Commission on Law and Social Action in November 1945). Headed by Will Maslow, the Commission on Law and Social Action combated discrimination in employment, education, and housing against blacks as well as Jews. By so doing, by seeking to promote civil rights for all minorities, Rabbi Wise wrote the NAACP's Thurgood Marshall, the fight against anti-Semitism is bound up "with the fight for the status and rights of all minority groups in this country." Thus, the 1945 platform of the AJC, "Full Equality in a Free Society," promised Negroes "that in all the causes for which they struggle they can count upon finding the Jews and the American Jewish Congress on the side of justice." Morality and self-interest had intersected. A marriage of convenience, said Will Maslow: "It was in our interest to help them. We had the staff, the money and the political muscle to do it."[23]

Convinced that they had a common enemy in Nazism, both at home and abroad, the NAACP also forged bonds with the more conservative American Jewish Committee and Anti-Defamation League of B'nai B'rith. Previously concerned solely with anti-Semitism and the threat to Jews, such groups now redefined their mission to creating a more pluralistic and egalitarian society for all, and reached out to work with the National Association of Colored Women,

the National Council of Negro Women, the Urban League and others. Together they promoted a liberal, reformist creed of equality. Believing that justice and social acceptance would come shortly after the war's end, they concentrated on appeals to conscience and on the political process, abjuring mass
pressure tactics. Far more than any comparable groups, they overwhelmingly
voted Democratic. They joined in testifying before legislative committees for
anti-discrimination and anti-KKK laws, as well as for higher quotas for Jewish
refugees. Along with other Jewish and African American organizations they
collaborated on celebrating diversity and inclusion, urging Hollywood to end
degrading stereotypes, seeking to analyze and cure prejudice, mobilizing public opinion against intolerance, lobbying in favor of the creation of a Jewish
state in Palestine, campaigning for civil rights legislation, especially a permanent Fair Employment Practices Committee, and challenging discrimination
in the law. Well before the Supreme Court's Brown decision in 1954, every single major Jewish civic organization had filed friends of the court briefs in behalf of the NAACP's suit to end segregation in public education. This was the
"democracy, liberalism, and freedom" that A. Philip Randolph lauded as the
enemies of anti-Semitism and "the hopes of the Negro."[24]

The Holocaust had both frightened Jews and blacks into a defensive alliance and emboldened them to capitalize on the revulsion and guilt engendered by Nazism's horrors. The descriptions by Private John Stribling Jr. in the
Chicago Defender, among many others, of the "horrible odor of burned human flesh," of "naked human bodies piled on top of each other," of "bodies
dissected for human experimentation," of prisoners "blind, crippled, and half-
insane, they could barely walk," brought increased sympathy for Jews and decreased "respectability" for racism. The shocking photographs and newsreels
of corpses stacked like cordwood, of boxcars heaped with the bones of dead
prisoners, of bulldozers shoving emaciated bodies into hastily dug ditches, of
the barely alive liberated, living skeletons, lying in their own filth, their vacant,
sunken eyes staring through barbed wire, proved a turning point in racial attitudes. The horror of what has occurred in its name demolishes the doctrine
of racial superiority, wrote Ralph McGill in an *Atlanta Constitution* editorial;
and the editor of the *Detroit Free Press*, after visiting the concentration camps,
stated, "I found in the hell that once was Germany an indictment of my own
beloved America." African American columnists elaborated upon this view
throughout the year. Moreover, the theme of a common oppression made its
way into the songs of William Grant Still, the fiction of Chester Himes, and
the scholarship of Oliver Cox. Du Bois, whose *Souls of Black Folk* had contained numerous references to Jews as sly, dishonest, and unscrupulous, omit-

ted them in a postwar edition, admitting that he "did not realize until the horrible massacre of German Jews, how even unconscious repetition of current folklore such as the concept of Jews as more guilty of exploitation than others, had helped the Hitlers of the world." The Holocaust, and all the depravity associated with it, had revealed the logical conclusion of prejudice, and many Jewish and African American commentators now made the "we're in the same boat" argument as justification for a civil rights alliance. "The barbaric excesses of Nazism have made it impossible to escape the full implications of racial and religious prejudice, no matter what its form," wrote Kenneth Clarke: enlightened African Americans and Jews must pool their efforts to overcome prejudice and discrimination. Much as a letter to the editor of the *Norfolk Journal and Guide* had prophesized, or hoped, in 1934: "When history is written a hundred years from now, Adolf Hitler of Germany will be given credit for showing the world the absurdity of race prejudice." The "Final Solution" would ultimately lead to the demise of racism being socially acceptable, intellectually justified, or legally permissible.[25]

The magnitude of the Holocaust gave racial reformers a powerful weapon, one that became yet stronger as nonwhite nations raised the issue of race in international relations and the Soviet Union sought to exploit American racism for its own ends. Momentum for racial changes in the United States flowed from all the official condemnations of the Holocaust and official declarations in favor of nondiscrimination accompanying the creation of the United Nations and the United Nations Educational, Scientific, and Cultural Organization (UNESCO), the establishment of the Commission on Human Rights and its special Sub-Commission on the Prevention of Discrimination and Protection of Minorities, and the UN's adoption in 1948 of the Universal Declaration of Human Rights and the Convention on the Prevention and Punishment of the Crime of Genocide. Concurrently, the racial awareness catalyzed by the Holocaust along with the necessity of keeping the two-thirds of the world's peoples who were nonwhite out of the Soviet orbit pushed liberal cold warriors into openly condemning racial discrimination and segregation in the United States—a process that would eventually result in the legal ending of those practices.[26]

Of course, it was not all onward and upward, not an unbroken line of progress from barbarism and indifference to compassion and liberality. Bursts of reform and of reaction alternated. While benign neglect, in the main, characterized relations between African Americans and Jews, particularized instances of conflict often made headlines. Prominent Jews bade farewell to their former allies and embraced neoconservative policies on affirmative action, voting rights, and the welfare state; and a new generation of African American scholars and demagogues employed anti-Semitism as a weapon in the battle for who will speak for Black America. Each often referred to the Holocaust, in one way or another, to make its case, as both anti-Semitism and racial prejudice and discrimination proved more resilient and pervasive than reformers had presumed.[27]

Accordingly, the lessons once learned, the impulses generated, the notion that justice and self-interest need not be opposites, become easier to forget as the Holocaust receded into the historical past. Who remembers Leon Bass? An African American in the 183rd Combat Engineer Battalion who helped bury the dead at Buchenwald, Bass consequently dedicated his remaining years to speaking out against anti-Semitism and racism. Or remembers Paul Parks? A black draftee ordered to go into Dachau as part of a burial squad, a stunned Parks wandered by the still-warm ovens and emaciated bodies until he encountered a Jewish prisoner who spoke English. Why? Why the Jews? What did they do? Nothing, said the prisoner, nothing, they were killed just because they were Jews. "I understand that," Parks slowly responded, "I understand that because I've seen people lynched just because they were black." He returned from Europe determined to make his own country a better country, becoming one of Martin Luther King's negotiators in the struggle to end racial discrimination in the South and a key leader in the effort to desegregate the public schools of Boston. Or recalls Paul Cowan's remembrance? One of the Jews who accounted for nearly two-thirds of the white volunteers who went south in 1964 for the Freedom Summer, Cowan would later write that "there was no doubt in any of our minds that we were risking our lives to achieve the very American goal of integration because our kinsmen had been slaughtered in Lithuania, Poland, and Germany." But, as James Baldwin reminds us in *Nobody Knows My Name*, too few Jews actually thought that way: "One can be disappointed in the Jew—if one is romantic enough—for not having learned from his history, but if people did learn from history, history would be very different." For African Americans as well as Jews the unlearned and forgotten haunts. "Who, after all, speaks today of the annihilation of the Armenians?" Adolf Hitler spoke confidently as the Nazis prepared for the Final Solution.[28]

NOTES

1. I use the term *Holocaust* to signify the systematic extermination of some six million European Jews by the Nazi regime. The use of the term by some to refer to

other examples of genocide, to other tragedies, to ecological disasters, and even to personal psychological pain, has led numerous Jews, and others, to prefer the Hebrew word *Shoah*. I do, too, but because most readers are more familiar with Holocaust, that is the term used in this essay for the specific Nazi effort to annihilate European Jewry.

2. Hugh Pearson, "Blacks and Jews View the Holocaust," *Wall Street Journal*, April 19, 1996; and Hasia Diner, *In the Almost Promised Land: American Jews and Blacks, 1915–1935* (Baltimore: Johns Hopkins University Press, 1977), 241–43.

3. Lunabelle Wedlock, *The Reaction of Negro Publications and Organizations to German Anti-Semitism* (Washington, D.C.: n.p., 1942), 91, 189; and Lenora Berson, *The Negroes and the Jews* (New York: Random House, 1971), 175.

4. Dennis Mack Smith, *Mussolini* (New York: Random House, 1982), 182; Paul Gordon Lauren, *Power and Prejudice, The Politics and Diplomacy of Racial Discrimination*, 2d ed. (Boulder, Colo.: Westview Press, 1996), 129–130. Various Jewish organizations associated with the Popular Front joined with black groups to support Ethiopia. See William R. Scott, *The Sons of Sheba's Race: African-Americans and the Italo-Ethiopian War, 1935-1941* (Bloomington: Indiana University Press, 1993) and Joseph E. Harris, *African-American Reactions to War in Ethiopia, 1936-1941* (Baton Rouge: Louisiana State University Press, 1994).

5. George Mosse, *Toward the Final Solution: A History of European Racism* (New York: Howard Fertig, 1978), 191; A. James Gregor, *The Ideology of Fascism* (New York: Free Press, 1969), 241–282, and Leni Yahil, *The Holocaust: The Fate of European Jewry, 1932–1945* (New York: American Philological Association, 1990). See also Lucy Dawidowicz, *The War against the Jews* (New York: Schocken Books, 1975).

6. Charles H. Stember et al., *Jews in the Mind of America* (New York: Basic Books, 1966), 53–62, 138; Leonard Dinnerstein, *Antisemitism in America* (New York: Oxford University Press, 1994), 203–207; David S. Wyman, *The Abandonment of the Jews: America and the Holocaust, 1941–1945* (New York: Pantheon, 1984), x–xi; Kenneth B. Clark, "Candor about Negro-Jewish Relations," *Commentary* I (February 1946): 8–14; Richard Wright, *Black Boy* (New York: Harper & Row, 1945), 70; James Baldwin, *Notes of a Native Son* (New York: Dial Press, 1955), 28, and "The Harlem Ghetto: Winter 1948," *Commentary* 5 (February 1948): 165–170; Rabbi Robert Gordis, "Negroes Are Anti-Semitic Because They Want a Scapegoat," in Leonard Dinnerstein, ed., *Antisemitism in the United States* (New York: International Thomson Publishing, 1971), 132–137; Brenda Gayle Plummer, *Rising Wind: Black Americans and U.S. Foreign Affairs, 1935–1960* (Chapel Hill: University of North Carolina Press, 1996), 67–68; Editorials, *Philadelphia Tribune*, April 6, October 12, 1933, July 5, 1934; Isabel B. Price, "Black Responses to Anti-Semitism: Negroes and Jews in New York, 1880 to World War II" (Ph.D. diss., University of New Mexico, 1973), 230; and W. E. B. Du Bois, "As

the Crow Flies," *Crisis* 40 (September 1933), 197. American Jewish Committee, *The Jews in Nazi Germany: The Factual Record of Their Persecution by the National Socialists* (New York: American Jewish Committee, 1933) is an early, largely ignored effort to alert Americans to what was happening in Germany.

7. *The Black Man* 1 (July 1935), 9; Roi Ottley, *New World A-Coming* (Boston: Houghton Mifflin, 1943), 118–119, 129, 334; Adam Clayton Powell Jr., *Marching Blacks* (New York: Dial Press, 1945), 75, 81; Wedlock, *The Reaction of Negro Publications,* 72–73, 171–173; "What the Black Belt Needs Is a Hitler to Fight for Our Race and Purge Us of the Exploiting Jew." *Dynamite,* May 28, October 22, 1938; Edward L. Israel, "Jew Hatred Among Negroes," *Crisis* 43 (February 1936): 39, 50. Also see S. A. Haynes, "Jews and Negroes," *Philadelphia Tribune,* July 26, 1934; Harold L. Sheppard, "The Negro Merchant: A Study of Negro Anti-Semitism," *American Journal of Sociology* 53 (September 1947), esp. 96–99; Ella Baker and Marvel Cooke, "The Bronx Slave Market," *Crisis* 42 (November 1935): 330; Lawrence D. Reddick, "Anti-Semitism Among Negroes," *Negro Quarterly* 1 (Summer 1942): 113; George Britt, "Poison in the Melting Pot," *Nation* 148 (April 1, 1939): 374–376; Oscar R. Williams Jr., "Historical Impressions of Black-Jewish Relations Prior to World War II," *Negro History Bulletin* 40 (July–August 1977): 728–731; and Box C-208, National Association for the Advancement of Colored People Papers, Library of Congress, Washington, D.C., for more on black anti-Semitism.

8. *Baltimore Afro-American,* June 17, 1933, August 24, 1935, February 22, 1936; *St. Louis Argus,* July 15, 1938; "From the Press," *Crisis* 46 (January 1939): 19, (March 1939): 83, and *Crisis* 45 (September 1938): 300; *Amsterdam News,* December 7, 1935, March 14 and 28, 1936, June 12, 1937; and Chandler Owen, "Should the Negro Hate the Jew," *Chicago Defender,* November 8, 1941.

9. J. A. Rogers columns in *Philadelphia Tribune,* September 21, 1933, July 26, 1934; Kelly Miller, "Race Prejudice in Georgia and in Germany," *Washington Tribune,* June 23, 1933, "Race Prejudice in Germany," *Opportunity* 14 (April 1936): 102–105, column in *Norfolk Journal and Guide,* April 1, 1933, December 17, 1938, January 21, 1939, and "Hitler Hits Back," *Chicago Defender,* December 10, 1938; George Schuyler to Walter White, December 22, 1935, NAACP Papers, II L 7, article in New York *World Telegram,* November 21, 1938, and columns in *Pittsburgh Courier,* January 23, February 20, 1937, November 26, December 3, 1938; Powell in *Amsterdam News,* March 7, 1936, January 23, February 20, 1937, April 9, 16, July 16, 23, 1938; and *Norfolk Journal and Guide,* December 17, 1938.

10. Wilkins in *Amsterdam News,* March 20, December 11, 1937, *Philadelphia Tribune,* December 22, 1937; White to William Hastie, July 20, 1939, White to Dr. Ames, November 18, 1938, White to Claude McKay, December 23, 1938, White to Hubert Delany, September 15, 1939, and White to George Mintzer, December 2, 1948,

NAACP Papers, II, A-325. Also see Cleophus Charles, "Roy Wilkins, the NAACP and the Early Struggle for Civil Rights" (Ph.D. diss., Cornell University, 1981).

11. Pickens to Du Bois, July 25, 1933, Du Bois Papers, University of Massachusetts, Reel 39; Pickens, "Why the Negro Must Be Anti-Fascist," *New Masses* (May 30, 1939): 29–30; Pickens, "Nine Hundred Jews on A Ship," *Norfolk Journal and Guide,* June 24, 1939; "Stay Out of Nazi Olympics," *Crisis* 42 (September 1935): 273; White to Max Yergan, November 30, 1938, NAACP Papers, C-208. Also see Pickens, "The Jewish People and Prejudice," *Norfolk Journal and Guide,* August 19, 1939. There are many examples in the Negro press of using the plight of German Jewry to call attention to the evils of racism in the United States. See, for example, the following editorials in the *Baltimore Afro-American*: "Jim Crow for Jews Now," October 14, 1933, "The German Cracker," December 21, 1935, and "The Nazis and Dixie," February 22, 1936.

12. Press release "N.A.A.C.P. Secretary Denounces Nazi Pogroms: Says All Must Unite to Protect Minority Rights Here and Save Democracy," November 18, 1938, White address to NAACP Annual Meeting, January 5, 1936, "Nazism and the Negro," a series of 1936 WMCA radio addresses by White, and "The Nazi Terror—My Reaction, White address of November 27, 1938, NAACP Papers, Box 208, "Anti-Semitism 1935–1938"; *Amsterdam News,* November 15, 1938; "Walter White Scores Persecution of Jews," *Crisis* 45 (December 1938): 399–400, Roy Wilkins to Walter White, March 25, 1938, and White to Cordell Hull, March 25, 1938, NAACP Papers, I, C208; also see *Crisis* 45 (September 1938): 339.

13. Conference resolutions appear annually in the September *Crisis*. "Walter White Scores Persecution of Jews," *Crisis* 45 (December 1938): 399–400; Editorials, *Crisis* 45 (September 1938): 301, (December 1938): 393, *Crisis* 42 (September 1935): 273, *Crisis* 47 (July 1940): 209, and *Crisis* 42 (September 1935): 273. Also see *Crisis* 43 (September 1936): 273 and 45 (April 1938): 113. Earlier efforts by African Americans to use the plight of the Jews to draw attention to racial abuses in the United States are mentioned in Arnold Shankman, "Brothers Across the Sea: Afro-Americans on the Persecution of Russian Jews, 1881–1917," *Jewish Social Studies* 37 (Spring 1975): 114–121.

14. Rabbi Stephen S. Wise, "Parallel Between Hitlerism and the Persecution of Negroes in America," *Crisis* 41 (May 1934): 127–129; Jacob J. Weinstein, "The Jew and the Negro" and "The Negro and the Jew," *Crisis* 41 (June 1934): 178–179 and (July 1934): 197–198; Harry Essrig, "Einhorn: Champion of Racial Equality," *Crisis* 47 (October 1940): 314–315, "John Brown's Jewish Associates," *Crisis* 47 (December 1940): 380–381, and "Jewish Friends of Negro Emancipation," *Crisis* 48 (January 1941): 16; *Crisis* 46 (January 1939): 29 and (October 1939): 308. Also see "Anti-Semitism among Negroes," *Crisis* 45 (June 1938): 177.

15. Norton Belth, "Problems of Anti-Semitism in the United States," *Contemporary Jewish Record* 2 (July 1939): 43–57; "Americans All," *National Jewish Monthly* 53

(April 1939): 298; *American Hebrew,* December 13, 1936; Joseph Roucek, "The Forgotten Man in Europe and America," *Opportunity* 11 (March 1933): 73–74; Verna Arvey, "Tolerance," *Opportunity* 18 (August 1940): 244; Elmer Carter, "The Way of Madness," *Opportunity* 16 (October 1938): 292; Lawrence Reddick, "What Hitler Says About the Negro," *Opportunity* 17 (April 1939): 108–110; and editorials, *Opportunity* 17 (January 1939): 2, (June 1939): 164, (November 1939): 324, and "The Negro and Nazism," *Opportunity* 18 (July 1940): 194–195.

16. Adam Clayton Powell Jr., "Soap Box," *Amsterdam News,* February 19, March 18, April 16, 1938; Ralph Bunche, "Forward," in Wedlock, *The Reaction of Negro Publications,* 3, 10; William Pickens, "German Fascists and Free Speech in America," *Norfolk Journal and Guide,* March 11, 1939; editorial, "Fascism Spreads," *Amsterdam News,* March 19, 1938; Chandler Owen, "Should the Negro Hate the Jew?" *Chicago Defender,* November 8, 1941; "Danger Is Seen in Anti-Jewish Onset as Probe Is Begun," *Atlanta Daily World,* August 15, 1938; M. Beaunorus Tolson, "Keep That Chin Up, My Jewish Brother!" *Philadelphia Tribune,* March 11, 1939; and Robert Bagnall, "Taken in Stride," *Philadelphia Tribune,* August 4, 1938.

17. Editorials in *Baltimore Afro-American,* February 22, 1936, August 24, and October 5, 1935, April 1, 1933, and April 11, May 2, 1936; Miller in *Washington Tribune,* June 23, 1933; editorials in *Amsterdam News,* February 11, April 8, 15, 1939; *Crisis* 45 (September 1938): 301, (December 1938): 393, *Crisis* 47 (August 1940): 232, and Thomas F. Doyle, "Gestapo in Memphis," *Crisis* 48 (May 1941): 152–154, 172–173; and *New York Times,* August 22, 1939.

18. Editorials, *Crisis* 48 (May 1941): 151, (July 1941): 215; "A Georgia Hitler," *Opportunity* 19 (August 1941): 226–227; Harold Preece, "The Klan's 'Revolution of the Right,'" and "Klan 'Murder, Inc.' in Dixie," *Crisis* 53 (July 1946): 202, 220, and (October 1946): 299–301, and editorial, *Crisis* (September 1946): 276. The sole African American in Congress, Arthur W. Mitchell, wrote to Roosevelt urging the U.S. government to take greater measures to protect European Jews. "October 12" in Janus Adams, *Freedom Days: 365 Inspirational Moments in Civil Rights History* (New York: Wiley, 1998).

19. *Amsterdam News,* February 14, 1942, and *Pittsburgh Courier,* October 23, 1943; Marie Syrkin, "Anti-Semitic Drive in Harlem," *Congress Weekly* 8 (October 31, 1941): 6–8; *Crisis* 51 (February 1944); Adam Clayton Powell Jr., "What Negroes Think of Jews," *New Currents* 1 (September 1943): 15–16; Langston Hughes column, *Chicago Defender,* March 10, 1945; Walter White and Rabbi Lou H. Silberman, "The Minority Problem from the Inside Looking Out," *Hebrew Union College Monthly* 30 (April 1943): 6–7; *Pittsburgh Courier,* August 4, 1945; and Randolph quote in Gunnar Myrdal, *An American Dilemma* (New York: Harper and Brothers, 1944), 852. See also editorial, "The Dangers of Anti-Semitism," *Chicago Defender,* March 17, 1945. More

examples of African American wartime efforts to combat anti-Semitism are found in the NAACP Papers, II A-325.

20. Minutes of the NAACP Board of Directors, February 1942, NAACP Papers, II A-134; *Congress Weekly,* December 4, 1942; Stephen Wise to Walter White, December 17, 1942 and Edwin C. Johnson to Walter White, June 23, 1943, NAACP Papers, II A-374; Walter White to American Jewish Congress, August 30, 1943, NAACP Papers, II A-325; Lester Granger to Walter White, June 21, 1943, NAACP Papers, II A-446. On what was known and what was reported see Deborah Lipstadt, *Beyond Belief: The American Press and the Coming of the Holocaust, 1933–1945* (New York: Free Press, 1986). The *New York Times* began printing stories on the slaughter of millions of Jews in June 1942, although the Allied governments did not publicly acknowledge it until December.

21. See articles and editorials from Jewish publications in NAACP Papers, II A-325, II A-361, II A-380, and II L-7; "Defend the Negro," and "Help Wanted—No Negroes, No Jews," in NAACP Papers, II A-325; *Jewish Survey* II, June 1942; *Year Book, Central Conference of American Rabbis* (New York: Central Conference of American Rabbis, 1942); on the activities of the American Jewish Congress see NAACP Papers, II C-300; and Lucille B. Morton, "On the Civil-Liberty Front," *New Republic,* June 26, 1944, 839–840, and Kenneth B. Clark, "Candor About Negro-Jewish Relations," *Commentary* 1 (February 1946)· 9. See also columns by Roy Wilkins, *Amsterdam News,* February 28, 1942, April 17, 1943.

22. Louis D. Reddick, "Anti-Semitism Among Negroes," *Negro Quarterly* (Summer 1942): 105; W. H. Jernigan, "Tolerance is Indivisible," *Jewish Survey* II (August 1942); New York *Jewish Forward,* March 3, 1942, and Louis Harap, "Anti-Negroism among Jews," *Negro Quarterly* (Summer 1942): 107; Walter White and Rabbi Lou H. Silberman, "The Minority Problem From the Inside Looking Out," *Hebrew Union College Monthly* 30 (April 1943): 6–7; and Jacob X. Cohen, "Fighting Together For Equality" and *The Negro and Anti Semitism,*" in NAACP Papers, II C-300. Also see Marshall F. Stevenson Jr., "Points of Departure, Acts of Resolve: Black-Jewish Relations in Detroit, 1937–1962" (Ph.D diss., University of Michigan, 1988).

23. Milton R. Konvitz, "Jews and Civil Rights," in Peter I. Rose, ed., *The Ghetto and Beyond: Essays on Jewish Life in America* (New York: Random House, 1969), 274–280; American Jewish Congress pamphlet "Accent on Action, A New Approach to Minority Group Problems in America," and Bernard Gittelson to Walter White, June 14, 1945, Alexander H. Pekelis to Thurgood Marshall, June 15, 1945, and Rabbi Stephen Wise to Thurgood Marshall, April 11, 1946, NAACP Papers, II C-300; and Maslow in Berson, *The Negroes and the Jews,* 96. Also see Jonathan Kaufman, *Broken Alliance, The Turbulent Times Between Blacks and Jews in America* (New York: Scribner, 1988), and Edward S. Shapiro, "Black-Jewish Relations Revisited," *Judaism* 44 (Summer 1995): 379.

24. Cheryl Greenberg, "Liberation and Liberalism: The Politics of Black-Jewish Relations in the 1960s," a paper presented at the Organization of American Historians 1996 annual meeting, is an indispensable account of the emerging alliance, as is Stuart Svonkin, *Jews Against Prejudice: American Jews and the Fight for Civil Liberties* (New York: Columbia University Press, 1997). Files "Negro Race Problems" and "Negro-Jewish Relations," and *ADL Bulletin*, Anti-Defamation League Papers, Anti-Defamation Library, New York City; "Negro Jewish Relations File," American Jewish Congress Papers, American Jewish Congress Library, New York City; 1945 platform of the Central Conference of American Rabbis, *Pittsburgh Courier*, February 3, 1945; Myron Harshhaw to George Schuyler, June 30, 1943, George Schuyler Papers, Schomburg Archives, New York Public Library; Kaufman, *Broken Alliance*, 97–100; and Walter White column and story on Randolph in *Chicago Defender*, January 27, 1945.

25. "Chicago GI Tells Horrors of Nazi 'Murder Factory' Prison Camp," *Chicago Defender*, May 12, 1945; *Atlanta Constitution*, August 8, 1945; "Editor Sees Parallel of Nazi Germany in America," *Pittsburgh Courier*, May 26, 1945; Joseph Bibb column, *Pittsburgh Courier*, March 31, 1945; Marjorie McKenzie column, *Pittsburgh Courier*, May 12, 1945; Horace R. Cayton column, *Pittsburgh Courier*, December 8, 1945; letter to the editor, *Norfolk Journal and Guide*, July 21, 1934; and Lauren, *Power and Prejudice*, 144. The overall impact of the news of the Holocaust is best covered in Robert H. Abzug, *Inside the Vicious Heart: Americans and the Liberation of Nazi Concentration Camps* (New York: Oxford University Press, 1985). See also William Grant Still's "Wailing Woman" (1946), Chester Himes, *If He Hollers Let Him Go* (New York: Doubleday, 1945), Oliver Cox, *Caste, Class and Race* (New York: Doubleday, 1948), W. E. B. Du Bois, *The Souls of Black Folk* (Milkwood, N.Y.: Bard, 1973), 42–43, Clarke, "Candor About Negro-Jewish Relations," as well as references to the Holocaust later made by Martin Luther King Jr., *A Testament of Hope: The Essential Writings and Speeches of Martin Luther King, Jr.* (San Francisco: HarperCollins, 1991), 50, 356.

26. Alphonse Heningburg, "What the Urban League Expects for All Races as a Result of the San Francisco Conference," *Opportunity* 23 (Summer 1945), 123; editorial, "The Jews Look Ahead," *Atlanta Daily World*, May 6, 1945; Brenda Gayle Plummer, *Rising Wind: Black Americans and U.S. Foreign Affairs, 1935–1960* (Chapel Hill: University of North Carolina Press, 1996), 164–165; and, especially, Jonathan Seth Rosenberg, "How Far the Promised Land? World Affairs and the American Civil Rights Movement from the First World War to Vietnam" (Ph.D. diss., Harvard University, 1997). See also Carol Anderson, "Eyes Off the Prize: African Americans, the United Nations, and the Struggle for Human Rights, 1944–1952" (Ph.D. diss., Ohio State University, 1995).

27. Roy Wilkins, "Jewish-Negro Relations: An Evaluation," *American Judaism* 12 (Spring 1963): 4–5; Eugene I. Bender, "Reflections on Negro-Jewish Relationships: The Historical Dimension," *Phylon* 30 (Spring 1969): 59–65; Marguerite Cartwright, "Do I Like Jews?" *Negro History Bulletin* 21 (November 1957): 38–39; and Murray Friedman, *What Went Wrong? The Creation and Collapse of the Black-Jewish Alliance* (New York: Free Press, 1995).

28. Kaufman, *Broken Alliance,* 5–6, 52–53; Paul Cowan, *An Orphan in History* (New York: Doubleday, 1982), 6; Baldwin quote in Dinnerstein, ed., *Antisemitism in the United States,* 131; Elie Wiesel commentary in Michael Freeman, "Can Social Science Explain Genocide?" *Patterns of Prejudice* 20 (1986): 10.

8

RACE, ROCK AND ROLL, AND THE RIGGED SOCIETY: THE PAYOLA SCANDAL AND THE POLITICAL CULTURE OF THE 1950S

Steven F. Lawson

On February 1, 1960, students in Greensboro, North Carolina, held a sit-in at a Woolworth's lunch counter in a demonstration much heralded in the annals of civil rights history. This momentous confrontation with racial segregation invigorated the African American freedom struggle and would substantially change the lives of blacks and whites throughout the South and the United States. A week later, on February 8, a seemingly unrelated event occurred in Washington, D.C. On that day, a committee of the House of Representatives convened public hearings on the subject of payola in the broadcasting industry, a practice that involved illicit payments to get music aired on radio and television programs.

Contemporary coverage of each made no mention of the other, and on the surface it was hard to see the connections. Yet the struggle for racial change, which inspired the sit-ins, also helped shape seemingly nonracial issues such as business ethics in broadcasting. In this case, rock and roll, a musical form that traced its origins to African Americans, became a surrogate target for opponents of civil rights in the South and for those who feared increasing black cultural influence over American youth throughout the country. The increased visibility of the black freedom movement, marked by the Supreme Court's 1954 ruling in *Brown v. Board of Education,* the 1955 Montgomery bus boycott, and the 1957 Little Rock school integration crisis, encouraged supporters and critics alike to find racial dimensions in political arenas not usually considered under the category of civil rights. Heightened racial agitation produced a highly charged atmosphere and the political and cultural fallout from these explosive issues landed in unexpected places.

The payola scandal of 1959–1960 was also part and parcel of the political culture of investigation that characterized the 1950s. Congressional committees served as the main vehicle for inquiry, and the new medium of television brought the drama of confrontation between scolding lawmakers and defensive witnesses into millions of homes. Though the need for corrective legislation provided the rationale for these inquiries, the impulse toward exposure and demonization drove them forward. Anticommunist inquisitions by the House Committee on Un-American Activities, Wisconsin Senator Joseph R. McCarthy, and Senator James Eastland of Mississippi have drawn the greatest attention from historians, furnishing textbook representations of the political tensions of the postwar period. Their importance notwithstanding, they formed only part of a larger structure of popular investigation. These included inquiries led by Tennessee Senator Estes Kefauver into organized crime and juvenile delinquency, John McClellan of Arkansas and John F. Kennedy of Massachusetts into labor racketeering, and Arkansas Representative Oren Harris into television quiz shows.[1]

Within the context of this culture of investigation, narrow economic rivalries and broad social tensions fueled the payola inquiry. Initially, charges of fraudulent payments for airplay on radio stations arose out of a power struggle between two competing agencies inside the business. The internal conflict between the American Society of Composers, Authors, and Publishers (ASCAP) and Broadcast Music International (BMI) over control of publishing and performance royalties escalated into an attack by the more tradition-oriented ASCAP on BMI-associated rock and roll music.

What started out as an internecine economic battle, however, soon took on the trappings of race. Following the landmark *Brown* decision, southern segregationists embarked on a campaign of massive resistance to racial equality that included attacks on black-inspired rock and roll. Joining them were northerners who believed that rock and roll, identified with working-class black and white youths, eroded middle-class values and standards of sexual conduct, thereby threatening the morality of their sons and, more important, their daughters. Congressional probes of payola gave voice to the economic and aesthetic complaints of music-business professionals as well as to fears over the erosion of racial and class boundaries by middle-class parents and their congressional representatives. The fact that the payola investigation did not continue as a significant component in the struggle over racial equality was a consequence not of the retreat by white politicians and their constituents, but rather of mass mobilization of black youths and their white allies, which shifted the battle from Congress and radio stations to the streets of America.

The practice of payola did not suddenly spring up with the appearance of rock and roll; it had a history as long as commercial, popular music. *Variety,* the music trade newspaper that first coined the term payola, reported in 1914 that vaudeville singers "tell the publisher what they want to sing, how much a week they must have for singing the song or songs, and if not receiving a stipulated weekly salary, think nothing of asking for an advance."[2] Although the shape of the music business changed over the next several decades, undisclosed commercial transactions for performances remained a constant. The growth of radio in the 1920s and 1930s brought live broadcasts and the possibility of reaching millions of listeners in a single sitting. Given this potentially wider audience, popular bandleaders commanded higher payments than had their vaudevillian predecessors.[3]

In the 1950s, the cast of characters changed, but payola persisted. The development and widespread appeal of television altered the character of radio. Live broadcasts of musical concerts virtually disappeared and programs of recorded music replaced them. Disk jockeys took over from bandleaders as maestros of musical selections. The decade also witnessed a proliferation of small, independent record companies that competed with the six majors (Columbia, Capitol, Decca, RCA, MGM, and Mercury) for airplay. The advent of 45 rpm single records, whose sale price was much cheaper than 33⅓ long-playing albums, inflated the number of records in circulation, increasing competition even further. Disk jockeys stood as gatekeepers in choosing songs from the burgeoning supply of records sent to the stations. What *Variety* called the "time-dishonored standard operating procedure in the music business," payola, now centered on payments from record companies and their distributors to disk jockeys.[4]

Throughout its considerable history, payola had spawned campaigns, largely unsuccessful, against it. For all the criticism it generated, payola was not a crime. No federal statute outlawed the practice, and the closest it came to a criminal offense appeared in state commercial bribery laws.[5] The main effort to combat payola came from elements within the music business. Spearheaded by *Variety* in 1916, the Music Publishers' Protective Association was formed "to promote and foster clean and free competition among music publishers by eradicating the evil custom of paying tribute or gratuities to singers or musicians."[6]

In the early 1950s, when the issue resurfaced amid the postwar obsession with moral decline and the growing prospects for racial change, *Variety* again led the campaign. In July 1954 the trade newspaper launched a series of editorials condemning the practice. The editors declared, "the music biz payola had reached ridiculous and dangerous proportions," and concluded, "it's about time it was curbed." Speaking for the denizens of "Tin Pan Alley" in New York City, where established music publishers and songwriters congregated, they raised a concern that would be repeated frequently in the years to come. "Private side-changing chicanery," as *Variety* referred to payola, lowered the quality of songs and decreased the likelihood that truly talented stars would get heard.[7]

The trade paper left little doubt about its taste in music. In February 1955, *Variety* issued a "Warning to the Music Business." Upset over the growing popularity of songs with sexually suggestive "leer-ics," the paper called for the industry to impose some self-restraint or face unwanted federal regulation. Their real target was rock and roll, which had burst on the scene during the previous few years and appealed almost exclusively to young people. Considering rock and roll a "raw musical idiom ... [that] smell[ed] up the environment," *Variety* condemned its "hug" and "squeeze" lyrics for "attempting a total breakdown of all reticences about sex."[8] These comments reflected the disdain traditional segments of the music business and the adult public held for rock and roll; opponents assumed that such inferior music could push its way into the marketplace only through the connivance of payola.

Historians do not dispute the existence of payola, but its significance lies in its political linkage with rock and roll and race. Rather than simply an objectionable business practice of interest mainly within the recording and broadcasting industries, payola became, for a short time, a heated subject of public debate. It involved more than private morality and individual greed and moved beyond the pages of trade paper whistle blowing. Following the *Brown* decision, the Supreme Court's clarion call for racial equality, payola became a topic for public scrutiny because it coincided with growing anxiety about the nation's youth and racial minorities. The association of rock and roll with these two groups turned the music from just another in a long line of popular, juvenile fads into a subject of intense national inquiry.

The behavior of teenagers had already aroused serious apprehension. "Never in our 180-year history," *Collier's* remarked in 1957, "has the United States been so aware of—or confused about—its teenagers."[9] The political response to this concern had already appeared in congressional hearings. In 1955, Senator Estes Kefauver, who had earlier investigated adult criminals, convened a legislative inquiry into the causes of juvenile delinquency. James Gilbert, the leading historian of this subject, concluded that "the delinquency hearings, the attack on youth culture, the crusade to censor culture expressed a deep malaise at what was emerging during the 1950s: a vastly different order of social, sexual, and cultural practices."[10] The perceived erosion of parental authority had serious implications for the vitality of the nuclear family during the Cold War period when domestic harmony was considered the first line of defense against Communism.[11]

The Kefauver Committee underscored the extent to which rock and roll had become contested ground between parents and their teenage offspring. Worse than its lack of aesthetics and professionalism, rock, according to its critics, was spreading antisocial, working-class values among America's youth. The words of the songs, even when they were cleaned up for popular radio consumption, combined with the throbbing sounds and pulsating performers, opened the way for sexual expression deemed unacceptable in polite society. Even if the emergent music did not turn unsuspecting middle-class youngsters into depraved delinquents, it might lead them down that path. As Jeff Greenfield, a New York City teenager in the mid-1950s, remarked, rock and roll spread the message "that our bodies were our own Joy Machines." Afraid that this was indeed the case, parents sought to curtail "the sounds of pain and joy now flooding the airwaves, infecting the bodies of their children."[12]

Middle-class worries over the unwanted influences of rock and roll were not confined to whites. Members of the black bourgeoisie also expressed their distaste. When asked by a seventeen-year-old in 1958 whether it was sinful to play rock and roll, the civil rights leader and pastor Dr. Martin Luther King Jr. replied that whether it was a sin or not, rock music "often plunges men's minds into degrading and immoral depths." In a similar vein, a columnist for the New York Amsterdam News had earlier attacked the music as "smut" and "tripe" and proclaimed that African Americans themselves should not listen to lyrics that "projected the idea that all Negro women longed for was barnyard-type romance."[13]

As the commentary in the Amsterdam News suggests, class concerns intersected with those of gender. The heightened sexuality of rock and roll both lyrically and musically was seen as posing a particular threat to young girls. According to middle-class social norms, adolescent females were primarily mothers-in-waiting, preparing themselves for marriage, raising children, and safeguarding the virtues of the nuclear family. Virginity was next to godliness, and sex was reserved for marriage. As moral caretakers of the home, wives and daughters were seen as strengthening the nation by combating evil conspiracies designed to undermine it. During the Cold War, communism stood at the top of the list of enemies, but any assault on pubescent, female chastity was seen as subversive.[14]

Rock and roll was regarded as posing such a threat. According to Jeff Greenfield, the "honking tenor sax and the vibrating electric guitar and the insistent drum beat," were considered by his parents' generation as "fearful engines of immorality, driving daughters to strange dance steps and God knows what else."[15] Although adults usually found the wild gyrations of the performers and the raucous quality of the sound distasteful if not unfathomable, they were just as alarmed by the slow music, known as doo-wop. Teenage dance shows on television gave adults a peek at the possible dangers as they watched young couples clutch each other trying to get as close as possible on the dance floor. "If you were a parent at home watching your daughter," a disk jockey admitted, "watching a guy all over a girl, you figure, 'Is this what my daughter does at record hops?' "[16]

Whether young female rock and rollers saw themselves as subverting the moral order is debatable. Charlotte Grieg contends that the music transformed "all the conventional ideas of love, romance and marriage . . . into visions of a steamy teenage paradise throbbing with erotic and sexual desire" that undermined adult notions of responsibility and domesticity.[17] Yet throughout the fifties most of the songs that teenage girls listened to had less to say about consummating sex than about longing for the boy of their dreams and marrying him. Nor did rock and roll overturn the double standard that distinguished "good girls" from "bad girls." Nevertheless, it did allow many young women to experience a forbidden sexual energy that their elders found dangerous. If not exactly revolutionary, the music allowed teenagers, girls and boys, to express themselves in a language and style removed from their parents' tight control.[18] This mixture of class and gender fears occasioned powerful anxieties about rock and roll and teen culture, but the addition of race proved explosive. The term *rock and roll* had evolved out of the rhythm and blues lyrical expression for sexual intercourse. As long as rhythm and blues remained "race music," separated from the popular tunes white audiences listened to, it aroused only minimal concern within the nonblack community. But when it began to enter the musical mainstream as rock and roll, which appealed largely to white youths, it alarmed the guardians of teenage morality. *Variety* undertook its crusade against sexually suggestive lyrics (or, as it called them, "leerics") with great urgency because rhythm and blues was no longer "restricted to special places and out and out barrelhouses." Transformed into rock and roll, it had broken out of the segregated confines of black venues and appeared "as standard popular music for general consumption, including consumption by teenagers."[19]

Rock and roll gave white teenagers the rare opportunity to come into cultural contact with African Americans in a nation that was still racially segregated. Particularly in the South, Jim Crow maintained a rigid wall to keep whites and black apart. Dixie's laws could keep schools and public accommodations racially restricted, but not the public airwaves. Radio stations targeted for blacks picked up a sizable white audience, some 20 to 30 percent of overall listeners.[20] In the privacy of their own rooms, young southern whites turned on their radios to hear the forbidden sounds of rhythm and blues or they took their portable transistor radios, which had just become available in the early 1950s, to gathering places for teens, away from their parents' watchful eyes. One white youth recalled that he loved to listen to the music on black-oriented stations "whenever and wherever I could. . . . I loved to dance to it. That got me into trouble with my parents and the schools, because we were not allowed to listen to this music openly." Some of the bolder youths attended live performances with blacks, and in spite of efforts to keep them apart, the excitement of the music frequently pulled them side by side in the aisles or on the dance floor.[21]

Moreover, white teen icons such as Elvis Presley stepped over the racial divide by incorporating the sounds and styles of African American music into his act. A Mississippian who achieved stardom in Memphis, Presley readily acknowledged his debt to blacks. "Colored folks have been singing and playing this music for more years'n anybody knows," the twenty-one-year-old Presley explained in 1956. "They played it in the shanties all 'round Tupelo, Mississippi, where I got it from them, and nobody paid 'tention till I goose it up."[22] Nelson George has written that the "young Presley came closer than any other rock and roll star to capturing the swaggering sexuality projected by many Rhythm and Blues vocalists."[23]

In the North and West, where de facto segregation and more subtly constructed patterns of racism kept blacks and whites apart, rock and roll likewise exerted the centripetal force that pulled teenagers of both races together. Colorful white radio disk jockeys such as Alan "Moondog" Freed in Cleveland and New York City, George "Hound Dog" Lorenz in Buffalo, and Hunter Hancock and Johnny Otis in Los Angeles exposed their predominantly white teenage listeners to black rhythm and blues and rock and roll artists. Not only did they feature the original records of black performers over versions covered by white artists, but they also talked in the hip street vernacular of the singers. As in the South, their live concerts and dances drew an interracial crowd, throwing together white and black youths who would otherwise have remained in their own neighborhoods. More than in any other setting in America at that time, these gatherings permitted teenagers to step over racial and class boundaries in defiance of their elders.[24]

Rock and roll served as a musical backdrop to the black freedom struggle that was breaking onto the national scene during the 1950s. Some have discerned a direct connection between the rise of rock and roll and racial change. A singer for the Platters, Harvey Weinger, looking back on that period remarked, "Because of our music, white kids ventured into black areas. They had a sense of fair play long before the civil rights movement." Herbie Cox of the Cleftones seconded this view, asserting that rock and roll "disk-jockeys and record distributors were doing more for integration than *Brown versus the Topeka Board of Education.*"[25] The journalist Robert Palmer perceived rock and roll as the cultural component of the black freedom struggle. "It's no mere accident of history," Palmer argues, "that Rosa Parks's refusal to move to the back of a segregated Alabama bus . . . occurred during the brief pop-music ascendancy of performers like Chuck Berry and Little Richard, black men whose very sound and sign communicated their refusal to respond to the racists' traditional 'C'mere, boy.' "[26]

Without doubt rock and roll contributed to changing patterns of racial and cultural interaction, but its impact should not be exaggerated. Because white youths listened to black-inspired music or attended concerts with African Americans did not mean that they shed the racial prejudices of their families and neighborhoods. The sensuality of the rhythms that attracted many white teens also served to reinforce stereotypical notions of black male and female sexuality, views that white society had historically used to demonize African Americans. Besides, most white kids listened to rock and roll within the confines of racially segregated environments—homes, social clubs, schools, and cars—without venturing into close proximity to blacks.[27] Moreover, although rock and roll energized young people and cast them in opposition to dominant styles, the teenagers who became the vanguard of the civil rights movement in places such as Little Rock and Greensboro owed their inspiration less to avant-garde music and more to their churches, youth groups, and other community organizations.

Nevertheless, opponents of racial change considered rock and roll as subversive. In the wake of the Supreme Court's ruling in *Brown,* segregationist watchdogs saw an increasing need to guard the South's white youth from all forms of race mixing. Schools occupied the primary political battleground because they offered the most likely space for white and black students to interact. But the war for racial purity did not end at the schoolhouse door. As the commercial marketplace, including the entertainment industry, directed more of its efforts toward gaining a share of rising teenage spending, segregationists turned their attention to youth culture. They perceived danger as coming from many directions—television, radio, motion pictures—and considered the national media, in the words of the *Shreveport Journal,* as "one of the South's greatest foes in its fight to maintain racial segregation."[28] The greatest threat came from images and sounds that might lure white and black youngsters together.

Hostility to rock and roll became part of the agenda for southern white massive resistance. In addition to other efforts to preserve segregation and disfranchisement, White Citizens Councils, a slightly more moderate counterpart of the Ku Klux Klan, campaigned against rock and roll. In 1956, Asa Carter, the head of the North Alabama White Citizens Council, called rock "the basic, heavy-beat music of Negroes." Allowed to go unchecked, he feared nothing less than the collapse of "the entire moral structure . . . the white man has built through his devotion to God." He and his followers did not consider their concern farfetched as they saw that "white girls and boys were turned to the level of animal" by the sensuous music."[29] In a racialized society rapidly coming under assault from the civil rights movement, music that promoted social intercourse also aggravated fears of miscegenation.[30]

Carter and segregationists like him contended that the proliferation of rock and roll had not occurred naturally; how could it given their view of the music's inherent worthlessness? Rather, they saw it as part of a sinister plot designed by integrationist groups such as the National Association for the Advancement of Colored People (NAACP) to contribute to the "moral degradation of children."[31] The *Brown* decision and rock and roll were just two sides of the same integrationist coin and segregationists responded to both by trying to beat them back.

Racism was not confined to the South, and similar assumptions guided opponents of rock and roll in the North. The thrust of the attack above the Mason-Dixon line was not so much to preserve the system of Jim Crow but to combat anxieties over the spread of juvenile delinquency, which the Kefauver Committee had publicized. In 1957, Senator John F. Kennedy, a Massachusetts Democrat, read into the *Congressional Record* an article from *Newsday,* a Long Island newspaper, connecting rock and roll with the designs of broadcasters, record companies, and music publishers to foist decadent music on an unsuspecting public. Nonetheless, the language used to link rock with the behavior of antisocial youths was couched in the same racial stereotypes. The *Music Journal* asserted that the "jungle rhythms" of rock incited juvenile offenders into "orgies of sex and violence" just as its forerunners did for the "savages." The New York *Daily News* derided the obscene lyrics set to "primitive jungle-beat rhythms." A week before Asa Carter traced rock and roll's penetration of the South to the NAACP, a New England psychiatrist disparaged the music as "cannibalistic and tribalistic." Similarly, a Catholic clergyman from Boston denounced the sexually suggestive lyrics for inflaming youths "like jungle tom-toms readying warriors for battle."[32]

As targets of this criticism, African Americans generally recognized the racial animus behind attacks on rock and roll. Although they too expressed dismay at the use of inappropriate lyrics aimed at youngsters and did not always find the music to their liking, many black adults softened in their reactions to the music as they witnessed the growing campaign against the civil rights movement.

As massive resistance swung into high gear in 1956, black commentators perceptively drew the connection between the South's efforts to defend segregation and to smear black-derived music. A writer for the *Amsterdam News* suggested "that the hate rock 'n' roll seems to inspire in some of its critics stems solely from the fact that Negro musicians predominate in the field, originated it, and are making the loot out of it." Even more forcefully, the *Pittsburgh Courier* editorialized that the war against rock and roll constituted "an indirect attack against Negroes, of course, because they invented rock 'n' roll (as they did all other distinctive U.S. music), and because it has so captivated the younger generation of whites that they are breaking down dance floors and gutting night clubs here and abroad."[33] A matter of racial pride, many black adults came to consider the harsh denunciation of rock and roll as an attempt to demean the contributions made by African Americans to American popular culture.

Although race and rock and roll set the stage for the congressional investigation of payola, the immediate stimulus for the probe grew out of an internal struggle for power in the music business. Until 1940 ASCAP controlled the licensing of performance rights and the collection of royalties due its members from any place music was sold or played. Locked in a bitter dispute with ASCAP over higher fees, in 1941, radio broadcasters transformed BMI, which they had created two years earlier, into a rival performance licensing group. For the next two decades, ASCAP sought to destroy BMI as a competitor through lawsuits and congressional action.[34]

In 1953, ASCAP songwriters filed a $150 million antitrust case charging BMI with engaging in monopolistic practices. They argued that because broadcasters operated BMI, they had a special interest in playing music licensed by their own organization to the detriment of songs contained in the ASCAP catalogue. In fact, radio stations contracted with both ASCAP and BMI and entered into standard financial arrangements with each. Indeed, ASCAP had continued to profit since the formation of BMI, its income nearly quadrupling to $25 million between 1939 and 1956. By the mid-1950s the older organization still licensed 85 percent of the music heard on radio and 75 percent of the songs distributed on record albums, which accounted for the largest proportion of sales in the record business. Nevertheless, BMI made significant inroads on the older organization's share of the market. Until 1955, ASCAP-licensed songs dominated the popular music charts and particularly the tunes ranked in the top ten of the highly regarded *Billboard* magazine listing. However, by the late 1950s, BMI-recorded hits appeared more frequently than those of ASCAP in the coveted top ten rankings.[35]

Rock and roll became the outlet for much of ASCAP's discontent. Major recording studios could adapt to changing tastes by signing up rock and roll performers. RCA did so in 1956, buying Elvis Presley's contract from Sun Records, one of the many independent companies providing unwelcome competition for the major firms. Tin Pan Alley songwriters, however, found it much more difficult to pen tunes for the changing youth-oriented market. Those who had crafted hits in the past for Broadway shows and Hollywood movies had little inclination to shift their efforts to a musical form that they despised and considered professionally inferior. In 1959, *Billboard* wrote that "many frustrated music men—out of step with current song and recording trends . . . sigh for the good old days."[36] Believing that payola spawned rock, songwriters of traditional music attacked the former in hope of curtailing the latter. The fact that BMI firms published most rock and roll songs stoked the fires of ASCAP's fury.

As ASCAP's lawsuit against BMI dragged on through the courts during the 1950s without success, the organization turned to Congress to press its case. In 1956, ASCAP received a sympathetic reception from the House Judiciary Committee, which held extensive hearings on the subject of broadcasting monopolies. The support provided by Emanuel Celler, the committee chairman, shows that outside of the South's massive resistance campaign, race operated in a more subtle fashion. On one hand, Celler, a liberal representative from Brooklyn, was a staunch supporter of black advancement and a leader of the successful effort to pass civil rights legislation in 1957. At the same time, the congressman did not have much appreciation for rock and roll. The music had a place in the culture because, as he explained patronizingly, it had given "great impetus to talent, especially among the colored people: it's a natural expression of their emotions and feelings."[37] This attitude did not keep Celler from fighting against legal segregation and disfranchisement, but it did line him up on the same side as those who viewed black-derived rock and roll as inferior music.[38]

Despite a lengthy inquiry into the dispute and clear sympathy with AS-CAP's position, nothing came out of the Celler Committee deliberations.[39] The Senate then took up the issue. George Smathers of Florida embraced ASCAP's cause as the South continued to combat school desegregation and attempts of blacks to register to vote. Shortly before passage of the Civil Rights Act of 1957, Smathers introduced a bill to force broadcast stations to divest themselves from BMI or lose their licenses from the Federal Communications Commission (FCC). The Senate Committee on Interstate and Foreign Commerce held hearings on the Smathers's measure beginning in March 1958.[40]

Chaired by John Pastore of Rhode Island, like Celler a liberal Democrat, the investigation traveled over familiar terrain. ASCAP supporters argued that without sponsorship of BMI and the constant plugging of disk jockeys, rock and roll would have collapsed. Perhaps the most vivid testimony of this sort was articulated by Vance Packard, who had been hired as an expert witness by the Songwriters Protective Association, whose membership overlapped with that of ASCAP. A popular magazine writer and author of a best-selling book exposing the practices of advertisers in manipulating the public's taste for consumer goods, Packard charged that many of the social problems that affected Americans stemmed from the techniques of "hidden persuasion" perfected by Madison Avenue. He warned the committee that the nation was becoming increasingly "standardized, homogenized, hypnotized, and sterilized," and was losing such core values "as respect for the dignity of the individual, freedom from conformity, and freedom of choice."[41] The notion of hidden persuaders fit in with prevailing perceptions—whether applied to communist infiltration, juvenile delinquency, labor racketeering, or civil rights protest—that clandestine forces rigged the country's institutions and sapped their moral strength.

Packard applied the same analysis to explain the teenage infatuation with rock and roll. Tracing it to the hidden hand of broadcasting corruption, he argued that the kind of music BMI mainly handled could not have possibly become successful unless the broadcasters themselves had pushed it upon the public. Like other critics of rock and roll, Packard disparaged its racial antecedents. "Inspired by what had been called race music modified to stir the animal instinct in modern teenagers," Packard informed Pastore, "its chief characteristics now are a heavy, unrelenting beat and a raw, savage tone." Music of this inferior sort, he suggested, could not have gained commercial success without the manipulation of juvenile tastes by unscrupulous disk jockeys under the sway of payola.[42] This notion of conspiratorial machination had far reaching implications. For example, it reinforced the thinking of southern white segregationists who believed that outside civil-rights agitators were conniving to upset time-honored Jim Crow practices in their region.

Packard's views did not go unchallenged. BMI supporters pointed out that far from engaging in a conspiracy to undermine American standards of decency, the appeal of rock and roll vindicated faith in democracy by demonstrating that people could choose what they wanted to hear. The testimony of individuals not associated with rock and roll proved most effective. The distinguished opera star Robert Merrill doubted that rock tunes harmed "the spiritual and emotional health of young people," and seriously questioned whether the problems attributed to teenagers "would disappear if our youngsters were exposed exclusively to Puccini and never to Presley."[43] Another witness took exception with Packard's characterization of rock and roll as lowlife music. The wife of Nat King Cole testified on behalf of her husband who was out on tour. Although her husband sang a different style of music, Maria Ellington Cole presented a spirited defense of rock and roll as "authentic music . . . [that] must stand or fall on its own merits." In a blunt rejoinder to opponents who denigrated rock as race music, she proudly noted that "just as country music grew up as the folk music of people in the hills of Tennessee and in the West, so did race music grow as a part of the folk music of American Negroes."[44]

After listening to the evidence over several months, Pastore and his committee decided not to intrude legislatively in what was essentially an economic battle between ASCAP and BMI. The Rhode Island senator was not convinced that BMI engaged in a conspiracy to deceive the public into accepting rock and roll and dismissed the notion that divorcing BMI from broadcasters would mean "the end of all rock and roll." Hardly a fan of the music, he nevertheless tolerated it as part of "a fashion and a fad that appeals to young people," including his fourteen-year-old daughter (who, he admitted with chagrin, liked the Coasters' hit "Yakety Yak"). To join in a battle to destroy rock and roll and what it stood for culturally, smelled to Pastore like a form of dreaded censorship and "thought control."[45]

As ASCAP continued to scuffle with BMI in the courts and to heap scorn upon rock and roll, hearings into television quiz show improprieties unexpectedly launched a full-blown congressional inquiry into payola. In 1959, the House Legislative Oversight Subcommittee, chaired by Representative Oren Harris, an Arkansas Democrat, conducted a highly publicized investigation into a scandal that had been brewing for several years. In the 1950s, quiz and other game shows had made the transition from radio to television and attracted huge audiences. Programs such as *The $64,000 Question* and *Twenty-One* awarded big cash prizes to contestants who competed to furnish information usually buried in the pages of encyclopedias. Producers of these shows heightened the level of their authenticity by keeping the participants in isolation booths and delivering the questions under armed guard. However, the facade of honesty collapsed when a few disgruntled contestants admitted that they had been coached and that the outcome of these televised matches of brain power were rigged. After a grand jury in New York City, where most of these programs originated, gathered considerable evidence of deception, Congress took up the matter.[46]

The quiz show scandal riveted public attention on Washington. It provided the Democratic majority in Congress with an opportunity to look ahead to the presidential campaign in 1960 and build a case that under the Republican administration of Dwight Eisenhower a climate of moral decay had set in. Already in 1958, the Legislative Oversight Subcommittee had probed federal regulatory commissions and uncovered influence peddling between federal regulatory agencies and Sherman Adams, Eisenhower's closest advisor, who was forced to resign. Planning his race for the presidency, Senator John F. Kennedy exploited the public disillusionment these scandals produced. A close friend of George Smathers and a moderate on civil rights, Kennedy was courting key southern Democrats to support his nomination for the presidency. Yet his strategy aimed beyond the South. Richard N. Goodwin, a staff lawyer on the Oversight Subcommittee during the quiz show probe, explained that the Massachusetts senator had "an intuitive belief that his fellow citizens were dissatisfied, that they expected more from their society and themselves, that they wanted to 'Get America Moving Again.' "[47]

The quiz show revelations reinforced the notion that the United States had lost its moral compass, and Charles Van Doren became a symbol of this concern. An English instructor at Columbia University and the son of a prominent professor there, Van Doren had achieved victory on *Twenty-One* through a combination of his own intelligence and the backstage manipulation of the show's producers. Until he admitted his guilt in testimony before the Legislative Oversight Subcommittee in 1959, the thirty-three-year-old academic was viewed as a worthy role model for youth to follow.[48] In contrast to rock stars whose performances aroused teenagers into an emotional frenzy, Van Doren offered his cool intellect as an attractive alternative. Adults embraced him as the counter-Elvis, "a new kind of T.V. idol of all things, an egghead . . . whom many a grateful parent regards as T.V.'s own health-restoring antidote to Presley."[49] His fall from grace before the House Committee removed Van Doren as a useful weapon in the generational culture wars. Deeply disturbed over the moral implications of Van Doren's fall from grace, in 1959, the writer John Steinbeck rued: "on all levels [society] is rigged. A creeping all-pervading nerve gas of immorality . . .starts in the nursery and does not stop before it reaches the highest offices, both corporate and governmental."[50]

The quiz show scandal also prompted lawmakers to mount another investigation into manipulation and deception in broadcasting and the music business. The Harris Committee thus turned its attention to payola as another example of the dangers lurking in the "rigged society." Indeed, ASCAP and its allies regarded the quiz show hearings as benefiting their continuing efforts to hamstring BMI. At the end of that investigation, in November 1959, Burton Lane, the president of the American Guild of Authors and Composers and a longstanding antagonist of BMI, informed the Legislative Oversight Subcommittee that the evidence it had uncovered with respect to quiz show fraud had "a counterpart in the promotion of music." He told lawmakers that commercial bribery in the form of payola "has become a prime factor in determining what music is played on many broadcast programs and what musical records the public is surreptitiously induced to buy."[51] Lane had leveled these charges without success many times before to Congress, the Federal Communications Commission, and the Federal Trade Commission. This time, however, he received a more favorable response. By the end of the year, the Oversight Subcommittee's preliminary inquiry revealed that payola was "rampant" and both the FCC and the FTC initiated their own probes.[52] In the wake of the widespread attention garnered by the quiz show hearings and in anticipation of the 1960 elections, lawmakers found the time right to tackle the century-old practice of payola.

Racial motives influenced some key congressmen. Representative Harris lined up with his southern colleagues in opposition to civil rights legislation. In 1950 he had served on the steering group that helped defeat passage of a bill establishing a Fair Employment Practice Committee (FEPC), a measure designed to check racial bias. Harris did not see it that way. According to the Arkansas congressman, "just as discrimination should not be practiced as affecting minorities, neither should the minorities arbitrarily control our political institutions against the best interest and real desires of the majority."[53]

Harris and his colleagues painted a dire if distorted picture of the FEPC acquiring "unlimited authority, the most far reaching powers [over] the business and economic life of this country ever given throughout our entire history."[54]

Throughout the rest of the decade, Harris's anxieties about federal involvement to promote civil rights only increased. In 1956, he signed his name to a manifesto of 101 southern congressional lawmakers challenging the legitimacy of the Supreme Court's desegregation decree in *Brown*. The following year, President Eisenhower vividly displayed Washington's commitment to the enforcement of federal court orders by sending troops into Little Rock. During the confrontation, Harris staunchly defended the segregationist stand taken by Governor Orval Faubus and distanced himself from any attempt to hammer out a peaceful compromise. "Stunned beyond expression" by Eisenhower's action, the congressman "deeply resented it, [and] thought it was unnecessary and unwarranted."[55]

To Harris and other proponents of massive resistance, the payola investigation offered an opportunity to check integrationist advances not only politically but also culturally. Harris endorsed the views of the *American Nationalist,* an extreme right-wing publication originating in southern California, which claimed that "Negroes have been raised to stardom and adulation as a result of the fictitious popularity of rock-and-roll music— popularly purchased through 'payola.'" Raising the specter of miscegenation, this prosegregationist and antirock tract recoiled over "teenage daughters . . . squealing and drooling over Negroidal crooners."[56] Harris fully agreed with these sentiments, and he replied to his hometown constituent who sent him the material: "I have the same views as you do on such distasteful propaganda to integrate the races." Vowing to make "every effort in opposition, either by legislation or Executive action," Harris assured his correspondent that his committee "would not shirk in any way or overlook" the subject of payola, and he did not consider its racial angle "too hot to handle."[57]

Actually, the white southern counteroffensive of massive resistance had already slowed down the civil rights momentum building after *Brown* and the Montgomery Bus Boycott, especially at the grassroots level. Throughout most of the Deep South, school desegregation made almost no progress, and bus boycotts expanded to very few southern cities. Although Martin Luther King Jr. established the Southern Christian Leadership Conference in 1957, an organization designed to mobilize nonviolent, direct-action protests, the group made little headway in promoting mass demonstrations or placing blacks on the voter rolls. In fact, the pace of black voter registration, which had grown steadily since World War II, leveled off far short of enfranchising a majority of black adults by the end of the 1950s.[58] Nevertheless, the persistent gap between actual civil rights breakthroughs and continued white domination only slightly moderated southern fears of losing control over fundamental racial matters.

Whatever the realities of the civil rights situation, Harris felt much more strongly about containing racial equality than he did about stamping out corruption in broadcasting. In the mid-1950s the Arkansas congressman had received a 25 percent interest in KRBB, a television station in his hometown of El Dorado. He paid a token amount of $500 for the investment and signed a promissory note for the much larger figure of $4,500, which the station never asked him to repay. In 1958 the FCC granted KRBB permission to expand its power output to a level the commission had denied before Harris became part owner. When the chief investigator for Harris's own Legislative Oversight Committee leaked the details of this story to the press, the congressman sold his interest in the station and at the same time fired the whistle-blower.[59] His own questionable behavior did not stop Harris from chairing investigations of unethical conduct relating to the FCC and FTC as well as television quiz shows; nor would it keep him from probing payola. In light of the enormous public drama surrounding the downfall of Charles Van Doren, it made good political sense for the committee to carry its probe in the related direction of the rigging of records for broadcast.

Most if not all of the nine legislators who sat on Harris's Legislative Oversight Committee had a dim view of the quality of rock and roll; however, this did not mean that race was foremost in all their minds.[60] No one paid greater attention to the proceedings than did John Moss, a California Democrat. Born a Mormon, Moss had ceased practicing the religion because of the church's "strong pattern of racial discrimination." Before entering politics, he owned a small appliance store, and his business outlook shaped his attitude toward payola. It did not matter that payola was frequently used by small, independent record companies to outmaneuver the giant firms. To Moss, payola constituted commercial bribery, which he identified with the kind of activity big business used to undermine competition. A believer in free enterprise in the populist and Progressive tradition, he favored governmental regulation to oversee "powerful interests that thwart opportunity and competition." His commitment to openness also emerged in Moss's sponsorship of freedom of information legislation to minimize government secretiveness.[61] As for rock and roll, Moss did not exhibit much of an open mind and expressed the typical reaction of his colleagues: hearing it played on the radio his response was "to snap the thing off, as quickly as possible." He complained that his own teenage children listened to this "trash" because disk jockeys pushed it on them.[62]

Some legislative action to curb payola appeared certain. The Eisenhower administration joined the chorus condemning the practice. Already stung by the scandal involving one of his closest aides, Sherman Adams, the Republican president sought to recapture higher moral ground. Following the public brouhaha over television quiz show deception, Eisenhower instructed Attorney General William Rogers to investigate the problem of fraud in broadcasting and report back to him.[63] Rogers issued his findings at the close of 1959, declaring there was "evidence of widespread corruption and lack of the personal integrity which is so essential to the fabric of American life." He proposed legislation to make the receipt of payola by station personnel a federal criminal offense.[64]

The Eisenhower administration had hoped to get out in front of the Democrat-controlled Legislative Oversight subcommittee, but Harris did not intend to relinquish the spotlight in a presidential election year. Harris did not need much additional incentive to turn up the political heat on the Eisenhower regime. The military intervention in Little Rock and the Republican administration's successful sponsorship of civil rights legislation in 1957 had irked the Arkansas congressman. Opening on February 8, 1960, the hearings confirmed what the trade press and industry insiders had known about for years—the widespread existence of payola. The Harris Committee paraded a lineup of witnesses consisting mainly of disk jockeys and record company executives and distributors. Most witnesses did not deny their part in the acceptance of gifts, but they adamantly rejected the notion that these payments affected their play selection.[65] According to this defense, at the very most disk jockeys took payments not to dictate what they played but to advise record companies on what kind of tunes would appeal to their listeners. Actually, the under-the-table gratuities did not ensure that a disk jockey could turn a particular record into a hit, but they did guarantee that of the hundreds of free records the radio station received each week, those furnished by companies dispensing payola would make it to the top of the pile for the disk jockey's review and increase the potential for airplay.[66]

Congressional inquisitors remained unconvinced by the denials. Influenced by Vance Packard's warnings of "hidden persuaders," they believed that consumers did not have a free choice and were more likely to have their desires shaped by advertisers and product merchandisers. In particular, they considered a teenage audience even more vulnerable to manipulation than adults. Harris asserted from the outset that "the quality of broadcast programs declines when the choice of program materials is made, not in the public interest, but in the interest of those who are willing to pay to obtain exposure of their records." Without payola, he declared, "we probably would not have a lot of stuff that the American people have had to listen to."[67]

The bad "stuff," undoubtedly, referred to rock and roll. Record spinners who accepted gifts but who did not play rock and roll escaped committee censure. A Boston disk jockey admitted receiving Christmas gifts from record distributors, but he continued to play "the type of music that an adult audience would enjoy . . . not . . . the raucous kind of sound that I had always associated payola with." Another disk jockey in the same city, Stan Richards, passed muster from the lawmakers by denouncing rock and roll as "junk music" that he refused to play. According to *Billboard* reporter Mildred Hall, who observed the hearing closely, such condemnations "won approving congressional smiles in each instance."[68]

Indeed, in condemning rock and roll and underscoring its connection to payola, disk jockeys who came clean received praise from the committee. This public process of denunciation resembled the role that ex-Communists played in the McCarthy era in providing justification for controversial investigations into unpopular political beliefs. The culture of investigation contained a ritual of forgiveness and redemption for those who cooperated, allowing them to receive the blessing of the committee. For example, Chairman Harris applauded Richards at the conclusion of his testimony, noting that while he had once engaged in "pathetic" conduct as a disk jockey, his presentation had proven him to be a "good fellow" entitled to continue his career.[69]

Rock and roll remained a focus of the deliberations, as it had in the Pastore hearings two years earlier, but this time the ASCAP-BMI war had shifted to another battleground. After its supporters had helped initiate the investigation with their complaints to the legislative committee, ASCAP turned its attention to the executive branch. Following the fallout from the quiz show scandal and Attorney General Rogers's recommendation for more vigorous federal regulation, ASCAP officials took their case against payola and BMI to the FCC and FTC.[70] Without the congressional spotlight on the ASCAP-BMI conflict, much of the discussion shifted away from private rivalries in the music business and centered on the decline in standards of public morality.[71]

In contrast with the often stated ties between rock and roll and the decline of public morality, race had a muted presence during the congressional probe. Unlike the situation in previous hearings, witnesses did not publicly refer to rock and roll in racially coded terms, for example, as "jungle" music arousing "savage" passions. The disappearance of such rhetoric, however, did not mean that racial fears had subsided. Rather it reflected two changes in the cultural and political environment. First, rock and roll music had become considerably whiter. The hard, raunchy edge of the original music turned softer as record companies, always sensitive to bad publicity, responded to the concerted attacks on suggestive lyrics. Black pioneers such as Chuck Berry and Little Richard passed from the scene, as had the white rocker Jerry Lee Lewis, who lost public favor after marrying his thirteen-year-old cousin. Moreover, the most popular of them all, Elvis Presley, had gone into the Army and returned as a toned-down balladeer and Hollywood movie star. From an alleged fomenter of juvenile delinquency, the black-inspired Presley had assumed the identity of a patriotic ex-GI and all-American boy.[72] In their places the rock scene attracted less threatening white crooners who seemed more cuddly than menacing.

Second, while rock and roll had functioned as a convenient symbol of racial anxieties in the 1950s, by 1960 the civil rights movement offered a more tangible target for racist attacks. White supremacists in the South had more direct problems facing them than "race music." Beginning in late 1959 and erupting in February 1960, they had to face a resurgent freedom struggle invigorated by African American high-school and college students who challenged racial inequality through sit-ins, freedom rides, and other forms of direct-action protest. Whatever notion segregationists may have had that in destroying rock and roll they could frustrate racial reform paled beside the visible threat posed by young black protesters and their white allies. In the heightened atmosphere of racial agitation that accompanied this new phase of the civil rights struggle, antirock and antipayola crusades lost much of their significance compared with the bruising battles that took place in cities and towns throughout America.

Besides, in the latter part of the 1950s, southern state governments directly launched their own investigations into subversive influence within the civil rights movement. Primarily targeting the NAACP in Florida and Louisiana, state legislative investigation committees attempted to link the civil rights group with Communist infiltration. For a time, Alabama managed to ban the NAACP from operating within its borders. In the wake of *Brown*, Mississippi created the State Sovereignty Commission, which monitored civil rights activists, planted informers within their ranks, and collaborated with local law enforcement agencies to harass them. Thus, on the state level, committees such as these mirrored the legislative culture of investigation in Washington, D.C., that in the 1950s sustained an array of inquisitorial forays into the "rigged society."[73]

Though race moved to the background of the payola hearings at the same time as it moved into the foreground of politics and social change, it still cast a shadow over the congressional investigation. The racial connotation of rock and roll, and hence their association with the black freedom struggle, played themselves out in the opposing fates of the two most prominent disk jockeys in the business: Dick Clark and Alan Freed. The "whitening" of rock and its movement into the musical mainstream, which had lessened somewhat the hysterical opposition to it, helps explain how Clark emerged relatively unscathed from the hearings. In contrast, Freed, who represented the early and less acceptable black-oriented version of the music, fared much worse.

In August 1957, when Dick Clark became host of *American Bandstand,* the nationally televised teenage dance show on the ABC network, the twenty-seven-year-old Syracuse University graduate with a degree in advertising was not yet a decade past his own teenage years. Clark considered himself more a businessman than a rock and roll enthusiast, and his own musical tastes ran along the lines of Glenn Miller. Convinced that if he could successfully market rock and roll to a broad teenage audience, Clark looked forward to making "a good deal of money."[74]

Clark packaged himself as an understanding mediator between adult society and the mysterious world of teenagers. Publishing an advice manual for teenagers, Clark pressed them on the need to understand their parents, who "have a strange way of being right most of the time."[75] Moreover, he sought to tone down the controversial aspects of rock and roll. He insisted that the kids on his program conform to a dress code, because "it made the show acceptable to adults." He came across as a "friend, adviser, older brother or young parent," the kind of man a teenage boy aspired to become and a teenage girl looked for in a husband. He domesticated the wilder features of rock and roll and consciously posed no threat to traditional family values. The music did not have to turn girls wild, it could also tame them. He encouraged young housewives, many of them not too far removed from their teenage years, "to roll up the ironing board and join us when you can."[76] He largely achieved his goal. Describing the participants on *American Bandstand* as an "attractive group of youngsters," the stately *New York Times* approvingly noted the absence of any "motorcycle jackets and hardly a sideburn in the crowd."[77]

Furthermore, Clark built his popularity on whiteness. Although he featured black performers on *Bandstand,* he strictly adhered to the network broadcasting policy of not stirring the racial brew. The dance party impresario did make an overture to bring black youths into his studio audience when he went on the air throughout the nation in 1957, but their presence was exceedingly thin and hardly visible in front of the cameras. As with rock and roll, he approached racial matters in a careful and practical manner. Acknowledging that he was not an "integrationist or pioneer," Clark broke the color barrier, however modestly, not out of any moral conviction but because he could "see it was going to happen, and there was no sense not doing it."[78] Nevertheless, African Americans remained largely invisible on his show. A black teenager from Philadelphia, where the show originated, complained: "When we have attempted to attend [Bandstand] . . . we've been given the run-around by officials of the show. And if a few of us manage to get inside, we're discouraged from dancing on the floor."[79]

However, it is too simple to dismiss Dick Clark as a racist. An impressive number of black performers first appeared on national television on *American Bandstand*, including Chuck Berry, Sam Cooke, Little Anthony and the Imperials, the Chantels, the Coasters, and Jackie Wilson. Clark also took many of them along with a group of white stars on integrated bus caravans touring the South.[80] Nevertheless, what Clark did best was not to promote African American culture or foster social integration but to help absorb black music into a popular format dominated by whites. He certainly did not discriminate against black performers and even helped some in their careers, but he was much more closely associated both in public perception and in reality with young white heartthrobs such as Frankie Avalon, Fabian, Bobby Rydell, and Bobbie Vinton. Clark acknowledged that he owed a great deal to the African American community for supplying the source of the music, but given his enormous popularity, he was more responsible than anyone else for refashioning that legacy into a whiter product.[81] At a time when African Americans were beginning to win battles in the courts, in Congress, in the schools of Little Rock, and on the streets of a few cities such as Montgomery, Alabama, Clark's orchestration of rock and roll lessened some of its perceived threat to white racial and cultural hegemony.

Clark's efforts stand in sharp contrast to those of Alan Freed, who by contrast appeared to challenge the racial status quo already under assault from the incipient civil rights movement. Whereas Clark appeared to represent "middle America, nice, a white-bread face," as one record company executive put it, "Freed was gruff, a street man, New York rock and roll, tough."[82] Eight years older than Clark, Freed first made his reputation in Cleveland before he moved on to New York City in 1954. Though he did not coin the label "rock and roll," he popularized it in concerts and on his frenetically paced radio shows, complete with sound effects, jive talk, and shouts of joy. If Clark appeared cool, calm, and collected if somewhat stiff and detached from the teenagers and their music, Freed acted just the opposite and got caught up in the energy and excitement of the programs he produced.[83]

At the heart of Freed's unique style was his association with the black roots of rock and roll. Freed's "Big Beat" concerts, starting in Cleveland in March 1952, showcased black performers and attracted largely African American audiences. Even as he increasingly attracted white fans, he insisted on playing the original recordings of rock songs by black artists. He considered the cover versions record companies put out by white artists as "anti-Negro." He served as a transmission belt for black-oriented rock seeping into the lives of white teenagers, and this made him dangerous to many. He reported receiving "batches of poison-pen letters calling me a 'nigger-lover.'"[84]

His association with blacks got him in trouble. When violence erupted outside one of his Big Beat concerts in Boston in 1958, his detractors blamed the attacks on black hoodlums, a charge that could not be substantiated. Nevertheless, local authorities indicted Freed for inciting a riot and his New York City radio station cut him loose.[85] The self-proclaimed "King of Rock 'n' Roll" also had his own dance party television program canceled by WABC in New York City the year before because of an incident with racial overtones. While *American Bandstand* managed to keep a low profile when it came to blacks, Freed's show spotlighted one of his vocal guests, Frankie Lymon of the Teenagers, dancing with a white girl in the audience. Distributed throughout the country, the show caused a furor in the South, and in 1957 the network dropped it.[86]

Freed was far from perfect. He was brash and arrogant, employed an agent with connections to organized crime, drank alcohol too heavily, and lived a lavish lifestyle that he supported in part with elaborate gifts from record companies that he explained away as consulting fees. His affinity for black talent did not prevent Freed from cutting himself in on the songwriting credits of Chuck Berry's "Maybelline" and the Moonglows' "Sincerely" and receiving royalties from their successes.[87]

However, as Freed steadfastly maintained his commitment to black performers and became a target of those who attacked rock and roll with racist smears, he gained even greater admiration among African Americans. The singer Jackie Wilson explained Freed's esteem among black entertainers: "Looking at it from an economic standpoint, I can say that because of him, hundreds of Negro musicians, singers, and arrangers got work." When Freed became a prime focus of the payola probe, the *Pittsburgh Courier* wondered if the investigations were "being used as a means of destroying the music that millions of teenagers have come to regard as their own."[88]

The payola scandal destroyed what was left of Freed's downwardly spiraling career. Even before the hearings commenced, Freed had lost jobs on both radio and television. Having moved from WINS to WABC after the Boston incident, Freed was asked by the latter station to sign an affidavit swearing that he had never taken payola. He refused, calling the demand "an insult to my reputation." Nevertheless, the flamboyant disk jockey hurt his case by issuing characteristically flippant remarks. "A man said to me," Freed commented, " 'if somebody sent you a Cadillac, would you send it back'? I said, 'It depends on the color.' " By way of clarification, Freed told reporters that he never accepted money in advance to play a record, "but if anybody wanted to thank him for playing a tune, he saw nothing wrong in accepting a gift."[89]

In contrast, Dick Clark held onto his lucrative job hosting *American Bandstand*. Employed by ABC, the parent company that owned Freed's New York City station, Clark did not have to sign the same kind of affidavit as did his fellow disk jockey. Instead, network executives permitted the Philadelphia broadcaster to fashion his own document that allowed him greater flexibility in denying that he had engaged in improper activities. Defining payola narrowly—the receipt of payments in exchange for playing a particular record—Clark asserted that he had never engaged in it. Yet Clark had to pay a price to keep his position. Heavily involved in an extensive array of enterprises including music publishing, marketing, manufacturing, and artist representation, Clark had to divest himself of these holdings to satisfy ABC's demand that he avoid any conflict of interest. This arrangement infuriated Freed, who howled that given the chance he could have truthfully signed the same statement as did Clark.[90]

Typically, Freed did not exit quietly. Griping that if he were "going to be a scapegoat" then Clark should "be one too," Freed got his wish. He even cooperated with the Harris Committee by appearing in executive session. Under the rules of the House this would keep him from incriminating himself with respect to other judicial action, but it also allowed him to help the committee build a case against Clark. On April 25, 1960, Freed testified in closed session that although he had been on the payroll of several record companies, he had never taken "a dime to play a record. I'd be a fool to. I'd be giving up control of my program."[91] He also criticized ABC officials for favoring Clark, a conclusion that the committee had also reached.

Indeed, Clark and not Freed became the primary target of the Harris Committee's inquiry. To Washington lawmakers, even those as racially sensitive as the Arkansas chairman, rock and roll was harmful whether the records were spun by Freed or Clark. The Philadelphian, however, provided the legislators with the opportunity to make headlines by exposing a star as bright as Charles Van Doren.[92] For those who believed in the continuing danger of a rigged society, Clark offered a shining example. He might appear clean cut and virtuous on the outside, but the committee intended to show him as corrupt and deceitful on the inside.

Harris's staff had not uncovered much evidence that Clark had accepted payola, narrowly defined as "play for pay." Rather committee investigators discovered that Clark profited from holdings in a network of enterprises related to the music he aired on his program. The popular image of a shadowy individual greasing the palm of a greedy disk jockey with payments did not fit Clark's operation. Through various companies in which he had invested, the proprietor of *American Bandstand* "played records he had an interest in more frequently than those with no interest." A statistical breakdown of his program selections revealed that he played the records he had a stake in earlier and longer.[93] Thus, *Billboard* concluded, the nation's premier disk jockey derived royalties from "every possible source of revenue in the music industry, from copyright to distribution."[94] Congressman Moss coined the word "Clarkola" to describe the Philadelphian's unique variation on the subject under investigation.[95] On this basis, the *New York Post* entertainment columnist Earl Wilson asserted that "Dick's on the edge of a precipice—and could easily be pushed off."[96]

These dire predictions notwithstanding, Clark turned in a virtuoso performance, one that saved his career, setting him apart from both Freed and Van Doren. Unlike Freed who presented his story behind closed doors in executive session, giving the appearance that he had something to hide, Clark faced the committee in open session on April 29 and May 2, with reporters and cameras recording his testimony. He proved that serving as a pitchman for rock and roll hardly made him an anti-establishment figure. Although he defended the music he played as a wholesome, recreational outlet for teenagers, he came across more as a shrewd businessman than a diehard fan of rock and roll. Pressed about his financial interests in thirty-three different companies that stood to gain from the popularity of *American Bandstand*, he explained his motive as trying to ensure his economic future by diversifying investments in "the recording, publishing, manufacturing [and] distribution fields." At most, he pleaded guilty with an explanation: "I would note that until the committee's activities, no one had really pointed out the inconsistency of performing records and owning an interest in record and music companies," a standard practice in the music industry. Besides, having sold off his outside musical holdings in agreement with ABC, Clark argued that the issue of improper influence had become moot.[97]

Despite the damaging evidence against him and his obvious tiptoeing around the meaning of the practice of payola, incredibly Clark walked away from the hearings with his reputation intact. The skepticism many committee members voiced about the disk jockey's questionable business arrangements proved not to have much depth. He proved neither a serious threat to traditional American values nor to the civil rights concerns of southern white lawmakers. Chairman Harris spoke for most of his colleagues before dismissing Clark when he said, "You have given us a different light on the use of the broadcast media than has been presented to us by the admitted payola people. . . . You have been very helpful to the committee in the consideration of its responsibility. And I want to compliment you for that." Later when Clark wrote Harris privately to thank him for his "kind consideration," the Arkansas representative replied: "I was pleased to have the privilege of knowing you. I thought you gave a very good account of yourself."[98] Rather than coming off as the "Baby Face Nelson of the music business," Clark performed before the committee in a polished, courteous manner that distinguished him from the popular image of the sordid disk jockey on the take. A fellow of great charm who continued to receive the firm backing of his network employer ABC, Clark was never in as much danger as he had anticipated. How could he have been? As he later recalled, the chief counsel for the committee, Robert Lishman, during a lunch break brought up his teenage son to Clark to get his autograph and have a picture snapped with him.[99]

Alan Freed did not fare as well. He was the anti-Clark, fostering an image of the untamed, rebellious, and dark (racially and socially) sides of rock and roll. No parents would want him to marry their daughter. If adults could consider Clark the likeable boy next door, they had no room for Freed in their neighborhood. Freed's cooperation with the Harris committee did not spare him from an indictment for commercial bribery by a grand jury in New York City. Whereas Clark's subsequent career has thrived for nearly four decades, after the hearings Freed accepted a plea bargain of a $500 fine and a suspended six-month jail sentence. He bounced around from job to job for a few years until his death from kidney failure in 1965.[100]

The final outcome of the Harris investigation produced mixed results. After Congress passed an antipayola bill, President Eisenhower signed it into law on September 13, 1960. The legislation required any station employee who accepted a payment for broadcasting material or the person making the payment to report it first to the station management. Failure to comply constituted a crime with a penalty of a year in jail and a $10,000 fine.[101]

Passage of the law may have given lawmakers an election-year victory to bring home to their constituents, but it did not kill payola. Endemic to the music business, the practice continued in even more clandestine form. At the end of the year, *Billboard* reported that the law had merely driven payola further underground. According to a survey conducted by the trade journal, the majority of disk jockeys believed that the payola investigation "was more of a political football than a practical cleanup." Music journalist Ralph Gleason observed that payola was "still alive and well" and that untraceable cash payments had replaced checks as the standard fare of conducting surreptitious business dealings.[102] Nevertheless, with the Justice Department, FCC, and Internal Revenue Service as an increased threat to those who dispensed or accepted illegal payments, payola no longer flourished as it had in the 1950s.[103]

After building throughout the 1950s, the antipayola campaign reached its peak in 1960. The timing mirrored a number of features of the decade's political culture. Consistent with the myriad investigations into communism, organized crime, juvenile delinquency, and television quiz show fraud, the payola probe sought to expose the dangers to an unsuspecting public, especially among American youth, that came from the manipulation of their musical choices. Genuine payola and real deception certainly existed in the music business, as it had for most of the century, but during the 1950s the subject became a serious political issue because it conformed to the popular view that conspiratorial elements were operating to produce a rigged society. In this context, payola became the "hidden persuader" that produced an inferior and decadent brand of music undermining the nation's cultural strength and vitality. The drive against payola—"musical McCarthyism" as one contemporary disparagingly called it[104]—smeared rock and roll with sinister influences and conveyed multiple fears related to youth, discipline, economic competition, race, and the Cold War. Some involved concerns over the decline of public morality and national purpose in an era of hostile relations with the Soviet Union; others grew out of a power struggle between professional associations in the music field. Moreover, rock and roll and payola mirrored the growing presence of the civil rights movement and racial confrontation on the American political landscape.

In the years after *Brown v. Board of Education*, rock and roll served as a symbolic target for those worried about the wrenching racial changes looming on the horizon. These fears accelerated with tangible examples of black protest such as the Montgomery bus boycott and the desegregation of Central High School in Little Rock. Yet for most of the half decade following *Brown,* civil rights efforts were scattered, nonconfrontational, and confined largely to Congress and the courts. This changed dramatically in 1960 with the rise of student activism and the sit-ins. The pace of black protest heightened as did awareness of direct attacks on the racial status quo. Those upset by the changes that the black freedom struggle promised to bring had more palpable areas for concern than rock and roll now furnished. Thus, by 1960, the chief threat to white supremacy came not from the musical transmission of black popular culture but from the mobilization of a mass movement of blacks and their white allies. Although rock and roll continued to provide the soundtrack for young activists in the struggle, it drifted away from the center of the contest for black advancement in the South and the nation. During the 1960s, payola persisted in the music industry and rock and roll transformed itself into a more powerful product even as their value as political and cultural signifiers of racial tensions diminished.[105]

NOTES

1. On congressional anticommunism, Robert Griffith, *Politics of Fear: Joseph Mc-Carthy and the Senate* (Amherst: University of Massachusetts Press, 1987); William Howard Moore, *The Kefauver Committee and the Politics of Crime, 1950–1952* (Columbia: University of Missouri Press, 1974); and James Gilbert, *A Cycle of Outrage: America's Reaction to the Juvenile Delinquent in the 1950s* (New York: Oxford University Press, 1986); Kent Anderson, *Television Fraud: The History and Implications of the Quiz Show Scandals* (Westport, Conn.: Greenwood, 1978).

2. Quoted in Kerry Seagrave, *Payola in the Music Industry: A History, 1880–1991* (Jefferson, N.C.: McFarland, 1994), 12. Seagrave dates the first appearance of the word *payola* to 1938 (p. 1). John A. Jackson, *Big Beat Heat: Alan Freed and the Early Years of Rock & Roll* (New York: Schirmer Books, 1991), 245, dates it to 1916, but gives no specific reference. Whenever the term formally appeared, it is clear that the concept was well known around the turn of the century. See also, R. H. Coarse, "Payola in Radio and Television Broadcasting," *Journal of Law and Economics* 22 (October 1979): 32; Marc Eliot, *Rockonomics: The Money Behind the Music* (New York: Citadel Press, 1993), 10; *Billboard,* November 23, 1959, p. 4.

3. Seagrave, *Payola,* 29; Coarse, "Payola," 286; Steve Chapple and Reebee Garofalo, *Rock 'n' Roll Is Here to Pay: The History and Politics of the Music Industry* (Chicago: Nelson-Hall, 1977), 55.

4. *Variety,* November 11, 1959, p. 55; Chapple, *Rock 'n' Roll,* 60; Eliot, *Rockonomics,* 42.

5. Jackson, *Big Beat,* 252; Dorothy Wade and Justin Picardie, *Music Man: Ahmet Ertegun, Atlantic Records, and the Triumph of Rock 'n' Roll* (New York: W. W. Norton, 1989), 89; Fredric Dannen, *Hit Men: Power Brokers and Fast Money Inside the Music Business* (New York: Times Books, 1990), 43 ff. For example, in 1909, New York made it illegal for anyone either to offer or accept a gratuity "with intent to influence" an employee's behavior without the employer's knowledge. However, this statute was aimed at department stores and not music industry practices.

6. Quoted in Coarse, "Payola," 276. See also Coarse, 278, 279, 280, 283, 285; Seagrave, *Payola,* 16; Hazel Meyer, *The Gold in Tin Pan Alley* (Philadelphia: Lippincott, 1958), 155. Over the years the MPPA proved ineffective in curbing payola; without enforcement power it could not stop publishers from trying to gain an advantage at the expense of their competitors by reviving payoffs. An abortive effort to curb the practice came with an antipayola provision inserted in the music business code under the New Deal's National Recovery Administration. Before the code could go into effect, the Supreme Court declared the NRA unconstitutional in 1935.

7. *Variety,* July 21, 1954, p. 35, July 28, 1954, p. 107, August 11, 1954, pp. 43, 49

8. *Variety,* February 23, 1955, p. 2.

9. Quoted in Gilbert, *Cycle,* 201; Grace Palladino, *Teenagers: An American History* (New York: Basic Books, 1996), 53, 156–157; Thomas Doherty, *Teenagers and Teenpics* (Boston: Unwin Hyman, 1988), 6, 54; David Szatmary, *Rockin' in Time: A Social History of Rock-and-Roll* (Englewood Cliffs, N.J.: Prentice-Hall, 1991), 24; Jonathan Kamin, "Parallels in the Social Reactions to Jazz and Rock," *Journal of Jazz Studies* 2 (1974): 121; Eliot, *Rockonomics,* 65.

10. Gilbert, *Cycle,* 176.

11. Gilbert, *Cycle,* 10, 13–14; Elaine Tyler May, *Homeward Bound: American Families in the Cold War Era* (New York: Basic Books, 1988), chaps. 4 and 5.

12. Greenfield, *No Peace, No Place* (Garden City, N.Y.: Doubleday, 1973), 29, 56. On high schools as an institution to keep working-class and ethnic influences away from middle class whites and at the same time promote values of tolerance, see William Graebner, *Coming of Age in Buffalo: Youth and Authority in the Postwar Era* (Philadelphia: Temple University Press, 1990); Gertrude Samuels, "Why They Rock 'n' Roll—And Should They?," *New York Times Magazine,* January 12, 1958, p. 19; Doherty, *Teenagers and Teenpics,* 81; Palladino, *Teenagers,* 124; Carl Belz, *The Story of Rock* (New York: Oxford University Press, 1972), 20.

13. King in *Ebony,* April 1958, p. 104; Joe Bostic in *Amsterdam News,* March 5, 1955, p. 26. On the belief that " 'bad' working-class teenagers were leading the rest

astray," see Simon Frith, *Sound Effects: Youth, Leisure, and the Politics of Rock 'n' Roll* (New York: Pantheon, 1981), 186. George Lipsitz, *Time Passages: Collective Memory and American Popular Culture* (Minneapolis: University of Minnesota Press, 1990), 123, and "Ain't Nobody Here but us Chickens: The Origins of Rock and Roll," in George Lipsitz, ed., *Rainbow at Midnight: Labor and Culture in the 1960s* (Urbana: University of Illinois Press, 1994), 330; Jackson Lears, "A Matter of Taste: Corporate Hegemony in Mass Consumption Society," in Lary May, ed., *Recasting America: Culture and Politics in the Age of Cold War* (Chicago: University of Chicago Press, 1989), 53; Palladino, *Teenagers*, 152; Michael Bane, *White Boys Singin' the Blues* (New York: Da Capo, 1982), 125–126; Wini Breines, *Young, White, and Miserable: Growing Up Female in the Fifties* (Boston: Beacon Press, 1992), 20.

14. May, *Homeward Bound*, chap. 5.

15. Greenfield, *No Peace*, 53.

16. John A. Jackson, *American Bandstand: Dick Clark and the Making of a Rock 'n' Roll Empire* (New York: Oxford University Press, 1997), 217, quoting Philadelphia disk jockey Hy Lit.

17. Charlotte Grieg, *Will You Still Love Me Tomorrow? Girl Groups from the Fifties On*, (London: Virago Press, 1989), 26.

18. For many teenagers rock and roll became, as Wini Breines asserts, "a symbol of youth rebellion against authority, with sex and race the not-so-hidden-narrative." Breines, *Young*, 155; Susan J. Douglas, *Where the Girls Are: Growing Up Female with the Mass Media* (New York: Times Books, 1994), 84.

19. "Warning to the Music Business," *Variety*, February 23, 1955, p. 2. As it developed in the 1950s, rock and roll evolved into a hybrid of rhythm and blues and the country-flavored sounds of rockabilly as exemplified in the music of Elvis Presley, Jerry Lee Lewis, Carl Perkins, and Buddy Holly.

20. Russell Sanjek, *American Popular Music and Its Business in the 20th Century* (New York: Oxford University Press, 1988), 326; Shane Maddock, "Whole Lotta Shakin' Goin' On: Racism and Early Opposition to Rock Music," *Mid-America* 78(Summer 1996): 182; Peter Guralnick, *Last Train to Memphis: The Rise of Elvis Presley* (Boston: Little, Brown, 1994), 39–40.

21. Breines, *Young*, 153–154; Jerry Wexler and David Ritz, *Rhythm and the Blues: A Life in American Music* (New York: St. Martin's Press, 1993), 286; Richard A. Peterson, "Why 1955? Explaining the Advent of Rock Music," *Popular Music* 9 (1990): 99, 101; Szatmary, *Rockin'*, 23; Palladino, *Teenagers*, 152; Chappell, *Rock 'n' Roll*, 41; *Variety*, July 6, 1955, p. 43.

22. Frye Gaillard, *Race, Rock, and Religion: Profiles from a Southern Journalist*, (Charlottesville: University Press of Virginia, 1982), 74; Charlie Gillett, *The Sound of the City: The Rise of American Rock and Roll* (New York: Pantheon, 1983), 38.

23. Nelson George, *The Death of Rhythm & Blues* (New York: Pantheon, 1988), 63.

24. Wexler, *Rhythm*, 90; Graebner, *Buffalo*, 29; George Lipsitz, "Land of a Thousand Dances: Youth, Minorities and the Rise of Rock and Roll," in May, *Recasting America*, 273; Jackson, *Big Beat*, 335; David Nasaw, *Going Out: The Rise and Fall of Public Amusements* (New York: Basic Books, 1993), 244; Trent Hill, "The Enemy Within: Censorship in Rock Music in the 1950s," in Anthony DeCurtis, ed., *Present Tense: Rock & Roll Culture* (Durham, N.C.: Duke University Press, 1992), 53. Otis, a musician as well as disk jockey, was an interesting case. Of Greek origin, he identified himself as culturally black, and his show in Los Angeles appealed to Latinos as well as blacks and whites.

25. Brian Ward, *Just My Soul Responding: Rhythm and Blues, Black Consciousness, and Race Relations* (Berkeley: University of California Press, 1998), 128.

26. Robert Palmer, "The '50s," *Rolling Stone*, April 19, 1989, p. 48; Richard Welch, "Rock 'n' Roll and Social Change," *History Today* 40 (February 1990): 32; Breines, *Young*, 152; Hill, "Enemy," 50.

27. Ward, *Just My Soul*, 129–130; Martha Bayles, *Hole in Our Soul: The Loss of Beauty and Meaning in American Popular Music* (New York: Free Press, 1994), 115.

28. *Shreveport Journal*, November 12, 1959, clipping, Box 1149, Oren Harris Papers, University of Arkansas, Fayetteville.

29. Ward, *Just My Soul*, 103; *Newsweek*, April 23, 1956, p. 32.

30. Gerald Early has written: "These were the years . . . in which America recognized and cringed before, the social reality . . . of a miscegenated culture in which, beneath the mask of inhuman racial etiquette where everyone supposedly was as separated as the twin beds in the bedroom of nearly every 1950s T.V. sitcom, there lurked an unquenchable thirst for mixing." Quoted in Breines, *Young*, 152; Lipsitz, "Land of a Thousand Dances," 273, 280–281; Robert Palmer, *Rock & Roll: An Unruly History* (New York: Harmony Books, 1995), 139; Frith, *Sound*, 24; Szatmary, *Rockin'*, 25.

31. Linda Martin and Kerry Seagrave, *Anti-Rock: The Opposition to Rock 'n' Roll*, (Hamden, Conn.: Archon Books, 1988), 41, 103. See *Christian Century*, April 11, 1956, p. 444, and *Chicago Defender*, April 14, 1956, p. 13, for critical responses to Carter's charges. Carter's group, extremist even by Alabama standards, went beyond mere words and resorted to violence to protect white virtue. On April 10, 1956, several of its members attacked Nat King Cole while he was performing to a whites-only audience in the Birmingham Municipal Auditorium. Cole was hardly a rock and roll crooner, but he shared the stage with a white woman singer, which according to Carter posed the same threat as authentic rock and roll performers who also took their shows to Birmingham. After all, Carter reasoned, it marked only "a short step . . . from the sly, nightclub technique vulgarity of Cole, to the openly animalistic obscenity of the horde of Negro rock and rollers. Ward, *Just My Soul*, 100.

32. *Congressional Record*, 85th Cong., 1st Sess., August 15, 1957, Appendix, 6288. John Charles Hajduk, "Music Wars: Conflict and Accommodation in America's Culture Industry, 1940–1960" (Ph.D. diss., State University of New York at Buffalo, 1995), 432; Martin, *Anti-Rock,* 37, 53; Maddock, "Whole Lotta Shakin'," 189–190; *Variety,* June 13, 1956, p. 51, September 5, 1956, p. 33; *Life,* "Rock and Roll," p. 168; *Time,* June 18, 1956, p. 54.

33. *Amsterdam News,* July 14, 1956, p. 12; *Pittsburgh Courier,* October 6, 1956, p. 9; *Ebony,* December 1956, p. 80.

34. Hajduk, "Music Wars," chap. 2.

35. The information on ASCAP and BMI in these two paragraphs comes from, Hill, "Enemy," 58–59; Sanjek, *American Popular Music,* 308, 328; Hajduk, "Music Wars," 481; Chapple, *Rock 'n' Roll,* 65; Eliot, *Rockonomics,* 57; Ward, *Just My Soul,* 119; Coarse, "Payola," 315.

36. Seagrave, *Payola,* 104–105.

37. Chapple, *Rock 'n' Roll,* 46; Hajduk, "Music Wars," 479; *Billboard,* April 7, 1958, p. 10.

38. House of Representatives, Antitrust Subcommittee of the Committee of the Judiciary, Hearings, "Monopoly Problems in Regulated Industries," 84th Cong., 2d Sess. (Washington, D. C., 1957), 4141, 4425, 4426, 4427, 4428.

39. In 1957 the Celler Committee issued a report concluding that as "disk jockeys are responsible for selecting much of the music played on the air . . . BMI has made the effort to influence them to favor its music." House of Representatives, Committee on the Judiciary, Hearings, "Television Broadcasting Industry, Report of the Antitrust Subcommittee," 85th Cong., 1st Sess., (Washington, D. C., 1957), 122.

40. The Smathers bill, S. 2834, sought to amend the Communications Act of 1934. At around the same time, Congressman James Roosevelt conducted hearings before the Select Committee on Small Business in the House into charges by dissident ASCAP members that the society favored a small group of large music publishing firms. Though proving inconclusive, the investigation heard ASCAP officials brag that ASCAP had few composers of rock and roll. House of Representatives, Subcommittee No. 5 of the Select Committee on Small Business, Hearings, "Policies of American Society of Composers, Authors, and Publishers," 85th Cong., 2d Sess. (Washington, D.C., 1958), 1, 16–17. Defensive about its internal management practices, ASCAP had another incentive for continuing its war with BMI and welcoming investigations into payola. Sanjek, *American Popular Music,* 421.

41. United States Senate, Committee on Interstate and Foreign Commerce, Subcommittee on Communication, Hearings, "Amendment to the Communications Act of 1934," [Pastore Hearings], 85th Congress, 2d Sess. (Washington, D.C., 1958), 107; Daniel Horowitz, *Vance Packard and American Social Criticism* (Chapel Hill: Uni-

versity of North Carolina Press, 1994), 199; Vance Packard, *The Hidden Persuaders* (New York: Simon & Schuster, 1957).

42. Pastore Hearings, 136.

43. Pastore Hearings, 995.

44. Pastore Hearings, 541.

45. Pastore Hearings, 150, 607, 1181, 1184, 1218; Hajduk, Music Wars," 494. Six months after the hearings ended, a federal court dismissed ASCAP's complaint that BMI had engaged in a conspiracy against it but upheld the plaintiff's right to sue BMI for discriminating against its members' compositions. In any event, the networks began to divest their ownership of BMI and left control in the hands of the independent stations. Sanjek argues that network executives did not want to become embroiled in the widening payola scandal and its association with "unsavory rock 'n' roll." Sanjek, *American Popular Music,* 431, 432.

46. Anderson, *Television Fraud*; Richard S. Tedlow, "Intellect on Television: The Quiz Show Scandals of the 1950s," *American Quarterly* 28 (Fall 1976): 483–495.

47. Richard N. Goodwin, *Remembering America: A Voice From the Sixties* (Boston: Little, Brown, 1988), 63. Goodwin soon joined Kennedy's staff as a speechwriter.

48. Stephen Whitfield, *The Culture of the Cold War* (Baltimore: Johns Hopkins University Press, 1991), 176–177, Greenfield, *No Peace,* 142.

49. Walter Karp, "The Quiz Show Scandal," in Leonard Dinnerstein and Kenneth T. Jackson, eds., *American Vistas 1877 to the Present,* 6th ed. (New York: Oxford University Press, 1991), 330; Hajduk, "Music Wars," 502 n. 66; Karal Ann Marling, *As Seen on TV: The Visual Culture of Everyday Life in the 1950s* (Cambridge, Mass.: Harvard University Press, 1994), 183.

50. Whitfield, *Culture,* 177. Steinbeck's concern about moral decline also emerged in his novel *The Winter of Our Discontent* (New York: Viking, 1961).

51. Coarse, "Payola," 291; House of Representatives, Subcommittee on Legislative Oversight, *Interim Report,* [No. 1258] "Investigation of Regulatory Commissions and Agencies," 86th Cong., 2d Sess., (Washington, D. C., 1960), 37; Sanjek, *American Popular Music,* 439; Seagrave, *Payola,* 100–101; *Variety,* November 11, 1959, p. 1.

52. Subcommittee on Legislative Oversight, *Interim Report,* 37.

53. Oren Harris to A. Reed, January 21, 1950, Box 1109; William Colmer to Oren Harris, February 24, 1950, and Harris to Colmer, February 27, 1950, Box 1109; Harris to B. W. Mitchell, June 14, 1949, Box 1109, Harris Papers, Special Collections Division, University of Arkansas Library, Fayetteville.

54. Harris Speech, February 22, 1950, Box 1109, Harris Papers.

55. Roy Reed, *Faubus: The Life and Times of An American Prodigal,* (Fayetteville: University of Arkansas Press, 1997), 249, 263; Oren Harris to O. D. Johnson, September 30, 1957, Harris to A.G. Davis, September 16, 1957, Harris to George F. Edwards,

October 21, 1957, Box 1136, Harris Papers. For other examples of Harris's racial views see Ward, *Just My Soul*, 169; *Arkansas Gazette*, August 14, 1960, p. A4; Oren Harris to Alvy Edwards, July 8, 1959, Box 1143, Harris Papers.

56. *American Nationalist* attached to Oren Harris to J. J. Babb, January 5, 1960, Box 1149, Harris Papers. Babb lived in Arkansas, but the *American Nationalist* originated from California.

57. Oren Harris to J. J. Babb, January 5, Box 1960, 1149, Harris Papers. On the bottom of the copy of the *American Nationalist*, Babb, from El Dorado, Arkansas, had penned: "Dear Oren: Is this angle too hot to handle?"

58. On the "fallow years" of King and civil rights protest, see Adam Fairclough, *To Redeem the Soul of America: The Southern Christian Leadership Conference and Martin Luther King, Jr.* (Athens: University of Georgia Press, 1987), chap. 2. On the unsteady progress toward the ballot during the 1950s, see Steven F. Lawson, *Black Ballots: Voting Rights in the South, 1944–1969* (New York: Columbia University Press, 1976).

59. Bernard Schwartz, *The Professor and the Commissions* (New York: Alfred A. Knopf, 1959), 9, 96. "Statement of Dr. Bernard Schwartz," February 10, 1958, Box 1298, Harris Papers. Harris declared that he fired Bernard Schwartz for insubordination. "Statement of Honorable Oren Harris Upon Assuming Chairmanship of Special Subcommittee on Legislative oversight, Wednesday, February 12, 1958," Box 1298, Harris Papers.

60. Besides Harris, Democrats included Peter Mack of Illinois, Walter Rogers of Texas, John J. Flynt of Georgia, and John Moss of California. On the Republican side were John B. Bennett of Michigan, William Springer of Illinois, Steven B. Derounian of New York, and Samuel L. Devine of Ohio.

61. John E. Moss interview by Donald B. Seney, State Government Oral History Program, copy in Bancroft Library, University of California at Berkeley, pp. 6, 12–13, 183. "Memo from Moss," April 14, 1960, June 16, 1960, Scrapbook clippings, John E. Moss Papers, University Archives, California State University at Sacramento.

62. U. S. House of Representatives, Subcommittee on Legislative Oversight, Committee on Interstate and Foreign Commerce, "Responsibilities of Broadcasting Licensees and Station Personnel," [Payola Hearings], 86th Cong., 2d Sess. (Washington, D.C., 1960), 192, 870.

63. *Public Papers of the President, Dwight David Eisenhower, 1959* (Washington, D. C.: U.S. Government Printing Office, 1960), 277. At the same time, Eisenhower tried to quell the public outcry over the decline of public morality by commenting at a news conference on November 4, 1959, that he did not think "that America has forgotten her own moral standards." He compared the quiz show scandal to the Chicago Black Sox scandal of the 1919 World Series.

64. "Report to the President by the Attorney General on Deceptive Practices in Broadcasting Media, December 30, 1959," in Subcommittee on Legislative Oversight, *Interim Report,* Appendix E, pp. 63, 65, 70. *New York Times,* January 1, 1960, p. 1; *Billboard,* January 11, 1960, p. 1; William Boddy, *Fifties Television: The Industry and its Critics* (Urbana: University of Illinois Press, 1990), 224.

65. Payola Hearings, 183, 620, for representative testimony of Cleveland's Wes Hopkins and Bob Clayton from Boston.

66. See testimony of Samuel Clark, Payola Hearings, 485, for the view of what the record company hoped to get from payola.

67. Payola Hearings, 1, 331–332.

68. Payola Hearings, 92, 247; *Billboard,* February 15, 1960, p. 2; Sanjek, *American Popular Music,* 448.

69. Payola Hearings, 247, 252; *Broadcasting,* February 15, 1960, p. 54. Lee Gorman to Oren Harris, March 14, 1960 and Harris to Gorman, March 19, 1960, Box 1297, Harris Papers about employment for Richards in the wake of the investigation. For two opposing views on the ritual of confession and anticommunism see Victor S. Navasky, *Naming Names* (New York: Viking Press, 1980) and William L. O'Neill, *A Better World: The Great Schism—Stalinism and the American Intellectuals* (New York: Simon & Schuster, 1982).

70. Both federal agencies conducted their own investigations of payola, with the FTC uncovering payoffs to 255 disk jockeys in twenty-six states and issuing complaints against more than a hundred record companies and distributors to cease engaging in the unfair practice. Nevertheless, ASCAP had no more success against its BMI adversary in the administrative realm than it had in the judicial. Although the Justice Department eventually filed an antitrust suit against BMI in 1964, the government accepted an agreement that allowed broadcasters to retain ownership of BMI. Jackson, *Big Beat,* 322. *Variety,* March 9, 1960, p. 61, March 23, 1960, p. 24; December 9, 1959, p. 53; *Billboard,* May 23, 1960, p. 2; *Broadcasting,* February 22, 1960, pp. 36, 40; *New York Times,* August 8, 1960, p. 13; *New York Post,* December 3, 1959, pp. 5, 64; Hajduk, "Music Wars," 513; Seagrave, *Payola,* 135, 138; Sanjek, *American Popular Music,* 449; Payola Hearings, 641.

71. During the hearings in mid-March, Eisenhower accepted the resignation of his appointed chairman of the FCC, John C. Doerfer, who had testified before the Harris Committee of taking a Florida vacation aboard the yacht of George Storer, a wealthy owner of radio and television stations licensed by the FCC. Republicans on the committee, led by John Bennett of Michigan sought to move up the timetable for bringing the disk jockey Dick Clark to the nation's capital to testify in order to deflect attention away from this scandal tainting the GOP administration. Harris and the Democrats, however, did not act for another month and a half. Payola Hearings,

March 4, 1960, pp. 652, 725; *New York Post,* March 13, 1960, p. 5; *New York Times,* March 21, 1960, pp. 1, 28; "Statement of John B. Bennett," March 21, 1960; "Statement by Congressman Peter F. Mack and Congressman John E. Moss, March 21, 1960; Robert Lishman to Oren Harris, March 16, 1960, miscellaneous, Moss Papers.

72. Berry had been convicted on a morals charge allegedly for transporting a fourteen-year-old girl across state lines in violation of the Mann Act. Little Richard turned to the ministry. Szatmary, *Rockin',* 56–59.

73. Steven F. Lawson, "The Florida Legislative Investigation Committee and the Constitutional Readjustment of Race Relations, 1956–1963," in Kermit L. Hall and James W. Ely Jr., eds., *An Uncertain Tradition: Constitutionalism and the History of the South* (Athens: University of Georgia Press, 1989), 296–325; John Dittmer, *Local People: The Struggle for Civil Rights in Mississippi* (Urbana: University of Illinois Press, 1994), 80–83.

74. Jackson, *American Bandstand,* 60; Davidson, "Dick Clark," 111.

75. Dick Clark, *Your Happiest Years* (New York: Rosho Corporation, 1959), 17; Dick Clark and Richard Robinson, *Rock, Roll, and Remember* (New York: Crowell, 1976), 146.

76. Clark and Robinson, *Rock, Roll, and Remember,* 67; *New York Times,* March 5, 1960, p. 40; Belz, *Story of Rock,* 104; Jackson, *American Bandstand,* 69; Henry Schipper, "Dick Clark Interview," *Rolling Stone,* April 19, 1990, p. 68.

77. Jackson, *American Bandstand,* 66. Even with his squeaky-clean visage, Clark could not entirely remove himself from the negative images identified with rock and roll. He was called "The Czar of the Switchblade Set," "The Kingpin of the Teen-age Mafia," and "the Pied Piper of Bedlam." Pete Martin, "I Call on Dick Clark," *Saturday Evening Post,* October 10, 1959, p. 27; Bill Davidson, "The Strange World of Dick Clark," *Redbook,* March 1960, p. 111.

78. Clark and Robinson, *Rock, Roll, and Remember,* 82; Martin, *Anti-Rock,* 107; Schipper, "Dick Clark," 126; Donald Clarke, *The Rise and Fall of Popular Music* (New York: Viking, 1995), 422–423.

79. Letter from Dorothy Simmons, *Pittsburgh Courier,* September 5, 1959, p. 22, quoted in G. E. Pitts column. See also Jackson, *American Bandstand,* 141.

80. Clark recalled: "You can't live and eat and sleep next to people in a bus . . . and not begin to feel these are my people, we are together." Clark and Robinson, *Rock, Roll, and Remember,* 58, 135–136; Jackson, *Bandstand,* 204–205; Schipper, "Dick Clark," 70; *Amsterdam News,* May 21, 1960, p. 17. However, in 1960 Clark suspended operation of the tours into the Southeast after encountering opposition from whites. Clark and Robinson, *Rock, Roll, and Remember,* 245.

81. Ward, *Just My Soul,* 168.

82. Eliot, *Rockonomics,* quoting Joe Smith, p. 86.

83. *New York Times,* May 20, 1960, p. 62; Greenfield, *No Peace,* 47; Martin, *Anti-Rock,* 95.

84. Jackson, *Big Beat,* 34, 42, 73; Ward and Picardie, *Music Man,* 76, 85; Martin, *Anti-Rock,* 95; Rick Sklar, *Rocking America: An Insider's Story* (New York: St. Martin's Press, 1984), 21. Reinforcing this image, the *Pittsburgh Courier* gave Freed a special Brotherhood Award for promoting black talent.

85. The charges were later dropped, but not before Freed incurred huge legal fees. Jackson, *Big Beat,* 200–212, 247; "Rock 'n' Riot," *Time,* May 19, 1958, p. 50; Palmer, *Rock & Roll,* 136.

86. Jackson, *Big Beat,* 168; Martin, *Anti-Rock,* 97.

87. Jackson, *Big Beat,* 105–106; Ward and Picardie, *Music Man,* 82; Palmer, *Rock & Roll,* 138; Wexler, *Rhythm,* 129–131; Chuck Berry, *The Autobiography* (New York: Simon & Schuster, 1987), 107; *Amsterdam News,* November 20, 1954, pp. 8, 27, July 7, 1956, p. 20, November 24, 1956, p. 14; George, *Death,* 91. When he first came to New York City he drew fire from Gotham's black press for slicing into the radio and concert market of black disk jockeys, including emceeing programs at the famed Apollo Theater in Harlem.

88. *Pittsburgh Courier,* December 19, 1959, pp. 1, 23; *Amsterdam News,* February 6, 1960, p. 15

89. "Now Don't Cry," *Time,* December 7, 1959, p. 47; *Variety,* November 25, 1959, p. 1; Chapple, *Rock 'n' Roll,* 63.

90. Jackson, *Big Beat,* 279–280; *New York Post,* November 23, 1959, p. 41. Freed attributed the different treatment to the fact that Clark appeared on some three hundred stations and earned $12 million for the television network, while he broadcast on one radio station and brought in only $250,000 in revenue.

91. Jackson, *Big Beat,* 285; *New York Post,* April 25, 1960, p. 5. Jackson was given access to Freed's testimony, which the committee never released as part of its published hearings. Such testimony is closed to researchers for fifty years unless the House clerk grants permission. After many attempts to obtain permission, my request was denied.

92. On the Clark–Van Doren comparison, *New York Post,* May 2, 1960, p. 4; Clark and Robinson, *Rock, Roll, and Remember,* 219; Payola Hearings, 1341.

93. Payola Hearings, testimony of Joseph Tryon, pp. 1013, 1015, 1017; Doherty, *Teenagers and Teenpics,* 224; R. Serge Denisoff, *Tarnished Gold: The Record Industry Revisited* (New Brunswick, N.J.: Transaction Books, 1986), 238.

94. *Billboard,* May 9, 1960, p. 1.

95. *Washington Post,* April 30, 1960, pp. A1, A3. The Republican Steven B. Derounian judged Clark guilty of "royola." Payola Hearings, 1159.

96. *New York Post,* March 31, 1960, p. 12.

97. Payola Hearings, 1168, 1169, 1170, 1176, 1182, 1211.

98. Payola Hearings, 1351; Dick Clark to Oren Harris, May 4, 1960, Harris to Clark, May 6, 1960, Box 1149, Harris Papers.

99. Schipper, "Dick Clark," 70; "Teen Agers' Elder Statesman," *TV Guide,* August 29–September 4, 1959, p. 21; *Variety,* May 4, 1960, pp. 1, 50; Mary McGrory, "No Business Like," *New York Post,* May 3, 1960, p. 2 (magazine). Despite his escape, Clark came away bitter. He said the experience taught him "to protect your ass at all times." Clark and Robinson, *Rock, Roll, and Remember,* 225; Leonard H. Goldenson with Marvin J. Wolf, *Beating the Odds* (New York: Scribner, 1991), 164–165.

100. Of the seven others indicted with Freed, three were local black disk jockeys. Two of the black disk jockeys also admitted wrongdoing, while the remaining African American and three whites had the charges dropped. In contrast, Clark avoided prosecution in an investigation into payola undertaken by the Philadelphia district attorney, which produced admissions of guilt from over twenty disk jockeys and several of Clark's business associates. Moreover, in cooperation with law enforcement officials, Clark agreed to head a local organization of disk jockeys that pledged to draw up a code of ethics to stamp out payola. Jackson, *Big Beat,* 298–315; Jackson, *American Bandstand,* 191; *Billboard,* August 29, 1960, p. 1; *Amsterdam News,* May 28, 1960, p. 1.

101. Seagrave, *Payola,* 157; Coarse, "Payola," 298; Eliot, *Rockonomics,* 83; *Billboard,* June 13, 1960, p. 1; Minutes, Committee on Interstate and Foreign Commerce, 86th Cong, 2d Sess., June 9, 1960, RG 233, Box 207, National Archives; House of Representatives, Committee on Interstate and Foreign Commerce, "Report to accompany S. 1898, Communication Act Amendments, 1960," 86th Cong., 2d Sess. (Washington, D. C., 1960), 47; *Broadcasting,* July 4, 1960, p. 60, August 29, 1960, p. 3; *New York Times,* August 26, 1960, p. 1, August 31, 1960, p. 19.

102. *Billboard,* December 19, 1960, pp. 1, 3, 4; *Variety,* October 26, 1960, p. 57.

103. The target of payola shifted from disk jockeys to program directors who compiled the play lists. Coarse, "Payola," 206; Hill, "Enemy," 67.

104. The phrase comes from a quote by an anonymous record company executive, *Billboard,* January 18, 1960, p. 2.

105. The introduction of rap and hip-hop music in the late 1980s and 1990s, with the civil rights movement in secular decline, revived attacks against black musical forms considered offensive to (white) middle-class standards of decency. Tricia Rose, *Black Noise: Rap Music and Black Culture in Contemporary America* (Hanover, N.H.: University Press of New England, 1994).

9

"A REVOLUTION BUT HALF ACCOMPLISHED": THE TWENTIETH CENTURY'S ENGAGEMENT WITH CHILD-RAISING, WOMEN'S WORK, AND FEMINISM

Cynthia Harrison

Nothing renders society more restless than a . . . revolution but half accomplished.
—Carl Shurz

In 1966, a group of politically active women gathered around a table at a government luncheon and created the National Organization for Women, the first avowedly feminist organization of the twentieth century's "second wave" of women's-rights activism. The new movement responded to an expansion in wage work for women, a phenomenon driven not by ideology but by economic circumstance. Within the decade, the women's movement had crafted a comprehensive package of reforms that, if adopted, would have modernized workplace practice as well as family roles to fit the changed wage-earning roles of women and ensure the proper care of children.

For the rest of the century, feminists sought a revision in public policy to make possible equal opportunities for women at work, to improve economic security and independence for women (and their children), and to support a revolution in personal relationships between women and men. Arguing that gender roles grew out of social influences rather than biology—a key departure from the older varieties of women's activism—feminists declared child-raising to be a responsibility of both men and women as well as the society at large.

At the twentieth century's end, the U.S. Code and the statutes of the various states reflected the stunning success of the women's movement in expunging the hoary laws that diminished women's legal capacity and subordinated married women to their husbands. Thanks in large measure to a renewed feminist consciousness, legislation proscribed the ubiquitous discrimination that had existed in the practices of employers and educational institutions. Other laws, such as those guaranteeing access to abortion or family leave, acknowledged women's need for control over their reproductive lives and offered some accommodation to their responsibility for raising children. But the new millennium had not yet arrived. For all the feminist successes, change occurred slowly with respect to family responsibilities. In the 1990s, women still provided most childcare, receiving modest help from fathers, and little from employers or state agencies. The average "working mother" worked two shifts,[1] usually located in separate sites. Moreover, her wages reflected the long-standing assumption that women's paid work occupied a position secondary to their child-raising role, despite a labor-force participation rate in 1998 of 63.7 percent for married mothers with children under six and a rate of 76.1 percent for those with children from ages six to thirteen.[2]

The attempt to transform childcare arrangements faltered on practical aspects such as cost, but the failure also reflected confusion about the "traditional" way in which children were raised in the "typical" American family. The discussion about childrearing proceeded as if the "traditional" American family consisted for most of America's history of a father who "went to work" and earned enough by himself to support the family comfortably, a mother who "stayed home" and devoted herself to nurturing her children, and children who went to school full-time at least until they graduated from high school. Departures from this model—whether the absence of the father, his failure to earn an adequate wage, or the mother at wage work—thus represented a decline from a healthier and long-standing practice. Wage work for women detracted from their "natural" role as full-time mothers.

This history of the family was, however, a myth. Promulgated in the early nineteenth century, the ideal urban family constituted a realistic goal for only a minority of families in the nineteenth century and most of the twentieth century. The moment when a "typical" nonprofessional family could aspire to the family ideal existed only briefly—in the period following World War II, an anomaly popularized by the new medium of television. Most families recognized their own substantial shortfalls from the level of economic security (not to mention emotional and social control) displayed by their television models. They nevertheless accepted the image as the norm and therefore an appropriate goal.

But the true "traditional American family" was not the white middle-class suburban family of the 1950s pictured on the television screen. Until the twentieth century, most Americans had grown up on farms, not in suburbs, and in families that differed dramatically in character from 1950s televised fiction, where mothers vacuumed in high heels and fathers went to work at a vague and indistinguishable locale known as "The Office." In the traditional American farm family, particularly the subsistence agricultural setting of the frontier but also in the commercial agricultural environment of the nineteenth century, mothers—and fathers—undertook childrearing and breadwinning simultaneously and in the same place, and with little glamour about it.

FAMILY LIFE IN PREINDUSTRIAL AMERICA

On the farm, women's work had a central relation to agricultural production. In addition to engaging in market exchange activities, farmwomen fed and clothed not only their own large families but also auxiliary workers on hand to help with the crops or the indoor work. Producing food comprised many steps: planting and maintaining a garden, harvesting the fruit and vegetables grown there, preserving them for future meals and cooking and serving them in due course. Food also came from the family dairy: farmwomen processed milk, butter, and cheese for the family table. They raised chickens as well, which would need to be slaughtered and dressed, and eggs, which needed to be collected, some to be eaten and some to grow into new livestock. Making and maintaining the family's clothing was similarly time-consuming and labor-intensive: acquiring cloth, cutting simple patterns, stitching new clothing, mending or altering outgrown clothing for a younger child, laundering (including making soap from lye and fat, maintaining the fires that would heat water, scrubbing, rinsing, and hanging them out), and ironing, performed with weighted flatirons heated on the stove. Her labors supplied family members with goods, and they counted on her surplus production to bring in cash. In addition to marketing cheese and eggs, farmwomen skilled as dressmakers or midwives could help earn family income by performing services for neighboring families. And all of these chores took second place to field work when the crop required it.

As an agricultural producer, the farm wife could not have made childcare her primary focus. Children perforce grew up without the close adult scrutiny adjudged essential by nineteenth- and twentieth-century childrearing experts. On the farm, raising children meant attention to their physical needs, spiritual training, primary education, and apprenticeship for adult work roles. Mothers might have supplied little of this care. Siblings of the parents and of the children helped satisfy the child's physical needs. Small children were commonly expected to keep an eye on even smaller ones, bringing infants to adults when they needed to be fed. Children themselves took on economic roles early in life, boys helping with the outdoor work and girls emulating their mother's roles, sometimes undertaking labor as backbreaking as factory work.[3] Childcare thus became synonymous with job training.[4]

Although most late-twentieth-century families could not reproduce the coherence intrinsic to farm life (and they would certainly have wanted no part of the backbreaking work), the dual subsistence-producing and nurturing roles women played in that earlier context would have represented a sounder model for late-twentieth-century mothers than the "angel of the hearth." And a fuller conversancy with this earlier family template might have enabled urban Americans to understand the long history of women's role in family economic support and its centrality to the family's well-being. Instead, throughout the twentieth century, income-earning mothers found themselves described almost continuously as a "problem."

The "problem of the working mother" emerged in the nineteenth century almost immediately upon the relocation of families from the farm to an urban setting. The transition from a predominantly agricultural society to a predominantly urban one did not take place until the half-century following the Civil War, but a small proportion of families, particularly along the eastern seaboard, had experienced it earlier in the century. Elite families solved its central conundrum—how to raise children with home and work sites located in separate places—by creating the doctrine of "separate spheres."[5] Men would work to earn income and would support the mothers of their children, who would withdraw from income-producing work for virtually all of their adult lives; women would instead devote themselves exclusively and intensively to raising their children. In 1830, however, such a model was irrelevant to the 90 percent of families still residing on farms. It also bore little resemblance to the lives of poor urban dwellers, since most nonprofessional occupations did not permit a man to earn enough to support a family comfortably on his own.

By 1900, however, 40 percent of the American population lived in urban settings, confronting the issue of child-raising off the farm. The nineteenth-century domestic ideal still proved elusive. Relatively few families in industrial America could follow the model because relatively few men could earn the income to support it. The average wage in 1900 of $490 a year (about $9600 in 1999 dollars[6]) for nonfarm employees meant that a "typical" urban family of six was most unlikely to meet basic needs from the wage-earning capacity of only one adult.[7] Those nonfarm families that stayed in rural communities would have earned even less. Most nonfarm families therefore had to supplement the father's wage with the wage-earning work of at least one other family member, constrained by the prevailing notion that married mothers should not work for wages outside the home.

Twentieth-century Americans thus began a series of unwitting experiments in earning income and raising children in an urban industrial society. Early reformers and policymakers focused on various solutions for the pressing problems of insufficient family income, child abuse and neglect, and the preparation and protection of the modern workforce: "a family wage" for male workers; bans on child labor; compulsory schooling; protective labor laws barring women from certain occupations or hours of work; minimum-wage laws to raise the lowest rates paid to women workers; stipends for mothers raising children alone. No solution, however, succeeded in making permanent that desideratum of family life, the full-time mother relieved of the necessity to contribute to the family income. To the contrary, as the century unfolded, more rather than fewer married mothers worked for wages and more families relied on mothers' wages to survive. Yet, having never been addressed directly, at the twentieth century's end as at its beginning, the question of how to care for children in a nonagricultural setting while earning adequate family support still beset the polity. And at the end as at the beginning, race, social class, and gender inflected the answers.

TWENTIETH-CENTURY EXPERIMENTS IN CHILDREARING

In roughly chronological order, we can identify five twentieth-century arrangements adopted or proposed to deal with the problem of raising children and earning income for families in an industrial/commercial economy. Initially, income, not childcare, proved to be the preeminent concern. Thus, strategies to cope in the new urban world varied chiefly by which family member would assist in earning cash wages necessary to support the family and under what circumstances.

MOTHERS AT HOME, CHILDREN AT WORK

At the beginning of the century, when most Americans still lived in rural communities, European immigrants presented the most visible and aggravated cases of families' adapting to urban spaces. More than three million immigrants had arrived in the last decade of the nineteenth century; in 1900, of sixty-seven million white Americans, some twenty-six million were either foreign-born or the child of a foreign-born parent—40 percent of the white population. Thirteen million more immigrants arrived between 1900 and 1915, the majority settling in cities. Already coping with drastic shifts from European peasant or village life, urban immigrant families tried various ways to stave off poverty, many of which included mothers' work. The practice of taking in boarders was ubiquitous, taking in washing and sewing common. Some immigrant mothers worked in home industries, making clothing, flowers, or cigars.[8] For others, family businesses offered employment and the option to live above the store, thus being at hand when children were about. As Sonya Michel has pointed out, those desperate mothers who had to leave home to find work often took small children with them, keeping them occupied with related tasks, in essence using child labor as a form of childcare.[9] In these ways, families replicated in an urban setting the farm way of life in which mothers melded childcare and subsistence-producing work, albeit without the salubrious aspects of farm life—fresh air and homegrown food.

But economics and convention limited the amount that mothers could earn, and most nonfarm families relied on the wages of another wage earner—an adult or minor child. The data are sparse and do not precisely address the question of family wage-earning structure, but it is possible to draw some inferences from those data available. By 1910 only eleven married women out of a hundred recorded themselves as working for wages, fewer than two million wives. Still, there were 25.8 million nonfarm workers and fourteen million nonfarm households. Some three million households—those with professional or managerial men as the husband/father—probably could have relied on only one wage earner. Thus, approximately twenty-three million workers supported eleven million households, slightly more than two workers per family on average.[10] Census enumerators were instructed to request the occupation of all residents ten years old and older, recognizing how commonly children worked for wages. In 1910, the Census counted 1.6 million children ten to fifteen years old in the labor force, about 15 percent of children that age, unquestionably an undercount.[11] Children over the age of fourteen had usually left school; in 1910, only 15 percent of fourteen- to seventeen-year-olds attended high school.[12] Many parents expected older children to leave school and pursue paid work as soon as they could reasonably anticipate finding a place.[13] Thus, we can infer that the first experiment in raising children in a nonagricultural setting consisted, for the "typical" urban family, of mothers at home (trying to add to the family income from there) and children from ten years old and up performing wage work to help support the family.[14]

An exception to this pattern appeared early among African American families. Although some also sought to emulate the ideal of having a mother withdraw from wage work (and the field labor necessary for agricultural families), many preferred to keep daughters in school if possible. Thus, mothers took on domestic work rather than sending the younger women to such jobs where they would be more vulnerable to the sexual depredations of white male employers.[15] In 1900, when 3 percent of white married women reported themselves as working for wages, the labor-force participation rate of black married women was 26 percent. In this adaptation as in later ones, the black family anticipated a change that would come later to white ones.

"Maternalist" Progressive reformers in the early decades of the twentieth century sought to limit the workplace participation of children by protective labor legislation and by enforcement and extension of compulsory schooling laws. The movement to withdraw children under fourteen from paid labor and to keep them in school took four decades to effect. States were slow to outlaw child labor: by 1923 only thirteen states imposed any significant legal restrictions on child labor and those laws tended to deal only with factory work, leaving children working in agriculture unregulated.[16] Congress passed child-labor laws in 1916 and 1919, but the U.S. Supreme Court ruled both unconstitutional. A constitutional amendment submitted to the states by Congress in 1924 won the support of only six states by 1930. By 1932, however, all states had some legislation affecting child labor (most barring factory work by those age fourteen and younger)[17] and the work of children under the age of sixteen in interstate commerce finally became illegal in 1938 with the passage of the federal Fair Labor Standards Act.

Progressives had an easier time with compulsory schooling laws. Massachusetts had enacted a school attendance law as early as 1852. Another twenty-two states followed suit between the end of the Civil War and 1890. Southern states waited until the twentieth century, but by 1918 all states had compulsory school laws, normally requiring attendance of children to age fourteen. Enforcement was a different matter. Many objected to the government's compelling children to attend school, arguing that children benefited from working and that, in any case, such a decision belonged to parents. Families that needed children's income had a powerful incentive to flout laws and school districts lacked both sufficient desks for all children and the capacity to police either the densely packed tenement districts or the sparsely settled rural areas.[18] School officials disliked dealing with rough, poorly prepared students from urban ghettos—the very ones Progressives hoped would gain most from education provided at public expense. But Progressives succeeded in improving enforcement and in extending both the number of required days in school each year and the number of years a child would attend. According to David Tyack, from 1890 to 1918 more than ten thousand new high schools were built and high school attendance increased more than 700 percent. New school administrators emerged for the specific purpose of monitoring school enrollment and enforcing attendance rules.[19] The expectation that children would attend high school worked in tandem with child-labor laws to withdraw children from industrial labor. The proportion of children aged fourteen to seventeen enrolled in high school doubled from 16 percent in 1910 to 32 percent in 1920.[20] But that figure left two-thirds of high school-age children likely at work.

Ultimately, whether a child could stay in school or not depended on the general state of the economy. The prosperity that marked the 1920s lifted the wages of working men and helped to shrink the numbers of children in the labor force. In the 1920 census, the ratio of nonfarm workers to nonfarm households had dropped from 1.84 overall in 1910 to 1.75, indicating that additional families probably were relying on the wages of one earner. Indeed, the average wage of workers in all industries, excluding farm labor, rose from $630 in 1910 to $1,500 in 1920 (farm laborers earned only $810). An annualized wage for factory workers in 1920 equaled about $1,350. No doubt fostered by the relative affluence, high school attendance increased. By 1930, just over half (51.4 percent) of the high school-age population attended school.[21]

But an annualized wage for factory workers in 1920 equaled about $1,350—approximately $11,000 in 1999 dollars—and most families still probably required a second income to maintain an adequate standard of living. In their study of Muncie, the Lynds found that only twenty-five out of one hundred working-class families earned the $1,920 deemed the minimum income necessary for a family of five. In 1920, of approximately twenty-three million male nonfarm workers, 3.9 million, who occupied professional and managerial positions or owned their own businesses, were potentially successful single-family earners, less than 18 percent. Removing their households from the total of eighteen million nonfarm households at the time, we find that nineteen million remaining male workers (of whom sixteen million worked at manual labor and three million in white-collar jobs) presumably supported the balance of fourteen million nonfarm households, assisted by 7.5 million nonfarm working women (including about 9 percent of wives), an average of 1.9 workers for each of these households. It is possible that more than half of these urban households managed on one income, but if they did so they likely suffered substantial economic duress.[22]

The Depression both accelerated the trend against child labor and impeded the growth of paid labor for married women. The scarcity of jobs led families to encourage children to stay in school in the hope that they would be better able to earn with more education. The combination of compulsory school laws through twelfth grade or age sixteen and legal barriers to the employment of children younger than fourteen removed many urban children from the labor force. By 1940, 73 percent of fourteen- to seventeen-year-olds attended school, and the ratio of nonfarm workers to nonfarm households fell to 1.64. With work scarce, little sentiment favored mothers at work. The Depression crisis had already threatened family stability in numerous ways; restoring fathers as the family breadwinner constituted a key policy goal of the New Deal. The pervasive unemployment of men led to a more intense commitment to the "traditional" family than had appeared in the 1920s, when careers for married women enjoyed something of a vogue. Animosity toward married women at work led to both private actions by employers and legislation to establish a policy against hiring married women in lieu of male breadwinners. One unemployed husband voiced a widespread sentiment among working-class men when he declared, "I would rather starve than let my wife work."[23] Yet, despite the hostility toward them, married women increased their work rates during the Depression (though their numbers remained small). In 1930, about 12 percent of wives were at work; by 1940, that proportion had risen to 17 percent. Black married women entered the labor force at a rate three times that of white women, reflecting the disadvantaged position of black men in the labor force.[24]

Wives undoubtedly worked because families with only one wage earner had a hard time of it. In the 1930s, a third of all families reported an income below $800 annually (about $9500 in 1999 dollars), more than 80 percent of them one-earner families. One-third of the 20 percent of American families in 1940 that earned a middle-class income (between $1,600 and $2,500, or between $19,000 to $30,000 in 1999 dollars) got there by benefit of two or more earners.[25] But during the 1930s, older children, rather than wives, remained the preponderant group bringing in additional wages. Of eighteen- and nineteen-year-olds, only 12 percent had married, although only 29 percent were enrolled in school; for the next age cohort, twenty to twenty-four, fewer than 7 percent were in school, about two-thirds were still single and 88 percent of the men and 46 percent of the women were in the labor force, most likely helping with family expenses.[26]

World War II had the potential for creating dramatic changes in family-wage-earning arrangements. Once the United States started building arms, the availability of jobs drew married women into the labor force. At the peak of the war, the female labor force had grown by almost 50 percent and, while policymakers expressed reservations, mothers who could find good care for their children could do their part to ease the labor shortage without opprobrium. The federal government even allocated a small portion of public funds to the support of childcare centers. The number of wives at work doubled.[27] But the welcome for married women at work and the public support for childcare turned out to be a brief aberration that the polity was not yet prepared to endorse. The next adaptation appeared in the postwar era.

MOTHERS AT HOME, CHILDREN IN SCHOOL

After the war ended, the economic dominance of the United States globally, pent-up consumer demand, and huge government investment in infrastructure, education, and industry launched a boom that, for the first time in American history, appeared to make it possible for an "average" working-class family to survive on the wages of a single (male) income earner. By one measure—the Current Population Survey, conducted by the U.S. Bureau of the Census—from 1948 to 1955 slightly more than half of American families sustained themselves on the wages of a single wage earner.[28] But while suggestive, these data are not dispositive because the definition of "wage earner" included both casual teenage workers as well as those who contributed to family support, and the definition of "family" included childless married couples. Closer analysis of census data between 1940 and 1980 refines the picture: Daniel Hernandez concludes that the number of children in "ideal" families peaked in 1950. In that year, the proportion of children between birth and age seventeen who lived in families in which the father had worked at least forty-eight weeks the previous year and thirty-five hours the previous week and in which the mother did not participate in the labor force amounted to 47.1 percent. The proportion of children so situated fell to 44.7 percent by 1960 and to 26.3 percent by 1980.[29] Thus, even in the 1950s, more than half of American children lived in families that departed from the ideal. Moreover, some of the ostensibly ideal families certainly had the assistance of a second wage earner. The labor-force participation rate of teenaged children remained high, including two-thirds of boys aged sixteen to nineteen and two-fifths of girls that age.[30] Although many teenagers no doubt used their earnings as personal discretionary income, others also surely helped pay family bills, especially among the 23 percent of fourteen- to seventeen-year-olds not attending school.

Still, the prosperous postwar economy allowed many new mothers, especially white mothers, to stay out of the labor force without the family's relying on the wages of a minor or adult child, the second adaptation to raising children in a nonagricultural setting in the twentieth century and the first time working-class husbands could anticipate earning a "family wage." With 3.4 million to 4.2 million births every year for a decade, the population grew to include some twenty million new families with small children, out of some 43.5 million total families. In 1960 only 18.6 percent of married mothers with children under six worked for wages, but more than 60 percent of families (with and without children) earned more than $5,000 (the average family income was $6,819, or $28,000 in 1999 dollars). Only 39 percent of male workers over the age of fourteen earned that amount, although another 23 percent earned between $3,000 and $5,000, again strongly indicating the presence of a second wage earner in many families.[31] But most families probably did rely on one wage earner: 66.6 million nonfarm workers supported 48.7 million households—1.36 workers per household.[32]

MOTHERS AT HOME AND AT WORK

The moment was brief: For the rest of the century, the numbers of mothers in the labor force would increase. In 1950, 21.6 percent of mothers with children under eighteen were at wage work; by 1960, their participation rate had grown to 30.4. By 1967, in two-parent families where all the children were between the ages of six and seventeen, 44 percent of white mothers—and 55 percent of nonwhite mothers—worked.[33] The labor-force participation rate for married mothers with children between six and seventeen passed the halfway mark in the 1970s; those with children under six reached the halfway mark during the following decade.[34] These women thus instated the wage work of mothers as a permanent feature of the U.S. economy, initiating the third experiment in income-earning and raising children: mothers routinely fitting wage work in around school schedules and childcare needs.

Ironically, at the very moment that growing numbers of women were joining the paid labor force, a new invention inscribed the image of the model white affluent suburban family on the American consciousness. Television brought the Nelson family, the Anderson family, the Stone family, the Cleaver family, the Reilly family, and the Williams family into American living rooms, shortly followed by numerous other families, most of which revolved around a mother devoting full time to family care rather than wage earning, regardless of the age of the children.[35] The power and prevalence of these images did not cloud the vision of those families who realized that they could not in fact afford the ongoing estrangement of one adult from paid work. They did, however, implicitly characterize the working mother as "deviant" and, quite possibly, neglectful.

In order not to neglect their children, mothers employed outside the home took jobs less than full-time or year-round. And they worked part-time. In 1967, of working mothers with children between the ages of six and seventeen, 39 percent worked full-time for the full year, about 14 percent worked more than six months but fewer than fifty weeks at full time, and 12 percent worked full-time fewer than six months of the year. About one-third of mothers worked part-time. Mothers with children younger than three were no more likely to work part-time than were mothers with older children, but they did work fewer weeks per year, perhaps reflecting the difficulty of getting jobs that required fewer than thirty-five hours per week.[36] Employers, meanwhile, justified discrimination against the married mother (and, by extension, every woman) on the very ground that she would be likely to put her family before her wage work, as indeed she was expected to do.

Fitting childcare and paid work together became even more difficult because experts had redefined what children required in the way of "raising." The twentieth century witnessed not merely a shift from farmland to cityscapes but a revision of what a family owed a child. Although the idea of children as unique individuals requiring special attention had gained currency by the early nineteenth century, in the latter part of the century Darwinian psychologist G. Stanley Hall expanded the notion to suggest that children's physical and mental well-being demanded specific treatment at different developmental stages, by a mother trained for motherhood.[37] John B. Watson, in *Psychological Care of Infant and Child* (1928), insisted on scientific principles for raising children. Women could not rely on instinct and in particular needed to guard against excessive attachment.[38] Freudians laid at mothers' feet blame for the neurotic child, and popular writers such as Philip Wylie (*Generation of Vipers,* 1942) launched vituperative attacks on overbearing mothers who suffocated their children to fulfill their own selfish needs.[39] Meanwhile, concerns about juvenile delinquency led to censuring mothers who left their children unattended. A modern woman could not "mother" carefully enough. Such obligations had not beset the mother on the farm.

Modern mothers also had new responsibilities concerning their children's education. In an agricultural world, children's formal schooling got short shrift. School schedules purposely permitted children to help with farming and, even though schools suspended operation during the summer, farm children attended much less often than city kids, most only from mid-November to early spring.[40] In 1870, when most families were still farm families, the average length of the school term was 132 days, but the average number of days attended per enrolled pupil was 78, the equivalent of sixteen weeks of school.[41] In 1898 a "typical young American" could anticipate five years of education.[42] Southern children, black children, sharecroppers' children, could look forward to even less schooling.[43] But an urban twentieth-century worker needed formal education, more so as the century wore on. When educational professionals came in contact with the work of child development experts, they expanded their recommendations concerning the range of stimulation that children needed in their early years to enhance their success in school (and, therefore, later at work). Standardized testing documented deficits when children failed to meet grade-level norms; educators held mothers accountable for lapses. By 1950, children were expected to stay in school until high school graduation and mothers were expected to shepherd their children throughout, supplying emotional sustenance and intellectual enrichment. For the rest of the century, childrearing experts ratcheted up the efforts ostensibly required to raise a healthy and successful child, while at the same time more mothers undertook childrearing as a part-time rather than a full-time occupation, exacerbating the tension between their roles as mothers and as workers.

Criticism notwithstanding, mothers' wage work facilitated their children's education. If, in the first half of the century, the labor of adult children had permitted their fourteen-year-old, fifteen-year-old, and sixteen-year-old siblings to finish high school, in the next half-century mothers replaced their older children as family earners, permitting them to go to college. School enrollment of eighteen- and nineteen-year-olds closely tracked the labor-force participation rates of mothers with children between the ages of six and seventeen; enrollments of those twenty to twenty-four also rose in concert with mothers' work. The wage work of mothers permitted children to stay in school long past the legal working age, acquiring the skills necessary to navigate an economy increasingly reliant on sophisticated technical and professional skills.

The work of women benefited not only their own families but also the national economy. Women's work on farms had sustained the agricultural economy; women's work in the paid labor force was no less essential to a modern economic system. World War II had intensified the trend of married women's joining the paid labor force: In 1940 (as noted earlier), 17 percent of wives worked; by 1960, 32 percent did.[44] Immediately after the war, the growth of women's wage work led to concern among policymakers, businesses, and unions over the prospect of competition between men and women for scarce jobs. But by the time of John Kennedy's inauguration in 1961, it had become clear that women would not replace men in the jobs traditionally identified as male. To the contrary, the need for clerical workers, nurses, and teachers made plain that both the public and the private sectors required women's paid work. In addition, the Cold War fueled anxieties about leaving women's talents unplumbed; in 1957 the National Manpower Council released a report called *Womanpower*, warning that women were essential workers: "Without their presence in the labor force we could neither produce and distribute the goods nor provide the educational, health, and other social services which characterize American society." The council also observed that women were underutilized, especially compared to the Soviet Union: "There are annually some 13,000 women graduating as engineers in the Soviet Union, compared to well under 100 in the United States." But, the council also noted, women's lives "are fundamentally determined by their functions as wives, mothers, and homemakers."[45]

Thus, in 1961 John F. Kennedy appointed a presidential commission to formulate recommendations to help women negotiate the two often conflicting roles of worker and mother. The commission appointed seven subcommittees, three of them dealing with employment and working conditions, one with family life, and one with education geared to lifelong paid work. Two more subcommittees considered the changes in the law and in tax and insurance schemes needed to adapt them to women's new roles. The commission accumulated data that documented women's relative disadvantage and the extent of the problem of adequate care for children. In 1963, by the time the commission issued its report, a national network of activists had formed to pursue the goals the national commission and its state offshoots had crafted.[46] No one had suggested that a presidential commission examine how fathers could perform their two roles, although industrialization had also vitiated the role of fathers as educators and guides of their children. This burden—of merging paid work and childcare to meet the demands of the late-twentieth-century economy—fell entirely on women; a feminist movement, fostered by federal policymakers, emerged in part to help women cope with its demands.

Congress had responded quickly to women mobilized by the President's Commission and energized by the prospect of recognition. In 1963 Congress passed the Equal Pay Act, an amendment to the 1938 Fair Labor Standards Act that barred employers from discriminating in pay rates based on sex. The first piece of federal legislation banning sex discrimination by private employers, the statute signaled the beginning of government's recognition of the permanent attachment of women—including married mothers—to the wage-labor force.[47] In 1964, Congress passed a civil rights act that included a wider ban on sex discrimination in employment. The legislation designated a new agency, the Equal Employment Opportunity Commission (EEOC), to enforce the law, but the EEOC gave short shrift to its responsibility to ensure equal treatment for women workers. Its disdain provoked a response from the women's network organized by the federal and state commissions. In 1966, a group of women attending a meeting of state commissions on women formed a new nongovernmental organization devoted to the full equality of women—NOW: the National Organization for Women. NOW took as its first order of business improving the performance of the EEOC,[48] but its wider mission included reordering social expectations about gender roles and it proposed a fourth system—a new ideal—for earning income and raising children in modern America.

MOTHERS AND FATHERS AT WORK AND AT HOME, CHILDREN IN THE BEST OF ALL POSSIBLE WORLDS

NOW constituted only the first of what would become a plethora of new women's organizations devoted to an explicitly feminist agenda based on freedom from stereotypical gender roles. Its program was much more comprehensive than the one Kennedy's commission had laid out. Not only would society help women resolve the role conflict produced by wage work done simultaneously with childcare, feminists now called upon men to adopt with women ownership of the full range of human responsibilities, to be divided on lines of individual preference and aptitude, not by sex. Thus, the new woman's movement proposed a new feminist system of childrearing in which women and men would again share all the work of the world, including family financial support and child-raising—as they had a century earlier. Both parents would negotiate with employers and make compromises in their work lives to provide their children with adequate parental care, supplemented by income replacement from employers or government. Public funding would support new institutions that would also provide childcare, both to accommodate parental work schedules and to expose the young child to experiences beyond those her parents could offer. The arrangement would permit men to develop the affective side of their nature and women to achieve both the satisfaction of instrumental work and the protection of economic autonomy. Such economic wherewithal for women would equalize power within the heterosexual family, would permit women to leave unhealthy or dangerous marriages and still care for their children, and would make possible a variety of new family forms, including same-sex partners with children.

Feminists also fought for reproductive freedom, including access to abortion. Birth control had become accepted during the Depression as a method of "family planning," and the oral contraceptive, available in the 1960s, made contraception reliable and accessible. But abortion gave women ultimate control over reproductive vicissitudes, essential in the modern era to both women and to their employers. In an agricultural setting, in which children contributed labor as farm hands and a woman raised her children while she worked, an additional child could have a positive economic impact. In a corporate business economy, an unplanned child could constitute an economic disaster for the woman and her family and uncertainties for employers. An expanded right to birth control and abortion gave a woman the ability to determine her work life as well as her reproductive choices, making childrearing a much more contingent activity, increasingly a decision women themselves were forced to justify.[49] Thus, although crafted to respond to the problems of the moment as experienced by women, the feminist program would have modernized family organization and public policy to fit a late-twentieth-century postindustrial economy with virtually every adult engaged in lifelong wage work.

The movement, consisting of national and local groups of all political stripes, had a powerful impact on public policy, including executive branch actions, legislation, and court decisions on the federal and state level. Although from the outset the women's movement demanded public support for childcare, the political community proved most amenable to the laws that banned discrimination rather than those that seemed likely to change childrearing practices and to require substantial federal expenditure.[50] By 1980, federal laws and executive orders banned discrimination in employment and job training against women (even when pregnant) and Congress had expanded the reach of Title VII of the Civil Rights Act to state and local governments. Lenders could no longer offer credit only to men; educational institutions could no longer discriminate among their students based on sex (although schools could continue to limit enrollments to a single sex). Congress also opened military academies to women and allocated money for special programs to achieve equity for women and to hold a National Women's Conference to set new goals for eliminating sex discrimination.

Concomitantly, the U.S. Supreme Court reversed its jurisprudence pertaining to sex-based classification in the law. By 1980, the Court had enunciated a new standard for such statutes: States would have to demonstrate that a sex-based classification had a substantial relationship to an important governmental objective.[51] Using this standard, the Court threw out almost all laws that distinguished on the basis of sex, including those that pertained to marital property, alimony, jury service, and age of majority. The Court further established and maintained the existence of a right to privacy that permitted physicians to terminate pregnancies during the first three months of gestation (the famous holding in *Roe v. Wade*, 1973). By virtue of these judicial decisions, the close—and surprising—defeat of the Equal Rights Amendment in 1982 had only a marginal impact on women's legal standing.

With new support for equal treatment, women's wage-earning roles continued to grow. In 1996, the labor-force participation rate of single women reached 65 percent, up from 53 percent in 1970. For married women, the rate had changed in the same time from 41 to 61 percent; for married women with children under six, from 30 to 63 percent; for married women with children from six to seventeen years old, from 49 to 77 percent.[52] By the end of the century, women were 29 percent of lawyers and judges, 26 percent of physicians, a third of professional athletes, half of all entry- and midlevel managers. Women received more than half the bachelor's degrees awarded annually and almost half of the doctorates.

But feminists' success was incomplete. Most women worked in traditional women's jobs and earned the wages to show for it. In 1996, 57 percent of working women earned their livings as service workers, sales women, or secretarial/clerical workers. Women made up more than 90 percent of nurses, 98 percent of nursery school teachers and childcare providers, 83 percent of elementary school teachers, 97 percent of secretaries and receptionists, 92 percent of bookkeepers, 90 percent of bank tellers, and 95 percent of household service workers. Few working-class women gained access to the higher-paid and traditionally male blue-collar jobs; in 1996, women constituted only 2 percent of firefighters, 1 percent of automobile mechanics, and 5 percent of truck drivers. Although the wage gap had closed more than 15 percentage points since 1960, women on average were still earning only 76 percent of men's wages.[53] Women's lower wages reflected the prevailing view that women were "secondary" earners because they still held the primary responsibility for raising children, although 75 percent of working mothers with children ages six to seventeen worked full time, as did nearly two-thirds of working women with younger children.[54]

The feminist proposal for childcare envisioned a partnership among mothers, fathers, employers, and government, but key components of this regime failed to appear. Feminists came within a hair of winning major federal support for institutional assistance with child-raising but quickly lost their leverage. In 1971, Congress passed the Comprehensive Child Development Act, which would have provided $4.5 billion dollars in subsidized childcare for poor families. Richard Nixon vetoed it, in keeping with the rightist view that such facilities would "Sovietize" American children.[55] The political and religious right stymied federal financial support for childcare and joined forces to mobilize against the feminist agenda, eventually adopting the rubric of "family values," citing with opprobrium collective childcare arrangements, access to abortion, and support for gay rights.[56] As a result, congressional support for publicly funded childcare never came close to meeting the need. Instead, in 1981, tax credit provisions allowed families to claim up to $480 for care for one child and $960 for two or more children. Beginning in 1982, the federal government allocated about $3 billion a year for a social services block grant that states could (but did not have to) use for childcare services. States responded with major cuts in childcare services.[57] A 1990 bill, the Act for Better Child Care, which Republican President George Bush signed, included both $2.5 billion over three years to states for childcare services and tax breaks for mothers at home. Further devolution of such programs to the states at the end of the century left childcare support uncertain.

After a Democratic president won election in 1992, feminists wrested a grudging accommodation to their parental responsibilities in the form of a national guaranteed period of leave for pregnancy, childbirth, and the care of sick family members. In 1993, President Clinton signed the Family and Medical Leave Act, which mandated twelve weeks of unpaid family or medical leave for workers in covered employment, a proposal twice vetoed by his Republican predecessor, George Bush. Family and medical leave assumed that women would remain attached to the labor force even during their childbearing years and for the first time national legislation offered some job security to women facing childbirth. The sex-neutral language of the statute—men as well as women were guaranteed family leave—retained the feminist ideal of shared family roles, although women primarily would take advantage of the benefit. While poor women would need to retain their jobs at least as much as middle-class women, only those with ample resources could take the full leave, stingy though it was, without pay. The question of who would care for the three-month-old infants at the end of the leave remained unaddressed.

MOTHERS AND FATHERS AT WORK, CHILDREN IN TRANSIT

At century's end, with more than three-quarters of single and married mothers with school-age children in the labor force, families received comparatively little assistance in paying for or in locating suitable care for their children. Such limited public financing for childcare, resistance to educational standards for private daycare providers, and the absence of paid leave, set the United States apart from its Western European counterparts, which routinely offered such benefits to working families. Private daycare providers filled the gap, many of them women who hoped to reconcile their own parental responsibilities with their need to earn money by caring for children in their homes. Lax standards left parents with a shortage of satisfactory choices, while daycare workers—usually women, often minority women— earned an average wage of $11,780, too low to support their own families adequately and less than the average bartender did.[58] Businesses showed little interest in helping. By 1998, only 9 percent of a thousand employers surveyed by the Families and Work Institute offered childcare services to their employees, although they advised other firms that doing so helped recruitment and led to increased rates of retention.[59] According to Sonya Michel, about 5,600 employer-supported childcare programs served about half a million youngsters in the 1990s.[60]

Parents nevertheless continued to work and to find help with childcare. In 1995, for all children under six, 40 percent were cared for only by their parents. When mothers were at work full time, one-third of young children were cared for by relatives, about 40 percent were in daycare or nursery school, and an additional 32 percent were in the care of nonrelatives, either inside or outside their own home. For 12 percent, even with mothers working full-time, their parents managed all childcare.[61]

These figures reveal that some fathers had stepped in to provide hands-on care for their children. In 1997, a CBS News poll reported that in 31 percent of families, husbands and wives shared childcare equally, up from 27 percent in 1983.[62] In 1994, fathers were the primary caregivers in 22 percent of families with preschool children, a dramatic increase from virtually none.[63] The ideal feminist lifestyle of two parents both working for wages and caring for their children seemed most likely to be pursued by working-class couples. Although they may have evinced little interest in feminist theory, they possessed fewer economic resources to support other options. In 1993, for fathers of children under five years of age, 42 percent of those who worked in service occupations cared for their children while their wives worked, compared to 20 percent of fathers in professional or managerial jobs.[64] The highly educated professional classes, more committed to feminist ideology, were least likely to adopt an egalitarian arrangement.[65] Rather, these couples hired another woman to take care of their children, or the professional wife temporarily dropped out of a promising career to devote herself full-time to child-raising, relying on the single substantial professional income of her husband.

Still, the onus of arranging nonparental childcare fell most often on mothers and the demands of the job, coupled with antiquated school schedules, meant that mothers frequently had to arrange more than one kind of care for a child—or for two children—and had to plan transportation to get them from one place to the other. According to a national survey of 45,000 families conducted in 1997, 38 percent of children younger than five in nonparental care with mothers at work spent time in two or more childcare settings each week. Thirteen percent of these three- and four-year-olds had three or more nonparental caregivers in a given week (19 percent in Minnesota and New York).[66] Family income levels had no bearing on the use of multiple childcare providers. So at the end of the twentieth century, fathers retained their full-time connection to the paid work, while mothers working full time arranged surrogate care for their children around the demands of their jobs—the most recent of the experiments to raise children in a modern, nonagricultural economy.

In 1996, the conservative right itself acknowledged implicitly the weakening hold of the ideal of the full-time mother in reformulating policy for the poor (and putatively black) mother. At the beginning of the century, reformers had identified households that lacked male breadwinners as urgent objects of assistance. Because of their commitment to mothers at home, these Progressive reformers sought and gained publicly funded "mothers' pensions" to permit mothers to eschew paid employment for the sake of providing care to their children. States did not provide much in the way of funding and state officials openly favored white mothers, but the more effective New Deal policies, incorporated in the Social Security Act of 1935 and its 1939 amendments, adopted the model of financial support to mothers of minor children to permit them to forgo work for wages indefinitely.[67] Until the 1960s this support was contingent on the mother's *not* working outside the home.

In the 1960s several trends merged to undermine such a policy. Thanks to both urban migration and to the movements for civil rights and social justice, more black mothers received aid previously limited in many states almost entirely to white women.[68] As the program of "aid to families with dependent children" became identified with black families living in urban ghettoes, critics assailed public assistance as the cause of familial disorder rather than its palliative. At the same time, (white) working mothers became the rule rather than the exception. Animosity therefore intensified over taxing those white women to help other—black—mothers stay home. The federal government thus simultaneously enacted laws explicitly supporting women at work by barring discrimination (the Equal Pay Act in 1963 and the Civil Rights Act in 1964), at the same time devising programs (such as the work requirements in the Public Welfare Amendments of 1962) that would encourage poor women to work for wages rather than to remain full-time mothers.[69]

Over the next three decades, the preference for work grew and the defense of spending public money to allow poor women with young children to stay home virtually disappeared. Opponents of federal aid to the poor argued that poor impoverished children would benefit from working mothers as effective role models, and poor mothers would benefit from the experience of wage earning and workplace interactions.[70] Although evidence demonstrated that most mothers on public assistance already worked for wages for a substantial number of hours, in 1996 a Republican Congress insisted on the necessity of a law that would force women to work.[71] New federal legislation, the Personal Responsibility and Work Opportunity Reconciliation Act, mandated work and removed the guarantee of public assistance to poor mothers. With the signature of a Democratic president, this so-called welfare reform law apparently signaled that neither both political party would now defend full-time mothering for women as either the practice or the goal.

But the 1996 welfare legislation had as its explicit objective not to compel single mothers to work but rather to promote marriage. Copious evidence showed that most poor women leaving welfare could not find jobs that would provide sufficient income to support their families adequately.[72] In its "findings," Congress noted in the law: "Marriage is the foundation of a successful society; Marriage is an essential institution of a successful society

which promotes the interests of children." The new welfare law had as its purpose therefore "to increase the flexibility of States ... to ... provide assistance
to needy families so that children may be cared for in their own homes or in
the homes of relatives; [to] end the dependence of needy parents on government benefits by promoting job preparation, work, and marriage [and to]
encourage the formation and maintenance of two-parent families."[73] Unwilling to provide a public subsidy to permit single women to stay at home while
married mothers went to work, conservative policymakers argued for the
chimera of father-supported families, with mothers at home, for children in
families at all income levels.

The decline in marriage rates in the United States and the increase in single-mother families mirrored transnational trends.[74] Nevertheless, conservative commentators reasserted the necessity for fathers to occupy gender-
based "leadership" roles in the family, invoking both nature and the
principles of traditional Christian theology. David Blankenhorn, in his book
Fatherless America: Confronting Our Most Urgent Social Problem, warned not
simply that children needed their fathers in residence and married to their
mothers but that the parents had to adopt gendered parental roles, a need
supposedly confirmed by "psychological and anthropological evidence from
a diversity of cultures." Children required a full-time stay-at-home mother
and a father-breadwinner, a role that "permits men to serve their families
through competition with other men." The "New Father" of the feminist
model, wrote Blankenhorn, "finally becomes no father."[75] In June 1998 the
Southern Baptist convention declared, as an addition to their fundamental
credo, that a husband "has the God-given responsibility to provide for, to
protect and to lead his family." In return, "a wife is to submit graciously to
the servant leadership of her husband even as the church willingly submits
to the headship of Christ."[76] The president of the denomination, Paige Patterson, explained that the declaration responded to "a time of growing crisis
in the family."[77]

Meanwhile, the mainstream press began to characterize the childrearing
problem repeatedly as a woman's issue, a parallel "back-to-the-home" movement. On February 15, 1998, *The Washington Post Magazine* offered a cover
story entitled "Dispatches From the Mommy Wars—To Work or to Stay
Home: A New Mother's Tour of a Cultural Battlefield," by Tracy Thompson.
Not two months later, on April 5, 1998, *The New York Times Magazine* devoted a special issue to the subject, entitled (accurately enough) "Mothers
Can't Win: A Special Issue on the Joy and Guilt of Modern Motherhood." The
cover photograph of a woman and three children on a stark white back-

ground conveyed the clear idea that children were women's problem. Super-imposed on the photo was a series of questions, the first: "Work or home?" "No matter what they choose, they're made to feel bad," the cover type ex-plained—without acknowledging that such a choice was available only to the affluent woman. "Elizabeth Munro, ex-lawyer." On the contents page, a pho-tograph of another woman, this time with five children, showed her posed in front of a window, also without a father in sight. In an article concerning support groups for full-time mothers, the reporter noted that one mother "has an MBA, a master's degree in economics and is fluent in Mandarin," but is staying home with her son, having given up "a career in China and a six-figure salary." The mother herself expressed ambivalence: "No matter what a woman decides, to stay at work or to stay at home, she feels conflicted." For such women, groups like Mothers First, FEMALE, and Parents and Commu-nity Education, gave women the opportunity to meet other women who had made the same decision.[78] The resignation of Brenda Barnes, chief of Pepsi-co's North American operation, to spend more time with her children made the lead in a story called "Women on the Tightrope: Two Views," reviewing two books on the subject: *When Mothers Work: Loving Our Children Without Sacrificing Our Selves* by Joan Peters and *When Work Doesn't Work Anymore; Women, Work, and Identity* by Elizabeth Perle McKenna.[79]

With surrogate care often replacing the care of both poor and more af-fluent mothers, feminists had to confront arguments about the adequacy of group arrangements in order to respond to those who labeled "working mothers" a problem. Unable to change the discussion to emphasize the con-tinuing hesitance of men to render actual physical care for their children and the refusal of the government and employers to do more to assist fam-ilies, feminists were reduced to defending a system in which poorly paid women offered substitute childcare in group settings that many claimed failed to provide sufficient attention to young children.[80] Such circum-stances divided women by class and race as families tried to keep daycare costs low by resisting raises in wages that necessitated raises in rates. Rather than abating, conflict over the effect of surrogate care for children intensi-fied, with some combatants offering damning evidence about deficits in children left in institutional care, while others reassured anxious parents that surrogate care was fine. In 1998, a front-page story in the *New York Times*, "Struggling for Personal Attention in Day Care," observed that "such care often forces the workers to change their emphasis from individual at-tention to group management." Noting that the demand for daycare was rising, the reporter cited studies showing that "more than 1 in 10 children are in care that is unsafe and harmful to their development."[81] In "Attachment Theory: The Ultimate Experiment," a reporter rehearsed the data about attachment theory and referred to children raised in a Romanian orphanage to warn against a cavalier attitude toward daycare.[82] (Parents' parking children in front of television sets engendered no cries to remove those children to good daycare centers, however.) Television news shows and newspapers bruited horror stories of murderous nannies and viewers blamed the mother—not the father—for leaving the child with the caregiver.[83] (News stories of mothers and fathers murdering their children, however, did not prompt arguments against parental care, nor did reporters point out that a child was much more likely to be harmed by a parent than by a daycare worker.) Some experts rode to the rescue: In the March 1999 issue of *Developmental Psychology,* a psychologist concluded that children at age twelve whose mothers had worked during their first three years showed no ill effects when compared with children the same age whose mothers had been home,[84] and a report from the National Institute of Child Health and Human Development deemed most childcare "fair" or "good," with only 8 percent identified as "poor."[85]

So while feminists insisted on the need for more and better publicly funded childcare and more public and social support for families, conservatives maintained that the solution to raising children in a nonagricultural society was to have one adult (which is to say, the mother) withdraw from wage work and devote herself solely to childrearing. The father of the children, they argued, should subsidize such a solution.[86] For women who were not married, they recommended marriage. Still, enough measurable change had occurred in both behavior and in the way the public viewed family responsibilities to suggest that such a conservative counterrevolution would win few adherents. Only 22 percent in a 1997 poll agreed that a husband's job was more important than the wife's,[87] and a stunning 91 percent of men and 94 percent of women polled by in March 1998 agreed with the statement: "Everything about the care of children should be shared equally by both parents."[88]

CARING FOR CHILDREN IN THE
TWENTY-FIRST CENTURY

The transition from an agricultural to an industrial economy took place at the beginning of the twentieth century, but the end of the century found Americans still struggling with the question of how to care adequately for young children and provide sufficient family income. Initially, policy-makers had advocated the withdrawal of mothers from waged labor for a substantial portion of their lives to devote themselves to childcare. But this strategy depended upon the availability of other workers to supplement family wages. Such a system deprived young people of educational chances, while the financial dependence of women on men left women and children vulnerable to economic deprivation. The insufficiency of wages paid to male workers as well as rising divorce rates indicated that the father's wage earning alone could not in the long run support most families. In addition, as the century progressed, women's income provided benefits to families (college education, dental care, vacations, homes) that women's unwaged work at home could not. Moreover, by mid-century it had become clear that the national economy required both the skills and talents that women possessed as well as the sheer labor power to fill essential positions. Thus, calls to reestablish the "traditional American family" had an anachronistic ring, a fruitless attempt to establish an idealized nineteenth-century system unsuited to the reality of a twentieth-first-century economy.

At the turn of the twenty-first century, with global competition creating more pressure for all adults to work for wages outside the home, a raft of new policy proposals seemed to herald the understanding that a concerted social response would have to emerge to ensure the proper care of children—and other family members—and to complete the transition from an agricultural to a postindustrial economy.[89] Some proposals implied the kind of massive governmental intervention that accompanied earlier economic transformations. In January 2000, the *New York Times* reported that "the explosion in after-school programs—federal financing alone has ballooned to $454 million this year from $1 million in 1997—represents nothing less than a reimagining of the school day for the first time in generations, as educators and policymakers seek to respond to the realities of working families and what may be missing from the classroom."[90] Universal preschool programs appeared in the Democratic presidential platform, "the educational issue du jour," while forty two states instituted preschool programs for poor children.[91] Labor unions and private corporations indicated a new emphasis on negotiating issues concerning family care. In May 2001, the Ford Motor Company, at the urging of the United Auto Workers, announced plans to create thirty "Family Service and Learning Centers" with programs for both children and parents of Ford workers.[92] Countless books appeared to advise policymakers to update government mandates for private employers so that workers, both male and female, might provide their children and, increasingly, their parents with appropriate care.[93] Feminist policymakers advised expansion of "social wages," such as paid family leave, to provide additional support for families without futile attempts to coerce family forms. They argued that the burden of accommodation to the global economy could not be placed solely on the shoulders of women.[94]

Contrary to prevailing wisdom, for most of American history, most American women did not engage in full-time childcare. When they did so, it was all too often at the cost of making family breadwinners of teenagers. For only a historical minute in the middle of the twentieth century could a majority of American women contemplate a life devoted to full-time homemaking and child-raising, supported solely by a male breadwinner. As they reassumed income-producing roles—in the twentieth century, outside the home—women encountered haphazard and makeshift policy responses that failed to address the needs of children adequately and that left women disadvantaged as wage earners, also to the detriment of children. Solving the problem of childcare in a postindustrial society thus must be the work of the twenty-first century and, with its resolution, may come as well the culmination of the feminist revolution begun in the 1960s.

NOTES

1. For a discussion of this phenomenon, see, for instance, Arlie Hochschild and Anne Machung, *The Second Shift: Working Parents and the Revolution at Home* (New York: Viking Penguin, 1989).

2. U.S. Census Bureau, *Statistical Abstract of the United States: 1999* (Washington, D.C.: U.S. Government Printing Office, 1999), table 660.

3. Walter I. Trattner, *Crusade for the Children: A History of the National Child Labor Committee and Child Labor Reform in America* (Chicago: Quadrangle Books, 1970), chap. 6.

4. Descriptions of work and childrearing on farms at various periods include Joan M. Jensen, *Loosening the Bonds: Mid-Atlantic Farm Women, 1750–1850* (New Haven: Yale University Press, 1986); Stephanie McCurry, *Masters of Small Worlds: Yeoman Households, Gender Relations, and the Political Culture of the Antebellum South Carolina Low Country* (New York: Oxford University Press, 1995); Jacqueline Jones, *Labor of Love, Labor of Sorrow: Black Women, Work and the Family, From Slavery to the Present* (New York: Basic Books, 1985); Marilyn Irvin Holt, *Linoleum, Better Babies & the Modern Farm Woman, 1890–1930* (Albuquerque: University of New Mexico Press, 1995). For a discussion of the ways in which mothers handled

childcare in a preindustrial setting, see Sonya Michel, *Children's Interests / Mother's Rights: The Shaping of America's Child Care Policy* (New Haven: Yale University Press, 1999), chap. 1.

5. See, for example, Nancy F. Cott, *The Bonds of Womanhood: A Woman's Sphere in New England, 1780–1835* (New Haven: Yale University Press, 1977), for a discussion of this ideology.

6. All 1999 figures are calculated using Robert C. Sahr, "Consumer Price Index (CPI) Conversion Factors to Convert to Dollars of the Year 2000," an updated version of which is available at http://www.orst.edu/dept/pol_sci/fac/sahr/sahr.htm. All numbers are estimates.

7. U.S. Bureau of the Census, *Historical Statistics of the United States, Colonial Times to 1970, Part 1* (Washington, D.C.: U.S. Government Printing Office, 1975), Series D 779-793, p. 168 (hereinafter cited as *Historical Statistics*).

8. On homework, see especially Eileen Boris, *Home to Work: Motherhood and the Politics of Industrial Homework in the United States* (New York: Cambridge University Press, 1994).

9. Michel, *Children's Interests*, 97.

10. *Historical Statistics*, Series A 119-134, p. 15; Series A 350-352, p. 43; Series D 49-62, p. 133; Series D 182-232, p. 139.

11. See Katharine DuPre Lumpkin and Dorothy Wolff Douglas, *Child Workers in America* (New York: Robert M. McBride, 1937), chap. 1, for a discussion of "hidden" child workers.

12. Harry G. Good and James D. Teller, *A History of American Education* (New York: Macmillan, 1973), table 8.1.

13. Trattner, *Crusade for the Children*, 38–40.

14. In 1910 an adequate income for a family of six, depending on location, ranged from about $700 to $1,000, according to a number of different observers. See discussion in Gordon M. Fisher, "From Hunter to Orshansky: An Overview of (Unofficial) Poverty Lines in the United States from 1094 to 1965," August 1997, pp. 13–17, at http://www.census.gov/hhes/poverty/povmeas/papers/hstorsp.4html# N_1_. At the time, the average annual wage for "all industries" excluding farm labor equaled $630. In manufacturing, the average amounted to $558; for schoolteachers, the average was $492. The average annual wage for farm labor totaled $336. *Historical Statistics*, Series D 779-793, p. 168.

15. Paula Giddings, *When and Where I Enter: The Impact of Black Women on Race and Sex in America* (New York: Bantam, 1985), 101; Jones, *Labor of Love*, 96–98.

16. Trattner, *Crusade for the Children*, 30, 153; Molly Ladd-Taylor, *Mother-Work: Women, Child Welfare, and the State, 1890–1930* (Urbana: University of Illinois Press, 1994), 96.

17. Edgar W. Knight, *Fifty Years of American Education, 1900–1950* (New York: Ronald Press, 1952), 69; Trattner, *Crusade for the Children,* 184.

18. Knight, *Fifty Years of American Education,* 58–70; David Tyack, *The One Best System: A History of American Urban Education* (Cambridge, Mass.: Harvard University Press, 1974), 70–71.

19. Tyack, *The One Best System,* 183–184.

20. Good and Teller, *A History of American Education,* 237.

21. Good and Teller, *A History of American Education,* 237.

22. Robert S. Lynd and Helen Merrell Lynd, *Middletown: A Study in Contemporary American Culture* (New York: Harcourt Brace, 1929), 83–85; *Historical Statistics* (see note 10).

23. Lois Scharf, *To Work and to Wed* (Westport, Conn.: Greenwood, 1980), 141.

24. Grace Palladino, *Teenagers: An American History* (New York: Basic Books, 1996), chap. 3; John Modell, *Into One's Own: From Youth to Adulthood in the United States, 1920–1975* (Berkeley: University of California Press, 1989), chap. 4.

25. Scharf, *To Work and to Wed,* 148.

26. *Historical Statistics,* Series H 442-476, p. 372; Series A 160-171, p. 20; Series D 29-41, p. 132.

27. William H. Chafe, *The Paradox of Change: American Women in the 20th Century* (New York: Oxford University Press, 1991), chap. 7.

28. Table F-12, "Earners—Families (All Races) by Median and Mean Income: 1947 to 1996." Based upon the Current Population Survey, at http://www.census.gov/hhes/income/histinc/incfamdet.html.

29. Daniel Hernandez with David E. Myers for the National Committee on the 1980 Census, *America's Children: Resources from Family, Government, and the Economy* (New York: Russell Sage Foundation, 1993), fig. 4.6. Hernandez's figure is actually overly inclusive in that the fathers who worked forty-eight weeks were not necessarily working full-time during those weeks. Moreover, this figure includes children living in families in which the couple had a child before this marriage, another deviation from the "ideal" family.

30. *Historical Statistics,* Series D29-41, p. 132.

31. *Historical Statistics,* Series G 257-268, p. 298; Series G 283-296, p. 300; Series 297-305, p. 300; Series G 306-318, p. 301.

32. *Historical Statistics,* Series A 350-352, p. 43; Series D 11-25, p. 127.

33. U.S. Department of Labor, Women's Bureau, *1969 Handbook on Women Workers* (Washington, D.C.: U.S. Government Printing Office, 1969), tables 17 and 18.

34. *Statistical Abstracts 1997,* table 631.

35. These families figured, respectively, in *Ozzie and Harriet, Father Knows Best, The Donna Reed Show, Leave It to Beaver, The Life of Reilly,* and *Make Room for Daddy.* See

Stephanie Coontz, *The Way We Never Were: American Families and the Nostalgia Trap* (New York: Basic Books, 1992), chap. 2, for a discussion of this phenomenon. Lynn Spigel, *Make Room for TV: Television and the Family Ideal in Postwar America* (Chicago: University of Chicago Press, 1992) examines the interaction of family ideals and television. See also Susan J. Douglas, *Where the Girls Are: Growing Up Female with the Mass Media* (New York: Random House, 1995).

36. U.S. Department of Labor, Women's Bureau, *1969 Handbook on Women Workers* (Washington, D.C.: U.S. Government Printing Office, 1969), table 20.

37. Ladd-Taylor, *Mother-Work,* 46–47; G. Stanley Hall, *Youth: Its Education, Regimen and Hygiene* (1904), discussed in Maxine L. Margolis, *Mothers and Such: Views of American Women and Why They Changed* (Berkeley: University of California Press, 1984), 48.

38. Margolis, *Mothers and Such,* 51–54.

39. Margolis, *Mothers and Such,* 72–84.

40. Trattner, *Crusade for the Children,* 152.

41. *Historical Statistics,* Series H 520-530, p. 376.

42. Tyack, *The One Best System,* 66.

43. Lumpkin and Douglas, *Child Workers in America,* chap. 5.

44. See *Historical Statistics,* H 442-476, pp. 370–372; *Statistical Abstracts,* 1995, table 631; *1969 Handbook on Women Workers,* table 18.

45. National Manpower Council, *Womanpower* (New York: Columbia University Press, 1957), 262–263.

46. Cynthia Harrison, *On Account of Sex: The Politics of Women's Issues, 1945–1968* (Berkeley: University of California Press, 1988); Jo Freeman, *The Politics of Women's Liberation* (New York: McKay, 1975).

47. Harrison, *On Account of Sex,* chaps 3 and 6.

48. Harrison, *On Account of Sex,* 177–182, 295 n. 20; Jo Freeman, "How 'Sex' Got Into Title VII: Persistent Opportunism as a Maker of Public Policy" *Law and Inequality* 9 (March 1991): 163–184.

49. For an extended discussion of the constraints on women's decision regarding reproductive decisions, see Rosalind Pollack Petchesky, *Abortion and Woman's Choice: The State, Sexuality, & Reproductive Freedom,* rev. ed. (Boston: Northeastern University Press, 1990), and Rickie Solinger, *Beggars and Choosers: How the Politics of Choice Shapes Adoption, Abortion, and Welfare in the United States* (New York: Hill and Wang, 2001).

50. Discussions of the impact of the women's movement on public policy include Joyce Gelb and Marian Lief Palley, *Women and Public Policies: Reassessing Gender Politics* (Charlottesville: University Press of Virginia, 1996) and Leslie Friedman Goldstein, *The Constitutional Rights of Women: Cases in Law and Social Change* (Madison: University of Wisconsin Press, 1988).

51. *Craig v. Boren,* 429 U.S. 190 (1976).

52. *Statistical Abstracts 1997,* table 631. The data refer to women sixteen years old and up.

53. *New York Times,* June 10, 1998, p. A20.

54. Cynthia B. Costello, Shari Miles, and Anne J. Stone. *The American Woman, 1999–2000* (New York: W. W. Norton, 1998), table 4-22.

55. Michel, *Children's Interests,* 247–251.

56. See, for example, Phyllis Schlafly, *The Power of the Christian Woman* (Cincinnati: Standard Publishers, 1981).

57. Michel, *Children's Interests,* 253.

58. *New York Times,* April 29, 1990, p. A14; Children's Defense Fund, "Facts about child care in America," July 8, 1998, at http://www.childrensdefense.org.

59. *Washington Post,* July 17, 1998, pp. F1, F4.

60. Michel, *Children's Interests,* 264.

61. *Statistical Abstracts: 1997,* table 612. The figures add up to more than 100 percent because some children participated in more than one arrangement.

62. CBS News Poll, October 4, 1997, "Major changes in women's status over past 25 years," September 18–20, 1997.

63. Gail Sheehy, "The Divorced Dad's Burden," *New York Times,* June 21, 1998, p. D15.

64. Julia Lawlor, "For Many Blue-Collar Fathers, Child Care is Shift Work, Too," *New York Times,* April 26, 1998, p. C11.

65. See Hochschild and Machung, *The Second Shift.*

66. Jeffery Capizzano and Gina Adams, "The Number of Child Care Arrangements Used by Children Under Five: Variation Across States," Number B-12 in Series, "New Federalism: National Survey of America's Families" (Washington, D.C.: Urban Institute, 2000), at http://newfederalism.urban.org/html/series_b/b12/b12.html.

67. See, for example, Linda Gordon, *Pitied but Not Entitled: Single Mothers and the History of Welfare, 1890–1935* (New York: Free Press, 1994), for a discussion of earlier public-assistance programs.

68. For a discussion of the influence of race on the redirection of the federal welfare program, see Winifred Bell, *Aid to Dependent Children* (New York: Columbia University Press, 1965).

69. Michel, *Children's Interests,* 244–245.

70. Charles Murray, *Losing Ground: American Social Policy, 1950–1980* (New York: Basic Books, 1984).

71. Roberta Spalter-Roth et al., *Welfare That Works: The Working Lives of AFDC Recipients* (Washington, D.C.: Institute for Women's Policy Research, 1995).

72. See, for example, Wendell Primus et al. *The Initial Impacts of Welfare Reform*

on the Income of Single-Mother Families (Washington, D.C.: Center on Budget and Policy Priorities, August 22, 1999), available at www.cbpp.org/8-22-99wel.pdf.

73. P.L. 104-193.

74. Single-mother families in the United States suffered greater want, however. In 1990, 44.5 percent of families with children maintained by women lived in poverty, ameliorated much less by government programs. See Harrell R. Rodgers Jr., *Poor Women, Poor Children: American Poverty in the 1990s* (Armonk, N.Y.: M. E. Sharpe, 1996), table 5.1; U.S. Department of Labor, Women's Bureau, *1993 Handbook on Women Workers* (Washington, D.C.: U.S. Government Printing Office, 1994), 84.

75. David Blankenhorn, *Fatherless America: Confronting Our Most Urgent Social Problem* (New York: Basic Books, 1995), 101, 103, 116.

76. Gustav Niebuhr, "Southern Baptists Declare Wife Should 'Submit' to Her Husband," *New York Times,* June 10, 1998, pp. A1, A24.

77. Niebuhr, "Southern Baptists Declare," p. A1.

78. Jennifer Lenhart, "Meeting Other Mothers," *Washington Post,* Feb. 3, 1998, pp. C1, C3.

79. Deborah Stead, "Off the Shelf," *New York Times,* October 5, 1997, p. C7.

80. See, for example, Tamar Levin, "Struggling for Personal Attention in Day Care," *New York Times,* April 27, 1998, pp. A1, A13.

81. Levin, "Struggling for Personal Attention."

82. *New York Times Magazine,* May 24, 1998.

83. One example of such coverage: Louise Woodward, who was convicted on October 31, 1997, of the murder of the child in her care. After extensive coverage at the time, the popular CBS television news magazine *60 Minutes* revisited the story on March 7, 1999 (exposing new evidence supposedly exculpating Woodward)

84. "Mother's Working Causes No Harm, Study Finds," *New York Times,* March 1, 1999.

85. Christine Russell, "Only 10% of Day Care is Rated Excellent," *Washington Post Health,* February 23, 1999, p. 8.

86. See Blankenhorn, *Fatherless America,* and David Popenoe, *Life Without Father* (New York: Free Press, 1996).

87. Richard Morin and Megan Rosenfeld, "With More Equity, More Sweat: Poll Shows Sexes Agree on Pros and Cons of New Roles," *Washington Post,* March 22, 1998, p. A16; the poll was conducted by the *Post,* the Henry J. Kaiser Family Foundation, and Harvard University.

88. Morin and Rosenfeld, "With More Equity, More Sweat."

89. Almost 25 percent of households in 1996 were offering care to a friend or relative age fifty or older. U.S. Department of Labor, Women's Bureau, *Facts on Working Women,* May 1998, No. 98- 1, "Work and Elder Care." Thirty percent of workers

interviewed by Jody Heymann, director of the Harvard University Center for Society and Health, cut back on work time to take care of a relative; Tamar Lewin, "Taking Care: It's Not Just for Mothers Anymore," *New York Times,* May 13, 2001, p. D14.

90. Jodi Wilgoren, "The Bell Rings but the Students Stay, and Stay," *New York Times,* January 24, 2000, p. D4.

91. Lynette Holloway, "For Preschool, a Wealth of Benefits and a Dearth of Space," *New York Times,* September 5, 2000, p. B3.

92. Steven Greenhouse, "Child Care, the Perk of Tomorrow?" *New York Times,* May 13, 2001, p. D14.

93. The literature on this subject is immense, with titles such as *Families and Work: New Directions in the Twenty-First Century* (Karen Fredriksen-Goldsen and Andrew Scharlach, published by Oxford University Press, 2001). For a sampling, see "Work and family—United States" in the Library of Congress catalog.

94. See, for example, Nancy Folbre, *The Invisible Heart: Economics and Family Values* (New York: New Press, 2001); Joan Williams, *Unbending Gender: Why Family and Work Conflict and What to Do About It* (New York: Oxford University Press, 2000); and the many position papers published by the Institute for Women's Policy Research at www.iwpr.org.

10

RACE, CLASS, AND GENDER IN SOUTHERN HISTORY: FORCES THAT UNITE, FORCES THAT DIVIDE

William H. Chafe

Many years ago, at a meeting of the Southern Historical Association in Dallas, I had the opportunity to comment on a session dealing with various women's movements that had grown out of southern soil. Presenting papers that day were Jacquelyn Dowd Hall and Sara Evans. The gist of the dialogue that ensued was how important it was to complicate our analysis of gender by considering how gender intersected with and was shaped by issues of race and class. That was the first occasion on which I recall such a discussion. Since then, of course, these issues have been at the center of the work of many scholars and have helped to transform our understanding of the past.

Over the past few decades, the words *race, class,* and *gender* have become a mantra of sorts. They are invoked in liturgical fashion to alert an audience that it is in the presence of people who are "politically correct," scholars who, by sharing certain code words, demonstrate their joint participation in a venture dedicated to reforming the canon, be it literary or historical. This modern-day reformation is driven, initially at least, by the unity it derives from being in a heretical mode. The "old" history, once venerated and orthodox, is now viewed with derision, suffering from the twin liabilities of being out of style and dogmatically flawed. Like all participants in a quasi-religious reformation, those of us who attend the church of the "new social history" derive our primary self-esteem from being the "other" to our antagonists. Simply by virtue of being "not-they," we are superior. When the pretensions that accompany being a deconstructionist or literary theorist are added to this fundamental premise of superiority, we reformers become almost unbearable—from the heaviness, not the lightness of our being.

But at some point it becomes necessary to locate our source of self-worth in the positive contribution we make to scholarship—not just in our disdain for those who write the meta-narrative of white men. What is it that makes invoking the mantra of race, class, and gender helpful to understanding the past? What insights develop as a result of using these three concepts as variable tools of analysis? Where do they take us? And for what ends?

The first thing to realize, I think, is that focusing on race, class, and gender is a way of relating to, but also departing from, the dominant discourse of American culture—a discourse that has revolved around the concepts of individualism and equal opportunity. Whatever else we may think of the "old" history, it was a craft that presumed some kind of agency on the part of individual historical actors. That agency, in turn, assumed that in America any individual could aspire to and could become an important figure in history. In short, there was an inextricable connection between the attention of historians to individual heroes and heroines and the belief that America was a society where access to such roles was free and open.

Among other things, redirecting attention to race, class, and gender—whether these are viewed as social and cultural constructs or as substantive categories—flowed from a rejection of the idea that America was either a society of individuals or one of equal opportunity. Rather, the premise—supported by overwhelming evidence—was that America was a deeply unequal society, and that its inequality was tied directly to the extent that group identification—not individual identity—shaped and determined life possibilities. In retrospect, it seems hard to imagine that proposition was ever in question. Obviously, people who were of African descent—however light the color of their skin due to forced sexual interaction with white masters—were systematically excluded from all individual rights of citizenship from 1619 until 1964, with only a few exceptions. The same biological fact deprived African Americans of any chance to join the free economic competition that allegedly animated the success story of America.

Similarly, women—by virtue of their sex—were denied the same citizenship rights, as well as opportunities to compete to become members of the business, legal, or political elite of the country. Although in no way similar to African Americans in the degree of physical and material oppression they suffered, women too were the victims of legal, physical, economic, and psychological oppression—stereotyped, prevented from pursuing individual desires and talents, forced to play roles and profess subservience, no matter how incompetent were the men they had to satisfy.

The only category of the three that was not tied to a physical characteristic was that of class. Although dress, bearing, accent, and living condition conveyed visible reminders of what class meant, there were not the same kind of ready-made symbols that could immediately identify someone as poor as there were for identifying women or African Americans. Still, class operated in much the same way as a vehicle for excluding whole groups of Americans from participating in the "American dream." Education was for the most part not available. Child labor was pervasive. Inadequate healthcare and lodging kept the poor from ever being able to get "a leg up" or even pull even; and the prevalence of ethnic prejudice against Italians, Irish, Poles, or Jews carried over to white ethnics the same kinds of racial disqualification that so impeded African Americans.

That left one other category of historical actors whose fate was also shaped by the variables of race, class, and gender—men who were rich and also white. As it turned out, they (or we, as the case may be) were the individuals who had thrived in the equal-opportunity story that was America. Whether through malice aforethought, conspiracy, or simple good fortune through accident of birth, such individuals could hardly fail, because everything in the society was structured to insure their success—whatever their individual talent or ability might be. And the fact that so many of the poor were also black and to an increasing degree female made it all the easier to know and to defend one's "place."

These then were the fundamental departure points from which practitioners of the "new history" started to rewrite the story of our past in the 1960s, '70s, '80s, and '90s. In some ways the task seemed very easy. The villains were clear. So too were the victims.

Yet as soon as scholars set to work to explore and elaborate what the race, class, and gender mantra meant, it all became much more complicated. What about the role of gender among the poor as well as the rich, the black as well as the white? Did black women face the same obstructions relating to black men as white women to white men? How did differences of class—or color, the two often being correlated—lead to divergent experiences for people otherwise unified by their common identity as African Americans? Was there a priority among oppressions? Did gender represent the original source of inequality, as argued by Gerda Lerner? Was it class, as many Marxists contended? Or was race the central oppression, especially in America?

And how did race, class, and gender intersect? The word "intersection" became its own code word, symbolizing the degree to which all these experiences of inequality were interactive. But which was the dependent, which the independent variable? Some scholars resorted to imaginative metaphors to deepen and enrich our understanding of the problem of intersection. Elsa Barkley Brown used the image of a jazz combo, interweaving, sometimes in harmony, other times in dissonance, a whole series of riffs contributed by one or another of the themes of race, class, and gender, culminating in a coherent musical experience where the listener had simply to be attentive to the instrument playing at any one time. Nancy Hewitt, in turn, talked about the intersection as akin to a chemical formula, different ingredients coming together—sometimes dissolving into each other, at other times separate and undissolved—but providing a laboratory for historians to dissect and analyze in an effort to determine how in a given situation race, class, and gender have interacted.

Whatever the metaphor, it was clear that the new focus on gender, race, and class was going to produce as many questions as it did answers, and that the resulting work would be worthwhile precisely to the extent that it was multitextured and multicolored rather than monochromatic. In partial pursuit of such results, what I would like to do in this essay is to share three case studies of how race, class, and gender have been important in understanding different moments of southern history. My point of departure is the thesis that just as race, class, and gender have been primary instruments of oppression in southern history, they have also been primary sources around which resistance has organized. Hence, the same force that works to suppress and contain can also be turned around and used as a force that rebels and breaks out. Yet even as that process unfolds, these case studies suggest that ultimate freedom and success is impeded by the continuing degree to which divisions over race, class, and gender persist in crippling the drive for change. Thus, although gender, race, and class are forces that unite, they are also forces that divide. In that paradox lies at least part of the explanation of where the South—and the nation—has been and where it is going.

The first case study grows out of the work of my colleague Jacquelyn Dowd Hall. In a prizewinning book that built on the scholarship of Anne Firor Scott and has since been expanded through new research by Jacqueline Rouse and Deborah Gray White, among others, Hall traced the origins and development of a campaign by southern women against lynching. With southern reformer and feminist Jessie Daniel Ames as her protagonist, Hall narrated a complicated tale of interracial cooperation and conflict between black and white women.

The period of cooperation began in the early 1920s as an experiment in interracial communication based on the premise that "a bond of common womanhood" would permit middle-class white and black women to unite around concerns grounded in their shared gender. Carrie Parks Johnson, director of the Women's Committee of the Commission on Inter-racial Cooperation, attended a meeting at Tuskegee Institute of the National Association of Colored Women. There, led by Lugenia Burns Hope and Charlotte Hawkins Brown—two prominent black women educators and organizers—the black women spoke candidly of the divisions separating black and white women and the need for respect and partnership to guide any ventures they engaged in together. At Tuskegee, and in a subsequent meeting in Memphis, women of both races were inspired by a shared evangelical sense of being part of a new alliance.

That alliance in turn built upon having participated in institutions that were woman-centered. Although the black and white women encountered these institutions separately, since the institutions were segregated, the experience of being involved in women's missionary societies, the YWCA, and settlement house activities—all defined by their being exclusively women's groups devoted to "women's" concerns—appeared to provide enough of a shared foundation to launch this new experiment in interracialism. Together, these white and black women would address problems of the treatment of domestic servants, problems of public transportation, education, and the need to end the horror of lynching. Shared bonds of womanhood would provide the basis for building a new and more just society.

As we shall see, that hope proved illusory. Nevertheless, these early departures by the Women's Committee of the CIC provided the core organizing concept for Jessie Daniel Ames when in 1930 she set out to build the Association of Southern Women for the Prevention of Lynching. Building on the CIC's efforts, Ames convened a group of women from various southern states to address the degree to which women acting in solidarity with each other could puncture the myth that lynching black men was a means of protecting white womanhood. Led by demagogues like South Carolina's Cole Blease, white male southerners insisted that blacks were lynched because they had violated the sexual purity of white women through the act of rape. The ravishing of white womanhood called for immediate and extreme reprisal, Blease and others argued.

Ames and the thousands of women who eventually signed the petitions of the ASWPL disagreed. Not only was rape not even mentioned in the case of most lynchings, they argued. More important, southern womanhood could be honored only by eliminating barbarity, upholding civilization, and making sure that law and order prevailed in all criminal situations. This was a woman's issue, Ames insisted, because those who committed the crime of lynching insulted womanhood by using the pretext of protecting women as the basis for their horrific behavior. Hence, women must stand up and commit themselves—as women—to the maintenance of law and order. Women's higher mission, based on their gender and their commitment to the values of Christian charity, must be to civilize humanity.

In the end, Ames's campaign to unite southern women to fight against lynching proved powerful and effective. By focusing on gender as a force that could unite women in opposition to barbarism, she forged an effective educational and political instrument for fighting one of the worst scourges of southern racism. In those counties where the ASWPL was most active and visible, it turned out, there was a significant decline in the number of blacks seized from law enforcement officials, and a comparable increase in the commitment of sheriffs to create a climate of opinion that would discourage lynchers.

Yet, in the end, this was an effort that included white women only and that self-consciously and calculatedly decided to exclude black women— even though black women had been the ones who had pioneered the anti-lynching crusade long before the CIC or the ASWPL came into existence. The failure of "bonds of common womanhood" to overcome barriers based on race went back to the early efforts of the CIC, and its fundamental inability to deliver on the promise of creating a partnership based on mutual respect and shared decision-making. Notwithstanding the evangelical spirit that infused the Tuskegee and Memphis meetings, the white women quickly abandoned their black coworkers when it came to rendering in public the program they had agreed to. Hence, the CIC's Carrie Johnson deleted from her written summation of those meetings an agreed-upon preamble affirming that black women deserved "all the privileges and rights granted to American womanhood." Even worse, she added to Lugenia Hope's denunciation of lynching a statement rejecting "any act on the part of Negro men which excites the mob spirit," thereby appearing to embrace the myth that black men incited lynching by sexually assaulting white women. Implicitly addressing what all this meant for the notion that a bond of common womanhood was at work, Lugenia Hope observed, "it is difficult for me to understand why my white sisters so strenuously object. . . .This is the Negro woman's viewpoint, and that is what you asked for. . . ." So much for "frank and open" communication.

Nothing confirmed the dimensions of the problem more than the way noted black educator Charlotte Hawkins Brown was introduced to a CIC meeting in North Carolina by Mrs. T. W. Bickett, chair of the woman's committee and wife of North Carolina's governor. "[It was] my old Negro mammy," she said, "[who] endeared [me to black people] . . . I cannot say anymore, Mrs. Brown, for your race today than . . . that you are as fine as was my Negro mammy." The heavy layers of history and of cultural and social racism made it difficult to eliminate such condescension. No matter how much Carrie Parks Johnson or other CIC white women *said* they wanted to share "frank and open" communications based on mutual respect, the presumptions that existed in a racist culture, and the cues that activated those presumptions, were almost impossible to overcome without a total and self-conscious commitment.

Although Jessie Daniel Ames may have had more capacity for such a commitment than most, she too failed the test of true interracialism. The women she gathered together in the ASWPL certainly shared the same kind of experience in YWCA's and Women's Missionary Societies that the CIC women had. This was a group shaped by a sense of gender solidarity. But that solidarity ended at the boundary of the color line. Despite black women's leadership in the anti-lynching campaign, they were not included or cited in the ASWPL's efforts. Rather, as Jacquelyn Hall shows so well, most ASWPL members were unable to transcend their own racial preconceptions. They too often assumed that black men *did* initiate sexual assaults on white women and that it was up to the black community to control those men. And in their demands for law and order, they frequently fell into the trap of suggesting that, in Hall's words, "blacks could be kept in their place more efficiently . . . by a legal system firmly under the control of whites than by extralegal lynchings." Under such interpretations, the antilynching campaign became less a commitment to racial justice and more an effort to make control of blacks more efficient.

The ultimate consequence of not heeding the black side of the antilynching agenda was that, in critical circumstances, the ASWPL operated to undermine black women's objectives. Thus, Ames's opposition to a federal antilynching law put her in direct opposition to the NAACP, leading black women's organizations, and even white allies like Eleanor Roosevelt. In the most embarrassing example of how subversive such attitudes could be, Texas Senator Tom Connally was able to use a letter from Ames to proclaim that the Association of Southern Women for the Prevention of Lynching actually opposed the federal bill—hence, there could not possibly be any merit in it.

Even as gender served as a rallying point to unite certain women activists at a critical moment in southern history, therefore, it also failed miserably to be inclusive enough to overcome the divisive forces of race prejudice. Just as many potential black supporters of the contemporary feminist movement have felt that white supporters of women's liberation were talking past them and ignoring their presence, so too in the 1930s, all the ennobling rhetoric of sisterhood implicit in the phrase "the bonds of common womanhood" could not disguise or overcome the powerful dividing line of race. Yet again, the potential of a social movement rooted in the organizing power of one of the triad of the gender, class, race combination failed to come to fruition because of its failure to address the other two parts.

The second case study I would like to discuss is from the lynching capital of the South—the state of Mississippi, where more than six hundred black people were lynched in the years 1880 to 1940 with not a single white person convicted for the crime. Nearly 100,000 black Mississippians had served in the U.S. armed forces during World War II. Yet Senator James Eastland had this to say of black soldiers: "The Negro was an utter and dismal failure in combat in Europe." Accusing blacks of being lazy and irresponsible and of raping white women, Eastland told his fellow senators in June 1945: "I am proud that the purest of white blood flows through my veins. I know that the white race is a superior race. . . . It has given us civilization. It is responsible for all the progress on earth."

The white race was also one that evidently could not tolerate independence on the part of black people. One year earlier, in the spring of 1944, a white man wanted to buy a plot of land from Rev. Isaac Simmons because the land had oil on it. When Simmons refused and dared to go to a white lawyer to protect his investment, the prospective white buyer took Rev. Simmons in his car, cut out his tongue, and killed him with three shots in the back—all in front of Rev. Simmons's son. This was a state that Allard Lowenstein, a 1960s activist who had encountered brutality in many places in the world, called "as bad as—maybe worse than—South Africa."

Yet if race was a razor-sharp instrument of oppression for black people in Mississippi, it also represented the unifying principle around which African American citizens in that state rallied to resist and to demand their freedom. John Dittmer has written a vivid testimonial to these freedom fighters and the struggle they waged in his book, *Local People: The Struggle for Civil Rights in Mississippi*. It is a story of those who refused to be intimidated by the terror that killed Isaac Simmons, Emmett Till, Mack Parker, and countless others. These local heroes were legion in number, among them World War II veterans such as Medgar Evers, Amzie Moore, and Vernando Collier who demanded their citizenship rights after coming back to Mississippi, who would not give up no matter what the pressures, and who talked about taking up arms to defend themselves if white people kept attacking them. These were the people who joined the NAACP, even though to do so put their lives at risk, or the Regional Council of Negro Leadership; and who continued to fight, notwithstanding the fact that the White Citizens' Council, organized in 1955, arranged for their mortgages to be called in, their automobile insurance cancelled, and their taxes audited. At a time when most Americans thought black Mississippians were quaking in submissiveness, ten thousand of these local people gathered in Mound Bayou in 1955 to demand the right to vote.

Although there were traditional leaders like doctors and ministers in this freedom struggle, it was the grassroots organizers who lie at the heart of Dittmer's story. Student activists with the Student Non-Violent Coordinating Committee (SNCC) came to Mississippi in the early 1960s to stimulate protest on behalf of racial justice, but most of the "local people" John Dittmer writes about were ordinary people—farmers, sharecroppers, small property owners. People like Fannie Lou Hamer, Victoria Gray, Hazel Palmer, C. C. Bryant, Hartman Turnbow, and Amzie Moore. And although these people were ordinary in their background, they were far from ordinary in the courage they displayed. For these were the men and women who provided the backbone of the movement that in the 1960s would help to transform both Mississippi and America.

It was a movement that used the institutions and loyalties of race as a vehicle for overcoming racism. Sometimes the institution was the black church; at other times the black school, whether it be a segregated high school in McComb or a college campus like Tougaloo. When white authorities frustrated voter registration efforts by consistently beating and imprisoning those who sought to claim their citizenship rights—all the while claiming that blacks did not really want to vote—civil rights groups conceived the idea of holding a "Freedom Vote" in November 1963 to prove that if given the chance to cast ballots, black Mississippians would respond with enthusiasm. Using institutions in the black community like lodge halls, churches, and clubs, the movement held its own election, with more than eighty thousand African Americans casting their votes for candidates of their choice. It was a pivotal moment of community-building and solidarity that helped to provide both an incentive to the decision to bring up to a thousand volunteers to Mississippi the next summer, and a model for organizing the Mississippi Freedom Democratic Party, an organization that would seek to represent all the people of Mississippi in the national Democratic Party as well as in the state.

With the onset of Freedom Summer, the movement in Mississippi achieved its greatest successes. Despite the brutal lynching of Michael Schwerner, Andrew Goodman, and James Chaney at the beginning of the summer and the burning of scores of black churches used as movement centers during the summer, the movement would not subside or be defeated. Joined by the mostly white student volunteers from the North, the "local people" John Dittmer writes about set out to reclaim and rebuild their state. They started Freedom Schools where young children could learn about black history and the heroes and heroines who could serve as role models for their lives. In some places health clinics were opened where for the first time there was a chance for black citizens to secure rudimentary healthcare. Other organizers worked to create day care and nursery programs that would eventuate later in the Child Development Group of Mississippi, one of the first and most successful programs of Operation Headstart. And the Mississippi Freedom Democratic Party (MFDP) gathered support and documentary evidence for challenging the exclusionary practices of the white Mississippi Democratic Party, with the hope of using that material to unseat the all-white Mississippi delegation at the 1964 Democratic convention in Atlantic City. In the midst of that summer, the U.S. Congress passed the Civil Rights Act of 1964, finally achieving one hundred years after emancipation the right of blacks to compete for jobs without discrimination on the basis of race, and to have access to such public accommodations as hotels, restaurants, and theatres. Arguably, none of this could have happened without the struggle organized by local black people in Mississippi, based on the strengths and loyalties of their own institutions.

And yet the story John Dittmer tells is also one of failure. The potential for still greater victories fell by the wayside as forces of division—based on race, gender, and class—overcame the forces of unity. The divisions of race surfaced in the summer of 1964 and became dominant by the spring of 1966. They initially had to do with tensions between white volunteers from the north and indigenous black workers in the movement. With no malice or intention to wound, some white students brought with them to Mississippi a presumption of expertise and authority based on their education and experience that then caused them to act in ways that seemed condescending and racist to black movement activists. In the cultural miscommunication that ensued, it was sometimes difficult to break through the barriers that racism had erected over time.

But the pivotal source of racial division grew out of the experience of the MFDP at the Democratic National Convention in Atlantic City in August 1964. Armed with affidavits and vivid testimony, the MFDP delegates had come to the credentials committee with high hopes. They had gathered all the legal evidence they were told was necessary to make their case. They had followed the rules. Most observers believed there were enough votes on the credentials committee to send the challenge to the floor of the convention, where it was believed the MFDP would prevail. With Fannie Lou Hamer leading off the hearings with dramatic tales of how she was beaten by jailers for even talking about voter registration, it seemed the MFDP was on the road to victory.

But then Lyndon Johnson intervened. He did not wish any group to disrupt "his" convention. Mobilizing Hubert Humphrey and Walter Reuther, he set out to derail the MFDP challenge. One woman delegate was told her husband would not be given a federal judgeship if she supported the MFDP; another male delegate was warned he would lose his job. Soon the core of MFDP support on the credentials committee dissolved. In its place came a compromise proposal. The MFDP would get two seats—not the twenty or forty they had believed likely—and four years hence all delegates would be chosen without regard to race.

Furious, the MFDP delegation rejected the compromise. "We didn't come all this way for no two votes," Fannie Lou Hamer declared. They had played by the rules. They had done what they were supposed to do. And now they felt they had been sold out—by white liberals who had told them to show due regard to established procedures, and then had ignored those procedures themselves. It was a bitter lesson. Alienation between white liberals and black activists became harder to overcome. Suspicions rankled that whites would welcome blacks to biracial coalitions only if whites could control events. Within a year and a half, Black Power became the dominant slogan of the movement, and national conflict over civil rights strategies replaced unity.

Divisions over gender grew out of, and reflected these divisions over race. If white women volunteers in Mississippi shared some of the same cultural blinders as their male compatriots, they also experienced the differential power imbalance that accompanied growing up female in a male world. In some instances, at least, complications of interracial sex sharpened a sense of difference and of division—both between women and men and between white women and black women. It is impossible to imagine two cultural concepts more freighted with volatile messages than race and sex. In the chemistry of the civil rights struggle in the summer of 1964, therefore, it is not surprising that divisions over gender followed the explosion of divisions over race—or that the emergence of Black Power as a movement was followed soon thereafter by the emergence of the women's liberation movement among some white women veterans of the civil rights struggle.

Nor were divisions of class absent from the denouement of the Mississippi movement. As John Dittmer shows so well, there had always been tensions within the Mississippi movement. The national NAACP bitterly protested any group that threatened its domination of civil rights politics, and on numerous occasions, made life nearly impossible for Aaron Henry and Medgar Evers by the conservatism of its posture and its refusal to cooperate with other civil rights groups. But the NAACP conflicts were not just turf wars among civil rights activists. They also reflected a class conflict between a black bourgeoisie led by ministers, businesspeople, and professionals, and more ordinary people who had less to lose and more to gain by challenging existing hierarchies.

Significantly, these divisions of class overlapped with divisions over race in the years after 1964, centering especially on Democratic politics in the state of Mississippi and on the issue of who would control the local antipoverty movement. The MFDP came back to Mississippi from Atlantic City with the hope initially of carrying forward its plan to transform Democratic Party politics in the state by throwing out the existing Democratic machine. Moderate white Democrats in the state, on the other hand, saw the handwriting on the wall and, especially in light of the Voting Rights Act of 1965, recognized the need to coalesce with black leaders who would agree to work with them. NAACP leaders such as Aaron Henry were willing to join such a moderate coalition. Poorer and more radical blacks, on the other hand, sought to pursue their own agenda.

The ultimate site of their political war with each other was control over the antipoverty program in Mississippi, in particular the Headstart program. The Child Development Group of Mississippi (CDGM) represented the community-based, grassroots organizing hopes of the original MFDP. With heavy involvement of volunteers and "ordinary" people, it sought to use Operation Headstart as the vanguard of a social and educational movement that would remake the state. More established politicians, allied with Senators James Eastland and John Stennis, recognized the CDGM for what it was—a political as well as educational threat. In an eventual alliance with the moderate Democratic coalition of Hodding Carter and Aaron Henry, these powerful officials persuaded the Johnson administration to withdraw funding from the CDGM and give it instead to Mississippians Against Poverty (MAP), a group that was economically and politically allied with the more moderate, established segments of the state's power structure. In this way, class as well as race alliances undermined and defeated the original goals of the movement in Mississippi.

The story is by no means simple, nor does virtue rest on one side only. Yet in ways that testify to the full complexity of the intersection of gender, class, and race, what happened in Mississippi seems to speak as powerfully as any one example can to the ways that division can prevail over unity in the struggle to unite people for social change.

The final example pertinent to this discussion begins with an effort to use class as the organizing basis around which black men and women, with some white participation, sought to remake their lives. Winston-Salem, North Carolina, provided the location for this struggle, tobacco workers for R. J. Reynolds the immediate focus of the organizing effort. The year was 1942— the stakes the opportunity to create the first interracial union in the south, committed to a program of not only economic dignity and self-determination but also political and social reform. In writing the history of Local 22 and its brief but dramatic ascendancy, Robert Korstad has offered an intriguing insight into what happens when the least visible and most elusive of our three concepts—social class—becomes a force for uniting people to demand justice.

More than ten thousand people were employed at the R. J. Reynolds factory in the late spring of 1943. Wartime production demands had stretched the workforce to the limits. The company could barely meet the existing market for its product, and a shortage of labor due to the draft and a full employment economy meant that the seasonal labor force that usually came on board in the early summer months would not be available. Still, R. J. Reynolds had done little to reward the workers already there. The labor force was primarily black and predominantly female. In the tobacco factories, as in textile mills, the best jobs were reserved for whites, while blacks held down the dirtiest and most arduous assignments. Most blacks were paid the minimum wage of forty cents an hour, with only a small percentage earning as much as fifty cents.

Such were the circumstances when events leading to the emergence of Local 22 unfolded in June 1943. As the heat in the factory grew alongside the increased pressures of production, workers had become ever more conscious of their working conditions. Representatives of the United Cannery Agricultural Packinghouse and Allied Workers of America (UCAPAWA) had been in the community for a few months recruiting support for a union organizing effort, but no action had yet been taken to request an NLRB election to certify the union as the workers' bargaining agent.

On June 17, a particularly hot day, a woman worker on the fifth floor complained of being ill. Her foreman responded by saying she could leave if she wished, but her departure would be permanent. Other women on the floor then decided to engage in a work stoppage. A black man who had also complained of being sick that week decided to support them. Shortly thereafter, he keeled over and died from a heart attack. Earlier, the nurse had said he was not sick enough to go home. More than two hundred women on the fifth floor then joined the work stoppage, soon to be joined by women workers on the other floors. When a management representative appeared to urge them to go back to work, Theodosia Simpson spoke up and challenged him about the state of work conditions in the factory. A woman leader generated further support for the stoppage from women workers. Some men joined as well, and a workers council was elected to represent the laborers in negotiations with management. The second and third shifts learned of what had happened and decided to join in.

Soon, communitywide meetings were held at a local black church, whose minister worked in the factory and was a union supporter. When the company tried to recruit Robert Black, an African American worker of long experience in the factory who had great prestige in the community, to persuade the workers to go back to their jobs, he refused, insisting that the company recognize the workers' grievances and agree to negotiations about them. For three days the workers met in mass meetings. Federal conciliation representatives came to town at the request of the union, but management still refused to acknowledge the grievances the workers had brought. Finally, when it became clear that the workers would stand together without tolerating a break in their ranks, the company signed a statement saying it would sit down and talk about the workers' concerns if they returned to the workplace. Six months later UCAPAWA won the right to have an NLRB election, The results created Local 22 of UCAPAWA as the officially designated representative of the workers. A new contract was signed in April 1944. In the meantime, the union organized literacy campaigns in the community, registered thousands of people to vote, and set forth on a campaign to create a different kind of community, one where racial and economic injustices could be addressed, with a better cultural and civic life provided for all. Partly as a result of these efforts, in 1947 Winston-Salem elected the first black alderman to be chosen in the twentieth century in the South.

There were many distinctive aspects to the organizing efforts of Local 22. First, it was a movement led by black people. But it involved white workers as well. They served in the ranks of the union, but occupied only 15 percent or so of the leadership positions, approximately proportionate to their numbers in the labor force. Thus, the first integrated union in the South was also one where black strength and leadership were recognized. There was no condescension by white participants.

Second, this was a movement led by black women. They worked in partnership with black and white men, but they were the ones who initiated the work stoppage. Moreover, they comprised a significant percentage of the union's leadership. The role they played in making possible the union's formation, and the ease with which they exercised community leadership, helped to facilitate the process of uniting the community around its common interests. In short, two of the potential barriers to successful organization—disdain of men for women and of whites for blacks—did not exist in Winston-Salem in 1943 and 1944. Instead, the degree to which black women filled the ranks of the movement's vanguard helped assure that the potentially most divisive forces could be contained and that the union could move forward.

Nevertheless, this struggle too ended in failure. Management retained significant power in the community. In subsequent campaigns, R. J. Reynolds forged alliances with more conservative union forces from the AFL and the CIO to challenge UCAPAWA. Management also fomented festering racial tensions, seeking to set whites against blacks and to raise the specter of radical black activists taking over the community. Finally, it deployed its most powerful weapon, red-baiting Local 22 and claiming that support for the union meant support for communism. Anyone who wished to stick with the union thus took the risk of being defined as anti-American and pro-black. Ultimately, such weapons brought victory to R. J. Reynolds and in 1950, Local 22 was unable to prevail in an NLRB certification vote.

What remains most notable in retrospect, however, is how effectively the UCAPAWA movement was able to overcome the most formidable obstacles to create a biracial alliance along class lines, at least for half a decade. The forces of division may eventually have prevailed, but gender and race were not as powerful sources of division as they had proven to be with the antilynching campaign or the Mississippi Freedom Movement. Ironically, it required the charge that Local 22 was un-American and a voice for communism to bring down the union.

In no way, of course, are these three case studies necessarily representative of how gender, race, and class have functioned as forces of unity and forces of division in southern history. One could consider a dozen other examples, with a different chemistry or interaction likely to be found in each. Nevertheless, these three instances are illustrative of the issues historians need to be aware of in trying to answer some of the questions raised earlier about which of these variables is dependent or independent, and how they operate in political and cultural interaction with each other.

The first conclusion I would venture is that in any social circumstance where sex or race is a dominant consideration, and where women or blacks are in a minority position, the potential for divisiveness is very great. This is partly because of the layers of cultural baggage that surround race and sex as issues of group and individual identity. It is difficult to imagine more powerful cultural symbols than these. However much we may have the right to expect whites to be able to shed racist preconceptions rooted in centuries of history, it is virtually impossible to imagine that happening without transforming personal experiences that can burn away the attitudes we have inherited. So accustomed are whites to being in a superior position to blacks, and assuming, at best, the role of benign rescuer, that it is a huge task to break through such preconceptions or have them dissolved. White women of the CIC might temporarily transcend their racism in the fervor of an evangelical moment of sharing, but within the cold light of day, that racism almost inevitably reappeared, reflected in the conventional wisdom that whites surely knew best what was good for blacks, that Negro men of course wanted to ravish white women, and that the key issue was the gentility of the forms of social control, not their existence.

Similarly, white powerbrokers had so often dictated terms of compromise to those petitioning for change that it is difficult to imagine Walter Reuther and Hubert Humphrey thinking they were doing anything unusual when they, in effect, told the MFDP what it was "best" for the black insurgent party to accept. How inconceivable that black petitioners for the MFDP, or black women in the CIC, should be treated with mutual respect as equal partners, especially in light of the history of presumptive power that whites had exercised. When the potent chemistry of race mixed with the equally powerful emotions associated with sex—as in the case of Freedom Summer volunteers in 1964—it became almost impossible to prevent painful and bitter divisiveness. Only in a circumstance where blacks and women comprised a majority—hence in a position to exercise control of the agenda—did it seem possible that the divisive potential of race and gender could be subsumed to the forces of unity.

A second conclusion based on these case studies is that class may provide the best focal point for organizing people across barriers of race and gender. The theoretical argument for this hypothesis goes back to Karl Marx. In an American context, precedents were mixed for whether it would be possible to transcend racial barriers in the interest of a common economic agenda. During the Populist period in the 1890s, tentative efforts were made to join the Colored Farmers Alliance and the Southern Farmers Alliance in a common campaign to secure freedom from the bondage of the crop lien system. That campaign proved so threatening to white rulers that they invoked the banner of race solidarity and succeeded in disenfranchising black voters and instituting the Jim Crow system. As Robert Korstad and Nelson Lichtenstein have shown, CIO unions were the next to attempt such a biracial class alliance. At least in the case of Local 22, they seem to have succeeded, although here, too, it is important to remember that the majority of the union members were black and female. Still, the Local 22 example seems promising as a model for social change, especially when merged with the kind of passion associated with the civil rights movement.

The advantage of focusing on class seems to be reinforced when we examine what has happened to blacks and women in the aftermath of victories achieved since 1964 in the civil rights and women's rights movements. To a significant extent, discrimination based solely on race or gender has been abolished in the laws of the land. As a result, enormous changes have occurred. The number of African Americans attending college leaped 500 percent from 1962 to 1976. The black middle class expanded rapidly, especially as African American college graduates found themselves earning the same salaries as their white counterparts and moving into high-level positions in corporations, educational institutions, and the government.

Similar changes occurred among women. The number of female members of the entering law-, business-, and medical-school classes at most universities multiplied more than tenfold in the 1970s and '80s. Women earned over 30 percent of the doctorates awarded by 1990, in contrast to 11 percent in 1970. The same corporations, law firms, and hospitals that welcomed blacks to their executive ranks welcomed women as well.

On closer examination, however, it became clear that these gains were limited to *individuals* who were sufficiently well prepared educationally and economically to take advantage of the new rights that had been gained. It might be true that lowering the legal barriers of race and sex discrimination could help those already on the edge of the middle class. But these gains were not accessible to those who lacked economic security and educational preparation. Hence, even as the ranks of the black middle class grew, so too did the ranks of the black poor. High school dropout rates accelerated at the same time college graduation rates grew. Teenage pregnancies and poverty among female-headed households went up even faster than did the numbers of the black middle class.

Among women, white or black, the story was the same. More women might be employed than ever before, but 80 percent of those women worked in just 5 percent of all jobs. More and more, these were dead-end jobs in the service sector of the economy, paying minimum wages and offering little chance for advancement. The growing number of women who were poor, moreover, heightened the paradox of women's liberation. The right to be free and independent of men might mean new autonomy and fulfillment for some, but it brought immiseration and hopelessness to others.

Even as barriers of race and gender discrimination dissolved for individuals, therefore, the barrier of class—intersecting with barriers of race and gender—still kept millions in bondage. *Individuals* could escape the stigma of race or sex, but poverty closed the door to those who sought freedom.

Understanding how much class has become a primary source of inequality, however, is different from generating strategies for replicating the success of Theodosia Simpson and the tobacco workers of Local 22. Nor should the progress that has occurred on issues of race and gender obscure the degree to which racism and sexism remain a powerful presence throughout American society, at the top even more than at the bottom. Still, there seems little question that economic inequality lies at the heart of the injustice that remains in American society.

Focusing on an economic agenda, therefore, seems one viable path to pursue in addressing the continued ability of gender, class, and race to deny equality of opportunity to American citizens. The issues engaged by the Freedom Summer volunteers are the same as those pursued by Local 22—to build schools, healthcare facilities, and workplaces that offer respect, as well as nurturance, to those who attend them. Institutions such as the MFDP and Local 22 will continue to emerge. But perhaps the time has come to make the force of unity that dominates them a focus on jobs and economic security first of all—believing and hoping that divisions of gender and race can be overcome in the process.

11

LIBERALISM AFTER THE SIXTIES:
A RECONNAISSANCE

Otis L. Graham Jr.

"One of the rudest things you can call an American politician nowadays is a liberal," editorialized *The Economist* in 1996, recalling (among other examples) how George Bush had drawn blood by associating opponent Michael Dukakis with the "L-word" in the 1988 presidential race.[1] "Liberals—usually the good guys of my visceral political calculus—are losing the battle of ideas," wrote columnist William Raspberry a year later. "They haven't had a bright new idea in ages."[2]

It was not always so—in particular, the year I entered graduate school in 1960, which was by chance an election year. Liberalism was a proud and politically dominating tradition of ideas and social reforms with roots in the progressive era, given mature form under Franklin Roosevelt and the New Deal, and in 1960 gathering moral force and political energy for a third phase of what Harvard historian Arthur M. Schlesinger Jr. would teach us to call the Schlesinger Cycle of corrective liberal reform. When William E. Leuchtenburg ended an early November graduate history class with the admonition "Now vote, and vote right!" we all knew what had been said. Everyone at Columbia, it seemed, was a liberal. Many had stood three hours in the rain days earlier to glimpse the nominee from Massachusetts on a motorcade through New York. We sensed that great events, restorative and corrective, once again lay ahead in American politics, and we were right—though that was not all that lay ahead.

Sometime in the second half of the sixties, historian Arthur Mann later wrote, "Suddenly, things turned upside down." Assassinations wrenched the constitutional order, campuses and cities were engulfed in violence, and the American people became "unhappy, confused, adrift, distrustful, and divided. . . . What went wrong?"[3] In politics, things certainly went substantially wrong for liberals—Richard Nixon elected twice, one term and out for a moderate Democrat from Georgia, then a Reagan-led and Bush-extended conservative reign. Democrats returned to the White House in 1993, only behind a candidate who received 43 percent of the vote and would not use the word *liberal*. Then two terms of erratic searching for a governing center, ending in impeachment-spiced confusion and the election of a Republican in 2000.[4]

How and why did liberalism lose its political and intellectual dominance?

"IT ALL STARTED IN THE SIXTIES"

When Barry Goldwater conceded defeat to Lyndon Johnson in November 1964, having carried six states, not only the political but also the intellectual and moral supremacy of liberalism in American politics seemed to have reached a crest, with a long season of dominance ahead. The central feature of the liberal program, hesitantly begun by Kennedy and boldly pursued by Lyndon Johnson, was their sponsorship of the drive for black equality and an end to Jim Crow. The central fact of liberal political life from the sixties forward was a deeply felt moral (and intellectual) superiority. The political opposition had fought the civil rights crusade, spoke the evasive banalities of "states' rights" and of communist plots to divide Americans. No wonder that the bright and the young were drawn to the neighborhoods left of center.

Yet as the Great Society rolled forward, one astute observer of American politics sensed that the liberals were headed for political trouble. Lyndon Johnson told Bill Moyers, after signing the Civil Rights Act of 1964 ending Jim Crow, that he believed he had "delivered the South to the Republican Party for a long time to come."[5] This reads like a shrewd guess about the future, but it was both premature and flawed. LBJ, who quoted Martin Luther King Jr.'s phrase "We shall overcome," still received a majority of southern votes in the 1964 election, Goldwater carrying only the five Deep South states.[6] Positions taken on civil rights in 1963–64 had some political cost, but had not yet "delivered the South" to the opposition. The white South (and many voters elsewhere) would eventually turn more decisively toward the Republicans (or away from politics), but because of events ahead of LBJ's comment to Moyers in 1964—things Johnson and his allies had yet to do, along with social turbulence and cultural trends that became associated, fairly or unfairly, with liberalism.

LBJ in his memoirs conceded that political defeat in 1968 owed to more than the signing of the 1964 Civil Rights Act (though he thought he would have won if nominated). "The Democratic Party had pressed too far out in front of the American people . . . too far too fast in social reform," he concluded. And "the disruptive methods of the radicals of the "new left," at the Chicago convention and on university campuses" had frightened voters. But "I would not have abandoned a single major program" or "postponed a single law."[7] The people had faltered, their government a bit too good for them, too soon.

Johnson's error here was to see the Great Society as a single whole. Only a portion of Democratic Party–sponsored reform measures accounted—along with social turbulence—for the political upheavals that sent Johnson and then Humphrey into retirement. Within the Great Society were sectors of special vulnerability where the potential for political trouble was high. On the legislative side, one could say that roughly half of the Great Society had been widely discussed, reasonably well understood by the public, and popular. The banishment of Jim Crow in schools and public facilities, as well as an end to voting discrimination by race, were well understood, thoroughly aired, and backed by a national consensus that the white South would join much more quickly than anyone anticipated. A strong base of public support also existed for Medicare, federal aid to education, the Wilderness Act, the beginnings of federal action on cleaner water and air, workplace safety and consumer protection, even control of highway billboards. But another large basket could be filled with measures only briefly debated before Congress and poorly understood by the public or, often, their liberal architects: certain augmentations of the welfare state, notably the war on poverty's "community action" component and the parallel expansion of AFDC as well as Medicaid, which was tacked onto the Medicare legislation by Wilbur Mills with little congressional scrutiny; the expanded public housing program of 1968, rushed through in six months; the Hart-Celler Immigration Act of 1965, which increased immigration and ended the advantage given to nationalities that had settled and built the nation before 1920; bilingual education.[8]

In addition to Great Society laws and programs there was the postlegislative cutting edge of liberal reform—the program building and rule-making activities of federal bureaucrats and judges, offstage, carrying on reform by taking initiatives liberals knew to be right even if not exactly demanded by huge lobbying coalitions or large majorities in the polls. These included the deinstitutionalization of the mentally ill, the "black empowerment" strategy of the war on poverty, school busing to engineer the proper racial mix of students, "affirmative action" preferences in hiring, college admissions, and contracting for blacks that were soon extended to a broad range of certified "minorities."

As it turned out, certain of Great Society liberalism's politically costly associations—with the war in Vietnam, the hippie and protester riots outside the Chicago convention hall, flag- and draft-card burning, Black Panthers with fists raised and automatic weapons brandished—would slowly wane, while liberal social engineering was a growing presence.[9]

LIBERAL RACE POLICY AFTER THE END OF JIM CROW

"Is the civil rights movement over, now that we have outlawed Jim Crow and voting discrimination?" To this question, liberals emphatically answered that they had just begun to fight. Legal equality achieved, social equality must come quickly or the urban crisis of the 1960s would be only a foretaste. In retrospect, it was easily the most ambitious government project in modern history. Daunting handicaps had become attached to black America, entrenched during slavery and extended by discrimination and bigotry for decades thereafter. Then came the great black migration out of the rural South, a trickle beginning in the late nineteenth century, accelerating in the 1920s with restrictions on immigration, and then cresting in a wave of 4.5 million people from the 1940s to the 1960s. The new urbanites brought with them mixed cultural resources—a blend of assets such as strong church and family affiliations and some middle-class work and saving habits, but also a sharecropper culture of illiteracy, loose family ties, and dependence on white landowners.[10] The timing of their migration was unfortunate. Most of these refugees with agricultural skills arrived just as the American economy was shifting away from heavy industry toward a postindustrial mix in which education and technical and social skills were at an increasing premium.

Thus black populations gathering at the center of urban America after mid-century were a mix of a small, tenacious black middle class with a growing underclass–urban residents with what William Julius Wilson called "a weak attachment to the labor force," characterized by out-of-wedlock births, single-parent families, crime, and welfare dependency. Most black Americans were not in the underclass. But the underclass was mainly black, and growing, as the sixties arrived.[11] Their presence was marked by the statistics of social pathology. The urban crime rate rose 60 percent from 1960 to 1966, then jumped another 83 percent in the five years between 1966 and 1971; the National Academy of Sciences found that a disproportionate share of crimes of violence were by blacks (and against blacks). Births to unmarried women rose from 2.3 to 5.7 percent among whites across the sixties, but from 21.6 to 34.9 percent among blacks.[12]

Liberals, now not just sympathetic to the cause of black advancement but politically committed to it, struggled to find policy leverage. One of their first ideas ran into fierce trouble and got its author fired, shutting down a whole sector for discussion. Daniel Patrick Moynihan, a sociologist who was assistant secretary in the Labor Department, in March 1965 produced a seventy-eight-page paper entitled "The Negro Family: The Case for National Action." Moynihan pointed to the increase of single black mothers and concluded, "the Negro family structure is crumbling." Male joblessness and desertion was producing an illegitimacy rate of one-quarter among blacks, leading to welfare dependency and "a tangle of pathology." Moynihan attributed all this to historic racism and economic pressures and spoke vaguely and briefly of solutions through family-strengthening federal programs, not even hinting at black moral regeneration [13] Black leaders, at first welcoming a government official's exploration of the black situation, by October were accusing Moynihan of saying in effect that blacks tolerated or were unusually inclined toward promiscuity, illegitimacy, and welfare dependency. "Blaming the victim," charged Boston civil rights activist and psychiatrist William Ryan; "fuel for a new racism," pronounced James Farmer of CORE.[14] The uproar from the liberal and civil rights community ostracized Moynihan and led to his resignation. "All public discussions in mainstream liberal circles of issues like the state of the black family simply ceased," reported Nicholas Lemann.[15]

What, then, could government do? Urban riots after 1965 lent urgency to the question. Nondiscrimination and universality of human rights were the philosophical core of the 1964 and 1965 civil rights statutes, and these measures were spectacularly successful in desegregating public accommodations and promoting the black franchise. But nondiscrimination did not turn public schools into engines of black upward mobility, and black economic advancement was slow. Was there a faster way to continue the civil rights movement?

A central new idea was to move beyond proving discrimination, which was difficult and expensive, to proving unequal social outcomes, which statistics could quickly confirm. Once discrimination in the form of unequal outcomes was established—"institutional discrimination" was the term invented for it, since no actual discriminator could be found—the remedy was black preferences in jobs, contracts, and university admissions until equal results were obtained. This was soon the operative meaning of "affirmative action."

When the term first appeared in President Kennedy's 1963 Executive Order 10925, it was understood to mean "keep your eyes open for a qualified black." That it might evolve into something more ambitious and polarizing—black preference, special treatment, quotas—had been suspected by some of the legislators moving toward the law that killed Jim Crow, and strenuously and categorically denied by the chief sponsors of the 1964 Civil Rights Act. Asked in 1964 hearings on the civil rights bill if the legislation would "require employers to establish quotas for non-whites," Senator Hubert Humphrey assured the body that "proponents of the bill have carefully stated on numerous occasions that Title VII does not require an employer to achieve any sort of racial balance in his work force by giving preferential treatment to any individual or group," and pledged to eat the bill page by page if it ever did so.[16] Just three years later, officials in the Labor Department's Office of Contract Compliance (OFCC), in a hurry for results, saw federal contract dollars as a lever for rapid black job growth. Their Philadelphia Plan of 1967–68 would have required bids for federal construction contracts to hire "minority employees" in proportion to their presence in the work force. Astonishingly, this plan for race-based quotas was adopted by Nixon in 1970 and was rapidly expanded to cover four categories of minorities—Asians and Pacific Islanders, African Americans, Hispanics, and Native Americans and Alaska natives—and applied to more than 300,000 firms doing business with the federal government, eventually affecting one-quarter of the American workforce. Affirmative action would be expanded by the entrenched liberal activists in the civil rights bureaucracies in the Justice Department, in a new independent regulatory commission (the Equal Employment Opportunity Commission, EEOC), and in the line agencies (twenty-seven rights-enforcement offices were at work in line agencies by 1969). The "original, Kennedy-Johnson meaning of affirmative action, which meant nondiscrimination enhanced by outreach programs," or "soft affirmative action," writes Hugh Davis Graham, had given way to "hard affirmative action," which insisted on equality of results and did not need to find discrimination in order to intervene to order race-based corrrection.[17] The transition "occurred quickly and quietly" between 1965 and 1968.[18] "The public had no idea," added Stephen and Abigail Thernstrom.[19]

Equally fraught with political danger to liberals was another, faster path chosen first by HEW bureaucrats in 1966 and strongly followed by judges. This was busing public-school students as a remedy for segregated schools.

When southern school authorities resisted integration and the 1965 law extending federal aid to secondary education gave HEW leverage, guidelines were written making compliance with the Brown decision dependent not on the absence of discrimination, but on actual mixed student populations. Impatient with the snail's pace of school integration, the Supreme Court insisted in 1968 on unspecified "affirmative steps" by school officials to achieve integration, and in 1971 it confirmed a District Court order that the Charlotte-Mecklenburg (North Carolina) Board of Education bus students between white suburbs and the black inner city to achieve a strict racial quota for all schools in the huge district. Race-based busing soon spread across the country, an "immense social experiment" of liberal parentage, two scholars wrote, and one that was "wildly unpopular everywhere."[20]

THE RIGHTS REVOLUTION

But something larger was in motion than the redefinition of civil rights as requiring "affirmative action" in the form of racial preferences and busing for correct racial proportions in public school populations. The civil rights movement was with good reason called a "revolution," a profound moral awakening and political drama falling only a little short of the national experience with civil war. The moral certainty, fervent and innovative style, language, and tactics of "the movement" swept away what had seemed an impregnable structure of southern law and custom and wrote a new chapter in the American narrative. The energy and success of this crusade lent irresistible momentum to a larger "rights revolution" that began much earlier.

Michael Sandel locates a turning point in FDR's 1944 State of the Union speech on a new "Economic Bill of Rights," in which Roosevelt proposed making the government responsible for providing the "right" to a job, food and clothing, education and much else.[21] This was aspiration only, but it led toward what was to be liberalism's central project in the second half of the century. The Warren Court took the lead in the rights revolution beginning in the 1950s, declaring new rights in the areas of race in the schools and procedures affecting the criminally accused. In the 1960s, the "rights revolution" spread outward through the agency of thousands of liberal-left lawyers, law professors, activists for minorities and women, judges, federal officials, and legislators, all responding to what Mary Ann Glendon has called "the romance of rights."[22]

One result, beginning in the 1960s and continuing through subsequent decades, was the construction by Congress of an enormous second tier of regulatory agencies upon the base established during the New Deal. But un-like the economic focus of 1930s regulation this new wave of "social regula-tion" created statutory language conferring rights "to clean air and water; safe consumer products and workplaces; a social safety net including adequate food, medical care, and shelter; and freedom from public and private dis-crimination on the basis of race, sex, disability, and age," in the words of Cass Sunstein, whose *After the Rights Revolution* (1990) lists six civil-rights laws, five occupational-safety laws, and six environmental laws enacted in the 1960s, with many more to come in the succeeding two decades.[23]

This broadening movement to enlarge individual and group rights built on the logic of the civil rights crusade and gained impetus from a growing family of well-organized lobbies with few vocal or organized opponents (with the large exception of the ERA rights drive). In the two sectors of rights expansion devised as faster paths to black equality, however—affirmative ac-tion and welfare entitlements—some divisions appeared between moderate liberals and those to their left.

Nathan Glazer, reviewing the Civil Rights Commission's 1970 report *The Federal Civil Rights Enforcement Effort,* objected to what he saw as a move from "equal opportunity . . . to an attempt to ensure a *full equality* of achieve-ment." The CRC made "scarcely a reference to any single case of discrimina-tion by anybody in this enormous report," and a small army of federal offi-cials"—570 in the CRC, 166 in the Department of Defense, and six thousand more being trained for agency deployment—was pursuing the "full equality of groups." This was "reverse discrimination," and "we have become involved in something entirely new," Glazer wrote.[24]

Uneasiness over the hardening of affirmative action was also expressed in the deliberations of the McGovern Reform Commission of the Democratic Party in November 1969 as it considered, in the words of member Austin Ranney, the idea of "our fellow black Democrats" that "something more is needed than a non-discrimination rule." They debated establishing quotas for blacks in state delegations, voted 10–9 for language requiring delegations to have the same racial proportions as the local population, and then added women and "young people" without much discussion. Writer Theodore White was dismayed when he read the transcript of the meeting, for it meant that the Democratic convention in 1972 would be shaped by quotas. The "liberating idea" that blacks should not be excluded had "changed to become an intellectual prison . . . [in which] certain groups must be included." This was for White "to plunge over a political cliff to disaster."[25]

THE WELFARE DILEMMA

Another policy arena where 1960s liberals sensed opportunity and reaped political trouble was indigent relief. The New Deal moved the "welfare" issue from local relief to a system dominated by federal payments to the unemployed, but Franklin Roosevelt more than once denounced "welfare" as a long-term policy. He persuaded Congress to replace these emergency measures with a permanent system of social security anchored in contributory old age pensions, with direct federal relief only for the blind and the uncovered, currently destitute elderly and with federal public works for the able-bodied. Aid to fatherless children—through their mothers, who could hardly be in the workforce—was attached as the AFDC program and was expected to be minor. Caseloads were insignificant for two decades, then unaccountably boomed upward to 3.1 million recipients in 1960, then to 4.3 million by 1965, and rising.[26] "Welfare" began to be condemned as a support system for female-headed families in which the mother and children were slum-dwelling dependents of the state, shielded from any work experience, while the fathers escaped responsibility.

The engagement of liberals with the welfare issue was briefly the story of a failure, the war on poverty. After it was dismantled, their legacy became more an attitude than any particular program structure. Liberal opinion in the 1960s and after shifted away from the New Deal's commitment to work and its wariness of the dependency effects of direct relief, toward the "guaranteed annual income" idea that Richard Nixon and Democratic 1972 presidential candidate George McGovern would espouse. LBJ resisted this leftward shift of liberal opinion on welfare but could not contain it. It was driven by the climate created by black urban riots in 1967–68 and a growing liberal sense, expressed most scoldingly in the 1968 Kerner Commission Report on urban riots, that nothing less than universal entitlement to welfare would quiet the black community and constitute "social justice" at last for the descendants of slaves.[27]

This shift in elite opinion was paralleled, it appears, by a sharp change in attitudes among the poor, who moved away from earlier feelings of shame. Caught up in what historian James Patterson calls "the enhanced sense of entitlement that pervaded those turbulent times," the black poor especially were becoming aggressive and litigious about their "welfare rights" and bottom jobs with their insulting wages.[28] "Reports of resistance on the job circulated orally in the black community, among employers, and in white working class neighborhoods" in the late 1960s, Michael Piore wrote, a phenomenon reported earlier in an urban ghetto by Elliot Liebow in *Tally's Corner*.[29]

Liberals and advocates of the poor by 1968 had failed in two attempts to enact their guaranteed annual income. But along the way they had presided over and to some degree caused an expansion of the AFDC clientele from 4.3 percent of American families in 1965 to 6.1% in 1969 to 10.8 percent in 1974, and in the population on public assistance from 7.1 million in 1960 to 14.4 million in 1974. This income transfer drove down the proportion of Americans in poverty in a dramatic, unprecedented way, and was seen by many liberals as second only to ending Jim Crow as liberalism's crowning achievement.[30] Liberals "clapped their hands with pride," writes Patterson, at this "phenomenal reduction of absolute poverty" from 22 percent of the population in 1959 to 11 percent in 1973. The Great Society, along with economic growth, had moved 60 percent of the pre-transfer poor out of poverty in 1970 and raised America's welfare expenditures toward—though hardly matching—the levels of the social democracies in Western Europe.[31]

What of FDR's fear that these dollars (and food stamps and public housing and free legal services) would prove "a narcotic, a subtle destroyer of the human spirit"?[32] Patterson observes that "few people paid much attention to the Cassandras," as welfare at the end of the sixties became one of the rights of citizenship.[33] The zeitgeist did not lend itself to talk of obligation or to concern over what happened to "the human spirit" in its absence.

THE GREAT SOCIETY AND THE SIXTIES AS A REPUBLICAN OPPORTUNITY

Whatever one thought then of the Great Society and the rights revolution it had fostered, it had coincided with and was to some extent seen as associated with an ambience of mass media-transmitted images of antiwar protests, countercultural weirdness, drugs, the Manson killings, Black Panther fist salutes, feminist rebellion, free love, and urban riots. "In the public perception," wrote James Sundquist of the Brookings Institution, looking back from the 1980s, "all these things merged. Ghetto riots, campus riots, street crime, anti-Vietnam marches, poor people's marches, drugs, pornography, welfarism, rising taxes, all had a common thread: the breakdown of family and social discipline, of concepts of duty, of respect for law, of public and private morality."[34] Liberals would have said that they had made an unmatched record in attacking the causes of such social unrest and rebellion.

But it was not long before they were depicted as the most important source of this social unraveling.

One Democrat had already sensed the possibilities opened by the party's recent record and image. This was Governor George Corley Wallace of Alabama, the public figure who first framed the language to exploit liberal vulnerabilities. In the presidential primaries of 1964, before urban riots broke out, Wallace, despite his unmistakably southern drawl and unimpressive physical appearance, won 34 percent of the vote in Wisconsin, 30 percent in Indiana, and 45 percent in Maryland. The numbers make him just another loser in the history of runs for the presidency, but both his biographers, who agree on little else, call him the most influential loser in American politics.[35] The years between 1964 and 1968 opened an opportunity to capitalize on the invisible discontent of Democratic voters. Republicans picked up forty-four House seats in 1966, and one heard a hinge of political history turn when the GOP that year ended the career of liberal icon Senator Paul Douglas of Illinois and popular liberal Governor Pat Brown lost to a second-rate movie actor, Ronald Reagan.[36]

Two years later Wallace, now candidate of his own American Independent Party, moved northward with a language of populist protest far removed from the old racial appeals of southern politics, but portable anywhere in America. He did not attack blacks, but rather the elite Democratic establishment in Washington—politicians, journalists, judges, intellectuals—who were reaching down into local schools and workplaces all over America, practicing "reverse discrimination" and imposing heavy costs on ordinary working people. His use of the "wedge" or "social issues"—court imposed busing, affirmative action, leniency on crime, welfare abuse creating a dependent class, rising illegal drug use, urban disorder, and elite domination from Washington and the eastern seaboard—moved a significant number of Democrats, in their view abandoned by their own party, to vote some other way.

Wallace polled ten million votes, putting Richard Nixon, with 43 percent of the total, in the White House. Liberals read the 43 percent as the true strength of their enemy, but 57 percent of the voters had voted against the liberals' beribboned warrior, Hubert Humphrey. And Nixon, surely listening to Wallace's language, had shown impressive skill in endorsing an end to segregation and discrimination while bristling with objections to using federal power to "force a local community to carry out what a federal administrator or bureaucrat may think is best."[37] Wallace had been blunter: "They say, 'We've gotta write a guideline. We gotta tell you when to get up in the morning.'"[38]

Two books pointed out the opportunity in all this for antiliberals, especially Republicans. A writer and activist in the Nixon campaign, Kevin Phillips, described a seismic political shift toward *The Emerging Republican Majority* (1969), "the end of the New Deal Democratic hegemony and the beginning of a new era in America politics." The Democrats had been repudiated by the voters, Phillips argued, for their "ambitious social programming ... [and] inability to handle the urban and Negro revolutions," and because the "Democratic and liberal record was one of failure—in global diplomacy, Asian warfare, domestic economics, social and welfare policy, and law enforcement." The 1968 election was not a momentary setback for the party of FDR, but the first sign of a substantial realignment. The liberal party's northeastern stronghold was on the losing end of a vast demographic shift of power to the Sunbelt, the South and West. Especially in the South, "obsolescent Democratic loyalties" opened up the colonization of a new Republican heartland that Wallace had only momentarily pulled into a fleeting third-party effort.[39]

A year later came Richard Scammon and Ben Wattenberg's *The Real Majority* (1970). They saw the electorate turning from the older economic issues toward "the Social Issue," a combination of concerns over what they fuzzily characterized as "law and order, [racial] backlash, antiyouth, malaise, change, or alienation." "The law-and-order issue can be finessed" by Democrats, but occasional remarks against crime will not be enough. They have to "*believe* that the Social Issue is important, is distressing to their constituents. . . . Rhetoric alone is never enough." Otherwise, "it could get worse for Democrats," who simply must "listen to the center."[40]

IT ALL CONTINUED IN THE SEVENTIES

Liberals did not derive the same lessons from the 1968 election as Phillips and Scammon and Wattenberg—quite the opposite. To them Wallace was a demagogue, playing upon the racism of a portion of the white working class in a bad year for clear thinking. And Nixon's election was an aberration in a country destabilized by the Vietnam War, the electorate denied by assassination the chance to choose that tough, antiwar liberal Bobby Kennedy.[41] The next time around the American public could be led to do the right thing.

And liberal thinking on the meaning of recent events was especially important, because the Democratic Party, perhaps for the first time, was coming under the control of one of its components, the liberals. Party reforms

launched in 1968 by the left wing of the party shifted selection of nominat-
ing convention delegates from party regulars to activists in antiwar or
women's or other "rights movements," and under the new rules 83 percent of
the delegates to the 1972 Democratic Party Convention were from the ranks
of reform activists, the rest from state-based party organizations, with a
shrinking congressional component. "We aren't going to let these Harvard-
Berkeley Camelots take over our party," said an AFL-CIO official—but they
did.[42] An ideological upheaval had produced structural changes within the
Democratic Party, moving its image and policies leftward.

The convention in 1972 bypassed moderates such as Senator Henry
"Scoop" Jackson of Washington and nominated Senator George McGovern,
whose views expanded the political problem. He urged withdrawal from
Vietnam and called for a $30 billion cut in defense spending, amnesty for
Vietnam war deserters, and a grant of $1,000 to every American to eliminate
poverty and redistribute income. Historian Ronald Radosh spoke for Democratic centrists when he charged that the party's left by the end of 1972 had
firmly "identified the party with the rise of crime, the influence of drugs, the
decline in moral standards, and the breakup of the traditional family structure."[43] When voting time came, the New Deal coalition had badly splintered.
The Republicans took a majority of Catholic voters for the first time in any
presidential election; Nixon was favored by Italian Americans and by voters
in union families and made huge inroads on other components of the old
Democratic assemblage, such as Jews. McGovern carried Massachusetts and
the District of Columbia.

WHY ARE WE LOSING?

There were stirrings of an intraparty debate on that question after the
1972 disaster.[44] But the prevailing interpretation survived McGovern's defeat
and seems to have been this: we Democrats lost in 1968 and 1972 because political demagogues (George Wallace first, Nixon and Agnew second) exploited the Vietnam War turmoil but also the deep-seated racism, fear of economic changes brought on by an onrushing globalization of capitalism, fear
of feminist and gay self-assertion, and generally reactionary impulses of the
average American. These voters and citizens failed the cause, misled into
"white backlash" by wicked demagogues playing the race card through the
use of code words such as "welfare queen," "forced busing," and "crime." But,
surely, time was on our side. Liberals must make the case for the better an-

gels of our nature, and after an interlude the public will once again turn to affirmative government. Keep the faith.

In the meantime, all that was lost was the presidency. Democrats held their lead in governorships (31), and by a narrowed margin controlled both houses of Congress in every year of Nixon-Ford rule. And they translated this into policy results, pushing through an extraordinary number of environmental and consumer-protection laws—including the National Environmental Policy Act (1969), Clean Air Amendments in 1970, pesticide and pollution controls laws in 1972, and the Occupational and Safety and Health Act of 1970.[45]

A dissenting view was mobilizing, finding voice in the pages of a new journal, *The Public Interest*, in those of *Commentary* and elsewhere, and in those of authors such as Irving Kristol, Moynihan, Norman Podhoretz, James Q. Wilson, Ben Wattenberg, Seymour Martin Lipset, Aaron Wildavsky, and Nathan Glazer. In this perspective, the Democratic Party had moved steadily leftward after 1964 along a broad front of unpopular and little debated rights-revolution initiatives led by hard affirmative action and the expansion of welfare. All of this was for the most noble of goals: racial reconciliation and social equality. But choosing these paths and means meant that Democrats lost not just the white South but also the party's New Deal nonsouthern white urban base and transformed themselves into the minority party, at least for presidential elections. The implication, for those who see the central task of politics as gaining and holding power through durable, broad-based coalitions so that good deeds can then follow, would be to move back toward the center until a winning base is reclaimed. And good deeds can then follow, perhaps at a slower pace.[46]

A pivotal issue was one's understanding of the career of George Wallace. Astonished by his warm reception in northern primaries in 1968, Wallace declared, "They all hate black people, all of them. They're all afraid, all of them. Great God! That's it! They're all Southern! The whole United States is Southern!"[47] If Wallace said it, and it is a judgment about prejudice, then it must be so. But Nathan Glazer registered an early dissent in an essay on "The White Ethnic Political Reaction." White "ethnic" voters were not, in his view, more racially prejudiced than Anglo-Saxon Protestants, but according to some polls, less so. They were, however, in the path of the black surge into northern urban neighborhoods and experienced firsthand what college-based and suburban liberals (and Republicans) have not—housing and job competition with blacks. White working-class families found their orderly neighborhoods and schools increasingly populated by blacks, who, in the older residents' view, brought female-headed and welfare-dependent families, crime, and an unreliable male workforce. Glazer cited a handful of sociological studies documenting these class and cultural conflicts, suggesting that the "real source of prejudice is not race at all" but "realities" that "cannot be wished away."[48]

This brief treatment suggested a more complex understanding of the message sent by Wallace's voters than the governor himself, and the liberals who disagreed with him on everything else, appeared to hold. It was all very easy for white liberals to condemn and label as racists the angry housewives shouting into TV cameras from South Boston or Chicago busing protests, but "real grievances of the lower-middle-class ethnic groups were overlooked," Michael Novak had argued in his 1971 book *The Rise of the Unmeltable Ethnics*. Blacks move into their neighborhoods, "everything begins to decline" from crime rates to garbage collection to the quality of neighborhood schools, "white flight" (and black middle class flight) begins and property values slide, the realtor offers only $14,000 for a home worth more, the man sells, an incoming black family pays $17,000, and "everyone feels bitter." "Ethnic workers," Novak went on, "have legitimate reasons for economic, social, and cultural anxiety about the black revolution." But faraway "intellectuals," Novak's term for liberal elites, "lose nothing at all. It is for them a moral gravy train."[49] By the 1990s a small library of neighborhood studies had richly described the concrete resentments of the Jews and Italians of Canarsie, the white ethnics of South Boston and New York, and others whose cherished neighborhoods and local schools lay in the path of a spreading black ghetto culture.[50] The political result of all this was vividly captured in Samuel Freedman's *The Inheritance* (1996), whose subtitle, *How Three Families and America Moved from Roosevelt to Reagan*, announces the book's story of the political journey to the right of key elements of FDR's Catholic, ethnic base, whose party had "left" them.

LIBERALISM: STILL LEFTWARD

Such perspectives were heresy within liberal thought. Many decided that people like Moynihan and Glazer were not liberals any longer, but "neoconservatives," thus no longer a part of the conversation. The liberal project had not reached the time for extended soul-searching; there was too much to be done. Liberal reform ideas and energies in the 1970s ran strongly and found many outlets. The planning idea had lacked a champion after FDR, but it revived in the late 1960s. Senator Humphrey and others sponsored a national planning bill, the idea of a national growth policy, and promoted metropolitan regionalism. A liberal-labor coalition was only blocked by the threat of a Ford veto from enacting the Humphrey-Hawkins Full Employment legislation in 1975–76.[51]

But with equal or more energy and creativity, and considerably more success, liberals pushed ahead with the work that had begun during "The Movement." A main thrust was to expand the system of race, ethnicity, and gender preferences that embodied hard affirmative action. Unchecked by Republicans in the White House, the liberal impulse worked through executive branch agencies, and increasingly the courts. Federal regulators in the EEOC and the departments of Labor and Education were bent on equality in the workplace and rapid minority progress up the mobility ladder of higher education.[52] Labor's regulators (in the Office of Federal Contract Compliance Programs (OFCCP) expanded the Philadelphia plan, issuing Order #4 in 1971 to push the requirement of racial preferences for black Americans in the jobs and subcontracts attached to federal contracts outward to all major cities and the 20 percent of the nation's firms contracting with the government. Federal aid to education was a lever to thrust racial preferences into university admissions, and pressure from ethnic and women's lobbies soon produced an expansion of those qualifying for compensatory advantage because of past discrimination. Women and most racial minorities, even very recent immigrants with no history of exposure to discrimination in the United States, were included.

Congress was passive during this expansion of hard affirmative action until 1977, when, without hearings in either house, a voice vote in the Democrat-controlled House authorized a new "minority contract set-aside" program (MSA), in which 10 percent of public-works funds would be set aside from competitive bidding and reserved for businesses owned by "Negroes, Spanish-speaking, Orientals, Indians, Eskimos, and Aleuts."[53] The Supreme Court somewhat uneasily upheld the contract set-aside concept in 1980 in *Fullilove v. Klutznick,* and such programs spread to more than 230 state and city governments (where black mayors were increasingly in power) by 1989. Inside the federal government, minority "set-sides" that began in the Small Business Administration (SBA) spread to the immense contracting budgets of departments such as Defense and Transportation. Without formal hearings and under ethnic lobbying pressure, the SBA's MSA program was extended to include persons with ancestry from Brunei, Cambodia, Guam, Laos, and other countries in an apparently arbitrary process that excluded, for some reason, Iranians and Afghans. By the mid-1990s the federal government was running 159 preference programs for businesses whose owners were certified as "disadvantaged." Illegal aliens were eligible for these as well as other entitlements.[54]

Thus hard affirmative action—racial-ethnic-nationality-sex preferences aimed (loosely) at filling quotas in jobs, contracts and admissions—had become a main track on which liberals carried on the civil rights struggle. They were commendably determined to hasten social equality, dangerously moving ahead as social engineers of a new spoils system, without broad public discussion and consent.

Although hard affirmative action originated outside Congress and was little discussed, the conferring of new rights on a broadening range of citizens became a main theme of Congress, which in the 1970s created legal entitlements, in Cass Sunstein's words, to "freedom from risks in the workplace and from defective consumer products, from poverty, from long hours and low wages, from fraud and deception, from domination by employers, from one-sided or purely commercial broadcasting, and from dirty air, dirty water, and toxic substances." The 1970s brought a major expansion of government's protective regulatory reach. The federal budget for the major regulatory agencies grew from $886 million in 1970 to over $5.5 billion in 1979, the pages of the Federal Register devoted to proposed or actual administrative regulations multiplied from 9,562 to 74,120 pages.[55]

The courts were active partners in this post-1960s expansion of the reach of government into the daily economic and social life of Americans. The rights revolution, called "the longest-lasting legacy of the sixties" by Samuel Walker, a historian of the American Civil Liberties Union (ACLU), was pressed ahead in the 1970s by cadres of activist lawyers working in public-interest lobbying groups often funded by the Ford Foundation after its 1970 decision to sponsor the growth of new advocacy organizations. The drive for women's equal rights appeared blocked during the long, state-by-state battle that eventually prevented ratification of the ERA, but a string of successes profoundly altered the legal status of women. These began with the 1963 Equal Pay Act, included a major political mobilizer in the form of the Supreme Court's 1973 *Roe v. Wade* decision establishing a legal regime for abortion, and added up to a series of laws and court decisions prohibiting sex discrimination in areas ranging from education, maternity leave, access to credit, and the sex-labeling of jobs. The rights of prisoners, gays, the mentally ill, illegal aliens, and farmworkers were expanded by lawsuits brought by groups such as the ACLU, La Raza, and the

National Gay and Lesbian Task Force. "Millions of ordinary people—students, prisoners, women, the poor, gays and lesbians, the handicapped, the mentally retarded and others—discovered their own voices and demanded fair treatment and personal dignity," wrote Walker, in understandably triumphant tones, since there had been in his view no losers and no costs.[56] A different tone came in the assessment of Thomas and Mary Edsall, seeking in the early 1990s to understand a series of Democratic presidential defeats. They described "a revolution that sought new civil and citizenship rights for a range of previously stigmatized groups—criminal defendants, atheists, prisoners, homosexuals, the mentally ill, illegal aliens, publishers of pornography, and others."[57] Liberal academic and activist Lawrence Fuchs, an early supporter of hard affirmative action who developed strong misgivings, heard U.S. Commission on Civil Rights vice-chair Mary Francis Berry insist in 1980 that the civil rights agenda included admission of Cuban and Haitian boat people, and was stunned by "just how loose the meaning of civil rights had become."[58]

However one saw the social and political impacts of the rights revolution, it was clear that Nixon's two electoral victories had not ended or even slowed that part of the liberal reform cycle broadening out from the civil rights movement. Roll on, liberal-left, with or without presidential leadership.

LIBERALISM FRUSTRATED

Nixon disgraced, a weak successor Republican, but liberals did not cycle back into power, with an opportunity for another national renovation. The Democrat's moderate Georgian president floundered in economic troubles and poor luck, and in 1980 a divided and history-encumbered Democratic Party lost the White House and the leadership role again, this time to the former B-movie actor radiating California's sunny expectations. Carter carried only six states, and the Democrats lost the Senate.

Carter's defeat after one term spurred what looked like a broad rethinking—establishment of a Democratic Party Council, Congressional retreats and seminars, a new Center for National Policy, and a flurry of books by presidential hopefuls. One historian of all this reformist soul-searching found it "highly random" and "not productive or constructive."[59] Two more failed runs at the White House seemed required, and along they came—1984 candidate Walter Mondale, Hubert Humphrey's heir, carrying one state and the District of Columbia; 1988 candidate Michael Dukakis losing forty-two states to George Bush, who liberally called him a liberal. The "L-word" now seemed the third rail of American politics, synonymous, in Reagan and Bush rhetoric, with ACLU softness on crime, suspicion of the military, "tax and spend" economics, indifference to the values of family and flag. "Liberalism," observed historian Fred Siegal, is a creed now "defined in the public mind in cultural rather than economic terms."[60] The Democratic base had eroded, analyst Gerald Pomper points out, by shrinkage (of the labor union component), and disaffection (chiefly of southerners and Catholics). Getting nonvoters to the polls, the left's favorite theme, would not have helped, for in 1988 polls showed them leaning toward the Republicans.[61]

EXPERIMENTING WITH THE MESSAGE AND THE LABEL: THE 1990S

The story of Clinton-era efforts to reposition the Democratic Party is too close at hand and too erratic with cross-currents to permit a guess as to whether it will be seen only as part of the declensionist past, or in some sense an anteroom to a "New Democrat" future. Working from a base of ideas and phrases generated by the "communitarian" movement emphasizing the need to rebalance rights with responsibilities, and by the Democratic Leadership Council formed by southern elected Democrats in 1985 to find ways to "recapture the middle," Bill Clinton won the White House twice without using the L-word—with 43 percent of the vote in 1992 and 49 percent in 1996.[62] But he and Hillary were liberals, hoping to lead the next cycle of reform in the line of FDR Eleanor and JFK-Jacquie. Historian Arthur Schlesinger Jr. thought their timing excellent: "The tide is plainly turning," he wrote in 1992, "Governor Clinton and Senator Gore are indeed JFK's children."[63] It was not to be. Only by "triangulating" away from early liberal positions was Clinton able to squeeze into a second term. He spoke of having found a "'Third Way,'" language used by center-tending former left parties in Europe, especially Labor in the United Kingdom under Prime Minister Tony Blair. The term developed no identity, the Clinton years no momentum. Vice President Gore, running a bit left of "the Third Way" though inexplicably making no use of the most unifying of the sixties' crusades, environmentalism, in 2000 lost the closest election in American history to Republican George W. Bush. At the close of the twentieth century the Democratic Party bore much resemblance to its nineteenth-century self, a minority party harbor for ethnic tribes with no compelling ideas or national business to transact.

THE LIBERALS' PAST AND FUTURE: ASSESSMENTS AND SPECULATIONS

How had liberalism come to this place?[64]

Here, as in so much else, most of the scholarship on the issue is drawn back to seminal developments in and expanding beyond the sixties. Even if one concedes the case made by some historians that modern liberalism wandered from its core (and winning) economic reform mission as early as the 1940s, the sixties seem in retrospect the watershed of liberal political misjudgments. Beginning in that era and gaining momentum into the 1970s and after, liberal policies on and communicated attitudes about welfare, crime, preferential treatment of blacks and other minorities and women, school busing, and national defense and patriotism, drove a wedge between liberal elites and the party's base as well as the broader electorate. A persistent theme is policy decisions made without full and candid public discussion, often outside the relatively open processes of Congress. These include the move from soft to hard affirmative action and the vast expansion of bilingual education that were launched within new and little-scrutinized federal bureaucracies; the relentless incremental expansion of welfare; the long busing experiment in federal management of local education through judges. Even when Congress deliberated openly, liberal programs later to be deeply unpopular were sometimes adopted with explicit expert assurances that the policies would not do certain unwelcome things that they subsequently did—as, for example, the Immigration Act of 1965 both vastly expanded incoming numbers and radically altered countries of origin after solemn assurances to the contrary.

A cluster of unpopular programs was only a part of the problem for post–Great Society liberals. If politics were a set of policy scales with weights marked "law" or "program," unpopular policies might have been balanced or even outweighed by measures with the LBJ signature that had broad support—Medicare, aid to education such as student loans, subsidies to agriculture and medical research and municipal sewage plants, wilderness protection. But Great Society liberalism had other negatives beyond a large part of its policy portfolio. Journalist Kevin Phillips in 1982 perceived a "second social-issue wave" that had built up during the 1970s, "pivoting on religious, moral and sexual controversies." There was underway, as he saw it, a "morals revolution" with which liberals had become identified, even if only partisans on the right thought them solely responsible. By "championing permissiveness, homosexuality and abortion while implicitly derogating the family, prayer and biblical teachings," Phillips wrote, they not only lost Democratic voters but also energized the Christian right and brought some conservative nonvoters into active political life.[65] What Phillips called the "morals revolution" James David Hunter (and then everybody else) called, with more subtlety, *The Culture Wars* (1991). America seemed increasingly dividing into traditional-religious-nationalist versus cosmopolitan-secular-globalist camps. Republicans liked to oversimplify and exploit these alignments, since liberals, and the rest of the left, were entirely in the latter camp (along with staunch Republicans from the top echelons of business whose outlook was cosmopolitan and international). Looking back from the end of the century, Francis Fukuyama pointed out that the United States and every other economically advanced society experienced what he called "the Great Disruption" as they passed from industrial to information-based economies. Beginning in the mid-sixties and continuing through the century, "seriously deteriorating social conditions" unexpectedly built in behind economic change. Crime, social disorder, and divorce and illegitimacy rates shot upward, while trust and confidence in core institutions and even in fellow citizens went into a "forty-year decline."[66] In Fukuyama's view, liberalism was not responsible for this values disruption. Liberals merely ignored or underestimated it, all the while parenting a welfare system that seemed an accomplice. This judgment seems indulgent. As the belief system attuned to expanding group and individual rights, embracing an almost universal cultural tolerance and seeing all worries about crime and illegitimacy as essentially racist, liberalism seemed to many observers—and apparently to much of the voting public—one of the Great Disruption's sponsors.

Another cultural dimension of late-twentieth century liberal policymaking was "identity politics," a recently minted term for a new version of something old. Both—more correctly, all—American political parties have long made appeals to ethnic and racial groups. But liberals in the 1960s began a politically sustained, policy-expressed emphasis on locating the victims of discrimination or disadvantage (the second would often suffice, as proxy for the first) on the basis of race, ethnicity, gender and sexual orientation, and providing governmental advantage to these client groups.

The impetus, of course, came from the civil rights movement. Its exhilarating example led to minority-group multiplication and mobilization—by feminists, Hispanics of various group names, American Indians, gays and lesbians, and the mentally and physically handicapped. A growing number of organizations and "leaders" speaking in their names emphasized their groups' victimhood and claimed entitlement to the benefits of affirmative action, reparations, and apologies. The debate over such policies is robust and growing. The political implications are clear—the image of the Democratic Party caught up in a corrupting relationship with client tribes expecting governmental largesse, an arrangement justified by the "moral high ground" slogan of historic former wrongs redressed by rights. Equally worrisome to some observers was the power of identity politics to reorient public discourse and therefore civic culture. Mary Ann Glendon complained of a "rapidly expanding catalogue of rights" accompanied by a "new version of rights discourse . . . set apart from rights discourse in other liberal democracies by its starkness and simplicity, its prodigality in bestowing the rights label . . . and its silence with respect to personal, civic, and collective responsibilities."[67] For Todd Gitlin, veteran of New Left activism in the Bay Area during the sixties, "today it is the conservatives who claim common culture and color blindness as their special causes." When Ronald Reagan spoke of national revitalization, "the Democrats offered no commonality . . . no political culture—only a heap of demands piled on demands." Even as George Bush in 1992 admitted that he lacked "the vision thing," Democrats "stared uncomprehending into America's post–Cold War identity crisis, barely aware that they lacked even the terms of unification. . . . They needed a whole that was more than a heap. . . . The Democrats [by the 1990s] were a loose, baggy party, the Left an aggregation of movements, grouplets, and ideological tendencies. . . . Since the McGovern convention of 1972, raggedly and selectively, the Democrats had taken much of their poetry from a Left that had no conviction that commonality was possible. . . . They trapped themselves in zero-sum programs—busing, affirmative action—that split their base . . . [and] could not agree on a common commonality."[68] And in the words of Alan Wolfe: "Speaking the language of a cultural elite committed to tolerance, relativism, and personal and group identity, liberals separated themselves off from the traditional moral views of hardworking middle-class Americans, becoming, in the process, a 'new class' committed to an 'adversary culture' of collectivist values, therapeutic remedies, hostility to corporations, and even anti-Americanism."[69]

Theodore White had sensed the buildup of centrifugal forces as early as 1978, wondering in his autobiography whether "America would be transformed, in the name of opportunity, simply into a Place, a gathering of discretely defined and entitled groups, interests, and heritages; or whether it could continue to be a nation. . . ."[70] Liberalism had bonded with "Diversity," a sometimes good thing that was increasingly being asked to serve as the central goal of national policy. Would America, worried Richard Morgan, become "simply a collection of ethnics huddled around a standard of living?"[71]

THE MOMENTUM OF GOOD INTENTIONS

Of course, occasionally going a bit out in front of public consensus, even in a democracy, has a lot to be said for it. Liberal elites in the 1960s were pushing hard for an end to the legal regime of racial discrimination. Steps in this direction had for decades been meeting massive resistance from the southern white electorate, and in the 1960s it appeared that the white resistance had taken root across the nation. A disconnect between elite and working-middle class attitudes on race policy was a new and deeply felt reality. To liberals who were finding themselves as the elite, the situation implied a moral warrant for imaginative, innovative government willing to be on occasion "countermajoritarian." It was one of those hopefully rare times in which it was necessary to coerce the bigoted or uncompassionate majority, using the courts, administrative rulemaking, and other pathways around wrongheaded arrangements. This is sometimes called political leadership, the high plateau of political life.

But if innovative countermajoritarian policy leads to a long ordeal of party weakness and defeat another way to say, to the coming to power of hated enemies such as Richard Nixon—then, in politics, as distinct from seeking the kingdom of God, there must be rethinking and course corrections. Especially if the policies themselves bring disappointing social as well as political results. Yet serious rethinking by liberals came only in the 1990s, and then haltingly, after two decades of political hemorrhaging, the presidencies of Nixon, Reagan, and Bush, and other Republican enjoyments. Why was recognition of political vulnerability and misjudgment so long delayed?

To disgruntled leftist Michael Tomasky, for example, there was always much to be taken seriously in the criticism of hard affirmative action, welfare, bilingual education, and mass immigration under (and illegally around) the 1965 act. But liberals tended to dismiss all criticism as racism and would not rethink policies that seemed the only available means of continuing the civil rights crusade. Rejecting "any attempt at self-examination," Tomasky concludes, the left "has taken itself out of the conversation."[72] "In sum, liberals," physically and socially remote from the urban churning, "were arrogant," writes Gordon MacInnes, "and showed no respect for middle class and working Americans."[73] Reaching deeper, Thomas and Mary Edsall drew up a list of reasons why liberals could not bear to open a discussion of their errors: "Fear of information damaging to liberal goals . . . a reluctance to further stigmatize blacks who were just emerging from centuries of legal oppression . . . an unwillingness to raise issues straining the fragile liberal coalition . . . [and] the confusion growing out of the upheaval in moral values among the white middle and upper-middle class."[74]

LOOKING AHEAD

There is still some optimism in liberal—now "progressive"—precincts. Demographic trends promise victory, goes one view, because immigration brings a surging Hispanic vote that will "flip . . . the lower, 'Latinized' Sunbelt back to the Democrats."[75]

Perhaps so, though President George W. Bush clearly thinks all Americans of Mexican descent are potential Republicans. Even if he is wrong and the Democrats inherit most of the Hispanic vote, winning by this arithmetic does not promise the challenge of nation-saving, brings no history-making moment. Liberalism had once aimed at more. How again to be more than a 43 percent or 50.1 percent winner but a *cause*, rallying majorities for social transformation? That dream has a firm grip.[76]

Billionaire financier George Soros, remembering the 1890s and 1930s, imagines a meltdown of the global economy offering an opening for capitalism-fixers—which means liberals under whatever name, with a mission of building a "global New Deal."[77] But the strains of globalization remain below crisis level, and nowhere could one see the intellectual building blocks of a coherent international and national reform program to deal with a collapse or sustained malfunction of the global economy. The tea leaves are in a dark, deep cup.

On September 11, 2001, Islamic terrorists seized four civilian aircraft and drove two of them into the World Trade Center in New York and one into the Pentagon in Washington, killing more than three thousand people. A fourth hijacked plane, apparently headed for another target in Washington, crashed in Pennsylvania when the passengers, realizing the nature of the hijacker's mission, attacked the terrorist at the controls. America was at war, President George W. Bush declared, and others called it the beginning of World War III.

These events supplied a decided sense of national crisis with no likelihood of early resolution, a lengthy struggle against global terrorism that was not at all what crisis speculators had envisioned. Where was any opportunity for liberal-progressives? Criticism of and disagreement with President George W. Bush had at first to be muted, even on domestic matters, but the opposition would eventually oppose. But with what message and effect? Big Government was back, but it was President Bush and his administration asking for increased spending for defense, strengthened intelligence capacities and border/immigration controls, and assistance to war-damaged facilities as well as crippled airlines. A distinctive progressive response to the deadly global terrorist impulse and apparatus was going to be very difficult to fashion, especially because a part of the left initially seemed to be taking pacifist and "America is the problem" positions.[78] Liberal writer George Packer nonetheless saw a silver lining, commenting that September 11 "made it safe for liberals to be patriots."[79] Perhaps so, but that pathway to leadership had been clogged by Republicans since the Democrats buried PT-boat skipper John F. Kennedy. The public had for two decades expressed more confidence in Republicans than Democrats in foreign affairs and national security issues, and by a large margin.

A few intellectuals, even before the 2001 attacks, had been reminding their readers that liberalism had in the first half of the century been wedded with nationalism, and labored to work their way back from a splintered multiculturalism toward a workable accommodation with national solidarity, the risky emotions of patriotism, even that discredited old idea, national identity.[80] For those who followed the discourse of the public intellectuals, it was a mark of how widespread were these end-of-century reconsiderations in liberal territory when the dean of the multicultural left, Richard Rorty, urged the cultural left to drop its "semi-conscious anti-Americanism" and "start trying to construct inspiring images of the country" so that it can "begin to form alliances with people outside the academy."[81]

Whatever is ahead, at the start of the twenty-first century the liberal narrative is fragmented into confusion, the connections to the mainstream public lost, along with a convincing vision of what the historic moment requires. Liberals had lost their story. Republicans, sensing an opportunity, had substituted a new narrative, the liberal as tax-and-spend moral idiot. But this language, too, will age. Returning to the word *Progressive* may have more significance than is realized. It suggests a recognition that recent misjudgments are not the whole of a political heritage, and reminds that, a century ago, the nonsocialist left built a winning story around nation-building, along with the conviction that capitalism, alone, should not be given the only role in planning, or steering, a country.

Wearier than most, Daniel Patrick Moynihan, thinking of the social pathologies that the welfare state had made worse, but perhaps also of four decades of public policy's muddles and unintended consequences, concluded that "it is time for small platoons" of family, church, and neighborhood.[82] That sounded like the end of a political era, without a hint of the shape of the future.

NOTES

1. "Liberalism Defined," *The Economist* (December 21, 1996), p. 17. The focus of this essay is on political liberalism, the liberal persuasion engaged in political effort associated with the Democratic Party since Franklin Roosevelt. It does not review other forms such as legal liberalism or liberal political theory, on which there is an immense literature.

2. William Raspberry, "Liberals: Out of Ideas," *Washington Post,* September 26, 1997, p. A25. See also Tom Hamburger, "How Did Liberal Get to Be Such a Dirty Word?" *Minneapolis Star Tribune,* September 30, 1996, p. A7.

3. Arthur Mann, *The One and the Many* (Chicago: University of Chicago Press, 1979), 9.

4. "What went wrong?" is also an absorbing question for the opposition. "What is a conservative?" asked the *Los Angeles Times* at the end of 1998, with GOP House Speaker Newt Gingrich's leadership repudiated and its majority feeble. No party, in 2000 and after, could assemble a working majority or decisively win the White House. But this opens a larger question.

5. Robert Dallek, *Flawed Giant: Lyndon Johnson and His Times, 1961–1973* (New York: Oxford University Press, 1998), 120.

6. Numan Bartley and Hugh Davis Graham, *Southern Politics in the Second Reconstruction* (Baltimore: Johns Hopkins University Press, 1975), 106–110.

7. Lyndon Baines Johnson, *The Vantage Point: Perspective of the Presidency, 1963–1969* (New York: Holt, Rinehart and Winston, 1971), 549.

8. For influential overviews of the Great Society, see Allen J. Matusow, *The Unraveling of America* (New York: Harper and Row, 1984), and James T. Patterson, *Grand Expectations: The United States, 1945–1974* (New York: Oxford University Press, 1996).

9. For two contrasting views of LBJ and his legacy, see Robert Caro, *The Years of Lyndon Johnson: Means of Ascent* (New York: Alfred A. Knopf, 1990), and Dallek, *Flawed Giant.* Lewis L. Gould, "The Revised LBJ," *Wilson Quarterly* (Spring 2000): 80–96, is a useful review of the biographical literature.

10. See the vivid migrant biographies collected in Nicholas Lemann, *The Promised Land: The Great Black Migration and How It Changed America* (New York: Vintage Books, 1991).

11. On the "underclass," see William Julius Wilson, *The Truly Disadvantaged: The Inner City, the Underclass and Public Policy* (Chicago: University of Chicago Press, 1987); Ken Auletta, *The Underclass* (New York: Random House, 1982); Lemann, *The Promised Land,* and the notes to chap. 7, "Welfare and the Underclass Threat," in Mickey Kaus, *The End of Equality* (New York: Basic Books, 1992).

12. Thomas Edsall and Mary Edsall, *Chain Reaction* (New York: W. W. Norton, 1991), 52; *Statistical Abstracts of the United States, 1987* (Washington, D.C.: U.S. Government Printing Office, 1988); Gerald David Jaynes and Robin M. Williams Jr., eds., *A Common Destiny: Blacks and American Society* (Washington, D.C.: National Academy Press, 1989).

13. The report is reprinted in Lee Rainwater and William L. Yancey, *The Moynihan Report and the Politics of Controversy* (Cambridge, Mass.: MIT Press, 1967), 41–124.

14. Gordon MacInnes, *Wrong for All the Right Reasons: How White Liberals Have Been Undone by Race* (New York: New York University Press, 1995), 46.

15. Lemann, *Promised Land,* 177. It almost ceased. Economist Andrew Brimmer, a governor of the Federal Reserve Board, made a speech at Tuskegee Institute in 1970 entitled "The Deepening Schism," in which he noted that "able . . . and well-prepared" Negroes were making economic progress, but "those with few skills" were not, the latter entangled in "the dramatic deterioration in the position of Negro families headed by females." There was no uproar, since Brimmer was black. See Godfrey Hodgson, *America In Our Time* (New York: Doubleday, 1976), 445.

16. Hugh Davis Graham, *The Civil Rights Era: Origins and Development of National Policy, 1960–1972* (New York: Oxford University Press, 1990), 106–109; Nathan Glazer, *Affirmative Discrimination: Ethnic Inequality and Public Policy* (New York: Basic Books, 1975), 44–45; Stephan Thernstrom and Abigail Thernstrom, *America in Black and White: One Nation, Indivisible* (New York: Simon & Schuster, 1997), 425.

17. Thernstrom and Thernstrom, *America in Black and White,* 424–429; Hugh Davis Graham, "Race, History and Policy: African Americans and Civil Rights since 1964," in Hugh Davis Graham, ed., *Civil Rights in the United States* (University Park: Pennsylvania State University Press, 1994), 17–20. See also John David Skrentny, *The Ironies of Affirmative Action* (Chicago: University of Chicago Press, 1996).

18. Hugh Davis Graham, "Unintended Consequences: The Convergence of Affirmative Action and Immigration Policy," *American Behavioral Scientist* 41 (April 1998): 903–904; and Graham, *Collision Course: The Strange Convergence of Affirmative Action and Immigration Policy in America* (New York: Oxford University Press,

2002). The terms "soft" and "hard" affirmative action were, to my knowledge, first suggested by Nathan Glazer when he spoke of "hard affirmative action." See Glazer, *Affirmative Discrimination,* 207.

19. Thernstrom and Thernstrom, *America in Black and White,* 173.

20. Thernstrom and Thernstrom, *America in Black and White,* 330. See also J. Harvey Wilkinson III, *From Brown to Bakke: The Supreme Court and School Integration, 1954–1978* (New York: Oxford University Press, 1979), Ronald P. Formisano, *Boston against Busing: Race, Class and Ethnicity in the 1960s and 1970s* (Chapel Hill: University of North Carolina Press, 1991), and James T. Patterson, *Brown v. Board of Education: A Civil Rights Milestone and Its Troubled Legacy* (New York: Oxford University Press, 2001).

21. Michael J. Sandel, *Democracy's Discontent: America in Search of a Public Philosophy* (Cambridge, Mass.: Harvard University Press, 1996), 281.

22. Mary Ann Glendon, *Rights Talk: The Impoverishment of Political Discourse* (New York: Free Press, 1991), xx–xxi.

23. Cass R. Sunstein, *After the Rights Revolution: Reconceiving the Regulatory State* (Cambridge, Mass.: Harvard University Press, 1990), 12–30.

24. Nathan Glazer, "A Breakdown in Civil Rights Enforcement?" *The Public Interest* (Winter 1971): 107. See also Glazer, *Affirmative Discrimination,* and Graham, *Civil Rights Era,* 456–458.

25. Theodore H. White, *The Making of the President 1972* (New York: Atheneum, 1973), 24–33.

26. James T. Patterson, *America's Struggle against Poverty, 1900–1980* (Cambridge, Mass: Harvard University Press, 1980), 171.

27. Gareth Davies, *From Opportunity to Entitlement: The Transformation and Decline of Great Society Liberalism* (Lawrence: University Press of Kansas, 1996).

28. Patterson, *America's Struggle,* 171, 179. See also Patterson, "Race Relations and the 'Underclass' in Modern America: Some Historical Observations," *Qualitative Sociology* 18 (1995): 237–260.

29. Michael J. Piore, *Birds of Passage: Migrant Labor and Industrial Societies* (New York: Cambridge University Press, 1979), 161–162. See Elliot Liebow, *Tally's Corner: A Study of Streetcorner Men* (Boston: Little, Brown, 1967), and the discussion in William Julius Wilson, *The Declining Significance of Race* (Chicago: University of Chicago Press, 1978), 104–109.

30. John Morton Blum, *Years of Discord: American Politics and Society, 1961–1974* (New York: W. W. Norton, 1991), 170–177; Patterson, *America's Struggle,* chap. 10.

31. Patterson, *America's Struggle,* 160, 165–170, and see chap. 10 generally.

32. FDR quoted in Samuel Rosenman, ed., *The Public Papers and Addresses of Franklin D. Roosevelt* (New York: Random House, 1938), 4:19–20.

33. Rosenman, ed., *Public Papers and Addresses of Franklin D. Roosevelt*, 4:183.

34. James Sundquist, *The Dynamics of the Party System* (Washington, D.C.: The Brookings Institution Press, 1983), 382.

35. A point of agreement pointed out by Hugh Davis Graham in his review of Stephan Lesher, *George Wallace: American Populist* (1994) and Dan T. Carter, *The Politics of Rage: George Wallace, the Origins of the New Conservatism and the Transformation of American Politics* (1995), *Reviews in American History* 24 (1996): 332–336.

36. Matthew Dallek, "Liberalism Overthrown," *American Heritage* (October 1996), pp. 39–60; Dallek, *The Right Moment: Ronald Reagan's First Victory and the Decisive Turning Point in American Politics* (New York: Free Press, 2000).

37. Stephen A. Ambrose, *Nixon: The Triumph of a Politician, 1962–1972*, vol. 2 (New York: Simon & Schuster, 1989), 187.

38. Jody Carlson, *George C. Wallace and the Politics of Powerlessness* (New Brunswick, N.J.: Transaction Books, 1981), 6.

39. Kevin P. Phillips, *The Emerging Republican Majority* (New Rochelle, N.Y.: Arlington House, 1969), 1–33.

40. Richard M. Scammon and Ben J. Wattenberg, *The Real Majority* (New York: Coward-McCann, 1970), 20, 284–289.

41. Arthur M. Schlesinger Jr., "What If RFK Had Survived?" *Newsweek*, June 8, 1998, p. 55. For a skeptical view of RFK's electoral prospects, see Nelson Polsby, ed., *What If?* (Lexington, Mass.: Lewis, 1982). For doubts that RFK was an ardent liberal, see Ronald Steel, *In Love with Night: The American Romance with Robert Kennedy* (New York: Simon & Schuster, 1999), and Evan Thomas, *Robert Kennedy: His Life* (New York: Simon & Schuster, 2000).

42. Theodore H. White, *The Making of the President 1972* (New York: Atheneum, 1973), 38. For the McGovern-Fraser Commission reforms of Democratic Party rules, see Byron Shafer, *Quiet Revolution: The Struggle for the Democratic Party and the Shaping of Post-Reform Politics* (New York: Russell Sage, 1983), and William Mayer (*The Divided Democrats: Ideological Unity, Party Reform, and Presidential Elections* (Boulder, Colo.: Westview Press, 1996).

43. Ronald Radosh, *Divided They Fell: The Demise of the Democratic Party, 1964–1996* (New York: Free Press, 1996), xi.

44. Ben Wattenberg reports that he "helped start" and was chairman of "a Democratic anti-McGovernite factional group called the Coalition for a Democratic Majority," but says no more about it in his *Values Matter Most* (New York: Free Press, 1995). For a brief account of the group and two other small forerunners of the DLC, see James M. Burns and Georgia J. Sorenson, *Dead Center: Clinton-Gore Leadership and the Perils of Moderation* (New York: Scribner, 1999), 151–153; see also Norman Podhoretz, "Life of His Party," *National Review* (September 13, 1999), p. 50. On Sen-

ator Jackson, see Robert G. Kaufman, *Henry M. Jackson: A Life in Politics* (Seattle: University of Washington Press, 2000).

45. See David Vogel, *Fluctuating Fortunes: The Political Power of Business in America* (New York: Basic Books, 1989), especially chap. 4, "Business on the Defensive, 1969–1972."

46. This perspective on things found early expression in Scammon and Wattenberg's *The Real Majority* and in the 1990s was vigorously expressed in Edsall and Edsall, *Chain Reaction*. For a review of the Democrats' internal feuds and self-assessments, see Jacob Weisberg, *In Defense of Government: The Fall and Rise of Public Trust* (New York: Scribners, 1996).

47. Carter, *The Politics of Rage,* 344.

48. Glazer, *Affirmative Discrimination,* 177–195.

49. Michael Novak, *The Rise of the Unmeltable Ethnics* (New York: Macmillan, 1971), 7, 12–13, 250.

50. Jonathan Rieder, *Canarsie: The Jews and Italians of Brooklyn against Liberalism* (Cambridge, Mass.: Harvard University Press, 1985); Formisano, *Boston against Busing*; Jim Sleeper, *The Closest of Strangers: Liberalism and the Politics of Race in New York* (New York: W. W. Norton, 1990); Lemann, *The Promised Land*; Fred Siegel, *The Future Once Happened Here: New York, D.C., L.A., and the Fate of America's Big Cities* (New York: Free Press, 1997); Samuel Freedman, *The Inheritance: How Three Families and America Moved from Roosevelt to Reagan and Beyond* (New York: Simon & Schuster, 1996). Alan Brinkley lists several studies of the urban "populist right" with "rational grievances" in *Liberalism and Its Discontents* (Cambridge, Mass.: Harvard University Press, 1998), 361.

51. See Otis L. Graham Jr., *Toward a Planned Society: From Roosevelt to Nixon* (New York: Oxford University Press, 1976), and *Losing Time: The Industrial Policy Debate* (Cambridge, Mass.: Harvard University Press, 1992), chap. 1.

52. On the rights-based effort to force schools and universities toward equal results, see Stephen C. Halpern, *On The Limits of the Law: The Ironic Legacy of Title VI of the 1964 Civil Rights Act* (Baltimore: Johns Hopkins University Press, 1995).

53. Public Works Employment Act of 1977, Section 103(f)(2).

54. Hugh Davis Graham, "Since 1964: The Paradox of American Civil Rights Regulation," in Morton Keller and H. Shep Melnich, eds., *Taking Stock: American Government in the Twentieth Century* (Washington, D.C.: Woodrow Wilson Center Press, 1999), 187–218; "Unintended Consequences," 898–912; and "Race, History, and Policy: African Americans and Civil Rights since 1964," *Journal of Policy History* 6 (1994): 24–27. See also George La Noue and John Sullivan, " 'Presumptions for Preferences: The Small Business Administration's Decisions on Groups Entitled to Affirmative Action," *Journal of Policy History* 6 (1994): 439–467; and La Noue, "Split Visions: Mi-

nority Business Set-Asides," *The Annals* 523 (September 1992): 104–116. At Senator Robert Dole's request, in February 1995 the Congressional Research Service compiled a thirty-three-page list of every "federal statute, regulation, program, and executive order that grants a preference to individuals on the basis of race, sex, national origin, or ethnic background." (Congressional Research Service to Honorable Robert Dole, February 17, 1995.)

55. Sunstein, *After the Rights Revolution*, 12–30; David Vogel, *Fluctuating Fortunes: The Political Power of Business in America* (New York: Basic Books, 1989), chaps. 3–4.

56. Samuel Walker, *In Defense of American Liberties: A History of the ACLU* (New York: Oxford University Press, 1990), 300.

57. Edsall and Edsall, *Chain Reaction*, 45. See also James T. Patterson, "The Rise of Rights and Rights Consciousness in American Politics, 1930s–1970s," in Bryon E. Shafer and Anthony J. Badger, eds., *Contesting Democracy: Substance and Structure in American Political History, 1775–2000* (Lawrence: University Press of Kansas, 2002), 237–263.

58. Lawrence H. Fuchs, "The Changing Meaning of Civil Rights, 1954–1994," in John Higham, ed., *Civil Rights and Social Wrongs* (University Park: Pennsylvania State University Press, 1997), 71.

59. Caroline Arden, *Getting the Donkey out of the Ditch: The Democratic Party in Search of Itself* (New York: Greenwood, 1988), 1. Journalists talked of a new centrist impulse they labeled "neo-liberalism," defined by *The New Republic* editor Morton Kondracke as "an attempt to combine the traditional Democratic compassion for the downtrodden . . . with different vehicles than . . . quota systems or new federal bureaucracies." He named a rising cluster of younger Democrats—Gary Hart, Paul Tsongas of Massachusetts, Bill Bradley of New Jersey, Jerry Brown of California. Morton Kondracke, "A Doubtful New Order," *The New Republic* (November 15, 1980). See also Randall Rothenberg, *The Neo-Liberals* (New York: Simon and Schuster, 1984).

60. Fred Siegel, "What Liberals Haven't Learned and Why," *Commonweal* (January 13, 1989), pp. 17–18. Cultural and *racial* terms, argues Peter Brown in *Minority Party: Why Democrats Face Defeat in 1992 and Beyond* (Washington, D.C.: Regnery Gateway, 1991).

61. Gerald M. Pomper, ed., *The Election of 1988: Reports and Interpretations* (New York: Chatham House, 1989), 110–137.

62. The DLC story is well told in Kenneth S. Baer, *Reinventing Democrats: The Politics of Liberalism from Reagan to Clinton* (Lawrence: University Press of Kansas, 1999).

63. Schlesinger, in Peter B. Kovler, ed., *Democrats and the American Idea: A Bicentennial Appraisal* (Washington, D.C.: Center for National Policy Press, 1992), 363–364.

64. Some scholars object to the form of the question. Define liberalism in terms of the values of individualism, political equality, and the consent of the governed, they ar-

gue, and it has steadily expanded its moral authority. See Robert Booth Fowler, *Enduring Liberalism: American Political Thought since the 1960s* (Lawrence: University Press of Kansas, 1999). The same sense of robust liberalism comes if one defines it as citizens lobbying networks supporting a "postmaterialist" agenda of environmental protection, consumerism, and minority group advancement: see Jeffrey M. Berry, *The New Liberalism: The Rising Power of Citizen Groups* (Washington, D.C.: The Brookings Institution Press, 1999).

65. Kevin P. Phillips, *Post-Conservative America* (New York: Vintage Books, 1992), 23.

66. Francis Fukuyama, *The Great Disruption: Human Nature and the Reconstitution of the Social Order* (New York: Free Press, 1999), 4. See also Daniel Yankelovich, *New Rules: Searching for Self-Fulfillment in a World Turned Upside Down* (New York: Random House, 1981); Bruce J. Schulman, *The Seventies: The Great Shift in American Culture* (New York: Free Press, 2001).

67. Mary Ann Glendon, *Rights Talk: The Impoverishment of Political Discourse* (New York: Free Press, 1991), xx–xxi, 5.

68. Todd Gitlin, *The Twilight of Common Dreams: Why America Is Wracked by Culture Wars* (New York: Henry Holt, 1995), 33, 79, 82–83, 100. See also Amitai Etzioni, *The Spirit of Community: Rights, Responsibilities, and the Communitarian Agenda* (New York: Crown, 1993).

69. Alan Wolfe, *One Nation, After All* (New York: Viking, 1998), 304.

70. Theodore H. White, *In Search of History* (New York: Harper & Row, 1978), 538.

71. Richard E. Morgan, *Disabling America* (New York: Basic Books, 1984), 269.

72. Michael Tomasky, *Left for Dead* (New York: Free Press, 1996), 9, 13. George McGovern, always more thoughtful than the image created for him in 1972, regretted sixteen years later that the antiwar movement called the war "immoral" rather than imprudent or otherwise mistaken, since the word "immoral" shut off dialogue with the other side. "If you disagree with us, you are immoral." Recalled by George F. Will in *Suddenly* (Washington, D.C.: Washington Post Press, 1990), 266.

73. MacInnes, *Wrong for All the Right Reasons,* 7. This would be no news to historians Christopher Lasch and Robert Wiebe, who argued in different ways that a "national class" of self-appointed experts emerged in the reform movements at the start of the twentieth century and thereafter the political participation of the public was steadily reduced. See Christopher Lasch, *The Revolt of the Elites and the Betrayal of Democracy* (New York: W. W. Norton, 1995), and Robert Wiebe, *Self-Rule: A Cultural History of American Democracy* (Chicago: University of Chicago Press, 1995).

74. Edsall and Edsall, *Chain Reaction,* 53. See also Brown, *Minority Party.*

75. Paul Starr, "An Emerging Democratic Majority," *The American Prospect* (November–December 1997), p. 21. This was a remarkable calculation. Oklahoma Sena-

tor Fred Harris based his 1972 and 1976 presidential runs on the 25 million young people newly eligible to vote in 1972. See Richard Lowitt, *Fred Harris: His Journey from Liberalism to Populism* (Lanham, Md.: Rowman and Littlefield, 2002), p. 183. Unfortunately, says William Mayer, this is an "empirically inaccurate premise." Nonvoters are not closet Democrats or liberals, but mostly independents whose turnout would not much alter the results (*Divided Democrats*, 164–165). On how the "Joe Sixpack" white middle class could be won back with government measures to deal with economic insecurities, see Ruy Teixeira and Joel Rogers, *America's Forgotten Majority* (New York: Basic Books, 2000).

76. See, for example, E. J. Dionne, *They Only Look Dead: Why Progressives Will Dominate the Next Political Era* (New York: Simon & Schuster, 1996), and Weisberg, *In Defense*, 158–192.

77. George Soros, *The Crisis of Global Capitalism* (Boston: Perseus Books, 1998), and *Open Society: Reforming Global Capitalism* (New York: Public Affairs, 2001). See also Paul Krugman, "The Return of Depression Economics," *Foreign Affairs* 78, no. 1 (January/February 1999): 56–74. The phrase "Global New Deal" appears, among other places, in W. Bowman Cutter, Joan Spero, and Laura D'Andrea Tyson, "New World, New Deal," *Foreign Affairs* 79, no. 2 (March–April 2000): 80–98.

78. See Michael Kazin, "After the Attacks, Which Side Is the Left On?" *New York Times*, October 7, 2001, p. A4.

79. George Packer, "Recapturing the Flag," *New York Times Magazine* (September 30, 2001), p. 15.

80. John B. Judis and Michael Lind, "For A New Nationalism," *The New Republic* (March 27, 1995), pp. 19–27. See also Jeff Faux, *The Party's Not Over: A New Vision for the Democrats* (New York: Basic Books, 1996); and David A. Hollinger, "National Solidarity at the End of the Twentieth Century," *Journal of American History* (September 1997): 559–569, along with the exchange with Gary Gerstle and others. See also David Miller, *On Nationality* (New York: Oxford University Press, 1995); Martin Marty, *The One and the Many* (Cambridge, Mass.: Harvard University Press, 1997); Yael Tamir, *Liberal Nationalism* (Princeton: Princeton University Press, 1993); Russell Hardin, *One For All: The Logic of Group Conflict* (Princeton: Princeton University Press, 1995); and Martha C. Nussbaum, *For Love of Country: Debating the Limits of Patriotism* (Boston: Beacon Press, 1996).

81. Richard Rorty, "The Dark Side of the Academic Left," *Chronicle of Higher Education* (April 3, 1998), pp. B4–B6. See also Rorty, *Achieving Our Country: Leftist Thought in Twentieth Century America* (Cambridge, Mass.: Harvard University Press, 1998).

82. Daniel Patrick Moynihan, *Miles to Go: A Personal History of Social Policy* (Cambridge, Mass.: Harvard University Press, 1996), 230.

INDEX

A SCANDAL IN BOHEMIA
FROM THE ADVENTURES OF SHERLOCK HOLMES (1892)

I.

To SHERLOCK HOLMES she is always *the* woman. I have seldom heard him mention her under any other name. In his eyes she eclipses and predominates the whole of her sex. It was not that he felt any emotion akin to love for Irene Adler. All emotions, and that one particularly, were abhorrent to his cold, precise but admirably balanced mind. He was, I take it, the most perfect reasoning and observing machine that the world has seen, but as a lover he would have placed himself in a false position. He never spoke of the softer passions, save with a gibe and a sneer. They were admirable things for the observer— excellent for drawing the veil from men's motives and actions. But for the trained reasoner to admit such intrusions into his own delicate and finely adjusted temperament was to introduce a distracting factor which might throw a doubt upon all his mental results. Grit in a sensitive instrument, or a crack in one of his own high-power lenses, would not be more disturbing than a strong emotion in a nature such as his. And yet there was but one woman to him, and that woman was the late Irene Adler, of dubious and questionable memory.

I had seen little of Holmes lately. My marriage had drifted us away from each other. My own complete happiness, and the home-centred interests which rise up around the man who first finds himself master of his own establishment, were sufficient to absorb all my attention, while Holmes, who loathed every form of society with his whole Bohemian soul, remained in our lodgings in Baker Street, buried among his old books, and alternating from week to week between cocaine and ambition, the drowsiness of the drug, and the fierce energy of his own keen nature. He was still, as ever, deeply attracted by the study of crime, and occupied his immense faculties and extraordinary powers of observation in following out those clues, and clearing up those mysteries which had been abandoned as hopeless by the official police. From time to time I heard some vague account of his doings: of his summons to Odessa in the case of the Trepoff murder, of his

clearing up of the singular tragedy of the Atkinson brothers at Trincomalee, and finally of the mission which he had accomplished so delicately and successfully for the reigning family of Holland. Beyond these signs of his activity, however, which I merely shared with all the readers of the daily press, I knew little of my former friend and companion.

One night—it was on the twentieth of March, 1888—I was returning from a journey to a patient (for I had now returned to civil practice), when my way led me through Baker Street. As I passed the well-remembered door, which must always be associated in my mind with my wooing, and with the dark incidents of the Study in Scarlet, I was seized with a keen desire to see Holmes again, and to know how he was employing his extraordinary powers. His rooms were brilliantly lit, and, even as I looked up, I saw his tall, spare figure pass twice in a dark silhouette against the blind. He was pacing the room swiftly, eagerly, with his head sunk upon his chest and his hands clasped behind him. To me, who knew his every mood and habit, his attitude and manner told their own story. He was at work again. He had risen out of his drug-created dreams and was hot upon the scent of some new problem. I rang the bell and was shown up to the chamber which had formerly been in part my own.

His manner was not effusive. It seldom was; but he was glad, I think, to see me. With hardly a word spoken, but with a kindly eye, he waved me to an armchair, threw across his case of cigars, and indicated a spirit case and a gasogene in the corner. Then he stood before the fire and looked me over in his singular introspective fashion.

"Wedlock suits you," he remarked. "I think, Watson, that you have put on seven and a half pounds since I saw you."

"Seven!" I answered.

"Indeed, I should have thought a little more. Just a trifle more, I fancy, Watson. And in practice again, I observe. You did not tell me that you intended to go into harness."

"Then, how do you know?"

"I see it, I deduce it. How do I know that you have been getting yourself very wet lately, and that you have a most clumsy and careless servant girl?"

"My dear Holmes," said I, "this is too much. You would certainly have been burned, had you lived a few centuries ago. It is true that I had a country walk on Thursday and came home in a dreadful mess, but as I have changed my clothes I can't imagine how you deduce it. As to Mary Jane, she is incorrigible, and my wife has given her notice, but there, again, I fail to see how you work it out."

He chuckled to himself and rubbed his long, nervous hands together.

"It is simplicity itself," said he; "my eyes tell me that on the inside of your left shoe, just where the firelight strikes it, the leather is scored by six almost parallel cuts. Obviously they have been caused by someone who has very carelessly scraped round the edges of the sole in order to remove crusted mud from it. Hence, you see, my double deduction that you had been out in vile weather, and that you had a particularly malignant boot-slitting specimen of the London slavey. As to your practice, if a gentleman walks into my rooms smelling of iodoform, with a black mark of nitrate of silver upon his right forefinger, and a bulge on the right side of his top-hat to show where he has secreted his stethoscope, I must be dull, indeed, if I do not pronounce him to be an active member of the medical profession."

I could not help laughing at the ease with which he explained his process of deduction. "When I hear you give your reasons," I remarked, "the thing always appears to me to be

so ridiculously simple that I could easily do it myself, though at each successive instance of your reasoning I am baffled until you explain your process. And yet I believe that my eyes are as good as yours."

"Quite so," he answered, lighting a cigarette, and throwing himself down into an armchair. "You see, but you do not observe. The distinction is clear. For example, you have frequently seen the steps which lead up from the hall to this room."

"Frequently."

"How often?"

"Well, some hundreds of times."

"Then how many are there?"

"How many? I don't know."

"Quite so! You have not observed. And yet you have seen. That is just my point. Now, I know that there are seventeen steps, because I have both seen and observed. By the way, since you are interested in these little problems, and since you are good enough to chronicle one or two of my trifling experiences, you may be interested in this." He threw over a sheet of thick, pink-tinted notepaper which had been lying open upon the table. "It came by the last post," said he. "Read it aloud."

The note was undated, and without either signature or address.

"There will call upon you to-night, at a quarter to eight o'clock," it said, "a gentleman who desires to consult you upon a matter of the very deepest moment. Your recent services to one of the royal houses of Europe have shown that you are one who may safely be trusted with matters which are of an importance which can hardly be exaggerated. This account of you we have from all quarters received. Be in your chamber then at that hour, and do not take it amiss if your visitor wear a mask."

"This is indeed a mystery," I remarked. "What do you imagine that it means?"

"I have no data yet. It is a capital mistake to theorise before one has data. Insensibly one begins to twist facts to suit theories, instead of theories to suit facts. But the note itself. What do you deduce from it?"

I carefully examined the writing, and the paper upon which it was written.

"The man who wrote it was presumably well to do," I remarked, endeavouring to imitate my companion's processes. "Such paper could not be bought under half a crown a packet. It is peculiarly strong and stiff."

"Peculiar—that is the very word," said Holmes. "It is not an English paper at all. Hold it up to the light."

I did so, and saw a large "E" with a small "g," a "P," and a large "G" with a small "t" woven into the texture of the paper.

"What do you make of that?" asked Holmes.

"The name of the maker, no doubt; or his monogram, rather."

"Not at all. The 'G' with the small 't' stands for 'Gesellschaft,' which is the German for 'Company.' It is a customary contraction like our 'Co.' 'P,' of course, stands for 'Papier.' Now for the 'Eg.' Let us glance at our Continental Gazetteer." He took down a heavy brown volume from his shelves. "Eglow, Eglonitz—here we are, Egria. It is in a German-speaking country—in Bohemia, not far from Carlsbad. 'Remarkable as being the scene of the death of Wallenstein, and for its numerous glass-factories and paper-mills.' Ha, ha, my boy, what do you make of that?" His eyes sparkled, and he sent up a great blue triumphant cloud from his cigarette.

3

"The paper was made in Bohemia," I said.

"Precisely. And the man who wrote the note is a German. Do you note the peculiar construction of the sentence—'This account of you we have from all quarters received.' A Frenchman or Russian could not have written that. It is the German who is so uncourteous to his verbs. It only remains, therefore, to discover what is wanted by this German who writes upon Bohemian paper and prefers wearing a mask to showing his face. And here he comes, if I am not mistaken, to resolve all our doubts."

As he spoke there was the sharp sound of horses' hoofs and grating wheels against the curb, followed by a sharp pull at the bell. Holmes whistled.

"A pair, by the sound," said he. "Yes," he continued, glancing out of the window. "A nice little brougham and a pair of beauties. A hundred and fifty guineas apiece. There's money in this case, Watson, if there is nothing else."

"I think that I had better go, Holmes."

"Not a bit, Doctor. Stay where you are. I am lost without my Boswell. And this promises to be interesting. It would be a pity to miss it."

"But your client—"

"Never mind him. I may want your help, and so may he. Here he comes. Sit down in that armchair, Doctor, and give us your best attention."

A slow and heavy step, which had been heard upon the stairs and in the passage, paused immediately outside the door. Then there was a loud and authoritative tap.

"Come in!" said Holmes.

A man entered who could hardly have been less than six feet six inches in height, with the chest and limbs of a Hercules. His dress was rich with a richness which would, in England, be looked upon as akin to bad taste. Heavy bands of astrakhan were slashed across the sleeves and fronts of his double-breasted coat, while the deep blue cloak which was thrown over his shoulders was lined with flame-coloured silk and secured at the neck with a brooch which consisted of a single flaming beryl. Boots which extended halfway up his calves, and which were trimmed at the tops with rich brown fur, completed the impression of barbaric opulence which was suggested by his whole appearance. He carried a broad-brimmed hat in his hand, while he wore across the upper part of his face, extending down past the cheekbones, a black vizard mask, which he had apparently adjusted that very moment, for his hand was still raised to it as he entered. From the lower part of the face he appeared to be a man of strong character, with a thick, hanging lip, and a long, straight chin suggestive of resolution pushed to the length of obstinacy.

"You had my note?" he asked with a deep harsh voice and a strongly marked German accent. "I told you that I would call." He looked from one to the other of us, as if uncertain which to address.

"Pray take a seat," said Holmes. "This is my friend and colleague, Dr. Watson, who is occasionally good enough to help me in my cases. Whom have I the honour to address?"

"You may address me as the Count Von Kramm, a Bohemian nobleman. I understand that this gentleman, your friend, is a man of honour and discretion, whom I may trust with a matter of the most extreme importance. If not, I should much prefer to communicate with you alone."

I rose to go, but Holmes caught me by the wrist and pushed me back into my chair. "It is both, or none," said he. "You may say before this gentleman anything which you may say to me."

4

The Count shrugged his broad shoulders. "Then I must begin," said he, "by binding you both to absolute secrecy for two years; at the end of that time the matter will be of no importance. At present it is not too much to say that it is of such weight it may have an influence upon European history."

"I promise," said Holmes.

"And I."

"You will excuse this mask," continued our strange visitor. "The august person who employs me wishes his agent to be unknown to you, and I may confess at once that the title by which I have just called myself is not exactly my own."

"I was aware of it," said Holmes dryly.

"The circumstances are of great delicacy, and every precaution has to be taken to quench what might grow to be an immense scandal and seriously compromise one of the reigning families of Europe. To speak plainly, the matter implicates the great House of Ormstein, hereditary kings of Bohemia."

"I was also aware of that," murmured Holmes, settling himself down in his armchair and closing his eyes.

Our visitor glanced with some apparent surprise at the languid, lounging figure of the man who had been no doubt depicted to him as the most incisive reasoner and most energetic agent in Europe. Holmes slowly reopened his eyes and looked impatiently at his gigantic client.

"If your Majesty would condescend to state your case," he remarked, "I should be better able to advise you."

The man sprang from his chair and paced up and down the room in uncontrollable agitation. Then, with a gesture of desperation, he tore the mask from his face and hurled it upon the ground. "You are right," he cried; "I am the King. Why should I attempt to conceal it?"

"Why, indeed?" murmured Holmes. "Your Majesty had not spoken before I was aware that I was addressing Wilhelm Gottsreich Sigismond von Ormstein, Grand Duke of Cassel-Felstein, and hereditary King of Bohemia."

"But you can understand," said our strange visitor, sitting down once more and passing his hand over his high white forehead, "you can understand that I am not accustomed to doing such business in my own person. Yet the matter was so delicate that I could not confide it to an agent without putting myself in his power. I have come *incognito* from Prague for the purpose of consulting you."

"Then, pray consult," said Holmes, shutting his eyes once more.

"The facts are briefly these: Some five years ago, during a lengthy visit to Warsaw, I made the acquaintance of the well-known adventuress, Irene Adler. The name is no doubt familiar to you."

"Kindly look her up in my index, Doctor," murmured Holmes without opening his eyes. For many years he had adopted a system of docketing all paragraphs concerning men and things, so that it was difficult to name a subject or a person on which he could not at once furnish information. In this case I found her biography sandwiched in between that of a Hebrew rabbi and that of a staff-commander who had written a monograph upon the deep-sea fishes.

"Let me see!" said Holmes. "Hum! Born in New Jersey in the year 1858. Contralto—hum! La Scala, hum! Prima donna Imperial Opera of Warsaw—yes! Retired from operatic

stage—ha! Living in London—quite so! Your Majesty, as I understand, became entangled with this young person, wrote her some compromising letters, and is now desirous of getting those letters back."

"Precisely so. But how—"

"Was there a secret marriage?"

"None."

"No legal papers or certificates?"

"None."

"Then I fail to follow your Majesty. If this young person should produce her letters for blackmailing or other purposes, how is she to prove their authenticity?"

"There is the writing."

"Pooh, pooh! Forgery."

"My private note-paper."

"Stolen."

"My own seal."

"Imitated."

"My photograph."

"Bought."

"We were both in the photograph."

"Oh, dear! That is very bad! Your Majesty has indeed committed an indiscretion."

"I was mad—insane."

"You have compromised yourself seriously."

"I was only Crown Prince then. I was young. I am but thirty now."

"It must be recovered."

"We have tried and failed."

"Your Majesty must pay. It must be bought."

"She will not sell."

"Stolen, then."

"Five attempts have been made. Twice burglars in my pay ransacked her house. Once we diverted her luggage when she travelled. Twice she has been waylaid. There has been no result."

"No sign of it?"

"Absolutely none."

Holmes laughed. "It is quite a pretty little problem," said he.

"But a very serious one to me," returned the King reproachfully.

"Very, indeed. And what does she propose to do with the photograph?"

"To ruin me."

"But how?"

"I am about to be married."

"So I have heard."

"To Clotilde Lothman von Saxe-Meningen, second daughter of the King of Scandinavia. You may know the strict principles of her family. She is herself the very soul of delicacy. A shadow of a doubt as to my conduct would bring the matter to an end."

"And Irene Adler?"

"Threatens to send them the photograph. And she will do it. I know that she will do it. You do not know her, but she has a soul of steel. She has the face of the most beautiful of

women, and the mind of the most resolute of men. Rather than I should marry another woman, there are no lengths to which she would not go—none."

"You are sure that she has not sent it yet?"

"I am sure."

"And why?"

"Because she has said that she would send it on the day when the betrothal was publicly proclaimed. That will be next Monday."

"Oh, then we have three days yet," said Holmes with a yawn. "That is very fortunate, as I have one or two matters of importance to look into just at present. Your Majesty will, of course, stay in London for the present?"

"Certainly. You will find me at the Langham under the name of the Count Von Kramm."

"Then I shall drop you a line to let you know how we progress."

"Pray do so. I shall be all anxiety."

"Then, as to money?"

"You have *carte blanche*."

"Absolutely?"

"I tell you that I would give one of the provinces of my kingdom to have that photograph."

"And for present expenses?"

The King took a heavy chamois leather bag from under his cloak and laid it on the table.

"There are three hundred pounds in gold and seven hundred in notes," he said.

Holmes scribbled a receipt upon a sheet of his note-book and handed it to him.

"And Mademoiselle's address?" he asked.

"Is Briony Lodge, Serpentine Avenue, St. John's Wood."

Holmes took a note of it. "One other question," said he. "Was the photograph a cabinet?"

"It was."

"Then, good-night, your Majesty, and I trust that we shall soon have some good news for you. And good-night, Watson," he added, as the wheels of the royal brougham rolled down the street. "If you will be good enough to call to-morrow afternoon at three o'clock I should like to chat this little matter over with you."

II.

At three o'clock precisely I was at Baker Street, but Holmes had not yet returned. The landlady informed me that he had left the house shortly after eight o'clock in the morning. I sat down beside the fire, however, with the intention of awaiting him, however long he might be. I was already deeply interested in his inquiry, for, though it was surrounded by none of the grim and strange features which were associated with the two crimes which I have already recorded, still, the nature of the case and the exalted station of his client gave it a character of its own. Indeed, apart from the nature of the investigation which my friend had on hand, there was something in his masterly grasp of a situation, and his keen, incisive reasoning, which made it a pleasure to me to study his system of work, and to follow the quick, subtle methods by which he disentangled the most inextricable

mysteries. So accustomed was I to his invariable success that the very possibility of his failing had ceased to enter into my head.

It was close upon four before the door opened, and a drunken-looking groom, ill-kempt and side-whiskered, with an inflamed face and disreputable clothes, walked into the room. Accustomed as I was to my friend's amazing powers in the use of disguises, I had to look three times before I was certain that it was indeed he. With a nod he vanished into the bedroom, whence he emerged in five minutes tweed-suited and respectable, as of old. Putting his hands into his pockets, he stretched out his legs in front of the fire and laughed heartily for some minutes.

"Well, really!" he cried, and then he choked and laughed again until he was obliged to lie back, limp and helpless, in the chair.

"What is it?"

"It's quite too funny. I am sure you could never guess how I employed my morning, or what I ended by doing."

"I can't imagine. I suppose that you have been watching the habits, and perhaps the house, of Miss Irene Adler."

"Quite so; but the sequel was rather unusual. I will tell you, however. I left the house a little after eight o'clock this morning in the character of a groom out of work. There is a wonderful sympathy and freemasonry among horsey men. Be one of them, and you will know all that there is to know. I soon found Briony Lodge. It is a *bijou* villa, with a garden at the back, but built out in front right up to the road, two stories. Chubb lock to the door. Large sitting-room on the right side, well furnished, with long windows almost to the floor, and those preposterous English window fasteners which a child could open. Behind there was nothing remarkable, save that the passage window could be reached from the top of the coach-house. I walked round it and examined it closely from every point of view, but without noting anything else of interest.

"I then lounged down the street and found, as I expected, that there was a mews in a lane which runs down by one wall of the garden. I lent the ostlers a hand in rubbing down their horses, and received in exchange twopence, a glass of half-and-half, two fills of shag tobacco, and as much information as I could desire about Miss Adler, to say nothing of half a dozen other people in the neighbourhood in whom I was not in the least interested, but whose biographies I was compelled to listen to."

"And what of Irene Adler?" I asked.

"Oh, she has turned all the men's heads down in that part. She is the daintiest thing under a bonnet on this planet. So say the Serpentine-mews, to a man. She lives quietly, sings at concerts, drives out at five every day, and returns at seven sharp for dinner. Seldom goes out at other times, except when she sings. Has only one male visitor, but a good deal of him. He is dark, handsome, and dashing, never calls less than once a day, and often twice. He is a Mr. Godfrey Norton, of the Inner Temple. See the advantages of a cabman as a confidant. They had driven him home a dozen times from Serpentine-mews, and knew all about him. When I had listened to all they had to tell, I began to walk up and down near Briony Lodge once more, and to think over my plan of campaign.

"This Godfrey Norton was evidently an important factor in the matter. He was a lawyer. That sounded ominous. What was the relation between them, and what the object of his repeated visits? Was she his client, his friend, or his mistress? If the former, she had probably transferred the photograph to his keeping. If the latter, it was less likely. On the

issue of this question depended whether I should continue my work at Briony Lodge, or turn my attention to the gentleman's chambers in the Temple. It was a delicate point, and it widened the field of my inquiry. I fear that I bore you with these details, but I have to let you see my little difficulties, if you are to understand the situation."

"I am following you closely," I answered.

"I was still balancing the matter in my mind when a hansom cab drove up to Briony Lodge, and a gentleman sprang out. He was a remarkably handsome man, dark, aquiline, and moustached—evidently the man of whom I had heard. He appeared to be in a great hurry, shouted to the cabman to wait, and brushed past the maid who opened the door with the air of a man who was thoroughly at home.

"He was in the house about half an hour, and I could catch glimpses of him in the windows of the sitting-room, pacing up and down, talking excitedly, and waving his arms. Of her I could see nothing. Presently he emerged, looking even more flurried than before. As he stepped up to the cab, he pulled a gold watch from his pocket and looked at it earnestly, 'Drive like the devil,' he shouted, 'first to Gross & Hankey's in Regent Street, and then to the Church of St. Monica in the Edgeware Road. Half a guinea if you do it in twenty minutes!'

"Away they went, and I was just wondering whether I should not do well to follow them when up the lane came a neat little landau, the coachman with his coat only half-buttoned, and his tie under his ear, while all the tags of his harness were sticking out of the buckles. It hadn't pulled up before she shot out of the hall door and into it. I only caught a glimpse of her at the moment, but she was a lovely woman, with a face that a man might die for.

"'The Church of St. Monica, John,' she cried, 'and half a sovereign if you reach it in twenty minutes.'

"This was quite too good to lose, Watson. I was just balancing whether I should run for it, or whether I should perch behind her landau when a cab came through the street. The driver looked twice at such a shabby fare, but I jumped in before he could object. 'The Church of St. Monica,' said I, 'and half a sovereign if you reach it in twenty minutes.' It was twenty-five minutes to twelve, and of course it was clear enough what was in the wind.

"My cabby drove fast. I don't think I ever drove faster, but the others were there before us. The cab and the landau with their steaming horses were in front of the door when I arrived. I paid the man and hurried into the church. There was not a soul there save the two whom I had followed and a surpliced clergyman, who seemed to be expostulating with them. They were all three standing in a knot in front of the altar. I lounged up the side aisle like any other idler who has dropped into a church. Suddenly, to my surprise, the three at the altar faced round to me, and Godfrey Norton came running as hard as he could towards me.

"'Thank God,' he cried. 'You'll do. Come! Come!'

"'What then?' I asked.

"'Come, man, come, only three minutes, or it won't be legal.'

"I was half-dragged up to the altar, and before I knew where I was I found myself mumbling responses which were whispered in my ear, and vouching for things of which I knew nothing, and generally assisting in the secure tying up of Irene Adler, spinster, to Godfrey Norton, bachelor. It was all done in an instant, and there was the gentleman

thanking me on the one side and the lady on the other, while the clergyman beamed on me in front. It was the most preposterous position in which I ever found myself in my life, and it was the thought of it that started me laughing just now. It seems that there had been some informality about their license, that the clergyman absolutely refused to marry them without a witness of some sort, and that my lucky appearance saved the bridegroom from having to sally out into the streets in search of a best man. The bride gave me a sovereign, and I mean to wear it on my watch chain in memory of the occasion."

"This is a very unexpected turn of affairs," said I; "and what then?"

"Well, I found my plans very seriously menaced. It looked as if the pair might take an immediate departure, and so necessitate very prompt and energetic measures on my part. At the church door, however, they separated, he driving back to the Temple, and she to her own house. 'I shall drive out in the park at five as usual,' she said as she left him. I heard no more. They drove away in different directions, and I went off to make my own arrangements."

"Which are?"

"Some cold beef and a glass of beer," he answered, ringing the bell. "I have been too busy to think of food, and I am likely to be busier still this evening. By the way, Doctor, I shall want your co-operation."

"I shall be delighted."

"You don't mind breaking the law?"

"Not in the least."

"Nor running a chance of arrest?"

"Not in a good cause."

"Oh, the cause is excellent!"

"Then I am your man."

"I was sure that I might rely on you."

"But what is it you wish?"

"When Mrs. Turner has brought in the tray I will make it clear to you. Now," he said as he turned hungrily on the simple fare that our landlady had provided, "I must discuss it while I eat, for I have not much time. It is nearly five now. In two hours we must be on the scene of action. Miss Irene, or Madame, rather, returns from her drive at seven. We must be at Briony Lodge to meet her."

"And what then?"

"You must leave that to me. I have already arranged what is to occur. There is only one point on which I must insist. You must not interfere, come what may. You understand?"

"I am to be neutral?"

"To do nothing whatever. There will probably be some small unpleasantness. Do not join in it. It will end in my being conveyed into the house. Four or five minutes afterwards the sitting-room window will open. You are to station yourself close to that open window."

"Yes."

"You are to watch me, for I will be visible to you."

"Yes."

"And when I raise my hand—so—you will throw into the room what I give you to throw, and will, at the same time, raise the cry of fire. You quite follow me?"

"Entirely."

"It is nothing very formidable," he said, taking a long cigar-shaped roll from his pocket. "It is an ordinary plumber's smoke-rocket, fitted with a cap at either end to make it self-lighting. Your task is confined to that. When you raise your cry of fire, it will be taken up by quite a number of people. You may then walk to the end of the street, and I will rejoin you in ten minutes. I hope that I have made myself clear?"

"I am to remain neutral, to get near the window, to watch you, and at the signal to throw in this object, then to raise the cry of fire, and to wait you at the corner of the street."

"Precisely."

"Then you may entirely rely on me."

"That is excellent. I think, perhaps, it is almost time that I prepare for the new role I have to play."

He disappeared into his bedroom and returned in a few minutes in the character of an amiable and simple-minded Nonconformist clergyman. His broad black hat, his baggy trousers, his white tie, his sympathetic smile, and general look of peering and benevolent curiosity were such as Mr. John Hare alone could have equalled. It was not merely that Holmes changed his costume. His expression, his manner, his very soul seemed to vary with every fresh part that he assumed. The stage lost a fine actor, even as science lost an acute reasoner, when he became a specialist in crime.

It was a quarter past six when we left Baker Street, and it still wanted ten minutes to the hour when we found ourselves in Serpentine Avenue. It was already dusk, and the lamps were just being lighted as we paced up and down in front of Briony Lodge, waiting for the coming of its occupant. The house was just such as I had pictured it from Sherlock Holmes' succinct description, but the locality appeared to be less private than I expected. On the contrary, for a small street in a quiet neighbourhood, it was remarkably animated. There was a group of shabbily dressed men smoking and laughing in a corner, a scissors-grinder with his wheel, two guardsmen who were flirting with a nurse-girl, and several well-dressed young men who were lounging up and down with cigars in their mouths.

"You see," remarked Holmes, as we paced to and fro in front of the house, "this marriage rather simplifies matters. The photograph becomes a double-edged weapon now. The chances are that she would be as averse to its being seen by Mr. Godfrey Norton, as our client is to its coming to the eyes of his princess. Now the question is, Where are we to find the photograph?"

"Where, indeed?"

"It is most unlikely that she carries it about with her. It is cabinet size. Too large for easy concealment about a woman's dress. She knows that the King is capable of having her waylaid and searched. Two attempts of the sort have already been made. We may take it, then, that she does not carry it about with her."

"Where, then?"

"Her banker or her lawyer. There is that double possibility. But I am inclined to think neither. Women are naturally secretive, and they like to do their own secreting. Why should she hand it over to anyone else? She could trust her own guardianship, but she could not tell what indirect or political influence might be brought to bear upon a business man. Besides, remember that she had resolved to use it within a few days. It must be where she can lay her hands upon it. It must be in her own house."

"But it has twice been burgled."

"Pshaw! They did not know how to look."

"But how will you look?"

"I will not look."

"What then?"

"I will get her to show me."

"But she will refuse."

"She will not be able to. But I hear the rumble of wheels. It is her carriage. Now carry out my orders to the letter."

As he spoke the gleam of the sidelights of a carriage came round the curve of the avenue. It was a smart little landau which rattled up to the door of Briony Lodge. As it pulled up, one of the loafing men at the corner dashed forward to open the door in the hope of earning a copper, but was elbowed away by another loafer, who had rushed up with the same intention. A fierce quarrel broke out, which was increased by the two guardsmen, who took sides with one of the loungers, and by the scissors-grinder, who was equally hot upon the other side. A blow was struck, and in an instant the lady, who had stepped from her carriage, was the centre of a little knot of flushed and struggling men, who struck savagely at each other with their fists and sticks. Holmes dashed into the crowd to protect the lady; but, just as he reached her, he gave a cry and dropped to the ground, with the blood running freely down his face. At his fall the guardsmen took to their heels in one direction and the loungers in the other, while a number of better dressed people, who had watched the scuffle without taking part in it, crowded in to help the lady and to attend to the injured man. Irene Adler, as I will still call her, had hurried up the steps; but she stood at the top with her superb figure outlined against the lights of the hall, looking back into the street.

"Is the poor gentleman much hurt?" she asked.

"He is dead," cried several voices.

"No, no, there's life in him!" shouted another. "But he'll be gone before you can get him to hospital."

"He's a brave fellow," said a woman. "They would have had the lady's purse and watch if it hadn't been for him. They were a gang, and a rough one, too. Ah, he's breathing now."

"He can't lie in the street. May we bring him in, marm?"

"Surely. Bring him into the sitting-room. There is a comfortable sofa. This way, please!"

Slowly and solemnly he was borne into Briony Lodge and laid out in the principal room, while I still observed the proceedings from my post by the window. The lamps had been lit, but the blinds had not been drawn, so that I could see Holmes as he lay upon the couch. I do not know whether he was seized with compunction at that moment for the part he was playing, but I know that I never felt more heartily ashamed of myself in my life than when I saw the beautiful creature against whom I was conspiring, or the grace and kindliness with which she waited upon the injured man. And yet it would be the blackest treachery to Holmes to draw back now from the part which he had intrusted to me. I hardened my heart, and took the smoke-rocket from under my ulster. After all, I thought, we are not injuring her. We are but preventing her from injuring another.

Holmes had sat up upon the couch, and I saw him motion like a man who is in need of air. A maid rushed across and threw open the window. At the same instant I saw him raise his hand and at the signal I tossed my rocket into the room with a cry of "Fire!" The word was no sooner out of my mouth than the whole crowd of spectators, well dressed and ill—

gentlemen, ostlers, and servant maids—joined in a general shriek of "Fire!" Thick clouds of smoke curled through the room and out at the open window. I caught a glimpse of rushing figures, and a moment later the voice of Holmes from within assuring them that it was a false alarm. Slipping through the shouting crowd I made my way to the corner of the street, and in ten minutes was rejoiced to find my friend's arm in mine, and to get away from the scene of uproar. He walked swiftly and in silence for some few minutes until we had turned down one of the quiet streets which lead towards the Edgeware Road.

"You did it very nicely, Doctor," he remarked. "Nothing could have been better. It is all right."

"You have the photograph?"

"I know where it is."

"And how did you find out?"

"She showed me, as I told you she would."

"I am still in the dark."

"I do not wish to make a mystery," said he, laughing. "The matter was perfectly simple. You, of course, saw that everyone in the street was an accomplice. They were all engaged for the evening."

"I guessed as much."

"Then, when the row broke out, I had a little moist red paint in the palm of my hand. I rushed forward, fell down, clapped my hand to my face, and became a piteous spectacle. It is an old trick."

"That also I could fathom."

"Then they carried me in. She was bound to have me in. What else could she do? And into her sitting-room, which was the very room which I suspected. It lay between that and her bedroom, and I was determined to see which. They laid me on a couch, I motioned for air, they were compelled to open the window, and you had your chance."

"How did that help you?"

"It was all-important. When a woman thinks that her house is on fire, her instinct is at once to rush to the thing which she values most. It is a perfectly overpowering impulse, and I have more than once taken advantage of it. In the case of the Darlington Substitution Scandal it was of use to me, and also in the Arnsworth Castle business. A married woman grabs at her baby; an unmarried one reaches for her jewel-box. Now it was clear to me that our lady of to-day had nothing in the house more precious to her than what we are in quest of. She would rush to secure it. The alarm of fire was admirably done. The smoke and shouting were enough to shake nerves of steel. She responded beautifully. The photograph is in a recess behind a sliding panel just above the right bell-pull. She was there in an instant, and I caught a glimpse of it as she half drew it out. When I cried out that it was a false alarm, she replaced it, glanced at the rocket, rushed from the room, and I have not seen her since. I rose, and, making my excuses, escaped from the house. I hesitated whether to attempt to secure the photograph at once; but the coachman had come in, and as he was watching me narrowly, it seemed safer to wait. A little over-precipitance may ruin all."

"And now?" I asked.

"Our quest is practically finished. I shall call with the King to-morrow, and with you, if you care to come with us. We will be shown into the sitting-room to wait for the lady, but

it is probable that when she comes she may find neither us nor the photograph. It might be a satisfaction to his Majesty to regain it with his own hands."

"And when will you call?"

"At eight in the morning. She will not be up, so that we shall have a clear field. Besides, we must be prompt, for this marriage may mean a complete change in her life and habits. I must wire to the King without delay."

We had reached Baker Street and had stopped at the door. He was searching his pockets for the key when someone passing said:

"Good-night, Mister Sherlock Holmes."

There were several people on the pavement at the time, but the greeting appeared to come from a slim youth in an ulster who had hurried by.

"I've heard that voice before," said Holmes, staring down the dimly lit street. "Now, I wonder who the deuce that could have been."

III.

I slept at Baker Street that night, and we were engaged upon our toast and coffee in the morning when the King of Bohemia rushed into the room.

"You have really got it!" he cried, grasping Sherlock Holmes by either shoulder and looking eagerly into his face.

"Not yet."

"But you have hopes?"

"I have hopes."

"Then, come. I am all impatience to be gone."

"We must have a cab."

"No, my brougham is waiting."

"Then that will simplify matters." We descended and started off once more for Briony Lodge.

"Irene Adler is married," remarked Holmes.

"Married! When?"

"Yesterday."

"But to whom?"

"To an English lawyer named Norton."

"But she could not love him."

"I am in hopes that she does."

"And why in hopes?"

"Because it would spare your Majesty all fear of future annoyance. If the lady loves her husband, she does not love your Majesty. If she does not love your Majesty, there is no reason why she should interfere with your Majesty's plan."

"It is true. And yet—! Well! I wish she had been of my own station! What a queen she would have made!" He relapsed into a moody silence, which was not broken until we drew up in Serpentine Avenue.

The door of Briony Lodge was open, and an elderly woman stood upon the steps. She watched us with a sardonic eye as we stepped from the brougham.

"Mr. Sherlock Holmes, I believe?" said she.

"I am Mr. Holmes," answered my companion, looking at her with a questioning and rather startled gaze.

"Indeed! My mistress told me that you were likely to call. She left this morning with her husband by the 5:15 train from Charing Cross for the Continent."

"What!" Sherlock Holmes staggered back, white with chagrin and surprise. "Do you mean that she has left England?"

"Never to return."

"And the papers?" asked the King hoarsely. "All is lost."

"We shall see." He pushed past the servant and rushed into the drawing-room, followed by the King and myself. The furniture was scattered about in every direction, with dismantled shelves and open drawers, as if the lady had hurriedly ransacked them before her flight. Holmes rushed at the bell-pull, tore back a small sliding shutter, and, plunging in his hand, pulled out a photograph and a letter. The photograph was of Irene Adler herself in evening dress, the letter was superscribed to "Sherlock Holmes, Esq. To be left till called for." My friend tore it open, and we all three read it together. It was dated at midnight of the preceding night and ran in this way:

"MY DEAR MR. SHERLOCK HOLMES,—You really did it very well. You took me in completely. Until after the alarm of fire, I had not a suspicion. But then, when I found how I had betrayed myself, I began to think. I had been warned against you months ago. I had been told that, if the King employed an agent, it would certainly be you. And your address had been given me. Yet, with all this, you made me reveal what you wanted to know. Even after I became suspicious, I found it hard to think evil of such a dear, kind old clergyman. But, you know, I have been trained as an actress myself. Male costume is nothing new to me. I often take advantage of the freedom which it gives. I sent John, the coachman, to watch you, ran upstairs, got into my walking clothes, as I call them, and came down just as you departed.

"Well, I followed you to your door, and so made sure that I was really an object of interest to the celebrated Mr. Sherlock Holmes. Then I, rather imprudently, wished you good-night, and started for the Temple to see my husband.

"We both thought the best resource was flight, when pursued by so formidable an antagonist; so you will find the nest empty when you call to-morrow. As to the photograph, your client may rest in peace. I love and am loved by a better man than he. The King may do what he will without hindrance from one whom he has cruelly wronged. I keep it only to safeguard myself, and to preserve a weapon which will always secure me from any steps which he might take in the future. I leave a photograph which he might care to possess; and I remain, dear Mr. Sherlock Holmes,

"Very truly yours,

"IRENE NORTON, née ADLER."

"What a woman—oh, what a woman!" cried the King of Bohemia, when we had all three read this epistle. "Did I not tell you how quick and resolute she was? Would she not have made an admirable queen? Is it not a pity that she was not on my level?"

"From what I have seen of the lady, she seems, indeed, to be on a very different level to your Majesty," said Holmes coldly. "I am sorry that I have not been able to bring your Majesty's business to a more successful conclusion."

"On the contrary, my dear sir," cried the King; "nothing could be more successful. I know that her word is inviolate. The photograph is now as safe as if it were in the fire."

"I am glad to hear your Majesty say so."

"I am immensely indebted to you. Pray tell me in what way I can reward you. This ring—" He slipped an emerald snake ring from his finger and held it out upon the palm of his hand.

"Your Majesty has something which I should value even more highly," said Holmes.

"You have but to name it."

"This photograph!"

The King stared at him in amazement.

"Irene's photograph!" he cried. "Certainly, if you wish it."

"I thank your Majesty. Then there is no more to be done in the matter. I have the honour to wish you a very good morning." He bowed, and, turning away without observing the hand which the King had stretched out to him, he set off in my company for his chambers.

And that was how a great scandal threatened to affect the kingdom of Bohemia, and how the best plans of Mr. Sherlock Holmes were beaten by a woman's wit. He used to make merry over the cleverness of women, but I have not heard him do it of late. And when he speaks of Irene Adler, or when he refers to her photograph, it is always under the honourable title of *the* woman.

THE RED-HEADED LEAGUE
FROM THE ADVENTURES OF SHERLOCK HOLMES (1892)

I HAD CALLED upon my friend, Mr. Sherlock Holmes, one day in the autumn of last year and found him in deep conversation with a very stout, florid-faced, elderly gentleman with fiery red hair. With an apology for my intrusion, I was about to withdraw when Holmes pulled me abruptly into the room and closed the door behind me.

"You could not possibly have come at a better time, my dear Watson," he said cordially.

"I was afraid that you were engaged."

"So I am. Very much so."

"Then I can wait in the next room."

"Not at all. This gentleman, Mr. Wilson, has been my partner and helper in many of my most successful cases, and I have no doubt that he will be of the utmost use to me in yours also."

The stout gentleman half rose from his chair and gave a bob of greeting, with a quick little questioning glance from his small fat-encircled eyes.

"Try the settee," said Holmes, relapsing into his armchair and putting his fingertips together, as was his custom when in judicial moods. "I know, my dear Watson, that you share my love of all that is bizarre and outside the conventions and humdrum routine of everyday life. You have shown your relish for it by the enthusiasm which has prompted you to chronicle, and, if you will excuse my saying so, somewhat to embellish so many of my own little adventures."

"Your cases have indeed been of the greatest interest to me," I observed.

"You will remember that I remarked the other day, just before we went into the very simple problem presented by Miss Mary Sutherland, that for strange effects and extraordinary combinations we must go to life itself, which is always far more daring than any effort of the imagination."

"A proposition which I took the liberty of doubting."

"You did, Doctor, but none the less you must come round to my view, for otherwise I shall keep on piling fact upon fact on you until your reason breaks down under them and acknowledges me to be right. Now, Mr. Jabez Wilson here has been good enough to call upon me this morning, and to begin a narrative which promises to be one of the most singular which I have listened to for some time. You have heard me remark that the strangest and most unique things are very often connected not with the larger but with the smaller crimes, and occasionally, indeed, where there is room for doubt whether any positive crime has been committed. As far as I have heard, it is impossible for me to say whether the present case is an instance of crime or not, but the course of events is certainly among the most singular that I have ever listened to. Perhaps, Mr. Wilson, you would have the great kindness to recommence your narrative. I ask you not merely because my friend Dr. Watson has not heard the opening part but also because the peculiar nature of the story makes me anxious to have every possible detail from your lips. As a rule, when I have heard some slight indication of the course of events, I am able to guide myself by the thousands of other similar cases which occur to my memory. In the present instance I am forced to admit that the facts are, to the best of my belief, unique."

The portly client puffed out his chest with an appearance of some little pride and pulled a dirty and wrinkled newspaper from the inside pocket of his greatcoat. As he glanced down the advertisement column, with his head thrust forward and the paper flattened out upon his knee, I took a good look at the man and endeavoured, after the fashion of my companion, to read the indications which might be presented by his dress or appearance.

I did not gain very much, however, by my inspection. Our visitor bore every mark of being an average commonplace British tradesman, obese, pompous, and slow. He wore rather baggy grey shepherd's check trousers, a not over-clean black frock-coat, unbuttoned in the front, and a drab waistcoat with a heavy brassy Albert chain, and a square pierced bit of metal dangling down as an ornament. A frayed top-hat and a faded brown overcoat with a wrinkled velvet collar lay upon a chair beside him. Altogether, look as I would, there was nothing remarkable about the man save his blazing red head, and the expression of extreme chagrin and discontent upon his features.

Sherlock Holmes' quick eye took in my occupation, and he shook his head with a smile as he noticed my questioning glances. "Beyond the obvious facts that he has at some time done manual labour, that he takes snuff, that he is a Freemason, that he has been in China, and that he has done a considerable amount of writing lately, I can deduce nothing else."

Mr. Jabez Wilson started up in his chair, with his forefinger upon the paper, but his eyes upon my companion.

"How, in the name of good-fortune, did you know all that, Mr. Holmes?" he asked. "How did you know, for example, that I did manual labour. It's as true as gospel, for I began as a ship's carpenter."

"Your hands, my dear sir. Your right hand is quite a size larger than your left. You have worked with it, and the muscles are more developed."

"Well, the snuff, then, and the Freemasonry?"

"I won't insult your intelligence by telling you how I read that, especially as, rather against the strict rules of your order, you use an arc-and-compass breastpin."

"Ah, of course, I forgot that. But the writing?"

"What else can be indicated by that right cuff so very shiny for five inches, and the left one with the smooth patch near the elbow where you rest it upon the desk?"

"Well, but China?"

"The fish that you have tattooed immediately above your right wrist could only have been done in China. I have made a small study of tattoo marks and have even contributed to the literature of the subject. That trick of staining the fishes' scales of a delicate pink is quite peculiar to China. When, in addition, I see a Chinese coin hanging from your watch-chain, the matter becomes even more simple."

Mr. Jabez Wilson laughed heavily. "Well, I never!" said he. "I thought at first that you had done something clever, but I see that there was nothing in it after all."

"I begin to think, Watson," said Holmes, "that I make a mistake in explaining. 'Omne ignotum pro magnifico,' you know, and my poor little reputation, such as it is, will suffer shipwreck if I am so candid. Can you not find the advertisement, Mr. Wilson?"

"Yes, I have got it now," he answered with his thick red finger planted halfway down the column. "Here it is. This is what began it all. You just read it for yourself, sir."

I took the paper from him and read as follows:

"TO THE RED-HEADED LEAGUE: On account of the bequest of the late Ezekiah Hopkins, of Lebanon, Pennsylvania, U.S.A., there is now another vacancy open which entitles a member of the League to a salary of £ 4 a week for purely nominal services. All red-headed men who are sound in body and mind and above the age of twenty-one years, are eligible. Apply in person on Monday, at eleven o'clock, to Duncan Ross, at the offices of the League, 7 Pope's Court, Fleet Street."

"What on earth does this mean?" I ejaculated after I had twice read over the extraordinary announcement.

Holmes chuckled and wriggled in his chair, as was his habit when in high spirits. "It is a little off the beaten track, isn't it?" said he. "And now, Mr. Wilson, off you go at scratch and tell us all about yourself, your household, and the effect which this advertisement had upon your fortunes. You will first make a note, Doctor, of the paper and the date."

"It is *The Morning Chronicle* of April 27, 1890. Just two months ago."

"Very good. Now, Mr. Wilson?"

"Well, it is just as I have been telling you, Mr. Sherlock Holmes," said Jabez Wilson, mopping his forehead; "I have a small pawnbroker's business at Coburg Square, near the City. It's not a very large affair, and of late years it has not done more than just give me a living. I used to be able to keep two assistants, but now I only keep one; and I would have a job to pay him but that he is willing to come for half wages so as to learn the business."

"What is the name of this obliging youth?" asked Sherlock Holmes.

"His name is Vincent Spaulding, and he's not such a youth, either. It's hard to say his age. I should not wish a smarter assistant, Mr. Holmes; and I know very well that he could better himself and earn twice what I am able to give him. But, after all, if he is satisfied, why should I put ideas in his head?"

"Why, indeed? You seem most fortunate in having an *employé* who comes under the full market price. It is not a common experience among employers in this age. I don't know that your assistant is not as remarkable as your advertisement."

"Oh, he has his faults, too," said Mr. Wilson. "Never was such a fellow for photography. Snapping away with a camera when he ought to be improving his mind, and then diving down into the cellar like a rabbit into its hole to develop his pictures. That is his main fault, but on the whole he's a good worker. There's no vice in him."

"He is still with you, I presume?"

"Yes, sir. He and a girl of fourteen, who does a bit of simple cooking and keeps the place clean—that's all I have in the house, for I am a widower and never had any family. We live very quietly, sir, the three of us; and we keep a roof over our heads and pay our debts, if we do nothing more.

"The first thing that put us out was that advertisement. Spaulding, he came down into the office just this day eight weeks, with this very paper in his hand, and he says:

"'I wish to the Lord, Mr. Wilson, that I was a red-headed man.'

"'Why that?' I asks.

"'Why,' says he, 'here's another vacancy on the League of the Red-headed Men. It's worth quite a little fortune to any man who gets it, and I understand that there are more vacancies than there are men, so that the trustees are at their wits' end what to do with the money. If my hair would only change colour, here's a nice little crib all ready for me to step into.'

"'Why, what is it, then?' I asked. You see, Mr. Holmes, I am a very stay-at-home man, and as my business came to me instead of my having to go to it, I was often weeks on end without putting my foot over the door-mat. In that way I didn't know much of what was going on outside, and I was always glad of a bit of news.

"'Have you never heard of the League of the Red-headed Men?' he asked with his eyes open.

"'Never.'

"'Why, I wonder at that, for you are eligible yourself for one of the vacancies.'

"'And what are they worth?' I asked.

"'Oh, merely a couple of hundred a year, but the work is slight, and it need not interfere very much with one's other occupations.'

"Well, you can easily think that that made me prick up my ears, for the business has not been over good for some years, and an extra couple of hundred would have been very handy.

"'Tell me all about it,' said I.

"'Well,' said he, showing me the advertisement, 'you can see for yourself that the League has a vacancy, and there is the address where you should apply for particulars. As far as I can make out, the League was founded by an American millionaire, Ezekiah Hopkins, who was very peculiar in his ways. He was himself red-headed, and he had a great sympathy for all red-headed men; so, when he died, it was found that he had left his enormous fortune in the hands of trustees, with instructions to apply the interest to the providing of easy berths to men whose hair is of that colour. From all I hear it is splendid pay and very little to do.'

"'But,' said I, 'there would be millions of red-headed men who would apply.'

"'Not so many as you might think,' he answered. 'You see it is really confined to Londoners, and to grown men. This American had started from London when he was young, and he wanted to do the old town a good turn. Then, again, I have heard it is no

use your applying if your hair is light red, or dark red, or anything but real bright, blazing, fiery red. Now, if you cared to apply, Mr. Wilson, you would just walk in; but perhaps it would hardly be worth your while to put yourself out of the way for the sake of a few hundred pounds.'

"Now, it is a fact, gentlemen, as you may see for yourselves, that my hair is of a very full and rich tint, so that it seemed to me that if there was to be any competition in the matter I stood as good a chance as any man that I had ever met. Vincent Spaulding seemed to know so much about it that I thought he might prove useful, so I just ordered him to put up the shutters for the day and to come right away with me. He was very willing to have a holiday, so we shut the business up and started off for the address that was given us in the advertisement.

"I never hope to see such a sight as that again, Mr. Holmes. From north, south, east, and west every man who had a shade of red in his hair had tramped into the city to answer the advertisement. Fleet Street was choked with red-headed folk, and Pope's Court looked like a coster's orange barrow. I should not have thought there were so many in the whole country as were brought together by that single advertisement. Every shade of colour they were—straw, lemon, orange, brick, Irish-setter, liver, clay; but, as Spaulding said, there were not many who had the real vivid flame-coloured tint. When I saw how many were waiting, I would have given it up in despair; but Spaulding would not hear of it. How he did it I could not imagine, but he pushed and pulled and butted until he got me through the crowd, and right up to the steps which led to the office. There was a double stream upon the stair, some going up in hope, and some coming back dejected; but we wedged in as well as we could and soon found ourselves in the office."

"Your experience has been a most entertaining one," remarked Holmes as his client paused and refreshed his memory with a huge pinch of snuff. "Pray continue your very interesting statement."

"There was nothing in the office but a couple of wooden chairs and a deal table, behind which sat a small man with a head that was even redder than mine. He said a few words to each candidate as he came up, and then he always managed to find some fault in them which would disqualify them. Getting a vacancy did not seem to be such a very easy matter, after all. However, when our turn came the little man was much more favourable to me than to any of the others, and he closed the door as we entered, so that he might have a private word with us.

"'This is Mr. Jabez Wilson,' said my assistant, 'and he is willing to fill a vacancy in the League.'

"'And he is admirably suited for it,' the other answered. 'He has every requirement. I cannot recall when I have seen anything so fine.' He took a step backward, cocked his head on one side, and gazed at my hair until I felt quite bashful. Then suddenly he plunged forward, wrung my hand, and congratulated me warmly on my success.

"'It would be injustice to hesitate,' said he. 'You will, however, I am sure, excuse me for taking an obvious precaution.' With that he seized my hair in both his hands, and tugged until I yelled with the pain. 'There is water in your eyes,' said he as he released me. 'I perceive that all is as it should be. But we have to be careful, for we have twice been deceived by wigs and once by paint. I could tell you tales of cobbler's wax which would disgust you with human nature.' He stepped over to the window and shouted through it

at the top of his voice that the vacancy was filled. A groan of disappointment came up from below, and the folk all trooped away in different directions until there was not a red-head to be seen except my own and that of the manager.

"'My name,' said he, 'is Mr. Duncan Ross, and I am myself one of the pensioners upon the fund left by our noble benefactor. Are you a married man, Mr. Wilson? Have you a family?'

"I answered that I had not.

"His face fell immediately.

"'Dear me!' he said gravely, 'that is very serious indeed! I am sorry to hear you say that. The fund was, of course, for the propagation and spread of the red-heads as well as for their maintenance. It is exceedingly unfortunate that you should be a bachelor.'

"My face lengthened at this, Mr. Holmes, for I thought that I was not to have the vacancy after all; but after thinking it over for a few minutes he said that it would be all right.

"'In the case of another,' said he, 'the objection might be fatal, but we must stretch a point in favour of a man with such a head of hair as yours. When shall you be able to enter upon your new duties?'

"'Well, it is a little awkward, for I have a business already,' said I.

"'Oh, never mind about that, Mr. Wilson!' said Vincent Spaulding. 'I should be able to look after that for you.'

"'What would be the hours?' I asked.

"'Ten to two.'

"Now a pawnbroker's business is mostly done of an evening, Mr. Holmes, especially Thursday and Friday evening, which is just before pay-day; so it would suit me very well to earn a little in the mornings. Besides, I knew that my assistant was a good man, and that he would see to anything that turned up.

"'That would suit me very well,' said I. 'And the pay?'

"'Is £ 4 a week.'

"'And the work?'

"'Is purely nominal.'

"'What do you call purely nominal?'

"'Well, you have to be in the office, or at least in the building, the whole time. If you leave, you forfeit your whole position forever. The will is very clear upon that point. You don't comply with the conditions if you budge from the office during that time.'

"'It's only four hours a day, and I should not think of leaving,' said I.

"'No excuse will avail,' said Mr. Duncan Ross; 'neither sickness nor business nor anything else. There you must stay, or you lose your billet.'

"'And the work?'

"'Is to copy out the *Encyclopædia Britannica*. There is the first volume of it in that press. You must find your own ink, pens, and blotting-paper, but we provide this table and chair. Will you be ready to-morrow?'

"'Certainly,' I answered.

"'Then, good-bye, Mr. Jabez Wilson, and let me congratulate you once more on the important position which you have been fortunate enough to gain.' He bowed me out of the room and I went home with my assistant, hardly knowing what to say or do, I was so pleased at my own good fortune.

"Well, I thought over the matter all day, and by evening I was in low spirits again; for I had quite persuaded myself that the whole affair must be some great hoax or fraud, though what its object might be I could not imagine. It seemed altogether past belief that anyone could make such a will, or that they would pay such a sum for doing anything so simple as copying out the *Encyclopædia Britannica*. Vincent Spaulding did what he could to cheer me up, but by bedtime I had reasoned myself out of the whole thing. However, in the morning I determined to have a look at it anyhow, so I bought a penny bottle of ink, and with a quill-pen, and seven sheets of foolscap paper, I started off for Pope's Court.

"Well, to my surprise and delight, everything was as right as possible. The table was set out ready for me, and Mr. Duncan Ross was there to see that I got fairly to work. He started me off upon the letter A, and then he left me; but he would drop in from time to time to see that all was right with me. At two o'clock he bade me good-day, complimented me upon the amount that I had written, and locked the door of the office after me.

"This went on day after day, Mr. Holmes, and on Saturday the manager came in and planked down four golden sovereigns for my week's work. It was the same next week, and the same the week after. Every morning I was there at ten, and every afternoon I left at two. By degrees Mr. Duncan Ross took to coming in only once of a morning, and then, after a time, he did not come in at all. Still, of course, I never dared to leave the room for an instant, for I was not sure when he might come, and the billet was such a good one, and suited me so well, that I would not risk the loss of it.

"Eight weeks passed away like this, and I had written about Abbots and Archery and Armour and Architecture and Attica, and hoped with diligence that I might get on to the B's before very long. It cost me something in foolscap, and I had pretty nearly filled a shelf with my writings. And then suddenly the whole business came to an end."

"To an end?"

"Yes, sir. And no later than this morning. I went to my work as usual at ten o'clock, but the door was shut and locked, with a little square of cardboard hammered on to the middle of the panel with a tack. Here it is, and you can read for yourself."

He held up a piece of white cardboard about the size of a sheet of note-paper. It read in this fashion:

"THE RED-HEADED LEAGUE IS DISSOLVED. October 9, 1890."

Sherlock Holmes and I surveyed this curt announcement and the rueful face behind it, until the comical side of the affair so completely overtopped every other consideration that we both burst out into a roar of laughter.

"I cannot see that there is anything very funny," cried our client, flushing up to the roots of his flaming head. "If you can do nothing better than laugh at me, I can go elsewhere."

"No, no," cried Holmes, shoving him back into the chair from which he had half risen. "I really wouldn't miss your case for the world. It is most refreshingly unusual. But there is, if you will excuse my saying so, something just a little funny about it. Pray what steps did you take when you found the card upon the door?"

"I was staggered, sir. I did not know what to do. Then I called at the offices round, but none of them seemed to know anything about it. Finally, I went to the landlord, who is an accountant living on the ground floor, and I asked him if he could tell me what had

become of the Red-headed League. He said that he had never heard of any such body. Then I asked him who Mr. Duncan Ross was. He answered that the name was new to him.

"'Well,' said I, 'the gentleman at No. 4.'

"'What, the red-headed man?'

"'Yes.'

"'Oh,' said he, 'his name was William Morris. He was a solicitor and was using my room as a temporary convenience until his new premises were ready. He moved out yesterday.'

"'Where could I find him?'

"'Oh, at his new offices. He did tell me the address. Yes, 17 King Edward Street, near St. Paul's.'

"I started off, Mr. Holmes, but when I got to that address it was a manufactory of artificial knee-caps, and no one in it had ever heard of either Mr. William Morris or Mr. Duncan Ross."

"And what did you do then?" asked Holmes.

"I went home to Saxe-Coburg Square, and I took the advice of my assistant. But he could not help me in any way. He could only say that if I waited I should hear by post. But that was not quite good enough, Mr. Holmes. I did not wish to lose such a place without a struggle, so, as I had heard that you were good enough to give advice to poor folk who were in need of it, I came right away to you."

"And you did very wisely," said Holmes. "Your case is an exceedingly remarkable one, and I shall be happy to look into it. From what you have told me I think that it is possible that graver issues hang from it than might at first sight appear."

"Grave enough!" said Mr. Jabez Wilson. "Why, I have lost four pound a week "

"As far as you are personally concerned," remarked Holmes, "I do not see that you have any grievance against this extraordinary league. On the contrary, you are, as I understand, richer by some £ 30, to say nothing of the minute knowledge which you have gained on every subject which comes under the letter A. You have lost nothing by them."

"No, sir. But I want to find out about them, and who they are, and what their object was in playing this prank—if it was a prank—upon me. It was a pretty expensive joke for them, for it cost them two and thirty pounds."

"We shall endeavour to clear up these points for you. And, first, one or two questions, Mr. Wilson. This assistant of yours who first called your attention to the advertisement—how long had he been with you?"

"About a month then."

"How did he come?"

"In answer to an advertisement."

"Was he the only applicant?"

"No, I had a dozen."

"Why did you pick him?"

"Because he was handy and would come cheap."

"At half wages, in fact."

"Yes."

"What is he like, this Vincent Spaulding?"

"Small, stout-built, very quick in his ways, no hair on his face, though he's not short of thirty. Has a white splash of acid upon his forehead."

Holmes sat up in his chair in considerable excitement. "I thought as much," said he. "Have you ever observed that his ears are pierced for earrings?"

"Yes, sir. He told me that a gipsy had done it for him when he was a lad."

"Hum!" said Holmes, sinking back in deep thought. "He is still with you?"

"Oh, yes, sir; I have only just left him."

"And has your business been attended to in your absence?"

"Nothing to complain of, sir. There's never very much to do of a morning."

"That will do, Mr. Wilson. I shall be happy to give you an opinion upon the subject in the course of a day or two. To-day is Saturday, and I hope that by Monday we may come to a conclusion."

"Well, Watson," said Holmes when our visitor had left us, "what do you make of it all?"

"I make nothing of it," I answered frankly. "It is a most mysterious business."

"As a rule," said Holmes, "the more bizarre a thing is the less mysterious it proves to be. It is your commonplace, featureless crimes which are really puzzling, just as a commonplace face is the most difficult to identify. But I must be prompt over this matter."

"What are you going to do, then?" I asked.

"To smoke," he answered. "It is quite a three pipe problem, and I beg that you won't speak to me for fifty minutes." He curled himself up in his chair, with his thin knees drawn up to his hawk-like nose, and there he sat with his eyes closed and his black clay pipe thrusting out like the bill of some strange bird. I had come to the conclusion that he had dropped asleep, and indeed was nodding myself, when he suddenly sprang out of his chair with the gesture of a man who has made up his mind and put his pipe down upon the mantelpiece.

"Sarasate plays at the St. James's Hall this afternoon," he remarked. "What do you think, Watson? Could your patients spare you for a few hours?"

"I have nothing to do to-day. My practice is never very absorbing."

"Then put on your hat and come. I am going through the City first, and we can have some lunch on the way. I observe that there is a good deal of German music on the programme, which is rather more to my taste than Italian or French. It is introspective, and I want to introspect. Come along!"

We travelled by the Underground as far as Aldersgate; and a short walk took us to Saxe-Coburg Square, the scene of the singular story which we had listened to in the morning. It was a poky, little, shabby-genteel place, where four lines of dingy two-storied brick houses looked out into a small railed-in enclosure, where a lawn of weedy grass and a few clumps of faded laurel bushes made a hard fight against a smoke-laden and uncongenial atmosphere. Three gilt balls and a brown board with "JABEZ WILSON" in white letters, upon a corner house, announced the place where our red-headed client carried on his business. Sherlock Holmes stopped in front of it with his head on one side and looked it all over, with his eyes shining brightly between puckered lids. Then he walked slowly up the street, and then down again to the corner, still looking keenly at the houses. Finally he returned to the pawnbroker's, and, having thumped vigorously upon the pavement with his stick two or three times, he went up to the door and knocked. It was instantly opened by a bright-looking, clean-shaven young fellow, who asked him to step in.

"Thank you," said Holmes, "I only wished to ask you how you would go from here to the Strand."

"Third right, fourth left," answered the assistant promptly, closing the door.

"Smart fellow, that," observed Holmes as we walked away. "He is, in my judgment, the fourth smartest man in London, and for daring I am not sure that he has not a claim to be third. I have known something of him before."

"Evidently," said I, "Mr. Wilson's assistant counts for a good deal in this mystery of the Red-headed League. I am sure that you inquired your way merely in order that you might see him."

"Not him."

"What then?"

"The knees of his trousers."

"And what did you see?"

"What I expected to see."

"Why did you beat the pavement?"

"My dear doctor, this is a time for observation, not for talk. We are spies in an enemy's country. We know something of Saxe-Coburg Square. Let us now explore the parts which lie behind it."

The road in which we found ourselves as we turned round the corner from the retired Saxe-Coburg Square presented as great a contrast to it as the front of a picture does to the back. It was one of the main arteries which conveyed the traffic of the City to the north and west. The roadway was blocked with the immense stream of commerce flowing in a double tide inward and outward, while the footpaths were black with the hurrying swarm of pedestrians. It was difficult to realise as we looked at the line of fine shops and stately business premises that they really abutted on the other side upon the faded and stagnant square which we had just quitted.

"Let me see," said Holmes, standing at the corner and glancing along the line, "I should like just to remember the order of the houses here. It is a hobby of mine to have an exact knowledge of London. There is Mortimer's, the tobacconist, the little newspaper shop, the Coburg branch of the City and Suburban Bank, the Vegetarian Restaurant, and McFarlane's carriage-building depot. That carries us right on to the other block. And now, Doctor, we've done our work, so it's time we had some play. A sandwich and a cup of coffee, and then off to violin-land, where all is sweetness and delicacy and harmony, and there are no red-headed clients to vex us with their conundrums."

My friend was an enthusiastic musician, being himself not only a very capable performer but a composer of no ordinary merit. All the afternoon he sat in the stalls wrapped in the most perfect happiness, gently waving his long, thin fingers in time to the music, while his gently smiling face and his languid, dreamy eyes were as unlike those of Holmes the sleuth-hound, Holmes the relentless, keen-witted, ready-handed criminal agent, as it was possible to conceive. In his singular character the dual nature alternately asserted itself, and his extreme exactness and astuteness represented, as I have often thought, the reaction against the poetic and contemplative mood which occasionally predominated in him. The swing of his nature took him from extreme languor to devouring energy; and, as I knew well, he was never so truly formidable as when, for days on end, he had been lounging in his armchair amid his improvisations and his black-letter editions. Then it was that the lust of the chase would suddenly come upon him, and

that his brilliant reasoning power would rise to the level of intuition, until those who were unacquainted with his methods would look askance at him as on a man whose knowledge was not that of other mortals. When I saw him that afternoon so enwrapped in the music at St. James's Hall I felt that an evil time might be coming upon those whom he had set himself to hunt down.

"You want to go home, no doubt, Doctor," he remarked as we emerged.

"Yes, it would be as well."

"And I have some business to do which will take some hours. This business at Coburg Square is serious."

"Why serious?"

"A considerable crime is in contemplation. I have every reason to believe that we shall be in time to stop it. But to-day being Saturday rather complicates matters. I shall want your help to-night."

"At what time?"

"Ten will be early enough."

"I shall be at Baker Street at ten."

"Very well. And, I say, Doctor, there may be some little danger, so kindly put your army revolver in your pocket." He waved his hand, turned on his heel, and disappeared in an instant among the crowd.

I trust that I am not more dense than my neighbours, but I was always oppressed with a sense of my own stupidity in my dealings with Sherlock Holmes. Here I had heard what he had heard, I had seen what he had seen, and yet from his words it was evident that he saw clearly not only what had happened but what was about to happen, while to me the whole business was still confused and grotesque. As I drove home to my house in Kensington I thought over it all, from the extraordinary story of the red-headed copier of the *Encyclopædia* down to the visit to Saxe-Coburg Square, and the ominous words with which he had parted from me. What was this nocturnal expedition, and why should I go armed? Where were we going, and what were we to do? I had the hint from Holmes that this smooth-faced pawnbroker's assistant was a formidable man—a man who might play a deep game. I tried to puzzle it out, but gave it up in despair and set the matter aside until night should bring an explanation.

It was a quarter-past nine when I started from home and made my way across the Park, and so through Oxford Street to Baker Street. Two hansoms were standing at the door, and as I entered the passage I heard the sound of voices from above. On entering his room, I found Holmes in animated conversation with two men, one of whom I recognised as Peter Jones, the official police agent, while the other was a long, thin, sad-faced man, with a very shiny hat and oppressively respectable frock-coat.

"Ha! Our party is complete," said Holmes, buttoning up his pea-jacket and taking his heavy hunting crop from the rack. "Watson, I think you know Mr. Jones, of Scotland Yard? Let me introduce you to Mr. Merryweather, who is to be our companion in to-night's adventure."

"We're hunting in couples again, Doctor, you see," said Jones in his consequential way. "Our friend here is a wonderful man for starting a chase. All he wants is an old dog to help him to do the running down."

"I hope a wild goose may not prove to be the end of our chase," observed Mr. Merryweather gloomily.

"You may place considerable confidence in Mr. Holmes, sir," said the police agent loftily. "He has his own little methods, which are, if he won't mind my saying so, just a little too theoretical and fantastic, but he has the makings of a detective in him. It is not too much to say that once or twice, as in that business of the Sholto murder and the Agra treasure, he has been more nearly correct than the official force."

"Oh, if you say so, Mr. Jones, it is all right," said the stranger with deference. "Still, I confess that I miss my rubber. It is the first Saturday night for seven-and-twenty years that I have not had my rubber."

"I think you will find," said Sherlock Holmes, "that you will play for a higher stake to-night than you have ever done yet, and that the play will be more exciting. For you, Mr. Merryweather, the stake will be some £ 30,000; and for you, Jones, it will be the man upon whom you wish to lay your hands."

"John Clay, the murderer, thief, smasher, and forger. He's a young man, Mr. Merryweather, but he is at the head of his profession, and I would rather have my bracelets on him than on any criminal in London. He's a remarkable man, is young John Clay. His grandfather was a royal duke, and he himself has been to Eton and Oxford. His brain is as cunning as his fingers, and though we meet signs of him at every turn, we never know where to find the man himself. He'll crack a crib in Scotland one week, and be raising money to build an orphanage in Cornwall the next. I've been on his track for years and have never set eyes on him yet."

"I hope that I may have the pleasure of introducing you to-night. I've had one or two little turns also with Mr. John Clay, and I agree with you that he is at the head of his profession. It is past ten, however, and quite time that we started. If you two will take the first hansom, Watson and I will follow in the second."

Sherlock Holmes was not very communicative during the long drive and lay back in the cab humming the tunes which he had heard in the afternoon. We rattled through an endless labyrinth of gas-lit streets until we emerged into Farrington Street.

"We are close there now," my friend remarked. "This fellow Merryweather is a bank director, and personally interested in the matter. I thought it as well to have Jones with us also. He is not a bad fellow, though an absolute imbecile in his profession. He has one positive virtue. He is as brave as a bulldog and as tenacious as a lobster if he gets his claws upon anyone. Here we are, and they are waiting for us."

We had reached the same crowded thoroughfare in which we had found ourselves in the morning. Our cabs were dismissed, and, following the guidance of Mr. Merryweather, we passed down a narrow passage and through a side door, which he opened for us. Within there was a small corridor, which ended in a very massive iron gate. This also was opened, and led down a flight of winding stone steps, which terminated at another formidable gate. Mr. Merryweather stopped to light a lantern, and then conducted us down a dark, earth-smelling passage, and so, after opening a third door, into a huge vault or cellar, which was piled all round with crates and massive boxes.

"You are not very vulnerable from above," Holmes remarked as he held up the lantern and gazed about him.

"Nor from below," said Mr. Merryweather, striking his stick upon the flags which lined the floor. "Why, dear me, it sounds quite hollow!" he remarked, looking up in surprise.

"I must really ask you to be a little more quiet!" said Holmes severely. "You have

already imperilled the whole success of our expedition. Might I beg that you would have the goodness to sit down upon one of those boxes, and not to interfere?"

The solemn Mr. Merryweather perched himself upon a crate, with a very injured expression upon his face, while Holmes fell upon his knees upon the floor and, with the lantern and a magnifying lens, began to examine minutely the cracks between the stones. A few seconds sufficed to satisfy him, for he sprang to his feet again and put his glass in his pocket.

"We have at least an hour before us," he remarked, "for they can hardly take any steps until the good pawnbroker is safely in bed. Then they will not lose a minute, for the sooner they do their work the longer time they will have for their escape. We are at present, Doctor—as no doubt you have divined—in the cellar of the City branch of one of the principal London banks. Mr. Merryweather is the chairman of directors, and he will explain to you that there are reasons why the more daring criminals of London should take a considerable interest in this cellar at present."

"It is our French gold," whispered the director. "We have had several warnings that an attempt might be made upon it."

"Your French gold?"

"Yes. We had occasion some months ago to strengthen our resources and borrowed for that purpose 30,000 napoleons from the Bank of France. It has become known that we have never had occasion to unpack the money, and that it is still lying in our cellar. The crate upon which I sit contains 2,000 napoleons packed between layers of lead foil. Our reserve of bullion is much larger at present than is usually kept in a single branch office, and the directors have had misgivings upon the subject."

"Which were very well justified," observed Holmes. "And now it is time that we arranged our little plans. I expect that within an hour matters will come to a head. In the meantime Mr. Merryweather, we must put the screen over that dark lantern."

"And sit in the dark?"

"I am afraid so. I had brought a pack of cards in my pocket, and I thought that, as we were a *partie carrée*, you might have your rubber after all. But I see that the enemy's preparations have gone so far that we cannot risk the presence of a light. And, first of all, we must choose our positions. These are daring men, and though we shall take them at a disadvantage, they may do us some harm unless we are careful. I shall stand behind this crate, and do you conceal yourselves behind those. Then, when I flash a light upon them, close in swiftly. If they fire, Watson, have no compunction about shooting them down."

I placed my revolver, cocked, upon the top of the wooden case behind which I crouched. Holmes shot the slide across the front of his lantern and left us in pitch darkness —such an absolute darkness as I have never before experienced. The smell of hot metal remained to assure us that the light was still there, ready to flash out at a moment's notice. To me, with my nerves worked up to a pitch of expectancy, there was something depressing and subduing in the sudden gloom, and in the cold dank air of the vault.

"They have but one retreat," whispered Holmes. "That is back through the house into Saxe-Coburg Square. I hope that you have done what I asked you, Jones?"

"I have an inspector and two officers waiting at the front door."

"Then we have stopped all the holes. And now we must be silent and wait."

What a time it seemed! From comparing notes afterwards it was but an hour and a quarter, yet it appeared to me that the night must have almost gone, and the dawn be

breaking above us. My limbs were weary and stiff, for I feared to change my position; yet my nerves were worked up to the highest pitch of tension, and my hearing was so acute that I could not only hear the gentle breathing of my companions, but I could distinguish the deeper, heavier in-breath of the bulky Jones from the thin, sighing note of the bank director. From my position I could look over the case in the direction of the floor. Suddenly my eyes caught the glint of a light.

At first it was but a lurid spark upon the stone pavement. Then it lengthened out until it became a yellow line, and then, without any warning or sound, a gash seemed to open and a hand appeared, a white, almost womanly hand, which felt about in the centre of the little area of light. For a minute or more the hand, with its writhing fingers, protruded out of the floor. Then it was withdrawn as suddenly as it appeared, and all was dark again save the single lurid spark which marked a chink between the stones.

Its disappearance, however, was but momentary. With a rending, tearing sound, one of the broad, white stones turned over upon its side and left a square, gaping hole, through which streamed the light of a lantern. Over the edge there peeped a clean-cut, boyish face, which looked keenly about it, and then, with a hand on either side of the aperture, drew itself shoulder-high and waist-high, until one knee rested upon the edge. In another instant he stood at the side of the hole and was hauling after him a companion, lithe and small like himself, with a pale face and a shock of very red hair.

"It's all clear," he whispered. "Have you the chisel and the bags? Great Scott! Jump, Archie, jump, and I'll swing for it!"

Sherlock Holmes had sprung out and seized the intruder by the collar. The other dived down the hole, and I heard the sound of rending cloth as Jones clutched at his skirts. The light flashed upon the barrel of a revolver, but Holmes' hunting crop came down on the man's wrist, and the pistol clinked upon the stone floor.

"It's no use, John Clay," said Holmes blandly. "You have no chance at all."

"So I see," the other answered with the utmost coolness. "I fancy that my pal is all right, though I see you have got his coat-tails."

"There are three men waiting for him at the door," said Holmes.

"Oh, indeed! You seem to have done the thing very completely. I must compliment you."

"And I you," Holmes answered. "Your red-headed idea was very new and effective."

"You'll see your pal again presently," said Jones. "He's quicker at climbing down holes than I am. Just hold out while I fix the derbies."

"I beg that you will not touch me with your filthy hands," remarked our prisoner as the handcuffs clattered upon his wrists. "You may not be aware that I have royal blood in my veins. Have the goodness, also, when you address me always to say 'sir' and 'please.'"

"All right," said Jones with a stare and a snigger. "Well, would you please, sir, march upstairs, where we can get a cab to carry your Highness to the police-station?"

"That is better," said John Clay serenely. He made a sweeping bow to the three of us and walked quietly off in the custody of the detective.

"Really, Mr. Holmes," said Mr. Merryweather as we followed them from the cellar, "I do not know how the bank can thank you or repay you. There is no doubt that you have detected and defeated in the most complete manner one of the most determined attempts at bank robbery that have ever come within my experience."

"I have had one or two little scores of my own to settle with Mr. John Clay," said

Holmes. "I have been at some small expense over this matter, which I shall expect the bank to refund, but beyond that I am amply repaid by having had an experience which is in many ways unique, and by hearing the very remarkable narrative of the Red-headed League."

"You see, Watson," he explained in the early hours of the morning as we sat over a glass of whisky and soda in Baker Street, "it was perfectly obvious from the first that the only possible object of this rather fantastic business of the advertisement of the League, and the copying of the *Encyclopædia*, must be to get this not over-bright pawnbroker out of the way for a number of hours every day. It was a curious way of managing it, but, really, it would be difficult to suggest a better. The method was no doubt suggested to Clay's ingenious mind by the colour of his accomplice's hair. The £ 4 a week was a lure which must draw him, and what was it to them, who were playing for thousands? They put in the advertisement, one rogue has the temporary office, the other rogue incites the man to apply for it, and together they manage to secure his absence every morning in the week. From the time that I heard of the assistant having come for half wages, it was obvious to me that he had some strong motive for securing the situation."

"But how could you guess what the motive was?"

"Had there been women in the house, I should have suspected a mere vulgar intrigue. That, however, was out of the question. The man's business was a small one, and there was nothing in his house which could account for such elaborate preparations, and such an expenditure as they were at. It must, then, be something out of the house. What could it be? I thought of the assistant's fondness for photography, and his trick of vanishing into the cellar. The cellar! There was the end of this tangled clue. Then I made inquiries as to this mysterious assistant and found that I had to deal with one of the coolest and most daring criminals in London. He was doing something in the cellar—something which took many hours a day for months on end. What could it be, once more? I could think of nothing save that he was running a tunnel to some other building.

"So far I had got when we went to visit the scene of action. I surprised you by beating upon the pavement with my stick. I was ascertaining whether the cellar stretched out in front or behind. It was not in front. Then I rang the bell, and, as I hoped, the assistant answered it. We have had some skirmishes, but we had never set eyes upon each other before. I hardly looked at his face. His knees were what I wished to see. You must yourself have remarked how worn, wrinkled, and stained they were. They spoke of those hours of burrowing. The only remaining point was what they were burrowing for. I walked round the corner, saw the City and Suburban Bank abutted on our friend's premises, and felt that I had solved my problem. When you drove home after the concert I called upon Scotland Yard and upon the chairman of the bank directors, with the result that you have seen."

"And how could you tell that they would make their attempt to-night?" I asked.

"Well, when they closed their League offices that was a sign that they cared no longer about Mr. Jabez Wilson's presence—in other words, that they had completed their tunnel. But it was essential that they should use it soon, as it might be discovered, or the bullion might be removed. Saturday would suit them better than any other day, as it would give them two days for their escape. For all these reasons I expected them to come to-night."

"You reasoned it out beautifully," I exclaimed in unfeigned admiration. "It is so long a chain, and yet every link rings true."

"It saved me from ennui," he answered, yawning. "Alas! I already feel it closing in

upon me. My life is spent in one long effort to escape from the commonplaces of existence. These little problems help me to do so."

"And you are a benefactor of the race," said I.

He shrugged his shoulders. "Well, perhaps, after all, it is of some little use," he remarked. *"'L'homme c'est rien — l'œuvre c'est tout,'* as Gustave Flaubert wrote to George Sand."

THE FIVE ORANGE PIPS

FROM THE ADVENTURES OF SHERLOCK HOLMES (1892)

WHEN I GLANCE over my notes and records of the Sherlock Holmes cases between the years '82 and '90, I am faced by so many which present strange and interesting features that it is no easy matter to know which to choose and which to leave. Some, however, have already gained publicity through the papers, and others have not offered a field for those peculiar qualities which my friend possessed in so high a degree, and which it is the object of these papers to illustrate. Some, too, have baffled his analytical skill, and would be, as narratives, beginnings without an ending, while others have been but partially cleared up, and have their explanations founded rather upon conjecture and surmise than on that absolute logical proof which was so dear to him. There is, however, one of these last which was so remarkable in its details and so startling in its results that I am tempted to give some account of it in spite of the fact that there are points in connection with it which never have been, and probably never will be, entirely cleared up.

The year '87 furnished us with a long series of cases of greater or less interest, of which I retain the records. Among my headings under this one twelve months I find an account of the adventure of the Paradol Chamber, of the Amateur Mendicant Society, who held a luxurious club in the lower vault of a furniture warehouse, of the facts connected with the loss of the British barque *Sophy Anderson*, of the singular adventures of the Grice Patersons in the island of Uffa, and finally of the Camberwell poisoning case. In the latter, as may be remembered, Sherlock Holmes was able, by winding up the dead man's watch, to prove that it had been wound up two hours before, and that therefore the deceased had gone to bed within that time—a deduction which was of the greatest importance in clearing up the case. All these I may sketch out at some future date, but none of them present such singular features as the strange train of circumstances which I have now taken up my pen to describe.

It was in the latter days of September, and the equinoctial gales had set in with exceptional violence. All day the wind had screamed and the rain had beaten against the windows, so that even here in the heart of great, hand-made London we were forced to

raise our minds for the instant from the routine of life and to recognise the presence of those great elemental forces which shriek at mankind through the bars of his civilisation, like untamed beasts in a cage. As evening drew in, the storm grew higher and louder, and the wind cried and sobbed like a child in the chimney. Sherlock Holmes sat moodily at one side of the fireplace cross-indexing his records of crime, while I at the other was deep in one of Clark Russell's fine sea-stories until the howl of the gale from without seemed to blend with the text, and the splash of the rain to lengthen out into the long swash of the sea waves. My wife was on a visit to her mother's, and for a few days I was a dweller once more in my old quarters at Baker Street.

"Why," said I, glancing up at my companion, "that was surely the bell. Who could come to-night? Some friend of yours, perhaps?"

"Except yourself I have none," he answered. "I do not encourage visitors."

"A client, then?"

"If so, it is a serious case. Nothing less would bring a man out on such a day and at such an hour. But I take it that it is more likely to be some crony of the landlady's."

Sherlock Holmes was wrong in his conjecture, however, for there came a step in the passage and a tapping at the door. He stretched out his long arm to turn the lamp away from himself and towards the vacant chair upon which a newcomer must sit.

"Come in!" said he.

The man who entered was young, some two-and-twenty at the outside, well-groomed and trimly clad, with something of refinement and delicacy in his bearing. The streaming umbrella which he held in his hand, and his long shining waterproof told of the fierce weather through which he had come. He looked about him anxiously in the glare of the lamp, and I could see that his face was pale and his eyes heavy, like those of a man who is weighed down with some great anxiety.

"I owe you an apology," he said, raising his golden pince-nez to his eyes. "I trust that I am not intruding. I fear that I have brought some traces of the storm and rain into your snug chamber."

"Give me your coat and umbrella," said Holmes. "They may rest here on the hook and will be dry presently. You have come up from the south-west, I see."

"Yes, from Horsham."

"That clay and chalk mixture which I see upon your toe caps is quite distinctive."

"I have come for advice."

"That is easily got."

"And help."

"That is not always so easy."

"I have heard of you, Mr. Holmes. I heard from Major Prendergast how you saved him in the Tankerville Club scandal."

"Ah, of course. He was wrongfully accused of cheating at cards."

"He said that you could solve anything."

"He said too much."

"That you are never beaten."

"I have been beaten four times—three times by men, and once by a woman."

"But what is that compared with the number of your successes?"

"It is true that I have been generally successful."

"Then you may be so with me."

"I beg that you will draw your chair up to the fire and favour me with some details as to your case."

"It is no ordinary one."

"None of those which come to me are. I am the last court of appeal."

"And yet I question, sir, whether, in all your experience, you have ever listened to a more mysterious and inexplicable chain of events than those which have happened in my own family."

"You fill me with interest," said Holmes. "Pray give us the essential facts from the commencement, and I can afterwards question you as to those details which seem to me to be most important."

The young man pulled his chair up and pushed his wet feet out towards the blaze.

"My name," said he, "is John Openshaw, but my own affairs have, as far as I can understand, little to do with this awful business. It is a hereditary matter; so in order to give you an idea of the facts, I must go back to the commencement of the affair.

"You must know that my grandfather had two sons—my uncle Elias and my father Joseph. My father had a small factory at Coventry, which he enlarged at the time of the invention of bicycling. He was a patentee of the Openshaw unbreakable tire, and his business met with such success that he was able to sell it and to retire upon a handsome competence.

"My uncle Elias emigrated to America when he was a young man and became a planter in Florida, where he was reported to have done very well. At the time of the war he fought in Jackson's army, and afterwards under Hood, where he rose to be a colonel. When Lee laid down his arms my uncle returned to his plantation, where he remained for three or four years. About 1869 or 1870 he came back to Europe and took a small estate in Sussex, near Horsham. He had made a very considerable fortune in the States, and his reason for leaving them was his aversion to the negroes, and his dislike of the Republican policy in extending the franchise to them. He was a singular man, fierce and quick-tempered, very foul-mouthed when he was angry, and of a most retiring disposition. During all the years that he lived at Horsham, I doubt if ever he set foot in the town. He had a garden and two or three fields round his house, and there he would take his exercise, though very often for weeks on end he would never leave his room. He drank a great deal of brandy and smoked very heavily, but he would see no society and did not want any friends, not even his own brother.

"He didn't mind me; in fact, he took a fancy to me, for at the time when he saw me first I was a youngster of twelve or so. This would be in the year 1878, after he had been eight or nine years in England. He begged my father to let me live with him and he was very kind to me in his way. When he was sober he used to be fond of playing backgammon and draughts with me, and he would make me his representative both with the servants and with the tradespeople, so that by the time that I was sixteen I was quite master of the house. I kept all the keys and could go where I liked and do what I liked, so long as I did not disturb him in his privacy. There was one singular exception, however, for he had a single room, a lumber-room up among the attics, which was invariably locked, and which he would never permit either me or anyone else to enter. With a boy's curiosity I have peeped through the keyhole, but I was never able to see more than such a collection of old trunks and bundles as would be expected in such a room.

"One day—it was in March, 1883—a letter with a foreign stamp lay upon the table in

front of the colonel's plate. It was not a common thing for him to receive letters, for his bills were all paid in ready money, and he had no friends of any sort. 'From India!' said he as he took it up, 'Pondicherry postmark! What can this be?' Opening it hurriedly, out there jumped five little dried orange pips, which pattered down upon his plate. I began to laugh at this, but the laugh was struck from my lips at the sight of his face. His lip had fallen, his eyes were protruding, his skin the colour of putty, and he glared at the envelope which he still held in his trembling hand, 'K. K. K.!' he shrieked, and then, 'My God, my God, my sins have overtaken me!'

"'What is it, uncle?' I cried.

"'Death,' said he, and rising from the table he retired to his room, leaving me palpitating with horror. I took up the envelope and saw scrawled in red ink upon the inner flap, just above the gum, the letter K three times repeated. There was nothing else save the five dried pips. What could be the reason of his overpowering terror? I left the breakfast table, and as I ascended the stair I met him coming down with an old rusty key, which must have belonged to the attic, in one hand, and a small brass box, like a cashbox, in the other.

"'They may do what they like, but I'll checkmate them still,' said he with an oath. 'Tell Mary that I shall want a fire in my room to-day, and send down to Fordham, the Horsham lawyer.'

"I did as he ordered, and when the lawyer arrived I was asked to step up to the room. The fire was burning brightly, and in the grate there was a mass of black, fluffy ashes, as of burned paper, while the brass box stood open and empty beside it. As I glanced at the box I noticed, with a start, that upon the lid was printed the treble K which I had read in the morning upon the envelope.

"'I wish you, John,' said my uncle, 'to witness my will. I leave my estate, with all its advantages and all its disadvantages, to my brother, your father, whence it will, no doubt, descend to you. If you can enjoy it in peace, well and good! If you find you cannot, take my advice, my boy, and leave it to your deadliest enemy. I am sorry to give you such a two-edged thing, but I can't say what turn things are going to take. Kindly sign the paper where Mr. Fordham shows you.'

"I signed the paper as directed, and the lawyer took it away with him. The singular incident made, as you may think, the deepest impression upon me, and I pondered over it and turned it every way in my mind without being able to make anything of it. Yet I could not shake off the vague feeling of dread which it left behind, though the sensation grew less keen as the weeks passed and nothing happened to disturb the usual routine of our lives. I could see a change in my uncle, however. He drank more than ever, and he was less inclined for any sort of society. Most of his time he would spend in his room, with the door locked upon the inside, but sometimes he would emerge in a sort of drunken frenzy and would burst out of the house and tear about the garden with a revolver in his hand, screaming out that he was afraid of no man, and that he was not to be cooped up, like a sheep in a pen, by man or devil. When these hot fits were over, however, he would rush tumultuously in at the door and lock and bar it behind him, like a man who can brazen it out no longer against the terror which lies at the roots of his soul. At such times I have seen his face, even on a cold day, glisten with moisture, as though it were new raised from a basin.

"Well, to come to an end of the matter, Mr. Holmes, and not to abuse your patience,

there came a night when he made one of those drunken sallies from which he never came back. We found him, when we went to search for him, face downward in a little green-scummed pool, which lay at the foot of the garden. There was no sign of any violence, and the water was but two feet deep, so that the jury, having regard to his known eccentricity, brought in a verdict of 'suicide.' But I, who knew how he winced from the very thought of death, had much ado to persuade myself that he had gone out of his way to meet it. The matter passed, however, and my father entered into possession of the estate, and of some £ 14,000, which lay to his credit at the bank."

"One moment," Holmes interposed, "your statement is, I foresee, one of the most remarkable to which I have ever listened. Let me have the date of the reception by your uncle of the letter, and the date of his supposed suicide."

"The letter arrived on March 10, 1883. His death was seven weeks later, upon the night of May 2nd."

"Thank you. Pray proceed."

"When my father took over the Horsham property, he, at my request, made a careful examination of the attic, which had been always locked up. We found the brass box there, although its contents had been destroyed. On the inside of the cover was a paper label, with the initials of K. K. K. repeated upon it, and 'Letters, memoranda, receipts, and a register' written beneath. These, we presume, indicated the nature of the papers which had been destroyed by Colonel Openshaw. For the rest, there was nothing of much importance in the attic save a great many scattered papers and note-books bearing upon my uncle's life in America. Some of them were of the war time and showed that he had done his duty well and had borne the repute of a brave soldier. Others were of a date during the reconstruction of the Southern states, and were mostly concerned with politics, for he had evidently taken a strong part in opposing the carpet-bag politicians who had been sent down from the North.

"Well, it was the beginning of '84 when my father came to live at Horsham, and all went as well as possible with us until the January of '85. On the fourth day after the new year I heard my father give a sharp cry of surprise as we sat together at the breakfast-table. There he was, sitting with a newly opened envelope in one hand and five dried orange pips in the outstretched palm of the other one. He had always laughed at what he called my cock-and-bull story about the colonel, but he looked very scared and puzzled now that the same thing had come upon himself.

"'Why, what on earth does this mean, John?' he stammered.

"My heart had turned to lead. 'It is K. K. K.,' said I.

"He looked inside the envelope. 'So it is,' he cried. 'Here are the very letters. But what is this written above them?'

"'Put the papers on the sundial,' I read, peeping over his shoulder.

"'What papers? What sundial?' he asked.

"'The sundial in the garden. There is no other,' said I; 'but the papers must be those that are destroyed.'

"'Pooh!' said he, gripping hard at his courage. 'We are in a civilised land here, and we can't have tomfoolery of this kind. Where does the thing come from?'

"'From Dundee,' I answered, glancing at the postmark.

"'Some preposterous practical joke,' said he. 'What have I to do with sundials and papers? I shall take no notice of such nonsense.'

"'I should certainly speak to the police,' I said.

"'And be laughed at for my pains. Nothing of the sort.'

"'Then let me do so?'

"'No, I forbid you. I won't have a fuss made about such nonsense.'

"It was in vain to argue with him, for he was a very obstinate man. I went about, however, with a heart which was full of forebodings.

"On the third day after the coming of the letter my father went from home to visit an old friend of his, Major Freebody, who is in command of one of the forts upon Portsdown Hill. I was glad that he should go, for it seemed to me that he was farther from danger when he was away from home. In that, however, I was in error. Upon the second day of his absence I received a telegram from the major, imploring me to come at once. My father had fallen over one of the deep chalk-pits which abound in the neighbourhood, and was lying senseless, with a shattered skull. I hurried to him, but he passed away without having ever recovered his consciousness. He had, as it appears, been returning from Fareham in the twilight, and as the country was unknown to him, and the chalk-pit unfenced, the jury had no hesitation in bringing in a verdict of 'death from accidental causes.' Carefully as I examined every fact connected with his death, I was unable to find anything which could suggest the idea of murder. There were no signs of violence, no footmarks, no robbery, no record of strangers having been seen upon the roads. And yet I need not tell you that my mind was far from at ease, and that I was well-nigh certain that some foul plot had been woven round him.

"In this sinister way I came into my inheritance. You will ask me why I did not dispose of it? I answer, because I was well convinced that our troubles were in some way dependent upon an incident in my uncle's life, and that the danger would be as pressing in one house as in another.

"It was in January, '85, that my poor father met his end, and two years and eight months have elapsed since then. During that time I have lived happily at Horsham, and I had begun to hope that this curse had passed away from the family, and that it had ended with the last generation. I had begun to take comfort too soon, however; yesterday morning the blow fell in the very shape in which it had come upon my father."

The young man took from his waistcoat a crumpled envelope, and turning to the table he shook out upon it five little dried orange pips.

"This is the envelope," he continued. "The postmark is London—eastern division. Within are the very words which were upon my father's last message: 'K. K. K.'; and then 'Put the papers on the sundial.'"

"What have you done?" asked Holmes.

"Nothing."

"Nothing?"

"To tell the truth"—he sank his face into his thin, white hands—"I have felt helpless. I have felt like one of those poor rabbits when the snake is writhing towards it. I seem to be in the grasp of some resistless, inexorable evil, which no foresight and no precautions can guard against."

"Tut! tut!" cried Sherlock Holmes. "You must act, man, or you are lost. Nothing but energy can save you. This is no time for despair."

"I have seen the police."

"Ah!"

"But they listened to my story with a smile. I am convinced that the inspector has formed the opinion that the letters are all practical jokes, and that the deaths of my relations were really accidents, as the jury stated, and were not to be connected with the warnings."

Holmes shook his clenched hands in the air. "Incredible imbecility!" he cried.

"They have, however, allowed me a policeman, who may remain in the house with me."

"Has he come with you to-night?"

"No. His orders were to stay in the house."

Again Holmes raved in the air.

"Why did you come to me?" he said, "and, above all, why did you not come at once?"

"I did not know. It was only to-day that I spoke to Major Prendergast about my troubles and was advised by him to come to you."

"It is really two days since you had the letter. We should have acted before this. You have no further evidence, I suppose, than that which you have placed before us—no suggestive detail which might help us?"

"There is one thing," said John Openshaw. He rummaged in his coat pocket, and, drawing out a piece of discoloured, blue-tinted paper, he laid it out upon the table. "I have some remembrance," said he, "that on the day when my uncle burned the papers I observed that the small, unburned margins which lay amid the ashes were of this particular colour. I found this single sheet upon the floor of his room, and I am inclined to think that it may be one of the papers which has, perhaps, fluttered out from among the others, and in that way has escaped destruction. Beyond the mention of pips, I do not see that it helps us much. I think myself that it is a page from some private diary. The writing is undoubtedly my uncle's."

Holmes moved the lamp, and we both bent over the sheet of paper, which showed by its ragged edge that it had indeed been torn from a book. It was headed, "March, 1869," and beneath were the following enigmatical notices:

"4th. Hudson came. Same old platform.

"7th. Set the pips on McCauley, Paramore, and John Swain of St. Augustine.

"9th. McCauley cleared.

"10th. John Swain cleared.

"12th. Visited Paramore. All well."

"Thank you!" said Holmes, folding up the paper and returning it to our visitor. "And now you must on no account lose another instant. We cannot spare time even to discuss what you have told me. You must get home instantly and act."

"What shall I do?"

"There is but one thing to do. It must be done at once. You must put this piece of paper which you have shown us into the brass box which you have described. You must also put in a note to say that all the other papers were burned by your uncle, and that this is the only one which remains. You must assert that in such words as will carry conviction with them. Having done this, you must at once put the box out upon the sundial, as directed. Do you understand?"

"Entirely."

"Do not think of revenge, or anything of the sort, at present. I think that we may gain that by means of the law; but we have our web to weave, while theirs is already woven.

The first consideration is to remove the pressing danger which threatens you. The second is to clear up the mystery and to punish the guilty parties."

"I thank you," said the young man, rising and pulling on his overcoat. "You have given me fresh life and hope. I shall certainly do as you advise."

"Do not lose an instant. And, above all, take care of yourself in the meanwhile, for I do not think that there can be a doubt that you are threatened by a very real and imminent danger. How do you go back?"

"By train from Waterloo."

"It is not yet nine. The streets will be crowded, so I trust that you may be in safety. And yet you cannot guard yourself too closely."

"I am armed."

"That is well. To-morrow I shall set to work upon your case."

"I shall see you at Horsham, then?"

"No, your secret lies in London. It is there that I shall seek it."

"Then I shall call upon you in a day, or in two days, with news as to the box and the papers. I shall take your advice in every particular." He shook hands with us and took his leave. Outside the wind still screamed and the rain splashed and pattered against the windows. This strange, wild story seemed to have come to us from amid the mad elements—blown in upon us like a sheet of sea-weed in a gale—and now to have been reabsorbed by them once more.

Sherlock Holmes sat for some time in silence, with his head sunk forward and his eyes bent upon the red glow of the fire. Then he lit his pipe, and leaning back in his chair he watched the blue smoke-rings as they chased each other up to the ceiling.

"I think, Watson," he remarked at last, "that of all our cases we have had none more fantastic than this."

"Save, perhaps, the Sign of Four."

"Well, yes. Save, perhaps, that. And yet this John Openshaw seems to me to be walking amid even greater perils than did the Sholtos."

"But have you," I asked, "formed any definite conception as to what these perils are?"

"There can be no question as to their nature," he answered.

"Then what are they? Who is this K. K. K., and why does he pursue this unhappy family?"

Sherlock Holmes closed his eyes and placed his elbows upon the arms of his chair, with his finger-tips together. "The ideal reasoner," he remarked, "would, when he had once been shown a single fact in all its bearings, deduce from it not only all the chain of events which led up to it but also all the results which would follow from it. As Cuvier could correctly describe a whole animal by the contemplation of a single bone, so the observer who has thoroughly understood one link in a series of incidents should be able to accurately state all the other ones, both before and after. We have not yet grasped the results which the reason alone can attain to. Problems may be solved in the study which have baffled all those who have sought a solution by the aid of their senses. To carry the art, however, to its highest pitch, it is necessary that the reasoner should be able to utilise all the facts which have come to his knowledge; and this in itself implies, as you will readily see, a possession of all knowledge, which, even in these days of free education and encyclopædias, is a somewhat rare accomplishment. It is not so impossible, however, that a man should possess all knowledge which is likely to be useful to him in his work, and

this I have endeavoured in my case to do. If I remember rightly, you on one occasion, in the early days of our friendship, defined my limits in a very precise fashion."

"Yes," I answered, laughing. "It was a singular document. Philosophy, astronomy, and politics were marked at zero, I remember. Botany variable, geology profound as regards the mud-stains from any region within fifty miles of town, chemistry eccentric, anatomy unsystematic, sensational literature and crime records unique, violin-player, boxer, swordsman, lawyer, and self-poisoner by cocaine and tobacco. Those, I think, were the main points of my analysis."

Holmes grinned at the last item. "Well," he said, "I say now, as I said then, that a man should keep his little brain-attic stocked with all the furniture that he is likely to use, and the rest he can put away in the lumber-room of his library, where he can get it if he wants it. Now, for such a case as the one which has been submitted to us to-night, we need certainly to muster all our resources. Kindly hand me down the letter K of the *American Encyclopædia* which stands upon the shelf beside you. Thank you. Now let us consider the situation and see what may be deduced from it. In the first place, we may start with a strong presumption that Colonel Openshaw had some very strong reason for leaving America. Men at his time of life do not change all their habits and exchange willingly the charming climate of Florida for the lonely life of an English provincial town. His extreme love of solitude in England suggests the idea that he was in fear of someone or something, so we may assume as a working hypothesis that it was fear of someone or something which drove him from America. As to what it was he feared, we can only deduce that by considering the formidable letters which were received by himself and his successors. Did you remark the postmarks of those letters?"

"The first was from Pondicherry, the second from Dundee, and the third from London."

"From East London. What do you deduce from that?"

"They are all seaports. That the writer was on board of a ship."

"Excellent. We have already a clue. There can be no doubt that the probability—the strong probability—is that the writer was on board of a ship. And now let us consider another point. In the case of Pondicherry, seven weeks elapsed between the threat and its fulfilment, in Dundee it was only some three or four days. Does that suggest anything?"

"A greater distance to travel."

"But the letter had also a greater distance to come."

"Then I do not see the point."

"There is at least a presumption that the vessel in which the man or men are is a sailing-ship. It looks as if they always send their singular warning or token before them when starting upon their mission. You see how quickly the deed followed the sign when it came from Dundee. If they had come from Pondicherry in a steamer they would have arrived almost as soon as their letter. But, as a matter of fact, seven weeks elapsed. I think that those seven weeks represented the difference between the mail-boat which brought the letter and the sailing vessel which brought the writer."

"It is possible."

"More than that. It is probable. And now you see the deadly urgency of this new case, and why I urged young Openshaw to caution. The blow has always fallen at the end of the time which it would take the senders to travel the distance. But this one comes from London, and therefore we cannot count upon delay."

"Good God!" I cried. "What can it mean, this relentless persecution?"

"The papers which Openshaw carried are obviously of vital importance to the person or persons in the sailing-ship. I think that it is quite clear that there must be more than one of them. A single man could not have carried out two deaths in such a way as to deceive a coroner's jury. There must have been several in it, and they must have been men of resource and determination. Their papers they mean to have, be the holder of them who it may. In this way you see K. K. K. ceases to be the initials of an individual and becomes the badge of a society."

"But of what society?"

"Have you never—" said Sherlock Holmes, bending forward and sinking his voice —"have you never heard of the Ku Klux Klan?"

"I never have."

Holmes turned over the leaves of the book upon his knee. "Here it is," said he presently:

"'Ku Klux Klan. A name derived from the fanciful resemblance to the sound produced by cocking a rifle. This terrible secret society was formed by some ex-Confederate soldiers in the Southern states after the Civil War, and it rapidly formed local branches in different parts of the country, notably in Tennessee, Louisiana, the Carolinas, Georgia, and Florida. Its power was used for political purposes, principally for the terrorising of the negro voters and the murdering and driving from the country of those who were opposed to its views. Its outrages were usually preceded by a warning sent to the marked man in some fantastic but generally recognised shape—a sprig of oak-leaves in some parts, melon seeds or orange pips in others. On receiving this the victim might either openly abjure his former ways, or might fly from the country. If he braved the matter out, death would unfailingly come upon him, and usually in some strange and unforeseen manner. So perfect was the organisation of the society, and so systematic its methods, that there is hardly a case upon record where any man succeeded in braving it with impunity, or in which any of its outrages were traced home to the perpetrators. For some years the organisation flourished in spite of the efforts of the United States government and of the better classes of the community in the South. Eventually, in the year 1869, the movement rather suddenly collapsed, although there have been sporadic outbreaks of the same sort since that date.'

"You will observe," said Holmes, laying down the volume, "that the sudden breaking up of the society was coincident with the disappearance of Openshaw from America with their papers. It may well have been cause and effect. It is no wonder that he and his family have some of the more implacable spirits upon their track. You can understand that this register and diary may implicate some of the first men in the South, and that there may be many who will not sleep easy at night until it is recovered."

"Then the page we have seen—"

"Is such as we might expect. It ran, if I remember right, 'sent the pips to A, B, and C'— that is, sent the society's warning to them. Then there are successive entries that A and B cleared, or left the country, and finally that C was visited, with, I fear, a sinister result for C. Well, I think, Doctor, that we may let some light into this dark place, and I believe that the only chance young Openshaw has in the meantime is to do what I have told him. There is nothing more to be said or to be done to-night, so hand me over my violin and let

us try to forget for half an hour the miserable weather and the still more miserable ways of our fellow men."

It had cleared in the morning, and the sun was shining with a subdued brightness through the dim veil which hangs over the great city. Sherlock Holmes was already at breakfast when I came down.

"You will excuse me for not waiting for you," said he; "I have, I foresee, a very busy day before me in looking into this case of young Openshaw's."

"What steps will you take?" I asked.

"It will very much depend upon the results of my first inquiries. I may have to go down to Horsham, after all."

"You will not go there first?"

"No, I shall commence with the City. Just ring the bell and the maid will bring up your coffee."

As I waited, I lifted the unopened newspaper from the table and glanced my eye over it. It rested upon a heading which sent a chill to my heart.

"Holmes," I cried, "you are too late."

"Ah!" said he, laying down his cup, "I feared as much. How was it done?" He spoke calmly, but I could see that he was deeply moved.

"My eye caught the name of Openshaw, and the heading 'Tragedy Near Waterloo Bridge.' Here is the account:

"'Between nine and ten last night Police-Constable Cook, of the H Division, on duty near Waterloo Bridge, heard a cry for help and a splash in the water. The night, however, was extremely dark and stormy, so that, in spite of the help of several passers-by, it was quite impossible to effect a rescue. The alarm, however, was given, and, by the aid of the water-police, the body was eventually recovered. It proved to be that of a young gentleman whose name, as it appears from an envelope which was found in his pocket, was John Openshaw, and whose residence is near Horsham. It is conjectured that he may have been hurrying down to catch the last train from Waterloo Station, and that in his haste and the extreme darkness he missed his path and walked over the edge of one of the small landing-places for river steamboats. The body exhibited no traces of violence, and there can be no doubt that the deceased had been the victim of an unfortunate accident, which should have the effect of calling the attention of the authorities to the condition of the riverside landing-stages.'"

We sat in silence for some minutes, Holmes more depressed and shaken than I had ever seen him.

"That hurts my pride, Watson," he said at last. "It is a petty feeling, no doubt, but it hurts my pride. It becomes a personal matter with me now, and, if God sends me health, I shall set my hand upon this gang. That he should come to me for help, and that I should send him away to his death—!" He sprang from his chair and paced about the room in uncontrollable agitation, with a flush upon his sallow cheeks and a nervous clasping and unclasping of his long thin hands.

"They must be cunning devils," he exclaimed at last. "How could they have decoyed him down there? The Embankment is not on the direct line to the station. The bridge, no doubt, was too crowded, even on such a night, for their purpose. Well, Watson, we shall see who will win in the long run. I am going out now!"

"To the police?"

"No; I shall be my own police. When I have spun the web they may take the flies, but not before."

All day I was engaged in my professional work, and it was late in the evening before I returned to Baker Street. Sherlock Holmes had not come back yet. It was nearly ten o'clock before he entered, looking pale and worn. He walked up to the sideboard, and tearing a piece from the loaf he devoured it voraciously, washing it down with a long draught of water.

"You are hungry," I remarked.

"Starving. It had escaped my memory. I have had nothing since breakfast."

"Nothing?"

"Not a bite. I had no time to think of it."

"And how have you succeeded?"

"Well."

"You have a clue?"

"I have them in the hollow of my hand. Young Openshaw shall not long remain unavenged. Why, Watson, let us put their own devilish trade-mark upon them. It is well thought of!"

"What do you mean?"

He took an orange from the cupboard, and tearing it to pieces he squeezed out the pips upon the table. Of these he took five and thrust them into an envelope. On the inside of the flap he wrote "S. H. for J. O." Then he sealed it and addressed it to "Captain James Calhoun, Barque *Lone Star*, Savannah, Georgia."

"That will await him when he enters port," said he, chuckling. "It may give him a sleepless night. He will find it as sure a precursor of his fate as Openshaw did before him."

"And who is this Captain Calhoun?"

"The leader of the gang. I shall have the others, but he first."

"How did you trace it, then?"

He took a large sheet of paper from his pocket, all covered with dates and names.

"I have spent the whole day," said he, "over Lloyd's registers and files of the old papers, following the future career of every vessel which touched at Pondicherry in January and February in '83. There were thirty-six ships of fair tonnage which were reported there during those months. Of these, one, the *Lone Star*, instantly attracted my attention, since, although it was reported as having cleared from London, the name is that which is given to one of the states of the Union."

"Texas, I think."

"I was not and am not sure which; but I knew that the ship must have an American origin."

"What then?"

"I searched the Dundee records, and when I found that the barque *Lone Star* was there in January, '85, my suspicion became a certainty. I then inquired as to the vessels which lay at present in the port of London."

"Yes?"

"The *Lone Star* had arrived here last week. I went down to the Albert Dock and found that she had been taken down the river by the early tide this morning, homeward bound to Savannah. I wired to Gravesend and learned that she had passed some time ago, and as

the wind is easterly I have no doubt that she is now past the Goodwins and not very far from the Isle of Wight."

"What will you do, then?"

"Oh, I have my hand upon him. He and the two mates, are as I learn, the only native-born Americans in the ship. The others are Finns and Germans. I know, also, that they were all three away from the ship last night. I had it from the stevedore who has been loading their cargo. By the time that their sailing-ship reaches Savannah the mail-boat will have carried this letter, and the cable will have informed the police of Savannah that these three gentlemen are badly wanted here upon a charge of murder."

There is ever a flaw, however, in the best laid of human plans, and the murderers of John Openshaw were never to receive the orange pips which would show them that another, as cunning and as resolute as themselves, was upon their track. Very long and very severe were the equinoctial gales that year. We waited long for news of the *Lone Star* of Savannah, but none ever reached us. We did at last hear that somewhere far out in the Atlantic a shattered stern-post of a boat was seen swinging in the trough of a wave, with the letters "L. S." carved upon it, and that is all which we shall ever know of the fate of the *Lone Star*.

THE ADVENTURE OF THE SPECKLED BAND

FROM THE ADVENTURES OF SHERLOCK HOLMES (1892)

On GLANCING over my notes of the seventy odd cases in which I have during the last eight years studied the methods of my friend Sherlock Holmes, I find many tragic, some comic, a large number merely strange, but none commonplace; for, working as he did rather for the love of his art than for the acquirement of wealth, he refused to associate himself with any investigation which did not tend towards the unusual, and even the fantastic. Of all these varied cases, however, I cannot recall any which presented more singular features than that which was associated with the well-known Surrey family of the Roylotts of Stoke Moran. The events in question occurred in the early days of my association with Holmes, when we were sharing rooms as bachelors in Baker Street. It is possible that I might have placed them upon record before, but a promise of secrecy was made at the time, from which I have only been freed during the last month by the untimely death of the lady to whom the pledge was given. It is perhaps as well that the facts should now come to light, for I have reasons to know that there are widespread rumours as to the death of Dr. Grimesby Roylott which tend to make the matter even more terrible than the truth.

It was early in April in the year '83 that I woke one morning to find Sherlock Holmes standing, fully dressed, by the side of my bed. He was a late riser, as a rule, and as the clock on the mantelpiece showed me that it was only a quarter-past seven, I blinked up at him in some surprise, and perhaps just a little resentment, for I was myself regular in my habits.

"Very sorry to knock you up, Watson," said he, "but it's the common lot this morning. Mrs. Hudson has been knocked up, she retorted upon me, and I on you."

"What is it, then—a fire?"

"No; a client. It seems that a young lady has arrived in a considerable state of excitement, who insists upon seeing me. She is waiting now in the sitting-room. Now, when young ladies wander about the metropolis at this hour of the morning, and knock sleepy people up out of their beds, I presume that it is something very pressing which

they have to communicate. Should it prove to be an interesting case, you would, I am sure, wish to follow it from the outset. I thought, at any rate, that I should call you and give you the chance."

"My dear fellow, I would not miss it for anything."

I had no keener pleasure than in following Holmes in his professional investigations, and in admiring the rapid deductions, as swift as intuitions, and yet always founded on a logical basis with which he unravelled the problems which were submitted to him. I rapidly threw on my clothes and was ready in a few minutes to accompany my friend down to the sitting-room. A lady dressed in black and heavily veiled, who had been sitting in the window, rose as we entered.

"Good-morning, madam," said Holmes cheerily. "My name is Sherlock Holmes. This is my intimate friend and associate, Dr. Watson, before whom you can speak as freely as before myself. Ha! I am glad to see that Mrs. Hudson has had the good sense to light the fire. Pray draw up to it, and I shall order you a cup of hot coffee, for I observe that you are shivering."

"It is not cold which makes me shiver," said the woman in a low voice, changing her seat as requested.

"What, then?"

"It is fear, Mr. Holmes. It is terror." She raised her veil as she spoke, and we could see that she was indeed in a pitiable state of agitation, her face all drawn and grey, with restless frightened eyes, like those of some hunted animal. Her features and figure were those of a woman of thirty, but her hair was shot with premature grey, and her expression was weary and haggard. Sherlock Holmes ran her over with one of his quick, all-comprehensive glances.

"You must not fear," said he soothingly, bending forward and patting her forearm. "We shall soon set matters right, I have no doubt. You have come in by train this morning, I see."

"You know me, then?"

"No, but I observe the second half of a return ticket in the palm of your left glove. You must have started early, and yet you had a good drive in a dog-cart, along heavy roads, before you reached the station."

The lady gave a violent start and stared in bewilderment at my companion.

"There is no mystery, my dear madam," said he, smiling. "The left arm of your jacket is spattered with mud in no less than seven places. The marks are perfectly fresh. There is no vehicle save a dog-cart which throws up mud in that way, and then only when you sit on the left-hand side of the driver."

"Whatever your reasons may be, you are perfectly correct," said she. "I started from home before six, reached Leatherhead at twenty past, and came in by the first train to Waterloo. Sir, I can stand this strain no longer; I shall go mad if it continues. I have no one to turn to—none, save only one, who cares for me, and he, poor fellow, can be of little aid. I have heard of you, Mr. Holmes; I have heard of you from Mrs. Farintosh, whom you helped in the hour of her sore need. It was from her that I had your address. Oh, sir, do you not think that you could help me, too, and at least throw a little light through the dense darkness which surrounds me? At present it is out of my power to reward you for your services, but in a month or six weeks I shall be married, with the control of my own income, and then at least you shall not find me ungrateful."

Holmes turned to his desk and, unlocking it, drew out a small case-book, which he consulted.

"Farintosh," said he. "Ah yes, I recall the case; it was concerned with an opal tiara. I think it was before your time, Watson. I can only say, madam, that I shall be happy to devote the same care to your case as I did to that of your friend. As to reward, my profession is its own reward; but you are at liberty to defray whatever expenses I may be put to, at the time which suits you best. And now I beg that you will lay before us everything that may help us in forming an opinion upon the matter."

"Alas!" replied our visitor, "the very horror of my situation lies in the fact that my fears are so vague, and my suspicions depend so entirely upon small points, which might seem trivial to another, that even he to whom of all others I have a right to look for help and advice looks upon all that I tell him about it as the fancies of a nervous woman. He does not say so, but I can read it from his soothing answers and averted eyes. But I have heard, Mr. Holmes, that you can see deeply into the manifold wickedness of the human heart. You may advise me how to walk amid the dangers which encompass me."

"I am all attention, madam."

"My name is Helen Stoner, and I am living with my stepfather, who is the last survivor of one of the oldest Saxon families in England, the Roylotts of Stoke Moran, on the western border of Surrey."

Holmes nodded his head. "The name is familiar to me," said he.

"The family was at one time among the richest in England, and the estates extended over the borders into Berkshire in the north, and Hampshire in the west. In the last century, however, four successive heirs were of a dissolute and wasteful disposition, and the family ruin was eventually completed by a gambler in the days of the Regency. Nothing was left save a few acres of ground, and the two-hundred-year-old house, which is itself crushed under a heavy mortgage. The last squire dragged out his existence there, living the horrible life of an aristocratic pauper; but his only son, my stepfather, seeing that he must adapt himself to the new conditions, obtained an advance from a relative, which enabled him to take a medical degree and went out to Calcutta, where, by his professional skill and his force of character, he established a large practice. In a fit of anger, however, caused by some robberies which had been perpetrated in the house, he beat his native butler to death and narrowly escaped a capital sentence. As it was, he suffered a long term of imprisonment and afterwards returned to England a morose and disappointed man.

"When Dr. Roylott was in India he married my mother, Mrs. Stoner, the young widow of Major-General Stoner, of the Bengal Artillery. My sister Julia and I were twins, and we were only two years old at the time of my mother's re-marriage. She had a considerable sum of money—not less than £ 1000 a year—and this she bequeathed to Dr. Roylott entirely while we resided with him, with a provision that a certain annual sum should be allowed to each of us in the event of our marriage. Shortly after our return to England my mother died—she was killed eight years ago in a railway accident near Crewe. Dr. Roylott then abandoned his attempts to establish himself in practice in London and took us to live with him in the old ancestral house at Stoke Moran. The money which my mother had left was enough for all our wants, and there seemed to be no obstacle to our happiness.

"But a terrible change came over our stepfather about this time. Instead of making friends and exchanging visits with our neighbours, who had at first been overjoyed to see

a Roylott of Stoke Moran back in the old family seat, he shut himself up in his house and seldom came out save to indulge in ferocious quarrels with whoever might cross his path. Violence of temper approaching to mania has been hereditary in the men of the family, and in my stepfather's case it had, I believe, been intensified by his long residence in the tropics. A series of disgraceful brawls took place, two of which ended in the police-court, until at last he became the terror of the village, and the folks would fly at his approach, for he is a man of immense strength, and absolutely uncontrollable in his anger.

"Last week he hurled the local blacksmith over a parapet into a stream, and it was only by paying over all the money which I could gather together that I was able to avert another public exposure. He had no friends at all save the wandering gipsies, and he would give these vagabonds leave to encamp upon the few acres of bramble-covered land which represent the family estate, and would accept in return the hospitality of their tents, wandering away with them sometimes for weeks on end. He has a passion also for Indian animals, which are sent over to him by a correspondent, and he has at this moment a cheetah and a baboon, which wander freely over his grounds and are feared by the villagers almost as much as their master.

"You can imagine from what I say that my poor sister Julia and I had no great pleasure in our lives. No servant would stay with us, and for a long time we did all the work of the house. She was but thirty at the time of her death, and yet her hair had already begun to whiten, even as mine has."

"Your sister is dead, then?"

"She died just two years ago, and it is of her death that I wish to speak to you. You can understand that, living the life which I have described, we were little likely to see anyone of our own age and position. We had, however, an aunt, my mother's maiden sister, Miss Honoria Westphail, who lives near Harrow, and we were occasionally allowed to pay short visits at this lady's house. Julia went there at Christmas two years ago, and met there a half-pay major of marines, to whom she became engaged. My stepfather learned of the engagement when my sister returned and offered no objection to the marriage; but within a fortnight of the day which had been fixed for the wedding, the terrible event occurred which has deprived me of my only companion."

Sherlock Holmes had been leaning back in his chair with his eyes closed and his head sunk in a cushion, but he half opened his lids now and glanced across at his visitor.

"Pray be precise as to details," said he.

"It is easy for me to be so, for every event of that dreadful time is seared into my memory. The manor-house is, as I have already said, very old, and only one wing is now inhabited. The bedrooms in this wing are on the ground floor, the sitting-rooms being in the central block of the buildings. Of these bedrooms the first is Dr. Roylott's, the second my sister's, and the third my own. There is no communication between them, but they all open out into the same corridor. Do I make myself plain?"

"Perfectly so."

"The windows of the three rooms open out upon the lawn. That fatal night Dr. Roylott had gone to his room early, though we knew that he had not retired to rest, for my sister was troubled by the smell of the strong Indian cigars which it was his custom to smoke. She left her room, therefore, and came into mine, where she sat for some time, chatting about her approaching wedding. At eleven o'clock she rose to leave me, but she paused at the door and looked back.

"'Tell me, Helen,' said she, 'have you ever heard anyone whistle in the dead of the night?'

"'Never,' said I.

"'I suppose that you could not possibly whistle, yourself, in your sleep?'

"'Certainly not. But why?'

"'Because during the last few nights I have always, about three in the morning, heard a low, clear whistle. I am a light sleeper, and it has awakened me. I cannot tell where it came from—perhaps from the next room, perhaps from the lawn. I thought that I would just ask you whether you had heard it.'

"'No, I have not. It must be those wretched gipsies in the plantation.'

"'Very likely. And yet if it were on the lawn, I wonder that you did not hear it also.'

"'Ah, but I sleep more heavily than you.'

"'Well, it is of no great consequence, at any rate.' She smiled back at me, closed my door, and a few moments later I heard her key turn in the lock."

"Indeed," said Holmes. "Was it your custom always to lock yourselves in at night?"

"Always."

"And why?"

"I think that I mentioned to you that the Doctor kept a cheetah and a baboon. We had no feeling of security unless our doors were locked."

"Quite so. Pray proceed with your statement."

"I could not sleep that night. A vague feeling of impending misfortune impressed me. My sister and I, you will recollect, were twins, and you know how subtle are the links which bind two souls which are so closely allied. It was a wild night. The wind was howling outside, and the rain was beating and splashing against the windows. Suddenly, amid all the hubbub of the gale, there burst forth the wild scream of a terrified woman. I knew that it was my sister's voice. I sprang from my bed, wrapped a shawl round me, and rushed into the corridor. As I opened my door I seemed to hear a low whistle, such as my sister described, and a few moments later a clanging sound, as if a mass of metal had fallen. As I ran down the passage, my sister's door was unlocked, and revolved slowly upon its hinges. I stared at it horror-stricken, not knowing what was about to issue from it. By the light of the corridor-lamp I saw my sister appear at the opening, her face blanched with terror, her hands groping for help, her whole figure swaying to and fro like that of a drunkard. I ran to her and threw my arms round her, but at that moment her knees seemed to give way and she fell to the ground. She writhed as one who is in terrible pain, and her limbs were dreadfully convulsed. At first I thought that she had not recognised me, but as I bent over her she suddenly shrieked out in a voice which I shall never forget, 'Oh, my God! Helen! It was the band! The speckled band!' There was something else which she would fain have said, and she stabbed with her finger into the air in the direction of the Doctor's room, but a fresh convulsion seized her and choked her words. I rushed out, calling loudly for my stepfather, and I met him hastening from his room in his dressing-gown. When he reached my sister's side she was unconscious, and though he poured brandy down her throat and sent for medical aid from the village, all efforts were in vain, for she slowly sank and died without having recovered her consciousness. Such was the dreadful end of my beloved sister."

"One moment," said Holmes, "are you sure about this whistle and metallic sound? Could you swear to it?"

"That was what the county coroner asked me at the inquiry. It is my strong impression that I heard it, and yet, among the crash of the gale and the creaking of an old house, I may possibly have been deceived."

"Was your sister dressed?"

"No, she was in her night-dress. In her right hand was found the charred stump of a match, and in her left a match-box."

"Showing that she had struck a light and looked about her when the alarm took place. That is important. And what conclusions did the coroner come to?"

"He investigated the case with great care, for Dr. Roylott's conduct had long been notorious in the county, but he was unable to find any satisfactory cause of death. My evidence showed that the door had been fastened upon the inner side, and the windows were blocked by old-fashioned shutters with broad iron bars, which were secured every night. The walls were carefully sounded, and were shown to be quite solid all round, and the flooring was also thoroughly examined, with the same result. The chimney is wide, but is barred up by four large staples. It is certain, therefore, that my sister was quite alone when she met her end. Besides, there were no marks of any violence upon her."

"How about poison?"

"The doctors examined her for it, but without success."

"What do you think that this unfortunate lady died of, then?"

"It is my belief that she died of pure fear and nervous shock, though what it was that frightened her I cannot imagine."

"Were there gipsies in the plantation at the time?"

"Yes, there are nearly always some there."

"Ah, and what did you gather from this allusion to a band—a speckled band?"

"Sometimes I have thought that it was merely the wild talk of delirium, sometimes that it may have referred to some band of people, perhaps to these very gipsies in the plantation. I do not know whether the spotted handkerchiefs which so many of them wear over their heads might have suggested the strange adjective which she used."

Holmes shook his head like a man who is far from being satisfied.

"These are very deep waters," said he; "pray go on with your narrative."

"Two years have passed since then, and my life has been until lately lonelier than ever. A month ago, however, a dear friend, whom I have known for many years, has done me the honour to ask my hand in marriage. His name is Armitage—Percy Armitage—the second son of Mr. Armitage, of Crane Water, near Reading. My stepfather has offered no opposition to the match, and we are to be married in the course of the spring. Two days ago some repairs were started in the west wing of the building, and my bedroom wall has been pierced, so that I have had to move into the chamber in which my sister died, and to sleep in the very bed in which she slept. Imagine, then, my thrill of terror when last night, as I lay awake, thinking over her terrible fate, I suddenly heard in the silence of the night the low whistle which had been the herald of her own death. I sprang up and lit the lamp, but nothing was to be seen in the room. I was too shaken to go to bed again, however, so I dressed, and as soon as it was daylight I slipped down, got a dog-cart at the Crown Inn, which is opposite, and drove to Leatherhead, from whence I have come on this morning with the one object of seeing you and asking your advice."

"You have done wisely," said my friend. "But have you told me all?"

"Yes, all."

"Miss Roylott, you have not. You are screening your stepfather."

"Why, what do you mean?"

For answer Holmes pushed back the frill of black lace which fringed the hand that lay upon our visitor's knee. Five little livid spots, the marks of four fingers and a thumb, were printed upon the white wrist.

"You have been cruelly used," said Holmes.

The lady coloured deeply and covered over her injured wrist. "He is a hard man," she said, "and perhaps he hardly knows his own strength."

There was a long silence, during which Holmes leaned his chin upon his hands and stared into the crackling fire.

"This is a very deep business," he said at last. "There are a thousand details which I should desire to know before I decide upon our course of action. Yet we have not a moment to lose. If we were to come to Stoke Moran to-day, would it be possible for us to see over these rooms without the knowledge of your stepfather?"

"As it happens, he spoke of coming into town to-day upon some most important business. It is probable that he will be away all day, and that there would be nothing to disturb you. We have a housekeeper now, but she is old and foolish, and I could easily get her out of the way."

"Excellent. You are not averse to this trip, Watson?"

"By no means."

"Then we shall both come. What are you going to do yourself?"

"I have one or two things which I would wish to do now that I am in town. But I shall return by the twelve o'clock train, so as to be there in time for your coming."

"And you may expect us early in the afternoon. I have myself some small business matters to attend to. Will you not wait and breakfast?"

"No, I must go. My heart is lightened already since I have confided my trouble to you. I shall look forward to seeing you again this afternoon." She dropped her thick black veil over her face and glided from the room.

"And what do you think of it all, Watson?" asked Sherlock Holmes, leaning back in his chair.

"It seems to me to be a most dark and sinister business."

"Dark enough and sinister enough."

"Yet if the lady is correct in saying that the flooring and walls are sound, and that the door, window, and chimney are impassable, then her sister must have been undoubtedly alone when she met her mysterious end."

"What becomes, then, of these nocturnal whistles, and what of the very peculiar words of the dying woman?"

"I cannot think."

"When you combine the ideas of whistles at night, the presence of a band of gipsies who are on intimate terms with this old doctor, the fact that we have every reason to believe that the doctor has an interest in preventing his stepdaughter's marriage, the dying allusion to a band, and, finally, the fact that Miss Helen Stoner heard a metallic clang, which might have been caused by one of those metal bars that secured the shutters falling back into its place, I think that there is good ground to think that the mystery may be cleared along those lines."

"But what, then, did the gipsies do?"

"I cannot imagine."

"I see many objections to any such theory."

"And so do I. It is precisely for that reason that we are going to Stoke Moran this day. I want to see whether the objections are fatal, or if they may be explained away. But what in the name of the devil!"

The ejaculation had been drawn from my companion by the fact that our door had been suddenly dashed open, and that a huge man had framed himself in the aperture. His costume was a peculiar mixture of the professional and of the agricultural, having a black top-hat, a long frock-coat, and a pair of high gaiters, with a hunting-crop swinging in his hand. So tall was he that his hat actually brushed the cross bar of the doorway, and his breadth seemed to span it across from side to side. A large face, seared with a thousand wrinkles, burned yellow with the sun, and marked with every evil passion, was turned from one to the other of us, while his deep-set, bile-shot eyes, and his high, thin, fleshless nose, gave him somewhat the resemblance to a fierce old bird of prey.

"Which of you is Holmes?" asked this apparition.

"My name, sir; but you have the advantage of me," said my companion quietly.

"I am Dr. Grimesby Roylott, of Stoke Moran."

"Indeed, Doctor," said Holmes blandly. "Pray take a seat."

"I will do nothing of the kind. My stepdaughter has been here. I have traced her. What has she been saying to you?"

"It is a little cold for the time of the year," said Holmes.

"What has she been saying to you?" screamed the old man furiously.

"But I have heard that the crocuses promise well," continued my companion imperturbably.

"Ha! You put me off, do you?" said our new visitor, taking a step forward and shaking his hunting-crop. "I know you, you scoundrel! I have heard of you before. You are Holmes, the meddler."

My friend smiled.

"Holmes, the busybody!"

His smile broadened.

"Holmes, the Scotland Yard Jack-in-office!"

Holmes chuckled heartily. "Your conversation is most entertaining," said he. "When you go out close the door, for there is a decided draught."

"I will go when I have had my say. Don't you dare to meddle with my affairs. I know that Miss Stoner has been here. I traced her! I am a dangerous man to fall foul of! See here." He stepped swiftly forward, seized the poker, and bent it into a curve with his huge brown hands.

"See that you keep yourself out of my grip," he snarled, and hurling the twisted poker into the fireplace he strode out of the room.

"He seems a very amiable person," said Holmes, laughing. "I am not quite so bulky, but if he had remained I might have shown him that my grip was not much more feeble than his own." As he spoke he picked up the steel poker and, with a sudden effort, straightened it out again.

"Fancy his having the insolence to confound me with the official detective force! This incident gives zest to our investigation, however, and I only trust that our little friend will not suffer from her imprudence in allowing this brute to trace her. And now, Watson, we

shall order breakfast, and afterwards I shall walk down to Doctors' Commons, where I hope to get some data which may help us in this matter."

It was nearly one o'clock when Sherlock Holmes returned from his excursion. He held in his hand a sheet of blue paper, scrawled over with notes and figures.

"I have seen the will of the deceased wife," said he. "To determine its exact meaning I have been obliged to work out the present prices of the investments with which it is concerned. The total income, which at the time of the wife's death was little short of £ 1,100, is now, through the fall in agricultural prices, not more than £ 750. Each daughter can claim an income of £ 250, in case of marriage. It is evident, therefore, that if both girls had married, this beauty would have had a mere pittance, while even one of them would cripple him to a very serious extent. My morning's work has not been wasted, since it has proved that he has the very strongest motives for standing in the way of anything of the sort. And now, Watson, this is too serious for dawdling, especially as the old man is aware that we are interesting ourselves in his affairs; so if you are ready, we shall call a cab and drive to Waterloo. I should be very much obliged if you would slip your revolver into your pocket. An Eley's No. 2 is an excellent argument with gentlemen who can twist steel pokers into knots. That and a tooth-brush are, I think, all that we need."

At Waterloo we were fortunate in catching a train for Leatherhead, where we hired a trap at the station inn and drove for four or five miles through the lovely Surrey lanes. It was a perfect day, with a bright sun and a few fleecy clouds in the heavens. The trees and wayside hedges were just throwing out their first green shoots, and the air was full of the pleasant smell of the moist earth. To me at least there was a strange contrast between the sweet promise of the spring and this sinister quest upon which we were engaged. My companion sat in the front of the trap, his arms folded, his hat pulled down over his eyes, and his chin sunk upon his breast, buried in the deepest thought. Suddenly, however, he started, tapped me on the shoulder, and pointed over the meadows

"Look there!" said he.

A heavily timbered park stretched up in a gentle slope, thickening into a grove at the highest point. From amid the branches there jutted out the grey gables and high roof-tree of a very old mansion.

"Stoke Moran?" said he.

"Yes, sir, that be the house of Dr. Grimesby Roylott," remarked the driver.

"There is some building going on there," said Holmes; "that is where we are going."

"There's the village," said the driver, pointing to a cluster of roofs some distance to the left; "but if you want to get to the house, you'll find it shorter to get over this stile, and so by the footpath over the fields. There it is, where the lady is walking."

"And the lady, I fancy, is Miss Stoner," observed Holmes, shading his eyes. "Yes, I think we had better do as you suggest."

We got off, paid our fare, and the trap rattled back on its way to Leatherhead.

"I thought it as well," said Holmes as we climbed the stile, "that this fellow should think we had come here as architects, or on some definite business. It may stop his gossip. Good-afternoon, Miss Stoner. You see that we have been as good as our word."

Our client of the morning had hurried forward to meet us with a face which spoke her joy. "I have been waiting so eagerly for you," she cried, shaking hands with us warmly. "All has turned out splendidly. Dr. Roylott has gone to town, and it is unlikely that he will be back before evening."

"We have had the pleasure of making the Doctor's acquaintance," said Holmes, and in a few words he sketched out what had occurred. Miss Stoner turned white to the lips as she listened.

"Good heavens!" she cried, "he has followed me, then."

"So it appears."

"He is so cunning that I never know when I am safe from him. What will he say when he returns?"

"He must guard himself, for he may find that there is someone more cunning than himself upon his track. You must lock yourself up from him to-night. If he is violent, we shall take you away to your aunt's at Harrow. Now, we must make the best use of our time, so kindly take us at once to the rooms which we are to examine."

The building was of grey, lichen-blotched stone, with a high central portion and two curving wings, like the claws of a crab, thrown out on each side. In one of these wings the windows were broken and blocked with wooden boards, while the roof was partly caved in, a picture of ruin. The central portion was in little better repair, but the right-hand block was comparatively modern, and the blinds in the windows, with the blue smoke curling up from the chimneys, showed that this was where the family resided. Some scaffolding had been erected against the end wall, and the stone-work had been broken into, but there were no signs of any workmen at the moment of our visit. Holmes walked slowly up and down the ill-trimmed lawn and examined with deep attention the outsides of the windows.

"This, I take it, belongs to the room in which you used to sleep, the centre one to your sister's, and the one next to the main building to Dr. Roylott's chamber?"

"Exactly so. But I am now sleeping in the middle one."

"Pending the alterations, as I understand. By the way, there does not seem to be any very pressing need for repairs at that end wall."

"There were none. I believe that it was an excuse to move me from my room."

"Ah! that is suggestive. Now, on the other side of this narrow wing runs the corridor from which these three rooms open. There are windows in it, of course?"

"Yes, but very small ones. Too narrow for anyone to pass through."

"As you both locked your doors at night, your rooms were unapproachable from that side. Now, would you have the kindness to go into your room and bar your shutters?"

Miss Stoner did so, and Holmes, after a careful examination through the open window, endeavoured in every way to force the shutter open, but without success. There was no slit through which a knife could be passed to raise the bar. Then with his lens he tested the hinges, but they were of solid iron, built firmly into the massive masonry. "Hum!" said he, scratching his chin in some perplexity, "my theory certainly presents some difficulties. No one could pass these shutters if they were bolted. Well, we shall see if the inside throws any light upon the matter."

A small side door led into the whitewashed corridor from which the three bedrooms opened. Holmes refused to examine the third chamber, so we passed at once to the second, that in which Miss Stoner was now sleeping, and in which her sister had met with her fate. It was a homely little room, with a low ceiling and a gaping fireplace, after the fashion of old country-houses. A brown chest of drawers stood in one corner, a narrow white-counterpaned bed in another, and a dressing-table on the left-hand side of the window. These articles, with two small wicker-work chairs, made up all the furniture in

the room save for a square of Wilton carpet in the centre. The boards round and the panelling of the walls were of brown, worm-eaten oak, so old and discoloured that it may have dated from the original building of the house. Holmes drew one of the chairs into a corner and sat silent, while his eyes travelled round and round and up and down, taking in every detail of the apartment.

"Where does that bell communicate with?" he asked at last pointing to a thick bell-rope which hung down beside the bed, the tassel actually lying upon the pillow.

"It goes to the housekeeper's room."

"It looks newer than the other things?"

"Yes, it was only put there a couple of years ago."

"Your sister asked for it, I suppose?"

"No, I never heard of her using it. We used always to get what we wanted for ourselves."

"Indeed, it seemed unnecessary to put so nice a bell-pull there. You will excuse me for a few minutes while I satisfy myself as to this floor." He threw himself down upon his face with his lens in his hand and crawled swiftly backward and forward, examining minutely the cracks between the boards. Then he did the same with the wood-work with which the chamber was panelled. Finally he walked over to the bed and spent some time in staring at it and in running his eye up and down the wall. Finally he took the bell-rope in his hand and gave it a brisk tug.

"Why, it's a dummy," said he.

"Won't it ring?"

"No, it is not even attached to a wire. This is very interesting. You can see now that it is fastened to a hook just above where the little opening for the ventilator is."

"How very absurd! I never noticed that before."

"Very strange!" muttered Holmes, pulling at the rope. "There are one or two very singular points about this room. For example, what a fool a builder must be to open a ventilator into another room, when, with the same trouble, he might have communicated with the outside air!"

"That is also quite modern," said the lady.

"Done about the same time as the bell-rope?" remarked Holmes.

"Yes, there were several little changes carried out about that time."

"They seem to have been of a most interesting character—dummy bell-ropes, and ventilators which do not ventilate. With your permission, Miss Stoner, we shall now carry our researches into the inner apartment."

Dr. Grimesby Roylott's chamber was larger than that of his step-daughter, but was as plainly furnished. A camp-bed, a small wooden shelf full of books, mostly of a technical character, an armchair beside the bed, a plain wooden chair against the wall, a round table, and a large iron safe were the principal things which met the eye. Holmes walked slowly round and examined each and all of them with the keenest interest.

"What's in here?" he asked, tapping the safe.

"My stepfather's business papers."

"Oh! you have seen inside, then?"

"Only once, some years ago. I remember that it was full of papers."

"There isn't a cat in it, for example?"

"No. What a strange idea!"

"Well, look at this!" He took up a small saucer of milk which stood on the top of it.

"No; we don't keep a cat. But there is a cheetah and a baboon."

"Ah, yes, of course! Well, a cheetah is just a big cat, and yet a saucer of milk does not go very far in satisfying its wants, I daresay. There is one point which I should wish to determine." He squatted down in front of the wooden chair and examined the seat of it with the greatest attention.

"Thank you. That is quite settled," said he, rising and putting his lens in his pocket. "Hullo! Here is something interesting!"

The object which had caught his eye was a small dog lash hung on one corner of the bed. The lash, however, was curled upon itself and tied so as to make a loop of whipcord.

"What do you make of that, Watson?"

"It's a common enough lash. But I don't know why it should be tied."

"That is not quite so common, is it? Ah, me! it's a wicked world, and when a clever man turns his brains to crime it is the worst of all. I think that I have seen enough now, Miss Stoner, and with your permission we shall walk out upon the lawn."

I had never seen my friend's face so grim or his brow so dark as it was when we turned from the scene of this investigation. We had walked several times up and down the lawn, neither Miss Stoner nor myself liking to break in upon his thoughts before he roused himself from his reverie.

"It is very essential, Miss Stoner," said he, "that you should absolutely follow my advice in every respect."

"I shall most certainly do so."

"The matter is too serious for any hesitation. Your life may depend upon your compliance."

"I assure you that I am in your hands."

"In the first place, both my friend and I must spend the night in your room."

Both Miss Stoner and I gazed at him in astonishment.

"Yes, it must be so. Let me explain. I believe that that is the village inn over there?"

"Yes, that is the Crown."

"Very good. Your windows would be visible from there?"

"Certainly."

"You must confine yourself to your room, on pretence of a headache, when your stepfather comes back. Then when you hear him retire for the night, you must open the shutters of your window, undo the hasp, put your lamp there as a signal to us, and then withdraw quietly with everything which you are likely to want into the room which you used to occupy. I have no doubt that, in spite of the repairs, you could manage there for one night."

"Oh, yes, easily."

"The rest you will leave in our hands."

"But what will you do?"

"We shall spend the night in your room, and we shall investigate the cause of this noise which has disturbed you."

"I believe, Mr. Holmes, that you have already made up your mind," said Miss Stoner, laying her hand upon my companion's sleeve.

"Perhaps I have."

"Then, for pity's sake, tell me what was the cause of my sister's death."

"I should prefer to have clearer proofs before I speak."

"You can at least tell me whether my own thought is correct, and if she died from some sudden fright."

"No, I do not think so. I think that there was probably some more tangible cause. And now, Miss Stoner, we must leave you for if Dr. Roylott returned and saw us our journey would be in vain. Good-bye, and be brave, for if you will do what I have told you, you may rest assured that we shall soon drive away the dangers that threaten you."

Sherlock Holmes and I had no difficulty in engaging a bedroom and sitting-room at the Crown Inn. They were on the upper floor, and from our window we could command a view of the avenue gate, and of the inhabited wing of Stoke Moran Manor House. At dusk we saw Dr. Grimesby Roylott drive past, his huge form looming up beside the little figure of the lad who drove him. The boy had some slight difficulty in undoing the heavy iron gates, and we heard the hoarse roar of the Doctor's voice and saw the fury with which he shook his clinched fists at him. The trap drove on, and a few minutes later we saw a sudden light spring up among the trees as the lamp was lit in one of the sitting-rooms.

"Do you know, Watson," said Holmes as we sat together in the gathering darkness, "I have really some scruples as to taking you to-night. There is a distinct element of danger."

"Can I be of assistance?"

"Your presence might be invaluable."

"Then I shall certainly come."

"It is very kind of you."

"You speak of danger. You have evidently seen more in these rooms than was visible to me."

"No, but I fancy that I may have deduced a little more. I imagine that you saw all that I did."

"I saw nothing remarkable save the bell-rope, and what purpose that could answer I confess is more than I can imagine."

"You saw the ventilator, too?"

"Yes, but I do not think that it is such a very unusual thing to have a small opening between two rooms. It was so small that a rat could hardly pass through."

"I knew that we should find a ventilator before ever we came to Stoke Moran."

"My dear Holmes!"

"Oh, yes, I did. You remember in her statement she said that her sister could smell Dr. Roylott's cigar. Now, of course that suggested at once that there must be a communication between the two rooms. It could only be a small one, or it would have been remarked upon at the coroner's inquiry. I deduced a ventilator."

"But what harm can there be in that?"

"Well, there is at least a curious coincidence of dates. A ventilator is made, a cord is hung, and a lady who sleeps in the bed dies. Does not that strike you?"

"I cannot as yet see any connection."

"Did you observe anything very peculiar about that bed?"

"No."

"It was clamped to the floor. Did you ever see a bed fastened like that before?"

"I cannot say that I have."

"The lady could not move her bed. It must always be in the same relative position to

the ventilator and to the rope—or so we may call it, since it was clearly never meant for a bell-pull."

"Holmes," I cried, "I seem to see dimly what you are hinting at. We are only just in time to prevent some subtle and horrible crime."

"Subtle enough and horrible enough. When a doctor does go wrong he is the first of criminals. He has nerve and he has knowledge. Palmer and Pritchard were among the heads of their profession. This man strikes even deeper, but I think, Watson, that we shall be able to strike deeper still. But we shall have horrors enough before the night is over; for goodness' sake let us have a quiet pipe and turn our minds for a few hours to something more cheerful."

About nine o'clock the light among the trees was extinguished, and all was dark in the direction of the Manor House. Two hours passed slowly away, and then, suddenly, just at the stroke of eleven, a single bright light shone out right in front of us.

"That is our signal," said Holmes, springing to his feet; "it comes from the middle window."

As we passed out he exchanged a few words with the landlord, explaining that we were going on a late visit to an acquaintance, and that it was possible that we might spend the night there. A moment later we were out on the dark road, a chill wind blowing in our faces, and one yellow light twinkling in front of us through the gloom to guide us on our sombre errand.

There was little difficulty in entering the grounds, for unrepaired breaches gaped in the old park wall. Making our way among the trees, we reached the lawn, crossed it, and were about to enter through the window when out from a clump of laurel bushes there darted what seemed to be a hideous and distorted child, who threw itself upon the grass with writhing limbs and then ran swiftly across the lawn into the darkness.

"My God!" I whispered; "did you see it?"

Holmes was for the moment as startled as I. His hand closed like a vice upon my wrist in his agitation. Then he broke into a low laugh and put his lips to my ear.

"It is a nice household," he murmured. "That is the baboon."

I had forgotten the strange pets which the Doctor affected. There was a cheetah, too; perhaps we might find it upon our shoulders at any moment. I confess that I felt easier in my mind when, after following Holmes' example and slipping off my shoes, I found myself inside the bedroom. My companion noiselessly closed the shutters, moved the lamp onto the table, and cast his eyes round the room. All was as we had seen it in the daytime. Then creeping up to me and making a trumpet of his hand, he whispered into my ear again so gently that it was all that I could do to distinguish the words:

"The least sound would be fatal to our plans."

I nodded to show that I had heard.

"We must sit without light. He would see it through the ventilator."

I nodded again.

"Do not go asleep; your very life may depend upon it. Have your pistol ready in case we should need it. I will sit on the side of the bed, and you in that chair."

I took out my revolver and laid it on the corner of the table.

Holmes had brought up a long thin cane, and this he placed upon the bed beside him. By it he laid the box of matches and the stump of a candle. Then he turned down the lamp, and we were left in darkness.

How shall I ever forget that dreadful vigil? I could not hear a sound, not even the drawing of a breath, and yet I knew that my companion sat open-eyed, within a few feet of me, in the same state of nervous tension in which I was myself. The shutters cut off the least ray of light, and we waited in absolute darkness.

From outside came the occasional cry of a night-bird, and once at our very window a long drawn catlike whine, which told us that the cheetah was indeed at liberty. Far away we could hear the deep tones of the parish clock, which boomed out every quarter of an hour. How long they seemed, those quarters! Twelve struck, and one and two and three, and still we sat waiting silently for whatever might befall.

Suddenly there was the momentary gleam of a light up in the direction of the ventilator, which vanished immediately, but was succeeded by a strong smell of burning oil and heated metal. Someone in the next room had lit a dark-lantern. I heard a gentle sound of movement, and then all was silent once more, though the smell grew stronger. For half an hour I sat with straining ears. Then suddenly another sound became audible—a very gentle, soothing sound, like that of a small jet of steam escaping continually from a kettle. The instant that we heard it, Holmes sprang from the bed, struck a match, and lashed furiously with his cane at the bell pull.

"You see it, Watson?" he yelled. "You see it?"

But I saw nothing. At the moment when Holmes struck the light I heard a low, clear whistle, but the sudden glare flashing into my weary eyes made it impossible for me to tell what it was at which my friend lashed so savagely. I could, however, see that his face was deadly pale and filled with horror and loathing. He had ceased to strike and was gazing up at the ventilator when suddenly there broke from the silence of the night the most horrible cry to which I have ever listened. It swelled up louder and louder, a hoarse yell of pain and fear and anger all mingled in the one dreadful shriek. They say that away down in the village, and even in the distant parsonage, that cry raised the sleepers from their beds. It struck cold to our hearts, and I stood gazing at Holmes, and he at me, until the last echoes of it had died away into the silence from which it rose.

"What can it mean?" I gasped.

"It means that it is all over," Holmes answered. "And perhaps, after all, it is for the best. Take your pistol, and we will enter Dr. Roylott's room."

With a grave face he lit the lamp and led the way down the corridor. Twice he struck at the chamber door without any reply from within. Then he turned the handle and entered, I at his heels, with the cocked pistol in my hand.

It was a singular sight which met our eyes. On the table stood a dark-lantern with the shutter half open, throwing a brilliant beam of light upon the iron safe, the door of which was ajar. Beside this table, on the wooden chair, sat Dr. Grimesby Roylott clad in a long grey dressing-gown, his bare ankles protruding beneath, and his feet thrust into red heelless Turkish slippers. Across his lap lay the short stock with the long lash which we had noticed during the day. His chin was cocked upward and his eyes were fixed in a dreadful, rigid stare at the corner of the ceiling. Round his brow he had a peculiar yellow band, with brownish speckles, which seemed to be bound tightly round his head. As we entered he made neither sound nor motion.

"The band! the speckled band!" whispered Holmes.

I took a step forward. In an instant his strange headgear began to move, and there

reared itself from among his hair the squat diamond-shaped head and puffed neck of a loathsome serpent.

"It is a swamp adder!" cried Holmes; "the deadliest snake in India. He has died within ten seconds of being bitten. Violence does, in truth, recoil upon the violent, and the schemer falls into the pit which he digs for another. Let us thrust this creature back into its den, and we can then remove Miss Stoner to some place of shelter and let the county police know what has happened."

As he spoke he drew the dog-whip swiftly from the dead man's lap, and throwing the noose round the reptile's neck he drew it from its horrid perch and, carrying it at arm's length, threw it into the iron safe, which he closed upon it.

Such are the true facts of the death of Dr. Grimesby Roylott, of Stoke Moran. It is not necessary that I should prolong a narrative which has already run to too great a length by telling how we broke the sad news to the terrified girl, how we conveyed her by the morning train to the care of her good aunt at Harrow, of how the slow process of official inquiry came to the conclusion that the doctor met his fate while indiscreetly playing with a dangerous pet. The little which I had yet to learn of the case was told me by Sherlock Holmes as we travelled back next day.

"I had," said he, "come to an entirely erroneous conclusion which shows, my dear Watson, how dangerous it always is to reason from insufficient data. The presence of the gipsies, and the use of the word 'band,' which was used by the poor girl, no doubt, to explain the appearance which she had caught a hurried glimpse of by the light of her match, were sufficient to put me upon an entirely wrong scent. I can only claim the merit that I instantly reconsidered my position when, however, it became clear to me that whatever danger threatened an occupant of the room could not come either from the window or the door. My attention was speedily drawn, as I have already remarked to you, to this ventilator, and to the bell-rope which hung down to the bed. The discovery that this was a dummy, and that the bed was clamped to the floor, instantly gave rise to the suspicion that the rope was there as a bridge for something passing through the hole and coming to the bed. The idea of a snake instantly occurred to me, and when I coupled it with my knowledge that the doctor was furnished with a supply of creatures from India, I felt that I was probably on the right track. The idea of using a form of poison which could not possibly be discovered by any chemical test was just such a one as would occur to a clever and ruthless man who had had an Eastern training. The rapidity with which such a poison would take effect would also, from his point of view, be an advantage. It would be a sharp-eyed coroner, indeed, who could distinguish the two little dark punctures which would show where the poison fangs had done their work. Then I thought of the whistle. Of course he must recall the snake before the morning light revealed it to the victim. He had trained it, probably by the use of the milk which we saw, to return to him when summoned. He would put it through this ventilator at the hour that he thought best, with the certainty that it would crawl down the rope and land on the bed. It might or might not bite the occupant, perhaps she might escape every night for a week, but sooner or later she must fall a victim.

"I had come to these conclusions before ever I had entered his room. An inspection of his chair showed me that he had been in the habit of standing on it, which of course would be necessary in order that he should reach the ventilator. The sight of the safe, the saucer of milk, and the loop of whipcord were enough to finally dispel any doubts which

may have remained. The metallic clang heard by Miss Stoner was obviously caused by her stepfather hastily closing the door of his safe upon its terrible occupant. Having once made up my mind, you know the steps which I took in order to put the matter to the proof. I heard the creature hiss as I have no doubt that you did also, and I instantly lit the light and attacked it."

"With the result of driving it through the ventilator."

"And also with the result of causing it to turn upon its master at the other side. Some of the blows of my cane came home and roused its snakish temper, so that it flew upon the first person it saw. In this way I am no doubt indirectly responsible for Dr. Grimesby Roylott's death, and I cannot say that it is likely to weigh very heavily upon my conscience."

THE MUSGRAVE RITUAL
FROM THE MEMOIRS OF SHERLOCK HOLMES (1894)

AN ANOMALY which often struck me in the character of my friend Sherlock Holmes was that, although in his methods of thought he was the neatest and most methodical of mankind, and although also he affected a certain quiet primness of dress, he was none the less in his personal habits one of the most untidy men that ever drove a fellow-lodger to distraction. Not that I am in the least conventional in that respect myself. The rough-and-tumble work in Afghanistan, coming on the top of a natural Bohemianism of disposition, has made me rather more lax than befits a medical man. But with me there is a limit, and when I find a man who keeps his cigars in the coal-scuttle, his tobacco in the toe end of a Persian slipper, and his unanswered correspondence transfixed by a jack-knife into the very centre of his wooden mantelpiece, then I begin to give myself virtuous airs. I have always held, too, that pistol practice should be distinctly an open-air pastime; and when Holmes, in one of his queer humours, would sit in an armchair with his hair-trigger and a hundred Boxer cartridges, and proceed to adorn the opposite wall with a patriotic V. R. done in bullet-pocks, I felt strongly that neither the atmosphere nor the appearance of our room was improved by it.

Our chambers were always full of chemicals and of criminal relics which had a way of wandering into unlikely positions, and of turning up in the butter-dish or in even less desirable places. But his papers were my great crux. He had a horror of destroying documents, especially those which were connected with his past cases, and yet it was only once in every year or two that he would muster energy to docket and arrange them; for, as I have mentioned somewhere in these incoherent memoirs, the outbursts of passionate energy when he performed the remarkable feats with which his name is associated were followed by reactions of lethargy during which he would lie about with his violin and his books, hardly moving save from the sofa to the table. Thus month after month his papers accumulated, until every corner of the room was stacked with bundles of manuscript which were on no account to be burned, and which could not be put away save by their owner. One winter's night, as we sat together by the fire, I ventured to suggest to him that,

as he had finished pasting extracts into his common-place book, he might employ the next two hours in making our room a little more habitable. He could not deny the justice of my request, so with a rather rueful face he went off to his bedroom, from which he returned presently pulling a large tin box behind him. This he placed in the middle of the floor and, squatting down upon a stool in front of it, he threw back the lid. I could see that it was already a third full of bundles of paper tied up with red tape into separate packages.

"There are cases enough here, Watson," said he, looking at me with mischievous eyes. "I think that if you knew all that I had in this box you would ask me to pull some out instead of putting others in."

"These are the records of your early work, then?" I asked. "I have often wished that I had notes of those cases."

"Yes, my boy, these were all done prematurely before my biographer had come to glorify me." He lifted bundle after bundle in a tender, caressing sort of way. "They are not all successes, Watson," said he. "But there are some pretty little problems among them. Here's the record of the Tarleton murders, and the case of Vamberry, the wine merchant, and the adventure of the old Russian woman, and the singular affair of the aluminium crutch, as well as a full account of Ricoletti of the club foot, and his abominable wife. And here—ah, now, this really is something a little *recherché*."

He dived his arm down to the bottom of the chest, and brought up a small wooden box with a sliding lid, such as children's toys are kept in. From within he produced a crumpled piece of paper, an old-fashioned brass key, a peg of wood with a ball of string attached to it, and three rusty old disks of metal.

"Well, my boy, what do you make of this lot?" he asked, smiling at my expression.

"It is a curious collection."

"Very curious, and the story that hangs round it will strike you as being more curious still."

"These relics have a history then?"

"So much so that they *are* history."

"What do you mean by that?"

Sherlock Holmes picked them up one by one, and laid them along the edge of the table. Then he reseated himself in his chair and looked them over with a gleam of satisfaction in his eyes.

"These," said he, "are all that I have left to remind me of the adventure of the Musgrave Ritual."

I had heard him mention the case more than once, though I had never been able to gather the details.

"I should be so glad," said I, "if you would give me an account of it."

"And leave the litter as it is?" he cried, mischievously. "Your tidiness won't bear much strain after all, Watson. But I should be glad that you should add this case to your annals, for there are points in it which make it quite unique in the criminal records of this or, I believe, of any other country. A collection of my trifling achievements would certainly be incomplete which contained no account of this very singular business.

"You may remember how the affair of the *Gloria Scott*, and my conversation with the unhappy man whose fate I told you of, first turned my attention in the direction of the profession which has become my life's work. You see me now when my name has become known far and wide, and when I am generally recognised both by the public and by the

official force as being a final court of appeal in doubtful cases. Even when you knew me first, at the time of the affair which you have commemorated in 'A Study in Scarlet,' I had already established a considerable, though not a very lucrative, connection. You can hardly realize, then, how difficult I found it at first, and how long I had to wait before I succeeded in making any headway.

"When I first came up to London I had rooms in Montague Street, just round the corner from the British Museum, and there I waited, filling in my too abundant leisure time by studying all those branches of science which might make me more efficient. Now and again cases came in my way, principally through the introduction of old fellow-students, for during my last years at the University there was a good deal of talk there about myself and my methods. The third of these cases was that of the Musgrave Ritual, and it is to the interest which was aroused by that singular chain of events, and the large issues which proved to be at stake, that I trace my first stride towards the position which I now hold.

"Reginald Musgrave had been in the same college as myself, and I had some slight acquaintance with him. He was not generally popular among the undergraduates, though it always seemed to me that what was set down as pride was really an attempt to cover extreme natural diffidence. In appearance he was a man of exceedingly aristocratic type, thin, high-nosed, and large-eyed, with languid and yet courtly manners. He was indeed a scion of one of the very oldest families in the kingdom, though his branch was a cadet one which had separated from the northern Musgraves some time in the sixteenth century, and had established itself in western Sussex, where the Manor House of Hurlstone is perhaps the oldest inhabited building in the county. Something of his birthplace seemed to cling to the man, and I never looked at his pale, keen face or the poise of his head without associating him with grey archways and mullioned windows and all the venerable wreckage of a feudal keep. Once or twice we drifted into talk, and I can remember that more than once he expressed a keen interest in my methods of observation and inference.

"For four years I had seen nothing of him until one morning he walked into my room in Montague Street. He had changed little, was dressed like a young man of fashion—he was always a bit of a dandy—and preserved the same quiet, suave manner which had formerly distinguished him.

"'How has all gone with you Musgrave?' I asked, after we had cordially shaken hands.

"'You probably heard of my poor father's death,' said he; 'he was carried off about two years ago. Since then I have of course had the Hurlstone estates to manage, and as I am member for my district as well, my life has been a busy one. But I understand, Holmes, that you are turning to practical ends those powers with which you used to amaze us?'

"'Yes,' said I, 'I have taken to living by my wits.'

"'I am delighted to hear it, for your advice at present would be exceedingly valuable to me. We have had some very strange doings at Hurlstone, and the police have been able to throw no light upon the matter. It is really the most extraordinary and inexplicable business.'

"You can imagine with what eagerness I listened to him, Watson, for the very chance for which I had been panting during all those months of inaction seemed to have come within my reach. In my inmost heart I believed that I could succeed where others failed, and now I had the opportunity to test myself.

"'Pray, let me have the details,' I cried.

"Reginald Musgrave sat down opposite to me, and lit the cigarette which I had pushed towards him.

"'You must know,' said he, 'that though I am a bachelor, I have to keep up a considerable staff of servants at Hurlstone, for it is a rambling old place, and takes a good deal of looking after. I preserve, too, and in the pheasant months I usually have a house-party, so that it would not do to be short-handed. Altogether there are eight maids, the cook, the butler, two footmen, and a boy. The garden and the stables of course have a separate staff.

"'Of these servants the one who had been longest in our service was Brunton the butler. He was a young schoolmaster out of place when he was first taken up by my father, but he was a man of great energy and character, and he soon became quite invaluable in the household. He was a well-grown, handsome man, with a splendid forehead, and though he has been with us for twenty years he cannot be more than forty now. With his personal advantages and his extraordinary gifts—for he can speak several languages and play nearly every musical instrument—it is wonderful that he should have been satisfied so long in such a position, but I suppose that he was comfortable, and lacked energy to make any change. The butler of Hurlstone is always a thing that is remembered by all who visit us.

"'But this paragon has one fault. He is a bit of a Don Juan, and you can imagine that for a man like him it is not a very difficult part to play in a quiet country district. When he was married it was all right, but since he has been a widower we have had no end of trouble with him. A few months ago we were in hopes that he was about to settle down again for he became engaged to Rachel Howells, our second housemaid; but he has thrown her over since then and taken up with Janet Tregellis, the daughter of the head gamekeeper. Rachel—who is a very good girl, but of an excitable Welsh temperament—had a sharp touch of brain fever, and goes about the house now—or did until yesterday—like a black-eyed shadow of her former self. That was our first drama at Hurlstone; but a second one came to drive it from our minds, and it was prefaced by the disgrace and dismissal of butler Brunton.

"'This was how it came about. I have said that the man was intelligent, and this very intelligence has caused his ruin, for it seems to have led to an insatiable curiosity about things which did not in the least concern him. I had no idea of the lengths to which this would carry him, until the merest accident opened my eyes to it.

"'I have said that the house is a rambling one. One day last week—on Thursday night, to be more exact—I found that I could not sleep, having foolishly taken a cup of strong *café noir* after my dinner. After struggling against it until two in the morning, I felt that it was quite hopeless, so I rose and lit the candle with the intention of continuing a novel which I was reading. The book, however, had been left in the billiard-room, so I pulled on my dressing-gown and started off to get it.

"'In order to reach the billiard-room I had to descend a flight of stairs and then to cross the head of a passage which led to the library and the gun-room. You can imagine my surprise when, as I looked down this corridor, I saw a glimmer of light coming from the open door of the library. I had myself extinguished the lamp and closed the door before coming to bed. Naturally my first thought was of burglars. The corridors at Hurlstone have their walls largely decorated with trophies of old weapons. From one of these I

picked a battle-axe, and then, leaving my candle behind me, I crept on tiptoe down the passage and peeped in at the open door.

"'Brunton, the butler, was in the library. He was sitting, fully dressed, in an easy-chair, with a slip of paper which looked like a map upon his knee, and his forehead sunk forward upon his hand in deep thought. I stood dumb with astonishment, watching him from the darkness. A small taper on the edge of the table shed a feeble light which sufficed to show me that he was fully dressed. Suddenly, as I looked, he rose from his chair, and walking over to a bureau at the side, he unlocked it and drew out one of the drawers. From this he took a paper, and returning to his seat he flattened it out beside the taper on the edge of the table, and began to study it with minute attention. My indignation at this calm examination of our family documents overcame me so far that I took a step forward, and Brunton, looking up, saw me standing in the doorway. He sprang to his feet, his face turned livid with fear, and he thrust into his breast the chart-like paper which he had been originally studying.

"'"So!" said I. "This is how you repay the trust which we have reposed in you. You will leave my service to-morrow."

"'He bowed with the look of a man who is utterly crushed, and slunk past me without a word. The taper was still on the table, and by its light I glanced to see what the paper was which Brunton had taken from the bureau. To my surprise it was nothing of any importance at all, but simply a copy of the questions and answers in the singular old observance called the Musgrave Ritual. It is a sort of ceremony peculiar to our family, which each Musgrave for centuries past has gone through on his coming of age—a thing of private interest, and perhaps of some little importance to the archaeologist, like our own blazonings and charges, but of no practical use whatever.'

"'We had better come back to the paper afterwards,' said I.

"'If you think it really necessary,' he answered, with some hesitation. 'To continue my statement, however: I relocked the bureau, using the key which Brunton had left, and I had turned to go when I was surprised to find that the butler had returned, and was standing before me.

"'"Mr. Musgrave, sir," he cried, in a voice which was hoarse with emotion, "I can't bear disgrace, sir. I've always been proud above my station in life, and disgrace would kill me. My blood will be on your head, sir—it will, indeed—if you drive me to despair. If you cannot keep me after what has passed, then for God's sake let me give you notice and leave in a month, as if of my own free will. I could stand that, Mr. Musgrave, but not to be cast out before all the folk that I know so well."

"'"You don't deserve much consideration, Brunton," I answered. "Your conduct has been most infamous. However, as you have been a long time in the family, I have no wish to bring public disgrace upon you. A month, however is too long. Take yourself away in a week, and give what reason you like for going."

"'"Only a week, sir?" he cried, in a despairing voice. "A fortnight—say at least a fortnight!"

"'"A week," I repeated, "and you may consider yourself to have been very leniently dealt with."

"'He crept away, his face sunk upon his breast, like a broken man, while I put out the light and returned to my room.

"'For two days after this Brunton was most assiduous in his attention to his duties. I

made no allusion to what had passed, and waited with some curiosity to see how he would cover his disgrace. On the third morning, however he did not appear, as was his custom, after breakfast to receive my instructions for the day. As I left the dining-room I happened to meet Rachel Howells, the maid. I have told you that she had only recently recovered from an illness, and was looking so wretchedly pale and wan that I remonstrated with her for being at work.

""'You should be in bed," I said. "Come back to your duties when you are stronger."

"'She looked at me with so strange an expression that I began to suspect that her brain was affected.

""'I am strong enough, Mr. Musgrave," said she.

""'We will see what the doctor says," I answered. "You must stop work now, and when you go downstairs just say that I wish to see Brunton."

""'The butler is gone," said she.

""'Gone! Gone where?"

""'He is gone. No one has seen him. He is not in his room. Oh, yes, he is gone, he is gone!" She fell back against the wall with shriek after shriek of laughter, while I, horrified at this sudden hysterical attack, rushed to the bell to summon help. The girl was taken to her room, still screaming and sobbing, while I made inquiries about Brunton. There was no doubt about it that he had disappeared. His bed had not been slept in, he had been seen by no one since he had retired to his room the night before, and yet it was difficult to see how he could have left the house, as both windows and doors were found to be fastened in the morning. His clothes, his watch, and even his money were in his room, but the black suit which he usually wore was missing. His slippers, too, were gone, but his boots were left behind. Where then could butler Brunton have gone in the night, and what could have become of him now?

"'Of course we searched the house from cellar to garret, but there was no trace of him. It is, as I have said, a labyrinth of an old house, especially the original wing, which is now practically uninhabited; but we ransacked every room and cellar without discovering the least sign of the missing man. It was incredible to me that he could have gone away leaving all his property behind him, and yet where could he be? I called in the local police, but without success. Rain had fallen on the night before and we examined the lawn and the paths all round the house, but in vain. Matters were in this state, when a new development quite drew our attention away from the original mystery.

"'For two days Rachel Howells had been so ill, sometimes delirious, sometimes hysterical, that a nurse had been employed to sit up with her at night. On the third night after Brunton's disappearance, the nurse, finding her patient sleeping nicely, had dropped into a nap in the armchair, when she woke in the early morning to find the bed empty, the window open, and no signs of the invalid. I was instantly aroused, and, with the two footmen, started off at once in search of the missing girl. It was not difficult to tell the direction which she had taken, for, starting from under her window, we could follow her footmarks easily across the lawn to the edge of the mere, where they vanished close to the gravel path which leads out of the grounds. The lake there is eight feet deep, and you can imagine our feelings when we saw that the trail of the poor demented girl came to an end at the edge of it.

"'Of course, we had the drags at once, and set to work to recover the remains, but no trace of the body could we find. On the other hand, we brought to the surface an object of

a most unexpected kind. It was a linen bag which contained within it a mass of old rusted and discoloured metal and several dull-coloured pieces of pebble or glass. This strange find was all that we could get from the mere, and, although we made every possible search and inquiry yesterday, we know nothing of the fate either of Rachel Howells or of Richard Brunton. The county police are at their wits' end, and I have come up to you as a last resource.'

"You can imagine, Watson, with what eagerness I listened to this extraordinary sequence of events, and endeavoured to piece them together, and to devise some common thread upon which they might all hang. The butler was gone. The maid was gone. The maid had loved the butler, but had afterwards had cause to hate him. She was of Welsh blood, fiery and passionate. She had been terribly excited immediately after his disappearance. She had flung into the lake a bag containing some curious contents. These were all factors which had to be taken into consideration, and yet none of them got quite to the heart of the matter. What was the starting-point of this chain of events? There lay the end of this tangled line.

"'I must see that paper, Musgrave,' said I, 'which this butler of yours thought it worth his while to consult, even at the risk of the loss of his place.'

"'It is rather an absurd business, this ritual of ours,' he answered. 'But it has at least the saving grace of antiquity to excuse it. I have a copy of the questions and answers here if you care to run your eye over them.'

"He handed me the very paper which I have here, Watson, and this is the strange catechism to which each Musgrave had to submit when he came to man's estate. I will read you the questions and answers as they stand.

"'Whose was it?'

"'His who is gone.'

"'Who shall have it?'

"'He who will come.'

"'Where was the sun?'

"'Over the oak.'

"'Where was the shadow?'

"'Under the elm.'

"How was it stepped?'

"'North by ten and by ten, east by five and by five, south by two and by two, west by one and by one, and so under.'

"'What shall we give for it?'

"'All that is ours.'

"'Why should we give it?'

"'For the sake of the trust.'

"'The original has no date, but is in the spelling of the middle of the seventeenth century,' remarked Musgrave. 'I am afraid, however, that it can be of little help to you in solving this mystery.'

"'At least,' said I, 'it gives us another mystery, and one which is even more interesting than the first. It may be that the solution of the one may prove to be the solution of the other. You will excuse me, Musgrave, if I say that your butler appears to me to have been a very clever man, and to have had a clearer insight than ten generations of his masters.'

"'I hardly follow you,' said Musgrave. 'The paper seems to me to be of no practical importance.'

"'But to me it seems immensely practical, and I fancy that Brunton took the same view. He had probably seen it before that night on which you caught him.'

"'It is very possible. We took no pains to hide it.'

"'He simply wished, I should imagine, to refresh his memory upon that last occasion. He had, as I understand, some sort of map or chart which he was comparing with the manuscript, and which he thrust into his pocket when you appeared.'

"'That is true. But what could he have to do with this old family custom of ours, and what does this rigmarole mean?'

"'I don't think that we should have much difficulty in determining that,' said I; 'with your permission we will take the first train down to Sussex, and go a little more deeply into the matter upon the spot.'

"The same afternoon saw us both at Hurlstone. Possibly you have seen pictures and read descriptions of the famous old building, so I will confine my account of it to saying that it is built in the shape of an L, the long arm being the more modern portion, and the shorter the ancient nucleus, from which the other had developed. Over the low, heavily-lintelled door, in the centre of this old part, is chiseled the date, 1607, but experts are agreed that the beams and stonework are really much older than this. The enormously thick walls and tiny windows of this part had in the last century driven the family into building the new wing, and the old one was used now as a storehouse and a cellar, when it was used at all. A splendid park with fine old timber surrounds the house, and the lake, to which my client had referred, lay close to the avenue, about two hundred yards from the building.

"I was already firmly convinced, Watson, that there were not three separate mysteries here, but one only, and that if I could read the Musgrave Ritual aright I should hold in my hand the clue which would lead me to the truth concerning both the butler Brunton and the maid Howells. To that then I turned all my energies. Why should this servant be so anxious to master this old formula? Evidently because he saw something in it which had escaped all those generations of country squires, and from which he expected some personal advantage. What was it then, and how had it affected his fate?

"It was perfectly obvious to me, on reading the Ritual, that the measurements must refer to some spot to which the rest of the document alluded, and that if we could find that spot, we should be in a fair way towards finding what the secret was which the old Musgraves had thought it necessary to embalm in so curious a fashion. There were two guides given us to start with, an oak and an elm. As to the oak there could be no question at all. Right in front of the house, upon the left-hand side of the drive, there stood a patriarch among oaks, one of the most magnificent trees that I have ever seen.

"'That was there when your Ritual was drawn up,' said I, as we drove past it.

"'It was there at the Norman Conquest in all probability,' he answered. 'It has a girth of twenty-three feet.'

"'Have you any old elms?' I asked.

"'There used to be a very old one over yonder but it was struck by lightning ten years ago, and we cut down the stump.'

"'You can see where it used to be?'

"'Oh, yes.'

"'There are no other elms?'

"'No old ones, but plenty of beeches.'

"'I should like to see where it grew.'

"We had driven up in a dog-cart, and my client led me away at once, without our entering the house, to the scar on the lawn where the elm had stood. It was nearly midway between the oak and the house. My investigation seemed to be progressing.

"'I suppose it is impossible to find out how high the elm was?' I asked.

"'I can give you it at once. It was sixty-four feet.'

"'How do you come to know it?' I asked, in surprise.

"'When my old tutor used to give me an exercise in trigonometry, it always took the shape of measuring heights. When I was a lad I worked out every tree and building in the estate.'

"This was an unexpected piece of luck. My data were coming more quickly than I could have reasonably hoped.

"'Tell me,' I asked, 'did your butler ever ask you such a question?'

"Reginald Musgrave looked at me in astonishment. 'Now that you call it to my mind,' he answered, 'Brunton *did* ask me about the height of the tree some months ago, in connection with some little argument with the groom.'

"This was excellent news, Watson, for it showed me that I was on the right road. I looked up at the sun. It was low in the heavens, and I calculated that in less than an hour it would lie just above the topmost branches of the old oak. One condition mentioned in the Ritual would then be fulfilled. And the shadow of the elm must mean the farther end of the shadow, otherwise the trunk would have been chosen as the guide. I had, then, to find where the far end of the shadow would fall when the sun was just clear of the oak."

"That must have been difficult, Holmes, when the elm was no longer there."

"Well, at least I knew that if Brunton could do it, I could also. Besides, there was no real difficulty. I went with Musgrave to his study and whittled myself this peg, to which I tied this long string with a knot at each yard. Then I took two lengths of a fishing-rod, which came to just six feet, and I went back with my client to where the elm had been. The sun was just grazing the top of the oak. I fastened the rod on end, marked out the direction of the shadow, and measured it. It was nine feet in length.

"Of course the calculation now was a simple one. If a rod of six feet threw a shadow of nine, a tree of sixty-four feet would throw one of ninety-six, and the line of the one would of course be the line of the other. I measured out the distance, which brought me almost to the wall of the house, and I thrust a peg into the spot. You can imagine my exultation, Watson, when within two inches of my peg I saw a conical depression in the ground. I knew that it was the mark made by Brunton in his measurements, and that I was still upon his trail.

"From this starting-point I proceeded to step, having first taken the cardinal points by my pocket-compass. Ten steps with each foot took me along parallel with the wall of the house, and again I marked my spot with a peg. Then I carefully paced off five to the east and two to the south. It brought me to the very threshold of the old door. Two steps to the west meant now that I was to go two paces down the stone-flagged passage, and this was the place indicated by the Ritual.

"Never have I felt such a cold chill of disappointment, Watson. For a moment it seemed to me that there must be some radical mistake in my calculations. The setting sun

shone full upon the passage floor, and I could see that the old, foot-worn grey stones with which it was paved were firmly cemented together, and had certainly not been moved for many a long year. Brunton had not been at work here. I tapped upon the floor, but it sounded the same all over, and there was no sign of any crack or crevice. But, fortunately, Musgrave, who had begun to appreciate the meaning of my proceedings, and who was now as excited as myself, took out his manuscript to check my calculation.

"'And under,' he cried. 'You have omitted the "and under."'

"I had thought that it meant that we were to dig, but now, of course, I saw at once that I was wrong. 'There is a cellar under this then?' I cried.

"'Yes, and as old as the house. Down here, through this door.'

"We went down a winding stone stair, and my companion, striking a match, lit a large lantern which stood on a barrel in the corner. In an instant it was obvious that we had at last come upon the true place, and that we had not been the only people to visit the spot recently.

"It had been used for the storage of wood, but the billets, which had evidently been littered over the floor, were now piled at the sides, so as to leave a clear space in the middle. In this space lay a large and heavy flagstone with a rusted iron ring in the centre to which a thick shepherd's-check muffler was attached.

"'By Jove!' cried my client. 'That's Brunton's muffler. I have seen it on him, and could swear to it. What has the villain been doing here?'

"At my suggestion a couple of the county police were summoned to be present, and I then endeavoured to raise the stone by pulling on the cravat. I could only move it slightly, and it was with the aid of one of the constables that I succeeded at last in carrying it to one side. A black hole yawned beneath into which we all peered, while Musgrave, kneeling at the side, pushed down the lantern.

"A small chamber about seven feet deep and four feet square lay open to us. At one side of this was a squat, brass-bound wooden box, the lid of which was hinged upwards, with this curious old-fashioned key projecting from the lock. It was furred outside by a thick layer of dust, and damp and worms had eaten through the wood, so that a crop of livid fungi was growing on the inside of it. Several discs of metal, old coins apparently, such as I hold here, were scattered over the bottom of the box, but it contained nothing else.

"At the moment, however, we had no thought for the old chest, for our eyes were riveted upon that which crouched beside it. It was the figure of a man, clad in a suit of black, who squatted down upon his hams with his forehead sunk upon the edge of the box and his two arms thrown out on each side of it. The attitude had drawn all the stagnant blood to the face, and no man could have recognised that distorted liver-coloured countenance; but his height, his dress, and his hair were all sufficient to show my client, when we had drawn the body up, that it was indeed his missing butler. He had been dead some days, but there was no wound or bruise upon his person to show how he had met his dreadful end. When his body had been carried from the cellar we found ourselves still confronted with a problem which was almost as formidable as that with which we had started.

"I confess that so far, Watson, I had been disappointed in my investigation. I had reckoned upon solving the matter when once I had found the place referred to in the Ritual; but now I was there, and was apparently as far as ever from knowing what it was

which the family had concealed with such elaborate precautions. It is true that I had thrown a light upon the fate of Brunton, but now I had to ascertain how that fate had come upon him, and what part had been played in the matter by the woman who had disappeared. I sat down upon a keg in the corner and thought the whole matter carefully over.

"You know my methods in such cases, Watson. I put myself in the man's place and, having first gauged his intelligence, I try to imagine how I should myself have proceeded under the same circumstances. In this case the matter was simplified by Brunton's intelligence being quite first-rate, so that it was unnecessary to make any allowance for the personal equation, as the astronomers have dubbed it. He knew that something valuable was concealed. He had spotted the place. He found that the stone which covered it was just too heavy for a man to move unaided. What would he do next? He could not get help from outside, even if he had some one whom he could trust, without the unbarring of doors and considerable risk of detection. It was better, if he could, to have his helpmate inside the house. But whom could he ask? This girl had been devoted to him. A man always finds it hard to realize that he may have finally lost a woman's love, however badly he may have treated her. He would try by a few attentions to make his peace with the girl Howells, and then would engage her as his accomplice. Together they would come at night to the cellar, and their united force would suffice to raise the stone. So far I could follow their actions as if I had actually seen them.

"But for two of them, and one a woman, it must have been heavy work the raising of that stone. A burly Sussex policeman and I had found it no light job. What would they do to assist them? Probably what I should have done myself. I rose and examined carefully the different billets of wood which were scattered round the floor. Almost at once I came upon what I expected. One piece, about three feet in length, had a very marked indentation at one end, while several were flattened at the sides as if they had been compressed by some considerable weight. Evidently, as they had dragged the stone up they had thrust the chunks of wood into the chink, until at last, when the opening was large enough to crawl through, they would hold it open by a billet placed lengthwise, which might very well become indented at the lower end, since the whole weight of the stone would press it down on to the edge of this other slab. So far I was still on safe ground.

"And now how was I to proceed to reconstruct this midnight drama? Clearly, only one could fit into the hole, and that one was Brunton. The girl must have waited above. Brunton then unlocked the box, handed up the contents presumably—since they were not to be found—and then—and then what happened?

"What smouldering fire of vengeance had suddenly sprung into flame in this passionate Celtic woman's soul when she saw the man who had wronged her—wronged her, perhaps, far more than we suspected—in her power? Was it a chance that the wood had slipped, and that the stone had shut Brunton into what had become his sepulchre? Had she only been guilty of silence as to his fate? Or had some sudden blow from her hand dashed the support away and sent the slab crashing down into its place? Be that as it might, I seemed to see that woman's figure still clutching at her treasure trove and flying wildly up the winding stair, with her ears ringing perhaps with the muffled screams from behind her and with the drumming of frenzied hands against the slab of stone which was choking her faithless lover's life out.

"Here was the secret of her blanched face, her shaken nerves, her peals of hysterical laughter on the next morning. But what had been in the box? What had she done with that? Of course, it must have been the old metal and pebbles which my client had dragged from the mere. She had thrown them in there at the first opportunity to remove the last trace of her crime.

"For twenty minutes I had sat motionless, thinking the matter out. Musgrave still stood with a very pale face, swinging his lantern and peering down into the hole.

"'These are coins of Charles the First,' said he, holding out the few which had been in the box; 'you see we were right in fixing our date for the Ritual.'

"'We may find something else of Charles the First,' I cried, as the probable meaning of the first two questions of the Ritual broke suddenly upon me. 'Let me see the contents of the bag which you fished from the mere.'

"We ascended to his study, and he laid the *débris* before me. I could understand his regarding it as of small importance when I looked at it, for the metal was almost black and the stones lustreless and dull. I rubbed one of them on my sleeve, however, and it glowed afterwards like a spark in the dark hollow of my hand. The metal work was in the form of a double ring, but it had been bent and twisted out of its original shape.

"'You must bear in mind,' said I, 'that the Royal party made head in England even after the death of the King, and that when they at last fled they probably left many of their most precious possessions buried behind them, with the intention of returning for them in more peaceful times.'

"'My ancestor, Sir Ralph Musgrave, was a prominent Cavalier and the right-hand man of Charles the Second in his wanderings,' said my friend.

"'Ah, indeed!' I answered. 'Well now, I think that really should give us the last link that we wanted. I must congratulate you on coming into the possession, though in rather a tragic manner of a relic which is of great intrinsic value, but of even greater importance as an historical curiosity.'

"'What is it, then?' he gasped in astonishment.

"'It is nothing less than the ancient crown of the Kings of England.'

"'The crown!'

"'Precisely. Consider what the Ritual says: How does it run? "Whose was it?" "His who is gone." That was after the execution of Charles. Then, "Who shall have it?" "He who will come." That was Charles the Second, whose advent was already foreseen. There can, I think, be no doubt that this battered and shapeless diadem once encircled the brows of the royal Stuarts.'

"'And how came it in the pond?'

"'Ah, that is a question that will take some time to answer.' And with that I sketched out to him the whole long chain of surmise and of proof which I had constructed. The twilight had closed in and the moon was shining brightly in the sky before my narrative was finished.

"'And how was it then that Charles did not get his crown when he returned?' asked Musgrave, pushing back the relic into its linen bag.

"'Ah, there you lay your finger upon the one point which we shall probably never be able to clear up. It is likely that the Musgrave who held the secret died in the interval, and by some oversight left this guide to his descendant without explaining the meaning of it.

From that day to this it has been handed down from father to son, until at last it came within reach of a man who tore its secret out of it and lost his life in the venture.'

"And that's the story of the Musgrave Ritual, Watson. They have the crown down at Hurlstone—though they had some legal bother and a considerable sum to pay before they were allowed to retain it. I am sure that if you mentioned my name they would be happy to show it to you. Of the woman nothing was ever heard, and the probability is that she got away out of England and carried herself and the memory of her crime to some land beyond the seas."

❧ 6 ❧

THE REIGATE SQUIRES

FROM THE MEMOIRS OF SHERLOCK HOLMES (1894)

It was some time before the health of my friend Mr Sherlock Holmes recovered from the strain caused by his immense exertions in the spring of '87. The whole question of the Netherland-Sumatra Company and of the colossal schemes of Baron Maupertuis are too recent in the minds of the public, and are too intimately concerned with politics and finance to be fitting subjects for this series of sketches. They led, however, in an indirect fashion to a singular and complex problem which gave my friend an opportunity of demonstrating the value of a fresh weapon among the many with which he waged his life-long battle against crime.

On referring to my notes I see that it was upon the 14th of April that I received a telegram from Lyons which informed me that Holmes was lying ill in the Hotel Dulong. Within twenty-four hours I was in his sick-room, and was relieved to find that there was nothing formidable in his symptoms. Even his iron constitution, however, had broken down under the strain of an investigation which had extended over two months, during which period he had never worked less than fifteen hours a day, and had more than once, as he assured me, kept to his task for five days at a stretch. Even the triumphant issue of his labours could not save him from reaction after so terrible an exertion, and at a time when Europe was ringing with his name and when his room was literally ankle-deep with congratulatory telegrams I found him a prey to the blackest depression. Even the knowledge that he had succeeded where the police of three countries had failed, and that he had outmanoeuvred at every point the most accomplished swindler in Europe, was insufficient to rouse him from his nervous prostration.

Three days later we were back in Baker Street together; but it was evident that my friend would be much the better for a change, and the thought of a week of spring time in the country was full of attractions to me also. My old friend, Colonel Hayter, who had come under my professional care in Afghanistan, had now taken a house near Reigate in Surrey, and had frequently asked me to come down to him upon a visit. On the last occasion he had remarked that if my friend would only come with me he would be glad to

extend his hospitality to him also. A little diplomacy was needed, but when Holmes understood that the establishment was a bachelor one, and that he would be allowed the fullest freedom, he fell in with my plans and a week after our return from Lyons we were under the Colonel's roof. Hayter was a fine old soldier who had seen much of the world, and he soon found, as I had expected, that Holmes and he had much in common.

On the evening of our arrival we were sitting in the Colonel's gun-room after dinner, Holmes stretched upon the sofa, while Hayter and I looked over his little armoury of fire-arms.

"By the way," said he suddenly, "I think I'll take one of these pistols upstairs with me in case we have an alarm."

"An alarm!" said I.

"Yes, we've had a scare in this part lately. Old Acton, who is one of our county magnates, had his house broken into last Monday. No great damage done, but the fellows are still at large."

"No clue?" asked Holmes, cocking his eye at the Colonel.

"None as yet. But the affair is a petty one, one of our little country crimes, which must seem too small for your attention, Mr. Holmes, after this great international affair."

Holmes waved away the compliment, though his smile showed that it had pleased him.

"Was there any feature of interest?"

"I fancy not. The thieves ransacked the library and got very little for their pains. The whole place was turned upside down, drawers burst open, and presses ransacked, with the result that an odd volume of Pope's 'Homer,' two plated candlesticks, an ivory letter-weight, a small oak barometer, and a ball of twine are all that have vanished."

"What an extraordinary assortment!" I exclaimed.

"Oh, the fellows evidently grabbed hold of everything they could get."

Holmes grunted from the sofa.

"The county police ought to make something of that," said he; "why, it is surely obvious that—"

But I held up a warning finger.

"You are here for a rest, my dear fellow. For Heaven's sake don't get started on a new problem when your nerves are all in shreds."

Holmes shrugged his shoulders with a glance of comic resignation towards the Colonel, and the talk drifted away into less dangerous channels.

It was destined, however, that all my professional caution should be wasted, for next morning the problem obtruded itself upon us in such a way that it was impossible to ignore it, and our country visit took a turn which neither of us could have anticipated. We were at breakfast when the Colonel's butler rushed in with all his propriety shaken out of him.

"Have you heard the news, sir?" he gasped. "At the Cunningham's sir!"

"Burglary!" cried the Colonel, with his coffee-cup in mid-air.

"Murder!"

The Colonel whistled. "By Jove!" said he. "Who's killed, then? The J.P. or his son?"

"Neither, sir. It was William the coachman. Shot through the heart, sir, and never spoke again."

"Who shot him, then?"

"The burglar, sir. He was off like a shot and got clean away. He'd just broke in at the pantry window when William came on him and met his end in saving his master's property."

"What time?"

"It was last night, sir, somewhere about twelve."

"Ah, then, we'll step over afterwards," said the Colonel, coolly settling down to his breakfast again. "It's a baddish business," he added when the butler had gone; "he's our leading man about here, is old Cunningham, and a very decent fellow too. He'll be cut up over this, for the man has been in his service for years and was a good servant. It's evidently the same villains who broke into Acton's."

"And stole that very singular collection," said Holmes, thoughtfully.

"Precisely."

"Hum! It may prove the simplest matter in the world, but all the same at first glance this is just a little curious, is it not? A gang of burglars acting in the country might be expected to vary the scene of their operations, and not to crack two cribs in the same district within a few days. When you spoke last night of taking precautions I remember that it passed through my mind that this was probably the last parish in England to which the thief or thieves would be likely to turn their attention—which shows that I have still much to learn."

"I fancy it's some local practitioner," said the Colonel. "In that case, of course, Acton's and Cunningham's are just the places he would go for, since they are far the largest about here."

"And richest?"

"Well, they ought to be, but they've had a lawsuit for some years which has sucked the blood out of both of them, I fancy. Old Acton has some claim on half Cunningham's estate, and the lawyers have been at it with both hands."

"If it's a local villain there should not be much difficulty in running him down," said Holmes with a yawn. "All right, Watson, I don't intend to meddle."

"Inspector Forrester, sir," said the butler, throwing open the door.

The official, a smart, keen-faced young fellow, stepped into the room. "Good-morning, Colonel," said he; "I hope I don't intrude, but we hear that Mr. Holmes of Baker Street is here."

The Colonel waved his hand towards my friend, and the Inspector bowed.

"We thought that perhaps you would care to step across, Mr. Holmes."

"The fates are against you, Watson," said he, laughing. "We were chatting about the matter when you came in, Inspector. Perhaps you can let us have a few details." As he leaned back in his chair in the familiar attitude I knew that the case was hopeless.

"We had no clue in the Acton affair. But here we have plenty to go on, and there's no doubt it is the same party in each case. The man was seen."

"Ah!"

"Yes, sir. But he was off like a deer after the shot that killed poor William Kirwan was fired. Mr. Cunningham saw him from the bedroom window, and Mr. Alec Cunningham saw him from the back passage. It was quarter to twelve when the alarm broke out. Mr. Cunningham had just got into bed, and Mr. Alec was smoking a pipe in his dressing-gown. They both heard William the coachman calling for help, and Mr. Alec ran down to see what was the matter. The back door was open, and as he came to the foot of the stairs

he saw two men wrestling together outside. One of them fired a shot, the other dropped, and the murderer rushed across the garden and over the hedge. Mr. Cunningham, looking out of his bedroom, saw the fellow as he gained the road, but lost sight of him at once. Mr. Alec stopped to see if he could help the dying man, and so the villain got clean away. Beyond the fact that he was a middle-sized man and dressed in some dark stuff, we have no personal clue; but we are making energetic inquiries, and if he is a stranger we shall soon find him out."

"What was this William doing there? Did he say anything before he died?"

"Not a word. He lives at the lodge with his mother, and as he was a very faithful fellow we imagine that he walked up to the house with the intention of seeing that all was right there. Of course this Acton business has put every one on their guard. The robber must have just burst open the door—the lock has been forced—when William came upon him."

"Did William say anything to his mother before going out?"

"She is very old and deaf, and we can get no information from her. The shock has made her half-witted, but I understand that she was never very bright. There is one very important circumstance, however. Look at this!"

He took a small piece of torn paper from a note-book and spread it out upon his knee.

"This was found between the finger and thumb of the dead man. It appears to be a fragment torn from a larger sheet. You will observe that the hour mentioned upon it is the very time at which the poor fellow met his fate. You see that his murderer might have torn the rest of the sheet from him or he might have taken this fragment from the murderer. It reads almost as though it were an appointment."

Holmes took up the scrap of paper, a facsimile of which is here reproduced.

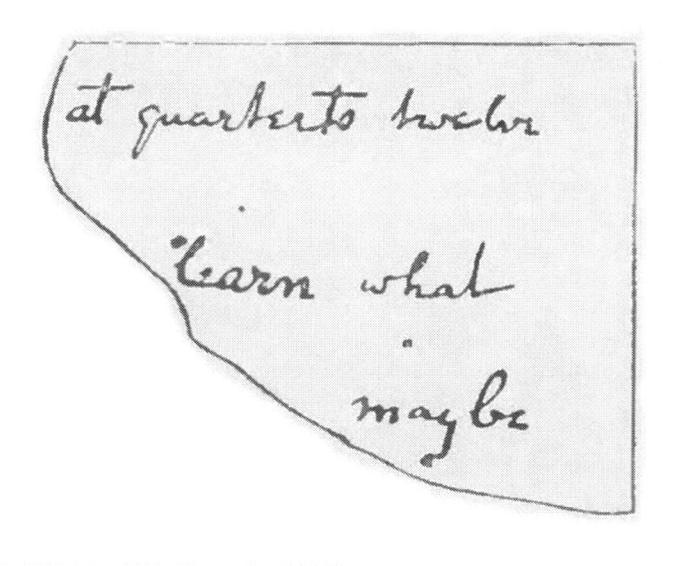

"Presuming that it is an appointment," continued the Inspector, "it is of course a

conceivable theory that this William Kirwan—though he had the reputation of being an honest man, may have been in league with the thief. He may have met him there, may even have helped him to break in the door, and then they may have fallen out between themselves."

"This writing is of extraordinary interest," said Holmes, who had been examining it with intense concentration. "These are much deeper waters than I had thought." He sank his head upon his hands, while the Inspector smiled at the effect which his case had had upon the famous London specialist.

"Your last remark," said Holmes, presently, "as to the possibility of there being an understanding between the burglar and the servant, and this being a note of appointment from one to the other, is an ingenious and not entirely impossible supposition. But this writing opens up—" He sank his head into his hands again and remained for some minutes in the deepest thought. When he raised his face again, I was surprised to see that his cheek was tinged with colour, and his eyes as bright as before his illness. He sprang to his foot with all his old energy.

"I'll tell you what," said he, "I should like to have a quiet little glance into the details of this case. There is something in it which fascinates me extremely. If you will permit me, Colonel, I will leave my friend Watson and you, and I will step round with the Inspector to test the truth of one or two little fancies of mine. I will be with you again in half an hour."

An hour and half had elapsed before the Inspector returned alone.

"Mr. Holmes is walking up and down in the field outside," said he. "He wants us all four to go up to the house together."

"To Mr. Cunningham's?"

"Yes, sir."

"What for?"

The Inspector shrugged his shoulders. "I don't quite know, sir. Between ourselves, I think Mr. Holmes had not quite got over his illness yet. He's been behaving very queerly, and he is very much excited."

"I don't think you need alarm yourself," said I. "I have usually found that there was method in his madness."

"Some folks might say there was madness in his method," muttered the Inspector. "But he's all on fire to start, Colonel, so we had best go out if you are ready."

We found Holmes pacing up and down in the field, his chin sunk upon his breast, and his hands thrust into his trousers pockets.

"The matter grows in interest," said he. "Watson, your country-trip has been a distinct success. I have had a charming morning."

"You have been up to the scene of the crime, I understand," said the Colonel.

"Yes; the Inspector and I have made quite a little reconnaissance together."

"Any success?"

"Well, we have seen some very interesting things. I'll tell you what we did as we walk. First of all, we saw the body of this unfortunate man. He certainly died from a revolver wound as reported."

"Had you doubted it, then?"

"Oh, it is as well to test everything. Our inspection was not wasted. We then had an interview with Mr. Cunningham and his son, who were able to point out the exact spot

where the murderer had broken through the garden-hedge in his flight. That was of great interest."

"Naturally."

"Then we had a look at this poor fellow's mother. We could get no information from her, however, as she is very old and feeble."

"And what is the result of your investigations?"

"The conviction that the crime is a very peculiar one. Perhaps our visit now may do something to make it less obscure. I think that we are both agreed, Inspector that the fragment of paper in the dead man's hand, bearing, as it does, the very hour of his death written upon it, is of extreme importance."

"It should give a clue, Mr. Holmes."

"It *does* give a clue. Whoever wrote that note was the man who brought William Kirwan out of his bed at that hour. But where is the rest of that sheet of paper?"

"I examined the ground carefully in the hope of finding it," said the Inspector.

"It was torn out of the dead man's hand. Why was some one so anxious to get possession of it? Because it incriminated him. And what would he do with it? Thrust it into his pocket, most likely, never noticing that a corner of it had been left in the grip of the corpse. If we could get the rest of that sheet it is obvious that we should have gone a long way towards solving the mystery."

"Yes, but how can we get at the criminal's pocket before we catch the criminal?"

"Well, well, it was worth thinking over. Then there is another obvious point. The note was sent to William. The man who wrote it could not have taken it; otherwise, of course, he might have delivered his own message by word of mouth. Who brought the note, then? Or did it come through the post?"

"I have made inquiries," said the Inspector. "William received a letter by the afternoon post yesterday. The envelope was destroyed by him."

"Excellent!" cried Holmes, clapping the Inspector on the back. "You've seen the postman. It is a pleasure to work with you. Well, here is the lodge, and if you will come up, Colonel, I will show you the scene of the crime."

We passed the pretty cottage where the murdered man had lived, and walked up an oak-lined avenue to the fine old Queen Anne house, which bears the date of Malplaquet upon the lintel of the door. Holmes and the Inspector led us round it until we came to the side gate, which is separated by a stretch of garden from the hedge which lines the road. A constable was standing at the kitchen door.

"Throw the door open, officer," said Holmes. "Now, it was on those stairs that young Mr. Cunningham stood and saw the two men struggling just where we are. Old Mr. Cunningham was at that window—the second on the left—and he saw the fellow get away just to the left of that bush. Then Mr. Alec ran out and knelt beside the wounded man. The ground is very hard, you see, and there are no marks to guide us." As he spoke two men came down the garden path, from round the angle of the house. The one was an elderly man, with a strong, deep-lined, heavy-eyed face; the other a dashing young fellow, whose bright, smiling expression and showy dress were in strange contrast with the business which had brought us there.

"Still at it, then?" said he to Holmes. "I thought you Londoners were never at fault. You don't seem to be so very quick, after all."

"Ah, you must give us a little time," said Holmes good-humoredly.

"You'll want it," said young Alec Cunningham. "Why, I don't see that we have any clue at all."

"There's only one," answered the Inspector. "We thought that if we could only find—Good heavens, Mr. Holmes! What is the matter?"

My poor friend's face had suddenly assumed the most dreadful expression. His eyes rolled upwards, his features writhed in agony, and with a suppressed groan he dropped on his face upon the ground. Horrified at the suddenness and severity of the attack, we carried him into the kitchen, where he lay back in a large chair, and breathed heavily for some minutes. Finally, with a shamefaced apology for his weakness, he rose once more.

"Watson would tell you that I have only just recovered from a severe illness," he explained. "I am liable to these sudden nervous attacks."

"Shall I send you home in my trap?" asked old Cunningham.

"Well, since I am here, there is one point on which I should like to feel sure. We can very easily verify it."

"What was it?"

"Well, it seems to me that it is just possible that the arrival of this poor fellow William was not before, but after, the entrance of the burglar into the house. You appear to take it for granted that, although the door was forced, the robber never got in."

"I fancy that is quite obvious," said Mr. Cunningham, gravely. "Why, my son Alec had not yet gone to bed, and he would certainly have heard any one moving about."

"Where was he sitting?"

"I was smoking in my dressing-room."

"Which window is that?"

"The last on the left next my father's."

"Both of your lamps were lit, of course?"

"Undoubtedly."

"There are some very singular points here," said Holmes, smiling. "Is it not extraordinary that a burglar—and a burglar who had had some previous experience—should deliberately break into a house at a time when he could see from the lights that two of the family were still afoot?"

"He must have been a cool hand."

"Well, of course, if the case were not an odd one we should not have been driven to ask you for an explanation," said young Mr. Alec. "But as to your ideas that the man had robbed the house before William tackled him, I think it a most absurd notion. Wouldn't we have found the place disarranged, and missed the things which he had taken?"

"It depends on what the things were," said Holmes. "You must remember that we are dealing with a burglar who is a very peculiar fellow, and who appears to work on lines of his own. Look, for example, at the queer lot of things which he took from Acton's—what was it?—a ball of string, a letter-weight, and I don't know what other odds and ends."

"Well, we are quite in your hands, Mr. Holmes," said old Cunningham. "Anything which you or the Inspector may suggest will most certainly be done."

"In the first place," said Holmes, "I should like you to offer a reward—coming from yourself, for the officials may take a little time before they would agree upon the sum, and these things cannot be done too promptly. I have jotted down the form here, if you would not mind signing it. Fifty pounds was quite enough, I thought."

"I would willingly give five hundred," said the J.P., taking the slip of paper and the

pencil which Holmes handed to him. "This is not quite correct, however," he added, glancing over the document.

"I wrote it rather hurriedly."

"You see you begin, 'Whereas, at about a quarter to one on Tuesday morning an attempt was made,' and so on. It was at a quarter to twelve, as a matter of fact."

I was pained at the mistake, for I knew how keenly Holmes would feel any slip of the kind. It was his specialty to be accurate as to fact, but his recent illness had shaken him, and this one little incident was enough to show me that he was still far from being himself. He was obviously embarrassed for an instant, while the Inspector raised his eyebrows, and Alec Cunningham burst into a laugh. The old gentleman corrected the mistake, however, and handed the paper back to Holmes.

"Get it printed as soon as possible," he said; "I think your idea is an excellent one."

Holmes put the slip of paper carefully away into his pocket-book.

"And now," said he, "it really would be a good thing that we should all go over the house together and make certain that this rather erratic burglar did not, after all, carry anything away with him."

Before entering, Holmes made an examination of the door which had been forced. It was evident that a chisel or strong knife had been thrust in, and the lock forced back with it. We could see the marks in the wood where it had been pushed in.

"You don't use bars, then?" he asked.

"We have never found it necessary."

"You don't keep a dog?"

"Yes, but he is chained on the other side of the house."

"When do the servants go to bed?"

"About ten."

"I understand that William was usually in bed also at that hour."

"Yes."

"It is singular that on this particular night he should have been up. Now, I should be very glad if you would have the kindness to show us over the house, Mr. Cunningham."

A stone-flagged passage, with the kitchens branching away from it, led by a wooden staircase directly to the first floor of the house. It came out upon the landing opposite to a second more ornamental stair which came up from the front hall. Out of this landing opened the drawing-room and several bedrooms, including those of Mr. Cunningham and his son. Holmes walked slowly, taking keen note of the architecture of the house. I could tell from his expression that he was on a hot scent, and yet I could not in the least imagine in what direction his inferences were leading him.

"My good sir," said Mr. Cunningham with some impatience, "this is surely very unnecessary. That is my room at the end of the stairs, and my son's is the one beyond it. I leave it to your judgment whether it was possible for the thief to have come up here without disturbing us."

"You must try round and get on a fresh scent, I fancy," said the son with a rather malicious smile.

"Still, I must ask you to humour me a little further. I should like, for example, to see how far the windows of the bedrooms command the front. This, I understand is your son's room"—he pushed open the door—"and that, I presume, is the dressing-room in which he sat smoking when the alarm was given. Where does the window of that look out

to?" He stepped across the bedroom, pushed open the door, and glanced round the other chamber.

"I hope that you are satisfied now?" said Mr. Cunningham, tartly.

"Thank you, I think I have seen all that I wished."

"Then if it is really necessary we can go into my room."

"If it is not too much trouble."

The J.P. shrugged his shoulders, and led the way into his own chamber, which was a plainly furnished and commonplace room. As we moved across it in the direction of the window, Holmes fell back until he and I were the last of the group. Near the foot of the bed stood a dish of oranges and a carafe of water. As we passed it Holmes, to my unutterable astonishment, leaned over in front of me and deliberately knocked the whole thing over. The glass smashed into a thousand pieces and the fruit rolled about into every corner of the room.

"You've done it now, Watson," said he, coolly. "A pretty mess you've made of the carpet."

I stooped in some confusion and began to pick up the fruit, understanding for some reason my companion desired me to take the blame upon myself. The others did the same, and set the table on its legs again.

"Halloa!" cried the Inspector, "where's he got to?"

Holmes had disappeared.

"Wait here an instant," said young Alec Cunningham. "The fellow is off his head, in my opinion. Come with me, father, and see where he has got to!"

They rushed out of the room, leaving the Inspector, the Colonel, and me staring at each other.

"'Pon my word, I am inclined to agree with Master Alec," said the official. "It may be the effect of this illness, but it seems to me that—"

His words were cut short by a sudden scream of "Help! Help! Murder!" With a thrill I recognised the voice of that of my friend. I rushed madly from the room on to the landing. The cries, which had sunk down into a hoarse, inarticulate shouting, came from the room which we had first visited. I dashed in, and on into the dressing-room beyond. The two Cunninghams were bending over the prostrate figure of Sherlock Holmes, the younger clutching his throat with both hands, while the elder seemed to be twisting one of his wrists. In an instant the three of us had torn them away from him, and Holmes staggered to his feet, very pale and evidently greatly exhausted.

"Arrest these men, Inspector!" he gasped.

"On what charge?"

"That of murdering their coachman, William Kirwan!"

The Inspector stared about him in bewilderment. "Oh, come now, Mr. Holmes," said he at last, "I'm sure you don't really mean to—"

"Tut, man, look at their faces!" cried Holmes, curtly.

Never, certainly, have I seen a plainer confession of guilt upon human countenances. The older man seemed numbed and dazed with a heavy, sullen expression upon his strongly-marked face. The son, on the other hand, had dropped all that jaunty, dashing style which had characterized him, and the ferocity of a dangerous wild beast gleamed in his dark eyes and distorted his handsome features. The Inspector said nothing, but, stepping to the door, he blew his whistle. Two of his constables came at the call.

"I have no alternative, Mr. Cunningham," said he. "I trust that this may all prove to be an absurd mistake, but you can see that—Ah, would you? Drop it!" He struck out with his hand, and a revolver which the younger man was in the act of cocking clattered down upon the floor.

"Keep that," said Holmes, quietly putting his foot upon it; "you will find it useful at the trial. But this is what we really wanted." He held up a little crumpled piece of paper.

"The remainder of the sheet!" cried the Inspector.

"Precisely."

"And where was it?"

"Where I was sure it must be. I'll make the whole matter clear to you presently. I think, Colonel, that you and Watson might return now, and I will be with you again in an hour at the furthest. The Inspector and I must have a word with the prisoners, but you will certainly see me back at luncheon time."

Sherlock Holmes was as good as his word, for about one o'clock he rejoined us in the Colonel's smoking-room. He was accompanied by a little elderly gentleman, who was introduced to me as the Mr. Acton whose house had been the scene of the original burglary.

"I wished Mr. Acton to be present while I demonstrated this small matter to you," said Holmes, "for it is natural that he should take a keen interest in the details. I am afraid, my dear Colonel, that you must regret the hour that you took in such a stormy petrel as I am."

"On the contrary," answered the Colonel, warmly, "I consider it the greatest privilege to have been permitted to study your methods of working. I confess that they quite surpass my expectations, and that I am utterly unable to account for your result. I have not yet seen the vestige of a clue."

"I am afraid that my explanation may disillusionize you but it has always been my habit to hide none of my methods, either from my friend Watson or from any one who might take an intelligent interest in them. But, first, as I am rather shaken by the knocking about which I had in the dressing-room, I think that I shall help myself to a dash of your brandy, Colonel. My strength has been rather tried of late."

"I trust that you had no more of those nervous attacks."

Sherlock Holmes laughed heartily. "We will come to that in its turn," said he. "I will lay an account of the case before you in its due order, showing you the various points which guided me in my decision. Pray interrupt me if there is any inference which is not perfectly clear to you.

"It is of the highest importance in the art of detection to be able to recognise, out of a number of facts, which are incidental and which vital. Otherwise your energy and attention must be dissipated instead of being concentrated. Now, in this case there was not the slightest doubt in my mind from the first that the key of the whole matter must be looked for in the scrap of paper in the dead man's hand.

"Before going into this, I would draw your attention to the fact that, if Alec Cunningham's narrative was correct, and if the assailant, after shooting William Kirwan, had *instantly* fled, then it obviously could not be he who tore the paper from the dead man's hand. But if it was not he, it must have been Alec Cunningham himself, for by the time that the old man had descended several servants were upon the scene. The point is a simple one, but the Inspector had overlooked it because he had started with the supposition that these county magnates had had nothing to do with the matter. Now, I

make a point of never having any prejudices, and of following docilely wherever fact may lead me, and so, in the very first stage of the investigation, I found myself looking a little askance at the part which had been played by Mr. Alec Cunningham.

"And now I made a very careful examination of the corner of paper which the Inspector had submitted to us. It was at once clear to me that it formed part of a very remarkable document. Here it is. Do you not now observe something very suggestive about it?"

"It has a very irregular look," said the Colonel.

"My dear sir," cried Holmes, "there cannot be the least doubt in the world that it has been written by two persons doing alternate words. When I draw your attention to the strong t's of 'at' and 'to', and ask you to compare them with the weak ones of 'quarter' and 'twelve,' you will instantly recognise the fact. A very brief analysis of these four words would enable you to say with the utmost confidence that the 'learn' and the 'maybe' are written in the stronger hand, and the 'what' in the weaker."

"By Jove, it's as clear as day!" cried the Colonel. "Why on earth should two men write a letter in such a fashion?"

"Obviously the business was a bad one, and one of the men who distrusted the other was determined that, whatever was done, each should have an equal hand in it. Now, of the two men, it is clear that the one who wrote the 'at' and 'to' was the ringleader."

"How do you get at that?"

"We might deduce it from the mere character of the one hand as compared with the other. But we have more assured reasons than that for supposing it. If you examine this scrap with attention you will come to the conclusion that the man with the stronger hand wrote all his words first, leaving blanks for the other to fill up. These blanks were not always sufficient, and you can see that the second man had a squeeze to fit his 'quarter' in between the 'at' and the 'to,' showing that the latter were already written. The man who wrote all his words first is undoubtedly the man who planned the affair."

"Excellent!" cried Mr. Acton.

"But very superficial," said Holmes. "We come now, however, to a point which is of importance. You may not be aware that the deduction of a man's age from his writing is one which has been brought to considerable accuracy by experts. In normal cases one can place a man in his true decade with tolerable confidence. I say normal cases, because ill-health and physical weakness reproduce the signs of old age, even when the invalid is a youth. In this case, looking at the bold, strong hand of the one, and the rather broken-backed appearance of the other, which still retains its legibility although the t's have begun to lose their crossing, we can say that the one was a young man and the other was advanced in years without being positively decrepit."

"Excellent!" cried Mr. Acton again.

"There is a further point, however, which is subtler and of greater interest. There is something in common between these hands. They belong to men who are blood-relatives. It may be most obvious to you in the Greek e's, but to me there are many small points which indicate the same thing. I have no doubt at all that a family mannerism can be traced in these two specimens of writing. I am only, of course, giving you the leading results now of my examination of the paper. There were twenty-three other deductions which would be of more interest to experts than to you. They all tend to deepen the impression upon my mind that the Cunninghams, father and son, had written this letter.

"Having got so far, my next step was, of course, to examine into the details of the crime, and to see how far they would help us. I went up to the house with the Inspector, and saw all that was to be seen. The wound upon the dead man was, as I was able to determine with absolute confidence, fired from a revolver at the distance of something over four yards. There was no powder-blackening on the clothes. Evidently, therefore, Alec Cunningham had lied when he said that the two men were struggling when the shot was fired. Again, both father and son agreed as to the place where the man escaped into the road. At that point, however, as it happens, there is a broadish ditch, moist at the bottom. As there were no indications of bootmarks about this ditch, I was absolutely sure not only that the Cunninghams had again lied, but that there had never been any unknown man upon the scene at all.

"And now I have to consider the motive of this singular crime. To get at this, I endeavoured first of all to solve the reason of the original burglary at Mr. Acton's. I understood, from something which the Colonel told us, that a lawsuit had been going on between you, Mr. Acton, and the Cunninghams. Of course, it instantly occurred to me that they had broken into your library with the intention of getting at some document which might be of importance in the case."

"Precisely so," said Mr. Acton. "There can be no possible doubt as to their intentions. I have the clearest claim upon half of their present estate, and if they could have found a single paper—which, fortunately, was in the strong-box of my solicitors—they would undoubtedly have crippled our case."

"There you are," said Holmes, smiling. "It was a dangerous, reckless attempt, in which I seem to trace the influence of young Alec. Having found nothing they tried to divert suspicion by making it appear to be an ordinary burglary, to which end they carried off whatever they could lay their hands upon. That is all clear enough, but there was much that was still obscure. What I wanted above all was to get the missing part of that note. I was certain that Alec had torn it out of the dead man's hand, and almost certain that he must have thrust it into the pocket of his dressing-gown. Where else could he have put it? The only question was whether it was still there. It was worth an effort to find out, and for that object we all went up to the house.

"The Cunninghams joined us, as you doubtless remember, outside the kitchen door. It was, of course, of the very first importance that they should not be reminded of the existence of this paper, otherwise they would naturally destroy it without delay. The Inspector was about to tell them the importance which we attached to it when, by the luckiest chance in the world, I tumbled down in a sort of fit and so changed the conversation.

"Good heavens!" cried the Colonel, laughing, "do you mean to say all our sympathy was wasted and your fit an imposture?"

"Speaking professionally, it was admirably done," cried I, looking in amazement at this man who was forever confounding me with some new phase of his astuteness.

"It is an art which is often useful," said he. "When I recovered I managed, by a device which had perhaps some little merit of ingenuity, to get old Cunningham to write the word 'twelve,' so that I might compare it with the 'twelve' upon the paper."

"Oh, what an ass I have been!" I exclaimed.

"I could see that you were commiserating me over my weakness," said Holmes, laughing. "I was sorry to cause you the sympathetic pain which I know that you felt. We

then went upstairs together, and having entered the room and seen the dressing-gown hanging up behind the door, I contrived, by upsetting a table, to engage their attention for the moment, and slipped back to examine the pockets. I had hardly got the paper, however—which was, as I had expected, in one of them—when the two Cunninghams were on me, and would, I verily believe, have murdered me then and there but for your prompt and friendly aid. As it is, I feel that young man's grip on my throat now, and the father has twisted my wrist round in the effort to get the paper out of my hand. They saw that I must know all about it, you see, and the sudden change from absolute security to complete despair made them perfectly desperate.

"I had a little talk with old Cunningham afterwards as to the motive of the crime. He was tractable enough, though his son was a perfect demon, ready to blow out his own or anybody else's brains if he could have got to his revolver. When Cunningham saw that the case against him was so strong he lost all heart and made a clean breast of everything. It seems that William had secretly followed his two masters on the night when they made their raid upon Mr Acton's, and having thus got them into his power, proceeded, under threats of exposure, to levy blackmail upon them. Mr. Alec, however, was a dangerous man to play games of that sort with. It was a stroke of positive genius on his part to see in the burglary scare which was convulsing the country side an opportunity of plausibly getting rid of the man whom he feared. William was decoyed up and shot, and had they only got the whole of the note and paid a little more attention to detail in the accessories, it is very possible that suspicion might never have been aroused."

"And the note?" I asked.

Sherlock Holmes placed the subjoined paper before us.

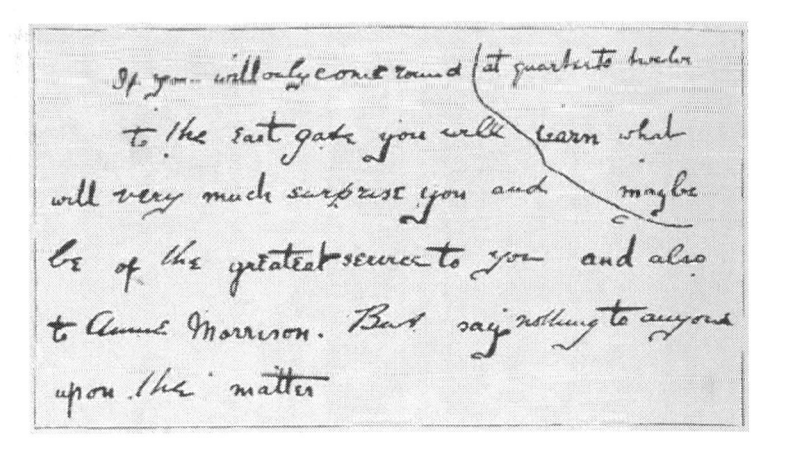

"It is very much the sort of thing that I expected," said he. "Of course, we do not yet know what the relations may have been between Alec Cunningham, William Kirwan, and Annie Morrison. The results shows that the trap was skillfully baited. I am sure that you cannot fail to be delighted with the traces of heredity shown in the p's and in the tails of the g's. The absence of the i-dots in the old man's writing is also most characteristic. Watson, I think our quiet rest in the country has been a distinct success, and I shall certainly return much invigorated to Baker Street to-morrow."

THE FINAL PROBLEM

FROM THE MEMOIRS OF SHERLOCK HOLMES (1894)

IT IS with a heavy heart that I take up my pen to write these the last words in which I shall ever record the singular gifts by which my friend Mr. Sherlock Holmes was distinguished. In an incoherent and, as I deeply feel, an entirely inadequate fashion, I have endeavoured to give some account of my strange experiences in his company from the chance which first brought us together at the period of the "Study in Scarlet," up to the time of his interference in the matter of the "Naval Treaty"—an interference which had the unquestionable effect of preventing a serious international complication. It was my intention to have stopped there, and to have said nothing of that event which has created a void in my life which the lapse of two years has done little to fill. My hand has been forced, however, by the recent letters in which Colonel James Moriarty defends the memory of his brother, and I have no choice but to lay the facts before the public exactly as they occurred. I alone know the absolute truth of the matter, and I am satisfied that the time has come when no good purpose is to be served by its suppression. As far as I know, there have been only three accounts in the public press: that in the *Journal de Genève* on May 6th, 1891, the Reuter's despatch in the English papers on May 7th, and finally the recent letter to which I have alluded. Of these the first and second were extremely condensed, while the last is, as I shall now show, an absolute perversion of the facts. It lies with me to tell for the first time what really took place between Professor Moriarty and Mr. Sherlock Holmes.

It may be remembered that after my marriage, and my subsequent start in private practice, the very intimate relations which had existed between Holmes and myself became to some extent modified. He still came to me from time to time when he desired a companion in his investigation, but these occasions grew more and more seldom, until I find that in the year 1890 there were only three cases of which I retain any record. During the winter of that year and the early spring of 1891, I saw in the papers that he had been engaged by the French government upon a matter of supreme importance, and I received two notes from Holmes, dated from Narbonne and from Nimes, from which I gathered

that his stay in France was likely to be a long one. It was with some surprise, therefore, that I saw him walk into my consulting-room upon the evening of the 24th of April. It struck me that he was looking even paler and thinner than usual.

"Yes, I have been using myself up rather too freely," he remarked, in answer to my look rather than to my words; "I have been a little pressed of late. Have you any objection to my closing your shutters?"

The only light in the room came from the lamp upon the table at which I had been reading. Holmes edged his way round the wall and flinging the shutters together, he bolted them securely.

"You are afraid of something?" I asked.

"Well, I am."

"Of what?"

"Of air-guns."

"My dear Holmes, what do you mean?"

"I think that you know me well enough, Watson, to understand that I am by no means a nervous man. At the same time, it is stupidity rather than courage to refuse to recognise danger when it is close upon you. Might I trouble you for a match?" He drew in the smoke of his cigarette as if the soothing influence was grateful to him.

"I must apologise for calling so late," said he, "and I must further beg you to be so unconventional as to allow me to leave your house presently by scrambling over your back garden wall."

"But what does it all mean?" I asked.

He held out his hand, and I saw in the light of the lamp that two of his knuckles were burst and bleeding.

"It is not an airy nothing, you see," said he, smiling. "On the contrary, it is solid enough for a man to break his hand over. Is Mrs. Watson in?"

"She is away upon a visit."

"Indeed! You are alone?"

"Quite."

"Then it makes it the easier for me to propose that you should come away with me for a week to the Continent."

"Where?"

"Oh, anywhere. It's all the same to me."

There was something very strange in all this. It was not Holmes's nature to take an aimless holiday, and something about his pale, worn face told me that his nerves were at their highest tension. He saw the question in my eyes, and, putting his finger-tips together and his elbows upon his knees, he explained the situation.

"You have probably never heard of Professor Moriarty?" said he.

"Never."

"Aye, there's the genius and the wonder of the thing!" he cried. "The man pervades London, and no one has heard of him. That's what puts him on a pinnacle in the records of crime. I tell you, Watson, in all seriousness, that if I could beat that man, if I could free society of him, I should feel that my own career had reached its summit, and I should be prepared to turn to some more placid line in life. Between ourselves, the recent cases in which I have been of assistance to the royal family of Scandinavia, and to the French republic, have left me in such a position that I could continue to live in the quiet fashion

which is most congenial to me, and to concentrate my attention upon my chemical researches. But I could not rest, Watson, I could not sit quiet in my chair, if I thought that such a man as Professor Moriarty were walking the streets of London unchallenged."

"What has he done, then?"

"His career has been an extraordinary one. He is a man of good birth and excellent education, endowed by nature with a phenomenal mathematical faculty. At the age of twenty-one he wrote a treatise upon the Binomial Theorem, which has had a European vogue. On the strength of it he won the Mathematical Chair at one of our smaller universities, and had, to all appearances, a most brilliant career before him. But the man had hereditary tendencies of the most diabolical kind. A criminal strain ran in his blood, which, instead of being modified, was increased and rendered infinitely more dangerous by his extraordinary mental powers. Dark rumours gathered round him in the university town, and eventually he was compelled to resign his chair and to come down to London, where he set up as an Army coach. So much is known to the world, but what I am telling you now is what I have myself discovered.

"As you are aware, Watson, there is no one who knows the higher criminal world of London so well as I do. For years past I have continually been conscious of some power behind the malefactor, some deep organizing power which forever stands in the way of the law, and throws its shield over the wrong-doer. Again and again in cases of the most varying sorts—forgery cases, robberies, murders—I have felt the presence of this force, and I have deduced its action in many of those undiscovered crimes in which I have not been personally consulted. For years I have endeavoured to break through the veil which shrouded it, and at last the time came when I seized my thread and followed it, until it led me, after a thousand cunning windings, to ex-Professor Moriarty of mathematical celebrity.

"He is the Napoleon of crime, Watson. He is the organizer of half that is evil and of nearly all that is undetected in this great city. He is a genius, a philosopher, an abstract thinker. He has a brain of the first order. He sits motionless, like a spider in the centre of its web, but that web has a thousand radiations, and he knows well every quiver of each of them. He does little himself. He only plans. But his agents are numerous and splendidly organized. Is there a crime to be done, a paper to be abstracted, we will say, a house to be rifled, a man to be removed—the word is passed to the Professor, the matter is organized and carried out. The agent may be caught. In that case money is found for his bail or his defence. But the central power which uses the agent is never caught—never so much as suspected. This was the organization which I deduced, Watson, and which I devoted my whole energy to exposing and breaking up.

"But the Professor was fenced round with safeguards so cunningly devised that, do what I would, it seemed impossible to get evidence which would convict in a court of law. You know my powers, my dear Watson, and yet at the end of three months I was forced to confess that I had at last met an antagonist who was my intellectual equal. My horror at his crimes was lost in my admiration at his skill. But at last he made a trip—only a little, little trip—but it was more than he could afford when I was so close upon him. I had my chance, and, starting from that point, I have woven my net round him until now it is all ready to close. In three days—that is to say, on Monday next—matters will be ripe, and the Professor, with all the principal members of his gang, will be in the hands of the police. Then will come the greatest criminal trial of the century, the clearing up of over forty

mysteries, and the rope for all of them; but if we move at all prematurely, you understand, they may slip out of our hands even at the last moment.

"Now, if I could have done this without the knowledge of Professor Moriarty, all would have been well. But he was too wily for that. He saw every step which I took to draw my toils round him. Again and again he strove to break away, but I as often headed him off. I tell you, my friend, that if a detailed account of that silent contest could be written, it would take its place as the most brilliant bit of thrust-and-parry work in the history of detection. Never have I risen to such a height, and never have I been so hard pressed by an opponent. He cut deep, and yet I just undercut him. This morning the last steps were taken, and three days only were wanted to complete the business. I was sitting in my room thinking the matter over, when the door opened and Professor Moriarty stood before me.

"My nerves are fairly proof, Watson, but I must confess to a start when I saw the very man who had been so much in my thoughts standing there on my threshhold. His appearance was quite familiar to me. He is extremely tall and thin, his forehead domes out in a white curve, and his two eyes are deeply sunken in his head. He is clean-shaven, pale, and ascetic-looking, retaining something of the professor in his features. His shoulders are rounded from much study, and his face protrudes forward, and is forever slowly oscillating from side to side in a curiously reptilian fashion. He peered at me with great curiosity in his puckered eyes.

"'You have less frontal development than I should have expected,' said he, at last. 'It is a dangerous habit to finger loaded firearms in the pocket of one's dressing-gown.'

"The fact is that upon his entrance I had instantly recognised the extreme personal danger in which I lay. The only conceivable escape for him lay in silencing my tongue. In an instant I had slipped the revolver from the drawer into my pocket, and was covering him through the cloth. At his remark I drew the weapon out and laid it cocked upon the table. He still smiled and blinked, but there was something about his eyes which made me feel very glad that I had it there.

"'You evidently don't know me,' said he.

"'On the contrary,' I answered, 'I think it is fairly evident that I do. Pray take a chair. I can spare you five minutes if you have anything to say.'

"'All that I have to say has already crossed your mind,' said he.

"'Then possibly my answer has crossed yours,' I replied.

"'You stand fast?'

"'Absolutely.'

"He clapped his hand into his pocket, and I raised the pistol from the table. But he merely drew out a memorandum-book in which he had scribbled some dates.

"'You crossed my path on the 4th of January,' said he. 'On the 23rd you incommoded me; by the middle of February I was seriously inconvenienced by you; at the end of March I was absolutely hampered in my plans; and now, at the close of April, I find myself placed in such a position through your continual persecution that I am in positive danger of losing my liberty. The situation is becoming an impossible one.'

"'Have you any suggestion to make?' I asked.

"'You must drop it, Mr. Holmes,' said he, swaying his face about. 'You really must, you know.'

"'After Monday,' said I.

"'Tut, tut,' said he. 'I am quite sure that a man of your intelligence will see that there can be but one outcome to this affair. It is necessary that you should withdraw. You have worked things in such a fashion that we have only one resource left. It has been an intellectual treat to me to see the way in which you have grappled with this affair, and I say, unaffectedly, that it would be a grief to me to be forced to take any extreme measure. You smile, sir, but I assure you that it really would.'

"'Danger is part of my trade,' I remarked.

"'That is not danger,' said he. 'It is inevitable destruction. You stand in the way not merely of an individual, but of a mighty organization, the full extent of which you, with all your cleverness, have been unable to realize. You must stand clear, Mr. Holmes, or be trodden under foot.'

"'I am afraid,' said I, rising, 'that in the pleasure of this conversation I am neglecting business of importance which awaits me elsewhere.'

"He rose also and looked at me in silence, shaking his head sadly.

"'Well, well,' said he, at last. 'It seems a pity, but I have done what I could. I know every move of your game. You can do nothing before Monday. It has been a duel between you and me, Mr. Holmes. You hope to place me in the dock. I tell you that I will never stand in the dock. You hope to beat me. I tell you that you will never beat me. If you are clever enough to bring destruction upon me, rest assured that I shall do as much to you.'

"'You have paid me several compliments, Mr. Moriarty,' said I. 'Let me pay you one in return when I say that if I were assured of the former eventuality I would, in the interests of the public, cheerfully accept the latter.'

"'I can promise you the one, but not the other,' he snarled, and so turned his rounded back upon me, and went peering and blinking out of the room.

"That was my singular interview with Professor Moriarty. I confess that it left an unpleasant effect upon my mind. His soft, precise fashion of speech leaves a conviction of sincerity which a mere bully could not produce. Of course, you will say: 'Why not take police precautions against him?' the reason is that I am well convinced that it is from his agents the blow will fall. I have the best proofs that it would be so."

"You have already been assaulted?"

"My dear Watson, Professor Moriarty is not a man who lets the grass grow under his feet. I went out about midday to transact some business in Oxford Street. As I passed the corner which leads from Bentinck Street on to the Welbeck Street crossing a two-horse van furiously driven whizzed round and was on me like a flash. I sprang for the foot-path and saved myself by the fraction of a second. The van dashed round by Marylebone Lane and was gone in an instant. I kept to the pavement after that, Watson, but as I walked down Vere Street a brick came down from the roof of one of the houses, and was shattered to fragments at my feet. I called the police and had the place examined. There were slates and bricks piled up on the roof preparatory to some repairs, and they would have me believe that the wind had toppled over one of these. Of course I knew better, but I could prove nothing. I took a cab after that and reached my brother's rooms in Pall Mall, where I spent the day. Now I have come round to you, and on my way I was attacked by a rough with a bludgeon. I knocked him down, and the police have him in custody; but I can tell you with the most absolute confidence that no possible connection will ever be traced between the gentleman upon whose front teeth I have barked my knuckles and the retiring mathematical coach, who is, I daresay, working out problems upon a blackboard

ten miles away. You will not wonder, Watson, that my first act on entering your rooms was to close your shutters, and that I have been compelled to ask your permission to leave the house by some less conspicuous exit than the front door."

I had often admired my friend's courage, but never more than now, as he sat quietly checking off a series of incidents which must have combined to make up a day of horror.

"You will spend the night here?" I said.

"No, my friend, you might find me a dangerous guest. I have my plans laid, and all will be well. Matters have gone so far now that they can move without my help as far as the arrest goes, though my presence is necessary for a conviction. It is obvious, therefore, that I cannot do better than get away for the few days which remain before the police are at liberty to act. It would be a great pleasure to me, therefore, if you could come on to the Continent with me."

"The practice is quiet," said I, "and I have an accommodating neighbour. I should be glad to come."

"And to start to-morrow morning?"

"If necessary."

"Oh yes, it is most necessary. Then these are your instructions, and I beg, my dear Watson, that you will obey them to the letter, for you are now playing a double-handed game with me against the cleverest rogue and the most powerful syndicate of criminals in Europe. Now listen! You will dispatch whatever luggage you intend to take by a trusty messenger unaddressed to Victoria to-night. In the morning you will send for a hansom, desiring your man to take neither the first nor the second which may present itself. Into this hansom you will jump, and you will drive to the Strand end of the Lowther Arcade, handing the address to the cabman upon a slip of paper, with a request that he will not throw it away. Have your fare ready, and the instant that your cab stops, dash through the Arcade, timing yourself to reach the other side at a quarter-past nine. You will find a small brougham waiting close to the curb, driven by a fellow with a heavy black cloak tipped at the collar with red. Into this you will step, and you will reach Victoria in time for the Continental express."

"Where shall I meet you?"

"At the station. The second first-class carriage from the front will be reserved for us."

"The carriage is our rendezvous, then?"

"Yes."

It was in vain that I asked Holmes to remain for the evening. It was evident to me that he thought he might bring trouble to the roof he was under, and that that was the motive which impelled him to go. With a few hurried words as to our plans for the morrow he rose and came out with me into the garden, clambering over the wall which leads into Mortimer Street, and immediately whistling for a hansom, in which I heard him drive away.

In the morning I obeyed Holmes's injunctions to the letter. A hansom was procured with such precaution as would prevent its being one which was placed ready for us, and I drove immediately after breakfast to the Lowther Arcade, through which I hurried at the top of my speed. A brougham was waiting with a very massive driver wrapped in a dark cloak, who, the instant that I had stepped in, whipped up the horse and rattled off to Victoria Station. On my alighting there he turned the carriage, and dashed away again without so much as a look in my direction.

So far all had gone admirably. My luggage was waiting for me, and I had no difficulty in finding the carriage which Holmes had indicated, the less so as it was the only one in the train which was marked "Engaged." My only source of anxiety now was the non-appearance of Holmes. The station clock marked only seven minutes from the time when we were due to start. In vain I searched among the groups of travellers and leave-takers for the lithe figure of my friend. There was no sign of him. I spent a few minutes in assisting a venerable Italian priest, who was endeavouring to make a porter understand, in his broken English, that his luggage was to be booked through to Paris. Then, having taken another look round, I returned to my carriage, where I found that the porter, in spite of the ticket, had given me my decrepit Italian friend as a traveling companion. It was useless for me to explain to him that his presence was an intrusion, for my Italian was even more limited than his English, so I shrugged my shoulders resignedly, and continued to look out anxiously for my friend. A chill of fear had come over me, as I thought that his absence might mean that some blow had fallen during the night. Already the doors had all been shut and the whistle blown, when—

"My dear Watson," said a voice, "you have not even condescended to say good-morning."

I turned in uncontrollable astonishment. The aged ecclesiastic had turned his face towards me. For an instant the wrinkles were smoothed away, the nose drew away from the chin, the lower lip ceased to protrude and the mouth to mumble, the dull eyes regained their fire, the drooping figure expanded. The next the whole frame collapsed again, and Holmes had gone as quickly as he had come.

"Good heavens!" I cried. "How you startled me!"

"Every precaution is still necessary," he whispered. "I have reason to think that they are hot upon our trail. Ah, there is Moriarty himself."

The train had already begun to move as Holmes spoke. Glancing back, I saw a tall man pushing his way furiously through the crowd, and waving his hand as if he desired to have the train stopped. It was too late, however, for we were rapidly gathering momentum, and an instant later had shot clear of the station.

"With all our precautions, you see that we have cut it rather fine," said Holmes, laughing. He rose, and throwing off the black cassock and hat which had formed his disguise, he packed them away in a hand-bag.

"Have you seen the morning paper, Watson?"

"No."

"You haven't seen about Baker Street, then?"

"Baker Street?"

"They set fire to our rooms last night. No great harm was done."

"Good heavens, Holmes! This is intolerable."

"They must have lost my track completely after their bludgeon-man was arrested. Otherwise they could not have imagined that I had returned to my rooms. They have evidently taken the precaution of watching you, however, and that is what has brought Moriarty to Victoria. You could not have made any slip in coming?"

"I did exactly what you advised."

"Did you find your brougham?"

"Yes, it was waiting."

"Did you recognise your coachman?"

"No."

"It was my brother Mycroft. It is an advantage to get about in such a case without taking a mercenary into your confidence. But we must plan what we are to do about Moriarty now."

"As this is an express, and as the boat runs in connection with it, I should think we have shaken him off very effectively."

"My dear Watson, you evidently did not realize my meaning when I said that this man may be taken as being quite on the same intellectual plane as myself. You do not imagine that if I were the pursuer I should allow myself to be baffled by so slight an obstacle. Why, then, should you think so meanly of him?"

"What will he do?"

"What I should do?"

"What would you do, then?"

"Engage a special."

"But it must be late."

"By no means. This train stops at Canterbury; and there is always at least a quarter of an hour's delay at the boat. He will catch us there."

"One would think that we were the criminals. Let us have him arrested on his arrival."

"It would be to ruin the work of three months. We should get the big fish, but the smaller would dart right and left out of the net. On Monday we should have them all. No, an arrest is inadmissible."

"What then?"

"We shall get out at Canterbury."

"And then?"

"Well, then we must make a cross-country journey to Newhaven, and so over to Dieppe. Moriarty will again do what I should do. He will get on to Paris, mark down our luggage, and wait for two days at the depôt. In the meantime we shall treat ourselves to a couple of carpet-bags, encourage the manufactures of the countries through which we travel, and make our way at our leisure into Switzerland, via Luxembourg and Basle."

At Canterbury, therefore, we alighted, only to find that we should have to wait an hour before we could get a train to Newhaven.

I was still looking rather ruefully after the rapidly disappearing luggage-van which contained my wardrobe, when Holmes pulled my sleeve and pointed up the line.

"Already, you see," said he.

Far away, from among the Kentish woods there rose a thin spray of smoke. A minute later a carriage and engine could be seen flying along the open curve which leads to the station. We had hardly time to take our place behind a pile of luggage when it passed with a rattle and a roar, beating a blast of hot air into our faces.

"There he goes," said Holmes, as we watched the carriage swing and rock over the points. "There are limits, you see, to our friend's intelligence. It would have been a *coup-de-maître* had he deduced what I would deduce and acted accordingly."

"And what would he have done had he overtaken us?"

"There cannot be the least doubt that he would have made a murderous attack upon me. It is, however, a game at which two may play. The question now is whether we should take a premature lunch here, or run our chance of starving before we reach the buffet at Newhaven."

We made our way to Brussels that night and spent two days there, moving on upon the third day as far as Strasburg. On the Monday morning Holmes had telegraphed to the London police, and in the evening we found a reply waiting for us at our hotel. Holmes tore it open, and then with a bitter curse hurled it into the grate.

"I might have known it!" he groaned. "He has escaped!"

"Moriarty?"

"They have secured the whole gang with the exception of him. He has given them the slip. Of course, when I had left the country there was no one to cope with him. But I did think that I had put the game in their hands. I think that you had better return to England, Watson."

"Why?"

"Because you will find me a dangerous companion now. This man's occupation is gone. He is lost if he returns to London. If I read his character right he will devote his whole energies to revenging himself upon me. He said as much in our short interview, and I fancy that he meant it. I should certainly recommend you to return to your practice."

It was hardly an appeal to be successful with one who was an old campaigner as well as an old friend. We sat in the Strasburg *salle-à-manger* arguing the question for half an hour, but the same night we had resumed our journey and were well on our way to Geneva.

For a charming week we wandered up the Valley of the Rhone, and then, branching off at Leuk, we made our way over the Gemmi Pass, still deep in snow, and so, by way of Interlaken, to Meiringen. It was a lovely trip, the dainty green of the spring below, the virgin white of the winter above; but it was clear to me that never for one instant did Holmes forget the shadow which lay across him. In the homely Alpine villages or in the lonely mountain passes, I could tell by his quick glancing eyes and his sharp scrutiny of every face that passed us, that he was well convinced that, walk where we would, we could not walk ourselves clear of the danger which was dogging our footsteps.

Once, I remember, as we passed over the Gemmi, and walked along the border of the melancholy Daubensee, a large rock which had been dislodged from the ridge upon our right clattered down and roared into the lake behind us. In an instant Holmes had raced up on to the ridge, and, standing upon a lofty pinnacle, craned his neck in every direction. It was in vain that our guide assured him that a fall of stones was a common chance in the spring-time at that spot. He said nothing, but he smiled at me with the air of a man who sees the fulfillment of that which he had expected.

And yet for all his watchfulness he was never depressed. On the contrary, I can never recollect having seen him in such exuberant spirits. Again and again he recurred to the fact that if he could be assured that society was freed from Professor Moriarty he would cheerfully bring his own career to a conclusion.

"I think that I may go so far as to say, Watson, that I have not lived wholly in vain," he remarked. "If my record were closed to-night I could still survey it with equanimity. The air of London is the sweeter for my presence. In over a thousand cases I am not aware that I have ever used my powers upon the wrong side. Of late I have been tempted to look into the problems furnished by nature rather than those more superficial ones for which our artificial state of society is responsible. Your memoirs will draw to an end, Watson, upon the day that I crown my career by the capture or extinction of the most dangerous and capable criminal in Europe."

I shall be brief, and yet exact, in the little which remains for me to tell. It is not a subject on which I would willingly dwell, and yet I am conscious that a duty devolves upon me to omit no detail.

It was on the 3rd of May that we reached the little village of Meiringen, where we put up at the Englischer Hof, then kept by Peter Steiler the elder. Our landlord was an intelligent man, and spoke excellent English, having served for three years as waiter at the Grosvenor Hotel in London. At his advice, on the afternoon of the 4th we set off together, with the intention of crossing the hills and spending the night at the hamlet of Rosenlaui. We had strict injunctions, however, on no account to pass the falls of Reichenbach, which are about half-way up the hill, without making a small détour to see them.

It is indeed, a fearful place. The torrent, swollen by the melting snow, plunges into a tremendous abyss, from which the spray rolls up like the smoke from a burning house. The shaft into which the river hurls itself is an immense chasm, lined by glistening coal-black rock, and narrowing into a creaming, boiling pit of incalculable depth, which brims over and shoots the stream onward over its jagged lip. The long sweep of green water roaring forever down, and the thick flickering curtain of spray hissing forever upward, turn a man giddy with their constant whirl and clamour. We stood near the edge peering down at the gleam of the breaking water far below us against the black rocks, and listening to the half-human shout which came booming up with the spray out of the abyss.

The path has been cut half-way round the fall to afford a complete view, but it ends abruptly, and the traveler has to return as he came. We had turned to do so, when we saw a Swiss lad come running along it with a letter in his hand. It bore the mark of the hotel which we had just left, and was addressed to me by the landlord. It appeared that within a very few minutes of our leaving, an English lady had arrived who was in the last stage of consumption. She had wintered at Davos Platz, and was journeying now to join her friends at Lucerne, when a sudden hemorrhage had overtaken her. It was thought that she could hardly live a few hours, but it would be a great consolation to her to see an English doctor, and, if I would only return, etc. The good Steiler assured me in a postscript that he would himself look upon my compliance as a very great favour, since the lady absolutely refused to see a Swiss physician, and he could not but feel that he was incurring a great responsibility.

The appeal was one which could not be ignored. It was impossible to refuse the request of a fellow-countrywoman dying in a strange land. Yet I had my scruples about leaving Holmes. It was finally agreed, however, that he should retain the young Swiss messenger with him as guide and companion while I returned to Meiringen. My friend would stay some little time at the fall, he said, and would then walk slowly over the hill to Rosenlaui, where I was to rejoin him in the evening. As I turned away I saw Holmes, with his back against a rock and his arms folded, gazing down at the rush of the waters. It was the last that I was ever destined to see of him in this world.

When I was near the bottom of the descent I looked back. It was impossible, from that position, to see the fall, but I could see the curving path which winds over the shoulder of the hill and leads to it. Along this a man was, I remember, walking very rapidly.

I could see his black figure clearly outlined against the green behind him. I noted him, and the energy with which he walked but he passed from my mind again as I hurried on upon my errand.

It may have been a little over an hour before I reached Meiringen. Old Steiler was standing at the porch of his hotel.

"Well," said I, as I came hurrying up, "I trust that she is no worse?"

A look of surprise passed over his face, and at the first quiver of his eyebrows my heart turned to lead in my breast.

"You did not write this?" I said, pulling the letter from my pocket. "There is no sick Englishwoman in the hotel?"

"Certainly not!" he cried. "But it has the hotel mark upon it! Ha, it must have been written by that tall Englishman who came in after you had gone. He said—"

But I waited for none of the landlord's explanations. In a tingle of fear I was already running down the village street, and making for the path which I had so lately descended. It had taken me an hour to come down. For all my efforts two more had passed before I found myself at the fall of Reichenbach once more. There was Holmes's Alpine-stock still leaning against the rock by which I had left him. But there was no sign of him, and it was in vain that I shouted. My only answer was my own voice reverberating in a rolling echo from the cliffs around me.

It was the sight of that Alpine-stock which turned me cold and sick. He had not gone to Rosenlaui, then. He had remained on that three-foot path, with sheer wall on one side and sheer drop on the other, until his enemy had overtaken him. The young Swiss had gone too. He had probably been in the pay of Moriarty, and had left the two men together. And then what had happened? Who was to tell us what had happened then?

I stood for a minute or two to collect myself, for I was dazed with the horror of the thing. Then I began to think of Holmes's own methods and to try to practise them in reading this tragedy. It was, alas, only too easy to do. During our conversation we had not gone to the end of the path, and the Alpine-stock marked the place where we had stood. The blackish soil is kept forever soft by the incessant drift of spray, and a bird would leave its tread upon it. Two lines of footmarks were clearly marked along the farther end of the path, both leading away from me. There were none returning. A few yards from the end the soil was all ploughed up into a patch of mud, and the branches and ferns which fringed the chasm were torn and bedraggled. I lay upon my face and peered over with the spray spouting up all around me. It had darkened since I left, and now I could only see here and there the glistening of moisture upon the black walls, and far away down at the end of the shaft the gleam of the broken water. I shouted; but only the same half-human cry of the fall was borne back to my ears.

But it was destined that I should after all have a last word of greeting from my friend and comrade. I have said that his Alpine-stock had been left leaning against a rock which jutted on to the path. From the top of this boulder the gleam of something bright caught my eye, and, raising my hand, I found that it came from the silver cigarette-case which he used to carry. As I took it up a small square of paper upon which it had lain fluttered down on to the ground. Unfolding it, I found that it consisted of three pages torn from his note-book and addressed to me. It was characteristic of the man that the direction was a precise, and the writing as firm and clear, as though it had been written in his study.

"My dear Watson," he said, "I write these few lines through the courtesy of Mr. Moriarty, who awaits my convenience for the final discussion of those questions which lie between us. He has been giving me a sketch of the methods by which he avoided the English police and kept

himself informed of our movements. They certainly confirm the very high opinion which I had formed of his abilities. I am pleased to think that I shall be able to free society from any further effects of his presence, though I fear that it is at a cost which will give pain to my friends, and especially, my dear Watson, to you. I have already explained to you, however, that my career had in any case reached its crisis, and that no possible conclusion to it could be more congenial to me than this. Indeed, if I may make a full confession to you, I was quite convinced that the letter from Meiringen was a hoax, and I allowed you to depart on that errand under the persuasion that some development of this sort would follow. Tell Inspector Patterson that the papers which he needs to convict the gang are in pigeonhole M., done up in a blue envelope and inscribed 'Moriarty.' I made every disposition of my property before leaving England, and handed it to my brother Mycroft. Pray give my greetings to Mrs. Watson, and believe me to be, my dear fellow,

"Very sincerely yours,

"Sherlock Holmes."

A few words may suffice to tell the little that remains. An examination by experts leaves little doubt that a personal contest between the two men ended, as it could hardly fail to end in such a situation, in their reeling over, locked in each other's arms. Any attempt at recovering the bodies was absolutely hopeless, and there, deep down in that dreadful caldron of swirling water and seething foam, will lie for all time the most dangerous criminal and the foremost champion of the law of their generation. The Swiss youth was never found again, and there can be no doubt that he was one of the numerous agents whom Moriarty kept in his employ. As to the gang, it will be within the memory of the public how completely the evidence which Holmes had accumulated exposed their organization, and how heavily the hand of the dead man weighed upon them. Of their terrible chief few details came out during the proceedings, and if I have now been compelled to make a clear statement of his career it is due to those injudicious champions who have endeavoured to clear his memory by attacks upon him whom I shall ever regard as the best and the wisest man whom I have ever known.

THE ADVENTURE OF THE EMPTY
HOUSE

FROM THE RETURN OF SHERLOCK HOLMES (1905)

IT WAS in the spring of the year 1894 that all London was interested, and the fashionable world dismayed, by the murder of the Honourable Ronald Adair under most unusual and inexplicable circumstances. The public has already learned those particulars of the crime which came out in the police investigation, but a good deal was suppressed upon that occasion, since the case for the prosecution was so overwhelmingly strong that it was not necessary to bring forward all the facts. Only now, at the end of nearly ten years, am I allowed to supply those missing links which make up the whole of that remarkable chain. The crime was of interest in itself, but that interest was as nothing to me compared to the inconceivable sequel, which afforded me the greatest shock and surprise of any event in my adventurous life. Even now, after this long interval, I find myself thrilling as I think of it, and feeling once more that sudden flood of joy, amazement, and incredulity which utterly submerged my mind. Let me say to that public, which has shown some interest in those glimpses which I have occasionally given them of the thoughts and actions of a very remarkable man, that they are not to blame me if I have not shared my knowledge with them, for I should have considered it my first duty to do so, had I not been barred by a positive prohibition from his own lips, which was only withdrawn upon the third of last month.

It can be imagined that my close intimacy with Sherlock Holmes had interested me deeply in crime, and that after his disappearance I never failed to read with care the various problems which came before the public. And I even attempted, more than once, for my own private satisfaction, to employ his methods in their solution, though with indifferent success. There was none, however, which appealed to me like this tragedy of Ronald Adair. As I read the evidence at the inquest, which led up to a verdict of willful murder against some person or persons unknown, I realized more clearly than I had ever done the loss which the community had sustained by the death of Sherlock Holmes. There were points about this strange business which would, I was sure, have specially appealed to him, and the efforts of the police would have been supplemented, or more probably

anticipated, by the trained observation and the alert mind of the first criminal agent in Europe. All day, as I drove upon my round, I turned over the case in my mind and found no explanation which appeared to me to be adequate. At the risk of telling a twice-told tale, I will recapitulate the facts as they were known to the public at the conclusion of the inquest.

The Honourable Ronald Adair was the second son of the Earl of Maynooth, at that time governor of one of the Australian colonies. Adair's mother had returned from Australia to undergo the operation for cataract, and she, her son Ronald, and her daughter Hilda were living together at 427, Park Lane. The youth moved in the best society had, so far as was known, no enemies and no particular vices. He had been engaged to Miss Edith Woodley, of Carstairs, but the engagement had been broken off by mutual consent some months before, and there was no sign that it had left any very profound feeling behind it. For the rest, the man's life moved in a narrow and conventional circle, for his habits were quiet and his nature unemotional. Yet it was upon this easy-going young aristocrat that death came, in most strange and unexpected form, between the hours of ten and eleven-twenty on the night of March 30, 1894.

Ronald Adair was fond of cards—playing continually, but never for such stakes as would hurt him. He was a member of the Baldwin, the Cavendish, and the Bagatelle card clubs. It was shown that, after dinner on the day of his death, he had played a rubber of whist at the latter club. He had also played there in the afternoon. The evidence of those who had played with him—Mr. Murray, Sir John Hardy, and Colonel Moran—showed that the game was whist, and that there was a fairly equal fall of the cards. Adair might have lost five pounds, but not more. His fortune was a considerable one, and such a loss could not in any way affect him. He had played nearly every day at one club or other, but he was a cautious player, and usually rose a winner. It came out in evidence that, in partnership with Colonel Moran, he had actually won as much as four hundred and twenty pounds in a sitting, some weeks before, from Godfrey Milner and Lord Balmoral. So much for his recent history as it came out at the inquest.

On the evening of the crime, he returned from the club exactly at ten. His mother and sister were out spending the evening with a relation. The servant deposed that she heard him enter the front room on the second floor, generally used as his sitting-room. She had lit a fire there, and as it smoked she had opened the window. No sound was heard from the room until eleven-twenty, the hour of the return of Lady Maynooth and her daughter. Desiring to say good-night, she attempted to enter her son's room. The door was locked on the inside, and no answer could be got to their cries and knocking. Help was obtained, and the door forced. The unfortunate young man was found lying near the table. His head had been horribly mutilated by an expanding revolver bullet, but no weapon of any sort was to be found in the room. On the table lay two banknotes for ten pounds each and seventeen pounds ten in silver and gold, the money arranged in little piles of varying amount. There were some figures also upon a sheet of paper, with the names of some club friends opposite to them, from which it was conjectured that before his death he was endeavouring to make out his losses or winnings at cards.

A minute examination of the circumstances served only to make the case more complex. In the first place, no reason could be given why the young man should have fastened the door upon the inside. There was the possibility that the murderer had done this, and had afterwards escaped by the window. The drop was at least twenty feet,

however, and a bed of crocuses in full bloom lay beneath. Neither the flowers nor the earth showed any sign of having been disturbed, nor were there any marks upon the narrow strip of grass which separated the house from the road. Apparently, therefore, it was the young man himself who had fastened the door. But how did he come by his death? No one could have climbed up to the window without leaving traces. Suppose a man had fired through the window, he would indeed be a remarkable shot who could with a revolver inflict so deadly a wound. Again, Park Lane is a frequented thoroughfare; there is a cab stand within a hundred yards of the house. No one had heard a shot. And yet there was the dead man and there the revolver bullet, which had mushroomed out, as soft-nosed bullets will, and so inflicted a wound which must have caused instantaneous death. Such were the circumstances of the Park Lane Mystery, which were further complicated by entire absence of motive, since, as I have said, young Adair was not known to have any enemy, and no attempt had been made to remove the money or valuables in the room.

All day I turned these facts over in my mind, endeavouring to hit upon some theory which could reconcile them all, and to find that line of least resistance which my poor friend had declared to be the starting-point of every investigation. I confess that I made little progress. In the evening I strolled across the Park, and found myself about six o'clock at the Oxford Street end of Park Lane. A group of loafers upon the pavements, all staring up at a particular window, directed me to the house which I had come to see. A tall, thin man with coloured glasses, whom I strongly suspected of being a plain-clothes detective, was pointing out some theory of his own, while the others crowded round to listen to what he said. I got as near him as I could, but his observations seemed to me to be absurd, so I withdrew again in some disgust. As I did so I struck against an elderly, deformed man, who had been behind me, and I knocked down several books which he was carrying. I remember that as I picked them up, I observed the title of one of them, *The Origin of Tree Worship*, and it struck me that the fellow must be some poor bibliophile, who, either as a trade or as a hobby, was a collector of obscure volumes. I endeavoured to apologize for the accident, but it was evident that these books which I had so unfortunately maltreated were very precious objects in the eyes of their owner. With a snarl of contempt he turned upon his heel, and I saw his curved back and white side-whiskers disappear among the throng.

My observations of No. 427, Park Lane did little to clear up the problem in which I was interested. The house was separated from the street by a low wall and railing, the whole not more than five feet high. It was perfectly easy, therefore, for anyone to get into the garden, but the window was entirely inaccessible, since there was no waterpipe or anything which could help the most active man to climb it. More puzzled than ever, I retraced my steps to Kensington. I had not been in my study five minutes when the maid entered to say that a person desired to see me. To my astonishment it was none other than my strange old book collector, his sharp, wizened face peering out from a frame of white hair, and his precious volumes, a dozen of them at least, wedged under his right arm.

"You're surprised to see me, sir," said he, in a strange, croaking voice.

I acknowledged that I was.

"Well, I've a conscience, sir, and when I chanced to see you go into this house, as I came hobbling after you, I thought to myself, I'll just step in and see that kind gentleman,

and tell him that if I was a bit gruff in my manner there was not any harm meant, and that I am much obliged to him for picking up my books."

"You make too much of a trifle," said I. "May I ask how you knew who I was?"

"Well, sir, if it isn't too great a liberty, I am a neighbour of yours, for you'll find my little bookshop at the corner of Church Street, and very happy to see you, I am sure. Maybe you collect yourself, sir. Here's *British Birds,* and *Catullus,* and *The Holy War*—a bargain, every one of them. With five volumes you could just fill that gap on that second shelf. It looks untidy, does it not, sir?"

I moved my head to look at the cabinet behind me. When I turned again, Sherlock Holmes was standing smiling at me across my study table. I rose to my feet, stared at him for some seconds in utter amazement, and then it appears that I must have fainted for the first and the last time in my life. Certainly a grey mist swirled before my eyes, and when it cleared I found my collar-ends undone and the tingling after-taste of brandy upon my lips. Holmes was bending over my chair, his flask in his hand.

"My dear Watson," said the well-remembered voice, "I owe you a thousand apologies. I had no idea that you would be so affected."

I gripped him by the arms.

"Holmes!" I cried. "Is it really you? Can it indeed be that you are alive? Is it possible that you succeeded in climbing out of that awful abyss?"

"Wait a moment," said he. "Are you sure that you are really fit to discuss things? I have given you a serious shock by my unnecessarily dramatic reappearance."

"I am all right, but indeed, Holmes, I can hardly believe my eyes. Good heavens! to think that you—you of all men—should be standing in my study." Again I gripped him by the sleeve, and felt the thin, sinewy arm beneath it. "Well, you're not a spirit anyhow," said I. "My dear chap, I'm overjoyed to see you. Sit down, and tell me how you came alive out of that dreadful chasm."

He sat opposite to me, and lit a cigarette in his old, nonchalant manner. He was dressed in the seedy frockcoat of the book merchant, but the rest of that individual lay in a pile of white hair and old books upon the table. Holmes looked even thinner and keener than of old, but there was a dead-white tinge in his aquiline face which told me that his life recently had not been a healthy one.

"I am glad to stretch myself, Watson," said he. "It is no joke when a tall man has to take a foot off his stature for several hours on end. Now, my dear fellow, in the matter of these explanations, we have, if I may ask for your cooperation, a hard and dangerous night's work in front of us. Perhaps it would be better if I gave you an account of the whole situation when that work is finished."

"I am full of curiosity. I should much prefer to hear now."

"You'll come with me to-night?"

"When you like and where you like."

"This is, indeed, like the old days. We shall have time for a mouthful of dinner before we need go. Well, then, about that chasm. I had no serious difficulty in getting out of it, for the very simple reason that I never was in it."

"You never were in it?"

"No, Watson, I never was in it. My note to you was absolutely genuine. I had little doubt that I had come to the end of my career when I perceived the somewhat sinister figure of the late Professor Moriarty standing upon the narrow pathway which led to

safety. I read an inexorable purpose in his grey eyes. I exchanged some remarks with him, therefore, and obtained his courteous permission to write the short note which you afterwards received. I left it with my cigarette-box and my stick, and I walked along the pathway, Moriarty still at my heels. When I reached the end I stood at bay. He drew no weapon, but he rushed at me and threw his long arms around me. He knew that his own game was up, and was only anxious to revenge himself upon me. We tottered together upon the brink of the fall. I have some knowledge, however, of baritsu, or the Japanese system of wrestling, which has more than once been very useful to me. I slipped through his grip, and he with a horrible scream kicked madly for a few seconds, and clawed the air with both his hands. But for all his efforts he could not get his balance, and over he went. With my face over the brink, I saw him fall for a long way. Then he struck a rock, bounded off, and splashed into the water."

I listened with amazement to this explanation, which Holmes delivered between the puffs of his cigarette.

"But the tracks!" I cried. "I saw, with my own eyes, that two went down the path and none returned."

"It came about in this way. The instant that the Professor had disappeared, it struck me what a really extraordinarily lucky chance Fate had placed in my way. I knew that Moriarty was not the only man who had sworn my death. There were at least three others whose desire for vengeance upon me would only be increased by the death of their leader. They were all most dangerous men. One or other would certainly get me. On the other hand, if all the world was convinced that I was dead they would take liberties, these men, they would soon lay themselves open, and sooner or later I could destroy them. Then it would be time for me to announce that I was still in the land of the living. So rapidly does the brain act that I believe I had thought this all out before Professor Moriarty had reached the bottom of the Reichenbach Fall.

"I stood up and examined the rocky wall behind me. In your picturesque account of the matter, which I read with great interest some months later, you assert that the wall was sheer. That was not literally true. A few small footholds presented themselves, and there was some indication of a ledge. The cliff is so high that to climb it all was an obvious impossibility, and it was equally impossible to make my way along the wet path without leaving some tracks. I might, it is true, have reversed my boots, as I have done on similar occasions, but the sight of three sets of tracks in one direction would certainly have suggested a deception. On the whole, then, it was best that I should risk the climb. It was not a pleasant business, Watson. The fall roared beneath me. I am not a fanciful person, but I give you my word that I seemed to hear Moriarty's voice screaming at me out of the abyss. A mistake would have been fatal. More than once, as tufts of grass came out in my hand or my foot slipped in the wet notches of the rock, I thought that I was gone. But I struggled upward, and at last I reached a ledge several feet deep and covered with soft green moss, where I could lie unseen, in the most perfect comfort. There I was stretched, when you, my dear Watson, and all your following were investigating in the most sympathetic and inefficient manner the circumstances of my death.

"At last, when you had all formed your inevitable and totally erroneous conclusions, you departed for the hotel, and I was left alone. I had imagined that I had reached the end of my adventures, but a very unexpected occurrence showed me that there were surprises still in store for me. A huge rock, falling from above, boomed past me, struck the path, and

bounded over into the chasm. For an instant I thought that it was an accident, but a moment later, looking up, I saw a man's head against the darkening sky, and another stone struck the very ledge upon which I was stretched, within a foot of my head. Of course, the meaning of this was obvious. Moriarty had not been alone. A confederate—and even that one glance had told me how dangerous a man that confederate was—had kept guard while the Professor had attacked me. From a distance, unseen by me, he had been a witness of his friend's death and of my escape. He had waited, and then making his way round to the top of the cliff, he had endeavoured to succeed where his comrade had failed.

"I did not take long to think about it, Watson. Again I saw that grim face look over the cliff, and I knew that it was the precursor of another stone. I scrambled down on to the path. I don't think I could have done it in cold blood. It was a hundred times more difficult than getting up. But I had no time to think of the danger, for another stone sang past me as I hung by my hands from the edge of the ledge. Halfway down I slipped, but, by the blessing of God, I landed, torn and bleeding, upon the path. I took to my heels, did ten miles over the mountains in the darkness, and a week later I found myself in Florence, with the certainty that no one in the world knew what had become of me.

"I had only one confidant—my brother Mycroft. I owe you many apologies, my dear Watson, but it was all-important that it should be thought I was dead, and it is quite certain that you would not have written so convincing an account of my unhappy end had you not yourself thought that it was true. Several times during the last three years I have taken up my pen to write to you, but always I feared lest your affectionate regard for me should tempt you to some indiscretion which would betray my secret. For that reason I turned away from you this evening when you upset my books, for I was in danger at the time, and any show of surprise and emotion upon your part might have drawn attention to my identity and led to the most deplorable and irreparable results. As to Mycroft, I had to confide in him in order to obtain the money which I needed. The course of events in London did not run so well as I had hoped, for the trial of the Moriarty gang left two of its most dangerous members, my own most vindictive enemies, at liberty. I travelled for two years in Tibet, therefore, and amused myself by visiting Lhassa, and spending some days with the head lama. You may have read of the remarkable explorations of a Norwegian named Sigerson, but I am sure that it never occurred to you that you were receiving news of your friend. I then passed through Persia, looked in at Mecca, and paid a short but interesting visit to the Khalifa at Khartoum the results of which I have communicated to the Foreign Office. Returning to France, I spent some months in a research into the coal-tar derivatives, which I conducted in a laboratory at Montpellier, in the south of France. Having concluded this to my satisfaction and learning that only one of my enemies was now left in London, I was about to return when my movements were hastened by the news of this very remarkable Park Lane Mystery, which not only appealed to me by its own merits, but which seemed to offer some most peculiar personal opportunities. I came over at once to London, called in my own person at Baker Street, threw Mrs. Hudson into violent hysterics, and found that Mycroft had preserved my rooms and my papers exactly as they had always been. So it was, my dear Watson, that at two o'clock to-day I found myself in my old armchair in my own old room, and only wishing that I could have seen my old friend Watson in the other chair which he has so often adorned."

Such was the remarkable narrative to which I listened on that April evening—a

narrative which would have been utterly incredible to me had it not been confirmed by the actual sight of the tall, spare figure and the keen, eager face, which I had never thought to see again. In some manner he had learned of my own sad bereavement, and his sympathy was shown in his manner rather than in his words. "Work is the best antidote to sorrow, my dear Watson," said he; "and I have a piece of work for us both to-night which, if we can bring it to a successful conclusion, will in itself justify a man's life on this planet." In vain I begged him to tell me more. "You will hear and see enough before morning," he answered. "We have three years of the past to discuss. Let that suffice until half-past nine, when we start upon the notable adventure of the empty house."

It was indeed like old times when, at that hour, I found myself seated beside him in a hansom, my revolver in my pocket, and the thrill of adventure in my heart. Holmes was cold and stern and silent. As the gleam of the street-lamps flashed upon his austere features, I saw that his brows were drawn down in thought and his thin lips compressed. I knew not what wild beast we were about to hunt down in the dark jungle of criminal London, but I was well assured, from the bearing of this master huntsman, that the adventure was a most grave one—while the sardonic smile which occasionally broke through his ascetic gloom boded little good for the object of our quest.

I had imagined that we were bound for Baker Street, but Holmes stopped the cab at the corner of Cavendish Square. I observed that as he stepped out he gave a most searching glance to right and left, and at every subsequent street corner he took the utmost pains to assure that he was not followed. Our route was certainly a singular one. Holmes's knowledge of the byways of London was extraordinary, and on this occasion he passed rapidly and with an assured step through a network of mews and stables, the very existence of which I had never known. We emerged at last into a small road, lined with old, gloomy houses, which led us into Manchester Street, and so to Blandford Street. Here he turned swiftly down a narrow passage, passed through a wooden gate into a deserted yard, and then opened with a key the back door of a house. We entered together, and he closed it behind us.

The place was pitch dark, but it was evident to me that it was an empty house. Our feet creaked and crackled over the bare planking, and my outstretched hand touched a wall from which the paper was hanging in ribbons. Holmes's cold, thin fingers closed round my wrist and led me forward down a long hall, until I dimly saw the murky fanlight over the door. Here Holmes turned suddenly to the right and we found ourselves in a large, square, empty room, heavily shadowed in the corners, but faintly lit in the centre from the lights of the street beyond. There was no lamp near, and the window was thick with dust, so that we could only just discern each other's figures within. My companion put his hand upon my shoulder and his lips close to my ear.

"Do you know where we are?" he whispered.

"Surely that is Baker Street," I answered, staring through the dim window.

"Exactly. We are in Camden House, which stands opposite to our own old quarters."

"But why are we here?"

"Because it commands so excellent a view of that picturesque pile. Might I trouble you, my dear Watson, to draw a little nearer to the window, taking every precaution not to show yourself, and then to look up at our old rooms—the starting-point of so many of your little fairy-tales? We will see if my three years of absence have entirely taken away my power to surprise you."

I crept forward and looked across at the familiar window. As my eyes fell upon it, I gave a gasp and a cry of amazement. The blind was down, and a strong light was burning in the room. The shadow of a man who was seated in a chair within was thrown in hard, black outline upon the luminous screen of the window. There was no mistaking the poise of the head, the squareness of the shoulders, the sharpness of the features. The face was turned half-round, and the effect was that of one of those black silhouettes which our grandparents loved to frame. It was a perfect reproduction of Holmes. So amazed was I that I threw out my hand to make sure that the man himself was standing beside me. He was quivering with silent laughter.

"Well?" said he.

"Good heavens!" I cried. "It is marvellous."

"I trust that age doth not wither nor custom stale my infinite variety," said he, and I recognized in his voice the joy and pride which the artist takes in his own creation. "It really is rather like me, is it not?"

"I should be prepared to swear that it was you."

"The credit of the execution is due to Monsieur Oscar Meunier, of Grenoble, who spent some days in doing the moulding. It is a bust in wax. The rest I arranged myself during my visit to Baker Street this afternoon."

"But why?"

"Because, my dear Watson, I had the strongest possible reason for wishing certain people to think that I was there when I was really elsewhere."

"And you thought the rooms were watched?"

"I *knew* that they were watched."

"By whom?"

"By my old enemies, Watson. By the charming society whose leader lies in the Reichenbach Fall. You must remember that they knew, and only they knew, that I was still alive. Sooner or later they believed that I should come back to my rooms. They watched them continuously, and this morning they saw me arrive."

"How do you know?"

"Because I recognized their sentinel when I glanced out of my window. He is a harmless enough fellow, Parker by name, a garroter by trade, and a remarkable performer upon the jew's-harp. I cared nothing for him. But I cared a great deal for the much more formidable person who was behind him, the bosom friend of Moriarty, the man who dropped the rocks over the cliff, the most cunning and dangerous criminal in London. That is the man who is after me to-night Watson, and that is the man who is quite unaware that we are after *him*."

My friend's plans were gradually revealing themselves. From this convenient retreat, the watchers were being watched and the trackers tracked. That angular shadow up yonder was the bait, and we were the hunters. In silence we stood together in the darkness and watched the hurrying figures who passed and repassed in front of us. Holmes was silent and motionless; but I could tell that he was keenly alert, and that his eyes were fixed intently upon the stream of passers-by. It was a bleak and boisterous night and the wind whistled shrilly down the long street. Many people were moving to and fro, most of them muffled in their coats and cravats. Once or twice it seemed to me that I had seen the same figure before, and I especially noticed two men who appeared to be sheltering themselves from the wind in the doorway of a house some distance up the

street. I tried to draw my companion's attention to them; but he gave a little ejaculation of impatience, and continued to stare into the street. More than once he fidgeted with his feet and tapped rapidly with his fingers upon the wall. It was evident to me that he was becoming uneasy, and that his plans were not working out altogether as he had hoped. At last, as midnight approached and the street gradually cleared, he paced up and down the room in uncontrollable agitation. I was about to make some remark to him, when I raised my eyes to the lighted window, and again experienced almost as great a surprise as before. I clutched Holmes's arm, and pointed upward.

"The shadow has moved!" I cried.

It was indeed no longer the profile, but the back, which was turned towards us.

Three years had certainly not smoothed the asperities of his temper or his impatience with a less active intelligence than his own.

"Of course it has moved," said he. "Am I such a farcical bungler, Watson, that I should erect an obvious dummy, and expect that some of the sharpest men in Europe would be deceived by it? We have been in this room two hours, and Mrs. Hudson has made some change in that figure eight times, or once in every quarter of an hour. She works it from the front, so that her shadow may never be seen. Ah!" He drew in his breath with a shrill, excited intake. In the dim light I saw his head thrown forward, his whole attitude rigid with attention. Outside the street was absolutely deserted. Those two men might still be crouching in the doorway, but I could no longer see them. All was still and dark, save only that brilliant yellow screen in front of us with the black figure outlined upon its centre. Again in the utter silence I heard that thin, sibilant note which spoke of intense suppressed excitement. An instant later he pulled me back into the blackest corner of the room, and I felt his warning hand upon my lips. The fingers which clutched me were quivering. Never had I known my friend more moved, and yet the dark street still stretched lonely and motionless before us.

But suddenly I was aware of that which his keener senses had already distinguished. A low, stealthy sound came to my ears, not from the direction of Baker Street, but from the back of the very house in which we lay concealed. A door opened and shut. An instant later steps crept down the passage—steps which were meant to be silent, but which reverberated harshly through the empty house. Holmes crouched back against the wall, and I did the same, my hand closing upon the handle of my revolver. Peering through the gloom, I saw the vague outline of a man, a shade blacker than the blackness of the open door. He stood for an instant, and then he crept forward, crouching, menacing, into the room. He was within three yards of us, this sinister figure, and I had braced myself to meet his spring, before I realized that he had no idea of our presence. He passed close beside us, stole over to the window, and very softly and noiselessly raised it for half a foot. As he sank to the level of this opening, the light of the street, no longer dimmed by the dusty glass, fell full upon his face. The man seemed to be beside himself with excitement. His two eyes shone like stars, and his features were working convulsively. He was an elderly man, with a thin, projecting nose, a high, bald forehead, and a huge grizzled moustache. An opera hat was pushed to the back of his head, and an evening dress shirt-front gleamed out through his open overcoat. His face was gaunt and swarthy, scored with deep, savage lines. In his hand he carried what appeared to be a stick, but as he laid it down upon the floor it gave a metallic clang. Then from the pocket of his overcoat he drew a bulky object, and he busied himself in some task which

ended with a loud, sharp click, as if a spring or bolt had fallen into its place. Still kneeling upon the floor he bent forward and threw all his weight and strength upon some lever, with the result that there came a long, whirling, grinding noise, ending once more in a powerful click. He straightened himself then, and I saw that what he held in his hand was a sort of gun, with a curiously misshapen butt. He opened it at the breech, put something in, and snapped the breech-lock. Then, crouching down, he rested the end of the barrel upon the ledge of the open window, and I saw his long moustache droop over the stock and his eye gleam as it peered along the sights. I heard a little sigh of satisfaction as he cuddled the butt into his shoulder; and saw that amazing target, the black man on the yellow ground, standing clear at the end of his foresight. For an instant he was rigid and motionless. Then his finger tightened on the trigger. There was a strange, loud whiz and a long, silvery tinkle of broken glass. At that instant Holmes sprang like a tiger on to the marksman's back, and hurled him flat upon his face. He was up again in a moment, and with convulsive strength he seized Holmes by the throat, but I struck him on the head with the butt of my revolver, and he dropped again upon the floor. I fell upon him, and as I held him my comrade blew a shrill call upon a whistle. There was the clatter of running feet upon the pavement, and two policemen in uniform, with one plain-clothes detective, rushed through the front entrance and into the room.

"That you, Lestrade?" said Holmes.

"Yes, Mr. Holmes. I took the job myself. It's good to see you back in London, sir."

"I think you want a little unofficial help. Three undetected murders in one year won't do, Lestrade. But you handled the Molesey Mystery with less than your usual—that's to say, you handled it fairly well."

We had all risen to our feet, our prisoner breathing hard, with a stalwart constable on each side of him. Already a few loiterers had begun to collect in the street. Holmes stepped up to the window, closed it, and dropped the blinds. Lestrade had produced two candles, and the policemen had uncovered their lanterns. I was able at last to have a good look at our prisoner.

It was a tremendously virile and yet sinister face which was turned towards us. With the brow of a philosopher above and the jaw of a sensualist below, the man must have started with great capacities for good or for evil. But one could not look upon his cruel blue eyes, with their drooping, cynical lids, or upon the fierce, aggressive nose and the threatening, deep-lined brow, without reading Nature's plainest danger-signals. He took no heed of any of us, but his eyes were fixed upon Holmes's face with an expression in which hatred and amazement were equally blended. "You fiend!" he kept on muttering. "You clever, clever fiend!"

"Ah, Colonel!" said Holmes, arranging his rumpled collar. "'Journeys end in lovers' meetings,' as the old play says. I don't think I have had the pleasure of seeing you since you favoured me with those attentions as I lay on the ledge above the Reichenbach Fall."

The colonel still stared at my friend like a man in a trance. "You cunning, cunning fiend!" was all that he could say.

"I have not introduced you yet," said Holmes. "This, gentlemen, is Colonel Sebastian Moran, once of Her Majesty's Indian Army, and the best heavy-game shot that our Eastern Empire has ever produced. I believe I am correct Colonel, in saying that your bag of tigers still remains unrivalled?"

The fierce old man said nothing, but still glared at my companion. With his savage eyes and bristling moustache he was wonderfully like a tiger himself.

"I wonder that my very simple stratagem could deceive so old a *shikari*," said Holmes. "It must be very familiar to you. Have you not tethered a young kid under a tree, lain above it with your rifle, and waited for the bait to bring up your tiger? This empty house is my tree, and you are my tiger. You have possibly had other guns in reserve in case there should be several tigers, or in the unlikely supposition of your own aim failing you. These," he pointed around, "are my other guns. The parallel is exact."

Colonel Moran sprang forward with a snarl of rage, but the constables dragged him back. The fury upon his face was terrible to look at.

"I confess that you had one small surprise for me," said Holmes. "I did not anticipate that you would yourself make use of this empty house and this convenient front window. I had imagined you as operating from the street, where my friend, Lestrade and his merry men were awaiting you. With that exception, all has gone as I expected."

Colonel Moran turned to the official detective.

"You may or may not have just cause for arresting me," said he, "but at least there can be no reason why I should submit to the gibes of this person. If I am in the hands of the law, let things be done in a legal way."

"Well, that's reasonable enough," said Lestrade. "Nothing further you have to say, Mr. Holmes, before we go?"

Holmes had picked up the powerful air-gun from the floor, and was examining its mechanism.

"An admirable and unique weapon," said he, "noiseless and of tremendous power: I knew Von Herder, the blind German mechanic, who constructed it to the order of the late Professor Moriarty. For years I have been aware of its existence though I have never before had the opportunity of handling it. I commend it very specially to your attention, Lestrade and also the bullets which fit it."

"You can trust us to look after that, Mr. Holmes," said Lestrade, as the whole party moved towards the door. "Anything further to say?"

"Only to ask what charge you intend to prefer?"

"What charge, sir? Why, of course, the attempted murder of Mr. Sherlock Holmes."

"Not so, Lestrade. I do not propose to appear in the matter at all. To you, and to you only, belongs the credit of the remarkable arrest which you have effected. Yes, Lestrade, I congratulate you! With your usual happy mixture of cunning and audacity, you have got him."

"Got him! Got whom, Mr. Holmes?"

"The man that the whole force has been seeking in vain—Colonel Sebastian Moran, who shot the Honourable Ronald Adair with an expanding bullet from an air-gun through the open window of the second-floor front of No. 427, Park Lane, upon the thirtieth of last month. That's the charge, Lestrade. And now, Watson, if you can endure the draught from a broken window, I think that half an hour in my study over a cigar may afford you some profitable amusement."

Our old chambers had been left unchanged through the supervision of Mycroft Holmes and the immediate care of Mrs. Hudson. As I entered I saw, it is true, an unwonted tidiness, but the old landmarks were all in their place. There were the chemical corner and the acid-stained, deal-topped table. There upon a shelf was the row of

formidable scrap-books and books of reference which many of our fellow-citizens would have been so glad to burn. The diagrams, the violin-case, and the pipe-rack—even the Persian slipper which contained the tobacco—all met my eyes as I glanced round me. There were two occupants of the room—one, Mrs. Hudson, who beamed upon us both as we entered—the other, the strange dummy which had played so important a part in the evening's adventures. It was a wax-coloured model of my friend, so admirably done that it was a perfect facsimile. It stood on a small pedestal table with an old dressing-gown of Holmes's so draped round it that the illusion from the street was absolutely perfect.

"I hope you observed all precautions, Mrs. Hudson?" said Holmes.

"I went to it on my knees, sir, just as you told me."

"Excellent. You carried the thing out very well. Did you observe where the bullet went?"

"Yes, sir I'm afraid it has spoilt your beautiful bust, for it passed right through the head and flattened itself on the wall. I picked it up from the carpet. Here it is!"

Holmes held it out to me. "A soft revolver bullet, as you perceive, Watson. There's genius in that, for who would expect to find such a thing fired from an airgun? All right, Mrs. Hudson. I am much obliged for your assistance. And now, Watson, let me see you in your old seat once more, for there are several points which I should like to discuss with you."

He had thrown off the seedy frockcoat, and now he was the Holmes of old in the mouse-coloured dressing-gown which he took from his effigy.

"The old *shikari's* nerves have not lost their steadiness, nor his eyes their keenness," said he, with a laugh, as he inspected the shattered forehead of his bust.

"Plumb in the middle of the back of the head and smack through the brain. He was the best shot in India, and I expect that there are few better in London. Have you heard the name?"

"No, I have not."

"Well, well, such is fame! But, then, if I remember right, you had not heard the name of Professor James Moriarty, who had one of the great brains of the century. Just give me down my index of biographies from the shelf."

He turned over the pages lazily, leaning back in his chair and blowing great clouds from his cigar.

"My collection of M's is a fine one," said he. "Moriarty himself is enough to make any letter illustrious, and here is Morgan the poisoner, and Merridew of abominable memory, and Mathews, who knocked out my left canine in the waiting-room at Charing Cross, and, finally, here is our friend of to-night."

He handed over the book, and I read:

Moran, Sebastian, Colonel. Unemployed. Formerly 1st Bangalore Pioneers. Born London, 1840. Son of Sir Augustus Moran, C.B., once British Minister to Persia. Educated Eton and Oxford. Served in Jowaki Campaign, Afghan Campaign, Charasiab (despatches), Sherpur, and Cabul. Author of *Heavy Game of the Western Himalayas* (1881); *Three Months in the Jungle* (1884). Address: Conduit Street. Clubs: The Anglo-Indian, the Tankerville, the Bagatelle Card Club.

On the margin was written, in Holmes's precise hand:

The second most dangerous man in London.

"This is astonishing," said I, as I handed back the volume. "The man's career is that of an honourable soldier."

"It is true," Holmes answered. "Up to a certain point he did well. He was always a man of iron nerve, and the story is still told in India how he crawled down a drain after a wounded man-eating tiger. There are some trees, Watson, which grow to a certain height, and then suddenly develop some unsightly eccentricity. You will see it often in humans. I have a theory that the individual represents in his development the whole procession of his ancestors, and that such a sudden turn to good or evil stands for some strong influence which came into the line of his pedigree. The person becomes, as it were, the epitome of the history of his own family."

"It is surely rather fanciful."

"Well, I don't insist upon it. Whatever the cause, Colonel Moran began to go wrong. Without any open scandal, he still made India too hot to hold him. He retired, came to London, and again acquired an evil name. It was at this time that he was sought out by Professor Moriarty, to whom for a time he was chief of the staff. Moriarty supplied him liberally with money, and used him only in one or two very high-class jobs, which no ordinary criminal could have undertaken. You may have some recollection of the death of Mrs. Stewart, of Lauder, in 1887. Not? Well, I am sure Moran was at the bottom of it, but nothing could be proved. So cleverly was the colonel concealed that, even when the Moriarty gang was broken up, we could not incriminate him. You remember at that date, when I called upon you in your rooms, how I put up the shutters for fear of air-guns? No doubt you thought me fanciful. I knew exactly what I was doing, for I knew of the existence of this remarkable gun, and I knew also that one of the best shots in the world would be behind it. When we were in Switzerland he followed us with Moriarty, and it was undoubtedly he who gave me that evil five minutes on the Reichenbach ledge.

"You may think that I read the papers with some attention during my sojourn in France, on the look-out for any chance of laying him by the heels. So long as he was free in London, my life would really not have been worth living. Night and day the shadow would have been over me, and sooner or later his chance must have come. What could I do? I could not shoot him at sight, or I should myself be in the dock. There was no use appealing to a magistrate. They cannot interfere on the strength of what would appear to them to be a wild suspicion. So I could do nothing. But I watched the criminal news, knowing that sooner or later I should get him. Then came the death of this Ronald Adair. My chance had come at last. Knowing what I did, was it not certain that Colonel Moran had done it? He had played cards with the lad, he had followed him home from the club, he had shot him through the open window. There was not a doubt of it. The bullets alone are enough to put his head in a noose. I came over at once. I was seen by the sentinel, who would, I knew, direct the colonel's attention to my presence. He could not fail to connect my sudden return with his crime, and to be terribly alarmed. I was sure that he would make an attempt to get me out of the way *at once*, and would bring round his murderous weapon for that purpose. I left him an excellent mark in the window, and, having warned the police that they might be needed—by the way, Watson, you spotted their presence in that doorway with unerring accuracy—I took up what seemed to me to be a judicious post for observation, never dreaming that he would choose the same spot for his attack. Now, my dear Watson, does anything remain for me to explain?"

"Yes," said I. "You have not made it clear what was Colonel Moran's motive in murdering the Honourable Ronald Adair?"

"Ah! my dear Watson, there we come into those realms of conjecture, where the most logical mind may be at fault. Each may form his own hypothesis upon the present evidence, and yours is as likely to be correct as mine."

"You have formed one, then?"

"I think that it is not difficult to explain the facts. It came out in evidence that Colonel Moran and young Adair had, between them, won a considerable amount of money. Now, Moran undoubtedly played foul—of that I have long been aware. I believe that on the day of the murder Adair had discovered that Moran was cheating. Very likely he had spoken to him privately, and had threatened to expose him unless he voluntarily resigned his membership of the club, and promised not to play cards again. It is unlikely that a youngster like Adair would at once make a hideous scandal by exposing a well-known man so much older than himself. Probably he acted as I suggest. The exclusion from his clubs would mean ruin to Moran, who lived by his ill-gotten card-gains. He therefore murdered Adair, who at the time was endeavouring to work out how much money he should himself return, since he could not profit by his partner's foul play. He locked the door lest the ladies should surprise him and insist upon knowing what he was doing with these names and coins. Will it pass?"

"I have no doubt that you have hit upon the truth."

"It will be verified or disproved at the trial. Meanwhile, come what may, Colonel Moran will trouble us no more. The famous air-gun of Von Herder will embellish the Scotland Yard Museum, and once again Mr. Sherlock Holmes is free to devote his life to examining those interesting little problems which the complex life of London so plentifully presents."

THE ADVENTURE OF THE DANCING MEN

FROM THE RETURN OF SHERLOCK HOLMES (1905)

HOLMES HAD BEEN SEATED for some hours in silence with his long, thin back curved over a chemical vessel in which he was brewing a particularly malodorous product. His head was sunk upon his breast, and he looked from my point of view like a strange, lank bird, with dull grey plumage and a black top-knot.

"So, Watson," said he, suddenly, "you do not propose to invest in South African securities?"

I gave a start of astonishment. Accustomed as I was to Holmes's curious faculties, this sudden intrusion into my most intimate thoughts was utterly inexplicable.

"How on earth do you know that?" I asked.

He wheeled round upon his stool, with a steaming test-tube in his hand, and a gleam of amusement in his deep-set eyes.

"Now, Watson, confess yourself utterly taken aback," said he.

"I am."

"I ought to make you sign a paper to that effect."

"Why?"

"Because in five minutes you will say that it is all so absurdly simple."

"I am sure that I shall say nothing of the kind."

"You see, my dear Watson,"—he propped his test-tube in the rack, and began to lecture with the air of a professor addressing his class—"it is not really difficult to construct a series of inferences, each dependent upon its predecessor and each simple in itself. If, after doing so, one simply knocks out all the central inferences and presents one's audience with the starting-point and the conclusion, one may produce a startling, though possibly a meretricious, effect. Now, it was not really difficult, by an inspection of the groove between your left forefinger and thumb, to feel sure that you did *not* propose to invest your small capital in the gold fields."

"I see no connection."

"Very likely not; but I can quickly show you a close connection. Here are the missing

links of the very simple chain: 1. You had chalk between your left finger and thumb when you returned from the club last night. 2. You put chalk there when you play billiards, to steady the cue. 3. You never play billiards except with Thurston. 4. You told me, four weeks ago, that Thurston had an option on some South African property which would expire in a month, and which he desired you to share with him. 5. Your check book is locked in my drawer, and you have not asked for the key. 6. You do not propose to invest your money in this manner."

"How absurdly simple!" I cried.

"Quite so!" said he, a little nettled. "Every problem becomes very childish when once it is explained to you. Here is an unexplained one. See what you can make of that, friend Watson." He tossed a sheet of paper upon the table, and turned once more to his chemical analysis.

I looked with amazement at the absurd hieroglyphics upon the paper.

"Why, Holmes, it is a child's drawing," I cried.

"Oh, that's your idea!"

"What else should it be?"

"That is what Mr. Hilton Cubitt, of Riding Thorpe Manor, Norfolk, is very anxious to know. This little conundrum came by the first post, and he was to follow by the next train. There's a ring at the bell, Watson. I should not be very much surprised if this were he."

A heavy step was heard upon the stairs, and an instant later there entered a tall, ruddy, clean-shaven gentleman, whose clear eyes and florid cheeks told of a life led far from the fogs of Baker Street. He seemed to bring a whiff of his strong, fresh, bracing, east coast air with him as he entered. Having shaken hands with each of us, he was about to sit down, when his eye rested upon the paper with the curious markings, which I had just examined and left upon the table.

"Well, Mr. Holmes, what do you make of these?" he cried. "They told me that you were fond of queer mysteries, and I don't think you can find a queerer one than that. I sent the paper on ahead, so that you might have time to study it before I came."

"It is certainly rather a curious production," said Holmes. "At first sight it would appear to be some childish prank. It consists of a number of absurd little figures dancing across the paper upon which they are drawn. Why should you attribute any importance to so grotesque an object?"

"I never should, Mr. Holmes. But my wife does. It is frightening her to death. She says nothing, but I can see terror in her eyes. That's why I want to sift the matter to the bottom."

Holmes held up the paper so that the sunlight shone full upon it. It was a page torn from a notebook. The markings were done in pencil, and ran in this way:

Holmes examined it for some time, and then, folding it carefully up, he placed it in his pocketbook.

"This promises to be a most interesting and unusual case," said he. "You gave me a few particulars in your letter, Mr. Hilton Cubitt, but I should be very much obliged if you would kindly go over it all again for the benefit of my friend, Dr. Watson."

"I'm not much of a story-teller," said our visitor, nervously clasping and unclasping his great, strong hands. "You'll just ask me anything that I don't make clear. I'll begin at the time of my marriage last year, but I want to say first of all that, though I'm not a rich man, my people have been at Riding Thorpe for a matter of five centuries, and there is no better known family in the County of Norfolk. Last year I came up to London for the Jubilee, and I stopped at a boarding-house in Russell Square, because Parker, the vicar of our parish, was staying in it. There was an American young lady there—Patrick was the name —Elsie Patrick. In some way we became friends, until before my month was up I was as much in love as a man could be. We were quietly married at a registry office, and we returned to Norfolk a wedded couple. You'll think it very mad, Mr. Holmes, that a man of a good old family should marry a wife in this fashion, knowing nothing of her past or of her people, but if you saw her and knew her, it would help you to understand.

"She was very straight about it, was Elsie. I can't say that she did not give me every chance of getting out of it if I wished to do so. 'I have had some very disagreeable associations in my life,' said she, 'I wish to forget all about them. I would rather never allude to the past, for it is very painful to me. If you take me, Hilton, you will take a woman who has nothing that she need be personally ashamed of, but you will have to be content with my word for it, and to allow me to be silent as to all that passed up to the time when I became yours. If these conditions are too hard, then go back to Norfolk, and leave me to the lonely life in which you found me.' It was only the day before our wedding that she said those very words to me. I told her that I was content to take her on her own terms, and I have been as good as my word.

"Well we have been married now for a year, and very happy we have been. But about a month ago, at the end of June, I saw for the first time signs of trouble. One day my wife received a letter from America. I saw the American stamp. She turned deadly white, read the letter, and threw it into the fire. She made no allusion to it afterwards, and I made none, for a promise is a promise, but she has never known an easy hour from that moment. There is always a look of fear upon her face—a look as if she were waiting and expecting. She would do better to trust me. She would find that I was her best friend. But until she speaks, I can say nothing. Mind you, she is a truthful woman, Mr. Holmes, and whatever trouble there may have been in her past life it has been no fault of hers. I am only a simple Norfolk squire, but there is not a man in England who ranks his family honour more highly than I do. She knows it well, and she knew it well before she married me. She would never bring any stain upon it—of that I am sure.

"Well, now I come to the queer part of my story. About a week ago—it was the Tuesday of last week—I found on one of the window-sills a number of absurd little dancing figures like these upon the paper. They were scrawled with chalk. I thought that it was the stable-boy who had drawn them, but the lad swore he knew nothing about it. Anyhow, they had come there during the night. I had them washed out, and I only mentioned the matter to my wife afterwards. To my surprise, she took it very seriously, and begged me if any more came to let her see them. None did come for a week, and then

yesterday morning I found this paper lying on the sundial in the garden. I showed it to Elsie, and down she dropped in a dead faint. Since then she has looked like a woman in a dream, half dazed, and with terror always lurking in her eyes. It was then that I wrote and sent the paper to you, Mr. Holmes. It was not a thing that I could take to the police, for they would have laughed at me, but you will tell me what to do. I am not a rich man, but if there is any danger threatening my little woman, I would spend my last copper to shield her."

He was a fine creature, this man of the old English soil—simple, straight, and gentle, with his great, earnest blue eyes and broad, comely face. His love for his wife and his trust in her shone in his features. Holmes had listened to his story with the utmost attention, and now he sat for some time in silent thought.

"Don't you think, Mr. Cubitt," said he, at last, "that your best plan would be to make a direct appeal to your wife, and to ask her to share her secret with you?"

Hilton Cubitt shook his massive head.

"A promise is a promise, Mr Holmes. If Elsie wished to tell me she would. If not, it is not for me to force her confidence. But I am justified in taking my own line—and I will."

"Then I will help you with all my heart. In the first place, have you heard of any strangers being seen in your neighbourhood?"

"No."

"I presume that it is a very quiet place. Any fresh face would cause comment?"

"In the immediate neighbourhood, yes. But we have several small watering-places not very far away. And the farmers take in lodgers."

"These hieroglyphics have evidently a meaning. If it is a purely arbitrary one, it may be impossible for us to solve it. If, on the other hand, it is systematic, I have no doubt that we shall get to the bottom of it. But this particular sample is so short that I can do nothing, and the facts which you have brought me are so indefinite that we have no basis for an investigation. I would suggest that you return to Norfolk, that you keep a keen lookout, and that you take an exact copy of any fresh dancing men which may appear. It is a thousand pities that we have not a reproduction of those which were done in chalk upon the window-sill. Make a discreet inquiry also as to any strangers in the neighbourhood. When you have collected some fresh evidence, come to me again. That is the best advice which I can give you, Mr. Hilton Cubitt. If there are any pressing fresh developments, I shall be always ready to run down and see you in your Norfolk home."

The interview left Sherlock Holmes very thoughtful, and several times in the next few days I saw him take his slip of paper from his notebook and look long and earnestly at the curious figures inscribed upon it. He made no allusion to the affair, however, until one afternoon a fortnight or so later. I was going out when he called me back.

"You had better stay here, Watson."

"Why?"

"Because I had a wire from Hilton Cubitt this morning. You remember Hilton Cubitt, of the dancing men? He was to reach Liverpool Street at one-twenty. He may be here at any moment. I gather from his wire that there have been some new incidents of importance."

We had not long to wait, for our Norfolk squire came straight from the station as fast as a hansom could bring him. He was looking worried and depressed, with tired eyes and a lined forehead.

"It's getting on my nerves, this business, Mr. Holmes," said he, as he sank, like a wearied man, into an armchair. "It's bad enough to feel that you are surrounded by unseen, unknown folk, who have some kind of design upon you, but when, in addition to that, you know that it is just killing your wife by inches, then it becomes as much as flesh and blood can endure. She's wearing away under it—just wearing away before my eyes."

"Has she said anything yet?"

"No, Mr. Holmes, she has not. And yet there have been times when the poor girl has wanted to speak, and yet could not quite bring herself to take the plunge. I have tried to help her, but I daresay I did it clumsily, and scared her from it. She has spoken about my old family, and our reputation in the county, and our pride in our unsullied honour, and I always felt it was leading to the point, but somehow it turned off before we got there."

"But you have found out something for yourself?"

"A good deal, Mr. Holmes. I have several fresh dancing-men pictures for you to examine, and, what is more important, I have seen the fellow."

"What, the man who draws them?"

"Yes, I saw him at his work. But I will tell you everything in order. When I got back after my visit to you, the very first thing I saw next morning was a fresh crop of dancing men. They had been drawn in chalk upon the black wooden door of the tool-house, which stands beside the lawn in full view of the front windows. I took an exact copy, and here it is." He unfolded a paper and laid it upon the table. Here is a copy of the hieroglyphics:

"Excellent!" said Holmes. "Excellent! Pray continue."

"When I had taken the copy, I rubbed out the marks, but, two mornings later, a fresh inscription had appeared. I have a copy of it here:"

Holmes rubbed his hands and chuckled with delight.

"Our material is rapidly accumulating," said he.

"Three days later a message was left scrawled upon paper, and placed under a pebble upon the sundial. Here it is. The characters are, as you see, exactly the same as the last one. After that I determined to lie in wait, so I got out my revolver and I sat up in my study, which overlooks the lawn and garden. About two in the morning I was seated by

the window, all being dark save for the moonlight outside, when I heard steps behind me, and there was my wife in her dressing-gown. She implored me to come to bed. I told her frankly that I wished to see who it was who played such absurd tricks upon us. She answered that it was some senseless practical joke, and that I should not take any notice of it.

"'If it really annoys you, Hilton, we might go and travel, you and I, and so avoid this nuisance.'

"'What, be driven out of our own house by a practical joker?' said I. 'Why, we should have the whole county laughing at us.'

"'Well, come to bed,' said she, 'and we can discuss it in the morning.'

"Suddenly, as she spoke, I saw her white face grow whiter yet in the moonlight, and her hand tightened upon my shoulder. Something was moving in the shadow of the tool-house. I saw a dark, creeping figure which crawled round the corner and squatted in front of the door. Seizing my pistol, I was rushing out, when my wife threw her arms round me and held me with convulsive strength. I tried to throw her off, but she clung to me most desperately. At last I got clear, but by the time I had opened the door and reached the house the creature was gone. He had left a trace of his presence, however, for there on the door was the very same arrangement of dancing men which had already twice appeared, and which I have copied on that paper. There was no other sign of the fellow anywhere, though I ran all over the grounds. And yet the amazing thing is that he must have been there all the time, for when I examined the door again in the morning, he had scrawled some more of his pictures under the line which I had already seen."

"Have you that fresh drawing?"

"Yes, it is very short, but I made a copy of it, and here it is."

Again he produced a paper. The new dance was in this form:

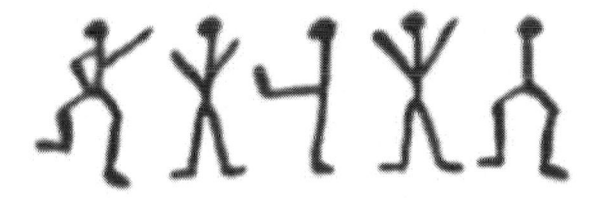

"Tell me," said Holmes—and I could see by his eyes that he was much excited—"was this a mere addition to the first or did it appear to be entirely separate?"

"It was on a different panel of the door."

"Excellent! This is far the most important of all for our purpose. It fills me with hopes. Now, Mr. Hilton Cubitt, please continue your most interesting statement."

"I have nothing more to say, Mr. Holmes, except that I was angry with my wife that night for having held me back when I might have caught the skulking rascal. She said that she feared that I might come to harm. For an instant it had crossed my mind that perhaps what she really feared was that *he* might come to harm, for I could not doubt that she knew who this man was, and what he meant by these strange signals. But there is a tone in my wife's voice, Mr. Holmes, and a look in her eyes which forbid doubt, and I am sure that it was indeed my own safety that was in her mind. There's the whole case, and now I

want your advice as to what I ought to do. My own inclination is to put half a dozen of my farm lads in the shrubbery, and when this fellow comes again to give him such a hiding that he will leave us in peace for the future."

"I fear it is too deep a case for such simple remedies," said Holmes. "How long can you stay in London?"

"I must go back to-day. I would not leave my wife alone all night for anything. She is very nervous, and begged me to come back."

"I daresay you are right. But if you could have stopped, I might possibly have been able to return with you in a day or two. Meanwhile you will leave me these papers, and I think that it is very likely that I shall be able to pay you a visit shortly and to throw some light upon your case."

Sherlock Holmes preserved his calm professional manner until our visitor had left us, although it was easy for me, who knew him so well, to see that he was profoundly excited. The moment that Hilton Cubitt's broad back had disappeared through the door my comrade rushed to the table, laid out all the slips of paper containing dancing men in front of him, and threw himself into an intricate and elaborate calculation. For two hours I watched him as he covered sheet after sheet of paper with figures and letters, so completely absorbed in his task that he had evidently forgotten my presence. Sometimes he was making progress and whistled and sang at his work; sometimes he was puzzled, and would sit for long spells with a furrowed brow and a vacant eye. Finally he sprang from his chair with a cry of satisfaction, and walked up and down the room rubbing his hands together. Then he wrote a long telegram upon a cable form. "If my answer to this is as I hope, you will have a very pretty case to add to your collection, Watson," said he. "I expect that we shall be able to go down to Norfolk tomorrow, and to take our friend some very definite news as to the secret of his annoyance."

I confess that I was filled with curiosity, but I was aware that Holmes liked to make his disclosures at his own time and in his own way, so I waited until it should suit him to take me into his confidence.

But there was a delay in that answering telegram, and two days of impatience followed, during which Holmes pricked up his ears at every ring of the bell. On the evening of the second there came a letter from Hilton Cubitt. All was quiet with him, save that a long inscription had appeared that morning upon the pedestal of the sundial. He inclosed a copy of it, which is here reproduced:

Holmes bent over this grotesque frieze for some minutes, and then suddenly sprang to his feet with an exclamation of surprise and dismay. His face was haggard with anxiety.

"We have let this affair go far enough," said he. "Is there a train to North Walsham to-night?"

I turned up the time-table. The last had just gone.

"Then we shall breakfast early and take the very first in the morning," said Holmes. "Our presence is most urgently needed. Ah! here is our expected cablegram. One moment,

Mrs. Hudson, there may be an answer. No, that is quite as I expected. This message makes it even more essential that we should not lose an hour in letting Hilton Cubitt know how matters stand, for it is a singular and a dangerous web in which our simple Norfolk squire is entangled."

So, indeed, it proved, and as I come to the dark conclusion of a story which had seemed to me to be only childish and bizarre, I experience once again the dismay and horror with which I was filled. Would that I had some brighter ending to communicate to my readers, but these are the chronicles of fact, and I must follow to their dark crisis the strange chain of events which for some days made Riding Thorpe Manor a household word through the length and breadth of England.

We had hardly alighted at North Walsham, and mentioned the name of our destination, when the station-master hurried towards us. "I suppose that you are the detectives from London?" said he.

A look of annoyance passed over Holmes's face.

"What makes you think such a thing?"

"Because Inspector Martin from Norwich has just passed through. But maybe you are the surgeons. She's not dead—or wasn't by last accounts. You may be in time to save her yet—though it be for the gallows."

Holmes's brow was dark with anxiety.

"We are going to Riding Thorpe Manor," said he, "but we have heard nothing of what has passed there."

"It's a terrible business," said the stationmaster. "They are shot, both Mr. Hilton Cubitt and his wife. She shot him and then herself—so the servants say. He's dead and her life is despaired of. Dear, dear, one of the oldest families in the county of Norfolk, and one of the most honoured."

Without a word Holmes hurried to a carriage, and during the long seven miles' drive he never opened his mouth. Seldom have I seen him so utterly despondent. He had been uneasy during all our journey from town, and I had observed that he had turned over the morning papers with anxious attention, but now this sudden realization of his worst fears left him in a blank melancholy. He leaned back in his seat, lost in gloomy speculation. Yet there was much around to interest us, for we were passing through as singular a countryside as any in England, where a few scattered cottages represented the population of to-day, while on every hand enormous square-towered churches bristled up from the flat green landscape and told of the glory and prosperity of old East Anglia. At last the violet rim of the German Ocean appeared over the green edge of the Norfolk coast, and the driver pointed with his whip to two old brick and timber gables which projected from a grove of trees. "That's Riding Thorpe Manor," said he.

As we drove up to the porticoed front door, I observed in front of it, beside the tennis lawn, the black tool-house and the pedestalled sundial with which we had such strange associations. A dapper little man, with a quick, alert manner and a waxed moustache, had just descended from a high dog-cart. He introduced himself as Inspector Martin, of the Norfolk Constabulary, and he was considerably astonished when he heard the name of my companion.

"Why, Mr. Holmes, the crime was only committed at three this morning. How could you hear of it in London and get to the spot as soon as I?"

"I anticipated it. I came in the hope of preventing it."

"Then you must have important evidence, of which we are ignorant, for they were said to be a most united couple."

"I have only the evidence of the dancing men," said Holmes. "I will explain the matter to you later. Meanwhile, since it is too late to prevent this tragedy, I am very anxious that I should use the knowledge which I possess in order to insure that justice be done. Will you associate me in your investigation, or will you prefer that I should act independently?"

"I should be proud to feel that we were acting together, Mr. Holmes," said the inspector, earnestly.

"In that case I should be glad to hear the evidence and to examine the premises without an instant of unnecessary delay."

Inspector Martin had the good sense to allow my friend to do things in his own fashion, and contented himself with carefully noting the results. The local surgeon, an old, white-haired man, had just come down from Mrs. Hilton Cubitt's room, and he reported that her injuries were serious, but not necessarily fatal. The bullet had passed through the front of her brain, and it would probably be some time before she could regain consciousness. On the question of whether she had been shot or had shot herself, he would not venture to express any decided opinion. Certainly the bullet had been discharged at very close quarters. There was only the one pistol found in the room, two barrels of which had been emptied. Mr. Hilton Cubitt had been shot through the heart. It was equally conceivable that he had shot her and then himself, or that she had been the criminal, for the revolver lay upon the floor midway between them.

"Has he been moved?" asked Holmes.

"We have moved nothing except the lady. We could not leave her lying wounded upon the floor."

"How long have you been here, Doctor?"

"Since four o'clock."

"Anyone else?"

"Yes, the constable here."

"And you have touched nothing?"

"Nothing."

"You have acted with great discretion. Who sent for you?"

"The housemaid, Saunders."

"Was it she who gave the alarm?"

"She and Mrs. King, the cook."

"Where are they now?"

"In the kitchen, I believe."

"Then I think we had better hear their story at once."

The old hall, oak-panelled and high-windowed, had been turned into a court of investigation. Holmes sat in a great, old-fashioned chair, his inexorable eyes gleaming out of his haggard face. I could read in them a set purpose to devote his life to this quest until the client whom he had failed to save should at last be avenged. The trim Inspector Martin, the old, grey-headed country doctor, myself, and a stolid village policeman made up the rest of that strange company.

The two women told their story clearly enough. They had been aroused from their sleep by the sound of an explosion, which had been followed a minute later by a second one. They slept in adjoining rooms, and Mrs. King had rushed in to Saunders. Together

they had descended the stairs. The door of the study was open, and a candle was burning upon the table. Their master lay upon his face in the centre of the room. He was quite dead. Near the window his wife was crouching, her head leaning against the wall. She was horribly wounded, and the side of her face was red with blood. She breathed heavily, but was incapable of saying anything. The passage, as well as the room, was full of smoke and the smell of powder. The window was certainly shut and fastened upon the inside. Both women were positive upon the point. They had at once sent for the doctor and for the constable. Then, with the aid of the groom and the stable-boy, they had conveyed their injured mistress to her room. Both she and her husband had occupied the bed. She was clad in her dress—he in his dressing-gown, over his night-clothes. Nothing had been moved in the study. So far as they knew, there had never been any quarrel between husband and wife. They had always looked upon them as a very united couple.

These were the main points of the servants' evidence. In answer to Inspector Martin, they were clear that every door was fastened upon the inside, and that no one could have escaped from the house. In answer to Holmes, they both remembered that they were conscious of the smell of powder from the moment that they ran out of their rooms upon the top floor. "I commend that fact very carefully to your attention," said Holmes to his professional colleague. "And now I think that we are in a position to undertake a thorough examination of the room."

The study proved to be a small chamber, lined on three sides with books, and with a writing-table facing an ordinary window, which looked out upon the garden. Our first attention was given to the body of the unfortunate squire, whose huge frame lay stretched across the room. His disordered dress showed that he had been hastily aroused from sleep. The bullet had been fired at him from the front, and had remained in his body, after penetrating the heart. His death had certainly been instantaneous and painless. There was no powder-marking either upon his dressing-gown or on his hands. According to the country surgeon, the lady had stains upon her face, but none upon her hand.

"The absence of the latter means nothing, though its presence may mean everything," said Holmes. "Unless the powder from a badly fitting cartridge happens to spurt backward, one may fire many shots without leaving a sign. I would suggest that Mr. Cubitt's body may now be removed. I suppose, Doctor, you have not recovered the bullet which wounded the lady?"

"A serious operation will be necessary before that can be done. But there are still four cartridges in the revolver. Two have been fired and two wounds inflicted, so that each bullet can be accounted for."

"So it would seem," said Holmes. "Perhaps you can account also for the bullet which has so obviously struck the edge of the window?"

He had turned suddenly, and his long, thin finger was pointing to a hole which had been drilled right through the lower window-sash, about an inch above the bottom.

"By George!" cried the inspector. "How ever did you see that?"

"Because I looked for it."

"Wonderful!" said the country doctor. "You are certainly right, sir. Then a third shot has been fired, and therefore a third person must have been present. But who could that have been, and how could he have got away?"

"That is the problem which we are now about to solve," said Sherlock Holmes. "You remember, Inspector Martin, when the servants said that on leaving their room they were

at once conscious of a smell of powder, I remarked that the point was an extremely important one?"

"Yes, sir; but I confess I did not quite follow you."

"It suggested that at the time of the firing, the window as well as the door of the room had been open. Otherwise the fumes of powder could not have been blown so rapidly through the house. A draught in the room was necessary for that. Both door and window were only open for a very short time, however."

"How do you prove that?"

"Because the candle was not guttered."

"Capital!" cried the inspector. "Capital!

"Feeling sure that the window had been open at the time of the tragedy, I conceived that there might have been a third person in the affair, who stood outside this opening and fired through it. Any shot directed at this person might hit the sash. I looked, and there, sure enough, was the bullet mark!"

"But how came the window to be shut and fastened?"

"The woman's first instinct would be to shut and fasten the window. But, halloa! What is this?"

It was a lady's hand-bag which stood upon the study table—a trim little handbag of crocodile-skin and silver. Holmes opened it and turned the contents out. There were twenty fifty-pound notes of the Bank of England, held together by an india-rubber band—nothing else.

"This must be preserved, for it will figure in the trial," said Holmes, as he handed the bag with its contents to the inspector. "It is now necessary that we should try to throw some light upon this third bullet, which has clearly, from the splintering of the wood, been fired from inside the room. I should like to see Mrs. King, the cook, again. You said, Mrs. King, that you were awakened by a *loud* explosion. When you said that, did you mean that it seemed to you to be louder than the second one?"

"Well, sir, it wakened me from my sleep, so it is hard to judge. But it did seem very loud."

"You don't think that it might have been two shots fired almost at the same instant?"

"I am sure I couldn't say, sir."

"I believe that it was undoubtedly so. I rather think, Inspector Martin, that we have now exhausted all that this room can teach us. If you will kindly step round with me, we shall see what fresh evidence the garden has to offer."

A flower-bed extended up to the study window, and we all broke into an exclamation as we approached it. The flowers were trampled down, and the soft soil was imprinted all over with footmarks. Large, masculine feet they were, with peculiarly long, sharp toes. Holmes hunted about among the grass and leaves like a retriever after a wounded bird. Then, with a cry of satisfaction, he bent forward and picked up a little brazen cylinder.

"I thought so," said he, "the revolver had an ejector, and here is the third cartridge. I really think, Inspector Martin, that our case is almost complete."

The country inspector's face had shown his intense amazement at the rapid and masterful progress of Holmes's investigation. At first he had shown some disposition to assert his own position, but now he was overcome with admiration, and ready to follow without question wherever Holmes led.

"Whom do you suspect?" he asked.

"I'll go into that later. There are several points in this problem which I have not been able to explain to you yet. Now that I have got so far, I had best proceed on my own lines, and then clear the whole matter up once and for all."

"Just as you wish, Mr. Holmes, so long as we get our man."

"I have no desire to make mysteries, but it is impossible at the moment of action to enter into long and complex explanations. I have the threads of this affair all in my hand. Even if this lady should never recover consciousness, we can still reconstruct the events of last night and insure that justice be done. First of all, I wish to know whether there is any inn in this neighbourhood known as 'Elrige's'?"

The servants were cross-questioned, but none of them had heard of such a place. The stable-boy threw a light upon the matter by remembering that a farmer of that name lived some miles off, in the direction of East Ruston.

"Is it a lonely farm?"

"Very lonely, sir."

"Perhaps they have not heard yet of all that happened here during the night?"

"Maybe not, sir."

Holmes thought for a little, and then a curious smile played over his face.

"Saddle a horse, my lad," said he. "I shall wish you to take a note to Elrige's Farm."

He took from his pocket the various slips of the dancing men. With these in front of him, he worked for some time at the study-table. Finally he handed a note to the boy, with directions to put it into the hands of the person to whom it was addressed, and especially to answer no questions of any sort which might be put to him. I saw the outside of the note, addressed in straggling, irregular characters, very unlike Holmes's usual precise hand. It was consigned to Mr. Abe Slaney, Elriges Farm, East Ruston, Norfolk.

"I think, Inspector," Holmes remarked, "that you would do well to telegraph for an escort, as, if my calculations prove to be correct, you may have a particularly dangerous prisoner to convey to the county jail. The boy who takes this note could no doubt forward your telegram. If there is an afternoon train to town, Watson, I think we should do well to take it, as I have a chemical analysis of some interest to finish, and this investigation draws rapidly to a close."

When the youth had been dispatched with the note, Sherlock Holmes gave his instructions to the servants. If any visitor were to call asking for Mrs. Hilton Cubitt, no information should be given as to her condition, but he was to be shown at once into the drawing-room. He impressed these points upon them with the utmost earnestness. Finally he led the way into the drawing-room, with the remark that the business was now out of our hands, and that we must while away the time as best we might until we could see what was in store for us. The doctor had departed to his patients, and only the inspector and myself remained.

"I think that I can help you to pass an hour in an interesting and profitable manner," said Holmes, drawing his chair up to the table, and spreading out in front of him the various papers upon which were recorded the antics of the dancing men. "As to you, friend Watson, I owe you every atonement for having allowed your natural curiosity to remain so long unsatisfied. To you, Inspector, the whole incident may appeal as a remarkable professional study. I must tell you, first of all, the interesting circumstances connected with the previous consultations which Mr. Hilton Cubitt has had with me in Baker Street." He then shortly recapitulated the facts which have already been recorded. "I

have here in front of me these singular productions, at which one might smile, had they not proved themselves to be the forerunners of so terrible a tragedy. I am fairly familiar with all forms of secret writings, and am myself the author of a trifling monograph upon the subject, in which I analyze one hundred and sixty separate ciphers, but I confess that this is entirely new to me. The object of those who invented the system has apparently been to conceal that these characters convey a message, and to give the idea that they are the mere random sketches of children.

"Having once recognized, however, that the symbols stood for letters, and having applied the rules which guide us in all forms of secret writings, the solution was easy enough. The first message submitted to me was so short that it was impossible for me to do more than to say, with some confidence, that the symbol XXX stood for E. As you are aware, E is the most common letter in the English alphabet, and it predominates to so marked an extent that even in a short sentence one would expect to find it most often. Out of fifteen symbols in the first message, four were the same, so it was reasonable to set this down as E. It is true that in some cases the figure was bearing a flag, and in some cases not, but it was probable, from the way in which the flags were distributed, that they were used to break the sentence up into words. I accepted this as a hypothesis, and noted that E was represented by

"But now came the real difficulty of the inquiry. The order of the English letters after E is by no means well marked, and any preponderance which may be shown in an average of a printed sheet may be reversed in a single short sentence. Speaking roughly, T, A, O, I, N, S, H, R, D, and L are the numerical order in which letters occur, but T, A, O, and I are very nearly abreast of each other, and it would be an endless task to try each combination until a meaning was arrived at. I therefore waited for fresh material. In my second interview with Mr. Hilton Cubitt he was able to give me two other short sentences and one message, which appeared—since there was no flag—to be a single word. Here are the symbols. Now, in the single word I have already got the two E's coming second and fourth in a word of five letters. It might be 'sever,' or 'lever,' or 'never.' There can be no question that the latter as a reply to an appeal is far the most probable, and the circumstances pointed to its being a reply written by the lady. Accepting it as correct, we are now able to say that the symbols stand respectively for N, V, and R.

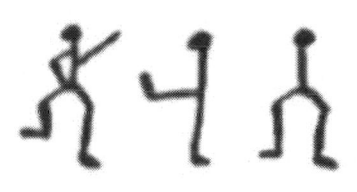

"Even now I was in considerable difficulty, but a happy thought put me in possession of several other letters. It occurred to me that if these appeals came, as I expected, from someone who had been intimate with the lady in her early life, a combination which contained two E's with three letters between might very well stand for the name 'ELSIE.' On examination I found that such a combination formed the termination of the message which was three times repeated. It was certainly some appeal to 'Elsie.' In this way I had got my L, S, and I. But what appeal could it be? There were only four letters in the word which preceded 'Elsie,' and it ended in E. Surely the word must be 'COME.' I tried all other four letters ending in E, but could find none to fit the case. So now I was in possession of C, O, and M, and I was in a position to attack the first message once more, dividing it into words and putting dots for each symbol which was still unknown. So treated, it worked out in this fashion:

.M .ERE ..E SL.NE.

"Now the first letter *can* only be A, which is a most useful discovery, since it occurs no fewer than three times in this short sentence, and the H is also apparent in the second word. Now it becomes

AM HERE A.E SLANE.

Or, filling in the obvious vacancies in the name:

AM HERE ABE SLANEY.

I had so many letters now that I could proceed with considerable confidence to the second message, which worked out in this fashion:

A. ELRI. ES.

Here I could only make sense by putting T and G for the missing letters, and supposing that the name was that of some house or inn at which the writer was staying."

Inspector Martin and I had listened with the utmost interest to the full and clear account of how my friend had produced results which had led to so complete a command over our difficulties.

"What did you do then, sir?" asked the inspector.

"I had every reason to suppose that this Abe Slaney was an American, since Abe is an American contraction, and since a letter from America had been the starting-point of all

the trouble. I had also every cause to think that there was some criminal secret in the matter. The lady's allusions to her past, and her refusal to take her husband into her confidence, both pointed in that direction. I therefore cabled to my friend, Wilson Hargreave, of the New York Police Bureau, who has more than once made use of my knowledge of London crime. I asked him whether the name of Abe Slaney was known to him. Here is his reply: 'The most dangerous crook in Chicago.' On the very evening upon which I had his answer, Hilton Cubitt sent me the last message from Slaney. Working with known letters, it took this form:

ELSIE .RE.ARE TO MEET THY GO.

The addition of a P and a D completed a message which showed me that the rascal was proceeding from persuasion to threats, and my knowledge of the crooks of Chicago prepared me to find that he might very rapidly put his words into action. I at once came to Norfolk with my friend and colleague, Dr. Watson, but, unhappily, only in time to find that the worst had already occurred."

"It is a privilege to be associated with you in the handling of a case," said the inspector, warmly. "You will excuse me, however, if I speak frankly to you. You are only answerable to yourself, but I have to answer to my superiors. If this Abe Slaney, living at Elrige's, is indeed the murderer, and if he has made his escape while I am seated here, I should certainly get into serious trouble."

"You need not be uneasy. He will not try to escape."

"How do you know?"

"To fly would be a confession of guilt."

"Then let us go arrest him."

"I expect him here every instant."

"But why should he come."

"Because I have written and asked him."

"But this is incredible, Mr. Holmes! Why should he come because you have asked him? Would not such a request rather rouse his suspicions and cause him to fly?"

"I think I have known how to frame the letter," said Sherlock Holmes. "In fact, if I am not very much mistaken, here is the gentleman himself coming up the drive."

A man was striding up the path which led to the door. He was a tall, handsome, swarthy fellow, clad in a suit of grey flannel, with a Panama hat, a bristling black beard, and a great, aggressive hooked nose, and flourishing a cane as he walked. He swaggered up a path as if the place belonged to him, and we heard his loud, confident peal at the bell.

"I think, gentlemen," said Holmes, quietly, "that we had best take up our position behind the door. Every precaution is necessary when dealing with such a fellow. You will need your handcuffs, Inspector. You can leave the talking to me."

We waited in silence for a minute—one of those minutes which one can never forget. Then the door opened and the man stepped in. In an instant Holmes clapped a pistol to his head, and Martin slipped the handcuffs over his wrists. It was all done so swiftly and deftly that the fellow was helpless before he knew that he was attacked. He glared from one to the other of us with a pair of blazing black eyes. Then he burst into a bitter laugh.

"Well, gentlemen, you have the drop on me this time. I seem to have knocked up

against something hard. But I came here in answer to a letter from Mrs. Hilton Cubitt. Don't tell me that she is in this? Don't tell me that she helped to set a trap for me?"

"Mrs. Hilton Cubitt was seriously injured, and is at death's door."

The man gave a hoarse cry of grief, which rang through the house.

"You're crazy!" he cried, fiercely. "It was he that was hurt, not she. Who would have hurt little Elsie? I may have threatened her—God forgive me!—but I would not have touched a hair of her pretty head. Take it back—you! Say that she is not hurt!"

"She was found badly wounded, by the side of her dead husband."

He sank with a deep groan on the settee and buried his face in his manacled hands. For five minutes he was silent. Then he raised his face once more, and spoke with the cold composure of despair.

"I have nothing to hide from you, gentlemen," said he. "If I shot the man he had his shot at me, and there's no murder in that. But if you think I could have hurt that woman, then you don't know either me or her. I tell you, there was never a man in this world loved a woman more than I loved her. I had a right to her. She was pledged to me years ago. Who was this Englishman that he should come between us? I tell you that I had the first right to her, and that I was only claiming my own."

"She broke away from your influence when she found the man that you are," said Holmes, sternly. "She fled from America to avoid you, and she married an honourable gentleman in England. You dogged her and followed her and made her life a misery to her, in order to induce her to abandon the husband whom she loved and respected in order to fly with you, whom she feared and hated. You have ended by bringing about the death of a noble man and driving his wife to suicide. That is your record in this business, Mr. Abe Slaney, and you will answer for it to the law."

"If Elsie dies, I care nothing what becomes of me," said the American. He opened one of his hands, and looked at a note crumpled up in his palm. "See here, mister! he cried, with a gleam of suspicion in his eyes, "you're not trying to scare me over this, are you? If the lady is hurt as bad as you say, who was it that wrote this note?" He tossed it forward on to the table.

"I wrote it, to bring you here."

"You wrote it? There was no one on earth outside the Joint who knew the secret of the dancing men. How came you to write it?"

"What one man can invent another can discover," said Holmes. There is a cab coming to convey you to Norwich, Mr. Slaney. But meanwhile, you have time to make some small reparation for the injury you have wrought. Are you aware that Mrs. Hilton Cubitt has herself lain under grave suspicion of the murder of her husband, and that it was only my presence here, and the knowledge which I happened to possess, which has saved her from the accusation? The least that you owe her is to make it clear to the whole world that she was in no way, directly or indirectly, responsible for his tragic end."

"I ask nothing better," said the American. "I guess the very best case I can make for myself is the absolute naked truth."

"It is my duty to warn you that it will be used against you," cried the inspector, with the magnificent fair play of the British criminal law.

Slaney shrugged his shoulders.

"I'll chance that," said he. "First of all, I want you gentlemen to understand that I have known this lady since she was a child. There were seven of us in a gang in Chicago, and

Elsie's father was the boss of the Joint. He was a clever man, was old Patrick. It was he who invented that writing, which would pass as a child's scrawl unless you just happened to have the key to it. Well, Elsie learned some of our ways, but she couldn't stand the business, and she had a bit of honest money of her own, so she gave us all the slip and got away to London. She had been engaged to me, and she would have married me, I believe, if I had taken over another profession, but she would have nothing to do with anything on the cross. It was only after her marriage to this Englishman that I was able to find out where she was. I wrote to her, but got no answer. After that I came over, and, as letters were no use, I put my messages where she could read them.

"Well, I have been here a month now. I lived in that farm, where I had a room down below, and could get in and out every night, and no one the wiser. I tried all I could to coax Elsie away. I knew that she read the messages, for once she wrote an answer under one of them. Then my temper got the better of me, and I began to threaten her. She sent me a letter then, imploring me to go away, and saying that it would break her heart if any scandal should come upon her husband. She said that she would come down when her husband was asleep at three in the morning, and speak with me through the end window, if I would go away afterwards and leave her in peace. She came down and brought money with her, trying to bribe me to go. This made me mad, and I caught her arm and tried to pull her through the window. At that moment in rushed the husband with his revolver in his hand. Elsie had sunk down upon the floor, and we were face to face. I was heeled also, and I held up my gun to scare him off and let me get away. He fired and missed me. I pulled off almost at the same instant, and down he dropped. I made away across the garden, and as I went I heard the window shut behind me. That's God's truth, gentlemen, every word of it, and I heard no more about it until that lad came riding up with a note which made me walk in here, like a jay, and give myself into your hands."

A cab had driven up whilst the American had been talking. Two uniformed policemen sat inside. Inspector Martin rose and touched his prisoner on the shoulder.

"It is time for us to go."

"Can I see her first?"

"No, she is not conscious. Mr. Sherlock Holmes, I only hope that if ever again I have an important case, I shall have the good fortune to have you by my side."

We stood at the window and watched the cab drive away. As I turned back, my eye caught the pellet of paper which the prisoner had tossed upon the table. It was the note with which Holmes had decoyed him.

"See if you can read it, Watson," said he, with a smile.

It contained no word, but this little line of dancing men:

"If you use the code which I have explained," said Holmes, "you will find that it simply means 'Come here at once.' I was convinced that it was an invitation which he

would not refuse, since he could never imagine that it could come from anyone but the lady. And so, my dear Watson, we have ended by turning the dancing men to good when they have so often been the agents of evil, and I think that I have fulfilled my promise of giving you something unusual for your notebook. Three-forty is our train, and I fancy we should be back in Baker Street for dinner."

Only one word of epilogue. The American, Abe Slaney, was condemned to death at the winter assizes at Norwich, but his penalty was changed to penal servitude in consideration of mitigating circumstances, and the certainty that Hilton Cubitt had fired the first shot. Of Mrs. Hilton Cubitt I only know that I have heard she recovered entirely, and that she still remains a widow, devoting her whole life to the care of the poor and to the administration of her husband's estate.

THE ADVENTURE OF THE PRIORY SCHOOL

FROM THE RETURN OF SHERLOCK HOLMES (1905)

WE HAVE HAD some dramatic entrances and exits upon our small stage at Baker Street, but I cannot recollect anything more sudden and startling than the first appearance of Thorneycroft Huxtable, M.A., Ph.D., etc. His card, which seemed too small to carry the weight of his academic distinctions, preceded him by a few seconds, and then he entered himself—so large, so pompous, and so dignified that he was the very embodiment of self-possession and solidity. And yet his first action, when the door had closed behind him, was to stagger against the table, whence he slipped down upon the floor, and there was that majestic figure prostrate and insensible upon our bearskin hearth-rug.

We had sprung to our feet, and for a few moments we stared in silent amazement at this ponderous piece of wreckage, which told of some sudden and fatal storm far out on the ocean of life. Then Holmes hurried with a cushion for his head, and I with brandy for his lips. The heavy, white face was seamed with lines of trouble, the hanging pouches under the closed eyes were leaden in colour, the loose mouth drooped dolorously at the corners, the rolling chins were unshaven. Collar and shirt bore the grime of a long journey, and the hair bristled unkempt from the well-shaped head. It was a sorely stricken man who lay before us.

"What is it, Watson?" asked Holmes.

"Absolute exhaustion—possibly mere hunger and fatigue," said I, with my finger on the thready pulse, where the stream of life trickled thin and small.

"Return ticket from Mackleton, in the north of England," said Holmes, drawing it from the watch-pocket. "It is not twelve o'clock yet. He has certainly been an early starter."

The puckered eyelids had begun to quiver, and now a pair of vacant grey eyes looked up at us. An instant later the man had scrambled on to his feet, his face crimson with shame.

"Forgive this weakness, Mr. Holmes, I have been a little overwrought. Thank you, if I might have a glass of milk and a biscuit, I have no doubt that I should be better. I came

personally, Mr. Holmes, in order to insure that you would return with me. I feared that no telegram would convince you of the absolute urgency of the case."

"When you are quite restored——"

"I am quite well again. I cannot imagine how I came to be so weak. I wish you, Mr. Holmes, to come to Mackleton with me by the next train."

My friend shook his head.

"My colleague, Dr. Watson, could tell you that we are very busy at present. I am retained in this case of the Ferrers Documents, and the Abergavenny murder is coming up for trial. Only a very important issue could call me from London at present."

"Important!" Our visitor threw up his hands. "Have you heard nothing of the abduction of the only son of the Duke of Holdernesse?"

"What! the late Cabinet Minister?"

"Exactly. We had tried to keep it out of the papers, but there was some rumour in the *Globe* last night. I thought it might have reached your ears."

Holmes shot out his long, thin arm and picked out Volume "H" in his encyclopædia of reference.

"'Holdernesse, 6th Duke, K.G., P.C.'—half the alphabet! 'Baron Beverley, Earl of Carston'—dear me, what a list! 'Lord Lieutenant of Hallamshire since 1900. Married Edith, daughter of Sir Charles Appledore, 1888. Heir and only child, Lord Saltire. Owns about two hundred and fifty thousand acres. Minerals in Lancashire and Wales. Address: Carlton House Terrace; Holdernesse Hall, Hallamshire; Carston Castle, Bangor, Wales. Lord of the Admiralty, 1872; Chief Secretary of State for——' Well, well, this man is certainly one of the greatest subjects of the Crown!"

"The greatest and perhaps the wealthiest. I am aware, Mr. Holmes, that you take a very high line in professional matters, and that you are prepared to work for the work's sake. I may tell you, however, that his Grace has already intimated that a check for five thousand pounds will be handed over to the person who can tell him where his son is, and another thousand to him who can name the man or men who have taken him."

"It is a princely offer," said Holmes. "Watson, I think that we shall accompany Dr. Huxtable back to the north of England. And now, Dr. Huxtable, when you have consumed that milk, you will kindly tell me what has happened, when it happened, how it happened, and, finally, what Dr. Thorneycroft Huxtable, of the Priory School, near Mackleton, has to do with the matter, and why he comes three days after an event—the state of your chin gives the date—to ask for my humble services."

Our visitor had consumed his milk and biscuits. The light had come back to his eyes and the colour to his cheeks, as he set himself with great vigour and lucidity to explain the situation.

"I must inform you, gentlemen, that the Priory is a preparatory school, of which I am the founder and principal. *Huxtable's Sidelights on Horace* may possibly recall my name to your memories. The Priory is, without exception, the best and most select preparatory school in England. Lord Leverstoke, the Earl of Blackwater, Sir Cathcart Soames—they all have intrusted their sons to me. But I felt that my school had reached its zenith when, weeks ago, the Duke of Holdernesse sent Mr. James Wilder, his secretary, with intimation that young Lord Saltire, ten years old, his only son and heir, was about to be committed to my charge. Little did I think that this would be the prelude to the most crushing misfortune of my life.

"On May 1st the boy arrived, that being the beginning of the summer term. He was a charming youth, and he soon fell into our ways. I may tell you—I trust that I am not indiscreet, but half-confidences are absurd in such a case—that he was not entirely happy at home. It is an open secret that the Duke's married life had not been a peaceful one, and the matter had ended in a separation by mutual consent, the Duchess taking up her residence in the south of France. This had occurred very shortly before, and the boy's sympathies are known to have been strongly with his mother. He moped after her departure from Holdernesse Hall, and it was for this reason that the Duke desired to send him to my establishment. In a fortnight the boy was quite at home with us and was apparently absolutely happy.

"He was last seen on the night of May 13th—that is, the night of last Monday. His room was on the second floor and was approached through another larger room, in which two boys were sleeping. These boys saw and heard nothing, so that it is certain that young Saltire did not pass out that way. His window was open, and there is a stout ivy plant leading to the ground. We could trace no footmarks below, but it is sure that this is the only possible exit.

"His absence was discovered at seven o'clock on Tuesday morning. His bed had been slept in. He had dressed himself fully, before going off, in his usual school suit of black Eton jacket and dark grey trousers. There were no signs that anyone had entered the room, and it is quite certain that anything in the nature of cries or a struggle would have been heard, since Caunter, the elder boy in the inner room, is a very light sleeper.

"When Lord Saltire's disappearance was discovered, I at once called a roll of the whole establishment—boys, masters, and servants. It was then that we ascertained that Lord Saltire had not been alone in his flight. Heidegger, the German master, was missing. His room was on the second floor, at the farther end of the building, facing the same way as Lord Saltire's. His bed had also been slept in, but he had apparently gone away partly dressed, since his shirt and socks were lying on the floor. He had undoubtedly let himself down by the ivy, for we could see the marks of his feet where he had landed on the lawn. His bicycle was kept in a small shed beside this lawn, and it also was gone.

"He had been with me for two years, and came with the best references, but he was a silent, morose man, not very popular either with masters or boys. No trace could be found of the fugitives, and now, on Thursday morning, we are as ignorant as we were on Tuesday. Inquiry was, of course, made at once at Holdernesse Hall. It is only a few miles away, and we imagined that, in some sudden attack of homesickness, he had gone back to his father, but nothing had been heard of him. The Duke is greatly agitated, and, as to me, you have seen yourselves the state of nervous prostration to which the suspense and the responsibility have reduced me. Mr. Holmes, if ever you put forward your full powers, I implore you to do so now, for never in your life could you have a case which is more worthy of them."

Sherlock Holmes had listened with the utmost intentness to the statement of the unhappy schoolmaster. His drawn brows and the deep furrow between them showed that he needed no exhortation to concentrate all his attention upon a problem which, apart from the tremendous interests involved must appeal so directly to his love of the complex and the unusual. He now drew out his notebook and jotted down one or two memoranda.

"You have been very remiss in not coming to me sooner," said he, severely. "You start

me on my investigation with a very serious handicap. It is inconceivable, for example, that this ivy and this lawn would have yielded nothing to an expert observer."

"I am not to blame, Mr. Holmes. His Grace was extremely desirous to avoid all public scandal. He was afraid of his family unhappiness being dragged before the world. He has a deep horror of anything of the kind."

"But there has been some official investigation?"

"Yes, sir, and it has proved most disappointing. An apparent clue was at once obtained, since a boy and a young man were reported to have been seen leaving a neighbouring station by an early train. Only last night we had news that the couple had been hunted down in Liverpool, and they prove to have no connection whatever with the matter in hand. Then it was that in my despair and disappointment, after a sleepless night, I came straight to you by the early train."

"I suppose the local investigation was relaxed while this false clue was being followed up?"

"It was entirely dropped."

"So that three days have been wasted. The affair has been most deplorably handled."

"I feel it and admit it."

"And yet the problem should be capable of ultimate solution. I shall be very happy to look into it. Have you been able to trace any connection between the missing boy and this German master?"

"None at all."

"Was he in the master's class?"

"No, he never exchanged a word with him, so far as I know."

"That is certainly very singular. Had the boy a bicycle?"

"No."

"Was any other bicycle missing?"

"No."

"Is that certain?"

"Quite."

"Well, now, you do not mean to seriously suggest that this German rode off upon a bicycle in the dead of the night, bearing the boy in his arms?"

"Certainly not."

"Then what is the theory in your mind?"

"The bicycle may have been a blind. It may have been hidden somewhere, and the pair gone off on foot."

"Quite so, but it seems rather an absurd blind, does it not? Were there other bicycles in this shed?"

"Several."

"Would he not have hidden *a couple*, had he desired to give the idea that they had gone off upon them?"

"I suppose he would."

"Of course he would. The blind theory won't do. But the incident is an admirable starting-point for an investigation. After all, a bicycle is not an easy thing to conceal or to destroy. One other question. Did anyone call to see the boy on the day before he disappeared?"

"No."

"Did he get any letters?"

"Yes, one letter."

"From whom?"

"From his father."

"Do you open the boys' letters?"

"No."

"How do you know it was from the father?"

"The coat of arms was on the envelope, and it was addressed in the Duke's peculiar stiff hand. Besides, the Duke remembers having written."

"When had he a letter before that?"

"Not for several days."

"Had he ever one from France?"

"No, never.

"You see the point of my questions, of course. Either the boy was carried off by force or he went of his own free will. In the latter case, you would expect that some prompting from outside would be needed to make so young a lad do such a thing. If he has had no visitors, that prompting must have come in letters; hence I try to find out who were his correspondents."

"I fear I cannot help you much. His only correspondent, so far as I know, was his own father."

"Who wrote to him on the very day of his disappearance. Were the relations between father and son very friendly?"

"His Grace is never very friendly with anyone. He is completely immersed in large public questions, and is rather inaccessible to all ordinary emotions. But he was always kind to the boy in his own way."

"But the sympathies of the latter were with the mother?"

"Yes."

"Did he say so?"

"No."

"The Duke, then?"

"Good Heavens, no!"

"Then how could you know?"

"I have had some confidential talks with Mr. James Wilder, his Grace's secretary. It was he who gave me the information about Lord Saltire's feelings."

"I see. By the way, that last letter of the Duke's—was it found in the boy's room after he was gone?"

"No, he had taken it with him. I think, Mr. Holmes, it is time that we were leaving for Euston."

"I will order a four-wheeler. In a quarter of an hour, we shall be at your service. If you are telegraphing home, Mr. Huxtable, it would be well to allow the people in your neighbourhood to imagine that the inquiry is still going on in Liverpool, or wherever else that red herring led your pack. In the meantime I will do a little quiet work at your own doors, and perhaps the scent is not so cold but that two old hounds like Watson and myself may get a sniff of it."

That evening found us in the cold, bracing atmosphere of the Peak country, in which Dr. Huxtable's famous school is situated. It was already dark when we reached it. A card

was lying on the hall table, and the butler whispered something to his master, who turned to us with agitation in every heavy feature.

"The Duke is here," said he. "The Duke and Mr. Wilder are in the study. Come, gentlemen, and I will introduce you."

I was, of course, familiar with the pictures of the famous statesman, but the man himself was very different from his representation. He was a tall and stately person, scrupulously dressed, with a drawn, thin face, and a nose which was grotesquely curved and long. His complexion was of a dead pallor, which was more startling by contrast with a long, dwindling beard of vivid red, which flowed down over his white waistcoat with his watch-chain gleaming through its fringe. Such was the stately presence who looked stonily at us from the centre of Dr. Huxtable's hearthrug. Beside him stood a very young man, whom I understood to be Wilder, the private secretary. He was small, nervous, alert with intelligent light-blue eyes and mobile features. It was he who at once, in an incisive and positive tone, opened the conversation.

"I called this morning, Dr. Huxtable, too late to prevent you from starting for London. I learned that your object was to invite Mr. Sherlock Holmes to undertake the conduct of this case. His Grace is surprised, Dr. Huxtable, that you should have taken such a step without consulting him."

"When I learned that the police had failed——"

"His Grace is by no means convinced that the police have failed."

"But surely, Mr. Wilder——"

"You are well aware, Dr. Huxtable, that his Grace is particularly anxious to avoid all public scandal. He prefers to take as few people as possible into his confidence."

"The matter can be easily remedied," said the brow beaten doctor; "Mr Sherlock Holmes can return to London by the morning train."

"Hardly that, Doctor, hardly that," said Holmes, in his blandest voice. "This northern air is invigorating and pleasant, so I propose to spend a few days upon your moors, and to occupy my mind as best I may. Whether I have the shelter of your roof or of the village inn is, of course, for you to decide."

I could see that the unfortunate doctor was in the last stage of indecision, from which he was rescued by the deep, sonorous voice of the red-bearded Duke, which boomed out like a dinner-gong.

"I agree with Mr. Wilder, Dr. Huxtable, that you would have done wisely to consult me. But since Mr. Holmes has already been taken into your confidence, it would indeed be absurd that we should not avail ourselves of his services. Far from going to the inn, Mr. Holmes, I should be pleased if you would come and stay with me at Holdernesse Hall."

"I thank your Grace. For the purposes of my investigation, I think that it would be wiser for me to remain at the scene of the mystery."

"Just as you like, Mr. Holmes. Any information which Mr. Wilder or I can give you is, of course, at your disposal."

"It will probably be necessary for me to see you at the Hall," said Holmes. "I would only ask you now, sir, whether you have formed any explanation in your own mind as to the mysterious disappearance of your son?"

"No, sir, I have not."

"Excuse me if I allude to that which is painful to you, but I have no alternative. Do you think that the Duchess had anything to do with the matter?"

The great minister showed perceptible hesitation.

"I do not think so," he said, at last.

"The other most obvious explanation is that the child has been kidnapped for the purpose of levying ransom. You have not had any demand of the sort?"

"No, sir."

"One more question, your Grace. I understand that you wrote to your son upon the day when this incident occurred."

"No, I wrote upon the day before."

"Exactly. But he received it on that day?"

"Yes."

"Was there anything in your letter which might have unbalanced him or induced him to take such a step?"

"No, sir, certainly not."

"Did you post that letter yourself?"

The nobleman's reply was interrupted by his secretary, who broke in with some heat.

"His Grace is not in the habit of posting letters himself," said he. "This letter was laid with others upon the study table, and I myself put them in the post-bag."

"You are sure this one was among them?"

"Yes, I observed it."

"How many letters did your Grace write that day?"

"Twenty or thirty. I have a large correspondence. But surely this is somewhat irrelevant?"

"Not entirely," said Holmes.

"For my own part," the Duke continued, "I have advised the police to turn their attention to the south of France. I have already said that I do not believe that the Duchess would encourage so monstrous an action, but the lad had the most wrong-headed opinions, and it is possible that he may have fled to her, aided and abetted by this German. I think, Dr. Huxtable, that we will now return to the Hall."

I could see that there were other questions which Holmes would have wished to put, but the nobleman's abrupt manner showed that the interview was at an end. It was evident that to his intensely aristocratic nature this discussion of his intimate family affairs with a stranger was most abhorrent, and that he feared lest every fresh question would throw a fiercer light into the discreetly shadowed corners of his ducal history.

When the nobleman and his secretary had left, my friend flung himself at once with characteristic eagerness into the investigation.

The boy's chamber was carefully examined, and yielded nothing save the absolute conviction that it was only through the window that he could have escaped. The German master's room and effects gave no further clue. In his case a trailer of ivy had given way under his weight, and we saw by the light of a lantern the mark on the lawn where his heels had come down. That one dint in the short, green grass was the only material witness left of this inexplicable nocturnal flight.

Sherlock Holmes left the house alone, and only returned after eleven. He had obtained a large ordnance map of the neighbourhood, and this he brought into my room, where he laid it out on the bed, and, having balanced the lamp in the middle of it, he began to smoke over it, and occasionally to point out objects of interest with the reeking amber of his pipe.

"This case grows upon me, Watson," said he. "There are decidedly some points of interest in connection with it. In this early stage, I want you to realize those geographical features which may have a good deal to do with our investigation.

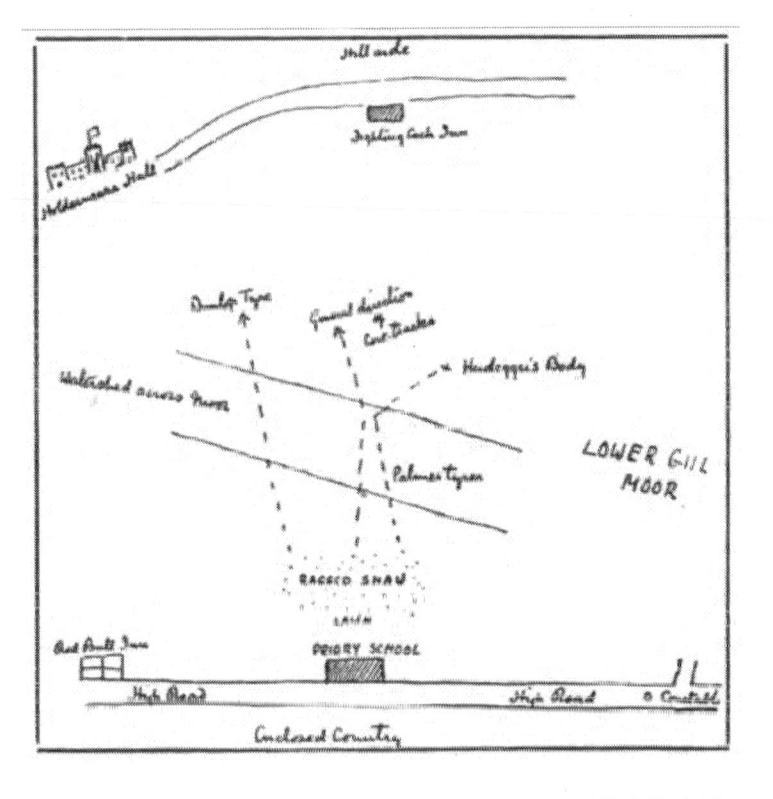

HOLMES' MAP OF THE NEIGHBOURHOOD OF THE SCHOOL.

"Look at this map. This dark square is the Priory School. I'll put a pin in it. Now, this line is the main road. You see that it runs east and west past the school, and you see also that there is no side road for a mile either way. If these two folk passed away by road, it was *this* road."

"Exactly."

"By a singular and happy chance, we are able to some extent to check what passed along this road during the night in question. At this point, where my pipe is now resting, a county constable was on duty from twelve to six. It is, as you perceive, the first cross-road on the east side. This man declares that he was not absent from his post for an instant, and he is positive that neither boy nor man could have gone that way unseen. I have spoken with this policeman to-night and he appears to me to be a perfectly reliable person. That blocks this end. We have now to deal with the other. There is an inn here, the Red Bull, the landlady of which was ill. She had sent to Mackleton for a doctor, but he did not arrive until morning, being absent at another case. The people at the inn were alert all night, awaiting his coming, and one or other of them seems to have continually had an

eye upon the road. They declare that no one passed. If their evidence is good, then we are fortunate enough to be able to block the west, and also to be able to say that the fugitives did *not* use the road at all."

"But the bicycle?" I objected.

"Quite so. We will come to the bicycle presently. To continue our reasoning: if these people did not go by the road, they must have traversed the country to the north of the house or to the south of the house. That is certain. Let us weigh the one against the other. On the south of the house is, as you perceive, a large district of arable land, cut up into small fields, with stone walls between them. There, I admit that a bicycle is impossible. We can dismiss the idea. We turn to the country on the north. Here there lies a grove of trees, marked as the 'Ragged Shaw,' and on the farther side stretches a great rolling moor, Lower Gill Moor, extending for ten miles and sloping gradually upward. Here, at one side of this wilderness, is Holdernesse Hall, ten miles by road, but only six across the moor. It is a peculiarly desolate plain. A few moor farmers have small holdings, where they rear sheep and cattle. Except these, the plover and the curlew are the only inhabitants until you come to the Chesterfield high road. There is a church there, you see, a few cottages, and an inn. Beyond that the hills become precipitous. Surely it is here to the north that our quest must lie."

"But the bicycle?" I persisted.

"Well, well!" said Holmes, impatiently. "A good cyclist does not need a high road. The moor is intersected with paths, and the moon was at the full. Halloa! what is this?"

There was an agitated knock at the door, and an instant afterwards Dr. Huxtable was in the room. In his hand he held a blue cricket-cap with a white chevron on the peak.

"At last we have a clue!" he cried. "Thank heaven! at last we are on the dear boy's track! It is his cap."

"Where was it found?"

"In the van of the gipsies who camped on the moor. They left on Tuesday. To-day the police traced them down and examined their caravan. This was found."

"How do they account for it?"

"They shuffled and lied—said that they found it on the moor on Tuesday morning. They know where he is, the rascals! Thank goodness, they are all safe under lock and key. Either the fear of the law or the Duke's purse will certainly get out of them all that they know."

"So far, so good," said Holmes, when the doctor had at last left the room. "It at least bears out the theory that it is on the side of the Lower Gill Moor that we must hope for results. The police have really done nothing locally, save the arrest of these gipsies. Look here, Watson! There is a watercourse across the moor. You see it marked here in the map. In some parts it widens into a morass. This is particularly so in the region between Holdernesse Hall and the school. It is vain to look elsewhere for tracks in this dry weather, but at *that* point there is certainly a chance of some record being left. I will call you early to-morrow morning, and you and I will try if we can throw some little light upon the mystery."

The day was just breaking when I woke to find the long, thin form of Holmes by my bedside. He was fully dressed, and had apparently already been out.

"I have done the lawn and the bicycle shed," said he. "I have also had a rumble

through the Ragged Shaw. Now, Watson, there is cocoa ready in the next room. I must beg you to hurry, for we have a great day before us."

His eyes shone, and his cheek was flushed with the exhilaration of the master workman who sees his work lie ready before him. A very different Holmes, this active, alert man, from the introspective and pallid dreamer of Baker Street. I felt, as I looked upon that supple figure, alive with nervous energy, that it was indeed a strenuous day that awaited us.

And yet it opened in the blackest disappointment. With high hopes we struck across the peaty, russet moor, intersected with a thousand sheep paths, until we came to the broad, light-green belt which marked the morass between us and Holdernesse. Certainly, if the lad had gone homeward, he must have passed this, and he could not pass it without leaving his traces. But no sign of him or the German could be seen. With a darkening face my friend strode along the margin, eagerly observant of every muddy stain upon the mossy surface. Sheep-marks there were in profusion, and at one place, some miles down, cows had left their tracks. Nothing more.

"Check number one," said Holmes, looking gloomily over the rolling expanse of the moor. "There is another morass down yonder, and a narrow neck between. Halloa! halloa! halloa! what have we here?"

We had come on a small black ribbon of pathway. In the middle of it, clearly marked on the sodden soil, was the track of a bicycle.

"Hurrah!" I cried. "We have it."

But Holmes was shaking his head, and his face was puzzled and expectant rather than joyous.

"A bicycle, certainly, but not *the* bicycle," said he. "I am familiar with forty-two different impressions left by tires. This, as you perceive, is a Dunlop, with a patch upon the outer cover. Heidegger's tires were Palmer's, leaving longitudinal stripes. Aveling, the mathematical master, was sure upon the point. Therefore, it is not Heidegger's track."

"The boy's, then?"

"Possibly, if we could prove a bicycle to have been in his possession. But this we have utterly failed to do. This track, as you perceive, was made by a rider who was going from the direction of the school."

"Or towards it?"

"No, no, my dear Watson. The more deeply sunk impression is, of course, the hind wheel, upon which the weight rests. You perceive several places where it has passed across and obliterated the more shallow mark of the front one. It was undoubtedly heading away from the school. It may or may not be connected with our inquiry, but we will follow it backwards before we go any farther."

We did so, and at the end of a few hundred yards lost the tracks as we emerged from the boggy portion of the moor. Following the path backwards, we picked out another spot, where a spring trickled across it. Here, once again, was the mark of the bicycle, though nearly obliterated by the hoofs of cows. After that there was no sign, but the path ran right on into Ragged Shaw, the wood which backed on to the school. From this wood the cycle must have emerged. Holmes sat down on a boulder and rested his chin in his hands. I had smoked two cigarettes before he moved.

"Well, well," said he, at last. "It is, of course, possible that a cunning man might change the tires of his bicycle in order to leave unfamiliar tracks. A criminal who was capable of

such a thought is a man whom I should be proud to do business with. We will leave this question undecided and hark back to our morass again, for we have left a good deal unexplored."

We continued our systematic survey of the edge of the sodden portion of the moor, and soon our perseverance was gloriously rewarded. Right across the lower part of the bog lay a miry path. Holmes gave a cry of delight as he approached it. An impression like a fine bundle of telegraph wires ran down the centre of it. It was the Palmer tires.

"Here is Herr Heidegger, sure enough!" cried Holmes, exultantly. "My reasoning seems to have been pretty sound, Watson."

"I congratulate you."

"But we have a long way still to go. Kindly walk clear of the path. Now let us follow the trail. I fear that it will not lead very far."

We found, however, as we advanced that this portion of the moor is intersected with soft patches, and, though we frequently lost sight of the track, we always succeeded in picking it up once more.

"Do you observe," said Holmes, "that the rider is now undoubtedly forcing the pace? There can be no doubt of it. Look at this impression, where you get both tires clear. The one is as deep as the other. That can only mean that the rider is throwing his weight on to the handle-bar, as a man does when he is sprinting. By Jove! he has had a fall."

There was a broad, irregular smudge covering some yards of the track. Then there were a few footmarks, and the tire reappeared once more.

"A side-slip," I suggested.

Holmes held up a crumpled branch of flowering gorse. To my horror I perceived that the yellow blossoms were all dabbled with crimson. On the path, too, and among the heather were dark stains of clotted blood.

"Bad!" said Holmes. "Bad! Stand clear, Watson! Not an unnecessary footstep! What do I read here? He fell wounded—he stood up—he remounted—he proceeded. But there is no other track. Cattle on this side path. He was surely not gored by a bull? Impossible! But I see no traces of anyone else. We must push on, Watson. Surely, with stains as well as the track to guide us, he cannot escape us now."

Our search was not a very long one. The tracks of the tire began to curve fantastically upon the wet and shining path. Suddenly, as I looked ahead, the gleam of metal caught my eye from amid the thick gorse-bushes. Out of them we dragged a bicycle, Palmer-tired, one pedal bent, and the whole front of it horribly smeared and slobbered with blood. On the other side of the bushes a shoe was projecting. We ran round, and there lay the unfortunate rider. He was a tall man, full-bearded, with spectacles, one glass of which had been knocked out. The cause of his death was a frightful blow upon the head, which had crushed in part of his skull. That he could have gone on after receiving such an injury said much for the vitality and courage of the man. He wore shoes, but no socks, and his open coat disclosed a nightshirt beneath it. It was undoubtedly the German master.

Holmes turned the body over reverently, and examined it with great attention. He then sat in deep thought for a time, and I could see by his ruffled brow that this grim discovery had not, in his opinion, advanced us much in our inquiry.

"It is a little difficult to know what to do, Watson," said he, at last. "My own inclinations are to push this inquiry on, for we have already lost so much time that we

cannot afford to waste another hour. On the other hand, we are bound to inform the police of the discovery, and to see that this poor fellow's body is looked after."

"I could take a note back."

"But I need your company and assistance. Wait a bit! There is a fellow cutting peat up yonder. Bring him over here, and he will guide the police."

I brought the peasant across, and Holmes dispatched the frightened man with a note to Dr. Huxtable.

"Now, Watson," said he, "we have picked up two clues this morning. One is the bicycle with the Palmer tire, and we see what that has led to. The other is the bicycle with the patched Dunlop. Before we start to investigate that, let us try to realize what we do know, so as to make the most of it, and to separate the essential from the accidental."

"First of all, I wish to impress upon you that the boy certainly left of his own free-will. He got down from his window and he went off, either alone or with someone. That is sure."

I assented.

"Well, now, let us turn to this unfortunate German master. The boy was fully dressed when he fled. Therefore, he foresaw what he would do. But the German went without his socks. He certainly acted on very short notice."

"Undoubtedly."

"Why did he go? Because, from his bedroom window, he saw the flight of the boy, because he wished to overtake him and bring him back. He seized his bicycle, pursued the lad, and in pursuing him met his death."

"So it would seem."

"Now I come to the critical part of my argument. The natural action of a man in pursuing a little boy would be to run after him. He would know that he could overtake him. But the German does not do so. He turns to his bicycle. I am told that he was an excellent cyclist. He would not do this, if he did not see that the boy had some swift means of escape."

"The other bicycle."

"Let us continue our reconstruction. He meets his death five miles from the school—not by a bullet, mark you, which even a lad might conceivably discharge, but by a savage blow dealt by a vigorous arm. The lad, then, *had* a companion in his flight. And the flight was a swift one, since it took five miles before an expert cyclist could overtake them. Yet we survey the ground round the scene of the tragedy. What do we find? A few cattle-tracks, nothing more. I took a wide sweep round, and there is no path within fifty yards. Another cyclist could have had nothing to do with the actual murder, nor were there any human foot-marks."

"Holmes," I cried, "this is impossible."

"Admirable!" he said. "A most illuminating remark. It *is* impossible as I state it, and therefore I must in some respect have stated it wrong. Yet you saw for yourself. Can you suggest any fallacy?"

"He could not have fractured his skull in a fall?"

"In a morass, Watson?"

"I am at my wits' end."

"Tut, tut, we have solved some worse problems. At least we have plenty of material, if

we can only use it. Come, then, and, having exhausted the Palmer, let us see what the Dunlop with the patched cover has to offer us."

We picked up the track and followed it onward for some distance, but soon the moor rose into a long, heather-tufted curve, and we left the watercourse behind us. No further help from tracks could be hoped for. At the spot where we saw the last of the Dunlop tire it might equally have led to Holdernesse Hall, the stately towers of which rose some miles to our left, or to a low, grey village which lay in front of us and marked the position of the Chesterfield high road.

As we approached the forbidding and squalid inn, with the sign of a game-cock above the door, Holmes gave a sudden groan, and clutched me by the shoulder to save himself from falling. He had had one of those violent strains of the ankle which leave a man helpless. With difficulty he limped up to the door, where a squat, dark, elderly man was smoking a black clay pipe.

"How are you, Mr. Reuben Hayes?" said Holmes.

"Who are you, and how do you get my name so pat?" the countryman answered, with a suspicious flash of a pair of cunning eyes.

"Well, it's printed on the board above your head. It's easy to see a man who is master of his own house. I suppose you haven't such a thing as a carriage in your stables?"

"No, I have not."

"I can hardly put my foot to the ground."

"Don't put it to the ground."

"But I can't walk."

"Well, then hop."

Mr. Reuben Hayes's manner was far from gracious, but Holmes took it with admirable good-humour.

"Look here, my man," said he. "This is really rather an awkward fix for me. I don't mind how I get on."

"Neither do I," said the morose landlord.

"The matter is very important. I would offer you a sovereign for the use of a bicycle."

The landlord pricked up his ears.

"Where do you want to go?"

"To Holdernesse Hall."

"Pals of the Dook, I suppose?" said the landlord, surveying our mud-stained garments with ironical eyes.

Holmes laughed good-naturedly.

"He'll be glad to see us, anyhow."

"Why?"

"Because we bring him news of his lost son."

The landlord gave a very visible start.

"What, you're on his track?"

"He has been heard of in Liverpool. They expect to get him every hour."

Again a swift change passed over the heavy, unshaven face. His manner was suddenly genial.

"I've less reason to wish the Dook well than most men," said he, "for I was head coachman once, and cruel bad he treated me. It was him that sacked me without a

character on the word of a lying corn-chandler. But I'm glad to hear that the young lord was heard of in Liverpool, and I'll help you to take the news to the Hall."

"Thank you," said Holmes. "We'll have some food first. Then you can bring round the bicycle."

"I haven't got a bicycle."

Holmes held up a sovereign.

"I tell you, man, that I haven't got one. I'll let you have two horses as far as the Hall."

"Well, well," said Holmes, "we'll talk about it when we've had something to eat."

When we were left alone in the stone-flagged kitchen, it was astonishing how rapidly that sprained ankle recovered. It was nearly nightfall, and we had eaten nothing since early morning, so that we spent some time over our meal. Holmes was lost in thought, and once or twice he walked over to the window and stared earnestly out. It opened on to a squalid courtyard. In the far corner was a smithy, where a grimy lad was at work. On the other side were the stables. Holmes had sat down again after one of these excursions, when he suddenly sprang out of his chair with a loud exclamation.

"By heaven, Watson, I believe that I've got it!" he cried. "Yes, yes, it must be so. Watson, do you remember seeing any cow-tracks to-day?"

"Yes, several."

"Where?"

"Well, everywhere. They were at the morass, and again on the path, and again near where poor Heidegger met his death."

"Exactly. Well, now, Watson, how many cows did you see on the moor?"

"I don't remember seeing any."

"Strange, Watson, that we should see tracks all along our line, but never a cow on the whole moor. Very strange, Watson, eh?"

"Yes, it is strange."

"Now, Watson, make an effort, throw your mind back. Can you see those tracks upon the path?"

"Yes, I can."

"Can you recall that the tracks were sometimes like that, Watson,"—he arranged a number of breadcrumbs in this fashion—: : : : :—"and sometimes like this"—: . : . : . : . —"and occasionally like this"—. · . · . · . "Can you remember that?"

"No, I cannot."

"But I can. I could swear to it. However, we will go back at our leisure and verify it. What a blind beetle I have been, not to draw my conclusion."

"And what is your conclusion?"

"Only that it is a remarkable cow which walks, canters, and gallops. By George! Watson, it was no brain of a country publican that thought out such a blind as that. The coast seems to be clear, save for that lad in the smithy. Let us slip out and see what we can see."

There were two rough-haired, unkempt horses in the tumble-down stable. Holmes raised the hind leg of one of them and laughed aloud.

"Old shoes, but newly shod—old shoes, but new nails. This case deserves to be a classic. Let us go across to the smithy."

The lad continued his work without regarding us. I saw Holmes's eye darting to right and left among the litter of iron and wood which was scattered about the floor. Suddenly,

however, we heard a step behind us, and there was the landlord, his heavy eyebrows drawn over his savage eyes, his swarthy features convulsed with passion. He held a short, metal-headed stick in his hand, and he advanced in so menacing a fashion that I was right glad to feel the revolver in my pocket.

"You infernal spies!" the man cried. "What are you doing there?"

"Why, Mr. Reuben Hayes," said Holmes, coolly, "one might think that you were afraid of our finding something out."

The man mastered himself with a violent effort, and his grim mouth loosened into a false laugh, which was more menacing than his frown.

"You're welcome to all you can find out in my smithy," said he. "But look here, mister, I don't care for folk poking about my place without my leave, so the sooner you pay your score and get out of this the better I shall be pleased."

"All right, Mr. Hayes, no harm meant," said Holmes. "We have been having a look at your horses, but I think I'll walk, after all. It's not far, I believe."

"Not more than two miles to the Hall gates. That's the road to the left." He watched us with sullen eyes until we had left his premises.

We did not go very far along the road, for Holmes stopped the instant that the curve hid us from the landlord's view.

"We were warm, as the children say, at that inn," said he. "I seem to grow colder every step that I take away from it. No, no, I can't possibly leave it."

"I am convinced," said I, "that this Reuben Hayes knows all about it. A more self-evident villain I never saw."

"Oh! he impressed you in that way, did he? There are the horses, there is the smithy. Yes, it is an interesting place, this Fighting Cock. I think we shall have another look at it in an unobtrusive way."

A long, sloping hillside, dotted with grey limestone boulders, stretched behind us. We had turned off the road, and were making our way up the hill, when, looking in the direction of Holdernesse Hall, I saw a cyclist coming swiftly along.

"Get down, Watson!" cried Holmes, with a heavy hand upon my shoulder. We had hardly sunk from view when the man flew past us on the road. Amid a rolling cloud of dust, I caught a glimpse of a pale, agitated face—a face with horror in every lineament, the mouth open, the eyes staring wildly in front. It was like some strange caricature of the dapper James Wilder whom we had seen the night before.

"The Duke's secretary!" cried Holmes. "Come, Watson, let us see what he does."

We scrambled from rock to rock, until in a few moments we had made our way to a point from which we could see the front door of the inn. Wilder's bicycle was leaning against the wall beside it. No one was moving about the house, nor could we catch a glimpse of any faces at the windows. Slowly the twilight crept down as the sun sank behind the high towers of Holdernesse Hall. Then, in the gloom, we saw the two side-lamps of a trap light up in the stable-yard of the inn, and shortly afterwards heard the rattle of hoofs, as it wheeled out into the road and tore off at a furious pace in the direction of Chesterfield.

"What do you make of that, Watson?" Holmes whispered.

"It looks like a flight."

"A single man in a dog-cart, so far as I could see. Well, it certainly was not Mr. James Wilder, for there he is at the door."

A red square of light had sprung out of the darkness. In the middle of it was the black figure of the secretary, his head advanced, peering out into the night. It was evident that he was expecting someone. Then at last there were steps in the road, a second figure was visible for an instant against the light, the door shut, and all was black once more. Five minutes later a lamp was lit in a room upon the first floor.

"It seems to be a curious class of custom that is done by the Fighting Cock," said Holmes.

"The bar is on the other side."

"Quite so. These are what one may call the private guests. Now, what in the world is Mr. James Wilder doing in that den at this hour of night, and who is the companion who comes to meet him there? Come, Watson, we must really take a risk and try to investigate this a little more closely."

Together we stole down to the road and crept across to the door of the inn. The bicycle still leaned against the wall. Holmes struck a match and held it to the back wheel, and I heard him chuckle as the light fell upon a patched Dunlop tire. Up above us was the lighted window.

"I must have a peep through that, Watson. If you bend your back and support yourself upon the wall, I think that I can manage."

An instant later, his feet were on my shoulders, but he was hardly up before he was down again.

"Come, my friend," said he, "our day's work has been quite long enough. I think that we have gathered all that we can. It's a long walk to the school, and the sooner we get started the better."

He hardly opened his lips during that weary trudge across the moor, nor would he enter the school when he reached it, but went on to Mackleton Station, whence he could send some telegrams. Late at night I heard him consoling Dr. Huxtable, prostrated by the tragedy of his master's death, and later still he entered my room as alert and vigorous as he had been when he started in the morning. "All goes well, my friend," said he. "I promise that before to-morrow evening we shall have reached the solution of the mystery."

At eleven o'clock next morning my friend and I were walking up the famous yew avenue of Holdernesse Hall. We were ushered through the magnificent Elizabethan doorway and into his Grace's study. There we found Mr. James Wilder, demure and courtly, but with some trace of that wild terror of the night before still lurking in his furtive eyes and in his twitching features.

"You have come to see his Grace? I am sorry, but the fact is that the Duke is far from well. He has been very much upset by the tragic news. We received a telegram from Dr. Huxtable yesterday afternoon, which told us of your discovery."

"I must see the Duke, Mr. Wilder."

"But he is in his room."

"Then I must go to his room."

"I believe he is in his bed."

"I will see him there."

Holmes's cold and inexorable manner showed the secretary that it was useless to argue with him.

"Very good, Mr. Holmes, I will tell him that you are here."

After an hour's delay, the great nobleman appeared. His face was more cadaverous than ever, his shoulders had rounded, and he seemed to me to be an altogether older man than he had been the morning before. He greeted us with a stately courtesy and seated himself at his desk, his red beard streaming down on the table.

"Well, Mr. Holmes?" said he.

But my friend's eyes were fixed upon the secretary, who stood by his master's chair.

"I think, your Grace, that I could speak more freely in Mr. Wilder's absence."

The man turned a shade paler and cast a malignant glance at Holmes.

"If your Grace wishes——"

"Yes, yes, you had better go. Now, Mr. Holmes, what have you to say?"

My friend waited until the door had closed behind the retreating secretary.

"The fact is, your Grace," said he, "that my colleague, Dr. Watson, and myself had an assurance from Dr. Huxtable that a reward had been offered in this case. I should like to have this confirmed from your own lips."

"Certainly, Mr. Holmes."

"It amounted, if I am correctly informed, to five thousand pounds to anyone who will tell you where your son is?"

"Exactly."

"And another thousand to the man who will name the person or persons who keep him in custody?"

"Exactly."

"Under the latter heading is included, no doubt, not only those who may have taken him away, but also those who conspire to keep him in his present position?"

"Yes, yes," cried the Duke, impatiently. "If you do your work well, Mr. Sherlock Holmes, you will have no reason to complain of niggardly treatment."

My friend rubbed his thin hands together with an appearance of avidity which was a surprise to me, who knew his frugal tastes.

"I fancy that I see your Grace's check-book upon the table," said he. "I should be glad if you would make me out a check for six thousand pounds. It would be as well, perhaps, for you to cross it. The Capital and Counties Bank, Oxford Street branch are my agents."

His Grace sat very stern and upright in his chair and looked stonily at my friend.

"Is this a joke, Mr. Holmes? It is hardly a subject for pleasantry."

"Not at all, your Grace. I was never more earnest in my life."

"What do you mean, then?"

"I mean that I have earned the reward. I know where your son is, and I know some, at least, of those who are holding him."

The Duke's beard had turned more aggressively red than ever against his ghastly white face.

"Where is he?" he gasped.

"He is, or was last night, at the Fighting Cock Inn, about two miles from your park gate."

The Duke fell back in his chair.

"And whom do you accuse?"

Sherlock Holmes's answer was an astounding one. He stepped swiftly forward and touched the Duke upon the shoulder.

"I accuse *you*," said he. "And now, your Grace, I'll trouble you for that check."

Never shall I forget the Duke's appearance as he sprang up and clawed with his hands, like one who is sinking into an abyss. Then, with an extraordinary effort of aristocratic self-command, he sat down and sank his face in his hands. It was some minutes before he spoke.

"How much do you know?" he asked at last, without raising his head.

"I saw you together last night."

"Does anyone else beside your friend know?"

"I have spoken to no one."

The Duke took a pen in his quivering fingers and opened his check-book.

"I shall be as good as my word, Mr. Holmes. I am about to write your check, however unwelcome the information which you have gained may be to me. When the offer was first made, I little thought the turn which events might take. But you and your friend are men of discretion, Mr. Holmes?"

"I hardly understand your Grace."

"I must put it plainly, Mr. Holmes. If only you two know of this incident, there is no reason why it should go any farther. I think twelve thousand pounds is the sum that I owe you, is it not?"

But Holmes smiled and shook his head.

"I fear, your Grace, that matters can hardly be arranged so easily. There is the death of this schoolmaster to be accounted for."

"But James knew nothing of that. You cannot hold him responsible for that. It was the work of this brutal ruffian whom he had the misfortune to employ."

"I must take the view, your Grace, that when a man embarks upon a crime, he is morally guilty of any other crime which may spring from it."

"Morally, Mr. Holmes. No doubt you are right. But surely not in the eyes of the law. A man cannot be condemned for a murder at which he was not present, and which he loathes and abhors as much as you do. The instant that he heard of it he made a complete confession to me, so filled was he with horror and remorse. He lost not an hour in breaking entirely with the murderer. Oh, Mr. Holmes, you must save him—you must save him! I tell you that you must save him!" The Duke had dropped the last attempt at self-command, and was pacing the room with a convulsed face and with his clenched hands raving in the air. At last he mastered himself and sat down once more at his desk. "I appreciate your conduct in coming here before you spoke to anyone else," said he. "At least, we may take counsel how far we can minimize this hideous scandal."

"Exactly," said Holmes. "I think, your Grace, that this can only be done by absolute frankness between us. I am disposed to help your Grace to the best of my ability, but, in order to do so, I must understand to the last detail how the matter stands. I realize that your words applied to Mr. James Wilder, and that he is not the murderer."

"No, the murderer has escaped."

Sherlock Holmes smiled demurely.

"Your Grace can hardly have heard of any small reputation which I possess, or you would not imagine that it is so easy to escape me. Mr. Reuben Hayes was arrested at Chesterfield, on my information, at eleven o'clock last night. I had a telegram from the head of the local police before I left the school this morning."

The Duke leaned back in his chair and stared with amazement at my friend.

"You seem to have powers that are hardly human," said he. "So Reuben Hayes is taken? I am right glad to hear it, if it will not react upon the fate of James."

"Your secretary?"

"No, sir, my son."

It was Holmes's turn to look astonished.

"I confess that this is entirely new to me, your Grace. I must beg you to be more explicit."

"I will conceal nothing from you. I agree with you that complete frankness, however painful it may be to me, is the best policy in this desperate situation to which James's folly and jealousy have reduced us. When I was a very young man, Mr. Holmes, I loved with such a love as comes only once in a lifetime. I offered the lady marriage, but she refused it on the grounds that such a match might mar my career. Had she lived, I would certainly never have married anyone else. She died, and left this one child, whom for her sake I have cherished and cared for. I could not acknowledge the paternity to the world, but I gave him the best of educations, and since he came to manhood I have kept him near my person. He surmised my secret, and has presumed ever since upon the claim which he has upon me, and upon his power of provoking a scandal which would be abhorrent to me. His presence had something to do with the unhappy issue of my marriage. Above all, he hated my young legitimate heir from the first with a persistent hatred. You may well ask me why, under these circumstances, I still kept James under my roof. I answer that it was because I could see his mother's face in his, and that for her dear sake there was no end to my long-suffering. All her pretty ways too—there was not one of them which he could not suggest and bring back to my memory. I *could* not send him away. But I feared so much lest he should do Arthur—that is, Lord Saltire—a mischief, that I dispatched him for safety to Dr. Huxtable's school.

"James came into contact with this fellow Hayes, because the man was a tenant of mine, and James acted as agent. The fellow was a rascal from the beginning, but, in some extraordinary way, James became intimate with him. He had always a taste for low company. When James determined to kidnap Lord Saltire, it was of this man's service that he availed himself. You remember that I wrote to Arthur upon that last day. Well, James opened the letter and inserted a note asking Arthur to meet him in a little wood called the Ragged Shaw, which is near to the school. He used the Duchess's name, and in that way got the boy to come. That evening James bicycled over—I am telling you what he has himself confessed to me—and he told Arthur, whom he met in the wood, that his mother longed to see him, that she was awaiting him on the moor, and that if he would come back into the wood at midnight he would find a man with a horse, who would take him to her. Poor Arthur fell into the trap. He came to the appointment, and found this fellow Hayes with a led pony. Arthur mounted, and they set off together. It appears—though this James only heard yesterday—that they were pursued, that Hayes struck the pursuer with his stick, and that the man died of his injuries. Hayes brought Arthur to his public-house, the Fighting Cock, where he was confined in an upper room, under the care of Mrs. Hayes, who is a kindly woman, but entirely under the control of her brutal husband.

"Well, Mr. Holmes, that was the state of affairs when I first saw you two days ago. I had no more idea of the truth than you. You will ask me what was James's motive in doing such a deed. I answer that there was a great deal which was unreasoning and fanatical in the hatred which he bore my heir. In his view he should himself have been

heir of all my estates, and he deeply resented those social laws which made it impossible. At the same time, he had a definite motive also. He was eager that I should break the entail, and he was of opinion that it lay in my power to do so. He intended to make a bargain with me—to restore Arthur if I would break the entail, and so make it possible for the estate to be left to him by will. He knew well that I should never willingly invoke the aid of the police against him. I say that he would have proposed such a bargain to me, but he did not actually do so, for events moved too quickly for him, and he had not time to put his plans into practice.

"What brought all his wicked scheme to wreck was your discovery of this man Heidegger's dead body. James was seized with horror at the news. It came to us yesterday, as we sat together in this study Dr. Huxtable had sent a telegram. James was so overwhelmed with grief and agitation that my suspicions, which had never been entirely absent, rose instantly to a certainty, and I taxed him with the deed. He made a complete voluntary confession. Then he implored me to keep his secret for three days longer, so as to give his wretched accomplice a chance of saving his guilty life. I yielded—as I have always yielded—to his prayers, and instantly James hurried off to the Fighting Cock to warn Hayes and give him the means of flight. I could not go there by daylight without provoking comment, but as soon as night fell I hurried off to see my dear Arthur. I found him safe and well, but horrified beyond expression by the dreadful deed he had witnessed. In deference to my promise, and much against my will, I consented to leave him there for three days, under the charge of Mrs. Hayes, since it was evident that it was impossible to inform the police where he was without telling them also who was the murderer, and I could not see how that murderer could be punished without ruin to my unfortunate James. You asked for frankness, Mr. Holmes, and I have taken you at your word, for I have now told you everything without an attempt at circumlocution or concealment. Do you in turn be as frank with me."

"I will," said Holmes. "In the first place, your Grace, I am bound to tell you that you have placed yourself in a most serious position in the eyes of the law. You have condoned a felony, and you have aided the escape of a murderer, for I cannot doubt that any money which was taken by James Wilder to aid his accomplice in his flight came from your Grace's purse."

The Duke bowed his assent.

"This is, indeed, a most serious matter. Even more culpable in my opinion, your Grace, is your attitude towards your younger son. You leave him in this den for three days."

"Under solemn promises——"

"What are promises to such people as these? You have no guarantee that he will not be spirited away again. To humour your guilty elder son, you have exposed your innocent younger son to imminent and unnecessary danger. It was a most unjustifiable action."

The proud lord of Holdernesse was not accustomed to be so rated in his own ducal hall. The blood flushed into his high forehead, but his conscience held him dumb.

"I will help you, but on one condition only. It is that you ring for the footman and let me give such orders as I like."

Without a word, the Duke pressed the electric bell. A servant entered.

"You will be glad to hear," said Holmes, "that your young master is found. It is the Duke's desire that the carriage shall go at once to the Fighting Cock Inn to bring Lord Saltire home.

"Now," said Holmes, when the rejoicing lackey had disappeared, "having secured the future, we can afford to be more lenient with the past. I am not in an official position, and there is no reason, so long as the ends of justice are served, why I should disclose all that I know. As to Hayes, I say nothing. The gallows awaits him, and I would do nothing to save him from it. What he will divulge I cannot tell, but I have no doubt that your Grace could make him understand that it is to his interest to be silent. From the police point of view he will have kidnapped the boy for the purpose of ransom. If they do not themselves find it out, I see no reason why I should prompt them to take a broader point of view. I would warn your Grace, however, that the continued presence of Mr. James Wilder in your household can only lead to misfortune."

"I understand that, Mr. Holmes, and it is already settled that he shall leave me forever, and go to seek his fortune in Australia."

"In that case, your Grace, since you have yourself stated that any unhappiness in your married life was caused by his presence I would suggest that you make such amends as you can to the Duchess, and that you try to resume those relations which have been so unhappily interrupted."

"That also I have arranged, Mr. Holmes. I wrote to the Duchess this morning."

"In that case," said Holmes, rising, "I think that my friend and I can congratulate ourselves upon several most happy results from our little visit to the North. There is one other small point upon which I desire some light. This fellow Hayes had shod his horses with shoes which counterfeited the tracks of cows. Was it from Mr. Wilder that he learned so extraordinary a device?"

The Duke stood in thought for a moment, with a look of intense surprise on his face. Then he opened a door and showed us into a large room furnished as a museum. He led the way to a glass case in a corner, and pointed to the inscription.

"These shoes," it ran, "were dug up in the moat of Holdernesse Hall. They are for the use of horses, but they are shaped below with a cloven foot of iron, so as to throw pursuers off the track. They are supposed to have belonged to some of the marauding Barons of Holdernesse in the Middle Ages."

Holmes opened the case, and moistening his finger he passed it along the shoe. A thin film of recent mud was left upon his skin.

"Thank you," said he, as he replaced the glass. "It is the second most interesting object that I have seen in the North."

"And the first?"

Holmes folded up his check and placed it carefully in his notebook. "I am a poor man," said he, as he patted it affectionately, and thrust it into the depths of his inner pocket.

THE ADVENTURE OF THE SECOND STAIN

FROM THE RETURN OF SHERLOCK HOLMES (1905)

I HAD INTENDED "The Adventure of the Abbey Grange" to be the last of those exploits of my friend, Mr. Sherlock Holmes, which I should ever communicate to the public. This resolution of mine was not due to any lack of material, since I have notes of many hundreds of cases to which I have never alluded, nor was it caused by any waning interest on the part of my readers in the singular personality and unique methods of this remarkable man. The real reason lay in the reluctance which Mr. Holmes has shown to the continued publication of his experiences. So long as he was in actual professional practice the records of his successes were of some practical value to him, but since he has definitely retired from London and betaken himself to study and bee-farming on the Sussex Downs, notoriety has become hateful to him, and he has peremptorily requested that his wishes in this matter should be strictly observed. It was only upon my representing to him that I had given a promise that "The Adventure of the Second Stain" should be published when the times were ripe, and pointing out to him that it is only appropriate that this long series of episodes should culminate in the most important international case which he has ever been called upon to handle, that I at last succeeded in obtaining his consent that a carefully guarded account of the incident should at last be laid before the public. If in telling the story I seem to be somewhat vague in certain details, the public will readily understand that there is an excellent reason for my reticence.

It was, then, in a year, and even in a decade, that shall be nameless, that upon one Tuesday morning in autumn we found two visitors of European fame within the walls of our humble room in Baker Street. The one, austere, high-nosed, eagle-eyed, and dominant, was none other than the illustrious Lord Bellinger, twice Premier of Britain. The other, dark, clear-cut, and elegant, hardly yet of middle age, and endowed with every beauty of body and of mind, was the Right Honourable Trelawney Hope, Secretary for European Affairs, and the most rising statesman in the country. They sat side by side upon our paper-littered settee, and it was easy to see from their worn and anxious faces that it was business of the most pressing importance which had brought them. The Premier's thin,

blue-veined hands were clasped tightly over the ivory head of his umbrella, and his gaunt, ascetic face looked gloomily from Holmes to me. The European Secretary pulled nervously at his moustache and fidgeted with the seals of his watch-chain.

"When I discovered my loss, Mr. Holmes, which was at eight o'clock this morning, I at once informed the Prime Minister. It was at his suggestion that we have both come to you."

"Have you informed the police?"

"No, sir," said the Prime Minister, with the quick, decisive manner for which he was famous. "We have not done so, nor is it possible that we should do so. To inform the police must, in the long run, mean to inform the public. This is what we particularly desire to avoid."

"And why, sir?"

"Because the document in question is of such immense importance that its publication might very easily—I might almost say probably—lead to European complications of the utmost moment. It is not too much to say that peace or war may hang upon the issue. Unless its recovery can be attended with the utmost secrecy, then it may as well not be recovered at all, for all that is aimed at by those who have taken it is that its contents should be generally known."

"I understand. Now, Mr. Trelawney Hope, I should be much obliged if you would tell me exactly the circumstances under which this document disappeared."

"That can be done in a very few words, Mr. Holmes. The letter—for it was a letter from a foreign potentate—was received six days ago. It was of such importance that I have never left it in my safe, but have taken it across each evening to my house in Whitehall Terrace, and kept it in my bedroom in a locked despatch-box. It was there last night. Of that I am certain. I actually opened the box while I was dressing for dinner and saw the document inside. This morning it was gone. The despatch-box had stood beside the glass upon my dressing-table all night. I am a light sleeper, and so is my wife. We are both prepared to swear that no one could have entered the room during the night. And yet I repeat that the paper is gone."

"What time did you dine?"

"Half-past seven."

"How long was it before you went to bed?"

"My wife had gone to the theatre. I waited up for her. It was half-past eleven before we went to our room."

"Then for four hours the despatch-box had lain unguarded?"

"No one is ever permitted to enter that room save the house-maid in the morning, and my valet, or my wife's maid, during the rest of the day. They are both trusty servants who have been with us for some time. Besides, neither of them could possibly have known that there was anything more valuable than the ordinary departmental papers in my despatch-box."

"Who did know of the existence of that letter?"

"No one in the house."

"Surely your wife knew?"

"No, sir. I had said nothing to my wife until I missed the paper this morning."

The Premier nodded approvingly.

"I have long known, sir, how high is your sense of public duty," said he. "I am

convinced that in the case of a secret of this importance it would rise superior to the most intimate domestic ties."

The European Secretary bowed.

"You do me no more than justice, sir. Until this morning I have never breathed one word to my wife upon this matter."

"Could she have guessed?"

"No, Mr. Holmes, she could not have guessed—nor could anyone have guessed."

"Have you lost any documents before?"

"No, sir."

"Who is there in England who did know of the existence of this letter?"

"Each member of the Cabinet was informed of it yesterday, but the pledge of secrecy which attends every Cabinet meeting was increased by the solemn warning which was given by the Prime Minister. Good heavens, to think that within a few hours I should myself have lost it!" His handsome face was distorted with a spasm of despair, and his hands tore at his hair. For a moment we caught a glimpse of the natural man, impulsive, ardent, keenly sensitive. The next the aristocratic mask was replaced, and the gentle voice had returned. "Besides the members of the Cabinet there are two, or possibly three, departmental officials who know of the letter. No one else in England, Mr. Holmes, I assure you."

"But abroad?"

"I believe that no one abroad has seen it save the man who wrote it. I am well convinced that his Ministers—that the usual official channels have not been employed."

Holmes considered for some little time.

"Now, sir, I must ask you more particularly what this document is, and why its disappearance should have such momentous consequences?"

The two statesmen exchanged a quick glance and the Premier's shaggy eyebrows gathered in a frown.

"Mr. Holmes, the envelope is a long, thin one of pale blue colour. There is a seal of red wax stamped with a crouching lion. It is addressed in large, bold handwriting to——"

"I fear, sir," said Holmes, "that, interesting and indeed essential as these details are, my inquiries must go more to the root of things. What *was* the letter?"

"That is a State secret of the utmost importance, and I fear that I cannot tell you, nor do I see that it is necessary. If by the aid of the powers which you are said to possess you can find such an envelope as I describe with its enclosure, you will have deserved well of your country, and earned any reward which it lies in our power to bestow."

Sherlock Holmes rose with a smile.

"You are two of the most busy men in the country," said he, "and in my own small way I have also a good many calls upon me. I regret exceedingly that I cannot help you in this matter, and any continuation of this interview would be a waste of time."

The Premier sprang to his feet with that quick, fierce gleam of his deep-set eyes before which a Cabinet has cowered. "I am not accustomed, sir," he began, but mastered his anger and resumed his seat. For a minute or more we all sat in silence. Then the old statesman shrugged his shoulders.

"We must accept your terms, Mr. Holmes. No doubt you are right, and it is unreasonable for us to expect you to act unless we give you our entire confidence."

"I agree with you," said the younger statesman.

"Then I will tell you, relying entirely upon your honour and that of your colleague, Dr. Watson. I may appeal to your patriotism also, for I could not imagine a greater misfortune for the country than that this affair should come out."

"You may safely trust us."

"The letter, then, is from a certain foreign potentate who has been ruffled by some recent Colonial developments of this country. It has been written hurriedly and upon his own responsibility entirely. Inquiries have shown that his Ministers know nothing of the matter. At the same time it is couched in so unfortunate a manner, and certain phrases in it are of so provocative a character, that its publication would undoubtedly lead to a most dangerous state of feeling in this country. There would be such a ferment, sir, that I do not hesitate to say that within a week of the publication of that letter this country would be involved in a great war."

Holmes wrote a name upon a slip of paper and handed it to the Premier.

"Exactly. It was he. And it is this letter—this letter which may well mean the expenditure of a thousand millions and the lives of a hundred thousand men—which has become lost in this unaccountable fashion."

"Have you informed the sender?"

"Yes, sir, a cipher telegram has been despatched."

"Perhaps he desires the publication of the letter."

"No, sir, we have strong reason to believe that he already understands that he has acted in an indiscreet and hot-headed manner. It would be a greater blow to him and to his country than to us if this letter were to come out."

"If this is so, whose interest is it that the letter should come out? Why should anyone desire to steal it or to publish it?"

"There, Mr. Holmes, you take me into regions of high international politics. But if you consider the European situation you will have no difficulty in perceiving the motive. The whole of Europe is an armed camp. There is a double league which makes a fair balance of military power. Great Britain holds the scales. If Britain were driven into war with one confederacy, it would assure the supremacy of the other confederacy, whether they joined in the war or not. Do you follow?"

"Very clearly. It is then the interest of the enemies of this potentate to secure and publish this letter, so as to make a breach between his country and ours?"

"Yes, sir."

"And to whom would this document be sent if it fell into the hands of an enemy?"

"To any of the great Chancelleries of Europe. It is probably speeding on its way thither at the present instant as fast as steam can take it."

Mr. Trelawney Hope dropped his head on his chest and groaned aloud. The Premier placed his hand kindly upon his shoulder.

"It is your misfortune, my dear fellow. No one can blame you. There is no precaution which you have neglected. Now, Mr. Holmes, you are in full possession of the facts. What course do you recommend?"

Holmes shook his head mournfully.

"You think, sir, that unless this document is recovered there will be war?"

"I think it is very probable."

"Then, sir, prepare for war."

"That is a hard saying, Mr. Holmes."

"Consider the facts, sir. It is inconceivable that it was taken after eleven-thirty at night, since I understand that Mr. Hope and his wife were both in the room from that hour until the loss was found out. It was taken, then, yesterday evening between seven-thirty and eleven-thirty, probably near the earlier hour, since whoever took it evidently knew that it was there and would naturally secure it as early as possible. Now, sir, if a document of this importance were taken at that hour, where can it be now? No one has any reason to retain it. It has been passed rapidly on to those who need it. What chance have we now to overtake or even to trace it? It is beyond our reach."

The Prime Minister rose from the settee.

"What you say is perfectly logical, Mr. Holmes. I feel that the matter is indeed out of our hands."

"Let us presume, for argument's sake, that the document was taken by the maid or by the valet——"

"They are both old and tried servants."

"I understand you to say that your room is on the second floor, that there is no entrance from without, and that from within no one could go up unobserved. It must, then, be somebody in the house who has taken it. To whom would the thief take it? To one of several international spies and secret agents, whose names are tolerably familiar to me. There are three who may be said to be the heads of their profession. I will begin my research by going round and finding if each of them is at his post. If one is missing—especially if he has disappeared since last night—we will have some indication as to where the document has gone."

"Why should he be missing?" asked the European Secretary. "He would take the letter to an Embassy in London, as likely as not."

"I fancy not. These agents work independently, and their relations with the Embassies are often strained."

The Prime Minister nodded his acquiescence.

"I believe you are right, Mr. Holmes. He would take so valuable a prize to headquarters with his own hands. I think that your course of action is an excellent one. Meanwhile, Hope, we cannot neglect all our other duties on account of this one misfortune. Should there be any fresh developments during the day we shall communicate with you, and you will no doubt let us know the results of your own inquiries."

The two statesmen bowed and walked gravely from the room.

When our illustrious visitors had departed Holmes lit his pipe in silence and sat for some time lost in the deepest thought. I had opened the morning paper and was immersed in a sensational crime which had occurred in London the night before, when my friend gave an exclamation, sprang to his feet, and laid his pipe down upon the mantelpiece.

"Yes," said he, "there is no better way of approaching it. The situation is desperate, but not hopeless. Even now, if we could be sure which of them has taken it, it is just possible that it has not yet passed out of his hands. After all, it is a question of money with these fellows, and I have the British treasury behind me. If it's on the market I'll buy it—if it means another penny on the income-tax. It is conceivable that the fellow might hold it back to see what bids come from this side before he tries his luck on the other. There are

only those three capable of playing so bold a game—there are Oberstein, La Rothiere, and Eduardo Lucas. I will see each of them."

I glanced at my morning paper.

"Is that Eduardo Lucas of Godolphin Street?"

"Yes."

"You will not see him."

"Why not?"

"He was murdered in his house last night."

My friend has so often astonished me in the course of our adventures that it was with a sense of exultation that I realized how completely I had astonished him. He stared in amazement, and then snatched the paper from my hands. This was the paragraph which I had been engaged in reading when he rose from his chair:

MURDER IN WESTMINSTER

A crime of mysterious character was committed last night at 16, Godolphin Street, one of the old-fashioned and secluded rows of eighteenth century houses which lie between the river and the Abbey, almost in the shadow of the great Tower of the Houses of Parliament. This small but select mansion has been inhabited for some years by Mr. Eduardo Lucas, well-known in society circles both on account of his charming personality and because he has the well-deserved reputation of being one of the best amateur tenors in the country. Mr. Lucas is an unmarried man, thirty-four years of age, and his establishment consists of Mrs. Pringle, an elderly housekeeper, and of Mitton, his valet. The former retires early and sleeps at the top of the house. The valet was out for the evening, visiting a friend at Hammersmith. From ten o'clock onward Mr. Lucas had the house to himself. What occurred during that time has not yet transpired, but at a quarter to twelve Police-constable Barrett, passing along Godolphin Street observed that the door of No. 16 was ajar. He knocked, but received no answer. Perceiving a light in the front room, he advanced into the passage and again knocked, but without reply. He then pushed open the door and entered. The room was in a state of wild disorder, the furniture being all swept to one side, and one chair lying on its back in the centre. Beside this chair, and still grasping one of its legs, lay the unfortunate tenant of the house. He had been stabbed to the heart and must have died instantly. The knife with which the crime had been committed was a curved Indian dagger, plucked down from a trophy of Oriental arms which adorned one of the walls. Robbery does not appear to have been the motive of the crime, for there had been no attempt to remove the valuable contents of the room. Mr. Eduardo Lucas was so well-known and popular that his violent and mysterious fate will arouse painful interest and intense sympathy in a widespread circle of friends.

"Well, Watson, what do you make of this?" asked Holmes, after a long pause.

"It is an amazing coincidence."

"A coincidence! Here is one of the three men whom we had named as possible actors in this drama, and he meets a violent death during the very hours when we know that that drama was being enacted. The odds are enormous against its being coincidence. No figures could express them. No, my dear Watson, the two events are connected—*must* be connected. It is for us to find the connection."

"But now the official police must know all."

"Not at all. They know all they see at Godolphin Street. They know—and shall know—nothing of Whitehall Terrace. Only *we* know of both events, and can trace the relation between them. There is one obvious point which would, in any case, have turned my suspicions against Lucas. Godolphin Street, Westminster, is only a few minutes' walk from Whitehall Terrace. The other secret agents whom I have named live in the extreme West End. It was easier, therefore, for Lucas than for the others to establish a connection or receive a message from the European Secretary's household—a small thing, and yet where events are compressed into a few hours it may prove essential. Halloa! what have we here?"

Mrs. Hudson had appeared with a lady's card upon her salver. Holmes glanced at it, raised his eyebrown, and handed it over to me.

"Ask Lady Hilda Trelawney Hope if she will be kind enough to step up," said he.

A moment later our modest apartment, already so distinguished that morning, was further honoured by the entrance of the most lovely woman in London. I had often heard of the beauty of the youngest daughter of the Duke of Belminster, but no description of it, and no contemplation of colourless photographs, had prepared me for the subtle, delicate charm and the beautiful colouring of that exquisite head. And yet as we saw it that autumn morning, it was not its beauty which would be the first thing to impress the observer. The cheek was lovely but it was paled with emotion, the eyes were bright but it was the brightness of fever, the sensitive mouth was tight and drawn in an effort after self-command. Terror—not beauty—was what sprang first to the eye as our fair visitor stood framed for an instant in the open door.

"Has my husband been here, Mr. Holmes?"

"Yes, madam, he has been here."

"Mr. Holmes. I implore you not to tell him that I came here." Holmes bowed coldly, and motioned the lady to a chair.

"Your ladyship places me in a very delicate position. I beg that you will sit down and tell me what you desire, but I fear that I cannot make any unconditional promise."

She swept across the room and seated herself with her back to the window. It was a queenly presence—tall, graceful, and intensely womanly. "Mr. Holmes," she said—and her white-gloved hands clasped and unclasped as she spoke—"I will speak frankly to you in the hopes that it may induce you to speak frankly in return. There is complete confidence between my husband and me on all matters save one. That one is politics. On this his lips are sealed. He tells me nothing. Now, I am aware that there was a most deplorable occurrence in our house last night. I know that a paper has disappeared. But because the matter is political my husband refuses to take me into his complete confidence. Now it is essential—essential, I say—that I should thoroughly understand it. You are the only other person, save only these politicians, who knows the true facts. I beg you then, Mr. Holmes, to tell me exactly what has happened and what it will lead to. Tell me all, Mr. Holmes. Let no regard for your client's interests keep you silent, for I assure you that his interests, if he would only see it, would be best served by taking me into his complete confidence. What was this paper which was stolen?"

"Madam, what you ask me is really impossible."

She groaned and sank her face in her hands.

"You must see that this is so, madam. If your husband thinks fit to keep you in the dark over this matter, is it for me, who has only learned the true facts under the pledge of

professional secrecy, to tell what he has withheld? It is not fair to ask it. It is him whom you must ask."

"I have asked him. I come to you as a last resource. But without your telling me anything definite, Mr. Holmes, you may do a great service if you would enlighten me on one point."

"What is it, madam?"

"Is my husband's political career likely to suffer through this incident?"

"Well, madam, unless it is set right it may certainly have a very unfortunate effect."

"Ah!" She drew in her breath sharply as one whose doubts are resolved.

"One more question, Mr. Holmes. From an expression which my husband dropped in the first shock of this disaster I understood that terrible public consequences might arise from the loss of this document."

"If he said so, I certainly cannot deny it."

"Of what nature are they?"

"Nay, madam, there again you ask me more than I can possibly answer."

"Then I will take up no more of your time. I cannot blame you, Mr. Holmes, for having refused to speak more freely, and you on your side will not, I am sure, think the worse of me because I desire, even against his will, to share my husband's anxieties. Once more I beg that you will say nothing of my visit."

She looked back at us from the door, and I had a last impression of that beautiful haunted face, the startled eyes, and the drawn mouth. Then she was gone.

"Now, Watson, the fair sex is your department," said Holmes, with a smile, when the dwindling *frou-frou* of skirts had ended in the slam of the front door. "What was the fair lady's game? What did she really want?"

"Surely her own statement is clear and her anxiety very natural."

"Hum! Think of her appearance, Watson—her manner, her suppressed excitement, her restlessness, her tenacity in asking questions. Remember that she comes of a caste who do not lightly show emotion."

"She was certainly much moved."

"Remember also the curious earnestness with which she assured us that it was best for her husband that she should know all. What did she mean by that? And you must have observed, Watson, how she manœuvred to have the light at her back. She did not wish us to read her expression."

"Yes, she chose the one chair in the room."

"And yet the motives of women are so inscrutable. You remember the woman at Margate whom I suspected for the same reason. No powder on her nose—that proved to be the correct solution. How can you build on such a quicksand? Their most trivial action may mean volumes, or their most extraordinary conduct may depend upon a hairpin or a curling tongs. Good-morning, Watson."

"You are off?"

"Yes, I will while away the morning at Godolphin Street with our friends of the regular establishment. With Eduardo Lucas lies the solution of our problem, though I must admit that I have not an inkling as to what form it may take. It is a capital mistake to theorize in advance of the facts. Do you stay on guard, my good Watson, and receive any fresh visitors. I'll join you at lunch if I am able."

All that day and the next and the next Holmes was in a mood which his friends would

call taciturn, and others morose. He ran out and ran in, smoked incessantly, played snatches on his violin, sank into reveries, devoured sandwiches at irregular hours, and hardly answered the casual questions which I put to him. It was evident to me that things were not going well with him or his quest. He would say nothing of the case, and it was from the papers that I learned the particulars of the inquest, and the arrest with the subsequent release of John Mitton, the valet of the deceased. The coroner's jury brought in the obvious Wilful Murder, but the parties remained as unknown as ever. No motive was suggested. The room was full of articles of value, but none had been taken. The dead man's papers had not been tampered with. They were carefully examined, and showed that he was a keen student of international politics, an indefatigable gossip, a remarkable linguist, and an untiring letter writer. He had been on intimate terms with the leading politicians of several countries. But nothing sensational was discovered among the documents which filled his drawers. As to his relations with women, they appeared to have been promiscuous but superficial. He had many acquaintances among them, but few friends, and no one whom he loved. His habits were regular, his conduct inoffensive. His death was an absolute mystery and likely to remain so.

As to the arrest of John Mitton, the valet, it was a council of despair as an alternative to absolute inaction. But no case could be sustained against him. He had visited friends in Hammersmith that night. The alibi was complete. It is true that he started home at an hour which should have brought him to Westminster before the time when the crime was discovered, but his own explanation that he had walked part of the way seemed probable enough in view of the fineness of the night. He had actually arrived at twelve o'clock, and appeared to be overwhelmed by the unexpected tragedy. He had always been on good terms with his master. Several of the dead man's possessions—notably a small case of razors—had been found in the valet's boxes, but he explained that they had been presents from the deceased, and the housekeeper was able to corroborate the story. Mitton had been in Lucas's employment for three years. It was noticeable that Lucas did not take Mitton on the Continent with him. Sometimes he visited Paris for three months on end, but Mitton was left in charge of the Godolphin Street house. As to the housekeeper, she had heard nothing on the night of the crime. If her master had a visitor he had himself admitted him.

So for three mornings the mystery remained, so far as I could follow it in the papers. If Holmes knew more, he kept his own counsel, but, as he told me that Inspector Lestrade had taken him into his confidence in the case, I knew that he was in close touch with every development. Upon the fourth day there appeared a long telegram from Paris which seemed to solve the whole question.

A discovery has just been made by the Parisian police (said the *Daily Telegraph*) which raises the veil which hung round the tragic fate of Mr. Eduardo Lucas, who met his death by violence last Monday night at Godolphin Street, Westminster. Our readers will remember that the deceased gentleman was found stabbed in his room, and that some suspicion attached to his valet, but that the case broke down on an *alibi*. Yesterday a lady, who has been known as Mme. Henri Fournaye, occupying a small villa in the Rue Austerlitz, was reported to the authorities by her servants as being insane. An examination showed she had indeed developed mania of a dangerous and permanent form. On inquiry, the police have discovered that Mme. Henri Fournaye only returned from a journey to London on Tuesday last, and there

is evidence to connect her with the crime at Westminster. A comparison of photographs has proved conclusively that M. Henri Fournaye and Eduardo Lucas were really one and the same person, and that the deceased had for some reason lived a double life in London and Paris. Mme. Fournaye, who is of Creole origin, is of an extremely excitable nature, and has suffered in the past from attacks of jealousy which have amounted to frenzy. It is conjectured that it was in one of these that she committed the terrible crime which has caused such a sensation in London. Her movements upon the Monday night have not yet been traced, but it is undoubted that a woman answering to her description attracted much attention at Charing Cross Station on Tuesday morning by the wildness of her appearance and the violence of her gestures. It is probable, therefore, that the crime was either committed when insane, or that its immediate effect was to drive the unhappy woman out of her mind. At present she is unable to give any coherent account of the past, and the doctors hold out no hopes of the reestablishment of her reason. There is evidence that a woman, who might have been Mme. Fournaye, was seen for some hours upon Monday night watching the house in Godolphin Street.

"What do you think of that, Holmes?" I had read the account aloud to him, while he finished his breakfast.

"My dear Watson," said he, as he rose from the table and paced up and down the room, "You are most long-suffering, but if I have told you nothing in the last three days, it is because there is nothing to tell. Even now this report from Paris does not help us much."

"Surely it is final as regards the man's death."

"The man's death is a mere incident—a trivial episode—in comparison with our real task, which is to trace this document and save a European catastrophe. Only one important thing has happened in the last three days, and that is that nothing has happened. I get reports almost hourly from the government, and it is certain that nowhere in Europe is there any sign of trouble. Now, if this letter were loose—no, it *can't* be loose— but if it isn't loose, where can it be? Who has it? Why is it held back? That's the question that beats in my brain like a hammer. Was it, indeed, a coincidence that Lucas should meet his death on the night when the letter disappeared? Did the letter ever reach him? If so, why is it not among his papers? Did this mad wife of his carry it off with her? If so, is it in her house in Paris? How could I search for it without the French police having their suspicions aroused? It is a case, my dear Watson, where the law is as dangerous to us as the criminals are. Every man's hand is against us, and yet the interests at stake are colossal. Should I bring it to a successful conclusion, it will certainly represent the crowning glory of my career. Ah, here is my latest from the front!" He glanced hurriedly at the note which had been handed in. "Halloa! Lestrade seems to have observed something of interest. Put on your hat, Watson, and we will stroll down together to Westminster."

It was my first visit to the scene of the crime—a high, dingy, narrow-chested house, prim, formal, and solid, like the century which gave it birth. Lestrade's bulldog features gazed out at us from the front window, and he greeted us warmly when a big constable had opened the door and let us in. The room into which we were shown was that in which the crime had been committed, but no trace of it now remained save an ugly, irregular stain upon the carpet. This carpet was a small square drugget in the centre of the room,

surrounded by a broad expanse of beautiful, old-fashioned wood-flooring in square blocks, highly polished. Over the fireplace was a magnificent trophy of weapons, one of which had been used on that tragic night. In the window was a sumptuous writing-desk, and every detail of the apartment, the pictures, the rugs, and the hangings, all pointed to a taste which was luxurious to the verge of effeminacy.

"Seen the Paris news?" asked Lestrade.

Holmes nodded.

"Our French friends seem to have touched the spot this time. No doubt it's just as they say. She knocked at the door—surprise visit, I guess, for he kept his life in water-tight compartments—he let her in, couldn't keep her in the street. She told him how she had traced him, reproached him. One thing led to another, and then with that dagger so handy the end soon came. It wasn't all done in an instant, though, for these chairs were all swept over yonder, and he had one in his hand as if he had tried to hold her off with it. We've got it all clear as if we had seen it."

Holmes raised his eyebrows.

"And yet you have sent for me?"

"Ah, yes, that's another matter—a mere trifle, but the sort of thing you take an interest in—queer, you know, and what you might call freakish. It has nothing to do with the main fact—can't have, on the face of it."

"What is it, then?"

"Well, you know, after a crime of this sort we are very careful to keep things in their position. Nothing has been moved. Officer in charge here day and night. This morning, as the man was buried and the investigation over—so far as this room is concerned—we thought we could tidy up a bit. This carpet. You see, it is not fastened down, only just laid there. We had occasion to raise it. We found——"

"Yes? You found——"

Holmes's face grew tense with anxiety.

"Well, I'm sure you would never guess in a hundred years what we did find. You see that stain on the carpet? Well, a great deal must have soaked through, must it not?"

"Undoubtedly it must."

"Well, you will be surprised to hear that there is no stain on the white woodwork to correspond."

"No stain! But there must——"

"Yes, so you would say. But the fact remains that there isn't."

He took the corner of the carpet in his hand and, turning it over, he showed that it was indeed as he said.

"But the under side is as stained as the upper. It must have left a mark."

Lestrade chuckled with delight at having puzzled the famous expert.

"Now, I'll show you the explanation. There *is* a second stain, but it does not correspond with the other. See for yourself." As he spoke he turned over another portion of the carpet, and there, sure enough, was a great crimson spill upon the square white facing of the old-fashioned floor. "What do you make of that, Mr. Holmes?"

"Why, it is simple enough. The two stains did correspond, but the carpet has been turned round. As it was square and unfastened it was easily done."

"The official police don't need you, Mr. Holmes, to tell them that the carpet must have

been turned round. That's clear enough, for the stains lie above each other—if you lay it over this way. But what I want to know is, who shifted the carpet, and why?"

I could see from Holmes's rigid face that he was vibrating with inward excitement.

"Look here, Lestrade," said he, "has that constable in the passage been in charge of the place all the time?"

"Yes, he has."

"Well, take my advice. Examine him carefully. Don't do it before us. We'll wait here. You take him into the back room. You'll be more likely to get a confession out of him alone. Ask him how he dared to admit people and leave them alone in this room. Don't ask him if he has done it. Take it for granted. Tell him you *know* someone has been here. Press him. Tell him that a full confession is his only chance of forgiveness. Do exactly what I tell you!"

"By George, if he knows I'll have it out of him!" cried Lestrade. He darted into the hall, and a few moments later his bullying voice sounded from the back room.

"Now, Watson, now!" cried Holmes with frenzied eagerness. All the demoniacal force of the man masked behind that listless manner burst out in a paroxysm of energy. He tore the drugget from the floor, and in an instant was down on his hands and knees clawing at each of the squares of wood beneath it. One turned sideways as he dug his nails into the edge of it. It hinged back like the lid of a box. A small black cavity opened beneath it. Holmes plunged his eager hand into it and drew it out with a bitter snarl of anger and disappointment. It was empty.

"Quick, Watson, quick! Get it back again!" The wooden lid was replaced, and the drugget had only just been drawn straight when Lestrade's voice was heard in the passage. He found Holmes leaning languidly against the mantelpiece, resigned and patient, endeavouring to conceal his irrepressible yawns.

"Sorry to keep you waiting, Mr. Holmes, I can see that you are bored to death with the whole affair. Well, he has confessed, all right. Come in here, MacPherson. Let these gentlemen hear of your most inexcusable conduct."

The big constable, very hot and penitent, sidled into the room.

"I meant no harm, sir, I'm sure. The young woman came to the door last evening—mistook the house, she did. And then we got talking. It's lonesome, when you're on duty here all day."

"Well, what happened then?"

"She wanted to see where the crime was done—had read about it in the papers, she said. She was a very respectable, well-spoken young woman, sir, and I saw no harm in letting her have a peep. When she saw that mark on the carpet, down she dropped on the floor, and lay as if she were dead. I ran to the back and got some water, but I could not bring her to. Then I went round the corner to the Ivy Plant for some brandy, and by the time I had brought it back the young woman had recovered and was off—ashamed of herself, I daresay, and dared not face me."

"How about moving that drugget?"

"Well, sir, it was a bit rumpled, certainly, when I came back. You see, she fell on it and it lies on a polished floor with nothing to keep it in place. I straightened it out afterwards."

"It's a lesson to you that you can't deceive me, Constable MacPherson," said Lestrade, with dignity. "No doubt you thought that your breach of duty could never be discovered, and

yet a mere glance at that drugget was enough to convince me that someone had been admitted to the room. It's lucky for you, my man, that nothing is missing, or you would find yourself in Queer Street. I'm sorry to have called you down over such a petty business, Mr. Holmes, but I thought the point of the second stain not corresponding with the first would interest you."

"Certainly, it was most interesting. Has this woman only been here once, constable?"

"Yes, sir, only once."

"Who was she?"

"Don't know the name, sir. Was answering an advertisement about typewriting and came to the wrong number—very pleasant, genteel young woman, sir."

"Tall? Handsome?"

"Yes, sir, she was a well-grown young woman. I suppose you might say she was handsome. Perhaps some would say she was very handsome. 'Oh, officer, do let me have a peep!' says she. She had pretty, coaxing ways, as you might say, and I thought there was no harm in letting her just put her head through the door."

"How was she dressed?"

"Quiet, sir—a long mantle down to her feet."

"What time was it?"

"It was just growing dusk at the time. They were lighting the lamps as I came back with the brandy."

"Very good," said Holmes. "Come, Watson, I think that we have more important work elsewhere."

As we left the house Lestrade remained in the front room, while the repentant constable opened the door to let us out. Holmes turned on the step and held up something in his hand. The constable stared intently.

"Good Lord, sir!" he cried, with amazement on his face. Holmes put his finger on his lips, replaced his hand in his breast pocket, and burst out laughing as we turned down the street. "Excellent!" said he. "Come, friend Watson, the curtain rings up for the last act. You will be relieved to hear that there will be no war, that the Right Honourable Trelawney Hope will suffer no setback in his brilliant career, that the indiscreet Sovereign will receive no punishment for his indiscretion, that the Prime Minister will have no European complication to deal with, and that with a little tact and management upon our part nobody will be a penny the worse for what might have been a very ugly incident."

My mind filled with admiration for this extraordinary man.

"You have solved it!" I cried.

"Hardly that, Watson. There are some points which are as dark as ever. But we have so much that it will be our own fault if we cannot get the rest. We will go straight to Whitehall Terrace and bring the matter to a head."

When we arrived at the residence of the European Secretary it was for Lady Hilda Trelawney Hope that Sherlock Holmes inquired. We were shown into the morning-room.

"Mr. Holmes!" said the lady, and her face was pink with her indignation. "This is surely most unfair and ungenerous upon your part. I desired, as I have explained, to keep my visit to you a secret, lest my husband should think that I was intruding into his affairs. And yet you compromise me by coming here and so showing that there are business relations between us."

"Unfortunately, madam, I had no possible alternative. I have been commissioned to

recover this immensely important paper. I must therefore ask you, madam, to be kind enough to place it in my hands."

The lady sprang to her feet, with the colour all dashed in an instant from her beautiful face. Her eyes glazed—she tottered—I thought that she would faint. Then with a grand effort she rallied from the shock, and a supreme astonishment and indignation chased every other expression from her features.

"You—you insult me, Mr. Holmes."

"Come, come, madam, it is useless. Give up the letter."

She darted to the bell.

"The butler shall show you out."

"Do not ring, Lady Hilda. If you do, then all my earnest efforts to avoid a scandal will be frustrated. Give up the letter and all will be set right. If you will work with me I can arrange everything. If you work against me I must expose you."

She stood grandly defiant, a queenly figure, her eyes fixed upon his as if she would read his very soul. Her hand was on the bell, but she had forborne to ring it.

"You are trying to frighten me. It is not a very manly thing, Mr. Holmes, to come here and browbeat a woman. You say that you know something. What is it that you know?"

"Pray sit down, madam. You will hurt yourself there if you fall. I will not speak until you sit down. Thank you."

"I give you five minutes, Mr. Holmes."

"One is enough, Lady Hilda. I know of your visit to Eduardo Lucas, of your giving him this document, of your ingenious return to the room last night, and of the manner in which you took the letter from the hiding-place under the carpet."

She stared at him with an ashen face and gulped twice before she could speak.

"You are mad, Mr. Holmes—you are mad!" she cried, at last.

He drew a small piece of cardboard from his pocket. It was the face of a woman cut out of a portrait.

"I have carried this because I thought it might be useful," said he. "The policeman has recognized it."

She gave a gasp, and her head dropped back in the chair.

"Come, Lady Hilda. You have the letter. The matter may still be adjusted. I have no desire to bring trouble to you. My duty ends when I have returned the lost letter to your husband. Take my advice and be frank with me. It is your only chance."

Her courage was admirable. Even now she would not own defeat.

"I tell you again, Mr. Holmes, that you are under some absurd illusion."

Holmes rose from his chair.

"I am sorry for you, Lady Hilda. I have done my best for you. I can see that it is all in vain."

He rang the bell. The butler entered.

"Is Mr. Trelawney Hope at home?"

"He will be home, sir, at a quarter to one."

Holmes glanced at his watch.

"Still a quarter of an hour," said he. "Very good, I shall wait."

The butler had hardly closed the door behind him when Lady Hilda was down on her knees at Holmes's feet, her hands outstretched, her beautiful face upturned and wet with her tears.

"Oh, spare me, Mr. Holmes! Spare me!" she pleaded, in a frenzy of supplication. "For heaven's sake, don't tell him! I love him so! I would not bring one shadow on his life, and this I know would break his noble heart."

Holmes raised the lady. "I am thankful, madam, that you have come to your senses even at this last moment! There is not an instant to lose. Where is the letter?"

She darted across to a writing-desk, unlocked it, and drew out a long blue envelope.

"Here it is, Mr. Holmes. Would to heaven I had never seen it!"

"How can we return it?" Holmes muttered. "Quick, quick, we must think of some way! Where is the despatch-box?"

"Still in his bedroom."

"What a stroke of luck! Quick, madam, bring it here!" A moment later she had appeared with a red flat box in her hand.

"How did you open it before? You have a duplicate key? Yes, of course you have. Open it!"

From out of her bosom Lady Hilda had drawn a small key. The box flew open. It was stuffed with papers. Holmes thrust the blue envelope deep down into the heart of them, between the leaves of some other document. The box was shut, locked, and returned to the bedroom.

"Now we are ready for him," said Holmes. "We have still ten minutes. I am going far to screen you, Lady Hilda. In return you will spend the time in telling me frankly the real meaning of this extraordinary affair."

"Mr. Holmes, I will tell you everything," cried the lady. "Oh, Mr. Holmes, I would cut off my right hand before I gave him a moment of sorrow! There is no woman in all London who loves her husband as I do, and yet if he knew how I have acted—how I have been compelled to act—he would never forgive me. For his own honour stands so high that he could not forget or pardon a lapse in another. Help me, Mr. Holmes! My happiness, his happiness, our very lives are at stake!"

"Quick, madam, the time grows short!"

"It was a letter of mine, Mr. Holmes, an indiscreet letter written before my marriage—a foolish letter, a letter of an impulsive, loving girl. I meant no harm, and yet he would have thought it criminal. Had he read that letter his confidence would have been forever destroyed. It is years since I wrote it. I had thought that the whole matter was forgotten. Then at last I heard from this man, Lucas, that it had passed into his hands, and that he would lay it before my husband. I implored his mercy. He said that he would return my letter if I would bring him a certain document which he described in my husband's despatch-box. He had some spy in the office who had told him of its existence. He assured me that no harm could come to my husband. Put yourself in my position, Mr. Holmes! What was I to do?"

"Take your husband into your confidence."

"I could not, Mr. Holmes, I could not! On the one side seemed certain ruin, on the other, terrible as it seemed to take my husband's paper, still in a matter of politics I could not understand the consequences, while in a matter of love and trust they were only too clear to me. I did it, Mr. Holmes! I took an impression of his key. This man, Lucas, furnished a duplicate. I opened his despatch-box, took the paper, and conveyed it to Godolphin Street."

"What happened there, madam?"

"I tapped at the door as agreed. Lucas opened it. I followed him into his room, leaving the hall door ajar behind me, for I feared to be alone with the man. I remember that there was a woman outside as I entered. Our business was soon done. He had my letter on his desk, I handed him the document. He gave me the letter. At this instant there was a sound at the door. There were steps in the passage. Lucas quickly turned back the drugget, thrust the document into some hiding-place there, and covered it over.

"What happened after that is like some fearful dream. I have a vision of a dark, frantic face, of a woman's voice, which screamed in French, 'My waiting is not in vain. At last, at last I have found you with her!' There was a savage struggle. I saw him with a chair in his hand, a knife gleamed in hers. I rushed from the horrible scene, ran from the house, and only next morning in the paper did I learn the dreadful result. That night I was happy, for I had my letter, and I had not seen yet what the future would bring.

"It was the next morning that I realized that I had only exchanged one trouble for another. My husband's anguish at the loss of his paper went to my heart. I could hardly prevent myself from there and then kneeling down at his feet and telling him what I had done. But that again would mean a confession of the past. I came to you that morning in order to understand the full enormity of my offence. From the instant that I grasped it my whole mind was turned to the one thought of getting back my husband's paper. It must still be where Lucas had placed it, for it was concealed before this dreadful woman entered the room. If it had not been for her coming, I should not have known where his hiding-place was. How was I to get into the room? For two days I watched the place, but the door was never left open. Last night I made a last attempt. What I did and how I succeeded, you have already learned. I brought the paper back with me, and thought of destroying it, since I could see no way of returning it without confessing my guilt to my husband. Heavens, I hear his step upon the stair!"

The European Secretary burst excitedly into the room. "Any news, Mr. Holmes, any news?" he cried.

"I have some hopes."

"Ah, thank heaven!" His face became radiant. "The Prime Minister is lunching with me. May he share your hopes? He has nerves of steel, and yet I know that he has hardly slept since this terrible event. Jacobs, will you ask the Prime Minister to come up? As to you, dear, I fear that this is a matter of politics. We will join you in a few minutes in the dining-room."

The Prime Minister's manner was subdued, but I could see by the gleam of his eyes and the twitchings of his bony hands that he shared the excitement of his young colleague.

"I understand that you have something to report, Mr. Holmes?"

"Purely negative as yet," my friend answered. "I have inquired at every point where it might be, and I am sure that there is no danger to be apprehended."

"But that is not enough, Mr. Holmes. We cannot live forever on such a volcano. We must have something definite."

"I am in hopes of getting it. That is why I am here. The more I think of the matter the more convinced I am that the letter has never left this house."

"Mr. Holmes!"

"If it had it would certainly have been public by now."

"But why should anyone take it in order to keep it in his house?"

"I am not convinced that anyone did take it."

"Then how could it leave the despatch-box?"

"I am not convinced that it ever did leave the despatch-box."

"Mr. Holmes, this joking is very ill-timed. You have my assurance that it left the box."

"Have you examined the box since Tuesday morning?"

"No. It was not necessary."

"You may conceivably have overlooked it."

"Impossible, I say."

"But I am not convinced of it. I have known such things to happen. I presume there are other papers there. Well, it may have got mixed with them."

"It was on the top."

"Someone may have shaken the box and displaced it."

"No, no, I had everything out."

"Surely it is easily decided, Hope," said the Premier. "Let us have the despatch-box brought in."

The Secretary rang the bell.

"Jacobs, bring down my despatch-box. This is a farcical waste of time, but still, if nothing else will satisfy you, it shall be done. Thank you, Jacobs, put it here. I have always had the key on my watch-chain. Here are the papers, you see. Letter from Lord Merrow, report from Sir Charles Hardy, memorandum from Belgrade, note on the Russo-German grain taxes, letter from Madrid, note from Lord Flowers——Good heavens! what is this? Lord Bellinger! Lord Bellinger!"

The Premier snatched the blue envelope from his hand.

"Yes, it is it—and the letter is intact. Hope, I congratulate you."

"Thank you! Thank you! What a weight from my heart. But this is inconceivable—impossible. Mr. Holmes, you are a wizard, a sorcerer! How did you know it was there?"

"Because I knew it was nowhere else."

"I cannot believe my eyes!" He ran wildly to the door. "Where is my wife? I must tell her that all is well. Hilda! Hilda!" we heard his voice on the stairs.

The Premier looked at Holmes with twinkling eyes.

"Come, sir," said he. "There is more in this than meets the eye. How came the letter back in the box?"

Holmes turned away smiling from the keen scrutiny of those wonderful eyes.

"We also have our diplomatic secrets," said he and, picking up his hat, he turned to the door.

12

THE ADVENTURE OF THE DEVIL'S FOOT

FROM HIS LAST BOW (1917)

In RECORDING from time to time some of the curious experiences and interesting recollections which I associate with my long and intimate friendship with Mr. Sherlock Holmes, I have continually been faced by difficulties caused by his own aversion to publicity. To his sombre and cynical spirit all popular applause was always abhorrent, and nothing amused him more at the end of a successful case than to hand over the actual exposure to some orthodox official, and to listen with a mocking smile to the general chorus of misplaced congratulation. It was indeed this attitude upon the part of my friend and certainly not any lack of interesting material which has caused me of late years to lay very few of my records before the public. My participation in some of his adventures was always a privilege which entailed discretion and reticence upon me.

It was, then, with considerable surprise that I received a telegram from Holmes last Tuesday—he has never been known to write where a telegram would serve—in the following terms: "Why not tell them of the Cornish horror—strangest case I have handled." I have no idea what backward sweep of memory had brought the matter fresh to his mind, or what freak had caused him to desire that I should recount it; but I hasten, before another cancelling telegram may arrive, to hunt out the notes which give me the exact details of the case and to lay the narrative before my readers.

It was, then, in the spring of the year 1897 that Holmes's iron constitution showed some symptoms of giving way in the face of constant hard work of a most exacting kind, aggravated, perhaps, by occasional indiscretions of his own. In March of that year Dr. Moore Agar, of Harley Street, whose dramatic introduction to Holmes I may some day recount, gave positive injunctions that the famous private agent lay aside all his cases and surrender himself to complete rest if he wished to avert an absolute breakdown. The state of his health was not a matter in which he himself took the faintest interest, for his mental detachment was absolute, but he was induced at last, on the threat of being permanently disqualified from work, to give himself a complete change of scene and air. Thus it was

that in the early spring of that year we found ourselves together in a small cottage near Poldhu Bay, at the further extremity of the Cornish peninsula.

It was a singular spot, and one peculiarly well suited to the grim humour of my patient. From the windows of our little whitewashed house, which stood high upon a grassy headland, we looked down upon the whole sinister semi-circle of Mounts Bay, that old death trap of sailing vessels, with its fringe of black cliffs and surge-swept reefs on which innumerable seamen have met their end. With a northerly breeze it lies placid and sheltered, inviting the storm-tossed craft to tack into it for rest and protection.

Then come the sudden swirl round of the wind, the blistering gale from the south-west, the dragging anchor, the lee shore, and the last battle in the creaming breakers. The wise mariner stands far out from that evil place.

On the land side our surroundings were as sombre as on the sea. It was a country of rolling moors, lonely and dun-coloured, with an occasional church tower to mark the site of some old-world village. In every direction upon these moors there were traces of some vanished race which had passed utterly away, and left as its sole record strange monuments of stone, irregular mounds which contained the burned ashes of the dead, and curious earthworks which hinted at prehistoric strife. The glamour and mystery of the place, with its sinister atmosphere of forgotten nations, appealed to the imagination of my friend, and he spent much of his time in long walks and solitary meditations upon the moor. The ancient Cornish language had also arrested his attention, and he had, I remember, conceived the idea that it was akin to the Chaldean, and had been largely derived from the Phœnician traders in tin. He had received a consignment of books upon philology and was settling down to develop this thesis when suddenly, to my sorrow and to his unfeigned delight, we found ourselves, even in that land of dreams, plunged into a problem at our very doors which was more intense, more engrossing, and infinitely more mysterious than any of those which had driven us from London. Our simple life and peaceful, healthy routine were violently interrupted, and we were precipitated into the midst of a series of events which caused the utmost excitement not only in Cornwall but throughout the whole west of England. Many of my readers may retain some recollection of what was called at the time "The Cornish Horror," though a most imperfect account of the matter reached the London press. Now, after thirteen years, I will give the true details of this inconceivable affair to the public.

I have said that scattered towers marked the villages which dotted this part of Cornwall. The nearest of these was the hamlet of Tredannick Wollas, where the cottages of a couple of hundred inhabitants clustered round an ancient, moss-grown church. The vicar of the parish, Mr. Roundhay, was something of an archæologist, and as such Holmes had made his acquaintance. He was a middle-aged man, portly and affable, with a considerable fund of local lore. At his invitation we had taken tea at the vicarage and had come to know, also, Mr. Mortimer Tregennis, an independent gentleman, who increased the clergyman's scanty resources by taking rooms in his large, straggling house. The vicar, being a bachelor, was glad to come to such an arrangement, though he had little in common with his lodger, who was a thin, dark, spectacled man, with a stoop which gave the impression of actual, physical deformity. I remember that during our short visit we found the vicar garrulous, but his lodger strangely reticent, a sad-faced, introspective man, sitting with averted eyes, brooding apparently upon his own affairs.

These were the two men who entered abruptly into our little sitting-room on Tuesday,

March the 16th, shortly after our breakfast hour, as we were smoking together, preparatory to our daily excursion upon the moors.

"Mr. Holmes," said the vicar in an agitated voice, "the most extraordinary and tragic affair has occurred during the night. It is the most unheard-of business. We can only regard it as a special Providence that you should chance to be here at the time, for in all England you are the one man we need."

I glared at the intrusive vicar with no very friendly eyes; but Holmes took his pipe from his lips and sat up in his chair like an old hound who hears the view-halloa. He waved his hand to the sofa, and our palpitating visitor with his agitated companion sat side by side upon it. Mr. Mortimer Tregennis was more self-contained than the clergyman, but the twitching of his thin hands and the brightness of his dark eyes showed that they shared a common emotion.

"Shall I speak or you?" he asked of the vicar.

"Well, as you seem to have made the discovery, whatever it may be, and the vicar to have had it second-hand, perhaps you had better do the speaking," said Holmes.

I glanced at the hastily clad clergyman, with the formally dressed lodger seated beside him, and was amused at the surprise which Holmes's simple deduction had brought to their faces.

"Perhaps I had best say a few words first," said the vicar, "and then you can judge if you will listen to the details from Mr. Tregennis, or whether we should not hasten at once to the scene of this mysterious affair. I may explain, then, that our friend here spent last evening in the company of his two brothers, Owen and George, and of his sister Brenda, at their house of Tredannick Wartha, which is near the old stone cross upon the moor. He left them shortly after ten o'clock, playing cards round the dining-room table, in excellent health and spirits. This morning, being an early riser, he walked in that direction before breakfast and was overtaken by the carriage of Dr. Richards, who explained that he had just been sent for on a most urgent call to Tredannick Wartha. Mr. Mortimer Tregennis naturally went with him. When he arrived at Tredannick Wartha he found an extraordinary state of things. His two brothers and his sister were seated round the table exactly as he had left them, the cards still spread in front of them and the candles burned down to their sockets. The sister lay back stone-dead in her chair, while the two brothers sat on each side of her laughing, shouting, and singing, the senses stricken clean out of them. All three of them, the dead woman and the two demented men, retained upon their faces an expression of the utmost horror—a convulsion of terror which was dreadful to look upon. There was no sign of the presence of anyone in the house, except Mrs. Porter, the old cook and housekeeper, who declared that she had slept deeply and heard no sound during the night. Nothing had been stolen or disarranged, and there is absolutely no explanation of what the horror can be which has frightened a woman to death and two strong men out of their senses. There is the situation, Mr. Holmes, in a nutshell, and if you can help us to clear it up you will have done a great work."

I had hoped that in some way I could coax my companion back into the quiet which had been the object of our journey; but one glance at his intense face and contracted eyebrows told me how vain was now the expectation. He sat for some little time in silence, absorbed in the strange drama which had broken in upon our peace.

"I will look into this matter," he said at last. "On the face of it, it would appear to be a case of a very exceptional nature. Have you been there yourself, Mr. Roundhay?"

"No, Mr. Holmes. Mr. Tregennis brought back the account to the vicarage, and I at once hurried over with him to consult you."

"How far is it to the house where this singular tragedy occurred?"

"About a mile inland."

"Then we shall walk over together. But before we start I must ask you a few questions, Mr. Mortimer Tregennis."

The other had been silent all this time, but I had observed that his more controlled excitement was even greater than the obtrusive emotion of the clergyman. He sat with a pale, drawn face, his anxious gaze fixed upon Holmes, and his thin hands clasped convulsively together. His pale lips quivered as he listened to the dreadful experience which had befallen his family, and his dark eyes seemed to reflect something of the horror of the scene.

"Ask what you like, Mr. Holmes," said he eagerly. "It is a bad thing to speak of, but I will answer you the truth."

"Tell me about last night."

"Well, Mr. Holmes, I supped there, as the vicar has said, and my elder brother George proposed a game of whist afterwards. We sat down about nine o'clock. It was a quarter-past ten when I moved to go. I left them all round the table, as merry as could be."

"Who let you out?"

"Mrs. Porter had gone to bed, so I let myself out. I shut the hall door behind me. The window of the room in which they sat was closed, but the blind was not drawn down. There was no change in door or window this morning, or any reason to think that any stranger had been to the house. Yet there they sat, driven clean mad with terror, and Brenda lying dead of fright, with her head hanging over the arm of the chair. I'll never get the sight of that room out of my mind so long as I live."

"The facts, as you state them, are certainly most remarkable," said Holmes. "I take it that you have no theory yourself which can in any way account for them?"

"It's devilish, Mr. Holmes, devilish!" cried Mortimer Tregennis. "It is not of this world. Something has come into that room which has dashed the light of reason from their minds. What human contrivance could do that?"

"I fear," said Holmes, "that if the matter is beyond humanity it is certainly beyond me. Yet we must exhaust all natural explanations before we fall back upon such a theory as this. As to yourself, Mr. Tregennis, I take it you were divided in some way from your family, since they lived together and you had rooms apart?"

"That is so, Mr. Holmes, though the matter is past and done with. We were a family of tin-miners at Redruth, but we sold our venture to a company, and so retired with enough to keep us. I won't deny that there was some feeling about the division of the money and it stood between us for a time, but it was all forgiven and forgotten, and we were the best of friends together."

"Looking back at the evening which you spent together, does anything stand out in your memory as throwing any possible light upon the tragedy? Think carefully, Mr. Tregennis, for any clue which can help me."

"There is nothing at all, sir."

"Your people were in their usual spirits?"

"Never better."

"Were they nervous people? Did they ever show any apprehension of coming danger?"

"Nothing of the kind."

"You have nothing to add then, which could assist me?"

Mortimer Tregennis considered earnestly for a moment.

"There is one thing that occurs to me," said he at last. "As we sat at the table my back was to the window, and my brother George, he being my partner at cards, was facing it. I saw him once look hard over my shoulder, so I turned round and looked also. The blind was up and the window shut, but I could just make out the bushes on the lawn, and it seemed to me for a moment that I saw something moving among them. I couldn't even say if it was man or animal, but I just thought there was something there. When I asked him what he was looking at, he told me that he had the same feeling. That is all that I can say."

"Did you not investigate?"

"No; the matter passed as unimportant."

"You left them, then, without any premonition of evil?"

"None at all."

"I am not clear how you came to hear the news so early this morning."

"I am an early riser and generally take a walk before breakfast. This morning I had hardly started when the doctor in his carriage overtook me. He told me that old Mrs. Porter had sent a boy down with an urgent message. I sprang in beside him and we drove on. When we got there we looked into that dreadful room. The candles and the fire must have burned out hours before, and they had been sitting there in the dark until dawn had broken. The doctor said Brenda must have been dead at least six hours. There were no signs of violence. She just lay across the arm of the chair with that look on her face. George and Owen were singing snatches of songs and gibbering like two great apes. Oh, it was awful to see! I couldn't stand it, and the doctor was as white as a sheet. Indeed, he fell into a chair in a sort of faint, and we nearly had him on our hands as well."

"Remarkable—most remarkable!" said Holmes, rising and taking his hat. "I think, perhaps, we had better go down to Tredannick Wartha without further delay. I confess that I have seldom known a case which at first sight presented a more singular problem."

Our proceedings of that first morning did little to advance the investigation. It was marked, however, at the outset by an incident which left the most sinister impression upon my mind. The approach to the spot at which the tragedy occurred is down a narrow, winding, country lane. While we made our way along it we heard the rattle of a carriage coming towards us and stood aside to let it pass. As it drove by us I caught a glimpse through the closed window of a horribly contorted, grinning face glaring out at us. Those staring eyes and gnashing teeth flashed past us like a dreadful vision.

"My brothers!" cried Mortimer Tregennis, white to his lips. "They are taking them to Helston."

We looked with horror after the black carriage, lumbering upon its way. Then we turned our steps towards this ill-omened house in which they had met their strange fate.

It was a large and bright dwelling, rather a villa than a cottage, with a considerable garden which was already, in that Cornish air, well filled with spring flowers. Towards this garden the window of the sitting-room fronted, and from it, according to Mortimer Tregennis, must have come that thing of evil which had by sheer horror in a single instant

blasted their minds. Holmes walked slowly and thoughtfully among the flower-plots and along the path before we entered the porch. So absorbed was he in his thoughts, I remember, that he stumbled over the watering-pot, upset its contents, and deluged both our feet and the garden path. Inside the house we were met by the elderly Cornish housekeeper, Mrs. Porter, who, with the aid of a young girl, looked after the wants of the family. She readily answered all Holmes's questions. She had heard nothing in the night. Her employers had all been in excellent spirits lately, and she had never known them more cheerful and prosperous. She had fainted with horror upon entering the room in the morning and seeing that dreadful company round the table. She had, when she recovered, thrown open the window to let the morning air in, and had run down to the lane, whence she sent a farm lad for the doctor. The lady was on her bed upstairs if we cared to see her. It took four strong men to get the brothers into the asylum carriage. She would not herself stay in the house another day and was starting that very afternoon to rejoin her family at St Ives.

We ascended the stairs and viewed the body. Miss Brenda Tregennis had been a very beautiful girl, though now verging upon middle age. Her dark, clear-cut face was handsome, even in death, but there still lingered upon it something of that convulsion of horror which had been her last human emotion. From her bedroom we descended to the sitting-room, where this strange tragedy had actually occurred. The charred ashes of the overnight fire lay in the grate. On the table were the four guttered and burned-out candles, with the cards scattered over its surface. The chairs had been moved back against the walls, but all else was as it had been the night before. Holmes paced with light, swift steps about the room; he sat in the various chairs, drawing them up and reconstructing their positions. He tested how much of the garden was visible; he examined the floor, the ceiling, and the fireplace; but never once did I see that sudden brightening of his eyes and tightening of his lips which would have told me that he saw some gleam of light in this utter darkness.

"Why a fire?" he asked once. "Had they always a fire in this small room on a spring evening?"

Mortimer Tregennis explained that the night was cold and damp. For that reason, after his arrival, the fire was lit. "What are you going to do now, Mr. Holmes?" he asked.

My friend smiled and laid his hand upon my arm. "I think, Watson, that I shall resume that course of tobacco-poisoning which you have so often and so justly condemned," said he. "With your permission, gentlemen, we will now return to our cottage, for I am not aware that any new factor is likely to come to our notice here. I will turn the facts over in my mind, Mr. Tregennis, and should anything occur to me I will certainly communicate with you and the vicar. In the meantime I wish you both good-morning."

It was not until long after we were back in Poldhu Cottage that Holmes broke his complete and absorbed silence. He sat coiled in his armchair, his haggard and ascetic face hardly visible amid the blue swirl of his tobacco smoke, his black brows drawn down, his forehead contracted, his eyes vacant and far away. Finally he laid down his pipe and sprang to his feet.

"It won't do, Watson!" said he with a laugh. "Let us walk along the cliffs together and search for flint arrows. We are more likely to find them than clues to this problem. To let the brain work without sufficient material is like racing an engine. It racks itself to pieces. The sea air, sunshine, and patience, Watson—all else will come.

"Now, let us calmly define our position, Watson," he continued as we skirted the cliffs together. "Let us get a firm grip of the very little which we *do* know, so that when fresh facts arise we may be ready to fit them into their places. I take it, in the first place, that neither of us is prepared to admit diabolical intrusions into the affairs of men. Let us begin by ruling that entirely out of our minds. Very good. There remain three persons who have been grievously stricken by some conscious or unconscious human agency. That is firm ground. Now, when did this occur? Evidently, assuming his narrative to be true, it was immediately after Mr. Mortimer Tregennis had left the room. That is a very important point. The presumption is that it was within a few minutes afterwards. The cards still lay upon the table. It was already past their usual hour for bed. Yet they had not changed their position or pushed back their chairs. I repeat, then, that the occurrence was immediately after his departure, and not later than eleven o'clock last night.

"Our next obvious step is to check, so far as we can, the movements of Mortimer Tregennis after he left the room. In this there is no difficulty, and they seem to be above suspicion. Knowing my methods as you do, you were, of course, conscious of the somewhat clumsy water-pot expedient by which I obtained a clearer impress of his foot than might otherwise have been possible. The wet, sandy path took it admirably. Last night was also wet, you will remember, and it was not difficult—having obtained a sample print—to pick out his track among others and to follow his movements. He appears to have walked away swiftly in the direction of the vicarage.

"If, then, Mortimer Tregennis disappeared from the scene, and yet some outside person affected the card-players, how can we reconstruct that person, and how was such an impression of horror conveyed? Mrs. Porter may be eliminated. She is evidently harmless. Is there any evidence that someone crept up to the garden window and in some manner produced so terrific an effect that he drove those who saw it out of their senses? The only suggestion in this direction comes from Mortimer Tregennis himself, who says that his brother spoke about some movement in the garden. That is certainly remarkable, as the night was rainy, cloudy, and dark. Anyone who had the design to alarm these people would be compelled to place his very face against the glass before he could be seen. There is a three-foot flower-border outside this window, but no indication of a footmark. It is difficult to imagine, then, how an outsider could have made so terrible an impression upon the company, nor have we found any possible motive for so strange and elaborate an attempt. You perceive our difficulties, Watson?"

"They are only too clear," I answered with conviction.

"And yet, with a little more material, we may prove that they are not insurmountable," said Holmes. "I fancy that among your extensive archives, Watson, you may find some which were nearly as obscure. Meanwhile, we shall put the case aside until more accurate data are available, and devote the rest of our morning to the pursuit of neolithic man."

I may have commented upon my friend's power of mental detachment, but never have I wondered at it more than upon that spring morning in Cornwall when for two hours he discoursed upon celts, arrowheads, and shards, as lightly as if no sinister mystery were waiting for his solution. It was not until we had returned in the afternoon to our cottage that we found a visitor awaiting us, who soon brought our minds back to the matter in hand. Neither of us needed to be told who that visitor was. The huge body, the craggy and deeply seamed face with the fierce eyes and hawk-like nose, the grizzled hair which nearly brushed our cottage ceiling, the beard—golden at the fringes and white near the

lips, save for the nicotine stain from his perpetual cigar—all these were as well known in London as in Africa, and could only be associated with the tremendous personality of Dr. Leon Sterndale, the great lion-hunter and explorer.

We had heard of his presence in the district and had once or twice caught sight of his tall figure upon the moorland paths. He made no advances to us, however, nor would we have dreamed of doing so to him, as it was well known that it was his love of seclusion which caused him to spend the greater part of the intervals between his journeys in a small bungalow buried in the lonely wood of Beauchamp Arriance. Here, amid his books and his maps, he lived an absolutely lonely life, attending to his own simple wants and paying little apparent heed to the affairs of his neighbours. It was a surprise to me, therefore, to hear him asking Holmes in an eager voice whether he had made any advance in his reconstruction of this mysterious episode. "The county police are utterly at fault," said he, "but perhaps your wider experience has suggested some conceivable explanation. My only claim to being taken into your confidence is that during my many residences here I have come to know this family of Tregennis very well—indeed, upon my Cornish mother's side I could call them cousins—and their strange fate has naturally been a great shock to me. I may tell you that I had got as far as Plymouth upon my way to Africa, but the news reached me this morning, and I came straight back again to help in the inquiry."

Holmes raised his eyebrows.

"Did you lose your boat through it?"

"I will take the next."

"Dear me! that is friendship indeed."

"I tell you they were relatives."

"Quite so—cousins of your mother. Was your baggage aboard the ship?"

"Some of it, but the main part at the hotel."

"I see. But surely this event could not have found its way into the Plymouth morning papers."

"No, sir; I had a telegram."

"Might I ask from whom?"

A shadow passed over the gaunt face of the explorer.

"You are very inquisitive, Mr. Holmes."

"It is my business."

With an effort Dr. Sterndale recovered his ruffled composure.

"I have no objection to telling you," he said. "It was Mr. Roundhay, the vicar, who sent me the telegram which recalled me."

"Thank you," said Holmes. "I may say in answer to your original question that I have not cleared my mind entirely on the subject of this case, but that I have every hope of reaching some conclusion. It would be premature to say more."

"Perhaps you would not mind telling me if your suspicions point in any particular direction?"

"No, I can hardly answer that."

"Then I have wasted my time and need not prolong my visit." The famous doctor strode out of our cottage in considerable ill-humour, and within five minutes Holmes had followed him. I saw him no more until the evening, when he returned with a slow step and haggard face which assured me that he had made no great progress with his investigation. He glanced at a telegram which awaited him and threw it into the grate.

"From the Plymouth hotel, Watson," he said. "I learned the name of it from the vicar, and I wired to make certain that Dr. Leon Sterndale's account was true. It appears that he did indeed spend last night there, and that he has actually allowed some of his baggage to go on to Africa, while he returned to be present at this investigation. What do you make of that, Watson?"

"He is deeply interested."

"Deeply interested—yes. There is a thread here which we had not yet grasped and which might lead us through the tangle. Cheer up, Watson, for I am very sure that our material has not yet all come to hand. When it does we may soon leave our difficulties behind us."

Little did I think how soon the words of Holmes would be realised, or how strange and sinister would be that new development which opened up an entirely fresh line of investigation. I was shaving at my window in the morning when I heard the rattle of hoofs and, looking up, saw a dog-cart coming at a gallop down the road. It pulled up at our door, and our friend, the vicar, sprang from it and rushed up our garden path. Holmes was already dressed, and we hastened down to meet him.

Our visitor was so excited that he could hardly articulate, but at last in gasps and bursts his tragic story came out of him.

"We are devil-ridden, Mr. Holmes! My poor parish is devil-ridden!" he cried. "Satan himself is loose in it! We are given over into his hands!" He danced about in his agitation, a ludicrous object if it were not for his ashy face and startled eyes. Finally he shot out his terrible news.

"Mr. Mortimer Tregennis died during the night, and with exactly the same symptoms as the rest of his family."

Holmes sprang to his feet, all energy in an instant.

"Can you fit us both into your dog-cart?"

"Yes, I can."

"Then, Watson, we will postpone our breakfast. Mr. Roundhay, we are entirely at your disposal. Hurry—hurry, before things get disarranged."

The lodger occupied two rooms at the vicarage, which were in an angle by themselves, the one above the other. Below was a large sitting-room; above, his bedroom. They looked out upon a croquet lawn which came up to the windows. We had arrived before the doctor or the police, so that everything was absolutely undisturbed. Let me describe exactly the scene as we saw it upon that misty March morning. It has left an impression which can never be effaced from my mind.

The atmosphere of the room was of a horrible and depressing stuffiness. The servant who had first entered had thrown up the window, or it would have been even more intolerable. This might partly be due to the fact that a lamp stood flaring and smoking on the centre table. Beside it sat the dead man, leaning back in his chair, his thin beard projecting, his spectacles pushed up on to his forehead, and his lean dark face turned towards the window and twisted into the same distortion of terror which had marked the features of his dead sister. His limbs were convulsed and his fingers contorted as though he had died in a very paroxysm of fear. He was fully clothed, though there were signs that his dressing had been done in a hurry. We had already learned that his bed had been slept in, and that the tragic end had come to him in the early morning.

One realised the red-hot energy which underlay Holmes's phlegmatic exterior when

one saw the sudden change which came over him from the moment that he entered the fatal apartment. In an instant he was tense and alert, his eyes shining, his face set, his limbs quivering with eager activity. He was out on the lawn, in through the window, round the room, and up into the bedroom, for all the world like a dashing foxhound drawing a cover. In the bedroom he made a rapid cast around and ended by throwing open the window, which appeared to give him some fresh cause for excitement, for he leaned out of it with loud ejaculations of interest and delight. Then he rushed down the stair, out through the open window, threw himself upon his face on the lawn, sprang up and into the room once more, all with the energy of the hunter who is at the very heels of his quarry. The lamp, which was an ordinary standard, he examined with minute care, making certain measurements upon its bowl. He carefully scrutinised with his lens the talc shield which covered the top of the chimney and scraped off some ashes which adhered to its upper surface, putting some of them into an envelope, which he placed in his pocketbook. Finally, just as the doctor and the official police put in an appearance, he beckoned to the vicar and we all three went out upon the lawn.

"I am glad to say that my investigation has not been entirely barren," he remarked. "I cannot remain to discuss the matter with the police, but I should be exceedingly obliged, Mr. Roundhay, if you would give the inspector my compliments and direct his attention to the bedroom window and to the sitting-room lamp. Each is suggestive, and together they are almost conclusive. If the police would desire further information I shall be happy to see any of them at the cottage. And now, Watson, I think that, perhaps, we shall be better employed elsewhere."

It may be that the police resented the intrusion of an amateur, or that they imagined themselves to be upon some hopeful line of investigation; but it is certain that we heard nothing from them for the next two days. During this time Holmes spent some of his time smoking and dreaming in the cottage; but a greater portion in country walks which he undertook alone, returning after many hours without remark as to where he had been. One experiment served to show me the line of his investigation. He had bought a lamp which was the duplicate of the one which had burned in the room of Mortimer Tregennis on the morning of the tragedy. This he filled with the same oil as that used at the vicarage, and he carefully timed the period which it would take to be exhausted. Another experiment which he made was of a more unpleasant nature, and one which I am not likely ever to forget.

"You will remember, Watson," he remarked one afternoon, "that there is a single common point of resemblance in the varying reports which have reached us. This concerns the effect of the atmosphere of the room in each case upon those who had first entered it. You will recollect that Mortimer Tregennis, in describing the episode of his last visit to his brother's house, remarked that the doctor on entering the room fell into a chair? You had forgotten? Well I can answer for it that it was so. Now, you will remember also that Mrs. Porter, the housekeeper, told us that she herself fainted upon entering the room and had afterwards opened the window. In the second case—that of Mortimer Tregennis himself—you cannot have forgotten the horrible stuffiness of the room when we arrived, though the servant had thrown open the window. That servant, I found upon inquiry, was so ill that she had gone to her bed. You will admit, Watson, that these facts are very suggestive. In each case there is evidence of a poisonous atmosphere. In each case, also, there is combustion going on in the room—in the one case a fire, in the other a

lamp. The fire was needed, but the lamp was lit—as a comparison of the oil consumed will show—long after it was broad daylight. Why? Surely because there is some connection between three things—the burning, the stuffy atmosphere, and, finally, the madness or death of those unfortunate people. That is clear, is it not?"

"It would appear so."

"At least we may accept it as a working hypothesis. We will suppose, then, that something was burned in each case which produced an atmosphere causing strange toxic effects. Very good. In the first instance—that of the Tregennis family—this substance was placed in the fire. Now the window was shut, but the fire would naturally carry fumes to some extent up the chimney. Hence one would expect the effects of the poison to be less than in the second case, where there was less escape for the vapour. The result seems to indicate that it was so, since in the first case only the woman, who had presumably the more sensitive organism, was killed, the others exhibiting that temporary or permanent lunacy which is evidently the first effect of the drug. In the second case the result was complete. The facts, therefore, seem to bear out the theory of a poison which worked by combustion.

"With this train of reasoning in my head I naturally looked about in Mortimer Tregennis's room to find some remains of this substance. The obvious place to look was the talc shelf or smoke-guard of the lamp. There, sure enough, I perceived a number of flaky ashes, and round the edges a fringe of brownish powder, which had not yet been consumed. Half of this I took, as you saw, and I placed it in an envelope."

"Why half, Holmes?"

"It is not for me, my dear Watson, to stand in the way of the official police force. I leave them all the evidence which I found. The poison still remained upon the talc had they the wit to find it. Now, Watson, we will light our lamp; we will, however, take the precaution to open our window to avoid the premature decease of two deserving members of society, and you will seat yourself near that open window in an armchair unless, like a sensible man, you determine to have nothing to do with the affair. Oh, you will see it out, will you? I thought I knew my Watson. This chair I will place opposite yours, so that we may be the same distance from the poison and face to face. The door we will leave ajar. Each is now in a position to watch the other and to bring the experiment to an end should the symptoms seem alarming. Is that all clear? Well, then, I take our powder—or what remains of it—from the envelope, and I lay it above the burning lamp. So! Now, Watson, let us sit down and await developments."

They were not long in coming. I had hardly settled in my chair before I was conscious of a thick, musky odour, subtle and nauseous. At the very first whiff of it my brain and my imagination were beyond all control. A thick, black cloud swirled before my eyes, and my mind told me that in this cloud, unseen as yet, but about to spring out upon my appalled senses, lurked all that was vaguely horrible, all that was monstrous and inconceivably wicked in the universe. Vague shapes swirled and swam amid the dark cloud-bank, each a menace and a warning of something coming, the advent of some unspeakable dweller upon the threshold, whose very shadow would blast my soul. A freezing horror took possession of me. I felt that my hair was rising, that my eyes were protruding, that my mouth was opened, and my tongue like leather. The turmoil within my brain was such that something must surely snap. I tried to scream and was vaguely aware of some hoarse croak which was my own voice, but distant and detached from myself. At the same

moment, in some effort of escape, I broke through that cloud of despair and had a glimpse of Holmes's face, white, rigid, and drawn with horror—the very look which I had seen upon the features of the dead. It was that vision which gave me an instant of sanity and of strength. I dashed from my chair, threw my arms round Holmes, and together we lurched through the door, and an instant afterwards had thrown ourselves down upon the grass plot and were lying side by side, conscious only of the glorious sunshine which was bursting its way through the hellish cloud of terror which had girt us in. Slowly it rose from our souls like the mists from a landscape until peace and reason had returned, and we were sitting upon the grass, wiping our clammy foreheads, and looking with apprehension at each other to mark the last traces of that terrific experience which we had undergone.

"Upon my word, Watson!" said Holmes at last with an unsteady voice, "I owe you both my thanks and an apology. It was an unjustifiable experiment even for one's self, and doubly so for a friend. I am really very sorry."

"You know," I answered with some emotion, for I have never seen so much of Holmes's heart before, "that it is my greatest joy and privilege to help you."

He relapsed at once into the half-humorous, half cynical vein which was his habitual attitude to those about him. "It would be superfluous to drive us mad, my dear Watson," said he. "A candid observer would certainly declare that we were so already before we embarked upon so wild an experiment. I confess that I never imagined that the effect could be so sudden and so severe." He dashed into the cottage, and, reappearing with the burning lamp held at full arm's length, he threw it among a bank of brambles. "We must give the room a little time to clear. I take it, Watson, that you have no longer a shadow of a doubt as to how these tragedies were produced?"

"None whatever."

"But the cause remains as obscure as before. Come into the arbour here and let us discuss it together. That villainous stuff seems still to linger round my throat. I think we must admit that all the evidence points to this man, Mortimer Tregennis, having been the criminal in the first tragedy, though he was the victim in the second one. We must remember, in the first place, that there is some story of a family quarrel, followed by a reconciliation. How bitter that quarrel may have been, or how hollow the reconciliation we cannot tell. When I think of Mortimer Tregennis, with the foxy face and the small shrewd, beady eyes behind the spectacles, he is not a man whom I should judge to be of a particularly forgiving disposition. Well, in the next place, you will remember that this idea of someone moving in the garden, which took our attention for a moment from the real cause of the tragedy, emanated from him. He had a motive in misleading us. Finally, if he did not throw the substance into the fire at the moment of leaving the room, who did do so? The affair happened immediately after his departure. Had anyone else come in, the family would certainly have risen from the table. Besides, in peaceful Cornwall, visitors did not arrive after ten o'clock at night. We may take it, then, that all the evidence points to Mortimer Tregennis as the culprit."

"Then his own death was suicide!"

"Well, Watson, it is on the face of it a not impossible supposition. The man who had the guilt upon his soul of having brought such a fate upon his own family might well be driven by remorse to inflict it upon himself. There are, however, some cogent reasons against it. Fortunately, there is one man in England who knows all about it, and I have

made arrangements by which we shall hear the facts this afternoon from his own lips. Ah! he is a little before his time. Perhaps you would kindly step this way, Dr. Leon Sterndale. We have been conducing a chemical experiment indoors which has left our little room hardly fit for the reception of so distinguished a visitor."

I had heard the click of the garden gate, and now the majestic figure of the great African explorer appeared upon the path. He turned in some surprise towards the rustic arbour in which we sat.

"You sent for me, Mr. Holmes. I had your note about an hour ago, and I have come, though I really do not know why I should obey your summons."

"Perhaps we can clear the point up before we separate," said Holmes. "Meanwhile, I am much obliged to you for your courteous acquiescence. You will excuse this informal reception in the open air, but my friend Watson and I have nearly furnished an additional chapter to what the papers call the Cornish Horror, and we prefer a clear atmosphere for the present. Perhaps, since the matters which we have to discuss will affect you personally in a very intimate fashion, it is as well that we should talk where there can be no eavesdropping."

The explorer took his cigar from his lips and gazed sternly at my companion.

"I am at a loss to know, sir," he said, "what you can have to speak about which affects me personally in a very intimate fashion."

"The killing of Mortimer Tregennis," said Holmes.

For a moment I wished that I were armed. Sterndale's fierce face turned to a dusky red, his eyes glared, and the knotted, passionate veins started out in his forehead, while he sprang forward with clenched hands towards my companion. Then he stopped, and with a violent effort he resumed a cold, rigid calmness, which was, perhaps, more suggestive of danger than his hot-headed outburst.

"I have lived so long among savages and beyond the law," said he, "that I have got into the way of being a law to myself. You would do well, Mr. Holmes, not to forget it, for I have no desire to do you an injury."

"Nor have I any desire to do you an injury, Dr. Sterndale. Surely the clearest proof of it is that, knowing what I know, I have sent for you and not for the police."

Sterndale sat down with a gasp, overawed for, perhaps, the first time in his adventurous life. There was a calm assurance of power in Holmes's manner which could not be withstood. Our visitor stammered for a moment, his great hands opening and shutting in his agitation.

"What do you mean?" he asked at last. "If this is bluff upon your part, Mr. Holmes, you have chosen a bad man for your experiment. Let us have no more beating about the bush. What *do* you mean?"

"I will tell you," said Holmes, "and the reason why I tell you is that I hope frankness may beget frankness. What my next step may be will depend entirely upon the nature of your own defence."

"My defence?"

"Yes, sir."

"My defence against what?"

"Against the charge of killing Mortimer Tregennis."

Sterndale mopped his forehead with his handkerchief. "Upon my word, you are getting on," said he. "Do all your successes depend upon this prodigious power of bluff?"

"The bluff," said Holmes sternly, "is upon your side, Dr. Leon Sterndale, and not upon mine. As a proof I will tell you some of the facts upon which my conclusions are based. Of your return from Plymouth, allowing much of your property to go on to Africa, I will say nothing save that it first informed me that you were one of the factors which had to be taken into account in reconstructing this drama—"

"I came back—"

"I have heard your reasons and regard them as unconvincing and inadequate. We will pass that. You came down here to ask me whom I suspected. I refused to answer you. You then went to the vicarage, waited outside it for some time, and finally returned to your cottage."

"How do you know that?"

"I followed you."

"I saw no one."

"That is what you may expect to see when I follow you. You spent a restless night at your cottage, and you formed certain plans, which in the early morning you proceeded to put into execution. Leaving your door just as day was breaking, you filled your pocket with some reddish gravel that was lying heaped beside your gate."

Sterndale gave a violent start and looked at Holmes in amazement.

"You then walked swiftly for the mile which separated you from the vicarage. You were wearing, I may remark, the same pair of ribbed tennis shoes which are at the present moment upon your feet. At the vicarage you passed through the orchard and the side hedge, coming out under the window of the lodger Tregennis. It was now daylight, but the household was not yet stirring. You drew some of the gravel from your pocket, and you threw it up at the window above you."

Sterndale sprang to his feet.

"I believe that you are the devil himself!" he cried.

Holmes smiled at the compliment. "It took two, or possibly three, handfuls before the lodger came to the window. You beckoned him to come down. He dressed hurriedly and descended to his sitting-room. You entered by the window. There was an interview—a short one—during which you walked up and down the room. Then you passed out and closed the window, standing on the lawn outside smoking a cigar and watching what occurred. Finally, after the death of Tregennis, you withdrew as you had come. Now, Dr. Sterndale, how do you justify such conduct, and what were the motives for your actions? If you prevaricate or trifle with me, I give you my assurance that the matter will pass out of my hands forever."

Our visitor's face had turned ashen grey as he listened to the words of his accuser. Now he sat for some time in thought with his face sunk in his hands. Then with a sudden impulsive gesture he plucked a photograph from his breast-pocket and threw it on the rustic table before us.

"That is why I have done it," said he.

It showed the bust and face of a very beautiful woman. Holmes stooped over it.

"Brenda Tregennis," said he.

"Yes, Brenda Tregennis," repeated our visitor. "For years I have loved her. For years she has loved me. There is the secret of that Cornish seclusion which people have marvelled at. It has brought me close to the one thing on earth that was dear to me. I could not marry her, for I have a wife who has left me for years and yet whom, by the

deplorable laws of England, I could not divorce. For years Brenda waited. For years I waited. And this is what we have waited for." A terrible sob shook his great frame, and he clutched his throat under his brindled beard. Then with an effort he mastered himself and spoke on:

"The vicar knew. He was in our confidence. He would tell you that she was an angel upon earth. That was why he telegraphed to me and I returned. What was my baggage or Africa to me when I learned that such a fate had come upon my darling? There you have the missing clue to my action, Mr. Holmes."

"Proceed," said my friend.

Dr. Sterndale drew from his pocket a paper packet and laid it upon the table. On the outside was written *"Radix pedis diaboli"* with a red poison label beneath it. He pushed it towards me. "I understand that you are a doctor, sir. Have you ever heard of this preparation?"

"Devil's-foot root! No, I have never heard of it."

"It is no reflection upon your professional knowledge," said he, "for I believe that, save for one sample in a laboratory at Buda, there is no other specimen in Europe. It has not yet found its way either into the pharmacopœia or into the literature of toxicology. The root is shaped like a foot, half human, half goatlike; hence the fanciful name given by a botanical missionary. It is used as an ordeal poison by the medicine-men in certain districts of West Africa and is kept as a secret among them. This particular specimen I obtained under very extraordinary circumstances in the Ubangi country." He opened the paper as he spoke and disclosed a heap of reddish-brown, snuff-like powder.

"Well, sir?" asked Holmes sternly.

"I am about to tell you, Mr. Holmes, all that actually occurred, for you already know so much that it is clearly to my interest that you should know all. I have already explained the relationship in which I stood to the Tregennis family. For the sake of the sister I was friendly with the brothers. There was a family quarrel about money which estranged this man Mortimer, but it was supposed to be made up, and I afterwards met him as I did the others. He was a sly, subtle, scheming man, and several things arose which gave me a suspicion of him, but I had no cause for any positive quarrel.

"One day, only a couple of weeks ago, he came down to my cottage and I showed him some of my African curiosities. Among other things I exhibited this powder, and I told him of its strange properties, how it stimulates those brain centres which control the emotion of fear, and how either madness or death is the fate of the unhappy native who is subjected to the ordeal by the priest of his tribe. I told him also how powerless European science would be to detect it. How he took it I cannot say, for I never left the room, but there is no doubt that it was then, while I was opening cabinets and stooping to boxes, that he managed to abstract some of the devil's-foot root. I well remember how he plied me with questions as to the amount and the time that was needed for its effect, but I little dreamed that he could have a personal reason for asking.

"I thought no more of the matter until the vicar's telegram reached me at Plymouth. This villain had thought that I would be at sea before the news could reach me, and that I should be lost for years in Africa. But I returned at once. Of course, I could not listen to the details without feeling assured that my poison had been used. I came round to see you on the chance that some other explanation had suggested itself to you. But there could be none. I was convinced that Mortimer Tregennis was the murderer; that for the sake of

money, and with the idea, perhaps, that if the other members of his family were all insane he would be the sole guardian of their joint property, he had used the devil's-foot powder upon them, driven two of them out of their senses, and killed his sister Brenda, the one human being whom I have ever loved or who has ever loved me. There was his crime; what was to be his punishment?

"Should I appeal to the law? Where were my proofs? I knew that the facts were true, but could I help to make a jury of countrymen believe so fantastic a story? I might or I might not. But I could not afford to fail. My soul cried out for revenge. I have said to you once before, Mr. Holmes, that I have spent much of my life outside the law, and that I have come at last to be a law to myself. So it was even now. I determined that the fate which he had given to others should be shared by himself. Either that or I would do justice upon him with my own hand. In all England there can be no man who sets less value upon his own life than I do at the present moment.

"Now I have told you all. You have yourself supplied the rest. I did, as you say, after a restless night, set off early from my cottage. I foresaw the difficulty of arousing him, so I gathered some gravel from the pile which you have mentioned, and I used it to throw up to his window. He came down and admitted me through the window of the sitting-room. I laid his offence before him. I told him that I had come both as judge and executioner. The wretch sank into a chair, paralysed at the sight of my revolver. I lit the lamp, put the powder above it, and stood outside the window, ready to carry out my threat to shoot him should he try to leave the room. In five minutes he died. My God! how he died! But my heart was flint, for he endured nothing which my innocent darling had not felt before him. There is my story, Mr. Holmes. Perhaps, if you loved a woman, you would have done as much yourself. At any rate, I am in your hands. You can take what steps you like. As I have already said, there is no man living who can fear death less than I do."

Holmes sat for some little time in silence.

"What were your plans?" he asked at last.

"I had intended to bury myself in central Africa. My work there is but half finished."

"Go and do the other half," said Holmes. "I, at least, am not prepared to prevent you."

Dr. Sterndale raised his giant figure, bowed gravely, and walked from the arbour. Holmes lit his pipe and handed me his pouch.

"Some fumes which are not poisonous would be a welcome change," said he. "I think you must agree, Watson, that it is not a case in which we are called upon to interfere. Our investigation has been independent, and our action shall be so also. You would not denounce the man?"

"Certainly not," I answered.

"I have never loved, Watson, but if I did and if the woman I loved had met such an end, I might act even as our lawless lion-hunter has done. Who knows? Well, Watson, I will not offend your intelligence by explaining what is obvious. The gravel upon the window-sill was, of course, the starting-point of my research. It was unlike anything in the vicarage garden. Only when my attention had been drawn to Dr. Sterndale and his cottage did I find its counterpart. The lamp shining in broad daylight and the remains of powder upon the shield were successive links in a fairly obvious chain. And now, my dear Watson, I think we may dismiss the matter from our mind and go back with a clear conscience to the study of those Chaldean roots which are surely to be traced in the Cornish branch of the great Celtic speech."

CONTENTS

❧❧❧

This collection draws from the four short story collections of Sherlock Holmes stories published from 1892 through 1917 respectively, as detailed below.

The Adventures of Sherlock Holmes: Originally published in 1892, this work is in the public domain.

The Memoirs of Sherlock Holmes: Originally published in 1894, this work is in the public domain.

The Return of Sherlock Holmes: Originally published in 1905, this work is in the public domain.

His Last Bow: Originally published in 1917, this work is in the public domain.

No copyright claim is made with respect to public domain works.

This work reflects minor editorial revisions to the original texts.

Cover design created using Canva.com and reproduced pursuant to its free media license agreement.

THE BEST OF SHERLOCK HOLMES COLLECTION

Twelve Classic Tales of Britain's Greatest Fictional Detective

ARTHUR CONAN DOYLE

What was Elkanah's other wife's name (v. 2)?

Based on what you've read, how would you describe Peninnah? Be honest!

What specific thing did Hannah want that Peninnah had?

What do you think Hannah was thinking and feeling about her situation? About Peninnah? About her husband? About God?

⌘ YOUR TURN ⌘

So far, how can you relate to what Hannah was going through? Have you ever had a difficult person in your life? Have they ever had something you wanted but couldn't have? Journal your answer.

All of us go through hard times. No matter what school you go to or what family you were born into, you will always encounter difficult people in your life. Relationships can be the most amazing treasures, but they can also be the root of our greatest pain. Sometimes they can cause so much stress that, like Hannah, we don't even want to eat. (But don't worry—we'll learn that Hannah starts eating again soon!)

A Bit Misunderstood

So far I think this story is pretty interesting. How about you? Are you relating to Hannah? You probably don't want to be pregnant. It'll be a long, long time before you think about having children. Although your situation isn't *exactly* like Hannah's, you still have a lot in common with her. Think about the things that are important to you now: the things that make you happy, the things that make you sad, and the things you want that other girls have. We might not be able to directly relate to the specifics of Hannah's life, but we can relate to her feelings.

Based on our earlier reading, who was Eli? (See v. 9.)
☐ The priest
☐ Her husband
☐ Peninnah's son
☐ Her brother

In verse 9, where was Hannah?
☐ Her house
☐ Peninnah's house
☐ The store
☐ The Lord's temple

Why do you think Hannah chose to go there? What was so significant about that place?

Okay, let's keep reading! **Take a look at 1 Samuel 1:12-16.**

What was Hannah doing that Eli the priest misunderstood?

How do you think Hannah felt in being accused by Eli?

Wow. There's a lot going on in this story so far. Struggling relationships. Multiple wives. A priest with false accusations. A woman who desperately wants a child but can't have one. A nasty woman named Peninnah who is a mean girl at heart. Does this sound anything like real life? Even though our culture is quite different from the one that Hannah lived in, I think we can still relate to a lot of what was happening to her. Think about the last chick flick you saw. Chance are, a thread of Hannah's story runs through it. Watch any TV show that features two women and you'll see the conflict. (You've probably experienced it yourself!) Pick up the paper or a magazine, and the advice columns probably touch these very topics from time to time. Misunderstanding, jealousy, girls fighting over a guy—it's the stuff of life today.

⌒ Your Turn ⌒

Have you ever been misunderstood before? We'll talk a lot more about this in chapter five, but for now, write about a really painful time when you were misunderstood.

So far, what connects you most to Hannah's character? How are you most like her?

Some Good News

Have you noticed Hannah's prayer life yet? One of the things that encourages me most about Hannah is her willingness to go to God in difficult times. As we've read, Hannah had a lot of pain in her life. She longed for a child but couldn't have one. Her husband was also married to another woman who happened to be a nightmare of a person. And even when Hannah wanted to escape to the LORD's temple to find encouragement, peace, and hope, Eli the priest—a man who was supposed to be a representative of God—accused her of being drunk! Yet, in all of that mess, Hannah still chose to turn to God in honesty and vulnerability.

Hannah's prayers are described in 1 Samuel 1:10-16. What about her prayers touch your heart the most?

We're about to get to the really good part. **Read 1 Samuel 1:17-20.**

I'm so happy to see Eli make a turnaround. Although he jumped to wrong conclusions about Hannah, he was willing to listen in order to get to the truth. How surprised Hannah must have been when Eli blessed her with the words, "May the God of Israel grant the petition you've requested from Him." Can you imagine what she must have been feeling? Thinking? After all she had been through—the years of hoping, praying, heartache, disappointment, and taunting—the cry of her heart had been heard. God had answered.

Sometimes I overlook the power of prayer. And just as often I can forget to be personal in my prayers. One thing I especially appreciate about my mom is her passion for prayer. She loves asking God for everything, from little things to big things. For instance, when my brother was young, he wanted tickets to an NBA basketball game. My mom told him to pray about it, and the next day someone offered two tickets to him and my dad! Even though that happened a long time ago, my brother always remembers that experience as a special answer to prayer.

In all of that mess, Hannah still chose to turn to God in honesty and vulnerability.

Please hear this: I'm not saying that God is like a genie in a magic lamp who simply grants our every request upon command—that distorts the point of prayer. But I do believe God cares about the desires of our hearts (check out Psalm 37:4 for proof!), and He wants us to be honest and real with Him in our prayers. Sometimes He will give us what we ask of Him, and other times He asks us to wait. Sometimes He says no because He knows it's not the best thing for us. Those are the hard times to accept. Regardless of what happens, you can know that God is good and wants good things for you.

∽ YOUR TURN ∾

Are you encouraged by how the story ends—that God gave Hannah a child after years of praying, hoping, longing, and waiting? Explain.

Losing Your Life

In a way, this story would make a great movie or novel. The elements are there—the hero (God), the main character (Hannah), the villain (Peninnah) the supporting roles (Eli and Elkanah). You can sense Hannah's desperation to have a son, the drama of her journey, and the "perfect ending" when she finally received what her heart longed for.

Name one of your favorite movies that contains some of the same elements as Hannah's story.

I appreciate that the Bible includes these real-life accounts for us to draw encouragement and strength from. It gives depth and strength to our faith when we see how God has worked in the lives of people who are a lot like us. But since the Bible is so realistic—and not a romantic comedy produced in Hollywood—we cannot ignore the more difficult elements of Hannah's life. Yes, she finally got her one wish, but she also faced great sacrifice in order to keep her vow to God. Intrigued yet? Good.

Read 1 Samuel 1:21-28.

My heart already aches for Hannah. It's hard to want something so desperately, only to give it up again when you finally receive what you wanted. And that's what happened to Hannah. She made a vow to God to give Samuel to Him in service. When the time came, she kept her vow, even though it must have broken her heart all over again.

> Since the Bible is so realistic, we cannot ignore the more difficult elements of Hannah's life.

A few years ago I really needed money to pay some bills. I was so excited when I got an email from a guy who wanted to hire me to come to an event and sing. He agreed to pay me a lot of money for this event. I was so happy to have a little money in the bank—finally. A couple of days after we agreed on the date, I got another email saying he was canceling. I think I was more heartbroken than before I got the job in the first place.

ᨑ YOUR TURN ᨑ

Have you ever wanted something, got it, and then lost it again? What was it? How did you feel in losing it?

The amazing thing about Hannah is that I don't think she viewed having to give up Samuel as a loss. Even though she would be away from him for most of his life, I think she understood something we all need to learn.

Read Matthew 16:24-25. In the space below, write out verse 25.

This verse almost sounds like a riddle doesn't it? It can be a bit confusing, but it's very important. In fact, these words are written in every one of the Gospels (Matthew, Mark, Luke, and John). It means that if we try to be our own boss and live by our own selfish choices and not God's, our lives will ultimately be lost. We won't be at peace or have true joy—things our heart needs no matter our age, gender, or situation in life. We won't be fulfilled in the depths of our souls. But, if we choose God's way and surrender our lives to Him and let Him lead us, we will find the most amazing life we could ever have. For a little more clarity, here's how *The Message* explains it:

> Then Jesus went to work on his disciples. "Anyone who intends to come with me has to let me lead. You're not in the driver's seat; I am. Don't run from suffering; embrace it. Follow me and I'll show you how. Self-help is no help at all. Self-sacrifice is the way, my way, to finding yourself, your true self. What kind of deal is it to get everything you want but lose yourself? What could you ever trade your soul for?" —Matthew 16:24-26

ᔕᕽ Your Turn ᕽᔕ

Describe a time when you gave up something and actually gained from your loss.

Think of something you need to do that goes against your own desires and selfishness. Maybe God has been speaking to you about something He wants you to do—like talk to your friend about her eating disorder or her partying lifestyle—but you've been putting it off because you don't want to make the sacrifice. Write a way you could "lose" your life like Hannah did.

Hannah understood that God was in charge of her life. If it was up to her, she probably would have chosen for Samuel to be near her for the rest of his life, not for him to live with Eli at the temple. But she knew that God had a bigger plan for Samuel. Even though it was painful to let go of something she loved dearly, she trusted that God would bless her obedience and that the life of faith and obedience was better than rebellion and disobedience. She knew that if she lost her life to His leadership and control, she would actually gain it. Pretty deep stuff, huh?

Hannah trusted that God would bless her obedience and that the life of faith and obedience was better than rebellion and disobedience.

A Little Recap

I feel like we've taken a major trip. Actually, we have. We've been through a lot with Hannah, and we're not even done. There's actually more to her story. But for now I think we have enough to process. We have seven more weeks to read about and discuss her inspiring life, so let's end this week's study with a mini recap.

☐ True ☐ False: Hannah was praying, but Eli thought she was sick with a fever.

☐ True ☐ False: Hannah took her pain to the Lord and poured out her heart to Him.

☐ True ☐ False: Even though Elkanah had another wife, he loved Hannah. (Read 1 Sam. 1:5 if you need help.)

Hannah finally got the child she always wanted and named him

_____.

    ☐ Richard
    ☐ Joseph
    ☐ Abraham
    ☐ Samuel

Hannah fulfilled her promise by giving Samuel back to _____ (1 Sam. 1:28)

    ☐ Her husband
    ☐ Peninnah
    ☐ The Lord
    ☐ Eli

Samuel was a little boy when he went to live in _____.

    ☐ A field
    ☐ The Lord's house (temple)
    ☐ The king's courts
    ☐ Heaven

I know this has been a lot of work. We've covered a lot of ground this week. Great job for sticking with it! Now you have a good working knowledge of Hannah's story. But, honestly, I'd be really disappointed if that's all we got out of the week—knowledge. The most important part about studying the Bible is allowing God to use it to change our hearts and make us more like His Son, Jesus. My prayer over the next seven weeks is that you'll allow Hannah's amazing story to change your life.

∽ YOUR TURN ∾

What's the most meaningful thing you learned this week? What did God show you about Himself and your relationship with Him?

What's one thing you're really struggling with?

CHAPTER 2

Just Go Away!

YOU'RE HANGING OUT WITH A GROUP of friends when in walks the guy you really like. He just so happens to sit down next to you, and you start talking. You can hardly believe it. You're hoping your hair looks good and that there's nothing in your teeth. You're trying not to say anything too dumb. So far, so good. He seems to be enjoying your company, and conversation is going smoothly. That is, until another girl (whom you've never liked) wedges herself in between the two of you and starts dominating the conversation. Everything about her says *Look at me!* She starts flirting and making jokes, some of which are at your expense. Cute Guy thinks she's funny and starts focusing his attention on her. Inside you are fuming. Not only is your big chance being hijacked, but you also feel humiliated in the process. Not to mention this isn't the first time this girl has stolen the attention from you. She acts like your friend one second but turns on you in the next. She's been getting under your skin for forever! If you wouldn't end up embarrassing yourself in front of everyone, you'd explode and let her know a few of your thoughts. But more than anything, you just wish she'd go away...

Or how about this one?

You just made the basketball team, and you're so excited. Not only are you on the team, but the coach says she's going to start you! You work hard in practice during preseason, but two weeks before the first game, a new girl moves to town. She's an all-star, which would be great—except she plays your position. All the other girls on the team love her. She's attractive, a strong leader, and the most athletic girl you've ever seen. It quickly becomes clear that you'll probably spend the bulk of the season warming the bench. All you can think about is the hard work you've put in and the time you've invested in your teammates. Now you feel like you're hardly needed. The coach pulls you aside and tries to tell you how important you are as a support player coming off the bench into the game. You fight back the tears. You're trying to be mature, but you really can't stand this girl. You know if she wasn't there you'd have your starting position and your friends back. All you can think about is how much you wish she'd just go away...

Do these situations sound familiar? Did you know that girl competition isn't a new concept? This problem existed a long time before you entered school. It was there well before I entered school, and that's been a while! It was even around in the Old Testament. Did you notice last week that it was a problem in Hannah's life? Let's take a closer look.

So You Want What Someone Else Has?
Read 1 Samuel 1:1-7 and look for the woman who made Hannah's life miserable.

There are a lot of really bizarre names in these few verses, so I hope you didn't get too bogged down. Those names seem foreign, but just remember that in those ancient times, names like "Mandy" or "Kaitlyn" or "Emily" would have raised some eyebrows.

Who was Hannah's rival?
- ☐ Elkanah
- ☐ Peninnah
- ☐ Zuph
- ☐ Tohu (cool name, huh?)

Who was Hannah's husband?

☐ Elkanah
☐ Eli
☐ Elihu
☐ Ezra

Who was Peninnah's husband?

☐ Elkanah
☐ Jeroham
☐ Ephraim
☐ Eli

Look back at verse two and fill in the blanks:

Peninnah had ___ _____, but Hannah was _____.

If you said Peninnah was Hannah's rival, you've got the right girl. And is it just me, or is even her name a little annoying? (Pih-niiiiiiii-nuh!) And if you picked Elkanah as Hannah and Peninnah's husband, you've got the right guy. Not only did Hannah share a husband with Peninnah (*never* a good thing), but Peninnah had children, while Hannah had none. And for a woman in the Old Testament, that was a bad, bad situation to be in.

ᔣᕽ YOUR TURN ᔣᕽ

What's something you really want that someone else has? Good looks? A glam wardrobe? A hot guy? Hannah wanted children. List your desires below.

How do you feel when you're around the person who has what you really, really, really want?

When We Hurt Others

It was hard enough that Hannah wanted children and had none while Peninnah had several. It was bad enough that Hannah had to be around Peninnah and her children, being constantly reminded of what she desperately wanted but didn't have. And if all this wasn't enough, the Bible tells us something even more painful about Hannah's story...

Look closely at 1 Samuel 1:6-7.

☐ True ☐ False: Verse six tells us that Peninnah was especially kind to Hannah because she felt so bad that Hannah couldn't have children.

Fill in the missing word from verse seven:
"**Whenever she [Hannah] went up to the LORD's house, her rival [Peninnah] _____ her.**"

Being sensitive and kind would have been the normal response, right? I mean, really, that's probably how you would have responded. At least you would have kept your mouth shut. But not Peninnah. She actually *taunted* Hannah! Perhaps she reminds you of some of the girls you try to avoid at school or youth group—girls who have things you don't and act snobby about it. Maybe she reminds you of some of the downright mean girls you know. It's possible that she might even remind you a little bit of *you*. After all, we've all been guilty of being mean.

⌁Your Turn⌁

Describe a recent time when you were really unkind to someone, either to his or her face or behind his or her back.

Make It Right

One of the wonderful things the Bible teaches is that Jesus Christ forgives us when we hurt one another. If you've asked God for forgiveness for the way you've treated someone, you can absolutely count on it. However, the Bible also says more about the subject.

Read Matthew 5:23-25.

What does Jesus tell us to do when we've hurt someone?

Why is doing that so important?

And why is that so hard for you and me to do?

Jesus was explaining to the people that before they came to worship, it was essential that they ask forgiveness from those they had wronged or hurt. Why? Because our relationship with God is hindered when we've hurt people and haven't sought forgiveness and reconciliation.

Is there anyone from whom you need to ask forgiveness? If so, write his or her name below.

Let's be honest. We've all gossiped. We've all said cruel things out of anger. We've all provoked our friends out of jealously or insecurity or just plain meanness. Because this is true, we all need to learn how to go to the people we've hurt and ask their forgiveness. It's vital in keeping our friendships healthy. It's also an important part of our relationship with God. Sometimes asking forgiveness can feel a little awkward, but it's always worth it! It takes practice, but it's one of the best things you can decide to do. You'll be amazed at what it does for you, your friendships, and your relationship with God.

Our relationship with God is hindered when we've hurt people and haven't sought forgiveness and reconciliation.

When I was growing up, my dad used to always tell us how important it was to ask forgiveness. One day I had done something really mean to my younger sister, Megan (a fairly common occurrence—I'm sure you can relate). I was feeling guilty about it but figured a little time would take care of it. But every time I thought about it, I got that sick feeling in my stomach. I knew I had to tell her I was sorry, but my pride wouldn't let me do it. All the way home from school I kept thinking to myself, *I'm going to do it now. Okay, now. No, I'll wait til we get to that red light, and then I'll do it.* But then...nothing would come out of my mouth. It was like my mouth didn't know how to form the words "I'm sorry"! Finally, when we were only a couple of turns away from our house, I mustered up the courage to say those tiny—but very powerful—words. Megan forgave me, and I was relieved.

Did you write a name down earlier of someone to whom you need to apologize? If so, spend some time praying that God would give you the courage and opportunity to make things right. It's one of the best things you can ever learn to do. Write down your prayer in the space provided below. If you're struggling with making things right, tell God why.

What's a Girl to Do?

Back to Hannah's story. If you recall, not only was she unable to have children, but her rival, Peninnah had several. That's got to hurt. And not only was Peninnah provocative and unkind, but we're about to find out something else that's rather discouraging...

According to verse seven, how long did Peninnah taunt Hannah?

☐ six months

☐ four years

☐ every year (year after year)

☐ a super long time

If you chose options three AND four, you're right. And if you're like me, your heart is breaking for Hannah. This extremely painful situation had been going on year after year!

⤫ YOUR TURN ⤬

You can probably relate to Hannah. Write about an uncomfortable or painful situation that's been going on for a very long time. It could be an unhealthy dating relationship, tension between your parents, a problem with a teacher, or even someone who taunts you. Be honest and write down how you feel about that person.

Lots of teens struggle with painful situations—dealing with people or circumstances they wish would just go away. Read the following fiction story of a girl like you who's faced her own Peninnah.

Amy's Story

I almost threw up when I saw him. I tried to stop staring and obey the nagging thoughts that bid me to return to the makeup room. It was only a half-hour until the curtain went up, but there he stood, a head and shoulders above everyone else. Looking rather put out, he waited in line at the ticket booth. I tried to bite back the hate that I knew was dangerously close to the surface. Seeing him made me want to vomit, but I could not tear my eyes away from him.

He's here...he's here...

I doubted he remembered me. The last time I was around him, I was about seven years old, and Lilly was eight. I hadn't understood then why everyone hated him. I knew that Lilly was sad, and somehow, it was his fault. I knew that she didn't talk as much, that I didn't see her at church, and that our play dates were becoming infrequent. But I didn't know what had happened. I didn't know how to fix it.

Lilly...

My thoughts flew to the girl who was still my best friend after all these years. She was still getting into costume, preparing for our high school's play. She hadn't thought he would come. Neither had anyone else. When he cut off her child support a few months before, he also cut off our hopes of his presence at the play.

I remembered being seven, and Lilly eight. She was happy once. They all were. I didn't know that things could change that fast.

I didn't know why her mother's eyes were so red. I didn't understand what had made Lilly cry so much. I tried to ask God to fix whatever was happening.

I know now that my mother was there during that awful year and a half. Some days she would hold Lilly's mother as she sobbed without stopping. Quietly my mother would rock her slowly back and forth for hours and pray to God in heaven—the only One we knew who could make any sense out of the mess. I did not recognize the dark feeling in the air when I went over to play with my best friend. I felt sad only because I felt I was losing a friend. I was neither wise, nor strong, nor selfless enough to know to help her like my mom helped her mom. To this day, I am mad at myself for what I didn't do.

Through the years, he continued to make things worse. Lilly was so young and didn't understand how to cope with the new woman and little girl in her childhood home or the worry and stress in her mother's life. She didn't understand why the new little girl got toys and clothes, while Lilly stayed in a small apartment in a scary part of town. Lilly became wary of relationships in her own quiet way, and after a while, she stopped talking about how much she hurt. But those of us who loved her knew that she didn't stop hurting. As we grew older, I saw a corner of her heart begin to harden—it was the only way to survive the disappointments, the forgotten birthdays, the cancelled trips to the zoo, and bounced child support checks. I wished that I could make it better, that I could be more than a helpless spectator. Every time he came back, I begged God, who was a million times the Father he was, to fix him and fix their family. But as I watched him leave time and again, I had to work hard to stop hating him. For those of us who love Lilly, it became a daily battle.

Eleven months before the play, she stopped talking to him. After so many years of being disappointed by a father she still yearned to trust, she couldn't take the hurt anymore. I was proud of her for holding out so long.

So when I saw him in the ticket line, I didn't know what to do. Does she know? Do I say something? If I say something, she might lose concentration on the play. If I don't say something and she sees him in the middle of the play, she'll be hurt anyway.

In the minutes before the curtain went up, those of us who loved Lilly exchanged glances. I told her boyfriend through clenched teeth.

"She knows," he said before mouthing, "I hate him, too."

I don't think the two of us had ever understood each other better.

Just before curtain, I gave Lilly a long, tight hug. Both of us tried to stop crying. We prayed frightened, watery prayers and tried to find courage. I found myself being seven again, completely unable to fix anything.

The play was spectacular. It was closing night, and the actors were at their best Lilly, who played a tragic part, was more brilliant than I'd ever seen her. Those who had seen the play before may have wondered why we refused to look toward the right half of the audience. We refused even to guess if the tall man looked proud.

After the curtain call, I searched everywhere. The makeup and green rooms were both empty, so was the catwalk. After a half hour, I saw her pacing alone. She was still in her costume, biting her nails, and trying to be brave.

I joined her at stage left, trying with all of my strength not to fail her like I did when I was seven.

"There you are. I've been looking for you."

"Here I am," she said.

And then she began to sob like she hadn't sobbed in many years. She cried and couldn't stop. Quietly, wishing I were strong and wise and selfless enough to know *what to do, I put my arms around my best friend, and we rocked back and forth as we cried. I prayed again to God in heaven the same prayer I'd prayed since I was seven years old. At that moment, it was my one and only wish.*

"Oh, Lord God, you love Lilly even more than I do. Please fix him. I can't. Please fix it. Make it better. Please fix it. Oh God, please fix it. Please."

It was the hardest prayer I'd ever prayed.

—AMY EVANS, Troutdale, Oregon

Your situation may be different, but I'm sure you can relate. Everyone faces tough times or tough people that just don't go away, no matter how much we want them to, no matter how much we pray for it. So what can you do?

Even though your Peninnah might seem like she has it all, she doesn't. No matter how confident or content a person may look on the outside, everyone has areas of struggle and dissatisfaction. No one has it all together all the time.

First, when you are faced with Peninnahs in your life, it's important to remember that even though your Peninnah might seem like she has it all, she doesn't. No matter how confident or content a person may look on the outside, everyone has areas of struggle and dissatisfaction. *No one* has it *all* together *all* the time. Second, if your Peninnah is always taunting you and is downright mean, I can promise you she's insecure. How do I know this? Because the girls who are confident in who they are in Christ don't hurt others in order to feel good. When we're at rest in the love of God, there's no reason for us to cut down others. On the other hand, when we feel insignificant or insecure, we provoke and make fun of others. So what am I saying? Your Peninnah isn't nearly as perfect as she wants you to think she is. More than anything, she needs you to love her and pray for her, even though it's the last thing you probably want to do!

Read Luke 6:27-36 and keep your personal Peninnah in mind.

What are the things we should do for our enemies, based on these verses?

List below some emotions you feel or questions you have when you think about Jesus' statements. These are tough commands to accept!

So how does this apply to you in the 21st century? In the space provided below, list some common teen girl problems in which the principles of Luke 6:27-36 would apply. A couple of examples are provided for you.

Posting suggestive pictures on a MySpace® page or Facebook® profile

Stealing a boyfriend

⤳ YOUR TURN ⤳

Now that you've been thinking about how Luke 6:27-36 can apply in the lives of teen girls, what are some specific ways that you can show love to someone who's been particularly hurtful to you? It could be inviting her to your house, sending a nice card, buying a small gift, or saying something nice. Be creative!

In light of this, why don't you spend some time praying specifically for the person who's been troubling you? It might be really hard at first, but God has a way of turning our hurt and anger into tender spots for those who have wounded us. Pray that God changes her heart. Pray that the hurts in his own life that cause him to be unkind would be healed. Pray that she would no longer feel pleasure from hurting others. Pray for his home life. You might even want to put yourself in that person's shoes and think about what he or she really needs. Then pray for those specific things. These are just some suggestions, so feel free to pray what's on your heart.

> If you are being abused by a teacher, parent, boyfriend, or anyone else, the Bible is not telling you to take the abuse. It is not telling you to bless those people and stay in the situation.

Before we move on, I want to make an important point: this passage is not talking about living in or accepting abusive situations. If you are being abused by a teacher, parent, boyfriend, or anyone else, the Bible is not telling you to take the abuse. It is not telling you to bless those people and stay in the situation. If you are experiencing abuse (mental, physical, emotional, or sexual), go to a trusted adult for help to get out of that situation immediately. If you suspect that someone is being abused, it's important that you speak to an adult as well. They will be able to help you take the steps necessary to help your friend.

Go to God

Sometimes we offer love to our enemies, and they still don't change. Sometimes we can do kind things for them, and for whatever reason, they continue to hurt us. Sometimes we do everything God has asked us to do, and we still find ourselves around that one person that we wish would just go away. So what do we do? When Hannah just couldn't take it any more, she went to God. And you can too! (We'll talk more about Hannah's prayer later.)

I love the Bible for many reasons, especially because it's so practical to my life every day. The people who wrote Scripture were just like you and me. They had sandals instead of high heels, camels for cars, and tunics for skirts, but their hearts were the same! They had all the same longings and hurts and desires and joys that you have.

Check out Psalm 31:9-24. If you're in a place where people won't think you're a little crazy, read all the verses out loud. Say them as if you're praying to God. Then, answer the following questions:

What were the most meaningful verses to you? Why?

How does this passage challenge the way you deal with the people who are causing you pain?

∽ YOUR TURN ∽

What's the most meaningful thing you learned this week? What did God show you about Himself and your relationship with Him?

What's one thing you're really struggling with?

I Don't Understand

WHEN I WAS IN HIGH SCHOOL, I played basketball. While my cheerleader friends were working on back tucks and dance moves, I was running suicides and doing defensive slides. If you were looking for me, you could always find me in the gym practicing my skills with a basketball. When the time came for me to choose a college, the best thing I could have hoped for happened. I was offered a full scholarship to play basketball at a school in South Carolina. The coach brought me down to visit, and I instantly fell in love. I knew it was the place for me!

After months of planning for college in South Carolina, you can imagine how disappointed I was when the coach called to tell me the whole thing was off. I couldn't believe it! I didn't understand how she could do this to me. She explained that some players had gotten hurt. She needed to use my scholarship money to replace them. I was devastated, hurt, and angry. I didn't know what to do without basketball. All my friends were going away to play college ball. *Why is God doing this to me?*, I thought.

I ended up staying home for a few years and commuting to a local university. It was hard at first, but gradually it got better. God brought other amazing things into my life. But more importantly, I began to understand something about God's sovereignty. *God's what?* God's sovereignty—it sounds like a big, churchy, "adult" word, I know. But here's a *very* simple definition: It means that God is in control. He is all-powerful. He doesn't need any help. He rules. He's in charge of everything. Yes, everything. God rules and works things out based on His purposes, even though some events and people may challenge or contradict Him. God is in control. We are not.

Understanding God's sovereignty is one of the most important things about God we can learn—and it's also one of the hardest things to accept sometimes. It's also one of the most important things Hannah learned. Let's keep reading...

Refresh your memory by reading 1 Samuel 1:1-7 again. If you want, choose a different translation of the Bible. It'll give you a different perspective on the story.

Who was responsible for closing Hannah's womb?
- ☐ The annoying Peninnah
- ☐ Elkanah
- ☐ God
- ☐ It was an accident

How do you feel knowing that God was the One who closed Hannah's womb and kept her from getting pregnant? What questions does it raise in your mind?

Now read verse 8. List some of the ways you can tell Hannah was really upset.

God's in Control!

All of us have gone through situations we didn't understand. Maybe you didn't get into a school you hoped you would. Or maybe you got cut from the soccer team. Perhaps your parents went through a divorce, your boyfriend broke up with you, or you crashed your car. When we think of a loving God, sometimes it's hard to understand why He doesn't always protect us from tough situations—situations that spark confusion, doubt, and even anger. It's also hard to understand why He sometimes doesn't give us the things we want so badly, like a new friend, more money, someone to go to the prom with, healing from a disease, or keeping our parents together.

> Understanding God's sovereignty is one of the most important things about God we can learn—but it's also one of the hardest things to accept sometimes.

I'm sure Hannah had similar questions about God's love and His sovereignty. It sounds so harsh to accept that God kept Hannah from having children, especially since she wanted them so badly. If you didn't take time to read the whole story, you might even infer that God wasn't very loving toward Hannah. He didn't seem very loving when I didn't get my basketball scholarship. Have you ever felt the same way?

༄ Your Turn ༄

Is there something you really wanted, but God chose not to give it to you? It could be a material possession, a change in circumstance, or even a person. Write about it.

Remember reading about God's sovereignty? Write down your own definition. How can you apply your understanding of God's sovereignty to the situation you wrote about in the previous question?

God is in control. He does whatever pleases Him. And sometimes what pleases Him is hard for us to understand. But—and this is an important "but"—we can be sure that He never does anything that isn't for our good! Let's read that one again—*God never does anything that isn't for our good.*

Read Psalm 84:11. Paraphrase this verse in your own words. How does this help you understand God's sovereignty?

Read Isaiah 55:9. Why do you think it's hard for us to understand God's ways sometimes?

After reading these verses, do you feel better about God's sovereignty? I grew up in a school that explained God's sovereignty in a way that scared me to death. I got this image of God as a stern policeman who did whatever He wanted just because He could. I now understand that, yes, God is in control, but His control is always expressed out of His love for us, not out of spite, bitterness, or for the sake of power. His ways are always best and for our good—even when we don't understand, even when our heart breaks, and even when life looks out of control.

His ways are always best and for our good—even when we don't understand, even when our heart breaks, and even when life looks out of control.

I'm one of those people who's always trying to fix the world around me. I struggle with worrying and carrying too much responsibility. I concern myself with situations I can't control. But understanding God's sovereignty has helped me. As my friends would say, God's helped me to chill out a little. The more I realize He's in control, the more I can relax. It's in His hands, not mine.

Do you see God's closing of Hannah's womb any differently now? I do. Even though Hannah was in a difficult situation, God loved her and His ways were higher than hers. He doesn't withhold good things from us forever, even when it seems like He is or we don't understand what He is doing. It's good to know we can always trust Him. That's what Hannah chose to do in her painful and confusing situation. And that's what we need to do in ours.

Just because we trust God doesn't mean our problems disappear. We still go through hard times while we trust Him. But 1 Peter 5:7 tells us to do something that will help. What does it say to do?

∽ Your Turn ∾

Remember the thing you really wanted, but God chose not to give you (at least not yet)? Now that you understand a little about God's sovereignty, how will you trust Him better with it? Write out a prayer of commitment to trust God in this situation, even though you can't see what He's doing in the midst of it.

A Bigger Plan

Have you ever watched those game shows in which you have to give up something good for the possibility of getting something better—the contests in which you must either walk away with a certain prize, or give it up for a chance to win something bigger? Sometimes the players lose big, and sometimes they win big. Either way, those shows always make me nervous.

I'm so glad that following God isn't like that. God doesn't leave us guessing. But sometimes God does ask us to give up a smaller dream for a bigger one. He asks us to trust Him with the things we don't understand so that He can do something even better. Remember, His ways are higher than our ways. Sometimes those bigger plans are easy to follow. Other times, following God's plans is tough. Hear one story of a girl who chose to trust Him even when it was tough.

Hannah's Story

THE SUMMER DIDN'T GO AS I HAD PLANNED. *I hadn't gotten out of bed in over a month. I hadn't even gotten up to take a shower. It had been even longer since I had eaten. My body was shutting down from a lousy combination of cancer and chemotherapy. The doctors sedated me for a number of reasons, but the result was that I was only coherent for a little while during those days.*

It had started out to be a normal teenage summer—a really good summer. It was the summer before my senior year, and I was looking forward to doing a lot of great things: going on a choir tour in Florida, a mission trip to Kentucky, a week in Colorado with YoungLife, and just hanging out with my friends like most students do.

But in March, I noticed a knot around where my appendix is. I ignored it for a while and then finally saw a couple of doctors who told me it was just an infected lymph node. I continued on with my busy life and schedule, trying to forget about the increasing size and occasional pain. In May, I ended up in the emergency room because I was in so much pain. After lots of blood tests and CAT scans through the night, my doctor told me that it looked like I had a tumor on my right ovary. He referred me to another doctor who decided to do surgery the next day. After the surgery my doctor told me that it wasn't my ovary. I had a malignant tumor, and he was able to remove about 90-95 percent of it. My fun summer was over just as it was getting started.

All of this was a pretty heavy reality, but I was very fortunate to have a solid foundation that was the rock that kept me steady. Both of my parents are Christians and have been sharing God's love with me since the day I was born. I accepted Christ into my life when I was six years old at a Backyard Bible Club. Then when I was eleven years old, I prayed and rededicated my life to Christ at a Fellowship of Christian Athletes rally. Since then God has continued to work in my life in so many different ways.

I know without a shadow of a doubt that if I didn't have Jesus Christ in my life, I would not be able to live with the overwhelming amount of peace, strength, and even joy that I have felt during this journey. In June, that painful journey continued, and I was sent to a special hospital in Houston, Texas, that specialized in treating cancer patients. I got there as things were starting to get pretty bad for me. I ended up spending what was supposed to be my fun summer in the hospital fighting this disease that was starting to take over my body.

<blockquote>
I know that God has a plan for my life.
As I go through this trial, I know that even this
sickness is all part of His good and perfect will.
I have put all of my trust in Jesus Christ.
</blockquote>

My condition continued to get worse, not better. The cancer moved quickly and aggressively. It robbed me of many things that I had previously taken for granted—like being able to eat or get out of bed and look out the window. It took me halfway across the country to a place far away from my two brothers and all of my friends that I love so much. But no matter what it stripped me of, the cancer could not take away my deep faith in Jesus Christ. In fact, as the cancer grew, so did my faith and the realization of how God works in our lives even when everything else around us seems to be slipping away.

In July, I was at my lowest point. The doctors had given up. They told my parents that there wasn't anything more they could do to help me. I was in bad shape. I couldn't even breathe on my own without the help of a ventilator. They said my body might not be able to hold up or fight much longer. But the doctors didn't know how many people were praying for me and that God was hearing and answering their prayers.

To all of the doctors' great amazement, my body started to get stronger. Each new day was a little better than the one before, and today I'm still getting better!

I know that God has a plan for my life. As I go through this trial, I know that even this sickness is all part of His good and perfect will. I have put all of my trust in Jesus Christ.

This summer was not what I expected. I may have lost out on the plans I had with my friends, but I gained some things that can never be taken away. I gained a whole new understanding of God's love and His perfect will for my life. While I *was in that hospital bed, I got to know God at a deeper level and learned how to depend on Him more. I've discovered that life may not always be what I expect it to be. But I also learned that no matter how tough the circumstances are, God will always be there and will always provide the strength I need.*

Maybe your life isn't going the way you expected. You can be sure that God will be there with you, and you can depend on Him. Put your trust in Him, and He will provide what you need for the journey—I know that to be true!

—HANNAH SOBESKI, Spartanburg, South Carolina

EDITOR'S NOTE: *On November 9, 2006, Hannah Sobeski passed away. She had written this story just months before she died. To read more about the legacy Hannah left behind, go to www.hannahshopeministries.org.*

When you read Hannah's story above, what questions do you have for God? Don't worry—God can handle your questions!

How do you feel when you read a story like the one above?

How do you think you would have responded if you had to face cancer and the possibility of death? What do you think you would feel and think?

When you talk with Hannah's parents, siblings, extended family, or friends, you don't hear anger, frustration, or doubt in their hearts. You hear trust—trust that even though they don't understand God's ways, they can still put their hope in Him.

Another person in the Bible had to trust God a lot like Hannah did. His name is Joseph, and I think you'll like his story. Joseph was one of twelve sons. The Bible tells us that he was his daddy's favorite. (My sisters and I used to tell our baby brother that he was our favorite brother, but he was also our only brother!) Anyhow, the other eleven brothers became very jealous of Joseph because he was always getting special treatment—like being a teacher's pet. His dad even made him a special coat. Joseph had amazing dreams from God, dreams in which he ruled over his brothers. After a while his brothers got so jealous (and tired of hearing Joseph's dreams) that they decided they would just get rid of him.

What the brothers did to Joseph to harm him, God made into something good. God was in control, even when others wanted to hurt Joseph.

Joseph's brothers decided they would throw him into a pit. After that, they sold him to some travelers as a slave. Then they went back to their dad and told him that an animal killed Joseph. Can you imagine being that jealous of someone? In the meantime, Joseph was taken to Egypt where he went through a lot of other hard stuff. (Check out Genesis 39-44 for the whole story. It reads like a story line from a drama on TV!) After many years though, he was promoted to the second highest position in all of Egypt.

While Joseph was ruling in Egypt, God told him that there was going to be a famine in the land and the shortage of food would affect Egypt and the surrounding nations. God also told Joseph to store lots of food ahead of time so the nation would be prepared for the famine. When that awful time happened, people started coming to Egypt from other countries looking for food. If you can believe it, Joseph's brothers came in need of food, but they didn't recognize their little brother after all these years. They had no idea that the boy they had sold into slavery would now decide whether they would get food!

Now read Genesis 45:1-8.

How did Joseph respond to his brothers?

How do you think you would have responded?

According to verses 5-7, why wasn't Joseph angry with his brothers?

From Joseph's perspective, who sent Joseph to Egypt?

Earlier in the story, the Bible tells us that Joseph's brothers were the ones who sent him to Egypt. But here it tells us that God was the One who sent him. Is anyone else confused?

Read Genesis 50:20. Maybe it will clear things up a bit.

What did the brothers want for Joseph?

What did God want for Joseph?

You see? It's all about God's sovereignty. What the brothers did to Joseph to harm him, God made into something good. God was in control, even when others wanted to hurt Joseph. What had seemed like a series of horrific events actually resulted in God using Joseph to save thousands of people from famine, including his own family.

God is good and what He does is good.
You can trust Him for that.

There's another verse in the New Testament that talks about the same thing. Romans 8:28 says, "We know that all things work together for the good of those who love God: those who are called according to His purpose." I can't give you answers about why God chooses to act in some situations but not others, like why some people are healed and others aren't. I can't tell you why He allows some of His followers to suffer (like so many Christians in other countries) while some Christians live in peace and comfort. I can't tell you how He'll work out the tough situations you face now. But I can tell you that God is good and what He does is good. You can trust Him for that.

A Big God

If I were Hannah, Peninnah would have driven me crazy. It would've been bad enough that she had everything I wanted, but she was mean about it! I would have been tempted to be like Joseph's brothers and sell her to some traveling salesmen. (Okay, that might be taking it a little too far, but you get my point.) It's hard when people have what we want and are mean about it on top of it. It's hard to suffer through hard times without understanding why it's happening to you. One of the things that I believe helped Hannah so much was her vision of how big and amazing God is. Even though Peninnah had what she wanted, ultimately Hannah knew that God had everything she needed.

Read Psalm 62:1-12.

According to the first verse, where did the psalmist's rest and salvation come from?

What names did David call God that give us clues about David's faith in God? Which name is most significant to you? Why?

Are you looking to someone or something (other than God) to be your salvation, strong place, or rest? If so, explain.

My favorite part of verse 12 says, "...faithful love belongs to You, LORD." Remember, God's sovereignty is always balanced with His faithful love. When you're going through difficult times, it's hard to remember that His love won't fail. He hasn't left you alone to suffer. He hasn't forgotten you. God's love is faithful.

Before we end the chapter, here's a little recap to jog your memory. First, God is sovereign. He is in control—even when your life seems to be spinning out of control! We also know that He acts out of love. Sometimes His love shows itself in ways that are painful or hard for us to understand, but we know we can trust Him. We can trust that God's ways are higher than ours. He sees things that we can't see and knows things we can't understand. Believing that God is in control also means we can relax. We don't need to take on every burden and weight because God is all-powerful and wants us to cast our worry on Him. Lastly, God alone is our rock, salvation, and place of rest. We can come to Him with anything and know He cares for and loves us.

Wow. What an amazing week of truth and encouragement. Keep up the good work!

ᑫᑐ YOUR TURN ᑭᑐ

What's the most meaningful thing you learned this week? What did God show you about Himself and your relationship with Him?

What's one thing you're really struggling with?

It's Not Fair

I MET MY FRIEND KIM IN ELEMENTARY SCHOOL and stayed friends with her all the way through high school. We played on sports teams together and carpooled back and forth to school a lot. One of my first memories of Kim was in the lunch line where she would steal french fries from other containers and put them in her own. I know, a french fry here or there doesn't seem like too big of a deal. But when we got to junior high, she began cheating on tests. By the time we were in high school, she lied to the coach about her time in the 600-yard dash because she wanted a starting position on the team. After college, I ran into her at a party where she had been drinking heavily. I could see the years of bad choices were wearing on her.

Although I don't see her often, I love Kim and would do anything for her. She's very funny and has some qualities I really enjoy. My prayer for her is that she would understand how much God loves her and that she would know God the way that Hannah did, the way that you and I are learning about. But I didn't always feel this way about Kim. When I was younger, it used to frustrate me to see her cheat, steal, and lie to get ahead. It didn't seem fair. I couldn't understand why doing the wrong thing always seemed to work out for her. She would get A's on the tests she cheated on, and she had lots of friends who liked her edgy style. She was super popular. Sometimes I wondered if doing the right thing was getting me anywhere.

ᝄ Your Turn ᝄ

Have you ever known someone who seemed to always get ahead by doing what was wrong? If so, write about how it made you feel.

Believe it or not, Hannah probably felt the same way I did being around Kim, the same way you have felt when others don't choose to follow God and still get everything they want. Even though she lived thousands of years ago, Hannah faced a similar struggle.

Take another look at 1 Samuel 1:2,6-7. (I know we've looked at these verses a lot, but there's so much here!) Describe why it must have been hard for Hannah to see Peninnah having so many children.

We've talked about how hard it must have been for Hannah to be around Peninnah because Peninnah had children—the very thing that Hannah wanted desperately. But there's more. Instead of being kind to Hannah and encouraging her, Peninnah provoked her. Peninnah kept making fun of Hannah for being barren until Hannah wept and wouldn't eat. Over and over, the taunting didn't stop until Hannah hit her breaking point. And did you notice *when* Peninnah provoked Hannah? When Hannah went to be with God—when she went to find solace in the One who could bring her peace. Talk about a mean girl.

Peninnah's actions reveal a lot about her character. She wasn't a godly woman. So not only did Hannah have to contend with a woman who had what she wanted, but she also had to wrestle with understanding why God would allow this mean woman to have children. Hannah was a faithful follower of God and couldn't have children, but evil Peninnah could. It just wasn't fair.

CHAPTER 4

It's Not Always As It Seems

It's easy to get mad and frustrated at people who get ahead by doing wrong, especially in today's world when it seems like evil wins all the time. And if you're like me, you've gotten really jealous of them before. You might have even gotten mad at God or your parents for challenging you to do what was right, especially when it didn't seem to be getting you anywhere.

> It's easy to get mad and frustrated at people who get ahead by doing wrong, especially in today's world when it seems like evil wins all the time.

The Apostle Paul, the writer of Galatians, has something to say to us girls who have felt jealous of the "bad girls" who prosper. He encourages those of us who have ever wondered whether following God was worth it when everyone else seems better off. Actually, he tells us three pretty amazing secrets.

Read Galatians 6:7-9 slowly and answer the following questions.
We reap what we _____.
God cannot be _____.
- ☐ blamed
- ☐ mocked
- ☐ made fun of

☐ True ☐ False. If we sow to sin, we will reap really good things.

What Paul is describing here is called "the law of the harvest." It contains the three secrets I mentioned. The first secret is simply this:

Secret #1—You reap what you sow.

Here's a quick agriculture lesson for you city girls: sowing means to plant seed in the ground. Reaping means to gather the crop that has

47

grown from the seed. Of course, Paul wasn't talking about literal seeds and literal crops. He was creating a metaphor. If you plant a watermelon seed, you'll get watermelons. If you plant tomato seeds, you'll get tomatoes. You get the point!

If you sow tomatoes, you're not going to get bananas. It's the same way in our lives. If a girl plants the seeds of meanness, lying, cheating, drinking, sex, or stealing in her life, she will not—cannot—reap good things from that, not anymore than a pumpkin seed will grow into a potato. But the reverse is true, too. If you plant the seeds of peace, kindness, love, encouragement, and honesty (even on tests!), you will absolutely reap blessings and good things from God.

◦◦ Your Turn ◦◦

How have you seen Secret #1 (you reap what you sow) come true in your own life? What bad things have you planted that resulted in bad consequences? What good things have you planted that resulted in good consequences?

How does Secret #1 (you reap what you sow) help you think differently about people who prosper from doing wrong?

It Takes Time

Remember that Paul shared three secrets in Galatians 6:7-9? Not only did he tell us that we reap what we sow, but he tips us off to two more secrets that are a little more subtle.

Time for another agriculture lesson. I talked with a friend whose parents are farmers in Missouri. They are experts in cotton and corn. She told me that cotton is planted in late April to mid-May and isn't harvested until late September and into October (harvesting takes a long time!) Corn is planted in March and isn't harvested until August. So what does this have to do with our study? It's the second secret:

Secret #2—The harvest takes time.

Look back at Galatians 6:9.

Keeping the second secret in mind, why do you think Paul tells us not to get tired of doing good?

When does he say we'll reap our harvest?

I think Paul encouraged us to keep doing good because he understood how easy it is to give up. In fact, the phrase "get tired" in verse 9 actually means "to give in to trouble; to become exasperated by difficulty; to be defeated in spirit, discouraged, or faint-hearted; to despair or lose heart."[1] He used some strong words, didn't he? Why? Because he was being truthful about living in this world. It's tough to keep doing good. It's easier to give into trouble than to fight against it. It's easy to get overwhelmed by difficulty, to get discouraged, and to lose heart. But Paul also knew that in time, the reward would come. And the reward would be worth the struggle.

Sometimes the people who make bad choices, like my friend Kim, don't experience the consequences of those decisions until much later. They succeed for a time, but not for long. Don't give up in doing good! God will not forget your love and faithfulness to Him. He promises to bless us in ways that we can't even imagine—if we don't give up.

It May Be Fun, BUT...

When I was growing up, some people told me that sinning or doing the "wrong" thing wasn't any fun. Meanwhile, my friends who were partying and drinking on the weekends were having lots of fun. I wasn't sure what to believe. I wanted to trust that I was doing the right thing by choosing to follow God, but it sure looked like I was missing out on a lot of fun.

Read Hebrews 11:24-25. Then write down below what these verses tell you about sin.

These verses refer to the Old Testament character Moses. If you'll remember, Moses was raised in the house of Pharaoh (Ex. 2) even though he was an Israelite—a group of people living as slaves. Later on, God called him to lead the Israelites away from Pharaoh and into freedom. He could have said no and gone back to being known as a child of the Pharaoh. But he didn't. He chose to identify himself as a child of God instead. He chose to follow God because sinning always ends badly.

See! We're back to this timing thing again. Yes, sin can be fun. But only for a time. And then we reap a harvest that is no fun at all. The law still applies—the consequences of good or bad choices may take time, but they *will* happen.

Bigger is NOT Always Better

For the third law of the harvest, let's look at an Old Testament verse.

Read Hosea 8:7 and summarize the verse in your own words.

Hosea was a prophet who married a prostitute. Why? To show the people that they were being unfaithful to God like Hosea's wife was being unfaithful to him. (It's actually a GREAT story of God's love for us. Check it out sometime.) Hosea wanted the people to understand that their efforts at finding happiness outside of God would be impossible—and would have devastating effects. He understood the third secret:

Secret #3—You always reap more than you sow.

Hosea told the people that they were sowing wind but would end up with a whirlwind. (A whirlwind is bigger than a gust of wind). Think about it in agricultural terms again: an apple and an apple tree are much larger than an apple seed. A pumpkin seed is small compared to the pumpkin. Get the point? You're always going to reap more than you sow—whether it's good or bad.

Let's be honest. Sin can be fun—otherwise we wouldn't be tempted to do it all the time! But here's the deal: sin always comes with an expensive price tag. Just ask the recovering alcoholic, the man on death row, or the teenage mother struggling to live on a minimum-wage income. Remember, whatever we sow, we reap. And we'll reap more than we sow. Here's a saying to remember: *sin will take you further than you want to go, keep you longer than you want to stay, and cost you more than you want to pay.* Don't be deceived into thinking that you can do whatever you want without any consequences down the road. While it may not seem like the friends you have are reaping any negative consequences for drinking, lying, cheating, or sexual activity, don't buy the lie. Sin always carries a high price tag, even if you can't see it at the time. Don't throw down any seeds that might be fun for a while but will bring you a lot of pain later. It's just not worth it.

A God Who Sees

As we close out the chapter, let's look back at Hannah's life for a minute. Read 1 Samuel 2:3 and summarize the warning there.

We'll examine this prayer later in the book, but I want you to see a sneak peek now. I don't know if Hannah was thinking about Peninnah when she said this, but I'm sure that her difficult experiences with Peninnah were at least in the back of her mind. Our takeaway truth from this verse is simple: We can be certain that God knows and weighs every deed. When we see people "secretly" getting away with evil, we can be sure God always sees. We can be sure that a whirlwind is on its way. It might not come for a while, but it will come. Evil will not win in the end.

There's one thing to be very careful about, though. It's important for you and me not to have an arrogant, smug, or satisfied attitude when people start reaping the consequences of their sin. Our job is not to judge—only God can do that because only He is perfect. Our job is to be people of mercy and love because that is how God has treated us. But, it is encouraging for us to know that the wicked never truly are prospering, even though it might look like it for a time. It's good to know that our faithfulness to God is worth it in the end.

∽ YOUR TURN ∽

What's the most meaningful thing you learned this week? What did God show you about Himself and your relationship with Him?

What's one thing you're really struggling with?

1. Spiros Zodhiates, ed., *Hebrew—Greek Key Study Bible* (Chattanooga: AMG Publishers, 1996), 1613.

CHAPTER 5

I've Got Something To Say

I DON'T MEAN TO USE STEREOTYPES, but we girls can *talk*. There are three girls in my family and one boy. Whenever I call my brother, he answers mostly in one-word replies—no sentences necessary. He says more in person, but he's just not a huge talker. Girls, on the other hand, can chat it up about everything from boys to movies to music to even sports (yes, there are some of us girls who can talk football). And when we get in groups? Forget about it. It's a talkfest. In fact, one of my favorite things to do in the whole world is sit down with a friend or two over dinner and talk. I love sharing back and forth, hearing and being heard by people who care about me. Though we can overdo it at times—I know I can—there's great value in talking.

It's possible that you're reading this and cannot relate. You might be a truly amazing girl who also happens to be on the quiet side. You like hanging out with your friends, but you like to listen rather than gab. Not to worry. You still have that "girl gene" that desires relationship. You appreciate communication and the need to express yourself, even if it's less than others. God wired us this way. We girls are all in this together—talkative or not.

But here's a great question: how often do we find ourselves talking to God? How much do we desire to be in relationship with Him? How much do we tell Him? How much do we listen? In today's study, we'll discover that Hannah learned the value in a good dialogue with God.

Read 1 Samuel 1:9-20.

List all the ways these verses describe Hannah praying to the Lord. Include as many adjectives and details as you can.

What detail is the most dramatic or surprising to you and why?

What vow did Hannah made?

How did Hannah respond to Eli's accusation?

☐ True or ☐ False: Eli didn't believe Hannah's explanation and threw her out of the temple.

What can you learn from Hannah's calm and respectful response to Eli's false accusation?

〜 YOUR TURN 〜

Have you ever made a promise to God? If so, what was it? Have you fulfilled that promise yet? Why or why not?

Don't Think I'm Crazy!

I hate to be misunderstood. It never feels good when people think something about you that's not true. I've had lots of experiences when someone took something the wrong way or believed something about me that wasn't true. I am so miserable when this happens! Sometimes I'm able to clear it up with a conversation; other times I have to just trust God with my reputation. Either way, it's never fun. Hannah can definitely relate—and I bet you can, too.

> The temple was supposed to be a safe place, a haven of hope and worship. And even here she was misunderstood and accused.

In this passage, Hannah was misunderstood. Remember, she desperately wanted a child. It's her heart's desire. She was taunted by the ultimate mean girl, Peninnah, so much that she didn't want to eat. Hannah did the right thing and went to the temple. She turned to God, the One who heard her cry and felt her pain. Yet, when she went to the temple, the priest accused her of being drunk! Can you imagine what that must have been like? The temple was supposed to be a safe place, a haven of hope and worship. And even here she was misunderstood and accused.

Most of us have never been accused of praying so hard that someone thought we were drunk. But you've probably been falsely accused of something else before. If you have a brother or sister, I bet you've been accused of starting a fight that you didn't. Or maybe you've been accused of starting a rumor that you had nothing to do with.

∾ YOUR TURN ∾

Explain a recent experience when you were falsely accused. How did you feel? How did you respond?

What's a Girl to Do?
Read Matthew 27:11-14. What's the most amazing thing about these verses?

Hannah responded with words of truth, while Jesus didn't respond at all. Both were perfectly good responses for two different circumstances. When we are falsely accused, sometimes the best thing to do is calmly explain the truth to the person accusing us. But sometimes people have hard hearts and they're determined not to hear us. In those cases, it might be good to remain silent and leave the results to God. Proverbs 9:8 says "Don't rebuke a mocker, or he will hate you; rebuke a wise man, and he will love you." See the difference? When you know you're wasting your time, it's best just to keep your mouth shut. Now, I'm not saying that you can't defend yourself or set the record straight. Scripture tells us to go to someone we've offended (check out Matthew 5:23-24). However, some people are just out to make trouble.

> When you know you're wasting your time,
> it's best just to keep your mouth shut.

No one likes to be falsely accused. Eli's bad call is a good reminder not to make assumptions. We don't want to gossip or spread rumors or jump to conclusions. They can only cause trouble. We don't want to be like Eli, who made a poor judgment based on the way things looked on the outside. Even if we clearly see someone acting in an unusual way, we don't always know what's going on behind the scenes. Take that girl in your science class. You think she's odd because she sleeps all the time. What you don't know is that her parents fight so much at home that she can't sleep. Or take the girl who wears warm clothes in the summer. You think she's just weird. But what you don't know is that she's wearing long clothes to cover up the scars from past abuses. The point? Don't judge; build up people instead.

A Little Practice

When Hannah faced the most painful thing in her life, she prayed. And it wasn't just a "bless my family, bless the food, and bless all the missionaries overseas" prayer. She poured her heart out to God. She held nothing back. Sounds great, doesn't it? But praying is not always easy. Sometimes it's the last thing we do. When things are hard, my natural reaction is to try to fix them myself, not to pray. When things are good, I stroll along in life and forget to pray. But prayer is not simply a practice for the super-spiritual. It's absolutely vital to our relationship with God. After all, how can we know Him if we never talk to Him?

Today we're going to practice pouring out our hearts to the Lord. This may seem scary to you because you think of God as big, holy, and majestic. You're right! He is all those things, but the Bible also tells us that He's our Friend, Shepherd, and Comforter. You might also feel uncomfortable because maybe you don't have anything as big to pray about as Hannah did. But guess what? God still wants to hear from you. Whether you're thanking Him for things He's done or you're pouring out your heart because you feel like your life is falling apart, He wants to hear your heart.

Write a prayer to the Lord. Pour out your soul to Him. Don't try to make it fancy or religious. Just be yourself. If you don't know where to start, look through the Book of Psalms. You'll find lots of prayers that can get you started.

God Answers Prayer

You've probably heard a million times that God answers prayer. But I bet you've also prayed a lot of times and heard nothing but silence on the other end. God didn't answer, no matter how long or hard you prayed. What about the times when we don't seem to get an answer? Sometimes God simply wants us to wait on Him. Sometimes He will give us what we've prayed for, but it's in His timing, not ours. That's always a hard one for me.

And, sometimes God says no. Those times aren't so fun either, but He always acts in His goodness (and that's hard to remember). For example, one of my sisters prayed that a guy named Derek would like her. They had dated on and off, but Derek never seemed to commit to their relationship. My sister kept praying that he would like her, even though his values were really different than my sister's. He wasn't following God and was self-absorbed. Her heart was broken for a time because he didn't like her, but later she was thankful. God protected her and didn't answer her with a "yes." She would have never met the great guy she married had God answered her prayer the way she wanted Him to then.

Sometimes He will give us what we've prayed for, but it's in His timing, not ours.

Learning to pour your heart out to God and to trust Him for the answers is tough—especially when things don't turn out like you'd hoped. Read the following story from a girl like you who learned to pray to God and trust His answers.

Caroline's Story

I was due to start high school in the fall, but the school I would attend was still a mystery. I wouldn't find out until late summer, so I went into the vacation slightly panicked. All my friends were going to Hume-Fogg, the high school I wanted to go to. In the back of my mind, I knew I would too. I began praying that God would place me in the school where He thought I would excel and be most happy.

As summer went by and most free time was spent with my friends, that prayer changed. I started asking God to place me at Hume-Fogg. I wasn't thinking about

God's plan for me. Summer began drawing to a close, and I became increasingly anxious. One afternoon my dad woke me up (sleeping until the early afternoon is my custom on days off). He asked if I would come to the kitchen and talk with him. When I walked into the room, he handed me a letter from the magnet school office. I don't think I had ever been happier. God had answered my prayer. I was going to the school I had wanted. The two weeks that followed were sheer joy. I told everyone. I called friends, family, and everyone at my church. I prayed and thanked God. It was the biggest relief, and I felt light.

The Friday before orientation, however, I got another letter. Once again I was called to the kitchen. This time, my dad told me that I wouldn't be going to Hume-Fogg. Everything stopped. (That cliché really is true!) I didn't understand. So I asked my dad to repeat himself. He did. Then the tears came. I turned around and flew to my room. The waterworks that followed were incomparable to any other time in my life. For days after, the reality of my life brought me to a soggy, squeaky mess. My feelings had been deeply hurt. I was so upset with God. I asked Him how He could do such a thing. I didn't know what to think, and I blamed Him.

Reluctantly, I went to church that week. I didn't think I could make it without bawling. When I arrived, my friend Kelly knew something was wrong. She asked if I was alright. I told her I was because I didn't want to go into the whole story during church. By the end of our talk, tears were pouring down my face. I finally told Kelly what had happened, and she began to tell me about a time like that in her own life and what she learned. I began accepting the idea that Hume-Fogg wasn't in my future and that God had a bigger and better plan for me. After all He was putting me where I had asked to be—the place where I would be most happy and productive.

Starting out at the new school was scary. I was convinced that I would spend my freshman year stuffed in a locker and being bullied for my lunch money. I dreaded making new friends. I certainly didn't want to try. But my preconceived notions turned out to be way off the mark. Looking back, it has been the best year of my academic career. The teachers are incredible, and my grades are outstanding. I have met some really great people that I would have never had the chance to know.

Getting to this point has been hard. Casting my worry onto the Lord is a great feeling, knowing that He wants it from me. God will provide me with everything I need. He will place me where He sees the best fit. I am taken care of completely and in every sense. God is in the driver's seat, and I am buckled in next to Him.

—CAROLINE FORTUNE, Nashville, Tennessee

When God Says YES!

A lot of times we think about God answering our prayers with a "no" or "wait." But guess what? God enjoys answering us with a "yes" when He sees that it's best for us.

Read Matthew 7:9-11. What do these verses tell you about God?

Read Ephesians 3:20. What does this verse tell you about prayer?

Now look back at 1 Samuel 1:17-20. How does Ephesians 3:20 tie into Hannah's story?

This is so cool! Finally, after all this time and after all the pain, God answered Hannah's prayer. And we'll learn later that she got more than she asked for. Go God! He still answers "yes!"

We Gotta Ask

This might seem obvious, but if we want something from God, we've gotta ask! Sometimes I get so obsessed with what's wrong in my life that I forget to ask God about it. I spend so much time trying to fix it myself that I forget to bring my requests and desires to Him.

Read James 4:2. Rewrite it in your own words below:

See the relationship between having and asking? We can't have unless we ask. But sometimes asking can be scary. What if God doesn't answer us the way we want? What if He says "no"? What if He wants us to be patient and says "wait"? I wonder if Hannah had some of the same fears. After all those years of asking, I wonder if she wanted to give up altogether.

ᕲᕳ Your Turn ᕲᕳ

Have you ever gotten discouraged while praying for something because it seemed like nothing changed? Write about it.

Jesus told two parables in Luke about being persistent in our prayers. I think you'll find them kind of surprising.

Read Luke 11:5-10; 18:1-5.

How are the two parables similar?

In Luke 18:1-5, why did the judge finally give the widow justice?
- ☐ Because she kept bothering him
- ☐ Because she only asked him once
- ☐ Because she threatened him
- ☐ Because she was so nice to him

Jesus was using these parables to teach us to keep praying and not give up. He used these metaphors to show us that sometimes people get what they want simply because they bug someone to death. Of course, the point is not to hound God like nagging children. But Jesus is telling us to keep asking, keep knocking, keep making our desires known to Him. He never wants us to stop coming to Him in prayer.

A Little Thanks

Isn't it amazing when God answers us with a "yes"? Those are my personal favorites! After all that time, Hannah finally got a "yes." God gave her a son. And what's more, she thanked God for Samuel. I don't know if you're like me, but sometimes when I finally get what I've been praying for, I forget to thank God. I move on to the next item on my grocery list of requests. The Bible tells us that it's good to remember the things God has done for us. One way we can do this is by keeping a journal of answered prayers.

ᴄᴏ Your Turn ᴄᴏ

End the week by writing a prayer of thanks to God for a time recently when He said "yes" to one of your prayers.

I'm glad you took the time to do that. It always feels good to thank the Lord for what He's done in our lives. It also reminds us of how much He's done! Sometimes we get so wrapped up in our needs that we forget all the ways God has already provided for us.

Just think of how prayer changed the life of Hannah in the few short weeks we've been reading about her: Peninnah was out of the picture, Eli stopped judging her, and most of all, she had been promised a son!

Great job this week, girls! You've spent precious time learning one of the most important aspects of being a believer—pouring your heart out before God. And speaking of prayer, my prayer for you is that this will be something you never stop doing. Always talk to God. He wants to be in relationship with you!

To close this chapter, read the following journal entries from a girl who's learning to pray.

Courtney's Story

"Why can't we see God when He seems to be holding our hands every step of the way? If You created us, why do we tend to turn our backs on You? We keep on searching even though deep down in the core of us, all we truly want is You. We can think that drugs, alcohol, relationships, materialism, partying, etc., will fill us or satisfy what we are looking for, but the only thing that can truly satisfy us is You. In the beginning, You were the One who created us. You thought of every small detail and designed our bodies so carefully. You even gave us a soul so we could know You forever and know that You are the only One who will make us truly happy."

One of my favorite things to do (and the most relieving) is to write in my journal and pour out my heart to God. Even though I may be completely and utterly frustrated or confused with Him, I know it still helps me to be able to pour out my heart to Him. When I am wondering if He is listening, I still want to tell Him what I'm thinking and feeling. I figure God knows me better than anyone.

For me personally—being 16, driving, living with a single parent, and going through high school—it's hard to watch my closest friends go through things that are difficult. And at times, I have felt completely helpless. I also wrote:

"I feel lost and lonely, like maybe it's just me and God, and He's the only One who understands. Sometimes it's hard to believe that He understands. It seems as if everyone hides, not wanting people to see their hurt and pain. So it's like they wear a mask every day to cover it all up, hoping people will not see their true identity. They want people to reach out and see their true colors so most times they do crazy things to get people to notice them and then maybe see them for who they are and help. I don't mean to blame people for doing this when I can play this game of pretend as well."

When I feel like that, when I am grieving or not trusting God, when I try to cover up how I feel so nobody knows I'm hurting, I find peace after being honest with Him. Deep down to the core of who I am, God loves me. When He took time to create me, He created me in love. Yet I still search. I think He wants me to pour out my heart to Him and invite Him to walk with me through life—through driving, through living with a single parent, and when I'm with my friends.

" ...Yes God, it's me again. I've come to you to share my life. You are real, so real; and even in these obstacles that I face daily, I realize that I cannot do this without You and Your guidance. I need Your perseverance and Your strength. I want to love you with passion and endurance. I want to love others the way You love me. Please help me, God. You are my wondrous Creator who loves me. There is nothing too big for You that I might face. I know You can do everything. You are always enough for me and for everyone else willing to cry out to You..."

—COURTNEY CRAVENS, Clifton, Virginia

ᠺ YOUR TURN ᠺ

What's the most meaningful thing you learned this week? What did God show you about Himself and your relationship with Him?

What's one thing you're really struggling with?

I Promise

DAD, IF YOU LET ME GO TO THE PARTY, *I promise I'll start doing my homework. And I'll start doing more around the house to help you. I swear.*

Mom, if you give me the money for the outfit at the mall, I promise I'll never ask for anything else this year.

God, if you let Ethan like me, I promise I'll go to church every week.

Jon, if you tell me what happened last night, I promise I'll never tell.

Kate, if you promise not to tell mom and dad about my date with Jeremy, I promise not to tell them about your F in English.

Do these promises sound familiar? I remember sitting in the doctor's office as a kid with a swollen finger. At the time I wasn't sure if it was broken or not. I knew that if the x-ray showed a break, the doctor would have to put it back in place, and I knew it would hurt like crazy. As I waited on the doctor's table, legs dangling off the edge, I begged God to make it just a sprain. (I was a little bit of a baby when it came to pain). I remember praying something like, "God, if this is just a sprain, I promise I will obey You for the rest of my life." I was very serious. It never occurred to me that I couldn't keep that promise.

Making and breaking promises are a part of our everyday life. For instance, a friend tells you a secret, and you promise you won't tell anyone. After a few days (or maybe a few minutes), you tell another friend and make them promise they won't tell anyone. Pretty soon the chain of people who promised they wouldn't tell is so long that your whole school knows the secret.

ᙅᙐ Your Turn ᙅᙐ

Write about a promise you made but didn't or couldn't keep.

In this chapter's study, we'll check out a big promise Hannah made, a promise she not only made but actually kept. Before we do, keep in mind that your Bible might use the word "vow" instead of promise. In the Bible, a vow is a promise made to God that is solemn and very serious in nature. In fact, it was better not to make a vow at all rather than make a vow and not keep it. Remember that while you're reading.

Read 1 Samuel 1:9-11. Just to refresh your memory, what was Hannah's plea to God?

What was the vow (or promise) she made in return for her request being answered?

Here's Hannah's vow as written in *The Message*:

> Then she made a vow: "Oh, God-of-the-Angel-Armies, If you'll take a good, hard look at my pain, If you'll quit neglecting me and go into action for me by giving me a son, I'll give him completely, unreservedly to you. I'll set him apart for a life of holy discipline." —1 Samuel 1:11

Did you catch that? Hannah vowed to give back her son in service to God if He would give her a son. This is serious stuff. Notice that she didn't offer to go to church more, to clean up her speech, or to treat Peninnah nicely (which would have been hard!). However, the depth of her desire for a son was matched with the depth of her commitment to complete her vow to God, as we'll see in a few minutes.

✿ Your Turn ✿

Have you ever made a promise or vow to God? If so, what was it?

Promises are easy to make but hard to keep.

A Promise Kept

Promises are easy to make but hard to keep. You've probably noticed that many commercials, magazine ads, and politicians make extreme promises that they never intend to keep. If you listen closely, you can hear messages like, "If you drive this car, everyone will admire you," "If you lose weight using our product, you'll be popular and beautiful," or "If I get elected, I promise to vote for what's right, no matter what." Sometimes you and I are guilty of the same thing. We make promises we never intend to keep. It's easy to say something, but it's much harder to deliver.

Unlike today's world, Hannah kept her vow. Read 1 Samuel 1:21-28 and write down every detail that shows that Hannah fulfilled her promise to God.

Read 1 Samuel 1:22 again. What did keeping her promise to God mean for her and Samuel?

God had granted Hannah's request and had given her a son. But the answered prayer was costly. In order for Hannah to keep her promise, she had to let Samuel grow up in the temple of the Lord at Shiloh. This meant that she would only see him when she made her journey to God's house.

ᕙ Your Turn ᕗ

If you were Hannah and had just given birth to your first child, would you be tempted to break your promise? Why?

Hannah promised God that if He gave her a son, she would give him back to God for the rest of his life. But she also made another interesting promise.

Look at 1 Samuel 1:11 and choose the correct answer.
Hannah promised never to:
- ☐ Give him wine
- ☐ Cut his hair
- ☐ Let him touch anything dead
- ☐ Let him come back home

Pretty strange by today's standards isn't it? She promised that his hair would never be cut. But why? A little explanation might help. In the Old Testament, a Nazarite was a person who was especially devoted to God's service. Sometimes they were dedicated to God's service for a short time, but sometimes their dedication was lifelong. And to demonstrate their devotion to God, Nazarites kept three disciplines: they didn't cut their hair, they didn't drink any alcoholic beverages, and they didn't come into contact with the dead. While these seem really random to you and me living in the 21st century, these were significant outward signs of an inner commitment to God.

> People from politicians to married couples and even television characters make and break promises on a regular basis without remorse or a second thought.

A Big Deal

Remember the last wedding you attended? If you're anything like me, you were probably swept up in the romance and sentiment of the ceremony. Maybe you got caught up in all the beautiful details: the bride, dress, groom, music, flowers, and, of course my favorite part—the cake at the reception. But what about the wedding vows? Did you catch the series of promises the bride and groom made to one another?

I've been to many weddings in my life and heard many wedding vows. But guess what? The divorce rate in America is right around 50 percent. This means that about half of the people who make these promises end up breaking them later. Why? Because we live in a country and a culture where promises and vows mean nothing. People from politicians to married couples and even television characters make and break promises on a regular basis without remorse or a second thought. For someone to break a promise is not all that surprising anymore. It's really not that big of a deal—or is it? The Bible has some interesting things to say about the promises we make.

Read Ecclesiastes 5:4-5 and Matthew 5:37 and complete the quiz below.

☐ True ☐ False: It's okay to say "yes" when you mean "no."

☐ True ☐ False: God would rather us make a vow that we don't keep (even though we tried) than not make any vow at all.

☐ True ☐ False: Breaking a promise in God's eyes is no big deal. It's the thought that counts.

☐ True ☐ False: After we've made a promise, we can take as long as we want to fulfill it.

Did you answer false to all of the questions? Sometimes these passages can seem harsh and even a little tricky. That is partly because our culture is so different than what the Bible wants. We're not used to people making grand oaths before God or lifetime vows like giving a child away or promising never to cut one's hair (like Hannah did with Samuel). But part of the problem is simply that our culture doesn't seem to value promises too much. In fact, one of the lies in our culture is that breaking a promise or a vow isn't a big deal. If you've ever had someone break a promise to you, you know the truth—breaking a promise *is* a big deal.

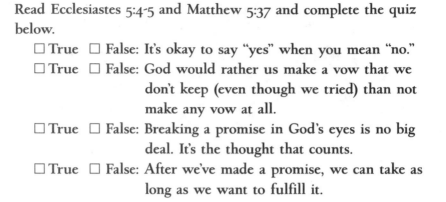

One of the lies in our culture is that breaking a promise or a vow isn't a big deal. If you've ever had someone break a promise to you, you know the truth— breaking a promise *is* a big deal.

Ecclesiastes tells us that it's better not to make a promise to God at all than to make one and break it later. When we make a promise to God, not only do we need to keep it, but we need to fulfill it quickly. Here's a small example: As I'm writing this study, I'm visiting my parents for the holidays. This morning I told my mom I would help her clean the house to get ready for a dinner party she's having. Because I told her I would help, I need to honor the word I've given. And I need to start helping her soon. Just picking up a few odds and ends at the last minute doesn't really help her at all. Like Ecclesiastes says, I shouldn't wait until the last minute to keep my promise. And, like the verse we read in Matthew, because I said "yes" to helping my mom, I need to also say "yes" with my actions.

∽ Your Turn ∾

What's a promise you haven't kept yet? It can be anything from promising to do your homework or promising to pray for someone. Stop and ask God to help you fulfill that promise in the near future and write out a plan of action below.

Keeping Tough Promises

It's hard enough to follow through on the little promises—like doing your homework when you told your parents you would, being home by curfew, and keeping secrets. But what about the really radical ones—the ones like Hannah made when she gave her son back to God? The big ones take a lot of loyalty and commitment. But God is happy when He sees us keep our promises even when it's hard.

Read Psalm 15:1-5 and fill in the blanks according to verse 2.

"The one who lives honestly, practices righteousness, and acknowledges the _____ in his _____."

So what does that verse mean? How does it relate to our study of keeping promises? It might be helpful to hear it in a different way. *The Message* translates it as, "Walk straight, act right, tell the truth." I love the imagery of speaking the truth from your heart. It's a little different than speaking the truth with your mouth. Words can be thrown around so easily sometimes. But when the truth comes from our hearts, it naturally flows out of our lives. When we keep a promise, it's like telling the truth from our heart.

Now look back at verse 4.
□ True □ False: **It's OK to break a promise if it hurts you to keep it.**

If you're still not sure, read Psalm 15:4b-5a from *The Message*: "...*Keep your word even when it costs you, make an honest living, never take a bribe...*" Get the point? Sometimes keeping our promises costs us something. It might even hurt us a little (or a lot!) to keep them. But as long as the promise was a good and healthy one in the first place, we should do our best to keep it no matter what.

When the truth comes from our hearts, it naturally flows out of our lives.
When we keep a promise, it's like telling the truth from our heart.

Before we move on, I need to mention an exception to this principle. Sometimes it's crucial to break a promise. For example, your best friend comes to you and makes you promise not to tell someone she's thinking about committing suicide. Or she tells you that she was raped on her date the night before. When someone comes to you and says, "I want to tell you something, but you've got to promise not to tell anyone," be very careful. You might need to say, "I appreciate your trusting me with this information. You need to trust me when I say that we need to tell an adult about this." Some serious matters like rape or abuse cannot stay a secret. You don't prove your loyalty by keeping quiet. You show your loyalty and love by doing what's best for your friend, even though she might get mad at you for a while.

Radical Promises

Sometimes I wonder why the Bible seems so serious about keeping promises. What's the big deal, really? If nobody gets hurt, then what difference does it make? Who cares? It recently occurred to me that one of the reasons God is so serious about us keeping our promises is because He is serious about keeping His. The Bible is full of God's promises to us. Just think about it. God promised that He would send His son Jesus to die for our sins. When it came time for Christ to die on the cross, can you imagine how much keeping that promise cost Him? As His children, we're supposed to follow in His footsteps, even as it pertains to making and keeping promises.

> One of the reasons God is so serious about us keeping our promises is because He is serious about keeping His.

I wish I could say I've kept every promise I've ever made. I would be lying if I said I did. But one of the things I love about God is that He *never* breaks a promise. Every promise He's ever made He's kept. There are no exceptions.

Read Romans 5:8. In what specific way did Jesus show us the love He promised?

Read 1 John 2:25. What radical promise did God make in this verse?

Did you get that? God has promised you the most amazing gift ever known. The God who flung the stars into the sky and knit you together in your mother's womb wants a relationship with you so badly that He gave His Son to make a way for us to know Him. He promises to give you eternal life if you turn to Him. If you've never trusted God to give you eternal life with Him, pray to Him and ask for this amazing gift. When you look at the rest of the Bible, it's clear that this promise of forgiveness and eternal life is freely offered to anyone who believes that God sent His Son Jesus Christ to die for our sins. He was resurrected on the third day and is now in heaven. If we believe that Jesus paid the penalty for our sins and we ask Him for forgiveness, we are promised to be in heaven with Him. If you haven't ever asked to receive this promise from God, pray to Him now. He promises to answer!

> Sometimes it's good and necessary to make a commitment to someone. On the other hand, I don't want to throw my words around lightly.

Living the Promise

One way I try to protect myself from breaking promises is by not making too many. After all, you can't break a promise that you haven't made. I'm not saying that I never make promises. Sometimes it's good and necessary to make a commitment to someone. On the other hand, I don't want to throw my words around lightly. And I don't want to set myself up to break a promise I shouldn't have made in the first place. But when it comes to my relationship with God, my whole life is a promise to Him. What do I mean? Let's look at some more Scripture to find out.

Read Romans 12:1-2. What do these verses ask of you and me?

In the Old Testament, God's people had to do lots of different things to show their commitment to God. They had a lot of vows and oaths that they were required to keep. But in the New Testament—after Christ came—it seems that God asks us to do less but be more. Sound confusing? It's not. The two verses you just read tell us that God wants our whole lives to be an offering to Him. We don't need to keep a million rules, we just have to offer ourselves to Him. I think *The Message* sums up how we're supposed to make our whole lives a living promise:

"So here's what I want you to do, God helping you: Take your everyday ordinary life—your sleeping, eating, going-to-work, and walking-around life—and place it before God as an offering. Embracing what God does for you is the best thing you can do for him."—Romans 12:1-2

You see, God wants you to live a life of love. He wants you to stand out, not because you never cut your hair like Samuel, but because you choose to live in purity, love others, respect your parents, and keep your promises. And you know what? You can't do any of this without God working in you! If you simply rely on yourself, you'll fall flat on your face. That's why it says, "God helping you."

Promises are a big deal to God. When you make promises to God or to your friends, it's important that you keep them with God's help.

In closing this chapter, look back at Romans 12:1-2. Journal below about how you can offer yourself as a living sacrifice to God. This is the ultimate response to a God who never breaks His promises!

∽ YOUR TURN ∽

What's the most meaningful thing you learned this week? What did God show you about Himself and your relationship with Him?

What's one thing you're really struggling with?

CHAPTER 7

It's All About You

R EADY FOR SOME STARTLING NEWS? You and I live in a self-centered world. Shocked? Probably not. Every day, you're bombarded with messages that encourage you to focus on yourself and your needs, no matter what the cost to you or somebody else. Need some examples? Check out the following T-shirt slogans:

"Let me drop everything and work on your problem."

"Here I am. Now what are your two other wishes?'"

"It's all about me. Deal with it."

Not only are these T-shirt slogans rude, but they also illustrate that many people in today's world are blind to the needs and feelings of others. Sad, but true. Just read the newspaper or watch the news and you'll see dozens of examples of people doing stupid things out of self-centeredness.

If you're honest with yourself, you'd admit that sometimes, you are self-centered, too. Maybe it shows up at school. Or at home. Or with your friends. Take the following quiz to determine your me-centered quota. Be honest!

Quiz Time

1. You're driving in a parking lot and notice a parking spot at the same time another driver does. You:
□ Whip into the space before the other person can get there.
□ Curse under your breath at the person who got there first.
□ Let the other driver have the spot and look for another one.

2. You and your best friend tried out for the volleyball team, something you've always wanted to do. She made the team, but you didn't. You:
□ Congratulate her and go to the games to watch her play.
□ Act nice on the outside but get jealous on the inside.
□ Stop hanging out with her since she took your spot on the team.

3. A friend makes fun of a nerdy girl at school. You:
□ Keep your mouth shut. You don't want her to make fun of you instead.
□ Secretly go back and apologize to the nerdy girl.
□ Make a point of saying something nice about the girl.

4. Your mom asks you to babysit your brother tonight since you'll be home. You:
□ Complain loudly, even though you don't have plans.
□ Agree to help out your parents.
□ Ask how much you'll get paid for the job.

5. Your youth minister asks you to mentor and disciple a younger girl in the group. You:
□ Don't really want to take the time, so you make excuses.
□ Think younger girls are lame, so you try to get out of it.
□ Wonder if this is a good idea, but you try it anyway.

How did you do? Did you see a pattern of self-centeredness? Did you see areas where you need to improve? Thinking about ourselves comes naturally. We don't have to try to remember to look out for number one. But the Bible tells us that we're not supposed to do anything out of selfishness or snobbishness. Instead God asks us to have an attitude of humility—an attitude Hannah demonstrated for us. I can't wait to see what you think of Hannah's prayer. After all you now know about her life, I think you'll enjoy this next step of her journey.

A Lot of God

Read 1 Samuel 2:1-4. What is the most meaningful part to you so far? Why?

In whom does Hannah say she rejoices?
- ☐ The Lord
- ☐ Samuel
- ☐ Her husband, Elkanah
- ☐ Eli, the priest

In verse 3, do you think Hannah is referring to anyone in particular? If so, whom do you think it is? Why? (There's no right or wrong answer, just give your opinion.)

Look back at all four verses again. List all the times Hannah references God. Write out each name she gives Him, even if it's simply "You." Then look for the number of times she talks about her son.

Part of me expected Hannah to start off her prayer by thanking God for Samuel. After all, wasn't he the one she wanted so badly? It would have been perfectly natural for her to be overly excited at the arrival of her son. (If you've ever been around new parents, you know how goofy they can act around their new child!) But she doesn't. In fact, she never specifically mentioned Samuel in her prayer. Although we know Hannah loved Samuel very much, it's cool to see how her joy for Samuel eventually expressed itself back to God. In fact, these verses show us that although she was thankful, her focus stayed on the God who answered her prayer, not the answer to the prayer itself.

Hannah was crazy about the Lord. She referenced Him at least eight times in just a few verses. I love seeing her passion for God because it encourages me to pursue a relationship like that with Him. So often I sing songs in church and do not really even think about the names of God I'm singing. I mumble prayers that are filled with my wants and requests without mentioning His name.

Hannah's focus stayed on the God who answered her prayer, not the answer to the prayer itself.

⤿ Your Turn ⤾

Write out a prayer of praise to God. Use different names for God that are significant to you, such as when Hannah used the adjective "rock."

It Can Turn Around

Things really turned around for Hannah. And as we keep reading about her, we'll see that things kept turning in ways she probably didn't expect. At one point she had no children, but now she had been given Samuel, who would be brought up in God's house. What an amazing turnaround—to go from being childless to having a child. And she did not have just any child, but a very special one who was set apart by God.

⌒ Your Turn ⌒

Journal about something you wanted for a really long time that God finally gave you. It can be a best friend, health for a relative, or even a job for your mom or dad. Tell about how you felt before God answered your prayer and how you felt when God finally answered.

Read 1 Samuel 2:4-7.

Hannah juxtaposes a lot of things in these few verses. To *juxtapose* something simply means to put two things together in order to show their obvious differences or similarities. In this case, Hannah put opposites together to illustrate that God is in charge of everything. In the columns on the next page, I want you to write each juxtaposition or pair of opposites. I'll fill in the first and the last ones as examples.

The bows of the warriors are broken	The feeble are clothed with strength
The Lord humbles	The Lord exalts

ᴄᴏ YOUR TURN ᴄᴏ

You've probably done your fair share of compare and contrast assignments in school. Assuming Hannah wasn't praying this for a school project, why do you think she compared and contrasted so much? Write the reasons that come to mind.

I would love to see what you wrote. To me, Hannah might have used the contrasts because of the change she'd already seen in her life. Once she was barren; now she is a mother. Through this ordeal, it seems that Hannah learned a lot about what God can do. If you're empty in a certain part of your life, ask God to fill it. If you're sad, ask Him to give you joy. If you're sick, ask Him for health. These verses teach us that God is about taking one thing and making it into something else.

We don't always get everything we ask for, but He will never stop listening to our requests.

> If you're empty in a certain part of your life, ask God to fill it. If you're sad, ask Him to give you joy. If you're sick, ask Him for health.

Raising the Poor

Finish Hannah's prayer by reading 1 Samuel 2:8-10. Before you begin ask God to show you something in your reading.

One of the first things that caught my attention is that God raises up the poor. What's the first thing that comes to your mind when you hear the word "poor"? Is it a starving child, a homeless person on the street, or someone begging for money? All of these things are certainly examples of the word "poor." But we can be poor in a lot of other areas too. How about when you feel like you don't have any friends? Or when your parents can't afford to pay for college? Or when you don't feel accepted by your family? All of these are examples of being poor in a certain area.

⌒ YOUR TURN ⌒

What's an area of life in which you feel poor or as if you're lacking something?

It is encouraging to know that God lifts up the needy and raises up the poor. Most of us are needy and poor every day—needing grace, needing hope, and maybe even needing money. But God requires something from us before He will lift us up. Turn to the New Testament to see what God is looking for in our hearts.

Read James 4:10 and 1 Peter 5:6. What do we need to do before God will lift us up?

How do you think Hannah demonstrated humility in her life? Peek back at chapter one of 1 Samuel if you need to be reminded.

It's not easy to be humble. We think we know what is best. We don't like it when others get ahead of us in line. We get jealous when someone else gets the glory—especially when we think we deserve it. We don't like to admit when we're wrong. Unfortunately, you and I are prone to arrogance.

> God can use His strength in my life and cause amazing things to happen, things that I couldn't achieve by myself.

One of my favorite verses in all of Scripture is 1 Samuel 2:9b: "...for a man does not prevail by his own strength." Lots of times, I've worked extremely hard on something but didn't succeed. These things have shown me my weaknesses, which is not a bad thing. I have learned that my own strength can only get me so far. God can use His strength in my life and cause amazing things to happen, things that I couldn't achieve by myself. Hannah's strength couldn't cure her barrenness. She knew that it was only because of God that she finally prevailed.

Becoming Less

We started off the chapter talking about our self-centered culture—the "it's all about me" mentality that you face every day. Then we looked into Scripture and saw that God teaches just the opposite: God helps the humble but cannot bless the proud. We're raised up when we humble ourselves. That's not exactly the message you would find in your favorite glamour mags.

Take a look at John 3:30. What does John the Baptist say?
He must _____, but I must _____.

That's not something you hear every day. John wasn't saying that you and I need to be self-critical, beating ourselves up or having low self-esteem. In a strange way, it's the opposite. When we bring ourselves before God and give our lives over to Him, when we serve other people, when we sacrifice for one another, and when we admit we're wrong, God promises to bless these acts of humility by actually lifting us up. In a way, we have to get small to get big!

Let's go back to Hannah for a minute. Look again at 1 Samuel 2:9. What does Hannah say God will do for His saints?

The Message puts it this way, *"He protectively cares for his faithful friends, step by step, but leaves the wicked to stumble in the dark."*

I don't know about you, but I had a lot of hard times in school. Whether it was a friend turning on me, the nervousness of trying out for a team, or the pressure of keeping up with schoolwork, it wasn't easy. Learning that God guards my steps is a big deal to me, especially when I think of difficult friendships or dating relationships. I'm so glad to know God is caring for and protecting me.

Hannah had to wait a long time before she had her son. But even in the middle of her pain, the Lord was protecting her steps. Hannah had a humble heart. She made her wishes known to the Lord but never demanded them of Him. She walked in humility, and the Lord raised her up.

God will lift you up for His glory and for His purposes because of your humility. He loves you, and He wants to bless you like He blessed Hannah. Maybe He will bless you in a different way, but the same love will be behind it! Another girl, Elizabeth, has learned that lesson. Read her story to close this chapter.

Elizabeth's Story

I love to be on the go. I sing and play the saxophone, piano, and guitar. I am also involved in ministry activities. I sing and play the piano on the worship team, lead a girls' Bible study with friends from school, and serve as a leader in my youth group. I have a passion for the lost and believe God is leading me into foreign missions. Grades and school are also important to me, so I study hard. Music, church, and school are enough to keep me busy, but in addition to it all is sports. I am 5 feet and 11 inches tall and still growing. I figure God made me tall for a reason, so I play basketball, volleyball, and run track. That is where my struggle really begins.

I love basketball; it is one of my deepest passions. As I approached my high school years, I had everything planned. I was going to play volleyball in the fall, basketball in the winter, and run track in the spring. I was going to practice hard because I wanted to make varsity as a freshman in basketball. In between those sports, I would continue in music and keep perfect grades. Nothing could hold me back. The world was at my fingertips, and nothing would stop me. Then I got sick.

A year ago, I came home from school running a high fever. My parents thought I had the flu. However, it didn't go away, and I ended up in the hospital. The doctors said that my white blood cell count had dropped to a dangerously low level, and they didn't know why. They tested me for leukemia. I was terrified, not because of death, but because I wasn't playing sports. All I was thinking was, "It's basketball season, and I'm not playing." During all the tests, I kept asking God, "Why?" I was supposed to be playing basketball, not lying in a hospital bed. I was supposed to be doing things normal teen girls do. I didn't understand. All I wanted to do was go back to school and play basketball.

When my leukemia test came back negative, I was thankful, but the doctors still didn't know what was wrong with me. Eventually, I was diagnosed with Chronic Fatigue Syndrome (CFS), which is a disease that causes high fevers, sore throats, swollen glands, and severe physical exhaustion from doing everyday things.

I was so grateful that I didn't have leukemia, but being diagnosed with CFS was not what I wanted to hear. A million questions ran through my head, but the biggest one of all was "Would I ever be able to play basketball again?" If I had to rest after brushing my teeth, how was I ever going to run up and down the basketball court?

What was God doing? Not only could I not play ball, but I was also missing school, backing out of church activities, and missing music lessons. My world was changing, and it seemed God was nowhere to be found.

After about six months, I felt stronger. I was back in school and slowly working my way back into sports. The summer before my freshman year, I was invited to go to team camp with the varsity basketball team. I was so excited because only two other freshmen were invited to go. This was my chance to show the coaches my skills. I ended up playing one and a half games back to back. In the middle of the second game, it hit me. My body completely shut down. I could barely walk up the court. My coaches took me out of the game, and that was the last of camp for me. I thought it was probably the last of basketball too. How could my team count on me if I couldn't finish a game? How could my coaches play me if I got really sick again?

Thankfully, my mom was there, and she took me back to the hotel. I couldn't do anything the rest of the week. Not only did my body ache, but my spirit hurt immensely. The struggle I felt inside was greater than any basketball game. Over the next few days while everyone else was playing, I sat in the hotel room, crying and pouring out my heart to God. I knew that my only comfort would be found in God, and I wanted desperately to feel His presence. I wanted Him to shine in my brokenness, but it was really tough to let go. So I spent my time journaling my deepest hurts and disappointments.

JULY 6

"I feel You here with me. You see the pain that alone I cannot bear. With each heartbeat You feel the pain I do. You catch my tears and calm my fear. But at this time it's different now. I need You more than the times before. I don't want to keep going on. Sustain my spirit now. Don't let my heart be discouraged. I can't go on without You. I'm in my deepest hour of need. Lord, come capture me! Let me rest in Your arms with each breath I take."

I admit I was angry with God. I didn't understand why this was happening. I knew I wouldn't be able to go on if I didn't surrender this to Him. I wish I could say that I surrendered my plans for my life to Him then, but I didn't. All I wanted to do was play basketball again. During my freshman year, I was able to play basketball, but it was a struggle. I missed a lot of practices and didn't get to start much. I continued to fight God about His plans for me. Then it happened—I grew tired of the fight. During a week of being sick and missing practice, I finally laid it all down.

DECEMBER 4

> *"God, You are lovesick about me! I am crying out to You because I'm tired. I am so scared. I desire to play basketball. Just fill me with your strength and renew my body! I truly surrender to You and Your plans for me!"*

I wish I could say it instantly got better, God healed me, and I went on to be the MVP, but I can't. It's still a daily battle, but once I finally surrendered to God, it made things so much easier. There are still many days when all I do is cry, but those days are the days God speaks to me the most. I have found such a peace. And I have begun to see how God is using my CFS to bring Him glory. I have opportunities to be a witness and have found peace and direction in my music. The worship is sweeter when you surrender. My walk with my Savior has gone to new and deeper levels. I'm beginning to experience His heart.

—ELIZABETH MOORE, Geering, Nebraska

⌒ YOUR TURN ⌒

What's the most meaningful thing you learned this week? What did God show you about Himself and your relationship with Him?

What's one thing you're really struggling with?

It Comes Full Circle

Hannah's Story

WHEN I WAS IN SEVENTH GRADE, my dad told my family that we had to move. I wasn't angry—just disappointed and scared. It's hard to leave everything behind. We moved right before I started eighth grade. I said good-bye to my best friends and the home I loved. I had to start all over. Every person and place I knew and loved was behind me, and I had to make a way for myself.

It was hard at first. Sure, people were nice, but I didn't become close friends with anyone right away. To make it even worse, my family hadn't found a church home. So not only did I not have any real friends at school, but I also didn't have that support from a group of people that cares about me that comes with being in church. I worried that I would never make any friends or feel like I belonged. I was really lonely, and I just didn't see God doing anything about it.

But God provided. I didn't expect it, but He did. He gave me a group of great friends. Now, in eleventh grade, I'm still close to many of the friends God provided for me in eighth grade. He also provided teachers and other adults who got involved in my life. They didn't just teach me academics; they truly cared about me.

That's not to say I was never lonely again. My best friend moved the summer after ninth grade. We had become close, and it felt like moving all over again when she left. Sure, I had other friends, but I wasn't as close to them. Plus, at the time, I was really insecure. I constantly compared myself to other girls, and of course I never measured up in my mind. I was never as pretty, as funny, or as well-liked as other girls. I began to look for approval from other people; if my friends were happy with me, then I was happy. And I got a lot of my sense of security from my best friend.

When my best friend moved, I was forced to face my problems. I realized how dependent on other people I had become for my identity. Instead of being grounded in who God said I was, I tried to make myself into the person that other people wanted me to be. When I realized how foolish I had been, I was so ashamed, but at the same time, I was relieved because I could have a fresh start.

Just like He did for Hannah in the Bible, God took what I thought was a problem and used it for His glory and my benefit. Now, instead of seeking the approval of my friends, I try to seek God. And He has stretched me and molded me. I have become more confident in myself—not because of my friends, looks, or popularity, but because I found my worth in Christ. As my relationship with God grew stronger, so did my relationships with other people. Once again, God provided new friends. I became close to a group of believers at school who encouraged me with the example of their own walks with the Lord.

You know, Hannah went for a long time without any evidence that God cared about her. She must have felt hopeless. But God did provide. When I was lonely and insecure, I thought that God wasn't concerned and wasn't involved. But I can see now that God did care, and He still had a plan for me even when things looked bad. God took situations that I thought would never get better, and He proved to me that He is in control...no matter what.

—HANNAH WAKEFIELD, Thompson Station, Tennessee

It Comes Full Circle

HERE WE ARE AT THE LAST WEEK. You've covered a lot of ground, and I hope you feel good about it. This was no easy task. You girls have really jumped in, and I'm so proud of you. I can't wait for you to get to the rest of the story this week. Yes, there's more! But first, here's a little review from the past seven weeks. Don't worry; you can do it. Plus, it's open-book so everyone should get an "A"!

Who was Hannah's husband?
- ☐ Peninnah
- ☐ Elkanah
- ☐ Brad Pitt
- ☐ Eli

CHAPTER 8

The reason a Nazarite never cut his hair was because:
- ☐ Not cutting his hair was against the cultural norm.
- ☐ Not cutting his hair was an outward symbol of a Nazarite's inner commitment to God.
- ☐ Short hair was a sign of God's displeasure.

What word means God is in control of everything in spite of how the situation appears?
- ☐ Authority ☐ Power
- ☐ Sovereignty ☐ Position

What are the three secrets of the harvest? (from Chapter 4)

1.

2.

3.

Keeping a promise is a big deal because...

What is the cure for being self-centered?

After all you've learned about Hannah, how are you similar to her, and how are you different? Give one example for each.

Great job! See how much you've learned over the past few weeks? Information can be a great thing, but only if we apply it in humility and love. The Bible says that knowledge can make us prideful, but love is the ultimate goal (check out 1 Corinthians 13). The point? Make sure that while you're learning new things, you're also remembering to be humble and full of love for others.

The Rest of the Story

Read 1 Samuel 2:18-21. Write down what makes you the happiest about this part of Hannah's story.

After Samuel, Hannah went on to have how many children?
- ☐ One
- ☐ Five
- ☐ Three
- ☐ Fourteen

According to Eli, why would God give Hannah and Elkanah more children?

I can't tell you how many times in my life I've tried to hurry God in the middle of something He was doing. When the college coach took away the basketball scholarship at the end of my senior year, I tried to hurry Him even then. I quickly tried to grab another scholarship at another school. I was sure it was somehow a mistake I had to fix. Actually, God was asking me to trust Him as the rest of the story unfolded. He wasn't asking me to do anything but just relax and believe that He had it under control.

We can see in Hannah's story that she didn't try to control or manipulate her situation. In biblical times, a woman who couldn't have children would hire a maidservant to have them for her. This happened in the Bible many times, but this wasn't God's best plan. Unlike so many other barren women, Hannah didn't choose this path. Instead, she waited on God.

⟋⟍ YOUR TURN ⟋⟍

In what area of your life are you tempted to get ahead of God or wish He would act more quickly?

A Similar Story

God brought Hannah's story full circle, but it was a test of her faith and trust in God. Maybe you can relate. Have you ever encountered a mean girl in your class? Someone who was making your life miserable? A popular girl who spread lies about you? Maybe you're in that situation right now, and you're wondering when God is going to make things right. Maybe it's been going on for several years now like Hannah's trial with Peninnah. But God was faithful and blessed Hannah beyond her wildest dreams.

> God is not a magic genie in the sky answering our every wish. But He does have the power—and promises to use it—to work out even the hard and painful things in our lives for good.

God is in the business of bringing good from bad. There are many other stories in the Bible that tell how someone was faithful in a struggle, and God brought it full circle in the end. Romans 8:28 says that "all things work together for the good of those who love God." Remember, God is not a magic genie in the sky granting our every wish. But He does have the power—and promises to use it—to work out even the hard and painful things in our lives for good.

A man in the Bible named Job is a great example of someone God honored after a lot of struggles. Job started out as a wealthy man. He had a wife and many children and was respected in his community. He was healthy and had a lot of cattle and land, which was the same as having lots of money today. He was also faithful to God. If you read the whole book, you would find that everything he had was destroyed, including his children and servants. Even his health was taken from him. He lost the respect of those around him. All he had left was a bitter wife and a few fairly lousy friends. It was tragic. But it doesn't end there—thankfully. I hate to be like someone who gives away the ending of a great movie, but go ahead and read the final few verses of Job. You can be mad at me later for ruining the end of Job's story.

Read Job 42:10-16.

    The Lord _____ his previous possessions.

    The Lord blessed the _____ part of Job's life even more than the _____.

Hang in there, girlfriend, if you're going through a hard time and it seems like it will never end. Your season of struggle will not last forever.

None of us wants to experience that kind of tragedy. I can't imagine what Job had to go through. For now, let's focus on the fact that God blessed Job even more in the end than he had been blessed before. I can guarantee—actually, God will guarantee—that if He takes something away or delays it for a time, it's only because He has something greater or better in store for you. The problem is that we miss out on it if we panic and become disobedient, thinking our trials will last forever. The Bible says that there is a season and a time for everything

(Eccl. 3:1). Hannah experienced a season of barrenness, but she also enjoyed a season of having many children. So what does that mean for you? Hang in there, girlfriend, if you're going through a hard time and it seems like it will never end. God will bring things full circle in due time. Your season of struggle will not last forever. In the meantime, hang on to the truth that God loves you deeply and wants the very best for your life.

A Little Secret

I'm about to show you one of the coolest things God has ever shown me in Scripture. Actually, you might have already seen it for yourself. Sometimes I have to read things over and over before I actually pick up on them.

Read 1 Samuel 1:7 again. How long did Peninnah's taunting of Hannah last?

Now read 1 Samuel 2:19. What did Hannah do for little Samuel? How often did she bring this robe up to him?

Do you see the parallel? Hannah had been tormented by Peninnah year after year. In the end, though, Hannah joyfully took a handmade robe to her son Samuel, year after year. What had been a miserable journey became a celebratory one!

Read Psalm 18:16-19. How do these verses relate to Hannah's story?

How do these verses apply in your own life right now?

Hannah's journey to the Lord's house used to be a painful one. But you know what? She kept making that journey, year after heartbreaking year. She remained faithful and loyal to God. After God's perfect time had passed, that very same journey became a blessing. No longer was Hannah's every step made with Peninnah's chiding voice in the background. Instead, she peacefully carried a robe that she had made for a son she had given back to God. Samuel was his name, and it is a beautiful name at that.

Why did Hannah name her first son Samuel? (See 1 Sam. 1:20.)

Don't be afraid to make your personal and desperate requests known to the Lord, no matter how big or small. Remember, He might ask you to wait like He asked Hannah, but when the time is right, He may give you your "Samuel"—or that which you have requested from the Lord. And even if He says no, you can trust that He wants the best for you.

More than Enough

This story still amazes me. The same Hannah who couldn't have children ends up with six! Remember the principle in week four about reaping more than you sow? This is an example of that. God honored Hannah's obedience and faithfulness to Him by giving her even more than she probably thought possible.

᙮᙮ YOUR TURN ᙮᙮

Write about a time in your life when you asked God for something and He gave you more than you asked.

I'm a sucker for happy endings. Not all the stories in the Bible have them, but Hannah's most definitely does. I think I'm a hopeless romantic that way. I love when everyone lives happily ever after like Hannah's story. Of course that's not without a lot of drama in between. But a little drama never hurt anyone, right?

At the End

We're at the end of our study, and I'd like to have a private word with you. Pretend we're sitting down to eat at your favorite restaurant. It's just you and me. Here's what I want to say:

You've done an amazing job studying God's Word these past few weeks. If you take anything away from this book, I want it to be this: God blesses obedience! Life is hard. There will be difficult people and struggles as you go through school. Some boys will break your heart. Some girls will betray you. Even wonderful parents will fail you sometimes. But don't despair. Don't give in to your own ways and don't take matters into your own hands. Wait on God. Obey Him in absolutely everything He tells you to do. And do you know what? In the end, when things come full circle, you'll have more "children" than you know what to do with. God will make good come from bad. In a sentence, your life will be God-sized. And there is nothing better my dear, sweet girl.

Much love from a grown-up one,
Kelly

LEADER HELPS

Dear Leader,

First, I want to thank you for the time and heart-energy you're about to put into the lives of some amazing teen girls. Those are two pretty awesome—and sometimes daunting—descriptions of the people you'll be leading: *teen* and *girls*. The two together can be, well, interesting to say the least. Let me put it this way: you won't be bored!

Perhaps some of you have been working with teens for years. Maybe this is your first time. Perhaps you have teens of your own or you're single. It's even possible that the only thing you know about teen girls is that you once were one. Regardless of your "expertise," I can assure you that if God has called you to this journey, you will be blessed.

If I can encourage you with a few things, I would humbly offer the following: First, pray, pray, pray. Pray for God's movement, His protection, and His purity in the lives of the girls. Second, get to know your girls. Ask about their family lives, their needs, and their passions. Most of them love to talk and be heard, so this shouldn't be hard. Third, encourage them with everything you've got. There's not a more insecure time in life than the ages in which your girls currently find themselves. Tell them you love their new shoes, their hairstyle, the way they laugh, the honesty in their questions, etc. Encourage them when you see them display the character of God. Finally, teaching God's Word is amazing, but living it is better. Simply put, show them what it means to be a Christ follower. I've found that being an example is stronger than almost anything you can tell them.

The following weekly guides are merely templates for you to use. You may have lots of creative ideas that are more suited for your group. It also might be that your group of girls is in unique circumstances that don't fit these guides as well. What follows are suggestions, discussion starters, and Scripture ideas for you to use. I hope you find these guides helpful, although I equally hope you will build upon or take away from them as needed. One helpful tip: Be sure to read the leader's guide for each week at least a few days before your gathering, as sometimes it will require you to do a few things in preparation.

Before you begin the study, raise interest in it by making posters to put up in the youth area, passing out sign up sheets to see how many girls are interested, and deciding on a time and place to have the introductory session. For the initial meeting, you'll want to know already how many girls are planning on being a part of the study so that you can have their books on hand. (If your church budget cannot provide the books for the girls, ask the girls to pay you up front for their book, before you order them. That way, you'll know who is really serious about attending.)

You'll probably want to have the introductory session wherever the group will meet for the remainder of the study. Although meeting in a room at the church will work, meeting in someone's home will be more comfortable and tends to create a more relaxed and intimate environment. Plus, it will give someone in your church with the spiritual gift of hospitality the opportunity to put it to good use! Decide on a day and time that works well for the girls in your group, and you're good to go!

Thank you from the bottom of my heart for the endeavor you are embarking upon. It is my privilege to assist you in the smallest of ways. After all, I've had the easy job of simply writing this thing. You're the one who will be living it out with these special girls who are dearly loved by God. Blessings to you as you journey with Hannah, your girls, and a little bit of me. I admire you!

Blessings,
Kelly

Optional Introductory Session

The bulk of this meeting is centered around group members getting to know each other. While this meeting is optional, it is highly encouraged. Because it takes girls a while to relax, get comfortable, and feel safe in sharing information, any additional time for fellowship that you can provide is good.

At this meeting, you'll want to have snacks available. Chips and salsa, veggies and dip, cookies, brownies, soft drinks, and bottled water always go over well with teen girls. Once everyone has arrived and has had a chance to snack and talk, send around a sheet of paper for girls to list their contact information (cell phone number and e-mail address are most important!). You may also want to pass around a sign-up sheet to have girls sign up to bring snacks each week.

To begin, instruct girls to stand if the statements listed below apply to them. The statements can be adapted to include any questions you want to ask, but they allow the girls to see some things they may have in common with someone unexpected. After each statement, allow girls to comment if they'd like. You may also want to ask follow-up questions like, "Which bones have you broken?" or "What second language can you speak?" Also feel the freedom to comment on the statements that apply to you (such as if you are an only child or have a bunch of pets). Again, the idea is to create a relaxed atmosphere and to allow you and the girls to get to know each other.

☐ You are an only child.
☐ You sleep in socks.
☐ You write in a journal.
☐ You hate science.
☐ You love math.
☐ You have more than two pets.
☐ You have a relative who is disabled.
☐ You like hanging out with your grandparents.
☐ You enjoy cooking or baking.
☐ You have ever broken a bone in your body.
☐ You speak another language fluently.

☐ You can text message faster than you can write.

☐ You check MySpace® or Facebook® more than twice a day.

☐ You help out with chores at home.

☐ You have a sibling under the age of 5.

☐ You are (or have been) the teacher's pet.

☐ You hope to play a sport in college.

☐ You detest coffee.

☐ You can juggle.

☐ You have ever been stood up for a date.

☐ You have tripped/fallen/slipped (or done anything else embarrassing) in front of a crush.

☐ You love dark chocolate.

Now that the girls have found out some unusual things they have in common, ask: **What do you know about the character Hannah in the Old Testament?** Allow girls to share what they know, even if it is very little. Then distribute the books and ask them to look through them and read the preface. Point out that there is space available for them to write their responses, thoughts, and feelings. Explain that much of the group discussion will come from what they write during the week as they study on their own. Assure them that they will never be forced to share information that they aren't comfortable sharing with the group. Also let them know that you are always available if they need to talk. Tell the girls to read and complete Chapter One in the coming week, and come back with questions, ready for discussion. Ask for prayer requests (or ask for a volunteer to be responsible for keeping the prayer list and e-mailing it out to everyone) and close the session in prayer.

In the next few days, you'll want to put together a list with everyone's e-mail address and phone number on it. E-mail it to the class and encourage them to really get into the first chapter. During the week, you'll want to do the study yourself, making notes of things that God reveals to you. Pray for each girl in your group and that God would use this study to deepen her faith and dependence on Him. May He bless you for your diligence and willingness to serve Him by leading this group!

Week 1: Group Meeting Ideas

OPENING ACTIVITY

Once everyone is settled, ask each girl to name her favorite song on the radio, favorite homemade meal she's eaten in the past month, and ultimate dream place to live. Give each girl only ten seconds to answer all three questions as if each girl is racing the clock on a game show. This will keep it moving and make it fun. After each girl has given her answers, start with the last girl and work backwards, allowing each girl to ask the girl on her left why she made the selection she did for one of her answers. For example, "Why is Song X your favorite song on the radio?" or "Why is City Z your dream place to live?" Again, give them each ten seconds to answer, and mostly, have fun with them!

POP QUIZ

Just to refresh their memory, open with a quick pop quiz. Throw each question out one at a time and have them yell out the answer as quickly as possible. This should be fun and lighthearted.

1. Eli was a _____. *(priest)*
2. True or False: Elkanah was Hannah's evil twin brother. *(False. Elkanah was her husband.)*
3. What was Elkanah's other wife's name? *(Peninnah)*
4. Hannah named her long awaited son _____. *(Samuel)*

DISCUSSION

Pick several of the following opening questions to get the discussion started. Throw them out one at a time and let a few of the girls share their thoughts. Do your best to get as many different girls as possible to share, as there will always be the natural talkers and those who are more quiet by nature. Discuss as many as time allows.

1. To what part of Hannah's story did you most closely relate?
2. In your opinion, what was the most painful part of her story? (Push them on this question. Don't just let them get away with saying

that she couldn't have children. Make them get beneath that answer. Remind them of the cultural ramifications in that time for not being able to bear children.)

3. What's one thing you really want to change in your life but don't have the power to change?
4. What about Peninnah do you find most difficult?
5. Without sharing names or intimate details, give an example of a way you've been misunderstood.

After asking the previous questions, direct girls to look back at their work and answer the following questions: **What was the most meaningful thing you learned this week? What's one thing you really struggled with?** Give girls plenty of time to share.

Scripture Focus

Call on a girl to read Matthew 16:24-25. Ask girls to read their paraphrase of verse 25 (from page 15 in the book). Ask: **How can a girl find her life by losing it? How did Hannah find her life by losing it? Do you think the message of these verses is fundamental to our lives as believers? Why or why not?** Then ask girls to share what they wrote as a way they could lose their lives like Hannah did (p. 16). As you talk together, drive home the point that when we try to grasp our own life, we lose it, but when we offer it to God, we gain it.

Closer

To close the group time, instruct girls to write their names on a piece of paper and put the paper in a cup you have provided. Direct girls to draw a name out of the cup (not their own). Challenge girls to pray for the girl whose name they drew. Pray with the girls and love on them as they leave.

Week 2: Group Meeting Ideas

OPENING ACTIVITY

There are lots of chick flicks that deal with female competition and rivalry. Find a clip (maybe three to five minutes long) of a scene in which a girl is jealous, in a fight with another girl, or feeling sad about not having what someone else has. Of course, be careful to only show something clean and appropriate. After all the girls have arrived, start off your time together by watching the clip. Afterward, ask: **how does this clip relate to your study this week?** If you can't find a video clip to show, ask the girls what television programs or movies they've recently seen that relate to this week of the study.

SCRIPTURE FOCUS

Read James 4:1-3,6-7 out loud and discuss the verses. Below are some questions to get the conversation rolling. Make sure to emphasize the fact that many girl fights stem from selfishness and pride. These Scripture verses are the key to setting us girls free!

1. According to these verses, what causes girl fights?
2. Have you ever asked God for something with wrong motives? If so, describe the situation to the group. (Be careful about not sharing intimate things about someone else.)
3. To whom does God give grace?
4. How have you been proud before? How has it contributed to girl quarrels?
5. What does it look like for you to submit yourself to God in the middle of jealousy or competition?

SCRIPTURE DISCUSSION

Say: **Even though Hannah was really hurting over not being able to have children, and even though Peninnah, her worst enemy, could have them, Hannah didn't respond in typical mean-girl fashion.** Direct girls to look back 1 Samuel 1:1-7 and point out ways that Hannah wisely dealt with her pain.

Ask: **Do you think you can be as honest and vulnerable before God with your struggles like Hannah was? Why or why not?**

REAL LIFE APPLICATION

More than likely, several of the girls are in a relationship that is causing them pain. Whether they've been hurt, are jealous, or are competing with someone, they need to work through their feelings in a healthy way. Now that they've reviewed Hannah's handling of her pain and read from James 4, discuss healthy and practical ways they can deal with the hurt they experience. Keep funneling them back to God's prescriptions.

REAL LIFE STORY

Forgiveness is one of the hardest but most freeing things we can do. Share a situation in which someone wronged you and you chose to forgive that person. Be honest about your feelings and the difficulty behind it, while describing your choice to obey and forgive. Call on girls to read Matthew 18:21-22, Luke 6:37, and Luke 17:4 out loud. Discuss what these verses say about forgiveness and how they can apply them to their own lives. Ask: **Do you think you could forgive the person in your life who is causing you frustration or pain? Explain. How do you know when you've forgiven someone? Is forgiveness an emotion or a choice? Explain.** *(It is both. You feel forgiveness in your heart; however, sometimes you don't feel like forgiving, but you still choose to forgive)* **Is forgiveness an event or a process? Explain.** *(It's both. You make the decision to forgive, which is an event. However, you must choose over and over not to allow unforgiveness creep into your heart, which is a process.)*

CLOSER

Take some time during prayer and give the girls the opportunity to forgive someone out loud (this is optional, not mandatory) without naming names. Girls can pray things like, "Lord, I forgive my friend who lied to me last week" or "God, I forgive someone who hurt my feelings." It will be a chance for them to publicly forgive before God and others. Then close in prayer, asking God to help the girls turn to Him when facing tough situations like Hannah's.

Week 3: Group Meeting Ideas

Note: This is a pivotal week as it deals with the issue of God's sovereignty. It is so important to learn at an early age the simple yet profound truth that God is in control. Though many godly scholars argue over the specifics of God's sovereignty, the bottom line is that God is in control of our lives and our world, even when our world seems chaotic or upside down. Grasping this truth will help anyone—specifically your teen girls—trust God through the hard things they can't always understand.

OPENING ACTIVITY

Prior to the meeting, write down the names of popular actresses on separate note cards. As each girl arrives, tape a note card to her back without allowing her to see the name. Explain that they are to discover whose name is on their back by asking each other yes or no questions to get clues. The first girl to correctly name the actress on her note card wins. Then ask: **If you were going to make a movie of Hannah's life, which Hollywood actress would you cast as Hannah? Why?** Then say: **Acting Hannah's part might be easy, but living the faith Hannah had is difficult, especially in light of what she went through.**

SCRIPTURE FOCUS

Call on a girl to read 1 Samuel 1:5-6 out loud. Below are some questions that should be asked in order. Throw them out one at a time and let girls share their thoughts.

1. What did you learn about Hannah's situation?
2. How do you feel about the fact that the Bible tells us the Lord closed Hannah's womb?
3. How would you describe or define God's sovereignty?
4. From what you know about Hannah, how did Hannah feel about God because He had not allowed her to have children?

5. Read Isaiah 55:9 to your girls. Explain to girls that our feelings are very important and valid, but it's not good for them to be our ultimate guide. Ask: How do you think Hannah's understanding of God's higher ways affected her response to her situation?
6. Can you name a time when you saw God's sovereignty even in something painful like Hannah's barrenness? If so, talk about it.
7. Do you think it's OK to question and doubt God in the midst of painful situations, even though you know He is sovereign?

Keep reminding them that God is always faithful, good, loving, and comforting, even though sometimes He might choose to do something or not do something that seems painful at the time. Give each girl the opportunity (without pressuring anyone to speak) to share an example of how they have trusted God's sovereignty in their lives. It can be about absolutely anything. Keep them within a time frame so no one runs away with the discussion. You might need to provide some examples from your own life so that you can spur girls' thinking.

CLOSER

To close this week's Bible study, instruct girls to reread Hannah Sobeski's story on pages 38-40. Allow girls to talk about how they felt about how Hannah's story ended. Ask: **How can you see God's goodness even in the midst of Hannah's illness and death? How does Hannah Sobeski's story challenge or encourage you?**

Explain that we have the privilege of knowing the rest of Hannah's story. We can see how her pain eventually gave way to great blessing from God. Close the prayer time today by allowing girls to voice their trust in God's sovereignty even though they don't always understand it. Then pray that God would allow the girls to see His goodness and power in the midst of situations that seem to lack both.

After today's study, you should remain afterward to talk with girls who may be struggling with God's sovereignty. Many girls face horrible situations, from divorce to molestation, and struggle with a loving God allowing such circumstances. Be sure to refer girls to professional help in areas where you may not be qualified to provide the best counsel.

Week 4: Group Meeting Ideas

Note: "It's not fair!" How many times do we catch ourselves saying or thinking that in a week? Even in adulthood, we're quick to cry "foul" when things aren't fair. My dad always used to say, "God's not fair, but He's always just." It used to drive me crazy, but I think I've finally begun to understand what he meant.

As best you can throughout your gathering, encourage the girls to remember that God's ways are higher than ours even when things aren't fair. He sees the bigger picture that we cannot.

OPENING ACTIVITY

Ask: **What's the biggest thing you used to think was so unfair when you were younger?** (For instance, when I was a child, my younger sisters always said it was so unfair that I got to stay up later than them.) Think of a few examples from your own childhood to help spark dialogue. This exercise should be light and fun! Ask: **What situation did Hannah face that could have made her say "That's not fair!"?**

SCRIPTURE FOCUS

Read Galatians 6:7-9 out loud. This should be a familiar passage for the girls, as they spent a lot of time on it this week. Then give them the following pop quiz. The answers are in parentheses.

The three parts to the "Law of the Harvest" are:
  a. You reap what you _____. *(sow)*
  b. The harvest _____ _____. *(takes time)*
  c. You always reap _____ _____ you sow *(more than)*
  d. Bonus question: When it comes to reaping and sowing, God will not be _____. *(mocked)*

SCRIPTURE DISCUSSION

Ask the girls to answer the following question: **How did last week's study on reaping what you sow change the way you looked at the prospering of "bad" girls?** Ask them to be specific with their perceptions but not with names. Then ask: **How does understanding** the "Law of the Harvest" help you deal with difficult people who often do the wrong thing to get ahead? How does understanding the "Law of the Harvest" encourage you to plant good seeds? What does it look like to plant good seeds in your life?

Scripture Focus

Call on one of your girls to read 1 Samuel 2:3. Ask: **Does it affect your choices to know that God knows and weighs every deed? Is it discouraging when you think of the mistakes that you've made? Why or why not? What role does grace play in light of the fact that God knows and weighs our choices and our actions?** Some of the teens might feel like they've already sown so much bad seed that it's hopeless. Encourage them with the reminder that God can restore even what we've messed up. Cap off their conversation by emphasizing that no sin or sowing of bad seed can outdo God's grace in our lives.

Explain that too often in Christian circles we're guilty of teaching that sin is no fun. The truth is that sin can be very fun, but the fun only lasts for a little while. And the consequences are never worth it, especially the ultimate consequence of having it cause distance between God and ourselves. Direct girls to complete the following from their study this week: Sin will _____ (*take*) you further than you want to _____ (*go*); sin will _____ (*keep*) you _____ (*longer*) than you want to _____ (*stay*); sin will _____ (*cost*) you more than you want to _____ (*pay*). Discuss with the girls the principle that sin can be fun, but it only lasts for a short time and carries great consequences.

Closer

Next week's study focuses on Hannah's prayer. Ask the girls to be thinking of at least one praise, one confession, and one request they can begin praying about throughout the week. Encourage them to come ready with these three aspects of prayer for a special prayer time next week. Close your time together by thanking God that He is both merciful and just.

Week 5: Group Meeting Ideas

Note: This week's study was all about prayer. And the only thing better than talking about prayer is actually doing it. That's why this week's small group session will focus on three elements of prayer: confession, praise, and requests. The following is merely a guide for you to use. You may have other ideas that are better suited to your group.

OPENING ACTIVITY

Distribute pens and three index cards to each girl. On the first card, direct them to write out a confession that God has laid on their hearts, or an area of their lives in which they need to confess sin. Challenge them to make it specific, i.e., *I yelled at my sister; I cheated on a test; I'm sexually active with my boyfriend.* (Reassure girls that this is private and will not be shared.) On the second card, direct them to write out a prayer of praise and thanks. Again, challenge them to be specific. On the third card, lead them to write out a special request or need. This will take some time.

CONFESSION

Direct girls to pull out their cards of confession. Lead them to close their eyes while you read the following verses. Encourage them to picture Christ's forgiveness for them personally.

> *"If we confess our sins, He is faithful and righteous to forgive us our sins and to cleanse us from all unrighteousness."* —1 John 1:9

> *"For You, Lord, are kind and ready to forgive, abundant in faithful love to all who call on You."* —Psalm 86:5

> *"As far as the east is from the west, so far has he removed our transgressions from us."* —Psalm 103:12

After you've read the verses, direct girls to tear their confession cards into tiny little pieces as a symbol of God's forgiveness. As they are tearing up the cards, explain in your own words God's grace and for-giveness for them. Direct them to place their torn-up cards in a trash bag you have provided.

PRAISE

Next, call attention to their cards of praise. Read the following verses to them. After you've read these verses, encourage them to read their praises out loud to the group. Emphasize the importance of prais-ing the Lord with one another! Explain that there is power in hear-ing God's character and work lifted up. God is glorified and we are encouraged.

> "But I will sing of Your strength and will joyfully proclaim Your faithful love in the morning. For You have been a stronghold for me, a refuge in my day of trouble." —Psalms 59:16

> "I will thank the LORD with all my heart; I will declare all Your wonderful works." —Psalms 9:1

> "The LORD is my strength and my shield; my heart trusts in Him, and I am helped. Therefore my heart rejoices, and I praise Him with my song." —Psalms 28:7

After your group has read its praises, provide a piece of poster board on which they can glue their praise cards. The idea is to make a praise collage. You can be as fancy or minimalistic with this as you wish.

REQUESTS

After you've made your collage, gather the girls back together for their final element of prayer. Only you will be able to tell how comfortable your group is with praying. If they are willing, direct the girls to swap their cards of request with one another so each girl ends up with someone else's prayer request. Once everyone is holding someone else's card, read the following verses to them:

*"Don't worry about anything, but in everything, through prayer and petition
with thanksgiving, let your requests be made known to God."*
—Philippians 4:6

"Carry one another's burdens; in this way you will fulfill the law of Christ."
—Galatians 6:2

Explain to them that when we pray for each other we are bearing one
another's burdens. Call on each girl to pray for the request on the card
she is holding. It should be a sweet time of lifting up one another's
needs.

Once this third prayer time is over, each girl should take home the
card she is holding and continue to pray for that request throughout
the week. This will also be an exercise in thinking about others and
not always focusing on self during prayer.

To clarify: At the end of the night, there should be one trash bag
of torn-up cards of confessions (which you will throw away), one collage full of praises, and each girl should be walking away with another
girl's request.

CLOSER
If you have time for discussion, consider asking some of the following
questions:
1. How do you think you'd have felt in Hannah's shoes when Eli
   falsely accused her? Have you ever been falsely accused? What
   happened?
2. How do you feel when you pour out your soul to God?
3. How do you know when God is telling you "no" or "not yet"
   when you pray for something?
4. Do you think God really wants to give you what your heart
   desires? Why or why not?

Week 6: Group Meeting Ideas

Note: Today's focus is all about promises: the promises God makes to us, the ones we make to one another, and the ones we entrust to others. As a leader, emphasize the importance of promises as Scripture portrays them, while also highlighting the areas in which our society doesn't value them. Before you meet with the girls this week, be thinking of modern-day examples of broken promises so you can help aid the discussion.

OPENING ACTIVITY

Prior to the group meeting, gather several print advertisements from current magazines and newspapers. If you have time, record some television commercials. As girls arrive, direct them to look at the ads to discover what each one promises. Ask: **Are the promises realistic?** Point out ways these products can't deliver, such as a car company making a guy popular with girls or a diet pill promising unrealistic weight loss. Then ask: **What are some other ways our culture disregards the value of a promise?** (*TV shows that glorify adultery, lying, cheating at work, etc.*) Challenge the girls to be specific with their examples. Ask: **Do you think our culture's view of a promise impacts the way you make and keep promises? Why or why not?**

SCRIPTURE FOCUS:

Call on two girls to read 1 Samuel 1:10-11 and 1 Samuel 1:24-28. Ask the following questions:

1. How hard do you think it was for Hannah to make that promise to God?
2. Have you ever promised God you would do something if He did something you wanted? If so, what was it? (*Example: I'll go to church if you heal my grandmother.*)
3. How hard do you think it was for Hannah to keep her promise once she had Samuel? Have them explain their answer in detail.
4. Have you broken a promise to someone? How did you feel? Have you ever broken a promise to God? How did you feel?

Stress how easy it is to make promises but how difficult it can be to keep them. Hannah could have easily gone back on her word to God, especially as she held Samuel in her arms. Yet, she still kept her promise and offered him to God at the temple. Discuss the difficulty of this decision, but highlight the fact that God blessed her for it. Ask: **How does this aspect of Hannah's life—her commitment to keep her vow to God—challenge you as a teen girl in the 21st century?**

REAL-LIFE APPLICATION

Say: **Now that we've discussed promises on a human level, let's turn our focus to God's divine promises that never fail.** Start at one end of the room and state this phrase: **God promises to...** Direct the first girl to finish the sentence with a promise that begins with the letter "A." Continue with the next girl naming a promise that begins with the letter "B." See how far in the alphabet the girls can get, and let them have fun with it. They can stretch the rules as broad as they want, i.e. God promises to... "Absolutely love us," "Be our only Savior," "Constantly give us mercy."

After you've completed the activity above, read 2 Peter 3:8-9 out loud to the group and discuss what it means. Explain that sometimes it seems as if God isn't keeping—or has forgotten—His promises to us. We can look around and see our pain and circumstances not changing, and wonder if God has broken His promise of love to us. Help girls understand that God's timetable is different than ours. He wants us to be patient and to trust Him, understanding that He is not slow in keeping His promises. Then ask: **Have you ever felt that God had broken a promise to you? If so, share. How does 2 Peter 3:8-9 give you a different perspective on your situation?**

CLOSER

As a closing activity, direct girls to spend time thanking God for His many promises to us. (They can think back to the ABC promises they did earlier.) Don't pressure girls to pray out loud, but challenge them to overcome this fear. As always, encourage girls and build them up as they leave. They will be stronger for it!

Week 7: Group Meeting Ideas

OPENING ACTIVITY

Before this week's gathering, collect some magazine ads or articles that essentially say, "It's all about me!" Distribute the articles and ads and challenge the girls to find the common theme among all of them. Gather as many as you can with as much variety as you can. You won't have any trouble finding these—just look at almost any ad, headline, or featured story in any popular magazine, and you should have what you need.

This exercise is especially good because it will help girls to see these ads and articles in a new light. They need to become more aware of things in culture that are contrary to God's Word. Ask: **How do you think you're influenced by these types of messages that culture is constantly advertising? If these things are all around us, is there any way to avoid them? If not, how can we combat the message that life is all about self?**

SCRIPTURE DISCUSSION

Call on a girl to read Romans 16:19. Ask: **How might this apply to our opening activity with the magazines?** Explain that God wants us to be wise about what is good, but innocent about what is evil. Sometimes we think that "bad" movies or racy magazines don't affect us. But Scripture tells us that these things *do* affect us. Help girls understand that believers cannot separate themselves from the world, but they can be aware of and be on guard against the notion of self-centeredness. Stress how God desires that we look to the interests of others, not always to our own needs. If they are dwelling solely on themselves, it is difficult to see and meet the needs of others. It is also difficult to live in humility before God, making His desires and plans your priority.

SCRIPTURE REVIEW

Direct girls to turn to 1 Samuel 2:1-10. Call on each teen to read one verse until Hannah's prayer has been read in its entirety. Then, group girls into teams of three or four, depending on the group size, and direct teams to rewrite the prayer as if Hannah was alive today. For instance, verse 4 discusses bows of warriors being broken and verse 5 talks about barren women. Verse 10 talks about God lifting up the horn of the anointed. Girls will need to think of modern-day parallels, substitutes, or paraphrases so that Hannah's prayer becomes more meaningful to girls in today's world. After several minutes, call on girls to read their everyday paraphrase. Then, ask the following questions:

1. What meant the most to you in Hannah's prayer and why?
2. How many times does Hannah mention her son Samuel? (*none*)
3. Were you surprised that Hannah's prayer was all about God? Why or why not? Why do you think Hannah's prayer was focused on God Himself and not the answer to prayer He provided?
4. Why do you think Hannah could praise God knowing that she would give up the son God had given her?
5. Have you ever been especially grateful for a prayer God answered? If so, talk about that time.

Scripture Focus

Say: **This chapter teaches us that it's not about us. It's all about God. We also learned that our lives should not be focused on ourselves.** Direct girls' attention to the quiz they completed on page 78. Ask: **How did you do on the quiz? In which area is it most difficult to think about others instead of thinking about yourself?** (*with friends, family, at church, at work*) Read aloud Philippians 2:3-5. Call on girls to name some practical ways they can look out for the interests of others. Direct them to be specific.

Real-Life Application

Read the following story to your girls:

Kate couldn't wait to get home from school because her mom had promised to take her shopping. Her first real date was just two days away, and she wanted a new outfit. Kate had saved up some shopping money, and her mom said she'd throw in some extra for accessories. Some of Kate's favorite moments were spent at the mall—especially when her mom helped pay. She couldn't wait to find some cool, funky jewelry and belts to accentuate her outfits. "Accessorize! Accessorize!" was Kate's motto. Her upcoming shopping trip caused her to check out mentally from her last class, Algebra, which wasn't that hard to do even when she wasn't going shopping! When Kate jumped off the bus, she raced home only to find her mom tending to her younger sister Jesse.

"Hey, Jesse, what's wrong?"

"I got sick at school and had to go to the nurse's office."

As Kate's mom felt Jesse's forehead, she added, "The school nurse called today and said that Jesse had a bad fever with chills. It looks like we might have to postpone our shopping trip."

Keeping in mind Philippians 2:1-5, challenge the girls in your small group to finish the story by elaborating on two possible endings: 1.) Kate handled the situation with selfishness, or 2) Kate handled the situation in humility that considered Jesse before herself. Again, challenge girls to be specific.

If you have time, continue to highlight Philippians 2:5-11, which portrays the model of Christ that we are to follow. Discuss His character and humility, pointing out the ways He desires for us to model that humility in our interactions with others.

CLOSER

To emphasize the interests of others, close in prayer this week by praying specifically for the needs of others. Allow girls to share prayer requests of those they know, not their own personal needs. Then direct girls to pair up or group in threes and pray for those requests. Close out your time together by praying for the girls to adopt an attitude of humility that looks to the interests of others.

Week 8: Group Meeting Ideas

Note: This is the final week. I hope you feel blessed, albeit probably tired, from your ministry to the girls over these past two months. My prayer is that your love for God and the girls has grown. If there is a message I could leave with you, it would be Hebrews 6:10, "For God is not unjust; He will not forget your work and the love you showed for His name when you served the saints—and you continue to serve them." What an awesome thing you've been doing with your time and heart's energy! I know it's a sacrifice, but I hope you've felt blessed as you've seen your group grow up in Jesus.

OPENING ACTIVITY

To close out the Bible study, make this week's group time one of celebration. Provide snacks and music as girls arrive. Allow them plenty of time to catch up on each other's weeks and lives. Since this is the last time to meet, I thought it would be cool to give the girls the opportunity to share some testimonies from their study over the past eight weeks—sort of like a sharing time around the campfire, except without the campfire. Say: **Today is our last time to meet together to talk about Hannah. As we do, I'd like us to reflect on Hannah's story and how it relates to our own lives.** Then ask the following questions, allowing plenty of time for discussion.

1. What do you remember knowing about Hannah before this Bible study began?
2. What is one of your favorite or most memorable things you've learned from our study together? What is a take-away truth that you will always remember? (Allow girls to look back over the previous weeks' studies to jog their memory.)
3. What is one way you've identified with Hannah? In other words, how is your life like hers? How is your life different than hers?
4. What's one thing you'll remember about being together as a group? It can be something funny that happened or something meaningful the group shared together.

Scripture Focus

Review this week's study by discussing the questions from page 104. Then review the story of Job and how God blessed Job's faithfulness. Call on girls to read 1 Samuel 15:22, Psalm 5:12, Psalm 84:11, and 1 John 5:3. Ask: **What do these verses have in common?** *(God blesses the faithful and obedient.)* **How has God blessed you for following Him?** Make sure that girls understand one truth this week: *God blesses obedience!*

Real-Life Story

Share a story with the girls about a time you chose obedience and God blessed you. It doesn't have to be a glossy, perfect story where everything turned around on a dime. In fact, the situation could have been very painful at the time. Help girls to understand that obedience can sometimes be very difficult, but God is always faithful to bless us when we obey.

Closer

To close out the Bible study, pray for each of the girls by name during a special prayer time. Prior to the Bible study, write out a special prayer for each girl, asking God to work in a specific way in her life based on what you have observed over the last few weeks. As you close, read the prayer you have written for each girl. Then as girls leave, give each one a copy of your prayer for her.

One Last Note

Again, thanks for making the effort and for selflessly depositing yourself into these girls' lives. Only God will know the impact that your graciousness and obedience will have.

Blessings from my heart,
Kelly

P.S. We'd love to hear how God worked in the lives of teen girls through this study. E-mail your stories to pam.gibbs@lifeway.com.